HOPE AND HEARTBREAK

Hope and Heartbreak

A Social History of Wales
and the Welsh, 1776–1871

Russell Davies

UNIVERSITY OF WALES PRESS
CARDIFF
2005

Learning Resources
Centre

1279211X

British Library Cataloguing-in-Publication Data
A catalogue record for this book is available from the British Library.

ISBN 0-7083-1932-7 (pb)
     0-7083-1933-5 (hb)

The right of Russell Davies to be identified as author of this work has been asserted by him in accordance with sections 77 and 79 of the Copyright, Designs and Patents Act 1988.

The publishers wish to acknowledge the financial support of the Higher Education Funding Council for Wales in the publication of this book.

Every effort has been made to contact the copyright holders of images reproduced in this book, in the event of a query, please contact the publishers.

Printed by Cromwell Press, Trowbridge, Wiltshire

I dair cenhedlaeth o Gymry – Mam a Dad, Nerys,
Betsan a Ffion – ac er cof am Adran Hanes Cymru,
Prifysgol Cymru, Aberystwyth.

Contents

Fantasies.   324

7   Happiness and Humour   *The Pursuit of Happiness. 'Gwlad y*
Gân': The Land of Song. The Lords of the Dance. Plays and Players.
Drugs, Drink and Dissolution. Sport and Society. Indoor Indulgences.
Welsh Wit and Wisdom. 'Collapse of Stout Party': Puns, Jokes and
Witticisms.   376

    Conclusion   434

    Notes   439

    Index   528

Acknowledgements

Acknowledgements sometimes have about them the insincerity of an Academy Awards acceptance speech. Only a fool would expect any recognition for writing for a public who never bothered to ask him to write for them in the first place, but it would be a greater fool who did not acknowledge his debts at the outset. Although this book sets out to demolish many traditions of Welsh history, the noble practice of a public expression of appreciation is not one which I would wish to decry or demean. During the course of the research for this book, I have accumulated several debts and received acts of generosity from many people and it would be churlish not to express my genuine appreciation.

The origins of this book can be traced back to the grey spring of 1975 when my diminutive history teacher, Marian Davies, forced me to read K. O. Morgan's *Wales in British Politics*. Like W. C. Fields, who was 'driven to drink by a woman, and I never had the courtesy to thank her', I never, until now, had the courtesy to thank Miss Davies for the equally intoxicating effects which Welsh history has had on me. That this book has been nearly thirty years in the making can principally be explained by the fact that I am not a professional historian. My time in archives and libraries has usually been restricted to the graveyard shifts. I am therefore deeply grateful to the staff of several institutions for the kindness and courtesy which they have always shown me, despite the fact that, inevitably and invariably, I arrived just before 'last orders'.

My post as Marketing Manager at the University of Wales, Aberystwyth does, however, have one great advantage for an aspiring Welsh historian. Over the years, I have been forced to travel the length and breadth of Wales – east, north, south and west. Sometimes experience is more important than book learning. Searching for a school in the Rhondda Fach when you should already be over the mountain in the Rhondda Fawr is probably the best introduction to the geography of Wales. 'Ysgol ddrud yw ysgol brofiad'. I have learnt the hard way that it is always wise to double check before departure as to whether an invitation to a meeting was in Newport, Pembrokeshire, or Newport, Monmouthshire, or to Pen-y-groes, Caernarfonshire, or Pen-y-groes, Carmarthenshire, or Pen-y-groes, Pembrokeshire. Unlike some current Welsh Assembly members who appear to believe that Wales stops at Rhiwbina, or some 1970s historians who seemed convinced that there was no history north or west of Merthyr Tydfil, this book attempts to be a history of Wales. During my travels, I have made use of the collections of the following repositories – the Nelson Museum, Monmouth, the Royal Welsh Fusiliers Museum, Caernarfon, the county archives at Caernarfon, Dolgellau, Denbigh, Llandrindod, Aberystwyth, Pembroke, Carmarthen, Swansea, Cardiff and Croesyceiliog, the local studies collection at Cardiff Central Library and the university libraries in Bangor, Cardiff and Swansea. My thanks to the staff of these institutions are great.

Aberystwyth's undoubted claim to fame is that it has the highest concentration of pubs and books per head of population in Britain. I hope my wife and family will accept this book as proof that I have spent nearly as much time in repositories that house the latter as I have in the former, jollier establishments. The staff of the University's Hugh Owen Library and the National Library of Wales combine courtesy and professionalism to such an extent that it is a pleasure to use these institutions. After twenty years in marketing, the National Library is one of the few institutions I know of which honours and merits its strap-line – 'Trysorfa Cenedl'. It is.

One of my greatest debts is to my tutors in the former Department of Welsh History at Aberystwyth. Emeritus Professor Ieuan Gwynedd Jones knows far more about this period than I ever will. I am deeply grateful to him for explaining this period to me in his special subject 'Victorian Wales' and for his encouragement to explore it for myself. The superlative 'excellent' is frequently used today in higher education to describe the quality of teaching. In the late 1970s, in the southern lecture theatres high up in Old College, Aberystwyth, against the crash of the sea, the roar of the westerly gales and the scream of the gulls, I was privileged to have encountered excellence in teaching. Looking back to those years, I realize why Ieuan's course was called a 'special subject'.

In recent years as the focus of this book sharpened, I sought help and assistance from a number of individuals who were working in areas which were new to me. Peter Goodall of Swansea Prison generously shared with me his sources on the history of punishment in Victorian Wales. Richard Ireland of the Department of Law at the University of Wales, Aberystwyth, provided me with a wealth of detail regarding the misdeeds and misdemeanours of my forefathers in Carmarthenshire. Dr E. G. Millward, formerly of the Department of Welsh in Aberystwyth, helped to locate and guided my interpretation of a wealth of non-traditional Welsh literary sources. Robin Gwyndaf of the Museum of Welsh Life in St Fagans took generosity to new bounds when he gave me free access to material on humour and superstition which he has accumulated over a lifetime. Dr Reg Davies of Lancaster put me on the trail of Welsh people in the East India Company's Army and those present at the Battle of Trafalgar. One day I hope to be able to answer the intriguing question set in one of his papers: 'Welshmen at the Battle of Trafalgar: "was your ancestor a one-legged survivor of the Battle"?'

Friends in the administrative departments of the University of Wales, Aberystwyth, have helped considerably in the preparation of this text. Miss Gill Parry, Mrs Denise Morgan, Mrs Nerys Hywel and Mrs Kylie Evans transformed pages of impenetrable scrawl into an orderly typescript. I am deeply grateful to them for their careful efforts and support. The trustees of the Sir David Hughes Parry Trust at the University of Wales, Aberystwyth have generously supported my work over the past twenty years. During the preparation of the typescript I have been humbled by the generosity of a number of friends who have made valuable corrections to the work. Dr Ian Salmon, Dr Huw Walters, Dr Lyn Davies, Dr John Davies, Mr Glyn Parry, Professor Geraint H. Jenkins, Emeritus Professor Ieuan Gwynedd Jones and Emeritus Professor Gareth Elwyn Jones read the entire manuscript and weeded out many of the most embarrassing errors. The errors which remain are mine, and mine alone. At the University of Wales Press I would like to thank Nia Peris and Leah Jenkins.

Perhaps the greatest burden of debt which this work carries is to other historians who have worked on this period. I must apologize to experts in particular fields who will feel, with just cause, that I have oversimplified their scholarship, misunderstood their interpretations and misinterpreted their views. The debt to local historians is even greater. Local historians are often regarded as the poorer brethren of the historical profession. The labours of these historical Cinderellas in local archives, published as books and as articles in county antiquarian and historical society journals, are a rich and fruitful source of the bizarre, the unusual, the idiosyncratic, the weird and the wonderful. I have sought to acknowledge my debts in the notes. I remain fearful however, that when I look over my shoulder I will see a thief's shadow.

Introduction

Portrait of an Age, 1776–1871 – the Welsh in their History

Two world-famous events, in both of which the Welsh had a significant role, mark the chronological boundaries of the period covered by this book. In 1776, sixteen, perhaps eighteen, Welshmen and men of Welsh descent, were amongst the signatories of the American Declaration of Independence. The Declaration commences with the resounding statement, 'all men are created equal, . . . they are endowed by their Creator with certain inalienable rights, among these are Life, Liberty and the pursuit of Happiness'. Characteristically, some would say, the Welsh placed emphasis on the Creator's role. Uncharacteristically, more would say, it was they who placed happiness in the declaration.[1] The second event is the most famous meeting in nineteenth-century history. On 10 November 1871, in Ujiji, Henry Morton Stanley, the illegitimate son of John Rowlands and Elizabeth Parry of Denbigh, who had spent his formative years in St Asaph workhouse, elbowed his way through a group of 'primitive' tribesmen. In the clearing ahead of him was a 71-year-old Scotsman. Stanley later recalled his momentous moment of destiny:

> My heart beats fast, but I must not let my face betray my emotions, lest it shall detract from the dignity of a white man appearing under such extraordinary circumstances. So I did that which I thought was most dignified. I pushed back the crowds, and, passing from the rear, walked down a living avenue of people, until I came . . . to . . . the white man with the grey beard. I would have run to him, only I was a coward in the presence of such a mob – would have embraced him, only he being an Englishman, I did not know how he would receive me.

Stanley stepped forward, took off his hat, and uttered the most famous words of the nineteenth century. A stark and simple questioning declaration, which still resounds across history: 'Dr Livingstone, I presume.'[2]

The emphasis on happiness by the Welsh people involved in formulating and framing the American Declaration of Independence reminds us that one sound, which is not often heard in Welsh historical studies, is that of laughter. Many portraits of eminent Welsh people show sombre, solemn men whose brows are furrowed in a permanent frown and rather grumpy and frumpy-looking old women in the black weeds of age, or widowhood, or both. Many look so formidable and forbidding that they could leach the light from any room they would enter. Like Howell Harris, the stern eighteenth-century evangelical, they resisted the devil's temptations and refused to smile. To these people, Jeremiah's book of Lamentations and the sterner pages of the Old Testament set the appropriate tone for Welsh society. In their short journey through the vale of tears on earth, people were advised to bear a rigid countenance. Laughter contained too many elements of envy, malice and rivalry to make it morally acceptable.

Yet, this is a distortion of the truth. The Welsh were a merry and mirthful people and even the Welsh religious tradition has a strong humorous element to it. Many of the hagiographic *cofiannau* published in the nineteenth century relate anecdotes which reveal the quick wit and ready repartee of Welsh religious leaders. Dafydd Evans, Ffynonhenri, Owen Owens, Cors-y-wlad and Stephen Jenkins are just three examples of Welsh religious leaders who offered a happy and humorous path to salvation. There is a touch of Mr Pickwick about these three characters, a charming mixture of geniality, innocence and whimsicality.[3] Some of the most spontaneous outbreaks of mass happiness in Wales took place in the name of religion. During the revivals in 1817, 1818, 1820, 1821, 1828 and 1829, crowds were described as being in a state of ecstatic happiness. Raucous laughter marked the convert's realization of the certainty of her or his salvation. Many ministers defended the cacophonous cackling of Nonconformist congregations.[4] Other Welsh people had to be assisted to look on the bright side of life. From the 1820s onwards, several joke books were published in Welsh to help Welsh speakers approach life with levity and laugh in the face of adversity. Some of the jokes contained in these guidebooks to *ffraethineb* are surprisingly modern and amusing, others are echoes of a gentler, simpler time.[5] Many of the jokes and stories, not always the amusing ones, are still heard on Welsh radio and television. In the nicknames given to individuals, in their instant dismissive and destructive responses to social pretension and hypocrisy, the Welsh reveal themselves as people who possessed a rich, rumbustious and malicious humour. To study Welsh humour is not to escape from the realities of daily life. Rather, the targets and topics the Welsh laughed at, and with, reveal another side to their emotions, fears and obsessions.

This book, concentrating on the years 1776–1871, is the first in a two-volume study of Wales in the period 1776–1945. Though it concentrates on the history of Wales between these dates, the study accepts that human lives are not confined to a particular period. Life and lives flow across the artificial boundaries created by historians. Some people born in the seventeenth century were still alive in our period. Many Welsh people born in the years 1776–1871 lived in the twentieth century. Ideas, experiences and emotions have histories which cannot be tied tightly to a single period. The historian must be aware of both the transient and the constant in human society. The study also accepts that the Welsh people, as the examples of the 'cowardly' but 'dignified' Henry Morton Stanley, and the 'happy' Welsh Americans show, did not confine themselves to Wales. Their disparate and desperate activities took them to all parts of the world. Though our focus is on the sedentary, stay-at-home Welsh, this study will also try, as far as possible, to follow the horizon-struck wanderers and the rainbow-chasers on their voyages of discovery and desperation.

Epic adventures are not often included in the history of Wales. During much of the nineteenth century it was an automatic assumption that adventurers, explorers or the doers of daring deeds would be English. The cultural inferiority complex which developed is encapsulated and exemplified in that remarkable meeting in Ujiji in 1871. Henry Morton Stanley's meeting with David Livingstone is indicative and illustrative of the tendency to subsume the Celtic into the English. In his best-selling memoirs, the Welshman, Stanley, presents himself as an American, while the Scot, Livingstone, is presented not only as an Englishman, but as a refined English gentleman. Even in darkest Africa enlightened sensitivities and sensibilities were strictly observed. Stanley suppressed and restrained his obvious inner joy at discovering the lost Livingstone and made no superficial gestures. Private joy was not tarnished through public jubilation. However, Stanley was anything but genuine. From a photograph taken in 1870, before he left on his intrepid journey, the moustachioed explorer gazes confidently at us. Pith-helmeted, he leans on his gun against a jungle background. Yet even in 1870, the camera lied. The whole scene had been composed in a studio, the ferns and the 'jungle' flora freshly picked in Dan-y-coed wood.[6]

One reason for the absence of these people from Welsh history is that the Welsh have often been very exclusive regarding who has been allowed to enter into their nation. Indeed, some definitions of Wales and the Welsh character have excluded the majority of the Welsh people. In the 1860s, for example, it was a truth universally acknowledged that the Welsh were a nation of Welsh-speaking Nonconformists. Gladstone, the church-going British Prime Minister who married into a wealthy Welsh family and himself lived in Flintshire, turned this myth into truth, when he declared 'the Nonconformists of Wales are the people of Wales'.[7] People who worshipped in church, or nowhere, those who did not speak Welsh, soldiers, industrialists, landowners with their 'claret and Havana Tory voices', indeed many who were prosperous or successful in the nineteenth century, are often excluded from the Welsh nation. Because of the narrow definitions adopted, the Welsh have been portrayed as unenterprising and unsuccessful, a people fearful of capitalism and resistant to change. In reality, the Welsh enterprised and ventured. Nor were they exempt, or immune, from some of the harsher aspects of capitalism and imperialism in the late eighteenth and early nineteenth centuries. They actively exploited themselves, their neighbours and people across the world. Large areas of South America were despoiled environmentally and deprived economically to feed the insatiable demands of the Welsh copper industry led by the remarkable Thomas Williams, Twm Chwarae Teg (Tom Fair Play), of Anglesey. Few traders in South America believed that this portly country solicitor, who controlled the world's copper industry, deserved his nickname. Boulton called him 'the despotic sovereign of copper'; James Watt considered Williams 'a perfect tyrant'.[8]

There are several uncomfortable and unpalatable aspects to the Welsh past which have been excluded from or ignored in our history. The Welsh have traditionally presented themselves as being firmly on the side of virtue in the campaign to abolish slavery in the early nineteenth century.[9] There were indeed a number of meetings held in Wales calling for an end to this evil trade. However, there was also a significant Welsh involvement in the slave trade. Like Captain William Williams, many of the captains and more of the crews of Bristol and Liverpool ships which carried slaves were Welsh. Nathaniel Phillips of Slebech, one of the founders of Milford Bank in 1810, made his fortune from the sale of rum and sugar grown by his slaves on his West Indian plantations. He also made substantial sums from speculating on the price of slaves. Like all keen capitalists, he bought when the price of slaves was low, and sold them when it was high.[10] Nathaniel Phillips was not an unique figure. As we shall see, several Welsh families owned slaves and slave plantations in the West Indies.[11] In Barbados, Demerara, Jamaica and St Thomas's, the names of several plantations have a Welsh resonance – 'Wales', 'Williams', 'Golden Grove' and 'Denbigh' – which betray the origins of their owners. The popularity of 'Williams' and 'Davies', as a surname amongst former slave families, is another echo of a link with Wales.[12]

In many encounters with native peoples across the world, the Welsh appear to have escaped censure and obloquy by hiding behind an 'English' empire. When they did amass sufficient courage to peep out from behind the back of their bigger neighbour, the Welsh fed their self-esteem by presenting themselves as the brave underdogs, heavily outnumbered by bold and barbaric savage warriors. After the so-called 'Indian Mutiny', *The Cambrian* and the *Monmouthshire Merlin* reported the horrific injuries inflicted on two Welsh women. Richard Jones, Ywain Meirion, Abel Jones, Levi Gibbon, E. Griffiths and J. W. Jones penned ballads that told the salacious details of the atrocities perpetrated against women and children. Ywain Meirion warned that:

Caiff terfysg India er cryfed fu,	Despite its strength, the Indian rising,
Cyn hir ei lethu i lawr	Before long will be suppressed,
Pob llwyddiant gaffo Lloegr lon	Happy England will enjoy success.
Er pob gelynion lu.[13]	Despite many enemies.

Yet the Welsh, like the English, Scots and Irish, were also capable of committing gross atrocities and appropriating land and valuables. In 1798, in Newry, the Ancient Britons, a Welsh regiment of fencible cavalry commanded by Sir Watkin Williams Wynn, showed how tenuous fellowship between fellow Celts was in a series of brutal battles and savage attacks on women and children.[14] Two of the most brutal governors of the West Indies were Welsh. Valentine Morris's governorship in St Vincent was marked by severe brutality, while Sir Thomas Picton's period as governor in Trinidad was one of the most bloodthirsty in that sad island's tragic history. Punishment was positively medieval.[15]

In the 1840s, in Kandahar, Sir William Nott's troops undertook a series of murderous reprisals against Afghan civilians.[16] It was the

Unknown artist, Captain Thomas Foley, of Narberth, Pembrokeshire. Foley was a captain of the *Elephant* when the ship was selected to be Nelson's flagship. Foley is representative of a rich military heritage which has almost been ignored in Welsh history. Whilst she has celebrated her saints, Wales has largely forgotten her sailors and soldiers.

'spoils of war', a contemporary euphemism for plunder and theft, greedily gathered by Captain Thomas Foley of Narberth, and Vice-Admiral John Thomas of Llandysul, that paid for their resplendent homes and luxurious lifestyles.[17] The stolen fortunes of John Thomas and Thomas Foley pale into insignificance when compared with the fabulous wealth appropriated by Admiral John Gell of Crickhowell. His ship truly came in when, in 1793, near Toulon, Gell captured the Spanish ship *Santiago*, valued at an amazing £1.5m. John Corbett, an American and Peninsular War veteran was less fortunate. His share of the prize money for the American War totalled £2. 14s. His Peninsular bounty was a less than bountiful £1. 4s.[18] One of the fundamental, but forgotten, aspects of Welsh history is of the Welsh people choosing to do unto others what had already been done unto them. In neither case, as the above episodes show, was that a matter of kind and tender mercies.

Historians, by the very nature of their 'sullen craft', are creatures consumed by and obsessed with dates. Their work explains, enhances and endows periods of past time with certain characteristics and caricatures, which distinguish various eras. The period chosen for this book, 1776–1871, cuts across certain well-established aspects of historiography. The study begins in 1776, which to some historians is part of the long eighteenth century. In this historiographical school, the eighteenth century includes the years from around 1688 to 1832. Others insist that our period is part of the long nineteenth century which they, with equal plausibility, argue runs from around 1750 or 1770, to 1860, or 1875, or 1880, or 1890, or 1901, or even 1914. This confusion over dates is mirrored in the contradictory titles that have been given to the period 1776–1871. This was the 'Age of Aristocracy', but it was also the 'Age of the Developing Democracies'. 'The Age of Scandal' and the 'Wickedest Age' were also the 'Age of Worship'. 'The Age of Elegance' was also the time of the 'First Industrial Revolution'. 'The Age of Improvement' was also the 'Age of Fear'.[19] Each of these titles reveals a part of the truth of the lives of Welsh people, but no single title can fully encompass the complex totality of the Welsh experience. Cutting up the past and labelling the snippets is one way of trying to impose order on the flex of history. But ages merge, and epithets mislead, so that it is probably wisest to accept that all ages are an amalgam of opposites. In this study many aspects of these descriptions are utilized to give a fuller portrait of the lives led by Welsh people. This might lead to the possibility that this study will make assertions which are contradictory, but then perhaps this only indicates that life was more complex than historical generalizations often allow.

Wales, as we shall see, developed into a complex society during the period 1776–1871. Parts of it were firmly locked in the past. The travellers who travelled into Wales came to discover, and consequently discovered, a verdant land which still in the early nineteenth century had about it the breath of Genesis's first morning. Their writings and paintings portray primitive, picturesque, wild, western lands that seemed to have only just emerged from original chaos, through which these brave explorers journeyed. Under the influence of the Romantic and Picturesque rediscovery of Wales, the land appears as God's masterpiece.[20] It was created by the Creator in a moment of special felicity, each mountain carved, each lake designed, each tree planted and each shoreline etched to achieve some particular pictorial or poetic effect. In contrast to the disorderly natural abundance of the romanticized, imagined land, Wales was far more complex in reality. Although some people remained in almost medieval simplicity and ignorance, Wales was not isolated or shut away from the rest of the world. This was a distinctive period in the making of modern Wales. The transformation to 'industrial' society had already commenced. Welsh society, in both urban and rural areas was capitalist, market orientated and materialist. It is fashionable now to condemn the denominational press of early nineteenth century Wales as being unworldly, concerned only with turgid discussions of obscure theological topics. Authors of articles in these journals, we are told, were more concerned with imagining the next world than with under-standing the realities of the world in which they wrote. Yet, open the proud volumes of *Seren Gomer*, *Y Beirniad*, *Yr Eurgrawn Wesleaidd* and many journals which now squat on the shelves of the cemeteries of forgotten books, and you will find that they are full of excited, breathless descriptions of mankind's discovery of the mysteries and miracles of God's creation.[21] These were people of the world. The press reports of the fervid activity of Welsh missionary societies linked the people of Maenclochog and Madagascar, and kept the primitive inhabitants of Hafod in touch with developments in Haiti.[22]

It was not just in spiritual matters that the Welsh were linked to the world. By the late eighteenth century, the Welsh economy marched to the beat of a global marketplace. The quays of Swansea were packed tight with battered ships which had braved the silences and storms of the seas, carrying copper ore from South America. Paintings of the port show ships tightly packed, hull to hull, below a dense forest of masts. On occasion it would have been easier to get a ship into a bottle than squeeze another into the surfeited port.[23] In the 1790s, some of the most valuable stock on the London stock exchange were those of companies which extracted lead ore from the windswept hills of Cardiganshire.[24] In February 1804, near Merthyr Tydfil, a new age was inaugurated when a steam engine was run on rails for the first time in world history.[25] By the 1860s, the rhythmic clip-clop of horse and mule transport would be drowned by the discordant clackety-clack of the clattering carriages of steam trains propelling people at a breakneck fifty miles an hour, hurtling the Welsh headlong into modernity. This study attempts to show how modernity coexisted with tradition, and change compromised with continuity. It also seeks to recapture something of the Bruegelian vigour of 'rural Wales', and the Lowrian slovenliness of 'industrial Wales'.

People are remarkably capable of living their lives inconsistently, maintaining different timescales for different aspects of their lives. Villages that were so lost in time that no map marked them existed a few miles from towns that were world leaders in a range of different industrial undertakings. Industrialists of incalculable wealth lived close to beggars dying of starvation, while world-leading mathematicians and scientists coexisted with bearded, messianic preachers, who believed, looked, sounded and smelt like Old Testament prophets. All these contrasting characters were housed and harboured in the land of Wales. Although they worked in modern industries, many Welsh people perpetuated the Middle Ages. In that most novel of industries, the railways, workers brought with them into their workplace older beliefs. If a bird, especially a robin, was seen in a carriage then it forewarned fearful tidings.[26] Thousands of Welsh people believed in the physical reality of unearthly beings such as angels and cherubs. Many of the most literate and the learned claimed to have seen them. In 1865, in *The Penitent's Vision*, Henry Clarence Whaite painted an angel, bathed in ethereal light.[27] In the dark corners of their lives which flickering candlelight could not enlighten, fairies, ghouls, ghosts, phantoms and spirits flourished. Contemporaneously with the technological inventions of the 'industrial revolution', the late eighteenth and early nineteenth centuries witnessed a cultural 'invention of tradition' which emphasized the longevity of Welsh traditions.[28] While the common people engaged in the age-old customs of singing, versifying and playing the harp competitively at *eisteddfodau*, wearing the national costume and marvelling at Iolo Morganwg's Druidic fantasies, the nouveaux riches of Wales gave architectural confirmation of their ideological return to Camelot. Between 1784 and 1824, Clyne, Cyfarthfa, Hensol, Margam, Penrhyn, Singleton and several other 'castles' were built to plans which would have met the approval of Wales's greatest castle builders – Edward I and Llywelyn ap Gruffydd. Other Welsh people openly admired and espoused the ideas and ideals of the eighth, thirteenth and fifteenth centuries. Hywel Dda and Owain Glyndŵr were heroes to many, while the Welsh gentleman's code of honour and behaviour was built on the firm, fictional foundations of Arthurian chivalry.[29] Many Welsh people made classical literature their model and taught their children Latin, Greek and ancient rhetoric. Some Welsh people were as well versed in Hebrew as they were in Welsh. The Revd R. Evans announced in *The Cambrian*, in 1824, that his school at 44 Orange Street, Swansea, was reopening for the tuition of youth in Greek, Latin and Hebrew classics.[30] To mould the plastic minds of Swansea's youth, Mr Evans read aloud Cicero, Tacitus and others of his Roman heroes in Latin, and Plato and Thucydides in the original Greek, which he considered the supreme language. An age of empire needed imperial role-models. Sons and daughters of wealthier Welsh families went abroad on their 'Grand Tours' in search of the glories that were Greece and the illustriousness that had been Italy. As with so much else, Sir Watkin Williams Wynn led the way with his spendthrift continental tour in 1768–9. He was quickly followed by his sister, Charlotte, Miss Harriet Lewis of Harpton Court, Sir Stephen Rich, Richard Glynne of Hawarden, Sarah Vivian of Swansea, William Earle of Glansevern and Connop Thirlwall.[31] To guide their way, many took with them Hugh William Williams's (1773–1849) *Travels in Italy, Greece and the Ionian Islands*, published in 1818. Born at sea in 1773 to a Welsh mother, Williams was so obsessed with all things Greek that he became known as 'Grecian Williams'.[32]

Wales has been well served by her historians. Historians have produced some of the most creative and entertaining work published in Wales in the last twenty-five years.[33] But historical writing, by its very nature, generalizes human experience. Over time some generalizations have acquired the imprint of truth. Fond white lies of the 1860s have become cherished truths in our historiography. Welsh historical writing seems to have settled into a comfortable groove. This study, by examining some of the fundamental aspirations, emotions and passions of the Welsh people, seeks to break out of the established pattern. This will no doubt disappoint and dismay those who come to this study expecting to find the traditional approach to Welsh history, commencing with a study of the 'primitive rebels' of the 1780s and 1790s, proceeding to discuss the emergence of industrial society in the 1790s, the death of 'Merrie Wales' in 1811, the creation of the working class between 1816 and 1831, the revolts of the working class in the 1830s and 1840s, and so on, in a carefully choreographed chronology.[34] This teleological approach to history has many advantages. However, it suffers the disadvantage of having a known or an expected ending. People who lived through these years did not have their future so clearly mapped out for them. Their lives were uncharted; they had no maps to follow. Often the most illuminating history is written to show how people acted in the expectation of a future that never happened. History is not about manifest destinies, but about unexpected and unforeseen futures; it is not a straight line.[35] Parts of the familiar story are included, but this is a study of the emotions and passions which drove the Welsh. Anger, ambition, envy, fear, hope, happiness, hatred, love and lust are powerful forces which shape human society. Their study can provide valuable new insights that question the stereotypes of Welsh history.[36]

Like all people, historians are victims of their prejudices and pre-occupations. Objectivity and impartiality, like virtue, are things which Welsh historians aspire to and aim at, but seldom reach. The polymath Iolo Morganwg made the point with characteristic lack of diplomacy: 'modern *Welsh historians*, gentlemen (if they may be so called) of *no conscience*, who are partial to everything but *Truth*'.[37] Welsh historians have often written Welsh history with a view to safeguard, or justify, a particular standpoint in the historian's present. The works of past masters tend to straitjacket subsequent historians into a particular chronological or ideological viewpoint. It would not be too much of a simplification to assert that there have been three major historical schools in Welsh historiography. First, the Nonconformist tradition emphasized the centrality of religion to Welsh life. Secondly, Labour historians have discovered a golden thread in our past, which leads on from the strike of 1816, to the reform crises of the 1830s, to Chartism in 1839, and so on to the emergence of the Labour Party.[38] Thirdly, nationalist-inspired authors have emphasized the creation of a Welsh national character and the survival of the Welsh language.[39] There are numerous examples of historians who write superbly in each of the three traditions. They have explored and explained the Welsh past, enriching and enhancing our understanding, but certain aspects of Welsh experience, for a number of reasons, are misrepresented or ignored in these traditions.

Thus one view of Welsh history is of heroic freedom fighters who formed a working-class culture and movement in Merthyr Tydfil in 1831. Those who attacked people and property are seen as heroes. But the evidence of three terrified children, barricaded behind a door in Joseph Coffin's house in Merthyr Tydfil, suggests that the rioters were not all heroic figures. Some were thugs and thieves who, after setting fire to the family's possessions, demanded, through threats of further violence, trifling amounts of money from children.[40] In the mid nineteenth century, so a number of historians and contempories tell us, Wales gloried in a golden age of strong morality and religious affili-ation. Wales, we are told, was 'God's Acre'. Horace Mann's census of religious worship, published in 1851, helps the historian to chart the ebb and flow of chapel and church building across Wales.[41] Building these simple and sublime buildings, these sermons in stone, with their eclectic architectural styles and their splendid carpentry, tongue in chiselled groove, was the work of true believers.[42] Yet, despite, or perhaps because of, the celestial standards that they set themselves, a nagging suspicion remains as to how religious the Welsh were in actual fact. Jan Morris, discussing the religiosity of the Venetians, noted acidly: 'the Venetians are not quite as religious as you might suppose from their multitude of churches and their mystical origins'.[43] Perhaps this comment is also apposite to describe the Welsh in the nineteenth century. Some historians have sought reverentially to guard the Welsh religious tradition by disqualifying and dismissing the work of others. In a review of Nigel Jenkins's *Gwalia in Khasia*, the late Revd Professor R. Tudur Jones dismisses the author's attempt to explain the motives of the missionaries with the cursory observation: 'he is not a Christian. So one cannot expect him to appreciate the spiritual motives of the missionaries'.[44] Only the elect, it appears, can comment on the Welsh religious tradition. If membership of a particular party or organiza-tion, or subscription to a certain interpretation of the world, is an essential prerequisite for the historian, then very few history books would ever be written. The value of those that were would surely, and rightly, be questioned.

Often current political or religious concerns dictate the view that a historian takes of the past. To some the Welsh language was doomed to decline and die as soon as industrialization commenced in Wales. In this view, Welsh people were more in tune with the Bowery than with Brechfa; they had more in common with Broadway than Bodorgan. Yet this, as the indefatigable Professor Hywel Teifi Edwards and Professor Geraint H. Jenkins's ably marshalled army of researchers have shown, ignores the buoyant Welsh-language cultural heritage of Wales.[45] The tendency amongst some historians to blame all the woes of the Welsh on the wiles of the English has given rise to an interpretation of the Welsh in their history as helpless and hapless, the gormless and guileless victims of a Machiavellian neighbour. Ever since the 'once upon a time', 'long ago', in hopeless skirmishes near streams in the snow when our princes were betrayed, beaten and beheaded, a cycle of abuser-abused-abuser-abused punctuates this nostalgic history. In the melodrama, the Welsh are always the passive victims, the English pernicious victimizers. In the period 1776–1871, the despoliation and exploitation of Wales through the industrial revolution, the so-called 'rape of the fair country', was the latest phase of this vicious cycle.[46] Such views ignore the ability of some Welsh people to fashion a future for themselves. Like those people, Welsh historical studies needs to stand on its own two feet.

Working to a preprepared template for works of historical scholarship has the disadvantage that important areas of people's lives are excluded if they do not conform to established preconceptions or generalizations. Things that do not fit neatly into a particular world view are excluded or forgotten from our history. But the prefixed, inflexible concepts of politics, sociology and dogma are of little use when confronted with the random and wilful patterns of personal style and behaviour. In the archives, this researcher often found himself in the position of expecting people to be living in one way, and discovering that, in fact, they were living in quite another. It might be pertinent to give just a few examples of people who do not appear to conform to the expected patterns. Each is an important figure who has been largely ignored in Welsh history. Robert Owen, the greatest socialist reformer and thinker that Wales has ever produced, was not the creation of 'industrial' south Wales. He was born in Newtown, a small town set at the heart of the rural vastness of the 'green desert' of mid Wales which, in view of its woollen manufacturing, immodestly named itself, 'the Leeds of Wales'.[47] David Davies, probably the most resourceful and rapacious, perhaps the richest, Welsh industrialist, was born and bred a few miles away in somnolent Llandinam.[48] Alfred Russel Wallace, the co-discoverer of the origin of species, was inspired in his researches into the mysteries of nature in the 'smoke-filled town' of Neath. His inspiration came during a visit to an exhibition of the orchid collection of J. Dillwyn Llewellyn. The tender flower *Epidendrum fragrans*, which so 'thrilled' Wallace was lovingly grown in the grim and grimy, copper-smoke-poisoned atmosphere of Swansea.[49] Few people in the period 1776–1871 got closer to royalty than the Welsh, for they enjoyed virtually a monopoly of the post of royal physician. The biblically named Sir Noah Thomas established the tradition in the 1770s, as the unenviably over-occupied doctor to George III. In the 1820s and 1830s, Sir David Davies was even busier, serving three monarchs, the drunken and dropsical William IV and Queens Adelaide and Victoria. If not amused by, Victoria was certainly enamoured of the Carmarthenshire Welsh, for two of her other doctors, David Lloyd Morgan and Sir John Williams, were from Llandeilo and Gwynfe. Each used his natural abilities and talents to escape from relative poverty and pauperism to reach the pinnacle of his chosen profession.[50] Another loyal and royal Welshman was Rear Admiral Sir Peter Puget, who gave his name to large tracts of coast in North America. His home was not along Wales's salt-dashed shores, but in landlocked Radnorshire, at Presteigne, probably the furthest point from the coast in Wales.[51]

Sir Peter Puget is representative of one of Wales's strongest traditions, which has been studiously ignored by our historians. The war heroes and their militaristic exploits are a sadly neglected aspect of our past. While remembering her saints, Wales has almost forgotten her sailors and soldiers. This is perhaps because the two main traditions of Welsh historical writing, for different reasons, dislike the military. The Nonconformist religious tradition has emphasized the strength of the pacifist movement in Wales, embodied in the stout person of the devout Henry Richard, one of the world leaders of the peace movement.[52] The traditional view is that the non-combative movement was a powerful force in the political and religious life of Wales. But if we examine the position closely the reality is different. Wales was not always against war. The response of the Welsh press, including the denominational, to the Crimean War was overwhelmingly anti-Russian and pro-war. Only two editors took an anti-war stand and only one, Eleazar Roberts, the modestly nom de plumed Meddyliwr (The Thinker), persisted with his opposition. John Jones,

Humilis, extended his vitriolic attacks on Russia, published in *Yr Eurgrawn Wesleaidd*, into a book entitled *Darlith ar Rwsia a'i Rhyfel*, published in 1854.[53] Hindsight shows us that the Crimean War was the first salvo of the struggle for mastery in Europe which ended when the lights of civilization went out all over the continent in August 1914.[54] In this sense it was the first modern war. Despite the fact that the 'anghredadun Twrcaidd' (infidel Turk) was now a supporter, and Christian Russia the enemy, the Welsh Nonconformist press portrayed the war for control of Jerusalem's Holy Places in terms of a struggle between infidels and Christendom – a depiction which would have been familiar to the Crusaders.

The labour tradition ignores the military heritage of Wales because of its role in the suppression of mob violence associated with popular protests for workers' rights. In this view, the Welsh volunteers and militia are portrayed as the lackeys of the forces of conservatism and authority. It is an uncomfortable fact that many Welsh riots in the late eighteenth and early nineteenth centuries were suppressed by well-aimed volleys fired by disciplined Welsh soldiers. In November 1814, the Royal Carmarthenshire militia shot to quell and to kill Welsh rioters, as did the Swansea Volunteer Cavalry at Merthyr Tydfil in October 1816, and the Mold Yeomanry and Royal Maylor Cavalry at Wrexham in 1826.[55] The military tradition of Wales was long, distinguished and strong. Generals Nott and Picton, the earl of Uxbridge and Lord Tredegar, Admirals Gell, Gower and Foley were accompanied by thousands of less well-known and esteemed, but no less heroic Welshmen, who also braved the battlefields of the Empire. These were the Welsh who never reasoned why, they just did and died. Thomas Burchlate, who died at Presteigne in 1850 at the advanced age for a foot-soldier of sixty-eight, is one of the forgotten fighters. Thomas served as a solider for over thirty years and survived battles in Egypt, the Iberian Peninsula and at Waterloo. He saw the wonders of the ancient world, helped to steal much of it, fought the 'Fuzzy-wuzzies' and the 'Frogs', and now lies an unquiet soul in the quiet earth of a mid Wales graveyard. Despite the ravages wrought by the weather, his message to posterity can still be read on his gravestone: 'Praise on tombs are titles vainly spent, a man's good name is his best monument'.[56] It is salutary to note that, between 1776 and 1871, only two years, 1826 and 1828, were untouched by 'the savage wars of peace' caused by an increasingly burdensome 'white man's burden'. In every other year, Wales was engaged in some form of the Empire's 'widow making'.[57] In far-flung, forlorn outposts of Africa and India, the Welsh mercenary was as formidable and ferocious as the Welsh missionary.

Considerable attention is given in this study to the history of the individual. The people we will meet include many of the best and the brightest, the great and the good of Wales. These are the people who pack the *Dictionary of Welsh Biography*, the closest that Wales has to a pantheon of heroes and, to a much lesser extent, heroines.[58] That stout volume has been much criticized for not only omitting many distinguished people, but for including too many divines. The Welsh nation comprised such a diverse cast of characters that it is mistaken to assume that some can be regarded as quintessential Welsh people, who adequately represent their generation or nation. In this study, readers will meet many Welsh people who can only be described as bad, base, evil and eccentric. People such as Jack Matthews, the entrepreneurial brothel keeper of Cardiff, the original tiger in the bay; Caddy Owens, the unscrupulous brothel madam of Holyhead who received young girls from the local Poor Law guardians into lives of squalor and sexual slavery; and the drunken, fornicating, masochistic Thomas Williams, Capelulo. There is a perceptible pungent whiff of sulphur present in archives when the historian reads details of the deeds of the serial killers Elizabeth 'Betsy' Gibbs of Laugharne, John Roberts of Caernarfon, John Ryan of Merthyr Tydfil, Isaac Davies of Salt Lake City and the vicious Susannah Rider of Llanymenech.[59] These and many more Welsh people should not be excluded from our history because their morals were suspect and their behaviour repugnant. It is hoped that a fuller portrait of Welsh society will emerge from discussing these forgotten characters alongside the more famous and industrious Welsh people. This is very much a biographical approach to history, written in the belief that, because of their common humanity, people matter. It is hoped that the work will not simply descend into an assemblage of anecdotes for, though the focus will be on the individual person – the constituent atom of human communities – attention will also be given to the broader experience of the society in which the individual lived. In many respects this study is modelled on the work of the *Annales* school of French historical writing who pioneered serial history.[60] Yet, it also echoes an older tradition. In 1931, that much misunderstood and maligned historian, Sir Lewis Namier, explained the challenges confronting the historian of a nation:

> The student has to be acquainted with the lives of thousands of individuals, with an entire ant-heap, see its files set out in various directions, understand how

they are connected and correlated, watch the individual ants, and yet never lose sight of the ant-hill.[61]

Through examining the role of the individual, evidence will emerge which questions and challenges some of the shibboleths of Welsh historiography. The traditional usage of 'industrial Wales' will be challenged. Despite the development of Merthyr Tydfil and its environs into the greatest iron-producing region on the planet, for much of our period 'industrial' enterprises were principally located in the rural areas of Wales. The late Professor L. J. Williams in his perceptive essays portrays early nineteenth-century Wales as a deprived, primary producing area, not an industrial society.[62] The split between master and worker, landlord and tenant, which has been dramatized by several historians, was not perhaps as intense as might be assumed. In order to function, industrial enterprises, as did landed estates, had to be the centres of class cooperation and collaboration. Chris Evans, in his splendid *'The Labyrinth of Flames': Work and Social Conflict in Early Industrial Merthyr Tydfil*, has shown that rivalry was often at its greatest, not between rival social classes, but between rival ironworks.[63]

Historians have been blind to the subtle gradations in Welsh society. Because people lived cheek by jowl in what is dismissed by the superficial observer as 'the terraces', the Welsh are assumed to be identical in all aspects of their lives. Many people were so poor that the possession, or non-possession, of petty and trivial things divided people cruelly into social categories. People frequently reminisce, fondly recalling long ago, 'slawer dydd', when morality was stronger and social bonds firmer. In those idyllic, halcyon days, doors were left open to welcome friends and strangers. Yet, some would say spitefully that the doors were kept open to reveal the treasures that the wealthier possessed. Some historians have emphasized that the Welsh people, especially in the nineteenth century, were divided not on class lines but on moral issues. Thus, we are told, Wales did not conform to any class model devised by sociologists; rather Wales split neatly, if not equally, into two. The Welsh people were either moral (*Buchedd A*) or immoral (*Buchedd B*).[64] The first group contained people who were religious, respectable, teetotal and successful, while the second group was composed of irreligious, unrespectable, dissolute losers. The two groups glared at each other across an unbridgeable social gulf. The tensions between the saintly and the sensualist can still be seen in many areas of Welsh life, and continues to influence the historiography of

Victorian Wales. Yet classes, like cultures, are rarely so hermetically sealed into separate, distinct, self-contained compartments. More often, due to the unpredictable nature of individual behaviour, they overlap and interrelate.[65]

Some historians have accepted the claims of contemporaries that, as a result of the stern sermons of Welsh Nonconformist ministers, the old *joie de vivre* of eighteenth-century 'Merrie Wales' had been killed stone dead by the mid nineteenth century. The joyful carousing of the fairs of Rhuthun, it has been claimed, ceased after a particularly stern sermon from the Christ-ravaged John Elias in 1811. Consultation of the court records reveals that chastity in the area continued to go the way of all flesh, long after Elias's stern rebukes. Indeed, the evidence presented in this study indicates that the 1850s and 1860s were not a period of severe sexual repression. These decades are usually regarded as a period of high Victorian respectability, reticence and restraint. Yet these years were probably the golden age of heterosexual activity in Wales. Prostitution flourished not just in the rowdy dock areas of Cardiff, Newport and Swansea, or 'China', the sin-soaked area of Merthyr Tydfil, but also in the cosy Bethel towns of Caernarfon and Carmarthen, in 'refined' Abergavenny and in Holywell, Rhyl and St Asaph. There is considerable evidence across Wales of the sale of abortificants, birth control mechanisms, pornography, 'toys and abominable devices for sexual gratification'.[66] Dildos were first sold in Swansea in 1820, and merkins, female genital wigs to hide the ravages of veneral diseases, were widely available throughout Wales. Two of the most celebrated lesbian couples in nineteenth-century Britain were based in Wales. The Welsh were either, like Queen Victoria, blissfully ignorant of such activities, or had a surprisingly modern tolerance of sexual differences.[67] However, 'Victorian', like 'Puritan', remains a derogatory term, overburdened with innuendoes of a paranoid prudery.[68] Some authors have claimed that so morbidly obsessive was the concern of Victorians for respectability that they insisted on covering table and piano legs to avoid upsetting sensitive ladies, shocking impressionable gentlemen or corrupting youth. But this custom, for which the Victorians are still ridiculed, developed for a practical purpose. Piano and table legs were covered by Welsh women to protect valuable furniture from damage inflicted by the hobnailed boots of the quarryman, collier and carter. Ironically, furniture leg covers were often removed to mark the visit of an important visitor. Thus the minister on a pastoral visit, while he sipped his tea and

Lady Leighton, *The Ladies of Llangollen. The Rt. Hon. Lady Eleanor Butler and Sarah Ponsonby* (Sir Michael Leighton). One of the most celebrated lesbian couples in Welsh history who settled at Plas Newydd, near Llangollen, and enjoyed 'pleasures unappreciated by the vulgar'.

gorged on sandwiches and cake, could admire the curvaceous, naked legs on wanton display.[69]

Welsh history has, until relatively recently, been the history of one half of society. Women have been excluded from much of our history. This study attempts to show the vital role which women played in the development of Welsh society. Thomas Charles, for example, one of the most powerful figures of Welsh religion, could not have achieved such prominence without the support of his wife Sally. This is not a statement based on the tokenism of the adage that behind every successful man is a greater woman, for Sally was the real power. It was her business acumen that kept their publishing ventures afloat, her drive, initiative and determination that made their commercial enterprises solvent. In comparison with Sally, Thomas appears ineffectual, unworldly and weak.[70] Other women made fortunes out of the physical weaknesses of men. In several of the paintings and photographs which survive from the years 1776–1871, indefatigable, ingenious women are often engaged in work. Wherever and whenever there was hard work, hard women engaged with the task, while weaker men looked on. The painting of weavers in Llangollen, by the grandiloquently named Julius Caesar Ibbetson, shows a world of work deserted by men.[71] In 1792, Ibbetson journeyed from the north to the south, where he produced two watercolours of coal mines. In both paintings horses and women are doing the hard, back-breaking work. In *Coal Staithe on the River Tawe*, the real beasts of burden are the women. In the foreground the women are leading ponies heavily burdened with large baskets of coal. The ponies carry only a single burden, but the women, in addition to helping the ponies, are also carrying latticed baskets on their heads. In the background men,

Julius Caesar Ibbetson, *Coal Staithe on the River Tawe*, 1792 (National Library of Wales). The painting seems to suggest that the real beasts of burden are the women of Wales. Whilst the men use machines to transport their burdens, the women not only have to look after the ponies, but also carry loads on their heads.

unencumbered with any additional burdens, use equipment to tip coal into the waiting ships. Ibbetson's portrayal of the power in the Welsh workforce is purely feminine.[72] This and similar evidence suggests that women were hard-working by nature, men by necessity. It is almost a truism of Victorian studies that 'separate spheres' existed for men and women. His was the dirty and dangerous world of work, hers the dainty and domesticated world of the home. The evidence provided in this study suggests that 'separate spheres' was just another Victorian ideal which had little basis in reality.[73]

The fact that they could not engage themselves in the political sphere, or that they were disadvantaged by law, should not blind us to the central place of women in Welsh society. To supplement meagre incomes, women took on a bewilderingly diverse range of employment. The celebrated *merched y gerddi* walked from the poverty-ravaged hills of Cardiganshire to harvest the fertile market gardens and orchards of England. Despite the dangers of cross-country travel, the girls' journey along the dew-splashed paths could be heard for miles around. Even in transit they sought to earn additional income. As they walked, they knitted stockings for sale in the markets which they passed on their way. The clackety-click, clackety-click of these double-stitchers set the rhythm for the journey.[74] Some women actively sought involvement in the traditional prerogatives and preserves of men. Jemima Nicholas and Elizabeth Davies (Betsy Cadwaladr) are just two ladies who distinguished themselves in times of war, traditionally regarded as a period of male posturing, bravado and machismo.[75] At the battle of the Nile in 1798, some of the most gut-wrenching tasks aboard Thomas Foley's ship *Goliath* were allocated to women and girls. It was they who undertook the dangerous and unpleasant work of helping the gunners and the gruesome task of assisting the surgeons. Years later, these brave women struck an early note for women's rights when they protested that they, unlike the men, had not been presented with campaign medals.[76] In 1795, when a French invasion seemed imminent, the women of Neath petitioned the Prime Minister for the right to form their own defence regiment. The seemingly unending wars against France would surely have ended sooner had the 'serious' *Amazones* of Neath been granted their request to receive light pikes and set free to defend their homelands.[77]

In order to pursue the history of the emotions and passions of the Welsh, this study utilizes a wide range of sources which reveal parts of the hidden world of the people. The major sources consulted include ballads, ceramics, diaries, folksongs, furniture, gravestones, hymns, letters, paintings, photographs, poems and songs. Each source, in its way, reveals a wealth of information on the personal lives of the Welsh people. Much of the poetry of the years 1776–1871 is regarded as execrable and overly sentimental. Yet this saccharine harvest helps us to understand the feelings and concerns of Welsh people. Despite the deprecation of cultural critics, the grief-obsessed poems of the graveyard school of Welsh poetry reveal that death was an unwelcome but constant companion to the Welsh people.[78] Death's arbitrary empire had a wealth of instruments with which to attack the under-nourished and overworked. Throughout the years 1776–1871, the first month of life was the most dangerous, the first year the hardest to survive. A person who survived the diseases which could debilitate or destroy and lived into his, but more usually her, sixties or seventies, was the exception. That journey into old age would have been a lonely voyage, along which the person would have lost family and friends. Quoting Oscar Wilde is often the refuge of the scoundrel or the unimaginative, but his touching and true comment, 'all bad poetry sprang from genuine feeling', is a useful reminder to cultural critics in their comfortable studies of the discomforts of Victorian life.[79]

Hymns are not often used as historical evidence. But pause to consider the words you are singing and hymns can open up a window revealing the highest joys and the deepest sadness which blessed and blighted people's lives. Welsh hymns reveal that religion was not simply the opiate of the people, but their poetry. The words of many Welsh hymns, these sublime works of literature, reveal a world in which fear and loneliness were powerful forces. The great hymn 'O! Fy Iesu Bendigedig' by Ebenezer Thomas, Eben Fardd, was written after the author lost two of his three daughters, his son, his nephew, his best friend and his wife, all within a painful few years of each other.[80] His hymn is eloquent testimony that hope is grief's best music. It is inter-esting to note that the hymns women wrote are in marked contrast to those written by men. Their style is more realistic and they have more regard for disappointment, pain and failure.[81] Indeed, in many of the archival sources, the historian is often struck by the fundamental differ-ences in the concerns of men and women. This reached even into deeper, spiritual matters. Men, especially in the early nineteenth century, tended to evoke a vengeful, psychotic God, who lashed the temporal world with strong winds, stinging rain and violent lightning, and promised unimaginable and unendurable tortures and terrors in an eternal hell. In contrast, women gossiped their daily woes of wayward children, wilful men and wanton neighbours to a gentler, more temperate God. This study will attempt to capture some of these differences.

The reader will quickly discern the heavy reliance of this work on contemporary newspapers and periodicals. These sources are fraught with difficulties and problems which are familiar to all historians. Even in our period, Welsh newspapers peddled scandal, crime, sex, sensationalism, hate, innuendo, and the political and financial uses of propaganda. Newspapers were also subject to bias, inaccurate reporting, prejudice and inefficiency. Their version of some events comes about as close to the truth as the Earth was to Neptune, the planet discovered in 1846 and excitedly reported in *Seren Gomer*. One of the most important skills for historians is to learn to read between the lies and the lines. Frustratingly, some historical events, which have acquired immense importance for posterity, receive no attention in the contemporary press. Historical study and hindsight have endowed certain events with significance, but in their day they were unremarked and uncelebrated. The Merthyr Rising of 1831, for example, merits little attention in many Welsh newspapers and magazines. Despite these enormous weaknesses, newspapers do enable the historian to capture something of the harsher reality of Wales in the period 1776–1871, and especially from 1804 onwards.[82] Comparison of stories in rival newspapers and magazines enables the historian to capture the complex, contradictory and conflicting nature of events. Careful and close reading of the newspapers over a period of time helps the historian to recapture the extraordinary capacity of the Welsh people to adapt themselves to massive changes of circumstances.

The documents and depositions of the Welsh courts are another vital source for the historian intent on plumbing the darker depths of Welsh society. In several of these tragic and terrible documents, the role of fear in ordinary lives comes powerfully to the fore. It is in the documents which police officers and officials of the petty, quarter and great sessions have left us that we come closest to the Welsh people alone in their nightmare hours. The personal testimonies contained in the court records, for example the 'true confession of the Clydach murderer' or the 'last dying speech and confession of Abel Ovans',[83] force the reader into a continuous reappraisal of the ambivalent nature of probity. Is a murderer necessarily evil? Can we believe his 'true confession'? Can a thief be honest? Can a brothel bully be believed? Does a drunkard deserve unredeemed derision? The personal histories

£100

REWARD

WHEREAS on the night of FRIDAY, the 27th of NOVEMBER instant, JOSEPH BUTLER, Keeper to the Right Honourable The Earl of Lisburne, was Shot dead by WILLIAM RICHARDS, of Cefncoch, in the Parish of Llangwryddon, in the County of Cardigan: the above Reward will be paid for the apprehension of the said William Richards.

The said William Richards is about 28 years of age, 5ft. 9in. or 10in. high, slight figure, long thin legs, with stooping gait, light hair slightly curled, thin sandy whiskers, long thin face, lower teeth overlapping upper teeth, long nose rather Roman, full grey eyes, speaks very little English; is supposed to be dressed in a dark home-made coarse coat, corduroy breeches and leggings, striped check shirt, and lace-up boots, clumsy feet, and has been operated upon for a bruise in the testicle.

All information to be addressed to the Superintendent of Police at Aberystwith.

Crosswood, 30th November, 1868.

J. COX, PRINTER AND STATIONER, PIER STREET, ABERYSTWITH.

Wanted poster for William Richards, Wil Cefn Coch, 1868. Some of the best descriptions of the Welsh people are to be found in the court and criminal records. In this case the final piece of information is probably more than one would need to identify the rustic rapscallion of a pre-orthodontic age.

of many simple people abound in several small acts of generosity and kindness, revealing that people who die drunk, in poverty and in squalor can still possess considerable moral fibre.[84]

The best descriptions of the physical characteristics of the Welsh people are provided in the documents of the criminal process. One fascinating example is the wanted poster for William Richards, Wil Cefn Coch, a rather ugly, 'Roman' nosed, 28-year-old, five foot nine or ten inch high, with 'long thin legs' farmer's son who murdered Joseph Butler, the earl of Lisburne's gamekeeper, in 1868. The poster gives a detailed description of this rustic rapscallion. Wil's physique and physiognomy is detailed down to the tiniest detail. We are even told that Wil 'has been operated upon for a bruise in the testicle' – obviously essential information for those who wished to apprehend him.[85] But the local people in Cardiganshire had no such intention. They harboured Wil for almost a year. On one occasion when the police arrived unannounced at a farm where Wil was being hidden, he was concealed in bed with his friend's pregnant wife. Victorian gentlemen to a man, social etiquette and protocol prohibited the police from searching this obvious hiding place. Wil eventually escaped to America, where he died in 1921. His escape to America was not unique. In 1840, the Revd Evan Thomas of Cricieth was shot and his unnamed but not unknown murderer also absconded to America.[86] The lives of these evil-working emigrants offers eloquent testimony that people's attitude to the law was complex and contradictory. Surely a moral, God-fearing land would yield, not shield, murderers?[87]

This type of evidence takes us into a darker corridor of history, not the history of famous people and great events, but that of the marginal and the ignored, the suppressed, the history of vice, of error, of confusion, of want, of intoxication, of vainglory, of delusion, of dissi-pation, of delirium and of violence. The mood that we encounter in the court documents is gloomy and pessimistic; patience is in short supply.[88] The documents reveal the cruelty of a society gone mad on its fringes: the foetuses floating in blood-soaked privies; babies scalded and scarred by cigarette burns; teenagers with vacant eyes and bleeding wrists; women with battered faces, pleading eyes and open stab wounds; the old, starved and tethered in their own excrement. All tragic victims of a savage and vicious world that existed throughout Wales. The pregnant woman who died after walking four miles to the midwife in a winter blizzard to seek help with her pregnancy, because her husband considered that there was 'no point tiring a horse for nothing', reveals how randomly, thoughtlessly and carelessly cruel this society could be. There are several picture-perfect, rose-covered, whitewashed cottages in Wales, whose every wall is stained with somebody's despair.[89]

The cruelty and violence inherent in Welsh society can be clearly seen in the popular disturbances which punctuate the years between 1776 and 1871. Historians have been exceptionally adroit in recapturing the crowds who took part in Welsh riots, revolts and risings.[90] Their work has established the poverty of the crowd, its pivotal role in the 'revolutionary' process and the level of political consciousness. The periods of greatest unrest are supposed to have been the era of the wars against France in the 1790s, the reform crisis of the 1830s, the Chartist rising in 1839 and the Rebecca riots of 1839–43. Thereafter, the history books concur with contemporaries; Wales, they say, entered a new era of peace and harmony which lasted until the 1880s.[91] Once the Chartists had filed away their Charter and Rebecca had hung up her dress, redress of public grievances though rioting is assumed to have ended. Careful examination of the court and newspaper archives across Wales challenges this view. In the 1850s and 1860s, Wales continued to be disturbed by outbreaks of unrestrained communal violence. One area that was exceptionally rowdy and riotous in the 1850s and 1860s was that forgotten area of Welsh history, the north-east.[92] During an industrial dispute in Mold in 1869, the Flintshire Yeomanry had to be supplemented with troops from Chester. As the tension intensified, the centre failed to hold, things rapidly fell apart, blood flowed. Four people were shot dead by the trigger-happy soldiers, two of them innocent women.[93] These are the tumultuous events in the background of the first great Welsh novel, Daniel Owen's *Rhys Lewis*, published in *Y Drysorfa* in instalments between 1882 and 1884. The *annus mirabilis* of Welsh politics, the 1868 election, occured against a background of mob violence.[94] One of the features which comes across strongly in the depositions and documents of the courts is the cruelty and brutality of these confrontations. Yet the historical narratives have been watered down and cruelty banished from their pages, horrific events have been covered up and some historians have almost engaged in a conspiracy with the men of the time to retain the good name of Welsh society in the mid-Victorian years. In our narrative we will attempt to confront cruelty as one of the underlying features of Welsh society.

The base cruelty of Welsh society is also shown by the large crowds which flocked to public hangings. Throughout Wales, thousands upon thousands gathered to watch infamous murderers drop to meet their maker. Even after 1868, when hanging ceased to be a public event, thousands of people still gathered outside Carmarthen, Caernarfon, Cardiff and Swansea jails and other places of execution to watch the lowering of a symbolic black flag. The largest crowd which gathered in nineteenth-century Wales came together not to pray, or to protest, or to perform. In 1858, over 25,000 people gathered quite early one morning on the sands in Swansea to watch two Greek sailors, Manoeli Selapatana, aged twenty-eight, and Panaotis Alepis, aged twenty-three, hang for the murder of another Greek, Atanasio Mitrepann, after a quarrel in Powell's Arms, High Street, one of the town's 'dancing houses'. Despite the ghastly and grisly nature of the event, the atmosphere on that chill March morning was carnivalesque. Food and drink were sold, enterprising people sold positions on wagons in order to enable people to see over the crowd, mothers held small children aloft to receive the ultimate visual lesson of why they should lead virtuous lives, ballad-mongers traded sensational songs specially and speedily written for the occasion, while pickpockets softly relieved the careless of their hard-earned money. As the corpses twitched and swung slowly side-by-side on the gibbets in a grotesque *danse macabre*, the crowd disappeared to work and dissipated to the pubs, content that justice had been seen to have been done in Swansea.[95] The only crowds in nineteenth-century Wales that come close to this number are the estimated 20,000–25,0000 who gathered in Brecon in 1845, to watch Thomas Thomas, 'a bold, bad man', hang and the 20,000 who assembled early one morning in Swansea to watch Robert Coe hang in 1866. 'The largest throng in Dolgellau's history' congregated on the morning of 17 April 1813 to watch Thomas Edwards, Yr Hwntw Mawr, die 'with an uncommon hardness'.[96] No political gathering, no religious revival, no cultural congress ever drew together as many people on a single day to a single place to watch a single event. Even the mass demonstrations in support of the Elementary Education Act, which took place in December 1870, failed to attract the mass of humanity who gathered inhumanely to watch men hang.[97] The size of these crowds requires Welsh historians to reassess the prominence given to political and religious issues as compared to popular preoccupations.[98]

It might be expected that a book that has a magpie's approach to sources should offer an explanation of the historical theory which supports and sustains it. Despite the fertility of structuralist and postmodernist approaches to historiography, this study resists the temptation to theorize, on the basis that a lack of knowledge of car mechanics does not prevent one from driving a car. How trouble-free the journey will be without a detailed explanation of the theoretical structure is for the reader to judge. Clearly this work is based on assumptions and theories of history. Those interested in such matters can themselves unravel the threads of theory from the tapestry. Without detailed theoretical explanations perhaps the story will be clearer to the reader.

Walter Benjamin wisely remarked that, 'nothing that has ever taken place should be lost to history', and he was even wiser not to attempt to turn his words into a work of total history.[99] Total history is an impossible task. The infinite variety of human activity cannot be compressed into a single volume, and no historian, however gifted and dedicated, can comprehend the complex totality of life. No one writing a general history can hope to attain the goal set at the outset. Traditional historians will undoubtedly and justifiably complain that subjects of immense importance to human society, such as politics, have been left at the fringes of this study. There is an obvious explanation. These topics have already received dedicated and detailed discussion in a number of seminal works. The subjects which are at the heart of this study were the emotions at the heart of the Welsh people. To study people's ambitions and anxieties, fears and phobias, loves and lusts, happiness and worries, joys and woes, their hopes and their heartbreaks, might enable future historians to penetrate the profound area of personal politics which is sadly often abandoned to the novelist or the biographer. The intention of this work is to provide a flavour of the infinite variety of life as it was experienced by the people of Wales between 1776 and 1871.

Part of the subtitle of this introduction is borrowed from that masterful chronicler of the Victorian age, G. M. Young, who once advised historians 'to go in reading until they can hear people talk'. As you will find in the following pages, much of the talk of the majority of the people of Wales in the years 1776–1871 was through the medium of Welsh. Accordingly quotations are given in their original language. To assist readers unfamiliar with the language contemporaries claimed was 'iaith y Nefoedd' (the language of Heaven), translations have been provided. Mindful of the fact that even skilled translators produce work which distorts and dislocates the nuances and subleties of the original, the author emphasizes that these translations are intended only as a guide. To hear the talk of the past, one needs to learn to read the original evidence.

1

The Reshaping of Everyday Life

Travellers' Tales

Someone, somewhere, some time towards the end of the eighteenth century, stated that 'Wales is a country in the world's arsehole'. Despite being so unfortunately located, Wales attracted many travellers in the late eighteenth century. Their impressions of, and reactions to, the country were written in books, journals and travelogues, sketched in drawings and etchings, and painted in oil and watercolour.[1] The tales these travellers told, and showed, provide historians with a bewildering body of evidence that Wales could, in equal measure, infuriate or inspire. Several authors vented their spleen on the savage barbarity of a 'poor, peripheral, peasant land'. When the self-regarding Lothario, Thomas Medwin, told friends in his London club that he was embarking on a fishing expedition to Wales, he was warned against the dangers of entering 'that *terra incognita* of goats and barbarians'.[2] In the 1790s, William Daniel and the flashily fashionable, umbrella-carrying Richard Ayton visited the south-western part of Llŷn. The local guide they engaged to steer them safely through this savage land warned them that they had entered 'a barbarous country' which Ayton referred to thereafter as 'ultima Thule'.[3]

Despite these supercilious voices, other travellers waxed lyrical on the beautiful vistas of Wales, insisting that England was east of Eden. The artist J. M. W. Turner confided in his diary in 1792: 'this combination of mountainous scenery is truly sublime and surpasses anything I have seen'. Wales inspired Turner's artistic and his less well-known and less talented poetic muse. In addition to his oils and watercolours of the 'striking emblem of solitude', Dolbadarn Castle, Turner offered a verse which encapsulates the sublime spirit of the north:

How awful is the silence of the waste,
Where nature lifts her mountains to the sky,
Majestic solitude, behold the tower,
Where hopeless Owen, long imprison'd pin'd,
And wrung his hands for liberty, in vain.

'Hopeless' Owen was the 'traitorous' Owen Goch, imprisoned for twenty years in Dolbadarn by his brother Llywelyn ap Gruffudd, the penultimate native prince of Wales.[4] Turner's sentiments were echoed twenty years later by the poet Percy Bysshe Shelley. In a letter to a friend he offered the following advice: 'steal, if possible, my revered friend one summer from the cold hurry of business, and come to Wales'.[5]

Rhapsodic or reprobative, travellers' tales often tell us as much about the travellers themselves as the land they traversed. Travellers came with firm ideas regarding what they would find in 'wild Wales'. They came in search of paradise, Arcadian and Edenic landscapes which had been unchanged for centuries. The basic rules of engagement had been firmly established in 1771 when the 'prince of north Wales', Sir Watkin Williams Wynn, spent the princely sum of £111. 7s. 6d. on the 'first Picturesque tour of Wales'.[6] Unable to visit continental Europe during the years of war against France, tourists and travellers poured into mid and north Wales and the Wye valley. So many artists arrived that contemporaries could be forgiven for feeling that they were living in a paintbox. The paintings generally portray landscapes that have only a few scattered people dotted about, inconsequential figures engaged in futile projects dwarfed by the immensities of nature. This was nature as culture. The only works of man worthy of note in these landscapes are the crumbling ruins of ancient abbeys and castles, from which the splendour had not only fallen but had long since departed. Ivy had reclaimed the walls for nature, and the corrosive and erosive effects of ice, rain and wind had given a more 'natural', irregular aspect to the walls. Dolbadarn Castle was a particular favourite of visitors and painters. In the late eighteenth century, views of the 'tragic citadel' were painted by John Glover, Moses Griffith, John Parker, Paul Sandby, J. M. W. Turner, William Turner and Richard Wilson.[7] Dolbadarn had a poignancy which appealed to the Picturesque, Romantic and Sublime movements principally because the human involvement was so ancient and epic.

The Welsh rapidly realized the economic value of their ancient history. In 1782, William Gilpin suggested that 'a mallet judiciously used' would render Tintern Abbey 'more delightfully irregular' and a greater attraction to visitors.[8] In the 1780s the enterprising David Pritchard, owner of the Royal Goat Inn, Beddgelert, erected a mound of stones near his hostelry. Here, he claimed, was buried Gelert, the fearless dog of Llywelyn ap Iorwerth. On returning home from a hunting trip, Llywelyn was greeted by his blood-stained dog. On finding his son's overturned cot and blood-strewn bedding, the impetuous and impatient Llywelyn, assuming that his dog had killed the infant, drew his sword and slew Gelert. The death pangs of the dying dog awoke the sleeping infant whom Llywelyn found unharmed underneath the bedclothes with the body of a wolf that had been killed by Gelert. In his remorse for his misdeed, the grieving Llywelyn allegedly erected the stones as a memorial to his best friend. The romance of the story drew droves of visitors, many of whom stayed in the storyteller's Royal Goat Inn.

When they were noticed at all, the people living amongst such natural splendour were depicted as 'noble savages', stoic creators of a static culture, frozen by immemorial primitivism, unchanged in an unchanging landscape. The Revd Richard Warner, during his tour of Wales in 1797, declared the Welsh 'Virgin descendants of the ancient Britons'.[9] In the same year Henry Wigstead declared that 'the people here are really almost in a state of simple nature'.[10] In the same decade, Samuel Jackson Pratt described the Welsh as 'a hardy and happy race of people rejoicing, like their country, in the simplest charms of nature'.[11] Others observed the Welsh in a different way. For every author who expressed envy of the Welsh for their natural accord and concord with nature, another described ignoble savages. Living alongside the elemental powers of nature, the Welsh were a base people, governed by the uncontrolled and uncivilized dictates of their emotions and passions. Part of this was fuelled by a genuine dislike of the Welsh, part of it was the wishful thinking of male travellers who viewed native women as suitable game for the sexual predator.[12]

In many of the books and paintings written and painted at the turn of the nineteenth century it is possible to detect an element of uncertainty. Several tours have as much an air of desperation about them as they do of discovery. It is as if the authors and painters believed that they were seeing the wonders of Wales for the last time. In many paintings artists appear to be fretting that paradise was being lost. The colours are often saturated with darker hues to create a sense of brooding. Threatening skies, broken trees, gathering storms and every

Paul Sandby, *View of the Copper Works at Neath*, 1779 (National Library of Wales). In the late eighteenth century industry was set in a bucolic setting in which nature dominates.

symbol of impending doom offered by the Welsh landscape characterize the paintings. The danger, which the painters were aware and fearful of, was that man's increasingly industrious activities threatened nature. As the nineteenth century progressed it became increasingly difficult to discover landscapes which were not dominated and scarred by man's labours. The first response of many painters was to portray industry within a rural perspective. Despite its subject matter, Paul Sandby's *View of the Copper Works at Neath* – a watercolour painted in 1779 – is positively bucolic. In the foreground, human figures tumble out of the picture across the frame. Amongst them a woman casts admiring glances at a man nimbly dancing a jig to a one-legged fiddler's tempo and tune. Although they are located in the centre of the picture, beneath billowing clouds of smoke, the copper works are set far away from the focus of attention, almost lost amid the rural vastness. The picture seems to suggest that this alien intrusive force into the natural environment will not conquer nature. Twenty years later, that certainty has been shattered.[13] In 1817, Thomas Hornor

Thomas Hornor, *The Tinplate Manufactory at Ynysygerwn*, *c*.1817 (National Library of Wales). Though the scene is almost the same as Sandby's, the certainty that nature would dominate industry has gone. The trees are depicted in dark forbidding hues, whilst the works bask under shafts of sunlight.

painted a similar watercolour of *The Tinplate Manufactory at Ynysygerwn*. The painting echoes the earlier watercolour, but the rustic figures have all departed. The danger to nature is shown in the fact that the trees and standing stones in the foreground are set in shadows, while the works bask under powerful shafts of bright sunlight beaming down from the heavens. Industry now, it seems, has divine sanction.

The search for the Picturesque, the Romantic and the Sublime became increasingly difficult in the nineteenth century. Yet this did not prevent many from undertaking the task. An interesting example of the difficulty of discovering unspoilt ancient landscapes is provided in *The Book of South Wales, the Wye and the Coast*, published by that devoted couple, Mr and Mrs S. C. Hall in 1861. In many respects they were a sad pair, born after their time, for the Romantic and Picturesque movements which they both adored had run their course long before they undertook their pilgrimage. Nevertheless the determinedly long-sighted Halls bravely sought beauty amongst the dirt and squalor of south Wales. Bridgend they tolerated, because it was 'on the way to scenery of a magnificent character, and to ancient castles, picturesque churches, and venerable abbeys'. They loathed

Neath, 'which is now a town of smoke, through which its rare and venerable antiquities are too often but dimly visible', and scuttled quickly on to Pont Nedd Fechan. Here 'the tour of the Vale properly commences amidst views of rare and surprising beauty – tree clad hills, looking down on the river, with vistas here and there, through rugged passes into charming glens'.[14]

The years between Sir Watkin Williams Wynn's profligate tour of 1771 and the Halls' presbyopic pilgrimage of the 1860s are regarded by some historians as an 'age of revolution'. Mr and Mrs Hall, during their peregrinations in search of the vestiges of the sublime, had to work hard to avoid the unpleasant effects of many of the revolutionary transformations which occurred in several aspects of Welsh life. It is important not to over-emphasize the pace of change, for the changes in the demographic, economic and social structure of Wales were as evolutionary as they were revolutionary. Changes took place over a period of years, not overnight. They were not sudden, unexpected or unheralded. A sensitive observer in the 1770s could draw attention to some prophetic factors – the development of industry, the growth in population in certain areas, improvements in transport, agricultural advances, enclosure of common land, technological advancements.

People and Places

The increase in the number of Welsh people is one of the most fundamental of the changes. In a sense the major purpose of this study is an attempt to explain this people problem and the problem people it generated. In 1780, it has been estimated that 530,000 people dug, dragged, scratched and scraped a living in Wales. By 1871, this figure had risen to 1,412,583. Each decade between these bookmark dates reveals an increase in Welsh population. The increase, as Table 1 shows, is gradual but inexorable.

Remarkably, in that dark decade of depression, distress and discontent, 1811–21, Wales experienced an increase in population of 17.93 per cent. Only that Klondike decade, 1901–11, experienced a higher decennial percentage increase. By 1801 Carmarthenshire and Glamorgan had the largest number of people, with 67,317 and 70,879 respectively, Radnorshire the fewest with 19,135. Already, the border county had more sheep than people. The census of 1871 revealed that

Table 1. Population growth, 1801–1861

1801	587,245
1811	673,340
1821	794,154
1831	904,400
1841	1,046,073
1851	1,163,139
1861	1,280,413

over half of the Welsh people lived in just three counties. Glamorgan outstripped all others with 397,859 people; Monmouthshire with 195,448 persons was the second most populous county, then came Carmarthenshire with 115,710 inhabitants. The phenomenal increase in Glamorgan's population meant that as many people lived within its borders as lived in seven rural counties combined.[15] Concealed within the general Welsh aggregate are the particularly distressing experiences of individual counties. Anglesey, Breconshire, Cardiganshire, Merionethshire, Montgomeryshire, Pembrokeshire and Radnorshire were in serious demographic decline. It is misleading to generalize on the basis of one example, but one county is indicative of wider trends. Montgomeryshire experienced its highest population in 1841, when 69,607 people lived in its rural vastness; thereafter, the county entered a period of continuous decline in population.

Historians have expended considerable effort in ascertaining the reason for the increase in population from the 1770s. Despite their ingenuity and inventiveness an adequate answer eludes. The explanation as to why the Welsh population increased is still lost in the intricacies of the mysterious interface between biology and behaviour. Some have drawn attention to the fact that from the late eighteenth century the annual number of births outnumbered the total of deaths; more people were cradled by the midwife than were carried by the undertaker. The reasons for the increase in the Welsh population are variously ascribed to the economic necessity of having a large family, improvements in agriculture, better diet, nutrition and sanitation.[16] Yet the timing of these developments varied enormously, and their effects were not always as great as has been implied. Even in the mid nineteenth century there were years of crisis, terror and disease – such as 1837, 1838, 1839 and 1840 – when deaths outnumbered births. The death rate continued to be exceptionally high throughout the nineteenth century. In every year from 1841, when we first have annual statistics for births and deaths, to 1871, the death rate was over 20 per 1,000 people. In the years when the Grim Reaper sent the terrors of cholera into Wales the rate increased dramatically to 25.8 in 1849, 23.9 in 1865 and 23.4 in 1866. Indeed, there was no significant decrease in the death rate until the 1880s.[17]

Ostensibly, ever since the first census was taken in 1801, the number of people resident in Wales increased decade on decade. But if we examine the situation in greater detail, the pattern is somewhat more complicated. For a population to increase it is obvious that more people need to be born than the number who die, but it is equally essential that a majority of the living reside within the county or national borders. The migration of people for adventure, freedom or work complicates the demographic profile. An examination of the relationship between the total change in population between each census, and the natural increase or decrease created by an excess or deficit of births over deaths, indicates the actual condition of a nation's population. The statistics gathered annually by the Registrar General from 1837 and decenially by the Census of Great Britain from 1801 enable us to calculate which counties were net winners or losers from the movement of people. Glamorgan is the only county that was consistently a net beneficiary from the movement of people. In 1841–51, the increase in Glamorgan was 35.44 per cent; between 1851 and 1861 the county witnessed an increase of 37.05 per cent in population and between 1861 and 1871 population expanded by 25.2 per cent. Despite the occasional increase elsewhere – in Anglesey in 1841–51 (+ 3.5 per cent), in Denbighshire in 1841–51 and 1851–61 (+ 1.69 and 0.38 per cent) and in Monmouthshire in 1841–51 (+ 6.36 per cent) – all other Welsh counties were net losers. The conclusion is inescapable. The vast majority of Welsh counties were exporting their most precious asset, their people. Many of these people undoubtedly went to Glamorgan and Denbighshire, for migration is often, initially, short-distance. This had important implications for the Welsh language. Without the ability of Glamorgan and, to a much lesser extent, Denbighshire, to attract Welsh migrants, the diaspora of Welsh speakers would have been much greater. Fewer Welsh speakers would have stayed in Wales. Extrapolated to an all-Welsh level, the figures reveal that, despite the phenomenal appeal and attractiveness of Glamorgan, Wales was exporting many of her people.[18] The numbers were never as great as those who were forced to flee the barbarities of the Highland Clearances in Scotland or the horrors of the Irish Famine, but the emigrants' experience is as vital an aspect of Welsh history as it was for their Celtic cousins.

The obvious answer as to why the Welsh population grew in some counties and not in others is that the introduction of industry and the exploitation of the mineral wealth of Wales favoured some counties more than others. It was the employment opportunities provided by industrial enterprises in Glamorgan, Monmouthshire and to a lesser extent Carmarthenshire that drew people to those counties like moths to bright lights. Within the county boundaries, the population history of individual parishes reflected this general ebb and flow. Again it is misleading to generalize on the basis of a few examples, but the contrasting demographic experiences of two neighbouring parishes are instructive. The population of Llanarth (Monmouthshire), a largely rural area, increased only gradually between 1801 and 1871, from 1,443 to 1,891. Tredegar's population in 1801 was only 1,132. By 1871, seduced by the siren calls of industry, 33,697 people were resident in the parish. Once more it is important to emphasize that the growth was not constant and consistent. Some decades experienced higher growth than others. Ten years is a long time in the life of a new community. Ten years, or even four or five, might be enough, in an uncertain economy, to witness both the rise and fall of a settlement. Caution should also be exercised to ensure that the predominance of industry in three counties does not distort the actual distribution of industry in Wales. The perception that industry was concentrated in and confined to three southern counties has affected the history of industry in Wales. In reality, industrial undertakings were widely distributed across Wales. Mr and Mrs Hall in the late 1850s managed to cross Wales from Monmouthshire, into Glamorgan and Carmarthenshire, to have their first serious confrontation with a coal mine at Saundersfoot, in Pembrokeshire. Parts of Cardiganshire, Caernarfonshire, Denbighshire, Flintshire and Montgomeryshire had significant concentrations of industry within their borders. The stereotypes of modern, progressive 'industrial' south Wales and medieval, regressive 'rural Wales' distort as much as they disclose. Indeed the first 'revolution' took place not in 'industrial Wales', wherever it was located, but in agriculture. Without the fundamental transformation in working the land which released resources from agriculture, it is debatable whether the much vaunted 'industrial revolution' would ever have taken place.[19]

Agricultural Advance

Agriculture was vital to Wales in two fundamental ways in the late eighteenth century. It enabled people to survive and provided the basis for future economic growth. Peasant men and women, toiling bent-backed, stunted in growth and so weatherbeaten that they looked like 'tawny Moors', are the mundane figures that people paintings and poems, yet the choice between economic stagnation or growth lay in their calloused hands. For industry to take off, many of the resources consumed by agriculture had to be freed. Labourers were required in the coal mines, ironworks, slate and stone quarries, and woollen factories, thus agriculture had to discover ways of producing enough food for an increasing population with fewer workers. Land had to be redeployed from agricultural activities to commercial, industrial, mining and transportation undertakings. Thus new land had to be enclosed from the commons and mountains, or reclaimed and drained from coastal tidelands. New husbandry techniques were utilized and innovations in equipment and implements introduced which constituted some of the most profound changes ever to take place in Welsh agriculture.[20] This transformation occurred between 1770 and 1871. The social costs in terms of the alienation, pain and suffering which these changes inflicted on Welsh people were extensive, but the extent of these changes was not uniform across Wales. Even in the mid nineteenth century, a run of bad harvests, such as in 1816, 1826, 1839 and 1842–3, could spell chaos and starvation for Welsh society. But these transformations laid the basis for a new capitalist-centred, market-oriented agriculture.

The transformation in ownership and use of Welsh land from the late eighteenth century was remarkable. In 1760 an Act had been introduced by Parliament to enclose large parts of the unenclosed lands north of Welshpool. This Act was followed by another five Acts by 1780 when the movement for enclosure really took off. By the 1840s, there had been over 120 Acts of Parliament relating to the enclosure of land in Wales. In one sense, the enclosure movement can be regarded as the restructuring of the Welsh agricultural economy, but in another it was a piece of blatant class legislation. In the 1840s, when he was engaged in surveying work in Llandrindod Wells, the unlikely class warrior, the naturalist Alfred Russel Wallace, expressed his disgust at the General Enclosure Act, which he described as 'obtaining land under false pretences – a legalised robbery of the poor for the aggrandisement of the rich, who are the law-makers'.[21]

In Wales, the beneficiaries of the enclosure Acts were the privileged. When 5,106 acres of Cors Fochno were enclosed in 1813, the major beneficiaries were Pryse Pryse of Gogerddan, lord of the manor of Genau'r Glyn and his near neighbour Matthew Davies of Cwmcynfelin.[22] The Acts to enclose the commons of Arwystli, Llanidloes and Caersws passed large tracts of land from public ownership into the possession of Sir Watkin Williams Wynn.[23] In 1843, an enclosure Act was passed relating to 935 acres of sheep walks around the small, but growing, village of Llandudno. The local lord of the manor, Edward Mostyn Lloyd Mostyn, received 832 acres.[24]

Land-lust was not confined to the gentry of Wales. Many poorer people coveted the common land of Wales. There was an erroneous, but widely held, belief in nineteenth-century Wales that if a person could build a cottage between sunset and sunrise on a single day, and have a fire lit in the hearth at dawn, then he or she could claim an acre of land surrounding the home. These were the so-called *tai unnos*, 'habitations of wretchedness and poverty' which appeared on the boundaries of the *ffriddoedd* – the upland grazing lands of Wales. In Cardiganshire in the 1830s and 1840s, such nocturnal erections appeared in increasing numbers in Ffair-rhos, Rhos Gelli-gron, Gors-neuadd, Blaencaron, Pentre-Richard, Clywedog, Cilcennin, Cellan, Mynydd Llanfair and Banc Siôn Cwilt. One visitor to the Brecon Beacons was so struck by these buildings that he considered 'it seemed as if an Irish estate had been transferred and filled in as a patchwork among the Welsh mountains'.[25] It appears that there was community approval for these popular incursions onto common land. In 1815, the parish vestry of Llanilar agreed to lend John Morgan of Rhosgron, Llangwyryfon, £8 to 'pay for the House of Rhosgron on wasteland'.[26]

But this reallocation and redistribution of land did not pass without protest. Across Wales walls and fences erected during the day to enclose common land were destroyed under the cover of darkness. On 4 September 1819 Elizabeth Parry wrote to her husband:

> . . . the lower class of people are inveterate against all the inclosure and pull down by night what is erected by day. Mr Powell, Nanteos, built on part allotted to him . . . the man who inhabited it received intimation that if he did not quit it they would burn it about his ears; they were as good as their word for during his absence they threw out all his furniture and burnt the house . . .[27]

Troops had to be called to Aberystwyth in 1812 to 'preserve the peace and to aid the civil power in dispersing the tumultuous assemblies of peasantry on the neighbouring hills, who are preventing the Commissioners under a certain Inclosure Act called "The Haminiog Act" from carrying their measures into execution'.[28] In the 1820s, the inhabitants of Mynydd Bach in Cardiganshire declared 'Rhyfel y Sais Bach' (the War of the Little Englishman) against Augustus Brackenbury, who had purchased enclosed local land.[29] Enclosure Acts were met with violent protests by local inhabitants determined to defend their time-honoured rights of grazing. The dispossessed fought openly to defend their hearths and homes from the insatiable land-greed of the gentry.[30] In response, the rich were subtle and surreptitious in their use of violence. William Edwards of Hindwell in Radnorshire testified to the Select Committee on Common Inclosure in 1844: 'I know men who have selected powerful men who were no sort of shepherds, but who were sent up the hill for the purpose of intimidation.'[31] But the most effective and brutal weapon was the gentry's ability to obtain parliamentary legislation to justify their usurpation of land. The legal and surveying costs incurred in this process were often paid from the sale of land which had recently been enclosed under the terms of the enclosure Act. Thus, the ferocious weapon of the law could be wielded at no personal financial cost to the gentry. Several Acts made it a condition that the inhabitants of smallholdings had to have been resident on their barren acres for over twenty years before they had a right of ownership. Even those who could claim this were unable to prove it at law and many were evicted from their humble homes. When the people protested, local militia, paid for from community rates, were called out to suppress popular riots.

The violence caused and created by this land war across Wales will be considered in greater depth later.[32] Some landlords, once they increased their acreage, set about maximizing the returns from their ill-gotten possessions. It is misleading to portray them as modernizers forcing a reluctant, backward-looking peasantry into modern agricultural practices. Not all landlords embraced the implications of the agricultural developments of the late eighteenth century. Many, like their peasants, continued to 'jog on the well-beaten path of their forefathers'.[33] Some never even trod those paths, for they were absentees who did not bother to visit the source of their income. Many made no improvement to the land they had acquired, letting it as rough pasture, or using it as game-coverts, until the land was needed for industrial development or railroad building, when a price equal to that of the best land in the district was often demanded and achieved.

However, several landlords did introduce modern agricultural practices into their estates, encouraged new methods of husbandry, rotated their crops to rest the land, and experimented with new breeds of cattle and sheep. Arthur Blainey of Gregynog forced his tenants to adopt a systematic rotation of crops when he let farms.[34] In 1814, in the *North Wales Gazette*, advertisements for farm bailiffs specified that applicants should be 'acquainted with the turnip and the green crop system'.[35] Richard Pennant, on succeeding through marriage to his Caernarfonshire estates in 1765, set about with gusto to improve agricultural conditions in one of the most backward counties. When he died over forty years later, it was claimed that he had been responsible for 'greater improvements than during several preceding centuries'.[36] The Erddig estate is often cited as an exemplar of good relations between landlord and tenant. In matters of agricultural improvement, however, the owner Philip Yorke was adamant that 'every field will be kept to the Culture I shall dictate'.[37] Others were less dictatorial, but agents and landowners throughout the nineteenth century exchanged letters carping about the unimaginative and medieval farming practices of their tenants.

Instead of complaining, some landlords offered incentives to persuade their tenants to improve their practices and stock. In 1837, Sir Charles Morgan gave prizes of £50 for the best fat cows under six years, three-year-old heifers and a number of other prizes for bovine beauties at his annual cattle show at Cwrt-y-Bella Farm at Newport.[38] In 1800, the remarkable Thomas Johnes of Hafod offered prizes to his tenants for growing high-quality crops, supported local agricultural and horticultural societies, and published *A Cardiganshire Landlord's Advice to his Tenants*. To ensure that his mostly monolingual Welsh tenants understood his blueprint for development, Johnes arranged a translation, *Cynghorion Priodor o Geredigion i Ddeiliaid ei Dyddynod*, by no less a wordsmith than William Owen Pughe. The advice was as much the result of Johnes's familiarity with the agricultural handbooks of ancient Rome as his passion for progress.[39] Indeed, one of the baffling things about European agriculture is why developments which had been known for centuries were not enacted until the early nineteenth century. From the late eighteenth century agricultural societies were founded all over Wales to exemplify and encourage good agricultural practice. Breconshire set the pattern in the 1750s, in part thanks to the efforts of the Methodist enthusiast Howell Harris.[40] By 1796, the improvement bug was contagious, especially in Flintshire and Denbighshire. Agricultural societies were founded in Wrexham and Montgomeryshire in 1796, and in 1807 Merionethshire, 'the most backward of all Welsh counties', established an agricultural society.[41] In 1806, inspired by the euphoria of improvement, the fifth baronet, Sir Watkin Williams Wynn, swept away the dilettantish fripperies of the fourth baronet, and converted the Wynnstay Theatre into a lecture hall for the agricultural society.[42]

Tenant farmers and smallholders are often portrayed by contemporaries and historians as frictive and restrictive forces in the agricultural development of Wales. The position of tenants and smallholders was unenviable, for their land, fertile of stones, fecund of thorns, was often unviable. Indeed, contrary to contemporary propaganda, tenants were not universally opposed to growing potatoes or turnips either for their own consumption or for market. Two powerful, insurmountable factors were firmly set against many Welsh farmers. Much of the land of Wales is over 500 feet above sea level, and across this the prevailing westerly winds blew, and blow, sheets of low, grey, rain-bearing clouds. In 1794, Robert Clutterbuck, on a visit to Aberglaslyn, noted in his journal, 'in the fever of heightened expectation we considered the rain, which continued to fall without intermission'.[43] Almost a century later, on 13 June 1871, Kilvert confided in his famous diary, 'the rain grew heavier'.[44] Both comments suggest that the rain had a permanence that would have been all too familiar to Welsh hill farmers. Much of their land was too high, too wet and too covered in rock for the growth of cereal or other cash crops. Many farmers practised a savage agriculture against a background of bald stone. All the collective wisdom of their oral tradition told them to continue with their time-tried and tested practices. But one fact, which is often overlooked in Welsh agricultural history, is that the increase in the number of tenancies and smallholdings in the early nineteenth century led to an intensification in farming and an increase in production. However inefficiently, Welsh agriculture reared more animals and grew greater quantities and varieties of crops in the early nineteenth century than it had done forty years previously.

The prize offered by the Glamorgan Agricultural Society for improvements to the threshing machine indicates that the Welsh were an inventive and industrious people. Between 1776 and 1871 there was a substantial increase in the use of technology in Welsh agriculture. In the 1770s, ploughmen trudged ponderously behind cumbersome oxen dragging heavy wooden ploughs. Some observers described the process as 'ripping rather than opening the earth'.[45] On a good day, when their songs of lamentation accelerated the oxen's tempo, they could cover almost half an acre. Charles Hassall described the effect of such ploughing techniques in Pembrokeshire in 1794: 'It seemed as if a drove of swine had been roiling the fields.' By the 1830s ploughboys followed horses drawing iron ploughs which corrugated the land swiftly into uniform strips.[46]

In 1830, an all-iron zigzag harrow was patented by a Welsh farmer. From 1756, Andrew Meikel's threshing drum became increasingly common on Welsh farms. In 1803, the 'father of the iron industry', the hyperactive John Wilkinson, became the first person to use a machine to thresh corn at his agricultural estate, Brymbo Hall.[47] Easing the burden on men's muscles, many of these machines were driven by water or horse power. Many farms used the *blwch nithio*, a wooden winnowing box, to separate the grain from the straw. One Presbyterian minister warned against the 'wickedness of the farmer who produces wind for his own particular use instead of waiting till it pleased the Lord to send one', but these machines were common on a number of farms. In the 1780s, a Pembrokeshire farmer invented a hand-cranked mill to grind gorse for horse feed. The invention resembled a medieval instrument of torture, but it was highly effective and widely used. It was also exported to Ireland. In 1815, in Breconshire, Walter Davies noted the preponderance of a particular type of wheeled cart 'convenient to carry grain to market or mill or . . . for harvest work', which had replaced the juddering *cart llusg* (drag cart). He added: 'we have seen it used as a sociable covered with tarpaulin and chairs placed inside it by a farmer conveying his family to town in rainy weather'.[48]

This ingenuity within agricultural communities is clearly shown in the vast range of tools and equipment created for local conditions.[49] In the 1780s, hoes, shovels, axes, rakes and scythes were heavy, cumbersome tools which might have been used in anger by Llywelyn ap Gruffudd's clanking knights. By the mid nineteenth century, it was clear that a new notion had dawned. Tools could save and lighten labour. Many tools were refined by farmers and local blacksmiths into highly effective and efficient equipment. The 'Aberaeron shovel' and billhook, designed for the particular needs of a hilly country, brought national acclaim and fortune to the local forge and the shovel factory established in 1850.[50] At the start of our period, farmers often paid the blacksmith in farm produce, but from the 1820s most transactions were in cash, revealing that the growth of banking in Wales and an increase in agricultural activity had boosted the flow of cash throughout Wales.[51]

One of the undoubted stimulants to agricultural change was the realization amongst farmers of the certainty of demand for the produce of their fields. Despite periods of agonizing depression, as after the Napoleonic Wars between 1815 and 1820, or the widespread depression in 1839 and 1842–3, farmers became increasingly aware of the potential of the markets of Wales. By the early nineteenth century, depending on their location and the quality of their land, Welsh farms were already commercial in their orientation. Around many Welsh towns, such as Carmarthen, Denbigh, Merthyr Tydfil, Swansea, Newport and Wrexham, the nature of farming was transformed to meet the initial requirements of town dwellers. By 1836, Lord Bute's unromantically named farm, Dobbin Pitts, fertilized by night soil, provided Cardiff and Merthyr Tydfil with much of their fresh vegetables.[52] From the Vale of Glamorgan and the Tywi valley, milk was quickly carried to local towns. Despite competition from Bristol, many workers in south Wales had a strong preference for the salted butter and cheese of Carmarthenshire. Animals in these towns were just as hungry as the people. Much to the annoyance of estate agents, pasture land around Merthyr Tydfil was depleted to feed the town's insatiable hunger for hay. By 1842, over 8,000 tons of hay were being sent to the iron town annually.[53] Elsewhere farmers continued to breed stock for sale in Welsh and English markets. The reason that the 'bachgen bach o Felin-y-wig, welodd e rioe'd tamed o gig' (little boy from Melin-y-wig, he never saw a piece of meat) was that the bulk of it was hoofed into England and Welsh towns. Much of the 'roast beef of Old England', the defining symbol of Englishness, had plodded a long, weary road from Wales. Anglesey was famous for the mooing herds of cattle, bleating flocks of sheep, grunting sounders of pigs and cackling gaggles of geese which regularly left the island for the markets of Denbigh, Rhuthun, Wrexham and further afield to England. When the Menai Bridge opened in 1825, amongst the major users of the new wonder of Wales were the animals of Anglesey.[54]

The drovers who drove this capital on the hoof were essential links between Welsh communities and the outside world. Very often their English was more a feat of memory than understanding, but they were important conduits for ideas, news and money to pass into rural areas.[55] One of their major services was financial. The drovers were amongst the few people who were accustomed to the use of paper money. In 1797, following a financial crisis caused by the wars against France, the Bank of England suspended the redemption of its notes. This created an incentive for the establishment of local banks across Wales. It was commonly believed that some of these fledgling financial houses were founded by drovers. But only a very few left the dusty roads for a musty office in a bank, where they kept track of other people's money in laborious copperplate.[56] One bank founded by drovers which survived the financial crisis of the 1820s was Banc y Ddafad Ddu (The Black Sheep Bank) in Aberystwyth. Animal dealers, however, had the resources to capitalize on the financial opportunity of 1797. In 1799, David Jones, a cattle dealer with the wisdom or good fortune to marry a wealthy heiress, established Bank yr Eidion Du (The Black Ox Bank) in the King's Head public house at Llandovery. Despite, or perhaps because, of its location, the bank prospered and also survived the crisis of 1825 when several Welsh banks collapsed, plunging people into panic. David Jones became a justice of the peace and high sheriff of Carmarthenshire and the owner of several substantial properties in the county. He had come a long way from his roving, droving, cattle-dealing days.[57]

Traditional Trades

Agriculture not only gave a livelihood to farmers and their workers, it also provided succour and support to a diverse range of crafts, trades and industries. The fortunes of villages and towns such as Brecon, Denbigh, Dolgellau, Llanybydder, Llandovery, Rhuthun and Narberth flourished or floundered according to the condition of their agricultural hinterlands. When the harsh winds of economic decline and depression blew through Welsh agriculture, the cold draughts were felt in many towns. Dr Johnson had considered Denbigh 'no mean town' in the late eighteenth century. By 1839 it was the centre for shoe-making, tailoring, cloth manufacturing (flannel, yarn, linsey-woolsey, plaids, tweeds), weaving, tanning, skin dyeing, candlemaking, flax dressing, turning and ropemaking. It also had wool and cloth factories and a corn mill at King's Mills, run by the patriotic Mr Edward Jones and later by his redoubtable widow.[58] Much of the industrial fabric of Anglesey was dependent upon agriculture. Tanneries were dependent on local farms for the supply of animal skins, but they in turn sustained several craftsmen – bootmakers, clogmakers and

saddlers – on the island. Cereal cultivation had assumed more importance in Anglesey than elsewhere in Wales, and corn mills, driven by
wind and water, were widely distributed over the surface of the county.
The sheep population of Anglesey provided the raw material for
domestic spinners and weavers and a large number of woollen mills
were established on the banks of the island's rivers.[59] Thomas Pennant,
the most perceptive traveller in eighteenth-century Wales, noted at
Llanfyllin the essential link between agriculture and industrial
manufacture: 'The abundance of sheep, which enliven the hills,
brought at the time I visited the country great wealth into it. The
flannel manufacture and that of the coarse cloth for the army, and for
the covering of the poor Negroes in the West Indies, is manufactured
in most parts.'[60]

One of the few industries in Wales, in the sense of taking a raw
material (wool) and transforming it through a manufacturing process
into another material (cloth), was the woollen industry that flourished
in mid and west Wales around Newtown and Welshpool and in the
Teifi valley. In the 1830s and 1840s, the production of wool in these
centres began to switch from a cottage-based industry to a factory
structure. Bontdolgadfan, Montgomeryshire, became a busy and
thriving centre of weaving factories. At Dolgellau fifteen fulling mills
were humming busily in the 1840s.[61]

Agriculture and industry, rural and urban communities, were not
the polarized opposites which many historians portray. They were not
separate and unrelated, but rather were connected and interrelated by
a wide range of activities. The interrelationships were clearly seen in
the fairs and markets of Wales. These were occasions when the civility
of the civic merged with the rumbustiousness of the rustic. In 1847, the
country artist Hugh Hughes painted *The Llanidloes Pig Fair* which
depicted a chaotic scene of bucolic business. Awkward, dung-stained,
heavily coated figures from the verses of Ceiriog have taken over the
town. In the centre of the town pigs lie prostrate, the mothers suckle
their young, whilst burly ham-fisted farmers strike deals with local
butchers. In the background, genteel ladies, all ribbons and silks and
Paris fashions, gently navigate a path between the porkers and their
excretions.[62]

In the 1870s, the American consul in Wales, Wirt Sikes, visited
several Welsh fairs and markets and remarked on the animation of the
events. The Carmarthen fair, he reported, began at dawn.[63] The pubs
and hotels opened early, for drinking was part of a ritual which eased

Hugh Hughes, *The Llanidloes Pig Fair* (Sothebys). The painting shows how the town was taken over by dung-coated figures from the verses of Ceiriog. Observe the lady, all frills and Paris fashion, trying to glide her way through the sprawling porcines.

the hundreds of little deals that were being sealed. Some farmers drank quickly so that they could proceed to their next meeting with the drovers. In one pub, Sikes noticed a man with a rope in his hand and at the end of it a cow drooling trails of spittle nearly inside the premises. In Carmarthen, he noticed that the people were conversing in the loveliest Welsh, at Llandaff more English was heard. Unsurprisingly, when these events finished villages and towns were filthy. Travellers and local carters had the unenvied, and often incompleted, task of clearing the dung, blood and guts from the butchers' yards, the human waste from the privies and the drunks from their cosy gutters. A notable feature of many localities were the hiring fairs for humans to which landless men and unmarried girls flocked in the hope of securing a better workplace. The master would feel the biceps of the young labourers, as cotton planters used to do with black boys and girls in the slave markets in Georgia. It particularly upset Sikes that children were given to the highest bidder, rather than the best master. The large hiring fair at Llanbadarn Fawr was sensationally described as a 'flesh market' by one sensitive observer in the 1770s.[64] At Pwllheli in May 1834 and May 1836, the hiring fairs, as opposed to the cattle markets, were deemed considerable successes.[65]

The chaos of the fairs is the feature which immediately strikes the superficial observer, but this is deceptive. The fairs and markets of Wales were not simply occasions for bucolic Bacchanalia. They were highly organized, essential and effective components in the transform-ation of Welsh agriculture. Here farmers obtained the inputs of labour and capital which were required by new agricultural techniques; they sold their produce profitably, and they bought goods which they no longer produced themselves. In different places at different times in nineteenth-century Wales, farmers realized that it was a more profitable use of their time and energies to purchase, rather than produce, certain products. Increasing numbers of Welsh farmers were farming intensively, rather than for subsistence. They began to use their time in a more 'industrious' way. Farmers devoted less time to producing things for household production and more to producing materials to sell at markets to earn income.

Industry and Industriousness

Increased industriousness is a marked feature of the years after 1780. These are the years to which the title 'industrial revolution' has been applied. Historians have expended considerable time and energy studying this phenomenon in Britain and Europe, so much so that the study of the industrial revolution is a veritable industry in itself. Despite this, an adequate explanation of this 'rather unhappy conjunction of adjective and noun' is still difficult.[66] It was not a unitary, progressive, integrated phenomenon. Several fortuitous circumstances coincided in Britain to trigger a take-off into industrial growth. The 'agricultural revolution' and an advanced financial system provided cheaper and easier sources of capital, while increasing agricultural productivity and mechanization released labour from the land. Farmers who profited from the changes in agriculture and the development of industry provided ready and willing consumers for the products of industries. A transformation in commerce and trade created better and more effective markets; novel and swifter transportation eased and speeded the flow of goods to consumers and also lowered prices. Together, these and a myriad other changes altered the consumer and commercial attitudes of people and gave an incentive to the spread of industry across Wales.[67] Consumers effectively had three choices in late eighteenth-century Wales. They could produce goods at home, support their local craftsmen or buy the products of new 'proto-industries', like the factories of Bontdolgadfan. With characteristic sarcasm, many characters in the *anterliwtiau* of Twm o'r Nant condemned the proclivity of the richer Welsh to purchase the latest consumer products from these 'fancy' new undertakings. Some historians have detected a quickening in the tempo of 'proto-industrial' activity as one of the causes of the 'industrial revolution'. In the Welsh context, despite the heroic labours of a number of historians in ploughing through vast fields of data provided by bills of fare, inventories and ledgers, it is still difficult to support this contention. In the late eighteenth and early nineteenth centuries, for a variety of reasons, there emerged in Wales an industrious, industrial nation.[68]

It is important not to over-emphasize the novelty of this development. Industry was not a totally new intrusion into Wales. Since Roman times the mineral wealth of Wales had been exploited by the Welsh and their conquerors. But from the 1770s the geological resources of Wales were exploited in a totally unprecedented fashion. Some of the most spectacular instances took place in the north. On a visit to Mynydd Parys in Anglesey, Thomas Pennant noted that: 'Nature has been profuse in bestowing her mineral favours on this spot'.[69] Others were also quick to realize the value of the copper and lead ore in the area.[70] Thomas Williams, a local solicitor, took charge of the company which had commenced mining operations and rapidly established a conglomeration of industrial enterprises.[71] These included smelting works in Denbigh, Flintshire, Liverpool and Swansea, as well as the mines of Mynydd Parys. The major demand for Anglesey copper came from the navy's need to provide a protective covering sheath for its 'men-o'-war'. As wars with America and France broke out from the 1770s this demand intensified. Desperate to find a scapegoat for its naval losses in the American War, the naval establishment blamed defective copper bolts used in its ships. To protect his industry, Thomas Williams perfected at Holywell bolts and nails which were above suspicion and impervious to the depredations of the teredo worm that had a devastating effect on ships' timbers. By 1785 his works were supplying bolts, nails, sheathing and copper-bands not just to the

Admiralty but also to the navies of France, Holland and Spain. At the height of the company's activities between 1790 and 1805, over 1,200 men, women and children were employed in raising copper ore from the cold, wet bowels of the earth. The metallic sound of the men's labours was often drowned by the thunderous discharge of gunpowder. During those years over 15,000 tons of gunpowder was fired annually, creating a stupendous gulch whose once ore-rich sides are today a riot of saffron.

In the 1770s, the Parys works became a frequent venue for artists on their tours through Wales. John Warwick Smith, Julius Caesar Ibbetson, William Havell and François Louis Thomas Francia all painted ground-level views to capture the immensity of the undertaking. After the death of Thomas Williams in 1802, the copper industry in Anglesey experienced alternating cycles of savage depression and partial revival until the works were abandoned around 1844. The real centre of the industry by that year was Swansea where nearly half of the copper smelting works in Great Britain were located. 1860 was the peak year for copper production in 'Copperopolis', when the town was obscured by the sulphurous smoke coughed out by over 600 chimneys.[72]

An even greater cavern was gouged at the Penrhyn slate quarry. Work commenced in 1762, when Richard Pennant leased the mineral rights of his land at Cae-braich-y-cafn to a number of quarrymen who dragged 1,000 tons of slate a year on back-breaking primitive drag-carts down to Bangor. In 1782, Pennant decided to involve himself more directly with the work and bought out the leases on the land and began investing. When he seized the initiative his estate had only four wheeled carts. Ten years later, the bridle paths leading from the quarry had been turned into roads and over a hundred carts were regularly employed in carrying slates down to the quay which the newly ennobled Lord Penrhyn had enlarged and immodestly named after himself. From there, the slate was exported to Ireland, to Flanders and to Pennant's estates in the West Indies. The immensity of this undertaking can perhaps be best seen in *The Penrhyn Quarry in 1832*, a painting by the English artist Henry Hawkins.[73] The painting is a paean of praise to the power of man. The whole scene is animated with fervent activity. In the foreground, men use iron rods to prise slabs of slate from the rock, while others dangle precariously from perpendicular crags. The only static figures are those of the genteelly dressed managerial classes who are giving instructions to the workers. Above the human ant-heap seagulls

Henry Hawkins, *The Penrhyn Quarry in 1832* (National Trust Photographic Library). A paean of praise to the power of mankind.

soar, their raucous cries echoing away into the immense vastness of the far distance. In 1832, on her only visit to Wales, Princess Victoria visited to see this wondrous Celtic Xanadu for herself. The total production of the neighbouring quarries at Blaenau Ffestiniog was 12,211 tons in 1832. By 1878, output had reached 119,279 tons. With increased demand for Welsh slate from England, Ireland and Wales, quarries were founded throughout the north – Rhosydd in 1833, Bugail and Bwlch in 1835, Graig-ddu in 1840, Drumin and Glan-y-pwll in 1840, Croesor and Foel-y-gron in 1846, Groesddwyafon in 1861, Pantmawr in 1865 and Cnicht in 1875.[74]

By 1850, the determination of the captains of industry to realize the mineral riches of Wales had created industrial enterprises in some of the most unlikely places. In the hills of mid and north Wales, where previously only buzzards had ventured, communities of workers were extracting copper, gold, iron, lead, slate, stone and zinc. In 1853–4, the hills around Dolgellau experienced a veritable 'gold rush' and by 1860 Gwynfynydd, Clogau and Glasdir were producing over 1,000 ounces of gold a year.[75] From Dylife in the Montgomery hills, over 1,000 tons of lead ore was carried down the heartbreakingly named Rhiw Saith Milltir (the seven mile hill) to Derwen-las and thence to the sea. This unlikely enterprise was owned by two local women, Jane Williams of Gellu Goch and Elizabeth Pughe of Aberdovey. In 1858, they sold their enterprise to the social reformer and radical Richard Cobden.[76]

In the 1750s, Lewis Morris had remarked that Cardiganshire was 'the richest country I ever knew'.[77] He based his judgement on the lead mining which scarred the hillsides east of Aberystwyth. The exploitation of this mineral wealth reached its zenith in the late 1840s when seventy-three companies were officially listed as working. Many others were unregulated and unregistered, engaging smaller groups of men who worked on tribute; the 'owners' often disappeared when the authorities sought them. The Lisburne mines achieved a profit of £7,378 in 1848 and were valued on the London stock market at £45,000, with the shares valued at £600 each. In 1850, the *Mining Journal* reported that at no time over the previous hundred years had the Cardiganshire mines been so prosperous.[78] At Rhandirmwyn in Carmarthenshire, 400 men mined lead in the hauntingly beautiful hill country. The owners, the Campbells of Golden Grove, amassed profits of over £300,000 over a sixty-year period. Throughout Wales the hills were alive to the sound of metal.[79]

Two industries – iron manufacturing and coal mining – dominated this cacophony which awoke the Welsh economy. Neither was a new phenomenon. They were both a cause and consequence of each other's existence and evolution. In the 1750s, much iron manufacture continued to operate on a scale which would have been familiar to the Lords Marcher. Small furnaces and forges were dotted across the length and breadth of Wales, at places where the confluence of energy, iron and power coincided. Near the mouth of the Mawddach estuary, a spectacularly located forge produced iron goods through harnessing water power. At Mathrafal in Montgomeryshire, Dolgain in Merionethshire and at Chirk, forges employed twenty men to produce a leisurely twenty tons of iron a week to meet local demand. From the 1750s, however, there was a transformation in the fortunes of iron manufacturing in Wales as larger, more intensive, integrated works were established in a flurry of speculation which had not been seen since the days of the South Sea Bubble. In 1753, the Bersham works was established in Denbighshire. This was the model which others quickly adopted or adapted. In 1757 a new ironworks was established at Hirwaun, quickly followed by others at Cyfarthfa in 1765, Sirhowy in 1778, Penydarren in 1784, Plymouth (Merthyr Tydfil) in 1788, Blaenavon and Ebbw Vale in 1789, Nant-y-glo in 1791, Tredegar,

Hugh Hughes, Frontispiece *Y Cymro*, 1830 (Hugh Owen Library, The University of Wales, Aberystwyth). The wonders of the modern world (steam ship, balloon, iron plough, factory, globe) are set within ancient traditions and values (castle, cromlech, countryside). The explanatory notes promise that the new paper would also reflect the needs and interests of the new society of emerging from the old.

Aberdare and Union in 1800, and Aber-nant in 1802. In 1788, a mere 12,500 tons of pig iron were cast in south Wales. By 1796, production reached 34,000 tons and in 1805 78,000 tons. By 1794, over 400 men, women and children were employed in the Dowlais works alone. According to one estimate in 1802, the larger Penydarren works gave employment to over 900, while Richard Crawshay's Cyfarthfa works was larger still, being the largest ironworks in Britain by the mid-1790s. The works appeared brazen in their disdain for the ordinary limits of human enterprise.[80] To these 'forges of Vulcan' trudged rootless armies of landless labourers from Carmarthenshire, Pembrokeshire, Cardiganshire, Breconshire and the west of England, thereby swelling the population of Merthyr Tydfil from 7,700 in 1801, to 11,100 in 1811 and 17,400 in 1827.[81] For a people well-versed in the scriptures, only one metaphor could describe this place 'of fires tended by blackened demons', 'it was a vision of hell'.

The stimulus for the explosive expansion of the Welsh iron industry was the insatiable demand for weapons of mass destruction created by the uncertain international situation of the late eighteenth century. When the dogs of war were unleashed, the order books of Bersham, Dowlais and Cyfarthfa multiplied. During the Seven Years War, John Wilkinson at Bersham made substantial profits from the sale of cannon. Following the war, he avoided a depression through reorganizing his works. Bersham was reconstructed and restructured between 1764 and 1768 so that cannon, grenades and shells of 4-inch calibre could be turned out in vastly increased numbers. When war broke out between the Russians and the Turks in 1768, he was ready to supply both sides with armaments. By the time war commenced with the Americans, he had taken out his patent for boring cannon, and zealously guarded it against interlopers.[82] It is uncertain whether even Wilkinson was foolhardy enough to supply armaments directly to Britain's enemies in the 1770s and 1790s. What is certain is that he set up works in other countries. When Arthur Young visited France in 1783, he found two such factories owned by 'Monsieur Wielkainsong' and the workers told him that the English ironmaster, who was brother-in-law to Dr Priestley, 'and therefore a friend of mankind', had 'taught them to bore cannon in order to give liberty to America'.[83] In 1777, Anthony Bacon and Richard Crawshay combined in partnership to supply cannon to the East India Company and to the Board of Ordinance. They rapidly acquired an international reputation as arms dealers and munitions suppliers. The Revolutionary and Napoleonic Wars proved an even greater bonanza for the producers of iron, dwarfing all previous struggles in their scope and intensity.[84]

Iron was not only used in anger; it was the wondrous fabric of the modern age. Its use in the production of bridges, rails and steam engines provided a steady demand for iron which helped to offset the dislocating effects of the outbreak of peace in 1815 on the industry. For twenty years, all but three or four of the engines supplied by Boulton and Watt had their cylinders made at Wilkinson's works.[85] Froncysyllte, 'the stream in the sky', a trough 1,020 feet long, 130 feet high, made of Welsh iron and supported by nineteen piers, was hailed by Sir Walter Scott as 'the finest work of art I have ever seen'.[86] Telford's superb suspension bridges at Conwy (1826) and Menai Bridge (1819–26) were other wonders of the iron age in Wales. A less dramatic but more consistent and persistent demand for iron came from the casting of domestic utensils and agricultural equipment. By the 1840s, many of the iron companies had become gigantic commercial enterprises. Their owners and shareholders had diversified into several interrelated industrial enterprises. Cwmavon Works was a typical example. In 1849, the colossal conglomeration included ironworks, copper works, chemical works, collieries, brickworks, workshops, lime and ore quarries and offered stabling for over 300 horses.[87]

The fires of the forges and furnaces were fired by coal which was mined in the vicinity of the ironworks. In the north-east the seams of coal were thinner, buried deeper and more fractured by faults than those of the south. Nevertheless, local ironmasters were swift to exploit coal reserves. In Ruabon and Chirk, William Hazeldine and Thomas Jones had both acquired collieries near to their ironworks by the time of the battle of Waterloo, while the unfortunate Edward Lloyd Rowland had sunk nearly thirty pits before he went bankrupt in 1823. John Wilkinson was even more enterprising. By 1829, there were forty-one pits on his Brymbo Hall estate, using up-to-date machinery to pump water from and air into the depths. In 1796, Thomas Pennant found the condition of the Deeside collieries 'the most flourishing I ever remember'.[88] In the south-east a similar relationship existed between coal and iron.[89] Although Crawshay considered that coal was a business 'fitted for lesser men', all the iron companies established collieries.[90] By 1840, the coal measures of Glamorgan were exploited more fully and extensively than they had been a century earlier.[91] The numbers, including labourers, employed in coal mines, according to the 1841 census, were 7,696 and no doubt some of the 3,465 miners 'branch not specified' and 6,945 'labourers' were also engaged in the coal industry. Those workers barehandedly raised over a million tons for the iron industry, 250,000 tons for the copper industry, 200,000 for other industries and household consumers, and 650,000 for export. These were the years of the birth of 'King Coal', who imperiously reigned over the Welsh economy from the late 1870s. But carboniferous capitalism had already extended its hold, and people marvelled at the magic and wonder of coal which provided heat, light and power in unprecedented abundance.

From the 1820s, the demand for coal also increased in other activities. In Flintshire, the Buckley potteries utilized the 'apparently inexhaustible' supplies of fireclay found in the local coal measures. Both potters and colliers flocked into the area from Staffordshire – 'many of them', complained the folk of Hawarden, 'hackneyed in vicious habits'. In Denbighshire, fireclay from the coal mines provided the raw material for the coarse earthenware produced at Cefn-mawr near Ruabon, and the bricks made at Llwyn Einion by the workers of the ironmaster Thomas Johnes.[92] In Carmarthenshire and Glamorgan, local supplies of fireclay and a plentiful supply of coal led to the establishment of potteries in Llanelli and Swansea, whose plates adorned the homes of the fashionable.[93] Agriculture also had its share in the development of coal mining. In order to improve the fertility of their land, farmers used increasing quantities of lime. It was a constant complaint of Thomas Johnes of Hafod, Cardiganshire, that he could not obtain limestone locally so that it had to be expensively carted over long distances to his Hafod estate. To fire the limestone he needed coal. Agriculture also benefited coal mining because the enclosure movement diminished the area from which people could take peat and brushwood, and so hastened the adoption of coal as a domestic fuel. In Anglesey the draining of the Malltraeth marsh prompted a vigorous but vain attempt to mine the coal seams lying beneath it. The venture's failure meant that the island had to depend on coastal imports of coal.[94]

Technological advances created an even greater demand for coal. The increasing use of steam engines in manufacturing produced a significant increase in the market for Welsh coal. In the 1820s, the perceptive could sense change in the air, as steam shipping started its slow conquest of sail. Steam packets such as the *Glamorgan* and the *Bristol*, which began a service in 1823 between the county and the city which gave the steamships their name, were a portent of this. On 30 August 1836, the *North Wales Chronicle* reported that 'the enterprising tradesmen of this spirited district have embarked considerable capital in building an elegant and powerful steamer' to trade between Conwy and Liverpool. The launch was a 'gala day' marked by 'civilised celebrations'.[95] In the 1830s, the East India Company sought supplies of coal for its steamers and the Admiralty established a network of coaling stations from Barbados to the Bay of Bengal. Both used high-quality Welsh coal.

The Character of Capitalism

The profound changes which transformed the Welsh economy and society after the 1780s did not escape the attention of contemporaries. Observers poured into Wales to ponder the effectiveness of feral capitalism.[96] To contemporaries, the sorcerers who wielded the protean powers which transfigured the economic structure of Wales from the semi-subsistence of the eighteenth century into a modern, capitalist economy had certain unquestioned characteristics. They were English, but, above all, they were male. It is unfortunate that the views of some misinformed visitors continue to distort our understanding of the operation of capitalism in Wales. The infamous comments of the *Report of the Commission of Inquiry into the State of Education in Wales*, the despised and derided 'Brad y Llyfrau Gleision' (The Treason of the Blue Books) have influenced the subsequent interpretation of nineteenth-century Wales. Lingen, in his caustic forty-two-page report on Carmarthenshire, Glamorgan and Pembrokeshire, offered the following observation:

> My district exhibits the phenomenon of a peculiar language isolating the masses from the upper portion of society . . . the Welsh element is never found at the top of the social scale, nor in its own body does it exhibit much variety of gradation . . . farmers are always smallholders; Welsh workmen never get into the office . . .'[97]

These assertions deserve to be analysed in closer detail, but that analysis still awaits its historian. Lingen's assertions have become assumptions in our history. Historians still argue that the Welsh did not lead in industry, that they were an unenterprising and unambitious people and that Wales did not have a middle class; its class structure consisted simply of a tiny upper class and a gigantic working class. Perhaps, for different reasons, movements within Welsh historiography have been content to accept this viewpoint. The communist and socialist tradition has emphasized the reckless irresponsibility of unregulated and uncontrolled capitalism which ruthlessly exploited people and resources after 1780. The nationalist school of Welsh historiography has tended to view Wales as England's first colony, which was ravaged and robbed of her riches by an unscrupulous oppressor. In both views the Welsh were victims who can be allowed no part in their own exploitation.

The iron industry provides considerable evidence to support Lingen's claims. The majority of the iron-willed men who created the iron industry in Wales originated from England.[98] John Wilkinson came to Bersham in 1753 to manage the ironworks leased to his father. He had considerable experience of operating ironworks in the north of England and under his leadership the works flourished. Richard Crawshay (1739–1810), after a characteristically bitter quarrel with his father, left Normanton, Yorkshire, for London. Penniless, he sold his house and obtained work at a smoothing iron manufacturer's works. For young Richard, the streets of London were not paved with gold but rather with a richer metal, iron. Crawshay married the owner's daughter and inherited the business. Learning of the potential of the iron industry in Wales he bought Homfray's lease of the Cyfarthfa ironworks and became sole owner in 1794. Eventually, he became as rich as Solomon, though perhaps not as wise. Francis Homfray (1726–98) had made a fortune for himself in the ironworks of Stafford and Worcester before he was drawn to the Merthyr Tydfil area. He decided to take out a share in a lease on the Penydarren works so that his talented sons, Jeremiah (1759–1833) and Samuel (d. 1822) could enter the industry. Their lives are almost polar opposites, oddly reminiscent of the lives of the biblical prophets after whom they were named. Samuel's speculations proved phenomenally successful. His marriage to Jane, the daughter of Sir Charles Morgan, the first baron of Tredegar Park, drew him into highly influential political circles and into ownership of lands with great mineral wealth. He invested £40,000 in the Glamorganshire Canal (which opened in 1795), the Monmouthshire Canal and the tramroad from Penydarren to Navigation (Abercynon). It was along this stretch that Richard Trevithick 'achieved the impossible' in getting an engine to pull five carriages, ten tons of iron and seventy men for nine miles. This also enabled Samuel to achieve an even more impossible feat and win a celebrated bet of £1,050 with the sceptical Richard Crawshay. In contrast to Samuel's industry and success, Jeremiah's life was one of inconsistency and squander. He enjoyed the adventure of speculation, being involved in developing the Ebbw Vale and Hirwaun works and collieries in the Pontypridd area, but he never possessed the persistence required to succeed in these ventures. In 1813, he was declared bankrupt and fled to Boulogne where he died in 1833.

The brothers Joseph (1783–1888) and Crawshay Bailey left Yorkshire to seek their fortunes in the Merthyr area under the patronage of their uncle, Richard Crawshay. They quickly won his favour and became partners in the Cyfarthfa ironworks. Joseph Bailey went on to establish his own ironworks at Nant-y-glo, the only ironworks to increase its order books during the industrial depression which followed the Napoleonic Wars. Crawshay Bailey had an almost pathological fear of the ostentation that followed wealth and deliber-ately dressed in old ragged clothes. When he negotiated the purchase of a works near Aber, the sceptical owner asked the shabbily dressed Bailey: 'How and when will you pay?' and received the swift, surprising response: 'Now, in cash.' John Guest left Borsley in Shropshire to supervise a small ironworks in Dowlais in 1759. Under his leadership the works flourished. They used the latest steam technology to drive the engines, built more efficient furnaces, purchased local coal-rich lands to provide their own coal supplies, and diversified in the sale of food. His son Sir John Josiah Guest (1785–1852) continued Dowlais's dominance of the world's iron industry. The Promethean energies unleashed by these men of iron had wide repercussions.

These remarkable men had the experience and knowledge which could persuade the world's financial investors that their venture capital would not be ventured in vain. Vast sums of between £70,000 and £100,000 were required for investment in the leviathans of the iron industry before a venture could produce a profit. Those sums could only come from the City of London, or slave-rich Bristol banks, and it was natural that those canny investors would seek only to part with their funds to men who had proved themselves.

Elsewhere, however, where trade was free of the chains of London capital, the Welsh proved themselves energetic enterprisers. John Hughes, born in Merthyr Tydfil in 1814 to an engineering family, attracted the attention of the tsar of Russia who invited him to establish the iron industry on the ice-bound wastes. By 1870 Hughes, together with seventy key workers who followed their leader to Russia, established a major industrial enterprise comprising coal mines and ironworks. The town which grew out of the works was named in honour of its father – Hughesovka, later Russified into Yuzovka. The hard-headed Hughes paid his female and child workers a pittance, housed them in huts on the frozen ground, but always ensured that shareholders received a dividend of 100 per cent. He became a major industrialist, landowner and a multi-millionaire from the profits of his coal and iron. The rails on which Tolstoy's fictitious tragic heroine Anna Karenina threw herself were most probably cast in one of John Hughes's foundries.

The copper industry also reveals that Wales had native-grown entrepreneurs. Thomas Williams, a Welsh-speaking country solicitor from Anglesey, through his legal and managerial work for the earl of Uxbridge and Lord Bulkeley of Beaumaris, rose to own and control almost half of the world's copper industry and to mastermind a major industrial empire. After he died in 1802 his heirs invested his fortune in the creation of a number of banks. The family's Anglesey country origins were quietly forgotten. Remarkably for the descendants of a north Wales solicitor, of Thomas Williams's granddaughters and great-granddaughters two married earls, one married a duke, and the two others the younger sons of an earl and a duke. His great-grandson Hwfa Williams, much to the disgust of Queen Victoria, who considered the Williamses 'a bad family', was influential in the Clarendon House set of Edward VII. His sister Edith was even closer to the burly prince. Thomas Williams was not a unique figure in Welsh industry. In the 1770s, the Welsh speaker Robert Morgan supplied the insatiable demands of the army and navy for armaments from his copper works, iron forges, and tinplate works in Carmarthenshire.

The mining of coal to supply domestic and international interests was predominantly undertaken by Welsh capitalists. When ironworks were established, local farmers were quick to take advantage. In May 1766, Phillip David, the tenant farmer of Wern Farm, Gelli-deg, applied to Charles Wood (via an interpreter) for rights to carry lime and coal to the new Cyfarthfa works. The Davies family of Gwernllwyn Isaf, prominent local Baptists, worked the mineral ore beneath their farm to their advantage, and grew rich in tandem with their main customer, the Dowlais Iron Company. Thomas Powell (b. 1779) began his working career as a timber merchant supplying collieries and ironworks in the Aberdare Valley and at Rhymney. Powell was once unfairly and unkindly described as 'not over-burdened with learning', yet he had the 'man of action's' perception to see that his current occupation could not last as the local tree cover was fast disappearing. In order to supply his mines with pit props he frequently purchased woodlands. On one occasion he agreed to pay for the wood 'when all the trees are felled'. To avoid paying, he kept six trees standing for several years. In the 1860s, he was at the height of his activity and prosperity. In 1886, he bought the Aberaman colliery, a blast furnace and 1,000 acres of land from Crawshay Bailey. In 1887, he bought the United Merthyr Colliery Company and three coal pits. The purchases of the 1880s laid the foundations of the Powell Duffryn combine which dominated the coal industry in the late nineteenth century. Robert Thomas, a native of west Wales, opened a mine at Waun Wyllt (Abercannaid). Through masterful marketing and astute advertising he established a thriving business selling house coal. When he died, his widow Lucy took over the business and expanded to include the sale of house coal to London. Some of the smog that atmospherically covered the city in the mid nineteenth century was the unwelcome by-product of burning coal from Lucy Thomas's Llety-Shenkin mine. Not only was she the metaphorical 'mother of the Welsh steam coal industry' but she was also related to the remarkable William Thomas Lewis, later Lord Merthyr. At thirteen he left Taliesin (ab Iolo) Williams's school in Merthyr Tydfil to work for the Bute estate. In the 1870s, he established several collieries in the Rhondda valley which later won fame under the name 'Lewis Merthyr'. Another who made a fortune from that coal-rich valley was Walter Coffin (1784–1867). In 1806, while gathering bark for his tannery, he became interested in coal, and purchased Dinas Rhondda farm. He then leased adjacent lands, sank new pits in 1815 and 1832 and built tramroads to link them to the canal. One of his few serious misjudgements was to underestimate the Rhondda's potential. Although he was a shareholder in the Taff Vale Railway in 1836, he opposed its expansion into the Rhondda because he was dubious of the depth and extent of the valley's coal reserves.

One who had no doubt about those riches was the redoubtable David Davies of Llandinam (1818–90), the 'Top Sawyer'. His was a real rags-to-riches story so beloved of the Smilesian self-help philosophy of the Victorian age. Davies's life provides ample evidence that the Welsh were astute businessmen. Leaving school at eleven, David Davies began work in the local sawpits, before he branched out into railway building, constructing the line between Llanidloes and Newtown in 1859. He then gambled his fortune on the existence of coal in the Rhondda Fawr. When his workers reached the coal, the success was spectacular. New pits were opened at Ocean Merthyr

(1867), Dare (1868), Western and Eastern (1872), Garw (1882) and Lady Windsor (1887). In 1887, his company, David Davies and Co., became the Ocean Coal Company Limited, one of the world's largest coal companies, and David Davies became a multi-millionaire.

Lucy Thomas was a remarkable, but not unique, figure in the history of industry in Wales. Other women were also active in industry. The japanning industry in Pontypool and Usk was run by a female dynasty, Mary Allgood I (1760–1822) and her daughter Mary Allgood II (1785–1848). Mary I had acquired the business after her husband William Allgood, alias 'Billy the Swagman', disappeared mysteriously in London. Obviously he, unlike his wife, did not live up to his surname. After her husband's brutal suicide, Mary Ann Lewis managed the family's tinplate works. To keep her workers in line, she carried a large stick which she freely used on the backs of any slackers. One of the pioneers of coal mining in the Birchgrove area of Swansea was a Mrs Morgans. She sold her mine in 1770, when she became too old and infirm to manage it. Thomas Charles's commercial ventures remained solvent because of the dedication and effort of his wife, Sally. She managed three shops and their publishing business. These and many other supposedly faint-minded females flourished in the masculine world of industrial management.

In west Glamorgan and Carmarthenshire, throughout the nineteenth century, Welsh entrepreneurs were busy opening new collieries and related enterprises. Evan Evans (1794–1871) began his working life as a confectioner in Neath.[99] In 1833, he realized that the locals had a thirst as well as a sweet tooth and opened the Garth Arms public house. In 1847, he purchased the Vale of Neath brewery and, in order to increase the demand for its ales, revived the Neath horse races. His brews were also served on his two steam ships, *Neath Abbey* and the *Liverpool*, which he purchased in 1846 and 1847, providing business and pleasure excursions between Briton Ferry and Bristol. In the 1860s, he opened four coal mines near the town and served as his own shipping merchant, exporting as much as 500 tons of coal a day to France. When the Congress of Welsh Independents visited Soar Chapel, Neath, in 1865, over a hundred ministers were treated to a free tea at the Neath Arms. Evans's greatest service to Neath was to buy lime and disinfectant to counteract a cholera outbreak in 1866 and in organizing his brewery workers to undertake the cleaning of the town. When the 'Grand Old Man' of Neath died in 1871, the town shut down for his funeral. The church bells tolled and his rifle volunteers led the cortege of this remarkable man and thousands of mourners to his well-earned rest. John Glasbrook, born and raised on Penybedw farm, through 'sheer industry and tenacity of purpose with neither wealth, nor family influence, to back him at the crucial parts of his career', became a substantial coal owner. He owned the Raven Hill, Gorseinon, Aberdare and Swansea collieries. This pattern of investment by local people of their hard-won income in coal-mining operations was a marked feature of the Carmarthenshire coalfield. Llewelyn Llewelyn invested the profit of his Amman ironworks in seven coal pits in 1868. David Lloyd of Blaina transferred his interests from land into the Glynmoch and Pant-y-ffynnon collieries. John Arthur and Herbert Lloyd, grocers, sank and developed the Tŷ'n-y-waun, New-Cae-Pont-Bren and Pontyates collieries.[100]

The list of such Welsh entrepreneurs and penny capitalists who realized the opportunities presented to them in the industrial transformations of the late eighteenth and early nineteenth centuries is not endless, but it is very long. The Welsh proved themselves to be remarkably capable of establishing capitalist enterprises; they were adept at taking their opportunities. The father of the iron industry in Middlesbrough was John Vaughan (1799–1868), a former manager at the Dowlais ironworks. Together with his German partner, Henry William Ferdinand Bolckow, Vaughan established the famous Vulcan works in 1841. Soon afterwards Vaughan discovered rich supplies of iron ore in the Cleveland area and he, above all others, was responsible for the industrial development of Teeside. To ensure the success of his ventures, Vaughan recruited highly skilled workers from Wales. Amongst them was the multi-talented Edward Williams, son of the dictatorially inspirational teacher Taliesin ab Iolo of Merthyr Tydfil and grandson of the literary colossus and forger Iolo Morganwg. Edward's ambitions and interests lay with iron forges not literary forgeries. In 1865, he was appointed general manager of Bolckow and Vaughan's ironworks. He eventually became Middlesbrough's major iron and steel magnate, chairman of the Iron and Steel Institute of Great Britain, an alderman, justice of the peace and much respected town mayor in 1873.[101]

The Welsh also revealed themselves to be inventive and adaptive people. It is a fact, often forgotten, that many of the inventions of the industrial revolution had to be refined and adapted for the particular geographic, geological or chemical circumstances of a region. Without local inventiveness, many industrial undertakings would not have been successful, for in their crude state many inventions were ineffective. Rees Jones of Penydarren, 'an ingenious self-taught mechanic', provided considerable assistance to Richard Trevithick in his experiments with engines and especially steam cranes. The steam-whistle, an important safety device, was invented by Adrian Stephens, an engineer at Samuel Hall's Plymouth ironworks. The device would have been of great assistance to Thomas Rees Morgan (1834–97),[102] one of the greatest engineers produced in Wales. As a ten-year-old child worker in the local ironworks he lost a leg. Unable to work, he decided to go to school. Inspired by the inspirational teaching of Taliesin (ab Iolo) Williams, he discovered that he possessed a gift for mathematics and mechanics. He returned to the local ironworks and was instrumental in adapting many processes. In 1865, he emigrated to America, where he established his own steam iron manufacturing company in 1868. His enterprise became a large undertaking, fulfilling several government contracts. It was his work that enabled the US government to bend and form large metal plates to cover warships.

Richard Roberts (1789–1864), the tall, gangly, monosyllabic son of toll gate keepers from Carreg-Hwfa, Llanymynech, 'one of the greatest inventors of the nineteenth century', took out at least one patent annually for twenty-eight years. He probably invented far more devices, but, since Roberts was not the most organized person, many of his creations were lost to others. Amongst his ingenious inventions are improvements to spinning and sowing machines, machine tools, steam machines, metal roadways, ships and ships' instruments, lighthouses, clocks and many other ingenious devices. Daniel Edwards (1835–1915) was the son of a stonemason and initially followed his father's trade. In the 1850s, he moved into tinplate manufacture, establishing his own works with two partners in 1868. He obtained his share of the funds needed to build the Worcester works near Swansea from one of his work initiatives. In the 1860s, he invented a tinning pot at the Duffryn works which used zinc chloride as a flux in place of palm oil. This achieved savings by increasing the amount of tin that was deposited on a plate and by reducing the number of workmen required in the tinhouse. Edwards has rather grandiloquently been christened 'Morriston's own Welsh Captain of Industry' and his presence can still be felt in the town. In 1870, he supervised the building of Tabernacl Chapel, the 'cathedral of Welsh nonconformity'. On numerous occasions in the building process, the tin-works owner proved that he had not forgotten his original trade.[103]

The careers of these individuals tells us much about the nature of capitalism in Wales. Many Welsh industries, such as copper, lead and tinplate manufacturing, were highly localized in the sense that finance was generated and control exercised locally. Many undertakings were of a scale which made it possible for people to form companies without any great personal capital. This fact is clearly seen in the shipping industry. Shipbuilding was a common activity along Wales's salt- and spray-dashed shores. Local people in Barmouth and Pwllheli were quick to see the possibilities of the increasing trade in slates. Between 1835 and 1855, William Jones (1793–1855) of Brynhyfryd, a druggist, expanded into shipbuilding and became a major shipowner. Instrumental in his success was his connection with prominent Liverpool merchants and shipowners, including John James Melhuish. Another entrepreneur-shipbuilder of note was the merchant, Robert Evans (1810–65). He built several vessels in his yard at Gadlys. These included the *Gwen Evans*, launched in 1842, which carried on her maiden voyage, along with cargo, forty-two local people in search of a better life in Boston, USA. Hugh Pugh (b. 1815), the inspiration for a famous Welsh sea-shanty, was another northern shipowner. His major interest was his banking enterprise in Caernarfon, Messrs Pugh Jones & Co., but he also controlled shares in several ships engaged in the timber trade with North America.[104]

Initially, many of these ships were owned on a share system. Shares were purchased by local solicitors, timber merchants, farmers, ministers and widows – indeed anyone with some spare money to venture in a promising enterprise.[105] In addition to local farmers and lawyers, one New Quay ship was partly owned by London 'cow keepers'. One reason for the lack of a 'revolution' in Wales in the early nineteenth century is that so many of the ordinary Welsh people had a financial interest in the capitalist system. People were acutely aware of the potential dividends which could be obtained from holding shares in successful ventures. On 30 October 1835, the *Carmarthen Journal* reported a frenzied scramble of thousands of people to obtain shares in the Taff Vale Railway Company. The share list was closed within a few hours of opening, for the people of Wales were conscious of the vast mineral reserves that bordered the railway line and the advantages of steam 'over the present tardy means of transport'.[106] But before people would invest, the venture had to possess credibility. Thomas Johnes of Hafod was deceiving himself in his assessment of his attempt to bring a railway to the hill country of north Cardiganshire:

Should I succeed, I shall do more good to these poor Counties than ever Howel Dha [sic] did. I really think I shall succeed and if I can show that subscribers will have from 6 to 8 per cent for their money, I trust this speculating age will soon find enough of the means to carry it on.[107]

His 'speculating age' would only speculate on winners. People's ambitions and aspirations were too precious to be squandered on idle speculation.

Transport and Transformation

The acceleration of economic activity was both a cause and a consequence of myriad improvements in transport. Novel methods of travel followed each other with remarkable rapidity. Before the implications of faster roads and canals had been fully realized, Wales was enmeshed in 'railway mania'. In 1817, there were even experiments with air transport. On 29 July, 'a massive crowd' gathered in Holyhead to greet Mr Sadler Junior, an 'aeronaut', who had left Dublin in his balloon at 2 p.m. before arriving to deafening cheers at 7 p.m.[108] Other developments were more mundane. Many of the crowd had travelled into Holyhead on the post road which had been improved twice since the 1770s.[109] Elsewhere in Wales, the quality of roads varied enormously. Walter Davies stole Daniel Defoe's joke by remarking that the road he used to get to Radnor was not a 'Brecknock road, but a Breakneck road'.[110] A Monmouthshire man recalled in 1839 that it had been customary for Welsh people to make their wills and make their peace with God before setting out on a journey.[111] Charles Heath recounted that the five-day journey from Monmouth to London on one of the eighteenth-century carrier wagons 'imposed a species of terror on the mind of the traveller'.[112] This feeling of terror at travelling in Wales comes through strongly in hymns and ballads. Several hymns yearn for heavenly release for 'weary travellers' and 'pilgrims in a savage land'. Despite the atrocious weather, the Revd Thomas Charles bravely decided to undertake a journey on horseback from Caernarfon to Bala to comfort his dying nephew in December 1799. Packed ice on the road and ruts as hard as iron made his journey extremely hazardous, and, mindful of his horse, Charles walked considerable distances. Crossing the Migneint, frostbite affected the thumb of his left hand. He came close to death himself and in November 1800 the thumb had to be amputated. The experience inspired Thomas to write his only hymn – 'Dyfais Fawr Tragwyddol Gariad' – in which the tired and terrified traveller glimpses the world beyond the grave.[113]

In the eighteenth century Welsh roads resembled forest pathways. The solution to the problem of improving these roads was the establishment, by Act of Parliament, of turnpike trusts. These companies built new roads or improved existing ones, recouping their costs through levying tolls on road users. The gentry of west Wales, anxious to get better and swifter access to lime to improve their land and to share in possible profits, were exceptionally active in the establishment of these trusts. The general attitude of common people towards them was one of deep suspicion and considerable irritation. Many people complained that the most inappropriate word in the title of these companies was 'trust'. They were rightly suspicious of jobbery, and believed that roads were only kept in good repair if they were near the homes of the gentry. A gate on the Three Commotts Trust road was alleged to have been placed so that Lord Cawdor could travel from Golden Grove to Llandeilo without paying.[114] By 1839, the south-west was firmly locked in a stranglehold by turnpike trusts. Virtually no movement was possible without paying a toll to one or other turnpike trust. In May that year, the gates and toll houses of the trusts became the symbolic targets of the Rebecca rioters. Yet, despite the abuses, the trusts did create an improvement in the condition of Welsh roads. The major arterial routes into Wales from England were the first roads to benefit from improvement. Already in 1830 the east to west flow of traffic across Wales, which has so distorted her economic development and history, was apparent. By 1836, the four-horse coach, *The Queen of Trumps*, could travel from Caernarfon to Liverpool in just under ten hours, stopping at a number of recently built coaching houses.[115] Better roads and easier travel encouraged tourism and led to the rise of spa towns and fashionable watering-places. By the 1780s, Llandrindod had emerged as a Mecca for hypochondriacs, boasting a hundred-bed hotel with its own shops, ballroom, concert and billiard rooms.[116] Many 'gay fashionables' caught the London stage-coach to Aberystwyth. In 1853, an awestruck commentator remarked that 'the Royal Mail runs every day throughout the year; you pay your two guineas in London and in twenty-four hours almost to the minute, you are in Aberystwyth. Who could have dreamed of this thirty years ago?'

The expanding road network increased the demand for bridges.[117] Fear of crossing a river was a recurring theme in the hymnology of Wales. This is not surprising, for rivers like the Teifi, Tywi, Mawddach,

Severn and Wye were impassable barriers for travellers to cross. Although a brave, or foolish, rider could find a fording place, a four-wheeled cart could not cross. Julius Caesar Ibbetson, in his painting *Colonel Greville at Briton Ferry*, captured the perils of the ford in poignant detail. Two men, under Colonel Greville's supervision, are attempting to load a carriage onto a boat which looks barely river-worthy, even before its cargo has been loaded.[118] Legally, the provision of bridges was the responsibility of justices at quarter sessions. No subject gave rise to greater acrimony. A bridge obviously enhanced the value of a landowner's property. In Carmarthenshire, William Chambers Jr roundly accused magistrates of building bridges at county cost for their own convenience. The bridge at Llandovery, completed in 1832, was not on the main road but was located purely for the magistrate's convenience.[119] The greatest bridge-building projects were those for the two crossings of the Menai Strait completed in 1826 and 1850. The activities of the bridge-builders of Wales created considerable opportunities for other trades. In 1818, thirty masons and over a hundred labourers and quarrymen were employed at Penmon in Anglesey to obtain stone for the new bridge over the Menai.[120]

In the 1790s, the solution to the ironworks' and collieries' problem of getting their products swiftly and cheaply to the ports came in the form of the canal. Between 1794 and 1797, four great canal lines had been opened for trade down the Welsh valleys to Swansea, Giant's Grave, Cardiff and Newport. They cost £420,000, covered 77 miles, utilized a total of 180 locks, rising at one point to over 500 feet above sea level.[121] In mid and north Wales picturesque canals were built between Brecon and Abergavenny (1799, 1812), near Llangollen (Ellesmere Canal, 1808) and in Montgomeryshire (1819). Canals were rightly seen as the midwives of a new age. Townspeople were keenly aware of their importance. To the accompaniment of the martial oomp-pah, oomp-pah of the Neath Brass Band, Mrs Elizabeth Davies, the lollipop-shop keeper of Wind Street, read her epic nineteen-verse poem to celebrate the opening of Neath's new canal.[122] In 1794, a letter written from Cardiff following the opening of the Glamorganshire Canal said, with a hint of superior racism:

> The Canal in this neighbourhood is completed . . . to the great exaltation, as you may imagine of the town. With the iron treasures of our hills, we hope to grow daily more truly rich than the Spaniards are, with their mines in Mexico and Peru; as ours occasion industry and population, whilst theirs purchase slothful dependence, and are destructive of both.[123]

It appeared that such high hopes were realistic. In 1814, 1815 and 1816 the Taff Vale Canal was so profitable that tolls were reduced and then abolished for half of the year.[124] Money, it appeared, was an embarrassment. These were rare years – the season of the smiling bank manager.

Canal construction was a complex engineering feat. Far more flexible and useful was the tramroad, 'the horse-worked railways of the pre-locomotion age'. Tramroads have been recorded as being in use in Wales since 1695. In the 1770s, in order to give greater durability to the tramroads, iron began to be used in their construction. By 1828, an estimated 1,800 miles of tramroads were operating in the South Wales Coalfield. In that year, the remarkable Brecon Forest tramroad was opened, its purpose to enable traffic to carry coal, timber, slate and seaborne goods into the interior, and limestone to be brought down to the Ynysygedwyn works.[125] The tramroads were an essential feature of the industrial history of Wales. Yet, despite their importance, they are often seen simply as the precursors of the modern railroad. Often their only mention in the history books is to record the world's first regular railway service which operated on the Oystermouth tramway in 1807, and the first ever use of a steam locomotive to haul a load on the Penydarren tramroad at Merthyr Tydfil in 1804.

Despite these early excursions in Wales, the proper inauguration of the Welsh railway age had to wait until at least the 1830s. By that decade, many companies were using locomotive engines to transport products and people. In 1830, a new engine, the *Eclipse*, built by Robert Stephenson and Co., was introduced by the Penydarren Iron Works to carry iron the seventeen miles to the Glamorganshire Canal in a record one hour forty-eight minutes. According to the highly impressed but zoologically confused reporter in *The Cambrian*, the *Eclipse* 'moved with the swiftness of a dolphin'.[126] In April 1836, the Ffestiniog railway was opened when a train and wagons left Mr Holland's quarries to Porthmadog. The red-ribbon event in the town's history was celebrated in typical style. Cannons were fired, a 'well-selected band from Caernarfon played a lively air', and the workmen proceeded through the town to enjoy a 'substantial repast' at Morfa Lodge where 'excellent *cwrw da* flowed plentifully'. The crowds noted the youth of the developers; Spooner was the oldest at forty-four, Archer and Pritchard were both thirty-three, while Smith was only twenty-three. None of them, like the town, had any experience of railways.[127] In the following eighteen years the Welsh people became familiar with this novel form of transport, and over twenty bills for Welsh railways were presented to Parliament.[128]

As the implications of the transport revolution were assessed, there was a rapid expansion in dock and port facilities throughout Wales. Between 1792 and 1880, Aberaeron, Aberystwyth, Pwllheli, Llanelli, Neath and Pembroke Dock all received parliamentary assent for bills to improve their harbours and docks. Of even greater significance was the opening of the West Bute Dock in Cardiff in 1839 and the Town Dock in Newport in 1842.

Transport begat trade, and trade in its turn begat transport. Contemporary French observers, jealous of the commercial success of Britain, stressed the importance of international trade. The deep-blue-water trade of Wales has considerable romance attached to it. The barques of Swansea, Cardiff and Newport took iron and coal to exotic places and carried home sugar from Mauritius, grain from America, timber from the Baltic, palm oil from West Africa and copper ore from Cuba and Chile. On their journeys, the waves were often taller than the tallest tales told in Swansea's Cuba public house. But despite the enormous value of the cargoes carried by these 'floating warehouses', the real boost to the Welsh economy came from less romantic coastal journeys. Schooners, sloops and steamers, built on a share basis with stakeholders in all sections of the community, sailed and steamed with a bewilderingly diverse range of goods into ports such as Llanelli, Tenby, Milford, New Quay, Cardigan, Aberystwyth, Bangor, Porth-madog, Beaumaris and Conwy. Much of this traffic came from Bristol and Liverpool, which still, in the mid nineteenth century, served as regional capitals for Wales.[129] Though these journeys did not appear to share the romance or the terrors of the storm-battered Cape Horn route, sailors also encountered dangers to bring their produce to port. Several parts of the Welsh coast were described as 'malignant', and the Irish Sea was deemed a 'psychotic sea'. Each year local church bells poignantly tolled over the waters for those lost at sea. In 1804, the people of Swansea were informed that, as from 7 January, they would have a new newspaper, *The Cambrian*. To considerable embar-rassment, the paper eventually appeared on 28 January. The delay had been caused by the fact that the paper needed to produce the newspaper was being carried by the sloop *The Phoenix* from Bristol, which, becalmed, was delayed for five days in port. When she eventually sailed, gales forced her across to Milford. Twenty-one days late the published paper carried news of the coastal-borne trade in its column 'The Shipping News'.[130]

Yet, despite revolutionary changes in transport, mid nineteenth-century Wales was still an equestrian and a pedestrian world. Many paintings portray people, especially women, walking to their occupations and preoccupations. It is almost as if the wheel had not been invented. Charles Morgan's watercolour of 1851, *Tenby*, depicts the weary trudge of a corpulent woman to the town's market.[131] Alongside her is her trusty steed. In the nineteenth century, mankind's best friend was not canine, it was equine. The mid nineteenth century was primarily 'oes aur y ceffylau' (the golden age of the horse).[132] Not only were they everywhere in the landscape – carrying loads, pulling carriages and machines – but they also gave work to a wide variety of people. Blacksmiths, saddlers, peripatetic stud men and *ysbaddwyr* (castrators), horse-breeders and many others derived a living from these noble beasts of burden.[133] In the early nineteenth century wagon trains of pack mules kept the villages and towns of Wales fed. Fresh butter, cheese, eggs and meat were brought in to Merthyr Tydfil in the simple *Cardi carts*. Each day, dozens of carts from Llandovery or Defynnog would wind their weary way into the town. The carters often left home at the paranoic hour of 3 a.m. in order to arrive in the town in time for market. The return journey was perilous, for the packmen and hucksters often carried as much as £70. On the lonely hills, such carts were easy prey. On 10 August 1845, Thomas Thomas was hanged for robbing and murdering David Lewis, a mid-Wales carter, in the wild hills above Cefn-Coed-y-Cymer.[134] Thomas had followed Lewis from Merthyr Tydfil market knowing that he carried a small fortune. The wagon trains continued into the canal and railway age. A visitor to the town in 1835 described the scene:

> The streets of Merthyr were enlivened by large troops of pack-horses, bringing wool and other goods ... pack horses were pouring in from Aberdare, Llanwono, Gellygaer, Llanvabon, and all the surrounding parishes ... the streets near the weighing-house were absolutely thronged with wagons, carts and carrying horses.[135]

Commerce and Consumption

The carts and wagons of the improving roads, the barges of the canals and the clattering carriages of the railways could carry far more goods and consumables to the towns than the means of transport they supplanted. Gradually the roughly carpented stalls, patchworked from bits and pieces salvaged from village waste tips, were transformed into decorous market halls. Swansea built a covered market in the 1770s and another in 1830, at a cost of £30,000. Large areas of the markets and certain days were devoted to specific items. There were fish, corn, hay, meat, poultry, fruit and vegetable markets. At each event, stalls selling cockles, laver-bread and faggots enjoyed a roaring trade.[136] Swansea's new marketplace, like the market house at Merthyr, had been principally built by private enterprise. The special correspondent of the *Morning Chronicle* offered a vivid portrait in 1851:

> The shops of Merthyr are numerous, well furnished, and show all the bustle and activity of a thriving trade. The market house, which is very capacious, may be termed a 'bazaar of shops'. The scene is one of the most extraordinary I have ever witnessed . . . the entire labouring population of Merthyr passes through its crowded halls . . . It is not only the field of supply, but evidently the promenade of the working classes . . . One division of the market is appropriated to butcher's meat; another to vegetables; a third to poultry and butter; a fourth to dried stores of bacon, cheese and herrings; a fifth to apples, eggs and fruit . . . There are also stalls of every description of hardware and other shop goods. Hatters, drapers, shoemakers, tinmen, ironmongers, and even booksellers, here derive an active and thriving trade . . . Outside the market-house are booths and shows, with their yellow-flaming lamps, flaunting pictures and obstreperous music.[137]

Though the Dowlais Company had tried to transform its now illegal and unprofitable truck shop into a market, the populace preferred the town market. Aberdare, Llanidloes, Newtown, Merthyr Tydfil, Cardiff and Newport also built market halls, each an overflowing cornucopia of practical, fashionable and desirable goods.

Markets and fairs were periodic activities which were still strongly tied to the seasonal demands of the agricultural calendar, but town and village people had constant demands which could not be satisfied or served by these episodic events. To meet this demand, increasing numbers of shops began to appear in the rapidly evolving commercial centres of Welsh towns. Swansea and Carmarthen had identifiable retail and commercial centres by the 1820s. In other towns, the establishment of shops was a more gradual process.[138] In 1860 the peripatetic painter Joseph Josiah Dodd painted *Castle Square, Caernarfon*.[139] The painting shows a town poised between two worlds. The partially paved street had become an extension of the store, a stage for the fashion conscious. Gentlemen in top hats and frock coats, silk-clad ladies carrying parasols and well-dressed, inquisitive children

Joseph Josiah Dodd, *Castle Square, Caernarfon, c.*1860 (National Library of Wales). A town poised between two worlds. In the centre of *Y Maes* the bedraggled ragamuffins are partying amongst the cattle and sheep, whilst on the pavement the better sort of people parade and window-shop.

are window-shopping. As they gaze in, the shopkeepers stare back stupidly through thick glass. By 1860, some had already acquired that ingratiating rictus of smarm shopkeepers called a smile. This street, with a hint of gentle irony, was christened 'Caernarfon's Regent Street'. In total contrast to the refined periphery of the street, in the centre of the dirt and dung-covered Maes, a bedraggled group sits and squats amongst the cattle, sheep and dung. One character is being followed by a dog, a gimcrack assemblage of bones which looks as if it would follow anything.

In their detailed study of Merthyr Tydfil in 1851, Harold Carter and Sandra Wheatley discovered that between 1822 and 1848 the town had the highest increase in the number of retail shops of any town or city in Britain.[140] Similar developments could be seen throughout Wales and were proudly listed in the town guides and directories which poured from the presses from the 1820s onwards. Shops offered a bewilderingly diverse assortment of products by the 1820s, ranging from simple materials – bread baskets, tea-caddies, books, clasped folio-Bibles – to the more costly and less portable items such as ornate pianofortes, chests of drawers, beds, looking-glasses. Much prized, especially in a society in which all travel meant exposure to the

elements, were barometers. The products of P. Maffia and Co. of
Monmouth, who had migrated from Italy in 1841, were highly regarded
for their prognostic powers.[141] In the 1820s, a new phenomenon, the
toyshop, enters Welsh retail history. In Swansea, the shops of Jonathan
Lundy, Mrs Richards, Mr Scott, Mrs Rowe and Jonathan Williams
seduced the tiny consumer with their magical window displays.[142] For
some fortunate souls, childhood commenced in Swansea in the 1820s.
Childhood became emotionally changed and charged from the 1820s.
The books and toys on sale in these miniature wonderlands in Swansea
taught valuable lessons to impressionable youth. Dolls instructed girls
into a matriarchal role, while swords and pistols taught boys the
bravery expected of a man. These emotions were further emphasized
in the books sold. Children's stories focused primarily on love and
affection for girls (but also for boys in relation to their mothers), and
bravery and righteous behaviour for boys. For thousands of children
who worked in the collieries and ironworks of Wales, such concepts
might have seemed alien and incomprehensible, but for thousands of
others these were ideals to aspire to and achieve. Capitalism was not
just a relentless machine crushing the wage-slaves at the bottom; it also
created a fantasy world of rapid social change, leisure and fairy tale.

Several shops were no more than country stores, but they acted as
an interface between the local disparate, dispersed agricultural
community and the global economy. To these outposts people brought
butter, eggs, oats, corn, axe handles, hats and anything they could use
to trade for commodities that they could not produce for themselves –
tea, coffee, sugar, molasses, 'dry goods'. The shopkeepers depended for
their survival on their shrewdness in dealing with thousands of small
transactions, on their facility for mental arithmetic and their gambling
instincts in allocating credit to their customers. In the stores, clerks
were 'boarded in' under a stifling and suffocating morality, but they
learnt the local arts of hard bargaining and sharp practices. Two of the
multitudes who began their working lives early in this environment
were the antiquarian Thomas Bexam, Caradawc y Fenni (1802–82),
who commenced his working life as a seven-year-old in the Clydach
Works Shop, and the musician David Pugh Evans (1866–1897), author
of the tear-jerking 'Hyd Fedd Hi Gâr yn Gywir' (To the grave she loves
correctly) and the epic 'Brad Dynrafon', who was a draper's apprentice
by his twelfth birthday. Lewis William Lewis (1831–1901), the
celebrated Llew Llwyfo, kept a shop for a period in Talsarn before
moving into newspaper editing.[143]

In Rhymney Andrew Buchan's shop began as a monopolistic company truck shop, but later flourished as a free enterprise. Supplies of butter, cheese, eggs and flour were carted in weekly from the farms which Buchan also owned. The bacon, beef, lamb and mutton he sold had been reared on his own land and slaughtered in his slaughter-houses. He also owned the Rhymney brewery. Buchan quickly realized the value of philanthropic generosity as a marketing tool. At a time of local famine and scarcity, it was said that he had sent a load of iron, at his own expense, to America, sold it and used the proceeds to purchase food which he distributed to his customers impoverished by the slump. Every time the Rhymney cricket team won, he presented each player with a gold sovereign. Fortunately for Buchan, the team had a poor season.[144] Buchan died in 1871, leaving a fortune of over £50,000. Another remarkable shopkeeper from Rhymney was David Morgan. He showed his understanding of the estate agent's monotonous advice of 'location, location, location', opening a corner shop within sight of three works in 1858. He rapidly expanded to own larger shops in Pontlotyn (1858), Brecon (1874), Abertillery (1875) and Cardiff (1879).[145] In 1837, Richard Owen of Caernarfon established the Nelson, which rapidly grew to be the most famous shop in the north. This Aladdin's cave of an emporium had swallowed several neigh-bouring properties by the time it was purchased by Richard Owen's fellow apprentice, Lewis Lewis, in 1851. In that year, the Nelson even published its own quarterly newspaper for staff, offering advice on behaviour and decorum as well as special offers on products. In Narberth the clothes shops of David Tudor Evans (1822–96) prospered and expanded. Evans later became a notable journalist and educationalist; he was one of the few Welsh people to be praised by the poison-tipped pen of R. R. W. Lingen.

David Morgan and Andrew Buchan prospered because they realized the value of adept advertising and mass marketing. Thomas Savin's shop in Oswestry was the talk of the county. Gentry and farmers flocked there to purchase flannel shirts, winter coats, 'jaquettes' and the latest Paris fashions. One heavily curtained room was gas-lit even in daylight to 'show the effect of the articles worn at night'.[146] Women were often employed in these shops. Managers liked them because they would discuss intimate items of apparel with female customers. They were more demure and less dishonest than men. Even better, they were paid less. Some shops offered the fail-safe device of a sale to entice customers across the threshold. On 6 January 1860, the

Piano-Forte and Music Establishment of 81 Oxford Street, Swansea, announced a sale in *The Cambrian* newspaper. Other establishments quickly appreciated that the Welsh enjoyed a bargain and offered their own special offers and sales. Surprisingly, the swarthy wine and beer shop of Rees and Stones, Waterloo Street, Swansea, much frequented by tough old ladies, also announced 'great reductions from this day in the prices of Spirits, Wines and Beers'.[147] Those who were engaged in the most competitive commercial environments quickly realized that the one who shouts loudest acquires most trade. The newspapers were crammed with advertisements for drapers and milliners, false teeth manufacturers and the ubiquitous ever-present patent-medicine sellers.

At the height of the cholera epidemic in 1849, David Morgan, chemist, High Street, Merthyr Tydfil, realized that even the worst winds could blow some good. He wrote to the *Cardiff and Merthyr Guardian* to defend his Cambrian Specific Medicine: 'the only ordinary medical still equal to the fearful mortality still prevailing'. This letter showed that Morgan had grasped two lessons of the new commercial world. The first was that you did not have to pay to publish a letter even if it advertised your product. The second was that your credibility increaases if you can persuade another to make outlandish claims on your behalf. In his support, David Morgan detailed quotations from the testimonials his medicine had received from Joseph Allen, a miner at the Plymouth Ironworks, G. E. Lomax, a temperance agent, Daniel Davies, a weaver of Caerphilly, and John Cole, a haulier from Merthyr Tydfil. Cole claimed that he had been ill with cholera for 108 hours, but after taking Cambrian Specific he had recovered his full health within an hour and a half. David Morgan's touch of genius included the endorsement of the Revd J. Jones, of Llangollen House, Victoria Street, Merthyr Tydfil. With such divine support, the paper's readers could not fail to believe that the Cambrian Specific was truly efficacious in every way.[148] The age of the newspaper in Wales, inaugurated from 1804, also introduced an 'age of fear'. Quack doctors and patent-medicine manufacturers exploited people's hopes and traded on their fear of disease and decline.

The power of advertising in the new Welsh press was quickly realized by the forces of law and order. Newspapers could carry inform-ation faster and further than the parish constable's plodding feet and primitive methods of communication. On 29 December 1832, *The Cambrian* congratulated itself on having helped to apprehend William

White who had robbed Mr Lloyd, a watchmaker at Brecon. White was apprehended in Cardiff after Constable David Evans had read a description of the delinquent in a previous edition of the paper.[149] Newspapers supported and sustained the commercial revolution which swept over Wales in the early nineteenth century. They linked different places together in ways that had not been possible previously, thereby creating a greater sense of regional identity and local pride.[150] Farmers read reports of the prices at different markets and chose to sell at the one in which they thought they would obtain the best price rather than the market they habitually attended. Merchants read the shipping news columns of the papers to ascertain where they could best obtain specialist goods and produce. But it was in the world of fashion that advertising played its greatest role. From the 1820s, the awareness of fashion penetrated further down the social scale in Wales than ever before. Paris fashions were no longer the proud preserve of the privileged. In the *North Wales Chronicle* on 1 November 1838, Lucy Hodgson of the Fashionable Millinery Company

> Begs to inform the Ladies of Bangor, Beaumaris, Caernarvon and their vicinities, that she has returned from Paris with a select assortment of goods, consisting of Millinery, Dresses, Cloaks, French Corsets, and other fashionable articles, which will be ready on Thursday next the third of November, when she requests the favour of an early inspection.[151]

The mention of 'French Corsets' had the prurient, as well as the fashionable, flocking to Ms Hodgson's emporium to inspect the fineries. Fashion undoubtedly changed the world for the better for some. Others were more cynical. One ballad singer in 1802 sang a spiteful song that strained to rhyme:

> If you'd seen the farmers' wives 'bout fifty years ago,
> In home-spun russet linsey clad from toe to toe;
> But now-a-days the farmers' wives are so puffed up with pride
> In 'Sunday habit' and green veil to the market they must ride.[152]

So fickle were fashions that clothes were rapidly discarded by the richer and wealthier members of society. Cast-offs were passed down the social scale so that a servant's best finery was often the master or mistress's former best. Some gentry would see several of their once favourite coats and gowns in the local fair or market. At times, some of the poorer members of Welsh society were dressed in a bizarre range of colour-clashing clothing. So rapidly did fashion change and so acute was the snobbery that some believed an item of clothing could be out of fashion even before it was worn. *Y Ffraethebydd* related the story of a certain William who was seen furiously running through his village. Upon being asked the reason for his haste, William explained that he had just purchased a new bonnet for his wife Marged, and he was terrified the fashion would change before he reached home.[153] Ministers and ballad-mongers might condemn the 'fripperies of fashion', but seasonally changing fashion provided job opportunities for milliners and dressmakers, some of whom claimed connections with London fashion houses and even affected fancy French names, though most were Welsh working girls. A cruel social stigma emerged which branded those wearing yesterday's vogue. Nevertheless, a flourishing business in second-hand clothes emerged in Wales from the 1820s as peddlers and traders traded old clothes for 'new' second-hand clothes in the hope of transforming rags into riches.[154]

Advertising and the wanton shop window displays proved too tempting for some. Shoplifting became a serious concern, for it brought a new type of criminal into the Welsh courts, people like Margaret Thomas, 'a pitiable case', a 'young woman of respectable character who cried bitterly while in the dock'. She was charged with stealing a silk parasol valued at 2s. 11d. and a roll of cotton from John Edwards, Draper, High Street, Swansea. She received a warning. Two years later the *Caernarvon and Denbigh Herald* reported that the court had shown less understanding and mercy to one Sarah Graham. Of Irish extraction, and living in 'Irish-Square', St Asaph, Sarah was imprisoned for three months with hard labour for stealing clothes from a local shop. To contemporaries, both got their just deserts. The Welsh deserved compassion, the Irish needed to be taught a lesson.[155]

The power of advertising and improved communications were the basis of the fortune amassed by Pryce Jones of Newtown. In 1846, the twelve-year-old Pryce had been apprenticed to a draper in the town. Eventually he acquired the shop in which he opened the world's first mail order business in 1859. An order in 1862 from Florence Nightingale gave him the essential oxygen of publicity that all businesses require. In the 1860s, after the railway reached the town, he prospered and expanded his business into the Royal Welsh Warehouse in 1879. In that year, his embossed letterheaded paper proudly proclaimed that he was patronized by HM Queen Victoria, HM the Empress of Austria, HM the Queen of Denmark, HM the Queen of Naples and 100,000 customers in Britain, Europe, America and Australia. A worldwide trading web had been spun by a small Welsh storekeeper aware of the opportunities presented by new technology and transport.[156]

By the 1850s, it was clear that consumerism had developed to such an extent that it offered and operated as an emotional surrogate for many people. Because they could not obtain comfort or pleasure in one area of their lives, people sought compensation in consumerist abandon. To many, especially women, conversation was characterized by emotionally invested discussion of their acquisitions.[157] In 1864, D. L. Jones, Cynalaw, included the following anecdote in his *Y Ffraethebydd*: 'Yn ddiweddar rhoddodd meddyg yn New York y cyngor meddygol i foneddigwraig: "Bonet newydd, shawl cashmere, a phâr o esgidiau." Ni rhaid dyweyd fod y foneddiges wedi gwella yn hollol' (Recently a doctor in New York gave the following medical advice to a female patient: 'New bonnet, cashmere shawl, and a pair of shoes.' Needless to say, the lady made a complete recovery). The anecdote might relate to a New York lady but its inclusion in a Welsh-language joke book indicates that the Welsh were familiar with the healing powers of retail therapy.[158]

The towns of Wales were the greatest beneficiaries of the advancing local and global capitalist economy. In 1801, Carmarthen, Merthyr Tydfil, Swansea and Wrexham were the only towns in Wales with more than 5,000 people; by 1851, there were over twenty such centres. The opinions of visitors to Welsh towns were almost universally unfavourable: Rhayader was 'a wild miserable town', Lampeter 'a miserable, poor market town'.[159] Against much competition, Newborough was described as 'the most miserable spot in Anglesey'. Newport was 'a vile town', and Merthyr Tydfil 'stank in the nostrils of the world'.[160] Yet, these and several other villages and towns became important centres after 1800. The scale of change varied enormously. Small, entirely local towns like Builth, Presteigne, Knighton and Lampeter, with populations of around 1,500 in 1831, were limited in their services and structures. Slightly larger than this group were towns such as Bala, Dolgellau, Machynlleth, Pwllheli, Llanidloes and Hay. These again were principally local in their nature and impact. Towns such as Denbigh, Holyhead, Pembroke, Welshpool, Bangor, Chepstow and Llandovery, with populations of between 2,000 and 5,000, developed, in addition to the commercial and industrial functions, regional administrative services. Above them were the larger market towns and industrial centres which offered a greater range of professional, banking and recreational services. In 1831 these included Carmarthen

(9,955 inhabitants), Caernarfon (7,642), Cardiff (6,187), Haverfordwest (5,787), Monmouth (5,446), Brecon (5,026), Abergavenny (4,953)
and Aberystwyth (4,128). Above them all towered Merthyr Tydfil, the
world centre for the iron industry.[161] Irrespective of size, most Welsh
towns in the early nineteenth century were charged with a new spirit of
enterprise and energy. In 1830, it was said of Aberaeron 'mae ysbryd
tra anturiaethus yn y lle' (there is a very adventurous spirit in this
place), while of Neath it was said 'mae masgnach [sic] y lle hwn, yng
nghyd â'i bwysfawrogrwydd ym mhob ystyr, trwy ei sefyllfa fanteisiol
a chyfleus yn swydd Forganwg, wedi cynnyddu yn rhyfeddol yn
ddiweddar' (the trade of this town and its importance in all meanings
because of its location in Glamorgan, has recently increased
remarkably).[162]

Some of the new towns of the early nineteenth century appear to
have originated through a process of creation as arbitrary as that
described in Genesis. Aberaeron was largely the work of Alban
Thomas Gwynne, Morriston of the Morris family, Tremadog and
Porthmadog of William Maddocks. In the 1790s, Robert Greville
persuaded twenty-five whaling families from Nantucket to transfer
their activities to Pembrokeshire. These driven ancestors of Ahab
created 'a new feeling of optimism' in Milford Haven, the place which
Greville possessively and proudly described as 'my town'.[163] Towns
such as Neyland were the creation of the railways, wholly dependent
upon the umbilical cord of the line. Pembroke Dock, which by 1850
dwarfed its near neighbour and namesake Pembroke, was the creation
of a parliamentary decision to establish a naval dockyard in 1814.
Holyhead also benefited from a parliamentary decision. In 1841 its
population stood at 3,869. In the 1840s, Parliament named the town as
the major port for crossing the Irish Sea. By 1851, its population had
risen to 8,863.[164]

One of the most remarkable achievements of the years between
1776 and 1871 was in housing Welsh people displaced by the vagaries
of capitalism. Industrial enterprises, established in inhospitable and
previously uninhabited parts of Wales, had to provide their own
housing for their workers. Today, in the hill country of Cwmrheidol,
Cwm Ystwyth, Rhandirmwyn, Dylife and Dolgoch, the ruins of the
barracks and small rows of terraced housing still stand, their roofs
vanished, their windows empty of glass are full of sky, reminders of
the 1830s and 1850s when they were home to workers at the mineral
mines. The most remarkable building boom took place between 1780

and 1830 at the heads of the valleys of the South Wales Coalfield. In an arc of land from Neath to Bryn-mawr, between 1790 and 1840, over 150,000 people found new homes in streets of terraces which clung tenaciously to the contours of the landscape. Many of the houses thrown up were primitive, one-room, one-loft constructions such as Bunkers Row, built in Blaenavon in 1789. Others were slightly larger three-roomed houses such as the Rhyd-y-car row built between 1810 and 1825 in Merthyr Tydfil, and Forge Row, Cwmafon.[165] In an unregulated building environment, the quality of construction was often poor. Builders whose profit margins were tight had little incentive to house people in no more than adequate structures. Jerry-building was rife. Worse still was the fact that the homes were soon overcrowded, and devoid of even the most basic sanitary provision. The building and construction industries expanded rapidly in the nineteenth century. By 1851, 26,102 men and 645 women were engaged full time in the building industry. Some builders achieved fame and notoriety in their areas.[166] The brothers William, David and James Hopkins, and David Thomas, alias Dai Cardi Bach, were the first builders in Tredegar. Their first projects were the erection of the furnaces. Then they moved on to the construction of several rows of houses in 1802, 1803 and 1804. They also built the Castle Hotel and Siloh Baptist Chapel, in that order. As towns grew, demand for building materials created other employment opportunities. The material for the building work of the Hopkins brothers and Dai Cardi Bach came initially from a local quarry behind Commercial Row, and from 1807 onwards, from Mr Thomas Amos's brickyard.[167]

It would be profoundly wrong to give the impression that the years between 1770 and 1871 were ones of continuous economic advance and development. The performance of the Welsh economy varied enormously throughout this period. Buoyant periods of economic boom were sandwiched between years of catastrophic collapse and deep depression. When one sector of the economy performed well and expanded, another slithered into apathy and stagnation. Retailers could not pay, industries and mines failed, banks suspended their activities and a vicious contraction radiated along the same trade routes upon which credit and capital had earlier flowed. The harsh winds of economic depression blew people around like snowflakes. Against this background the drama of people's ambitions and anxieties was enacted. The *cri de cœur* of two voices, separated by almost a century but united in suffering, can, perhaps, be allowed to speak for thousands of Welsh people whose lives of heartache and heartbreak were lived in an economic purgatory. In 1790, a native of Anglesey decried despairingly the harsh conditions at Mynydd Parys: 'O Arglwydd paham y gwnaethost bwyd mor ddrud, a chnawd ac enaid mor rhad' (O Lord why have you made food so dear and blood and souls so cheap).[168] In 1862, a lady named Jane wrote to her sister reflecting on her life: 'I have seen little besides pain, sorrow, darkness and trouble. We are wearing out a miserable existence, anxiously looking for something we may never attain.'[169]

2

Ambition, Adventure and Anxiety

Hierarchy and Hegemony

Sailors, soldiers and vicars are not the only people who wear uniforms
to differentiate themselves from others and to define their group. In
Wales, during the years 1776–1871, the streets of hamlets, villages and
towns were crowded with people whose gait and clothing reflected the
individual's class, rank and status as effectively as any livery. Any event
that drew the multitudes out onto the streets – a fair, a hanging, a riot,
or an *eisteddfod* – provides the historian with an opportunity to view
the social structure of Welsh society. Such an event was the funeral of
Christmas Evans, one of the most charismatic figures in Welsh
Nonconformity. This one-eyed minister cast his Cyclopean gaze on the
Welsh people for the last time in Swansea in July 1839. A preacher of
exceptional eloquence, his sermons were liberally laced with startling
similes and memorable metaphors. He had left his Christian citadel of
Caernarfon, on a mission to preach a gospel of grace to the graceless
people of the south. His funeral at Bethesda chapel drew droves of
people onto the sorrowful streets of Swansea.

 Among the crowds that bright summer's morning, who made slow,
steady progress to Bethesda chapel, behind a slow and stately hearse,
were several noteworthy characters. The shuffling stumbling figure
with a mouthful of teeth like broken flints and dressed in pungent rags
was John O'Sullivan, one of several vagrants and vagabonds who
'infest the town'.[1] John had been attracted to the scene in the vain hope
that sympathy was infectious and would extend to the living. The cap-
carrying, grime-encrusted, hob-nailed booted battalion were copper
workers plodding their weary way from work, too late for the service.
The portly, self-important man deep into the portly important matters
of Nonconformist politics, with the gold chain of his timepiece
stretched across his ballooning waistcoat, was Mr S. Rogers, a local

draper drawn to the event because funerals were good for business. The girl with the coarse, unintelligent features dressed in her 'dirty finery', and a face painted with the boldness of a doll-maker's, was Catherine Williams, one of the town's 'bats' – a prostitute who usually only appeared at night. The quick, sharp-eyed man in a Bible-black three-piece suit, with a complexion the colour of parchment, was the Revd Joshua Watkins of Carmarthen, one of several ministers who had arrived to bury one of his profession's stars. The bow-legged, strictly and impeccably dressed gentleman in ink-black trousers and jacket and a dark grey waistcoat, who had the air of an aloof penguin, was John Evans, one of countless clerks paying his last respects to the departed. The two men incongruously dressed in blue dungarees, clean white jumpers, with gold earrings, and clutching white caps with ornamental stitching, were sailors on their way back to port after their shore-leave. The tall, thin, well yet somehow carelessly dressed figure, with arms crossed behind him, and who seemed absorbed by a problem that was a little too hard for him was Mr W. M. Jones, one of Swansea's leading lawyers.[2] The small round man attired in an impeccable 'London business suit', with a crop of white hair above a fine forehead and a kindly intelligent face, was Mr W. M. Borrodale, owner of the Cambrian Iron and Spelter Co. These people and hundreds of others had been attracted to the spectacle that was a Victorian funeral. Their clothes and characters reflected and represented their position in Welsh society. Although there was a vast social distance between John O'Sullivan and W. M. Borrodale, it was not an empty void. It was filled with different social classes who merged and melded into each other. The social landscape between them consisted of gentle gradients rather than giant steps.

Yet many observers, whenever they observed Welsh society, saw a society that was torn between a small, grasping and greedy privileged class and an infinitely larger, deprived and depraved unprivileged mass. 'The poor', John Ellis declared in Machynlleth in 1796, are 'oppressed by the rich'.[3] A decade later and twenty miles further south, Walter Davies regretfully observed the 'want of confidence between higher and lower ranks in society'.[4] In 1842, a witness to the *Commissioners into the Employment of Children in Mines* remarked that his area of south Wales has 'no middle-class of trades' people'.[5] T. W. Rammell reached the same conclusion about Merthyr Tydfil, dividing the population into two groups, 'the iron masters and their agents and the workmen'. He did, however, as an afterthought add: 'and such professional men and tradesmen as are necessary for supplying the wants of the former'.[6] Three years later in the same town Dr William Kay confirmed the existence of this professional group and presented a three-tiered model of society, which consisted of the 'working classes, the middle rank of trades-people, shopkeepers and others, and the upper-class of iron masters, professional gentlemen, clerical and lay'.[7]

The two- and the three-class models of society were of great concern to contemporaries, and have received considerable attention from subsequent historians. The battle between the rival classes for financial resources, social prestige and political power has figured in several superb works of history.[8] One of the seminal features of this historiography is the making of the Welsh working class. The bitter experiences of the years of food and militia riots in the 1790s, the enclosure disturbances of the 1800s and 1820s, the serious industrial unrest in 1800 and 1816 and political unrest in the 1830s, it is argued, forged an unified working class in Wales. From the Merthyr Rising of 1831 onwards, this class acted in a consistent, unified and structured way.[9] Conscious of the inequalities that fractured Welsh society, the working class began to assert its rights pugnaciously. The journey of this class to political representation has been powerfully articulated and passionately argued by several historians. But the portrayal conceals as much as it reveals about Welsh society. The aims and aspirations of the rioters in the period 1790–1820 were more concrete than has hitherto been presented. They demanded the alleviation of a fixed grievance – the restitution of old corn prices, an end to the hoarding of grain, the abolition of unfair recruitment practices by the army and navy and so on. Once those rights were reinstated, protests subsided and protesters returned to the difficult business of keeping body and soul together. The hopes and aspirations of the workers who protested in the 1830s for an extension of the political franchise were shattered by the realisation that the victors of the 1832 Reform Act were the upper ranks of the middle classes. They were also the victors of the reform of the municipal corporations in 1835 and the repeal of the hated Corn Laws in 1846. Indeed, the seminal and salient fact of the early nineteenth century may well be the making of the Welsh middle class.[10]

The emphasis upon conflict and competition between the classes has clouded a number of aspects of Welsh society in the nineteenth century. One feature, which historians have only recently addressed, is the class position of women. Their protests over food and grain in the

1790s, are often categorized and characterized as 'primitive' rebel-lions.[11] But their fight for the basic right to have food and a minimum quality of life are amongst the most fundamental issues of politics. Another aspect which has been largely ignored is that different occupations were not always antagonistic to one another. The blind ballad singer Richard Williams, Dic Dywyll (1811–62), saw this more clearly than many of his contemporaries and subsequent historians, when he sang of the mutual suffering of different classes in times of economic decline and depression:

Mae'r miner cu, a'r collier	The miner and the collier,
A'r lab'rer yn ddi-lwydd;	Are as poor as the labourer;
A digon gwael yw cyflwr	And as far as we know
Pob gweithiwr yn ein gŵydd,	So are all workers,
Y gof, a'r gw'ydd a'r siopwr'	The blacksmith and the shopkeeper,
Sydd leni'n dod i lawr,	Have this year been cast down,
A llawer hen dafarnwr,	As have many a publican,
Fu'n magu boliau mawr.[12]	Who once grew fat.

Another aspect which remains obscure is that Welsh society continued to be hierarchical in its structure and stratification. To one minister, writing in the early nineteenth century, society was a bewil-dering honeycomb, cell built on cell, full of interest and contradiction. In the late eighteenth century, the worldview of the *anterliwtiau* of Thomas Edwards, Twm o'r Nant (1739–1810), presents society as a great chain, with links interlocking from the lowliest to the richest person. Some could use these chains to climb out of the confines of their social position, for this was not a closed system. The Traethydd in 'Tri Chryfion Byd' explained:

> Does fai ar neb am godi'n raddol,
> Fel bo'n sefyllfa'n gyfatebol.
>
> No one is to blame for gradually rising,
> So that their position is equitable.[13]

Such opinions were also articulated in the mid nineteenth century. At a time when class lines were supposed to have been firmly drawn, commentators continued to describe society as graded and ranked in a great chain. William Davies remarked that 'the strongest links in the chain of society, which connect the rich and the poor together, are the middling classes'.[14] It was almost universally acknowledged that upper and middling classes were ordered according to a system of complex gradations based on status, prestige and power, and further complicated by the notions of 'gentility' and 'respectability'.[15] But the working and lower classes were also graded and grouped according to the practice and prestige of the workplace. Hierarchy had not been swept away by the dual impact of the French Revolution, which stressed equality and fraternity, and the industrial revolution, which 'made' the working class. The process of industrialization as it developed in Wales ensured that hierarchical social structures were not ended; indeed they flowered and flourished. Even within those communities which, like a chemical process, 'condensed' around the ironworks, coal mines and quarries, there continued to be gradations within the workforce which were immensely important to people.

Superficial observers saw 'ironworkers', but the communities of workers were acutely aware of the gradations which existed within the workforce. The keeper and the puddler – highly skilled workers – could not have operated without the assistance of a wide range of 'lesser' workers. Sand-carriers and cinder-wheelers carted materials to and fro, 'pull-up-boys' held upright the door of the puddling furnace while the master turned molten metal into iron. Each ironworks had armies of smiths, millwrights, moulders, brickmakers, stonecutters, carpenters and masons who were charged with tasks essential for the maintenance and operation of the enterprise. Although hidden by the masculine language of these trades – 'workmen', 'forgemen' – women and girls did much of the work. In parts of Wales as many as one in ten of the workforce could be female. Ambition did not mock their useful toil, for each category of worker aspired to drag themselves upwards. 'Pull-up-boys' yearned to become underhands in their youth, and puddlers by their early manhood. To protect their position each group of workers attempted to erect barriers. It was said that the furnace keeper was confronted by powers of such volatility and elemental force as to make the forging of iron a mystical if not a magical process that the uninitiated could never hope to master. Many of the higher skilled workers were acutely conscious of their value and demanded remuneration and benefits equivalent to their worth. One engineer wrote to the Dowlais works from Cornwall offering his services. His transfer terms were almost as demanding as those expected by the masters of the transfer market – Nonconformist ministers. He wanted wages of twenty-five shillings a week, a house, a garden and firing, and he expressed a preference for working the morning shifts.[16]

Coal mines were also hierarchical in their stratification and structure. There were significant differences between surface and

underground workers and between craftsmen and labourers. One of
the most profound divisions was the manner in which rival workers
were paid.[17] Those who were paid on piece-work rates found that their
wages increased as the volume of coal they cut increased. Day-wage
men found that they were working harder for the same pay. This group
tended to be rawer recruits, young men straight off the farms of
Cardiganshire, Carmarthenshire, Denbighshire, Ireland and the west
of England. Their aim was to be given their own stall and entry to the
aristocracy of the mines, the piece-workers. Divisions between miners
were accentuated by differences in wages paid by different mines. In a
period when several mines were developed simultaneously, certain pits
paid higher wages as inducements to attract workers. In the 1830s,
mines in the Merthyr Tydfil area paid most. In the 1840s, Aberdare
was the area of highest wages. In the 1860s, the Rhondda was the
region of greatest remuneration. At no time would the highest-paid
workers support the efforts of miners in rival areas to increase pay to
the level offered in their area. Nor would they tolerate attempts to
lower wages. In the lead and slate mining industries, the subcontractor
who held 'Y Fargen' had considerable advantages over other workers
on the bare rock.[18] In the slate-dressing sheds, those who possessed the
aptitude and ability to dress the slate dexterously were treated as the
aristocracy of the workforce. In mockery of social pretensions, some
characters were given the title 'arglwydd' (lord). The paintings and
photographs of the crews of Welsh ships reveal strict segregation
between the ranks. The captains appear to be all braid and stern looks,
the first and second mates have less braid but even sterner looks, whilst
the cabin-boys with no braid have more smiles than all the other
ranks.[19]

   In rural areas, similar hierarchical structures were observed within
the workforce. Agricultural work was strictly ranked according to the
abilities and skills of the servants.[20] The 'gwas mawr' (chief servant)
had precedence in a whole range of activities and human relationships.
He could even control the time others spent eating. When he closed his
clasp-knife at meal times it signified that the meal was ended and the
workers had to return to their labours. When employed at a hiring fair
to join a new farm, many a 'gwas bach' hoped that the senior servant
was a slow masticator. The stud men and horse traders who travelled
across Wales had a strident machismo that derived from the importance of the equine in a horse-powered economy. Those who led a
rampant Arab stallion were especially regarded, for they were working

for the leisure and pleasure industries, not just for the continuation of plodding drones. When David Davies, Llandinam, was taunted for being a 'backwoods sawyer' he retorted: 'Ay!, but I was always Top Sawyer, wasn't I'.[21] The reply indicates that even within a work task that involved only two people, there was fierce competition based on skill and ability. To be top dog and to work in the open air, rather than down a sawdust-filled pit, was the simple ambition of many. Women who took in washing were also graded. In the early nineteenth century, Marged Ifans of Caernarfonshire, who could handle all the washing delivered to her by local people in the confines of her own home, acquired a higher social standing than Marged Jones who still had recourse to washing outside and in the river.[22]

It is impossible now to ascertain how far down through society work-based prestige reached. The drivers of the 'Night-Chariots', collectors of human waste in towns, and the 'urine-gatherers' of Swansea (liquid waste was collected from the houses to clean copper sheets in the copper works) must have been towards the bottom of the social scale. But below them were 'pure-gatherers', old women who, back-bent, scoured the byways and bridleways of Wales in search of dog excrement which they sold to the tanneries as purifying agents. It is hard to imagine a more degrading and demeaning trade, although Iolo Morganwg argued that there was a lower class – 'the Dogs Order' – who 'minister to the depraved passions and habits of men . . . Hairdressers, preparers of Cosmetics, Card makers, perfumers, Jewellers, Snuff-makers, Tobacconists, pipe makers, Lords, Knights of the Garter, Leaders of Dancing Bears, and Kings'.[23]

The underclass, which caused such fear and loathing among contemporaries, does not feature in many analyses of class structure in Britain. But this class, which existed just below the lower reaches of working people, was also hierarchical in its nature and a mirror image of working society. This was a fatalistic world characterized by a harsh humour, opportunism, a savage contempt for do-gooders and 'God-botherers' and a rebellious, resentful attitude to figures of authority. Around the poorer quarters where the ragged people lived in Bangor, Cardiff, Caernarfon, Newport, Swansea, parts of Anglesey, Mon-mouthshire, Radnorshire and the Gower, criminal communities flourished. As in language, so in life, crime and grime were never far apart. At the pinnacle of this world were the forgers, revered for their skill, and renowned for their ability to earn large profits.[24] The best-known area was the infamous, sin-drenched Pont-y-storehouse community in Merthyr Tydfil,[25] fondly and famously referred to as 'China', or 'The Celestial Empire', with its very own 'Emperor' and 'Empress' ruling over chaos. Those at the fringes of the respectable and unrespectable worlds – beggars and cripples who had neither the guts nor the gumption to steal for a living – were in a no man's land despised by both worlds.[26]

Nineteenth-century governments were certain that society was hierarchical in its structure. Statistics gathered every decade by the census since 1801 provide a wealth of evidence which enables the historian to trace the respective strength of the social classes in Wales. From 1851, details of the occupations of people were gathered with greater reliability and presented more consistently, allowing meaningful comparisons over time. The major trends which buffeted and battered the Welsh economy, transforming people's lives, are clearly seen in these tidy tables. The flight from the land continued unabated. Between 1851 and 1871, the number of males employed in agriculture declined from 135,443 to 111,815. During the same period, the employment of females in agriculture and related activities declined from 33,748 to 13,541. The consequent social disruption and dislocation was intense and was only partially cushioned by a rise in the employment opportunities in 'working metals' which increased from 35,659 to 53,717, 'mining and quarrying' which grew from 65,398 males employed in 1851 to 89,656 in 1871, and 'building' which rose from 26,102 to 33,603. Women, displaced from the agricultural tasks which had occupied their foremothers since medieval times, found new but hardly less burdensome tasks in 'domestic offices and services', which increased in number from 41,948 women employed in 1851 to 83,896 in 1871.[27] This would seem to suggest that there had been an increase in those classes and groups within society who could afford to keep servants, or hire women to undertake some of the more mundane chores – washing, cleaning, childminding or cooking. An examination of the occupational tables partly confirms this supposition. Those trades which were deemed to be 'middle class' by contemporaries, such as 'general and local government', 'professional', 'commercial', 'paper, printing and books', increased from 32,547 men employed in 1851 to 45,851 in 1871, and from 1,870 women in 1851 to 3,862 in 1871. But it is important to remember that many wealthier members of the working classes, the so-called 'aristocracy of labour', also had servants to help relieve them of drudgery.

Those 45,851 males and 3,862 females engaged in 'professional' occupations in 1871 lay at the heart of the rising and expanding middle classes in Wales. The middle class was an amorphous stratum encompassing a wide range of conditions and occupations. The boundaries with other classes were vague. At its less affluent end lay growing numbers of shopkeepers, school teachers, nurses, clerks and salespeople. At this bottom end, the line between clerks, teachers and the more prosperous members of the skilled working class could be hard to discern, especially since clerical workers – bank tellers, accountants, book-keepers, cashiers and teachers – could earn less than puddlers or stonemasons. The stern but inspirational teacher, Taliesin (ab Iolo) Williams (1787–1847), founder of one of the finest schools in Wales, consistently earned less than his former charges.[28] The class position of some women is almost impossible to ascertain. The novelist Ann Julia Hatton (Ann of Swansea, 1764–1838) by education, social aspiration and attitudes was obviously an epitome of the middling classes. These people were idealized as enjoying a monopoly of decency, piety, charity, good judgement, sobriety, refinement and responsibility in mid nineteenth century Wales. But the dipsomaniac Ann, a 'debased . . . exhibitionist' who had 'lectured' on 'the most unbecoming of bawdy subjects' at Doctor Graham's notorious Temple of Health and the Hymen, could not have been further in character from the respected and respectful bastions of Victorian morality, the middle class.[29] Her career was in stark contrast to that of another celebrated Swansea contemporary, Thomas Bowdler (1754–1825), 'censor' of Shakespeare, Gibbon and even the Bible.[30]

At its upper end, the middling classes bled imperceptibly into the great landowners and the upper classes, with the border peopled by independently wealthy professionals descended from industrial, mercantile and landholding families. Its upper ranks were composed of professionals and managers: successful doctors, lawyers, editors, architects, civil servants, reporters, engineers, advertising executives, corporate administrators, merchants, dentists, retailers, ministers, entrepreneurs and department store buyers.[31] In the ranks of these people were highly talented individuals who, through their diligence and dedication, prospered. They included industrial agents and contractors like John Llewellyn of Abercarn House, Newbridge, and Richard Johnson of Rhymney. The Brecon lawyer, Hugh Bold (1731–1809), much praised by John Wesley for his 'dependability and resolution', established a legal dynasty of considerable influence in the town and county.[32] John Jones (1787–1856), Talhaiarn, one of the

staunchest Tories in the north, the infamous adjudicator who awarded
the 1849 *eisteddfod* chair to 'Nicander', rather than the more talented
'Emrys', was a steward in the Mynydd Parys copper mines, the
founder of Melin Adda flour works in Amlwch, and the manager of
copper works at Drws-y-coed and Llanberis.[33] The career of Sir John
Williams (1840–1926) was the *locus classicus* of the self-made man
who rose from humble origins to a position of influence. Born the son
of a minister and farmer at Gwynfe, he became Queen Victoria's
doctor and one of the founders of the National Library.[34] Sir Henry
Jones (1852–1922) had a similar trajectory from obscurity to fame.
Apprenticed as a cobbler, he laboured long and hard to gain an
education and emerged in the 1890s as the Professor of Moral
Philosophy in Glasgow, decorated with an array of academic
honours.[35] Medicine was a vocation in which the Welsh excelled and
greedily gathered the glittering prizes. The post of royal physician was
held with almost nepotistic fervour by five Welshmen. Timothy
Richards Lewis (1841–86) was another Welsh doctor of distinction,
who achieved considerable success in bacteriology, especially in
countering the ravages of cholera. His life's work is commemorated in
an unusual way, for the bacilli which cause sleeping sickness carry a
Welsh name – *Trypanozoma Lewisili.*[36] Richard Morris Lewis
(1847–1918) was born in abject poverty, but raised himself to the
position of the chief clerk in the Inland Revenue offices in Swansea.
He is remembered for his translation of Grey's 'Elegy Written in a
Country Churchyard', which was considered to be a major
improvement on the original.[37] Many relied on luck in order to climb
the social ladder. Sir Thomas Bonsal began work in a lead mine in
Cwmystwyth. Through enclosure and speculations on land prices in
Aberystwyth, he made a fortune of £40,000. But perhaps his greatest
piece of good fortune was his marriage to Winifred Williams, heiress
of Fronfraith, which gave him entry into new social circles and, in
1795, the lord lieutenancy of Cardiganshire.[38] The careers of these
people proved that ambition, talent and perseverance could help
people rise to the top of Welsh society.

High Society

At, and above, this border between the very rich and the not quite so
rich, the awareness of power, prestige, status and social standing had

the sensitivity of an exposed nerve. In 1873, Parliament set out to document land ownership throughout England and Wales. *The Return of the Owners of Land*, popularly named the 'New Domesday Book', documented the stark realities of the profound inequalities still inherent in Welsh society.[39] A total of 60.78 per cent of the land of Wales was held by a mere 672 owners. This acreocracy, like all Welsh social groups, was deeply riven with profound internal divisions. The 'great landowners' placed themselves above the 'lower men', who had estates of fewer than 3,000 acres, and an annual rental under £3,000. Despite their vaunted social ambitions, personal connections and wealth, people like Robert Davies of Bodlondeb, Anglesey, William Davys Harries Campbell-Davys of Neuadd-Fawr, William Peel of Taliaris, Carmarthenshire, John Morgan Jenkin Harris of Tref-y-rhyg, and Henry Nathaniel Miers of Ynys-pen-llwch, Glamorgan, were excluded from this golden elite.[40] Only 163 individuals formed this inner elite of the super rich in Wales. Collectively, they owned 1,702,057 acres or 41.3 per cent of the land of Wales and luxuriated on a total rental income of £1,910,850. Although this group had an unassailed and unassailable position at the top of the Welsh social scale, it was not an unified class but riven with divisions, for even within the elite there were hierarchies. In terms of land owned, the real acreocracy were a select group of twenty people who each owned over 20,000 acres. At the top was Sir Watkin Williams Wynn of Wynnstay, the proud and privileged owner of 141,909 acres. His closest rivals were the earl of Cawdor, holder of 51,538 acres, Lord Penrhyn, owner of 43,974 acres, the earl of Lisburne, possessor of 42,706 acres, and Lord Tredegar with 38,750 acres.

Yet, despite the enormous prestige implicit in the ownership of such enormous expanses of land, the real test for many was in the rental that their acres achieved.[41] Some land was more valuable than others. At the pinnacle of this list was the wealthiest man in Wales, the fabulously wealthy marquess of Bute, with an annual rental income of £203,613. Immortalized by Disraeli as Lothair, his wealth enabled him to engage in his eccentric, mystical, medieval fantasies on a prodigious scale. He had no serious rival. In second place, with a rental of £124,598, was Lord Tredegar. Third in this list of the mega rich was Lord Penrhyn, who enjoyed an annual rental of £63,373; then came Christopher Price Mansel Talbot of Margam Castle with rents valued at £44,175, who narrowly pipped Sir Watkin Williams Wynn into fifth place with his rentals of £43,274. Below them, the riches dwindled until we reach those who just scraped over the £3,000 per annum threshold of the super rich. Like everything in Victorian society except the aristocracy, land was expected to work.[42] At a time when land was expected to yield a rental of £1 per acre, there was an enormous variation between the profitability of different estates. In 1873, the lands of the marquess of Bute earned over £9 per acre, while those of John Herbert of Llanarth Court, the earl of Jersey and Thomas Charlton-Meyrick of Bush, Pembrokeshire, each yielded over £5 an acre. In contrast, Thomas Pryce Lloyd of Nannau, the earl of Lisburne, Baroness Willoughby de Eresby and W. T. R. Powell of Nanteos barely achieved in excess of two shillings an acre. The explanation lies in the nature of the land owned. Industrial and urban acres were far more profitable than rural properties.

As the titles of the landowners suggest, this was not just a Welsh elite, but a supra-national British phenomenon.[43] Many of these people were also major landowners in Ireland, England and Scotland. Some of them only rarely or never troubled to visit their Welsh estates, preferring instead to enjoy the pleasures of high society in London and Paris. One fact which has been often overlooked by historians is that a significant portion of this patrician class was female. In all, eleven of the great landowners of Wales were women. In terms of land owned, the greatest female landowners were Baroness Willoughby de Eresby (30,688 acres), Sarah Kirkby of Maesyneuadd in Merionethshire (16,023 acres), Clara Thomas of Llwyn Madog, Breconshire (14,332 acres), Anna Maria Eleanor Gwynne-Holford of Buckland, Breconshire (12,728 acres), and Mary Anne Jane Corbett-Winder of Vaynor (6,693 acres). There would have been more women amongst the ranks of the great landowners of Wales had not the rights of ten women recently passed to their husbands upon marriage in the 1860s. These included Juliana Isabella Dawkins Pennant, the heiress of Penrhyn, whose titles passed to her husband in 1866, and Mary Dorothea Phillips, heiress of Slebech, whose rights had passed to her exotically titled husband, Baron de Rutzen of Riga. Women with great fortunes were not single for long. In the nineteenth century, it was a truth universally acknowledged that a single woman in possession of a good fortune must have been in want of a husband.

The bonds of marriage and the implications of cousinage were particularly powerful for these families. They tied families together in self-reinforcing and reinvigorating ways that saw a few fortunate people inherit vast fortunes. When Richard Gwynne died in 1874, his

estates passed to his nephew, W. H. Gladstone, eldest son of
W. E. Gladstone. Upon the death of the Revd Lord Dynevor in 1868,
the lands and title passed to his grandson E. R. Wingfield. Hugh
Robert Hughes of Kinmel Park succeeded to the fortune of his cousin
William, second Lord Dinorben, in 1852. Another lucky cousin was
Elisabeth Sophie Chetwode who, in 1856, inherited the Welsh lands of
her cousin, Sir Thomas Bigley Aubrey Bt, of Llantrithydd. When the
demons of demography conspired against certain families, it paid to
keep up relationships, however distant. At all costs, families sought to
avoid the complex and costly trustee arrangements which the inheritors of the estates of Lord and Lady Mostyn suffered in the 1870s.

Next to land, the greatest obsession of the great landowners of
Wales was status.[44] The high-flown honorifics of royal titles were
status designations, signifying precise degrees of rank which the Welsh
gentry coveted and collected. Of the 163 individuals included amongst
the great landowners in 1873, fourteen were baronets, two knights,
sixteen lords, six earls and five marquesses and one a duke. In the early
1870s, another four members of the class were raised to the title of
baronies, four to lordships, one to an earldom and one to a dukedom.
These were the status elite of Wales, acutely conscious of their
preferment and prestige, their pride and their panache. The fortunate
who reached the rank of a knight looked down on common, lowly
commoners. The blessed who crossed the next threshold into the
peerage considered themselves a cut above their knighted peers.[45]
Their status was reinforced through a veneration of ancestry which,
some people suggested, came close to necrophilia. John Junior jested
in *Vanity Fair* that the head of the Price family of Rhiwlas could 'show
a written pedigree tracing his descent back to the original Adam'.[46]
The Rices, Lords Dynevor, through some dubious genealogy, could
trace their lineage back to Hywel Dda. The longevity of family
heritage was exemplified in a bewildering display of heraldry. Family
crests were a jostle of crossed swords and crosiers, shields with closed
crowns, coronets, mitres on top, and electoral caps lined with ermine.
Around them pranced reclining or rampant red and golden lions,
wolves and a host of mythical creatures such as mermaids and,
patriotic Welsh that they were, roaring red dragons. In assembling their
imagery, the Welsh gentry were greatly assisted by the work of the
antiquarian and historian of Cardiganshire, Sir Samuel Rush
Meyrick's *Heraldic Visitations of Wales and Part of the Marches,
between the years 1586 and 1613*, published in 1846. Meyrick was the

expert who had organized the royal collection of ancient armour, thereby precipitating a rush amongst the Welsh gentry to salvage their armour from the family scrapheap.[47]

Generations of some families had reposed in resplendent splendour on their boundless acres for centuries. So rooted were the Williams Wynn dynasty of Wynnstay and the Philippses of Picton Castle, that they appeared almost to be a physical part of the landscape. But this was deceptive. Many families stumbled over the hazards of biology and only survived through their female line. To give the impression of continuity through the male line, many dynasties resorted to the substitution or hyphenization of surnames, hence the complexities of Davys Campbell-Davys, Williams-Drummond, Griffith Wynne-Griffiths, Battersby-Harford and Gwynne-Holford. These partners in hyphenization adopted convoluted titles and linguistic gymnastics to strengthen the appearance of continuity.

Yet, no group is ever immune or impervious to the torrents of change. The landed elite were no exception. Despite their carefully controlled marriages and their manipulation of the laws of succession, this in many respects was an open as well as a resilient elite.[48] Families like those of the Wilkinsons, the Guests and the Talbots, who had made fortunes in the industrial development of Wales, had only entered the gilded elite in the early nineteenth century. New wealth, derived from several sources, could buy into the privileged world of the landed elite. Piercefield in Monmouthshire was purchased by Valentine Morris with part of the fortune he had acquired in slave plantations in Antigua. After lavish expenditure, the house was sold in 1785 to George Smith who promptly engaged John Soane to build a new home. In 1794, the roofless shell and estates were purchased from the bankrupt Smith by Lieutenant-Colonel Mark Wood. Thereafter Piercefield entered a period of gradual, graceful decline until it reached a state of sad disrepair in the 1880s.[49] In the 1850s, the Liverpool banker, John Naylor, purchased the Leighton estate. Amongst his developments were an inclined railway which took him from his semi-Gothic house to his summer-house on nearby Moel-y-mab hill.[50] With a fortune from a prosperous legal practice John Lloyd Davies purchased the Alltyrodyn estate, and later crowned his social position by becoming Tory MP for Cardigan Boroughs in 1855. Unlike parts of England, Wales does not appear to have suffered the impassable and impenetrable barriers of social snobbery which prevented men of 'new' industrial and commercial wealth from entering high society. Great landowners like the Morgans of Tredegar, the Stepneys in Llanelli, the Dillwyns in Swansea and the Butes in Cardiff had long realized the value to them of the exploitation of their mineral rights. Riches were respected, however *nouveaux*.

The prodigality and profligacy of some ensured that their sojourn in elite ranks would be brief. The evocatively named estate of Pengwern was subsumed into more successful neighbouring estates. Aberllefenni shared a similar fate. Meol-y-glo, once a dowager house of the Wynn family of Glyn, was annexed to the Maesyneuadd estate, and reduced to the status of a farmhouse. Even in extreme misfortune, some squires were reluctant to economize. Henry Vaughan of Hengwrt never grasped the simple realities of Micawberian economics. Although nearly bankrupt, he maintained a household staff of 'fifty servants, not fewer Horses, Dogs, Cocks, Tradesmen of every sort'.[51] In the 1820s, it appeared that there were more Cardiganshire gentry in Calais avoiding their creditors than there were in their home county. The manic-impressive dowager Mrs Powell of Nanteos died there in 1826 as she had lived – beyond her means. Her 'psychopathic' son-in-law, Roderick Richards of Penglais, had to escape there twice to avoid his debts.[52] William Powell of Nanteos, the playboy of western Wales, only managed to avoid imprisonment for debt on account of his membership of the House of Commons, an immunity denied to Colonel John Vaughan of Trawsgoed once he left the House.[53] Between 1808 and 1813, the poet Walter Savage Landor spent over £70,000 on his estate near the scenic priory of Llanthony. The intransigence of his tenants and his impetuosity led rapidly to bankruptcy.[54] Powis Castle was abandoned for a period in the eighteenth century and deteriorated to a poor condition before it passed by marriage to the son of Lord Clive of India, who spent a fortune to untarnish its grandeur. In 1816, *The Cambrian* related the sad tale of an unnamed son of a wealthy family who had entered the care of the Poor Law authorities, after dissipating his farms and fortune 'and spending forty years of his life in fruitless endeavours to create a perpetual motion machine'.[55]

Others were equally tormented by the bees which they kept in their bonnets. The greatest of these obsessions were gentry houses and gardens. The century from 1776 saw a remarkable flurry of building of large houses to house and home the great landowners and gentry of Wales. Margam Castle, Cyfarthfa Castle, Singleton Abbey, Talacre Abbey, Woodlands (later Clyne) Castle, Hawarden Castle, Bryn Castle,

Maesllwch Castle, Hensol Castle and two Penrhyn Castles were either built, or largely rebuilt, during this century. They were called 'castles' in order to prove that the upper classes still held the upper hand. The decor, like the architecture, belonged more to Grimm's fairy tales than nineteenth-century Wales. These buildings of pharonic scale and Babylonian splendour were much more than houses or homes. They were symbols of authority and dignity, centres of administration and power, and pleasure domes for leisure, recreation and sport. In some parts of Wales, splendid stately homes were common. Along the Tywi valley, Golden Grove, Middleton Hall, Dinefwr and Aberglasney made stately progress upstream. In Pembrokeshire, Picton Castle, Slebech and Stackpole Court shared borders with one another and with Lawrenny, one of the 'finest houses in Wales'. In Anglesey, after Lord Bulkeley had constructed a road from the 'new' Menai bridge to Beaumaris, there emerged 'Millionaire's Mile'. Within this exclusive expanse, new homes – Craig-y-Don, Rhianfa, Glan Menai and Glyn Garth – were constructed, enjoying spectacular views over the Menai Strait and of Snowdonia.

Nature had done her best to provide the appropriate setting for these palatial palaces, but the gentry had to improve upon her efforts. 'Elegant seats' deserved to be 'set in parks of rich groves and rambling lawns' not 'dumped amongst the rubbish of creation'.[56] The period 1776–1830 witnessed a renaissance in Welsh gardens. At Hafod, that 'peacock in paradise', Thomas Johnes, created a garden of almost legendary splendour.[57] His efforts were rivalled by Mr Grove at Cwm Elan. Thomas Jones, Pencerrig, drew on his experience as a landscape painter in the 1790s to create panoramic vistas that included a six-acre lake complete with an artificial island. At Plas Glynamel, Richard Fenton created a 'Paradise of Landscape' and planted rare plants which included Mexican aloe, Indian Himalayan bamboo, figs, oranges and eucalyptus, all growing in the open. In Merthyr Mawr between 1806 and 1808, Henry Wood created fine landscaped parks for Sir John Nicholl. The effects of the Picturesque and Romantic movements were felt in the gardens of Wales, for gardening had become a form of landscape painting. Houses which had been standing for centuries were also swept up in this gardening mania. The grounds of Dinefwr Park, Wynnstay and Cardiff Castle were fundamentally transformed by the gardening fashions of the 1780s and 1790s, and transformed again by new fads in the 1840s and 1850s, as the 'old' features were deemed to be passé. The Welsh heritage was also

brutally adapted to the scenic sensibilities of the age. Abergavenny
Castle was relaid out as a place of recreation by the first marquis of
Abergavenny, as was Raglan Castle by the duke of Beaufort in 1830
and Newport Castle, Pembrokeshire, by Thomas Lloyd. In the 1830s,
the old village of Margam was demolished and the inhabitants
rehoused in Groes to provide room for a new kitchen and a garden for
Margam Castle. To obtain a better view, Golden Grove was demolished in 1826 and rebuilt in a more scenic position in 1832. This was
also the fate of Clytha. Perhaps the most remarkable achievements of
this period were the creation of superb vistas of Stackpole Court in
Pembrokeshire, complete with a man-made lake and the 'romantic'
garden of Plas Newydd, Llangollen. This was the idyllic retreat of the
famed 'Ladies of Llangollen', Eleanor Butler and Sarah Ponsonby.
Their celebrated garden drew a host of celebrity visitors including
Wordsworth, Southey, Shelley, Dr Darwin and his son Charles,
Sheridan, Sir Walter Scott and the duke of Wellington. Around the
grounds, the gentry paraded with peacock vanity.[58]

The landscaped grounds were packed with temples, belvederes,
towers, eye-catchers, grottoes, baths, hot-houses, ha-has and other
constructions of a whimsical nature. At Nerquis Hall in 1814, a
spectacular orangery and a two-dimensional castellated eye-catcher
were constructed. At Sketty Park, a stone-vaulted Gothic belvedere
was built in 1816. Downing, Trefor, Maenen Halls and Pontypool Park
had spectacular castellated towers. The owners of Soughton Hall
abandoned the conventional Gothic for a flamboyant Spanish-style
tower. At Castle Hall in Milford Haven, the American Quaker banker,
Benjamin Rotch, built a superb orangery in the 1770s. This was
eclipsed by the 327 foot (100 metre) orangery constructed for Thomas
Mansel Talbot between 1786 and 1790. The tender trees were heated
by hot air blown in through underfloor flues. Glynllifon even had two
forts – Fort Williamsburg and Fort Belan – constructed in the 1790s.
Hafod, Erddig and Chirk Castles had an impressive range of statuary
scattered around their grounds. Most surprisingly, the grounds of
Treveca, the centre of the religious community established by the
revivalist Howell Harris, were embellished with 'architectural absurd-
ities . . . Here a Gothic arch! there a Corinthian capital! Towers,
battlements and bastions'.[59] Animals were often housed in better
housing than the tenants. When the Revd Richard Mytton returned to
Wales with a fortune from India in 1811, he commissioned John Nash
to build stables and kennels in the same 'Strawberry Hill Gothic style

as the house'. Nanteos had a kennel disguised as a temple.[60] Rhiwlas
had a cemetery for the family's dogs where they gave their best friends
the touchingly respectful burials they denied their tenants. At Hafod,
Mariamne Johnes erected a marble urn as a memorial to her pet robin.
Over the Price family vault in Llanfor churchyard is the surprising
epitaph: 'I bless the good horse Bendigo that built this tomb for me'.[61]

An expected part of the job of having no job was the expectation
that one governed. Gentry families had for generations served as
justices of the peace, the workhorses of county administration.[62] Any
sense of enlightened public duty was tempered by acute self-interest.
The building of bridges, roads or public buildings could be, and was,
a remunerative and profitable undertaking for many people. Though
they lived ostentatiously, the gentry were a tough and resourceful
social group who loved money and power and tenaciously held on to
them for as long as possible. Their letters occasionally reveal that they
worried about what the future might bring.[63] Thus they sought to
ensure that they took every advantage of their positions of power. The
ubiquitous Williams Wynn family took full advantage of the
patronage of their uncle Lord Greville. Charlotte (1807–69) lived with
him and toured Europe, enjoying the life of a highly cultured lady of
leisure. The brothers Charles and Henry, cruelly characterized by the
press as 'Bubble and Squeak', on account of the peculiarity of their
voices, were advanced by Greville into profitable government positions
such as Secretary of State for War, 'Envoy Extraordinaire' to several
European courts, and senior board positions in the East India
Company.[64]

Despite the hopes of the protestors in support of 'reform' in the
early 1830s, and the fears of reactionaries, that any extension of the
franchise would lead to an end of the established order, the gentry
maintained their stranglehold over political power until the late 1860s
and beyond.[65] By December 1832, the Welsh electorate had increased
to only 42,516.[66] Of these, a mere 14,466 were able to cast their vote
since there were only nine contests in twenty-seven seats during the
1832 election. This pattern was repeated in successive elections. In
1865, there were only six contests in thirty-one seats. The parliamentary seat for Caernarfonshire was virtually the property of the
Tories, the Asserton-Smiths and the Pennants of Penrhyn. Cardiganshire saw no electoral contest until 1859, being the domain of the
Powells of Nanteos. William Edward Powell held the seat uninter-
rupted between 1816 and 1854. Denbighshire saw several contests

between 1832 and 1868, but only between the dominant families, of which the Williams Wynn interest usually held sway. Sir Watkin Williams Wynn held the seat as a Tory from 1796 until his death in 1840. Montgomeryshire was even deeper within the Williams Wynn fiefdom. In 1799, the Honourable Charles Watkin Williams Wynn abandoned the apparent security of the 'rotten borough' of Old Sarum for the safety of Montgomeryshire. He held the seat for fifty-one years until his death in 1850, when he was replaced by his nephew, Herbert, who held the seat until 1862 when, upon his death, a cousin, Charles, continued the custom of being elected unopposed.[67]

In Glamorgan where industry had become of paramount import-ance, parliamentary seats such as Swansea took on a Liberal, as opposed to a Tory, political leaning.[68] But the personnel of politics continued to be recruited from the wealthier members of the Welsh ruling elite. John Henry Vivian was the member from 1832 until his death in 1855. The new member was another industrialist, Lewis Llewelyn Dillwyn, son of L. W. Dillwyn, formerly member for Glamorgan. Between 1832 and 1863, Walter Coffin, who represented Cardiff from 1852 to 1857, was the only Dissenting MP, but he himself was a prominent Welsh industrialist and so ineffective and inarticulate in Parliament that his election did not signify any real break in Welsh political representation. The 1868 election, the famous *annus mirabilis*, allegedly saw the 'cracking of the ice of landlord domination'.[69] But careful study of the results reveal that the landlord and wealthy classes continued to dominate both political parties. The evictions of tenants for voting against their landlords – forty-three cases were proven in Cardiganshire and twenty-six in Carmarthenshire – set a bell ringing in the night which was prophetic of the changes that would occur in the 1870s and 1880s. Until then, power still resided with the status and wealth elites.

The stately homes were centres for feasts and regattas, race meetings, hunting parties and house parties on summer nights, when a young bachelor could go to several balls on the same evening. Night after night during the season, the beautiful people returned home in broad daylight to see other people tending their gardens and harvesting their crops. After dark, rainbowed in chandelier-reflecting tiaras, with their swan-necks clasped in cylinders of pearls against the magical tinkling of cutlery and glasses, ladies gossiped and gyrated their way to dawn. In September 1816, the *Carmarthen Journal* reported an Indian summer 'Thursday Evening Ball' in which 'there was a numerous assemblage of fashion and beauty, who tripped on the fantastic toe until an early hour'.[70]

Often they tripped before paintings of immeasurable value. At Penrhyn Castle, two generations of the Pennant family gathered a glorious gallery that included work by Cuyp, Ruysdall, Rembrandt, several Canaletto landscapes and a Gainsborough portrait.[71] Although a few of the great landowners patronized and promoted the works of Welsh artists, men like William Vaughan of Hengwrt had proven to be a rare breed, a lone echo to the old tradition of the *uchelwyr* – the enlightened supporters of Welsh culture. The majority invested their immense wealth, or their greater debts, in imagery which gave no recognition to its source. George Powell of Nanteos spent a fortune promoting the customs and heritage of Iceland, but for the culture and history of the land that gave him his wealth, his heart was just as ice.[72]

Life and Labour

The gentry were not the only people anxious to preserve their image for posterity. The rising middle class of Wales paid peripatetic painters to paint their family portraits. These portraits tell us much about the lives of these prosperous and progressive people. *The Family of John Evans of Carmarthen at Breakfast*, painted in oils by Hugh Hughes in or around 1823, is one such remarkable portrait. Confidently, the family stare at the viewer, surrounded by the trappings of a comfortable existence. Their faces radiate the values of earnestness, probity and diligence. They sit on modern chairs, their feet firmly and comfortably planted on carpeted and matted floors, taking their breakfast on a table beautifully laid with an arctic white cloth and a glacially blue china crockery set. In his hand, John Evans, the emblematic self-made man, holds a sealed letter that had been delivered to him that morning. At the other end of the family group, his son is reading the *Carmarthen Journal*, the newspaper on which the family fortune was based. The newspaper carried John Evans, if not from rags to riches, then at least to respectability. The men are clearly men of the world – information technology keeps them informed of the events and news of their age. Symbolically, Mrs Evans is seated in the centre of the picture since she was the focus and fulcrum of family life – the angel on the hearth. Remarkably, her hare-lip is portrayed, as

Hugh Hughes, *The Family of John Evans of Carmarthen at Breakfast*, c.1823 (Sothebys). The thoroughly modern family in their comfortable and well-furnished home. Note the letter and the newspaper – symbols of the mens' awareness of the outside world. The mother is at the centre of the picture as she was at the heart of the family.

is her daughter's curved and deformed spine. This family had obviously overcome considerable hardships in order to achieve their respectable repose. Another notable painting by Hugh Hughes, painted in 1813, was *The Family of Hugh Griffith of Bodwrda*, a tenant farmer on the Nanhoron estate.[73] This family was so keen to bequeath its image to posterity that it later posed for a daguerreotype in 1848. Hugh Griffith has aged, his daughter grown and graduated from dolls to drudgery, for she now holds a water bucket. One daughter stares, with her neck at the same disjointed angle as she did thirty-five years earlier, though, in the effort of holding the awkward pose for so long, the peaceable, equitable smile has become a snarl.

These and other paintings produced by the growing army of Welsh artisan painters provide valuable windows into the lives of the Welsh people.[74] The fads and fashions, the social changes which transformed the lives of countless individuals, can be clearly traced. In the nineteenth century, home-spun clothes were replaced by shop-bought fashion. Clothes which had been laboriously produced were discarded for cheaper factory-made cotton and woollen items. The women of the

Welsh middle class were wrapped in lashings of crinoline, and their frocks literally consisted of yards of yarn. Their clothes billowed out, so that the women of the 1840s resemble beetles. Women were often in real danger of being blown over and once toppled, had to be assisted to get upright.[75] *Y Punch Cymraeg* published a cartoon which graphically illustrated the practical problems middle-class couples had courting. This age did not need contraceptives, for males could not get close to the ladies because of their voluminous skirts.[76] Women seemed to move mysteriously, as if on castors. Their houses became more decorous and furnished. Power looms produced more carpets more cheaply for Welsh parlours in the 1830s and 1840s. Cheaper machine-made textiles meant that some houses had window curtains, and advancing technology could also produce wallpaper for parlour walls. Within these parlours was one of the most distinctive pieces of Welsh parlour furniture, the pianoforte – the true badge or emblem of gentility.[77] These have often been condemned as snobbish status symbols, but they gave genuine pleasure and inculcated a lasting love of music. Tall case and carriage clocks chimed away the hours in the parlours of a society that was both more affluent and time-conscious.[78]

The trappings of wealth gradually trickled down the social scale. With clothes being produced in greater abundance, it became possible for all classes to own more shirts and dresses, which led to an improvement in the cleanliness of the Welsh, particularly from the 1840s. Gradually, all classes had access to tables, chairs and utensils so that meal-times became more important social occasions.[79] More people had their own knives, forks, glasses, bowls and plates. The old communal practice of sharing a one-pot meal became a sin against the gospel of domestic decency, as espoused by Mrs Beaton and Lady Llanover in their celebrated cookery and household management books, and in the inspirational poetry of Felicia Hemans.[80]

It is important not to exaggerate the extent of such changes, for the poor still ate meagrely. Bread and potatoes were staple; a thin watery gruel and cawl were the culinary high point for many poor households. Meat seldom appeared on the tables of tenant and small farmers, for the produce of the farms was used to pay the rent. In Merionethshire, there were often no cattle, for the drovers had driven them away to market. In the towns, poor housewives spent much of their time trying to feed their families by searching for cheaper food in the markets, scavenging edible scraps from more prosperous neighbourhoods, foraging for fruit and berries in nearby fields, and, on occasion,

Unknown artist, *Y Punch Cymraeg*, 3 March 1860 (National Library of Wales). The cartoon pokes fun at the tall man who had lost his heart to a short woman. It also suggests that the female fashion of the age made it unnecessary for people to invest in contraceptive devices.

stealing food. Hard times produced harsh tasks. In 1839, 1842–3 and 1849, seasons of desperation and suffering exhausted food supplies, extinguished credit with grocers and shopkeepers, and forced many people in Wales close to starvation. Consumer goods flooded streets which were awash with people suffering the most abject poverty and pauperism. During the cholera epidemic of 1849, the *Cardiff and Merthyr Guardian* contained several advertisements for 'elegant drawing room, dining room and library fenders' and a host of exclusive items of furniture.[81]

Life for the poor was darker, wetter and colder than for the social classes above them. Their homes were sparsely furnished and they lived on damp, hard earth or mud floors. Entire families shared a single-roomed cottage and often a single bed. In the 1810s, Walter

Davies described the mud-walled and thatched roof cottages in the south as 'huts of the most humble plans and materials' and those of the north as 'smoky, soot encrusted hovels awash with wet muck . . . the habitations of wretchedness'. Sixty years later, the indefatigable social investigator Daniel Lleufer Thomas found that little had changed.[82] Winters were unbelievably cold. A Hook miner in the 1860s claimed that, to free his shoeless feet, frozen solid to the floor: 'I had to pee on them. It was all I could do.' The railway and coal tycoon David Davies remembered the urine freezing in the chamberpot under his bed. The atmosphere in the houses of the very poor was as fetid and rank as a chicken-pen in summer. The domestic interiors of Wales provided images of vast contrast and variety. The small, crowded, scantily furnished dwellings of the poor contrasted with the roomy, comfortable, well-furnished houses of the middling classes, which contrasted again with the palatial splendours of upper class houses.[83] Yet the poor had also benefited from the consumer revolution of the early and mid nineteenth century. In comparison with their parents and grandparents, they had more furniture, food, clothing and more light at night.

Many of the more fortunate practised philanthropy in order to relieve the suffering of the unfortunate, and ease troubled consciences. Much of this was undoubtedly motivated by a genuine compassion for the afflicted, but it was not enough just to do good, the deed had to be seen to have been done.[84] The creation of a good reputation was assisted by press notices. In the bitter winter of 1822, *The Cambrian* reported that 'Sir John Aubrey Bart has given twenty guineas to the minister of Llantrithyd to distribute to the deserving poor of the parish'.[85] Lord Milford sent beef to prisoners in Haverfordwest gaol, while Lord Clive, 'with his customary generosity', presented gifts of food and clothing.[86] Five years later, the same newspaper carried a notice that 'the prisoners in the Castle Gaol, Haverfordwest, beg to return their grateful thanks to Sir H. Mathias of the town, for a donation of a quantity of beef and potatoes which they received'.[87] In Wrexham, the game caught by several gentry in 1832 were sent to one dealer and the profits shared by the poor.[88] At Swansea, the Charity for the Distribution of Fuel and Provision provided assistance during the arctic conditions of the 1830 winter.[89] At Neath, in the same season of woe, the Rector's Benevolent Society 'cheered the feelings of many a despondent heart amongst the afflicted children of poverty' with their gifts.[90] Very often, it was the afflicted who helped each other, for the basic generosity of those who had little or nothing, the ragged trousered philanthropists, was almost legendary.

Perhaps the greatest contrast between rich and poor was in their complexions. Diet and deformity meant that, by his or her middle age, a worker's face had often collapsed into the shapeless form of a melting snowman's or a village idiot's. Eyes were bleary, noses were distorted. Teeth, even of the very young, were discoloured, yellowed and blackened like antique piano keys. By adolescence, most people had lost most of their teeth. Those who could afford them used false teeth produced from elephant ivory. In 1824, Mr Wallace, a surgeon dentist, 'respectfully announces to the nobility and gentry at Swansea and its vicinity that he could be consulted . . . to . . . fill hollow teeth with gold in five minutes'. The poor had to be content to have their gums on mumbling display. The skins of the rich were often white, transparent and translucent, whereas those of many workers were bright red from the heat or tanned and seamed like old leather from exposure to the sun and wind. It is no surprise that there was still a fervent belief in the 1810s and 1820s that a race of Welsh-speaking Indians existed in America; one only had to look at a Welsh worker for evidence of the anthropological links.[91] For the women of the upper classes, to acquire a sun tan was to plummet from gentility to coarseness. Sun-burnt skin suggested manual labour and even carried connotations of racial inferiority.

In order to ensure their survival, every member of working-class families had to work. Theirs was the world of the terse proverb – 'gwell ŵy heddiw na iâr yfori' (today's egg is better than tomorrow's hen). Women's work was essential, since every household needed a great deal of domestic labour to survive at all, and required heroic efforts to be considered 'genteel' or 'decent'.[92] Women had to be as brave as lionesses, and as frugal as ants, for their families to survive. Women clothed and fed Welsh families, but they also did far, far more. They helped their husbands in the fields, gathered bark, firewood, lichen, food and berries from the trees and hedges, gleaned wool from hedgerows, milked cows, and harvested the crops alongside men. They hauled water, killed and plucked chickens and looked after their children. On Banc Siôn Cwilt in Cardiganshire, women dug peat and carried it home and to market in baskets on their heads.[93] Their work was never done. Before sunrise they commenced their chores, not stopping until long after sunset. The moaning wail of the spinning wheel was a poignant background noise to many family histories. A skilled dairywoman who could produce clean, flavoursome butter provided well for her family's table and was a powerful economic asset. Good butter, packed in tubs or crocks and stamped with a distinctive print, was highly valued. The salted butter produced by Carmarthenshire women was probably the most popular and was in great demand in coalfield communities. Cheese was a valued source of dietary protein and cash. Both were products created through the arts of transformation and, consequently, throughout the period 1776–1871, had an aura of magic about them. When butter would not set, it was frequently said to have been 'witched' by some malignant force.[94]

Wash day was often held in dread by many women. The night before, many would collect a quantity of sheep's dung to which they would add boiling water, which they left standing overnight to produce an effective soap-jelly. To achieve the whiteness sought in their families' clothes – 'mor wyn â'r eira' (as white as snow) – women plunged their arms up to the elbows in tubs of near-boiling water until their fingers were bleached and par-boiled.[95] In the 1790s, as the painting *Llanrwst Bridge* by J. C. Ibbetson shows, women still waded into the rivers to wash their clothes.[96] Many caught their death for daring to venture into the icy water while in a sweat. Clothes were set out to dry on hedges, or preferably on gorse bushes. Gradually, by the 1850s, wash-day technology developed. First came washing dollies, then greater availability of washing machines, then mangles for drying clothes.[97] Throughout the tasks, tongues never stopped wagging, not just with gossip but with harmony. In his biography of Ann Griffiths, the Revd William Williams, Caledfryn (1801–69), claimed that: 'arferai y genethod ganu yn hyfryd wrth eu gwaith, fel dywed yr hen bennill: "Wrth y droell, a than y fuwch / Yn canu'n uwch na'r tanau"' (girls used to sing sweetly at their tasks, as the old verse says: 'At the spinning wheel, and under the cow / Singing louder than the strings'). In Monmouthshire, one in ten of the industrial labour force was female. Young women, childless wives and widows worked as limestone-breakers, sand-girls, coke-feeders, or as fillers and draggers in the mines. At the Ebbw Vale ironworks, Charlotte Chiles and Hannah Hughes claimed they earned more in a month than they had done in half a year as kitchen maids.[98]

Children were early acquainted with work.[99] They had to run errands, take care of younger children, undertake endless weeding, throw stones at crows and other pests to protect crops and help at harvests. Gradually, as they grew, children assumed increasing burdens

Julius Caesar Ibbetson, *Llanrwst Bridge*, c.1789–1792 (National Library of Wales). Wash day in Llanrwst, and the ladies of the town are busy washing in the waters of the river Conwy. One woman is boiling water in a large basin, whilst three others are washing clothes in large tubs using a soap mixture made from sheep's dung.

in their families. The industrial revolution did not create child labour, but it greatly increased the exploitation of the very young. In Merthyr Tydfil in 1841, between 500 and 600 boys and girls worked for Josiah John Guest and his colleagues. In Monmouthshire, one-fifth of the employees of the collieries and ironworks were under eighteen years of age. It was not uncommon in the sale-coal collieries for children as young as four and six years of age to be carried to work on their father's back. They started work opening and closing doors.[100] At twelve years of age, they graduated to being horse-drivers or haulers and by fifteen years, they had worked their way to being coal cutters. Most seventeen-year-olds were regarded as adult workmen. Economic necessity forced parents to send their children out to work. Edward Jenkins, an Independent minister in Bedwellty parish, was well aware of the intense economic pressure.[101] He kept a poorly attended school, but even then two of his own children were working down the pits. *The Commission into Employment of Women and Children*, which reported to Parliament in 1842, revealed the frightening and brutalizing conditions which

faced children during their working lives. Mary Richard, who had
started work at nine years of age helping her father fill a furnace, told
the Commissioners:

> I have been breaking limestone for three years. I work in all kinds of weather
> from seven in the morning until seven at night. The work is very hard, especially
> when the furnace goes fast. I earn between £2 and £3 a month. One of my
> friends lost an eye a while ago when a stone flew into it.[102]

Eight-year-old Evan Evans, who worked at Ebbw Vale raising a
furnace door, revealed an innocence, or ignorance, which could be
easily exploited: 'I work in the forge and my father does too. I think I
am eight years old. I work the same time as the men but I don't know
how much I earn.'[103] Fifteen-year-old Henry Thomas and his nine-
year-old brother James gave joint evidence of their twelve-hour day at
the Tredegar ironworks:

> Our father is a puddler and we have a brother who works with him. They earn
> £2. 4s. 0d. a week between them. Our time is from six to six and we get very tired
> by the end of the turn. We have good clothes at home. We get burned a little now
> and then. We have never been to school so we cannot read.[104]

Children as young as eight were sent out to earn their way through
life. Many highly talented individuals were locked into apprenticeships
which were little short of slavery.[105] William Williams (1738–1817), the
author and genealogist, was born to poor parents in Trefdraeth,
Anglesey. At seven years of age, he was apprenticed to a weaver and
then a saddler. John Thomas, Ifor Cwmgws (1813–66), of
Pentregwenlais, Llandybïe, was working in Job Davies's woollen
factory by his tenth birthday. His written works revealed that his
master had none of his namesake's patience, for conditions at the
works were brutal. John William Thomas, Arfonwyson (1805–40), a
gifted mathematician, author of *Elfennau Rhifyddiaeth*, began his
working life in the slate quarry at ten years of age. The poet and
novelist Lewis William Lewis, Llew Llwyfo (1831–1901), was a child
labourer on Mynydd Parys, the Anglesey copper mountain, and then
an apprentice to a draper. The radical Unitarian minister Thomas
Evans, Tomos Glyn Cothi (1764–1833), had worked as both a farm
labourer and a weaver before his fifteenth birthday.[106] Richard Griffith
Humphreys, Rhisiart o Fadog (1848–1924), was sent away to sea by his
seafaring father on his thirteenth birthday. Thomas Evans, Telynog
(1840–65), a precocious poet who tragically died before his considerable promise was fulfilled, was a ship's mate by his eleventh birthday.

The historian and litterateur Charles Ashton (1848–99) was working in the windswept lead mines at Dylife by his twelfth birthday. Perhaps the strangest apprenticeship of all was that of Henry Harries of Pant-cou, Carmarthenshire (d. 1862). From his earliest days, he was groomed to follow his father John's career as a wizard.[107]

The working class were not unique in sending their children out to work. John Daniel (1755–1823), 'one of the best printers that Wales ever produced' according to J. Ifano Jones, was apprenticed to the king's printer in London by his seventh birthday, and Thomas Elias, Bardd Coch (1792–1855), was working for a tailor in Llanwrtyd at the age of ten.[108] John Gwenogvryn Evans (1852–1930), a minister and editor of several Welsh manuscripts, was working for his uncle's grocery business in Lampeter at the tender age of twelve. In order to prosper, each of these had to overcome considerable hardships and make untold sacrifices to acquire an education and broaden their horizons from the narrow confines of their workplace.[109] The Victorians have been vilified for the gross exploitation of children, but they did not start the practice and indeed they were the first to legislate against the employment of the very young. The Factory Acts of 1844, limiting the hours and increasing the age of work for women and children, are landmark legislation, passed against the wishes of many workers who valued the income child labour brought to impoverished parents. However, as the careers of Richard Griffith Humphreys and John Gwenogvryn Evans show, the young continued to labour in laborious circumstances even after the enactment of the legislation.[110]

Beneath the legitimate world of work, a plethora of trades flourished or floundered according to the condition of the Welsh economy. Many women were forced into prostitution, while others chose the second oldest profession since it offered higher wages and better working conditions than many trades.[111] They entered the trade for excitement or independence from family, or for the lure of fashionable clothes and fripperies which their earnings could yield. A pretty girl, and some were so attractive that it was claimed they could turn the head of a minister by lifting an eyelash, in Pont-y-Storehouse in Merthyr Tydfil, or Mill Lane, Caernarfon, could earn three times as much as 'respectable' working girls. Although they wanted freedom, they were on the threshold of a darker, harsher sexual world of vulnerability, exploitation and commerce. By their thirties, though a few were handsome or seasoned viragos, many were monsters, some beldams. Descriptions give them the torpid solidity of the bovine, rather than the tremulous sensuality of the bohemian.[112] Two seasoned prostitutes were known unaffectionately as 'The Great Western' and 'Buffalo',[113] the latter of whom featured in one of Dic Dywyll's ballads. Jane Evans ignored her friend's warnings and insulted the ballad-singer, who took a terrible revenge by naming her in his ballad, making her a laughing stock for years. Some girls could effortlessly pick a man's pocket while gazing lustily and lovingly into his eyes. Elizabeth Jones, alias 'Neathy', robbed men while they copulated upright against back alley and pub walls.[114] Emily Atkins, Mary Williams and Anne Williams were three hardened habitual 'nymphs of the pave', whose nocturnal adventures in the 1840s were often chronicled with admiration, if not affection, in the *Cardiff and Merthyr Guardian*.

Although much Welsh lawlessness was undoubtedly opportunistic, others made careers from crime. John Baptista Bozette was one such character. In January 1824, after years of thieving, he was imprisoned for theft in Cardiff gaol. In February, he escaped over a twenty-four foot wall. In March, he was recaptured and in April, Bozette was sentenced at the Glamorgan Assizes to be transported to Van Diemen's Land for life.[115] The wives of such men might as well have been widows, for their husbands were more often confined at His and Her Majesty's pleasure than at home. Adelaide, wife of Augustus Robert Seymour, Anglesey's 'major criminal', was left to raise their four children through her dressmaking skills. When Augustus eventually got out of jail, he found that all his old cronies had either died, or were too decrepit to 'work'.[116] The characters who never appear in the criminal history of Wales are the successful ones. How many there were we cannot even hazard to guess. In 1860, it was estimated by the police, on what basis it is unclear, that there were 8,537 known criminals and 'suspected persons' at large in Wales.[117]

Around the fringes of this underworld there was a rootless, restless class of wandering beggars, vagrants and gypsies who criss-crossed Wales. Kilvert's diary for the years 1865–72 reveals the extent of rural poverty and desperation; he complained bitterly that children of a local cripple were constantly to be seen around Clyro begging 'for a bit of bread'.[118] Others turned begging into an art form. In 1817, *The Cambrian* complained that all the towns of south Wales were 'infested with beggars':

> Their tales of woe are gross falsehoods. The men assume the character of shipwrecked sailors – the women of distressed soldier's wives . . . Be warned, do not give these people money, it is by no means uncommon for them to actually

hire deformed children for the purpose of exciting sympathy and commiseration.[119]

The *Cardiff and Merthyr Guardian* warned that, through 'their artful ruses, professional beggars can earn more than honest people'.[120] The extent of this 'infestation' was revealed by a reporter in the *Carmarthen Journal*. In refined and genteel Brecon, a police officer in March 1832 'inspected the fourteen low lodging houses in the town and found that 868 persons, men, women and children, travellers of the lowest descriptions, were accommodated in the houses'.[121] The sea ports of Cardiff, Swansea and Newport had 570 lodging houses, and seventy-four homes of known receivers where 'thieves, prostitutes, their protectors, receivers, tramps and vagrants congregated'.[122] Such numbers meant that competition was tough between vagrants. Many beggars rolled up their sleeves and trouser legs to expose weeping patches of violet scar tissue, growths, amputations and suppurating sores. These malodorous people were almost anthropologically distinct, with their revolting skin eruptions, their wasted figures, poor hair, bony faces and weather-beaten skins. Like their lives, many were nasty, brutish and short.

In complex ways, the world of the vagrant merged into that of the travelling showmen, circuses, menageries, puppet shows, and bizarre, grotesque and exotic freak shows, which wandered across Wales. Pedlars, showmen and tinkers roamed the countryside. In one sense, the hundreds of pedlars were an advanced guard of Welsh commerce, helping both to create and supply growing rural markets for consumer goods.[123] In another, they were further evidence of the threat posed to settled society by unsettled elements. Gypsy encampments were another source of uncertainty and vexation. Here beautiful and sinuous fortune-tellers, with large earrings, flounced in luridly coloured flowing robes, and perfunctorily shuffled cards that would tell the fortune of people who clearly had none, while muscular sunburnt men, 'as dark as sin', went about their lawful and unlawful pursuits. The Ingrams, Boswells and Lovells were famous Welsh gypsy families. The most celebrated of all were the Wood family. Thomas Wood, born in a barn in Llanybydder, fathered nine children, many of whom were skilful harpists. Despite the hardships of the open road, Thomas died at the age of ninety-five, weary and full of years.[124]

Wales and the World

Ambition and aspirations are powerful, almost ungovernable emotions, which help to shape the nature of society. The character of societies is greatly influenced by the extent to which they are satisfied or frustrated. People's responses and reactions to the economic forces which transformed Wales from a medieval, primitive economy to a modern, commercial economy partly explain the fact that the years between 1776 and 1871 were probably the most unsettled in Welsh demographic history. The ebb and flow of powerful economic currents drew Welsh people in their slipstream into mines, quarries and a variety of works – a whole nation shimmering upstream like elvers.

These forces were not confined to Welsh or even to British borders, for Wales, by the early nineteenth century, was deeply enmeshed in a global economy. The loss of a donkey-train carrying copper ore down a canyon in South America reverberated in the profit ledgers of copper works in Swansea. The Welsh were conscious of the fact that they were citizens of the world. When they went outside into their gardens, many walked among fragrant flora that had been shipped from Asia, Africa, the Americas and even Australia. The growing newspaper and periodical press of Wales was filled with open-eyed reports of the wonders of the world. *Seren Gomer* in the 1830s and 1840s had special features, lavishly illustrated, of the animals which the voyages of exploration were constantly discovering. Throughout Wales, in the most unusual ways, people revealed that they were aware of worldwide developments. The Swansea oyster beds were christened 'California', 'Dutch', 'India' and 'Metz', and, because one bed was so far from the fishing village of Mumbles, it was deemed appropriate to call it 'Abyssinia'.

With such an acute awareness of the world, it is no surprise that many Welsh people sought to achieve their economic ambitions, honour their personal ideals and fulfil their spiritual aspirations outside Wales. Others had no choice, for they were forced to leave Wales for America, Africa and Australia as convicted criminals. John Frost, the Chartist leader, and the Rebecca rioter John Jones (1811–58), Sguborfawr – 'a half-witted and inebriate ruffian', as the historian David Williams unkindly described him – were amongst the most famous enforced emigrants.[125] Frost returned a bitter but a respectable and respected figure, proof to some contemporaries that the use of Australia as a prison could achieve positive results. The careers of other transported Welsh convicts had no redeeming respectability. Daniel Morgan, Mad Dog Morgan (*c*.1830–65), was one of the second wave of bushrangers (escaped convicts) who terrorized Victoria and New South Wales. Morgan was so afraid of poison that he would accept no food, except hard-boiled eggs, from the settlers he robbed.[126] John Jenkins was accused of shooting a man in the Australian outback, in court he assumed a

> threatening and unbecoming attitude, and remarked that he had not been given a fair trial, a bloody old woman had been palmed on him for a Counsel; he did not care a bugger for dying, or a damn for anyone in court . . . he struck the other defendant . . . as the judge sat in mute astonishment, it took a dozen constables to secure and handcuff him.[127]

Welsh women, like the pretty, petty thieves and prostitutes Ann Roberts and Margaret Insell of Montgomery, were also transported 'beyond the seas' to life in a wretched purgatory, relieved only by stretches of pure hell.[128] In this remarkable environment there was an 'efficiency for evil and futility for good'. Even those who were meant to uphold the law were corrupted. Edward Lord (1781–1859) was a Welsh marine officer who, in 1803, built the first private house in Hobart. The second most powerful man in the settlement, Lord was 'an arrogant land-grabbing troublemaker who burnt all the Government House papers in 1810 to cover his business tracks'.[129]

There was one overwhelming influence that pulled the Welsh to the far corners of the globe. Between 1776 and 1871, the British, those defenders and lovers of liberty, created an empire which enslaved and exploited 450,000,000 people.[130] The Welsh are often portrayed as troglodytes, toiling in the subterranean depths for coal, the fuel that powered the British to imperial grandeur. But their contribution to the Empire was much more diverse and distinct. The Welsh were not immune from the lust to exploit. In a sense, this was a natural development, for the Empire had been created, not in 'a fit of absence of mind', but by the plundering and pillaging of the Welsh privateer, Henry Morgan, in the 1650s.[131] From then on Welsh merchants, missionaries, mariners and marauders sought to commercialize, civilize, Christianize and conquer the heathen masses. Even if it was in the shadows cast by their larger and more powerful neighbour, the Welsh also sought their place in the sun.

Emigrants and Empire

The emigrant's tale of farewell and freedom has long been a part of Welsh society. For generations the Welsh have been wandering stars. Following the Acts of Union of 1536 and 1543, Welsh people were drawn increasingly into the orbit of England. In Welsh history, the scene was often played: the emigrant with his or her bags, putting on his or her best face for the occasion, the anxious family waving to a receding handkerchief-holding hand, watching and weeping as the stage-coach creaked away into the distance.

To further their administrative, commercial, educational and legal careers, Welsh people flocked to the bright lights of the border cities of Chester, Shrewsbury, Bristol and Liverpool. Above all, they answered the siren calls of London.[132] The city held a powerful attraction to wanderers who, bewildered in a cloud of fables, were prepared to believe marvels of the metropolis. One traveller from Cardiganshire, accustomed to parsimony, wrote home of the prodigality of the city, where he 'counted no fewer than twenty-two candles lit in one shop'. Welsh communities were rapidly established in London and in other English cities. Gradually, they evolved and expanded, and took on characteristics that were uniquely Welsh. Their presentation in the Victorian press is of a devout, self-righteous people whose cultural lives revolved around the *eisteddfod* and the chapel. The career of David Davies (1849–1923), a Baptist minister in Bristol, London and then Brighton, who was actively involved in the reform of the *eisteddfod*, is emblematic of many of these clichéd characters. Born in poverty in Rhydargaeau, Carmarthenshire, he followed wise advice and went east as a young man.[133]

The flowering of the Welsh cultural world in London was notable. Here in the late eighteenth century, the Cymmrodorion Society and the Gwyneddigion Society flourished. But the contribution of the Welsh to the cultural and ideological development of Britain was far more diverse than that which could be accommodated within the narrow stereotype of a cultured, but prudishly pious people, which became so influential during the years 1776–1871. In the ideological ferment and fervour created by the American and French Revolutions, many Welsh people made significant contributions.[134] The philosopher Dr Richard Price (1723–91) had been born into a family of devout Nonconformist tendencies in Llangeinor. But piety does not of necessity breed parochialism. Price moulded the ideological tendencies of his home milieu to become an intellectual colossus, a Renaissance man for the Enlightenment. Reading him today, you can still feel his energy and enthusiasm, his immense curiosity, on your face like sunburn. His *Review of the Principal of Morals* of 1753 foresaw the basic ideas of Kant on morality. Elected FRS in 1765, his 'Northampton Tables' set the basis for actuarial science and his *Appeal . . . on the National Debt* (1772) was quickly adopted by Pitt's government. Despite his prodigious achievements, freedom was the flame which burnt brightest for Price. In 1776, he published *Observations on Civil Liberty*, a work that gained him the freedom of the city of London and the degree of LLD from Yale alongside George Washington.[135] His sermon, *On the Love of our Country*, delivered in London in November 1789 to welcome the French Revolution, sparked one of the most remarkable political exchanges. In opposition to Price, Edmund Burke fired off his *Reflections on the Revolution in France*. In support of Price, Thomas Paine replied with *Rights of Man* (1791). In his own sermon, Price sounded a note of apocalyptical revolutionary prophecy: 'Tremble all ye oppressors of the world! . . . Restore to mankind their rights, and content to the correction of abuses, before they and you are destroyed together.'[136]

The clarion calls of Price sparked a torrent of discussion and dispute in the taverns and coffee houses of Britain. But some contemporaries were untouched by his apocalyptic warnings. At the same time as Price was playing the prophet, other Welsh young bloods were acting the prodigal sons. Gwin Lloyd of Hendwr, in the course of an eventful career, was rumoured to have married a barmaid in the Fleet. His life appeared a round of high jinks, and long louche weekends, filled with wine, women, song and sport. In order to indulge his extravagant tastes, he had to mortgage his estate. The censorious John Wynne branded him 'a profligate young rake, who, notwithstanding affects gaiety of dress beyond any woman'.[137] Lloyd's sartorial strutting was eclipsed by the raffish ramblings of another Merionethshire dandy, John Pugh Pryse, heir to the estates of Gogerddan, Mathafarn and Rug. Peroxided, powdered and rouged, he dressed up (or rather was dressed by his valet) in the green silk pantaloons and fantastic garments of comic opera uniforms. In a savage caricature drawn by Darley in 1772, he was depicted all frills and fallals, in outrageous Italianate garb as 'the Merionethshire Macaroni'.[138] Both Lloyd and Pryse were supporters of John Wilkes and his political campaign, and were founders of the 'Lunatic Club', a slightly more respectable version of the Hell Fire Club.

Other Merionethshire characters, such as Rhys Jones of Blaenau and Robert Wynne of Garthmeilo and Cwm-main, were more reserved in their dress but thoroughly unreserved in their love of London life.[139] Captain Gronow, a veteran of the wars against Napoleon, employed the resources of his Welsh estate to fund his enjoyment of London and Parisian high society until 1856, and dined out for fifty years on tales of his heroism.[140]

Between the extremes of the spiritualists and the sensualists, others sought to make friends and influence people in the archetypal middle-class careers of teaching and law. Dr Charles John Vaughan (1816–97) was appointed headmaster of Harrow in 1844. Within two years, he had transformed the fortunes of the school. After fifteen years of distinguished service, Vaughan, in the face of a dumbfounded public, resigned his headmastership in 1859, and thereafter refused the offer of several bishoprics, because 'I was afraid of ambition'. The truth, however, was more sordid. In Harrow he had at least one homosexual affair with a pupil. His sexual orientation and predations were exposed by the young John Addington Symonds, whose father demanded Vaughan's resignation from public life. Although in later life Vaughan served as dean of Llandaff, the stain of his early sins remained.[141] John Humphreys Parry (1816–80) was the son of a famous Welsh antiquary and lawyer who had taken an active part in the revival of the Cymmrodorion in 1820. Orphaned young, after his father's murder in a tavern brawl, Parry was harshly reared and took a succession of jobs, studying law in his spare time. Called to the Bar in 1843, he was reputed to possess the 'considerable forensic talents' of the 'born advocate'. His most celebrated case was the libel action which Whistler brought against Ruskin in 1878, when he famously accused the American painter of flinging 'a pot of paint into the public's face'. Sir William Robert Grove (1811–96) had the advantage over Parry of a formal education at Swansea Grammar School and at Oxford. He took silk in 1853. His legal career, however, was compromised by his poor health and his outstanding scientific abilities. These were confirmed by his election as FRS in 1840, for his pioneering work in the new field of electrochemistry and his development of the gas-voltaic battery, the evil-smelling battery that still bears his name.[142]

Following Dr Richard Price's praise for America, the American dream of freedom enticed thousands of Welsh people across the Atlantic. To many people in Wales, ideological conditions worsened during the wars against France. Persecution followed the treason trials

Mat Darley, *The Merionethshire Macaroni*, *c.*1772 (National Library of Wales). A caricature of John Pugh Pryse, heir of the estates of Gogerddan, Mathafarn and Rug, in one of his less comic opera uniforms.

of 1794 and the Fishguard landing of 1797. Many Dissenters were pushed into the republican fold. In the 1790s, America witnessed a remarkable series of social experiments to establish liberty settlements, utopian centres where people could be free to behave and worship as they wished.[143] A notable part was played by ministers in this transatlantic transplantation of people. In 1793, the Baptist Dr Enoch

Edwards preached a new Cambria in Wales. His letters depicted America as a land of boundless opportunity. 'Well, here we are in the Land of Liberty,' another Welsh emigrant wrote home in 1799, 'Now, where do we ground it?' Ezekiel Hughes and Edward Bebb sought to ground it along the Whitewater in 1800, in what would become the Welsh settlement of Paddy's Run. Morgan John Rhys sought to ground it on the waters of the Blacklick and the Connemaugh, about 250 miles west of Philadelphia. Here, Rhys and his wife Ann bought an entire county, 17,400 acres, to found the short-lived social experiment Beulah and the longer lived settlement of Cambria.[144] Robert Owen (1771–1858), the utopian, took the socialistic religion-free principles that had prospered at New Lanark to New Harmony, Indiana.[145]

During the depression which followed peace in 1815, increasing numbers of Welsh workers sailed to America. In 1818, *The Cambrian* reported that hundreds of ironworkers from Merthyr Tydfil had left for America. The newspaper also rekindled speculation about the existence of a tribe of Welsh-speaking Indians, the Madogwys, survivors of an earlier Welsh exodus.[146] Though some might have been attracted by the exoticism of this tale, the majority were drawn across the ocean by the positive proselytizing of the correspondence of relatives and friends. In November 1818, Elizabeth Johns of Llanvrechiva, Monmouthshire, took her family of twenty to join her son who was 'doing well' in America.[147] In the 1840s, another period of economic depression, reports of Welsh people fleeing economic hell at home for the earthly paradise intensified. Some never reached the promised land. In March 1849, the *Florida* carrying 171 emigrants, many from Wales, was lost off the Essex coast.[148] On 21 July 1849, the *Cardiff and Merthyr Guardian* reported that 'over 200 persons – men, women and children, passed through Newport on Monday last, from Nantyglo and Tredegar, for a steamer to Bristol, en-route for Pittsburg'.[149] The paper added that 'there are three or four very fine vessels advertising to sail from Newport with passengers to Boston in the USA, in the dock at the present time'.[150] In 1850, over 300 people from Bangor sailed on the *Forest Queen* to New York. During the month-long journey, emigrants had to endure terrific storms, mourn a death and celebrate two births. Although the *North Wales Chronicle* boasted that these were 'superior types' of emigrants, 'for they even included three ministers', the majority were a crew of people dingy enough to take a little of the magic out of the word emigration. Within their ranks were the long out of work, the illiterate, and the chronically drunk who had been offered the costs of the voyage by the Poor Law authorities, desperate to economize. In their ranks were also hopeless optimists, bankrupt adventurers and religious idealists.[151]

In 1866, *The Cambrian* reported that a large number of Mormons had emigrated from Merthyr Tydfil. The editor railed against the tactics of the Mormons.[152] 'First they gathered together a flock and then they emigrate with their Apostle. Fully 5,000 of our people have been drafted off to leave their whitened bones on the track, or live in wretchedness in the land of the Mormon.' During his career, the charismatic Mormon convert Dan Jones (1811–61) was credited with persuading 4,700 people to cross the Atlantic to a better life in Utah. When he died in 1861, 'having lived several lifetimes in his forty nine years, he left three wives'.[153] Although the Book of Mormon was chloroform in print for many, for other Welsh people it represented an ideal for which it was worth enduring unimaginable dangers and hardships. Some of the Welsh emigrants simply walked across the plains, pack on back, to Salt Lake City. Fortunate people travelled part of the way by rail, but one determined woman took a highly unusual form of transport: she bundled all her possessions into a wheelbarrow and walked with her two children, footsore in search of freedom.[154]

The trail contained many terrors. There were floods, fevers, fires and typhoons. Mosquitoes stung to madness, and polluted creeks poisoned people and beasts. Wild buffalo provoked stampedes. Women and children were drowned in raging torrents, or crushed beneath wagon wheels. But the least of their woes became the greatest of their worries. The most feared of all dangers were attacks by Indians displaced from their lands.[155] In 1862, the *Caernarvon and Denbigh Herald* reported 'Atrocious Indian Outrages' committed by Indians in Minnesota upon British settlers. In sensationalist language, the paper reported that the Indians had 'butchered innocent mothers and babes and taken over 200 white prisoners'. The editor reported that letters had been received by three, unnamed, local families detailing the horrors. The language of the report had a tone and attitude which would become familiar. The Indian attacks were 'cowardly', 'unprovoked', 'murderous'. The posse of whites who were sent to rescue the prisoners acted with 'bravery', showed 'necessary vigour' and 'defended their interests with fortitude'.[156] The Welsh soon became familiar with the language of conquest. But not all Welsh people were so ill-disposed towards the Indians. Robert Owen Pugh left the precipitous countryside of

Dolgellau in 1863 for the wider wilderness of Wyoming. There he married a niece of Blue Horse of the Oglala Sioux who fought and killed Custer at the battle of Little Big Horn. Robert Pugh was renamed *Istachtonka* or 'Big Eyes' by the Oglalas, and mixed in the company of Crazy Horse, Spotted Tail and Man Afraid of His Horse.[157]

By 1850, there were just under 30,000 foreign-born Welsh people living in the United States.[158] In 1890, the figure had more than trebled to reach a peak of 100,079. The passage of these people across the Atlantic proved to be a profitable enterprise for many companies. At Aberystwyth, Porthmadog and Bangor, local companies competed with each other to carry the emigrants. Often people were packed in amongst the cargoes of slate and coal. Following an industrial dispute in 1857, David Stephen Davies (1841–98), a steam engine operator in Aberdare, emigrated to America. In New York, he established an emigration company with its own ship, the *Rush*. His venture was not a success, for three of his ships sank before reaching Montevideo, Brazil and Patagonia. Following the loss of the *Electric Spark*, Davies had the unsettling experience of reading his own obituary in the American press. Disappointed at the assessment of his life, he returned to Wales and became minister of a chapel in Union Street, Carmarthen.[159]

The portrayal of the Welsh in the United States has tended to depict industrial workers in coal and iron, devoutly Nonconformist in religion, who sought cultural release in the literary and musical competitive milieu of the *eisteddfod*. There was, of course, a remarkable flowering of Welsh religion and culture in the United States from the early nineteenth century onwards. Armies of ministers crossed the Atlantic to save the souls of the heathen Indians and immigrants. In the early 1800s, Johnny Edwards, a scale-beam maker, was a familiar figure on the streets of New York, haranguing sinners from the back of his wagon, shouting through a three foot tin trumpet for the money-lenders on Wall Street to repent.[160] Despite the doom-laden howlings of Edwards and his devotees, others were devout and dedicated followers of Mammon. When gold was discovered in Colorado in 1859, the Welsh were amongst the fastest of rainbow chasers. George W. Griffith discovered substantial gold and silver deposits in Colorado and the settlement, which grew rapidly around his camp, was named Georgetown in his honour. The bard Cynfelin later managed the Mary Murphy Mine in the region. Morris Thomas and his partner Davies, were 'ymhlith rhai o brif olchwyr aur Gregory's Gulch' (amongst the

major gold washers of Gregory's Gulch). In 1863, Morris married
Hannah Thomas in the first all-Welsh wedding to be held in Colorado.
They then retired to Denver to enjoy a comfortable retirement free of
financial worries.[161]
     Mining communities were notoriously lawless places and those of
the American Wild West were particularly so. To control the wilder
elements, many Welsh people served as sheriffs and marshals. In
Canon City, W. S. Jones succeeded his fellow Welshman J. M. Davies
as marshal. In Coal Creek, Morgan Griffith was sheriff, while in Erie,
the marshal was Tom Williams.[162] In the 1860s, patrolman Alexander
S. Williams ruled the much feared 'Gangs of New York' with a savage
severity encapsulated in his motto: 'There is more law in the end of a
policeman's nightstick than in a decision of the Supreme Court.' The
Welsh were not only the enforcers of law and order, they also lived on
the fringes and frequently broke the law. Peter Williams ran a
notorious saloon at Slaughter House Point in New York where the
feared Daybreak Boys gang had its headquarters.[163] Further west, the
Welsh were even more prone to lawlessness. *Y Drych*, with the sancti-
monious condemnation that characterized the press in Wales, reported
that in Scranton:

> Ar Main Street mae yna Cymry . . . yn cadw bar bron yn ail dy. Os ydych . . . am
> grogshops Cymreig, whiskey holes, gin mills, rum cellars, ac ati ewch i
> Lackawanna Avenue, Main Street a Hyde Park . . . Os ydych am glywed iaith
> uffern . . . o gegau Cymreig, ewch am hanner awr ar hyd y strydoedd Cymreig,
> ac i'r salwns Cymreig.[164]

> On Main Street, there are Welsh people keeping bars almost every other house.
> If you want Welsh grogshops, whiskey holes, gin mills, rum cellars and so forth,
> go to Lackawanna Avenue, Main Street and Hyde Park . . . If you want to hear
> Hell's language . . . from Welsh lips, go for a half hour stroll on the Welsh streets,
> and to the Welsh saloons.

Some of the most infamous Americans were of Welsh origin. Frank
and Jesse James, the celebrated outlaws, were the grandchildren of a
Pembrokeshire minister who emigrated to Pennsylvania.[165] Isaac
Davies, the son of parents from Kidwelly, was a psychopathic mass
murderer and rapist, who terrorized the environs of Salt Lake City in
the 1840s, killing over a hundred people. As in North America so in
the South, the Welsh settled down to lives of dissipation and evil, as
well as to discipline and duty. The intensifying copper trade between
Wales and Chile drew people from the brothels around Swansea's

Cuba public house to cater for sailors in Shit Street, Santiago. John Porter was one of many who enjoyed a picturesque life among the ladies and knife-wielders.[166]

Missionaries and Missions

The imperious, imperial and impure trinity of merchant, military hero and missionary were the forces by which the British built their empire. Traditionally, the Welsh were deemed to have made their greatest contribution to the Empire through the Christianization of the heathen masses. They often claimed a monopoly of virtue, and the history of the Welsh missionaries is indeed a remarkable one.[167] Despite the profound problems which beset their home communities, hundreds of Welsh men and women preferred to travel the world propagating and propounding the gospel. Many went under the aegis of the London Missionary Society, but several others were trained in Wales. At the old Academy, Neuaddlwyd in Cardiganshire, a spider-infested ruin of a building, Dr Thomas Phillips, a part-time farmer but a full-time enthusiast, trained a remarkable group of people for service in missionary work. David Jones (1797–1841) entered the school at fourteen. Following further training at an academy in Llanfyllin, he began preaching at sixteen and became the first missionary to visit Madagascar. Thomas Bevan (1796–1829), one of his contemporaries in Neuaddlwyd, followed David Jones to Mauritius and Madagascar in August 1818. Today, three schools in Toamasina carry Thomas Bevan's name, testimony to the high regard still paid to his contribution to the island.[168]

Dr Thomas Phillips could scarcely have prepared the pliable young men under his care for all the dangers and perils they would encounter in their missionary work. The life of a missionary was undoubtedly harsh and dangerous, demanding determination, dedication and luck to survive. Many faced death from opponents. Robert Jermain Thomas (1840–66), of Monmouth, became the first Christian martyr in Korea when he was killed by local soldiers.[169] A Mrs Coultart from Breconshire fought against considerable opposition and oppression to help her husband establish a successful mission in Jamaica in the 1820s.[170] David Griffiths (1792–1863) had to flee for his life from Madagascar during the murderous onslaught of Queen Ranavalona in the 1820s.[171] John Williams was less fortunate. He was killed and eaten in 1839 by natives of Erromanga in the unsuitably named Society Islands.[172] But the greatest danger came in microscopic form. Daniel Jones (1813–46), a missionary for the Calvinistic Methodists in the rain-drenched Khasia hills, died after just a few months in India from jungle fever. He was buried with his small daughter in the missionary graveyard in Cherappoonjee. Thomas Jones (1810–49), the stubborn and proud missionary to Khasia, died after eight years in India aged thirty-nine.[173] Jacob Davies (1716–1849), Baptist missionary in Ceylon, died there of a horrible and horrific wasting sickness. John Penry (1854–83) of Llandeilo died after less than a year of his mission to Zanzibar. Death also came in larger natural forms than the microbe.[174] Above Jamalpur, Gwilym Roberts lies beneath a tombstone which simply records that he 'died from the effects of an encounter with a tiger near this place, AD 1864'.

Perhaps the greatest contribution of the Welsh missionaries to countless thousands of people around the globe was not their spiritual salvation, but the formalization of their indigenous languages. The Welsh showed that they had learned one of the lessons of their own history – in order to enable people to understand your spiritual message you must translate the scriptures into their language. Although their aim was spiritual salvation, many Welshmen have been credited with linguistic rescue. Missionaries laboured long and hard to publish the Bible and the gospels in native tongues. John Davies (1772–1855), who served the London Missionary Society in the South Sea Islands for fifty-four years, translated *The Pilgrim's Progress*, large sections of the New Testament and the Psalms, Brown's and the Westminster Catechism into Tahitan.[175] He also prepared a dictionary of the language. David Johns (1796–1843) took a printing press with him to Madagascar and despite persecution helped to translate the Bible and *The Pilgrim's Progress* into the Malagasi language and to compile a Malagasi–English dictionary.[176] In China, Griffith John (1831–1912) translated the New Testament into the Wen-li language.[177] In India, John Ceredig Evans (1855–1936) was instrumental in preparing and publishing a version of the Bible in the Khasi language and a new edition of the hymn book. The 'mortal remains' of Thomas Jones still lie in Calcutta, beneath a headstone which proclaims him to be 'the father of the Khasi language'. A greater gift than language was freedom. This, allegedly, was the gift of Mrs Mary Knibb (d. 1886) to a group of slaves in Jamaica. As the slaves were being led past her, the spiritual and saintly lady asked permission of

the captors to feed the captives. Her devout demeanour so impressed
the slave owners that they freed the slaves.[178]

Slavery and Slavers

This melodramatic redemption struck a chord in a Wales which, by the
1820s, had become strongly anti-slavery.[179] *Greal y Bedyddwyr* and the
Nonconformist press were overwhelmingly in favour of the abolition
of the slave trade. Since 1805, *The Cambrian* had published a series of
letters which outlined 'the horrors of West Indian slavery'.[180] In 1826,
the paper declared against slavery with editorial self-righteousness:
'He who allows oppression, shares the crime.'[181] In 1818, *Seren Gomer*
was highly critical of the US government for selling 139 slaves, 'people
who had fought for Liberty'.[182] Meetings were held in several towns,
condemning the trade in slaves, and several petitions were presented to
Parliament, calling for abolition. Benjamin Evans organized sugar
'boycotts'. The 'campaigner for freedom' Thomas Clarkson toured
Wales generating momentum for the anti-slave movement.[183] Despite
the strength of Welsh anti-slavery sentiment, there also existed a significant pro-slavery body within Wales. During his tour of the north,
Clarkson frequently complained that the gentry were hampering his
work. At Bala and Dolgellau, he complained of the 'malicious'
opposition of the estates of Nannau, Hengwrt, Ystumcolwyn and
Meillionydd and the 'pernicious influence' of Sir Robert Vaughan, MP
for Merionethshire between 1796 and 1835.

After abolition, many families drew attention away from the fact
that their fortunes rested on the profits of the slave trade. Over the
years, guilt has covered the traces of this 'sin' as a scab eventually
covers a festering wound. These guilty secrets, like Mrs Rochester, the
most famous Creole heiress, have been hidden away in shuttered attics.
But many families had strong links to the slave trade. The Pennants of
Penrhyn Castle, the Glynnes and the Gladstones of Hawarden, the
Stapletons of Bodrhyddan, John Jones Walsh, the Morrises of
Piercefield, Nathaniel Phillips of Slebech, the Yorkes of Erddig and
even the family of Adam Ottley, registrar of St David's diocese, all had
links with the slave trade in the West Indies, Africa and America.

The 1780s and 1790s were the high point of the infamous 'Triangular
Trade'. Manufactured textile and metal goods, including 'copper rods',
'manillas', and 'neptunes', were shipped to West Africa.[184] There, they

were exchanged for slaves who were brutally taken along the 'Middle Passage' to the West Indies, Central and North America. Cotton, sugar, rum and tobacco, all of which were infinitely more valuable than the original items, were then imported back to Britain. Those trinkets which were exchanged for lives were manufactured at the Penclawdd works, the White Rock works near Swansea and the Holywell works in Flintshire. The White Rock works even had a section dedicated to the production of short 'copper rods' and 'bronze manillas' – small pieces of copper shaped like horseshoes – which were used as currency in Africa for the purchase of slaves. In 1788, Thomas Williams, 'the Copper King', claimed that he had invested over £70,000 in these works; Williams was vigilant in his petitions to Parliament for compensation should one of the abolitionist bills become law.[185]

Many of the ships which carried slaves to the West Indies were captained or crewed by Welshmen. John Sinclair of Swansea, master of the brigantine *The Two Sisters*, John Roberts of Cardiff, a 'wicked man', and Thomas Stroud, captain of *The African Queen*, were three such characters.[186] When *The African Queen* was sunk in 1793, and Nathaniel Phillips's slave ship, *Mary Ann*, was lost in December 1772, the owners complained about the loss of revenue, not the loss of lives.[187] To them, slavery was simply a matter of economics. Slaves were not considered human. Like rum, sugar and tobacco, slaves were commodities. They were afforded no better comfort or care than cattle. In the correspondence between Lord Penrhyn and his Jamaican estate supervisor, Alexander Falconer, as much interest was evinced in the condition of cattle as in that of the negroes.[188] This was a trade devoid of sentiment. Hard as it is for people today to accept, to many people in the late eighteenth and early nineteenth centuries, slavery made sound economic sense. John Warlow, a bankrupt wine merchant from Haverfordwest, made a fortune after he emigrated to the West Indies in 1804 to run a business whose economic success was based on slavery.[189]

The papers of Nathaniel Phillips of Slebech in the National Library of Wales provide a fascinating insight into the world of a slave owner.[190] Phillips owned two large plantations in Jamaica. His correspondence is a litany of complaint about harsh economic realities. Nathaniel was sandwiched between incompetent slaves, who were poor workers ruining crops and over-burning rum and sugar, and grasping merchants who sought discounts for the allegedly 'inferior' quality of the rum and sugar produced on his plantations. Despite this, he achieved profits of over £10,000 a year in the 1790s and early 1800s.[191] This enabled him not only to pay the £20,000 price for the Slebech estate in 1793, in cash, but also to purchase a large town house in London, which he filled with fine furniture, art and Broadwood pianos. It also supplemented a lavish lifestyle which included mistresses, frequent resort to prostitutes, and all the other pleasures and peccadilloes to which Georgian gentlemen were prone. Most profitably, Nathaniel speculated in the price of slaves. His diaries for the 1790s contain calculations of the price that slaves would command in different markets. The ships he organized from Africa were always sent to where he calculated the market would provide the highest price.[192]

The Jamaica of Nathaniel Phillips was almost paradisiacal when compared to Trinidad under the governorship of Sir Thomas Picton. In that island's sad history this was surely the saddest moment.[193] Capri under Tiberius could not have been much worse than Trinidad under Picton. A professional soldier from Pembrokeshire, and a giant of a man, standing well over six foot, and with 'a repulsive expression which sometimes hung on his brow',[194] Picton set out to rule Trinidad with a brutality which has seldom been seen even in the bloody annals of Empire. In the 1790s, Trinidad, with no laws or lawyers and only a distant memory of Spanish forces, was Picton's kingdom. He was the law and his law was draconian. Picton increased the limit on the floggings of negroes from twenty-five to thirty-nine lashes, implemented a curfew, increased their hours of work and reduced the modest rights that they had. Picton created a fortune for himself and his mistress, the luscious and promiscuous Rosette Smith. He acquired lands, houses and enjoyed the profitable work of hunting down runaway slaves and selling them in America. When slaves threatened to revolt or indulged in sorcery, Picton acted with a medieval brutality. He had negroes burned at the stake, hanged and then beheaded. Their ashes were scattered to the winds and their heads spiked and displayed around the island. His nemesis came in the form of a young girl, Louise Calderdon.[195] Wrongly accused of theft, she was imprisoned. Picton authorized her torture. This outraged liberal opinion in Britain. Picton was recalled to Britain and imprisoned in Newgate, on the exceptionally high bail of £40,000. Although he was exonerated on the technicality that Spanish law, which still operated in Trinidad, allowed torture to extract confessions from prisoners, his reputation did not recover until his heroics in the Napoleonic Wars.[196] But his cruel legacy lasted. In 1825, ten years after Picton's death, his brother, a Pembrokeshire rector, was fined £164 for mistreating two negroes on the family's Trinidad estates.

Slavery was ended with the Emancipation Bill of 1833 and was enforced by the might of the British Navy. The bill authorized the payment of compensation, not to the slaves but to plantation owners. This proved highly profitable to some Welsh families. George Hay Dawkins Pennant received £14,683. 17s. 2d. in 1838, for his 764 emancipated slaves.[197] But emancipation did not close an infamous chapter in Welsh history. Slavery was institutionalized in America and the Welsh could be found in both the pro- and the anti-slavery lobbies. Robert Watson and Jeb Stuart both fought for the South during the Civil War. Although *Trysorfa'r Plant* described the Civil War as a divine visitation and a punishment to the United States for tolerating slavery for too long, many figures condemned the North. The insensitive but influential Talhaiarn criticized the North for its scorched earth policies and practices. Henry Morton Stanley, the adventurer, hedged his bets and fought for both sides. In the early 1850s, his involvement with the South foresaw his later involvement in the murderous campaigns of King Leopold II of Belgium in the Congo.[198] One who was deeply involved with the cause of slavery was the infamous William H. Williams.[199] From 1836, he was purchasing between 300 and 400 slaves each spring for further sale in the markets of the South. Like Nathaniel Phillips, he had the nous to purchase in a buyer's market and sell at the highest profit. He ran his business from the 'yellow house' in Washington, a three-storey brick building covered with plaster and painted the most garish shade of yellow. The house was described as 'that infernal hell'. In it, in 1850, the anti-slavery campaigner Fredrika Bremer found a large number of children, 'kept here', so Williams explained, 'for a short time to fatten'. Williams also selected out the prettiest 'fancy girls' for sale to northern brothels. With his considerable experience of incarceration, it was a natural development for Williams to diversify into private jails.

Welsh involvement in slavery was not simply a matter of enlightened abolitionists against uncivilized slavers, as the remarkable history of Nathaniel Wells showed. Nathaniel was one of five children fathered by William Wells, a Cardiff slave owner, from his slaves. William was not simply a lustful master enjoying his *droit du seigneur*, for he appeared to have a genuine regard for his slave lovers. Nathaniel was given his

freedom, educated in Britain, and inherited a large portion of William's
wealth. With this he purchased the Piercefield estate near Chepstow in
1802. Though he had escaped labour in his father's plantation, this did
not prevent Nathaniel from keeping his relatives slaves even after the
Abolition of Slavery Act in 1807. The mixed-race Nathaniel was one of
the richest men in Wales, enjoying influential positions as a magistrate
and as deputy lieutenant of Monmouthshire.[200]

Wales at War

Soldiers and sailors were ranked and regimented within a strict
hierarchy governed by practice and protocol. The navy of Georgian
and Victorian Britain has been portrayed as being crewed by an undisciplined rabble, scoured from the dregs of harbour-front society, afloat
on a sea of rum and satiated by sodomy.[201] As with all characteriza-
tions and caricatures, there is an element of truth in this view. But it is
hard to believe that such a force would have enabled Britain to create
and conquer an empire. It was only through ruling the waves that
Britannia could rule. Many of the Welsh who chose a life at sea were
capable, conscientious, charismatic characters. But the prospect of a
life at sea terrified many. In order to escape the brutal and brutalizing
conditions, John Jones, Jac Glan-y-gors (1766–1821), poet and writer
of tender love songs, fled to London in 1789, with the dreaded press
gang hot on his heels.[202] But others relished the prospect of a life on
the ocean's wave.

Sir William Jones (1721–83) of Breton Hill Mill in Pembrokeshire
ran away to sea as a twelve-year-old. Despite the fact that he had no
relation or patron to further his career, he rose to become commander-
in-chief of marine forces of the East India Company. Brave, prompt
and vigilant, Jones fought many battles against the French, Indian
princes and pirates.[203] Sir Erasmus Gower (1742–1815) was another
Pembrokeshire lad who left home at a tender age for a life at sea. In the
1760s, he was an officer in two voyages of exploration to the northern
oceans. In the 1800s, following his support of Cornwallis and
Macartney in China, Gower was promoted to the rank of admiral.[204]
Thomas Foley (1757–1833) of Ridgeway in Pembrokeshire worked his
way through the ranks until he became one of Nelson's captains. A
diligent, determined but shy man, he fought at Toulon (1795), Cape St
Vincent (1797) and the Battle of the Nile (1798), where his ship, the

Goliath, led the British fleet. Foley played a part in one of the most famous of military exchanges. He was the captain of Nelson's flagship when the famous hero was given an order not to engage the enemy. Nelson turned to Foley and remarked: 'You know, Foley, I have only one eye – and I have a right to be blind sometimes.' Putting his small telescope to his blind eye, Nelson exclaimed 'I really do not see the signal'. With the prize money he gained from plundering French and Spanish ships, Foley purchased the Abermarlais estate in Carmarthenshire.[205] Foley's wealth, however, was a mere pittance in comparison to that appropriated by Admiral John Gell, 'a rough swearing tar with a good heart', owner of Llanwysg, an elegantly eccentric Italianate house on the banks of the river Usk, near Crickhowell. In 1793, in an aggressive act that transferred Spanish enmity from France to Britain, Gell captured the treasure ship *Santiago*, estimated to be worth £1.5m.[206]

Foley, Gell, Sir Edward Hughes and Admiral Edward Campbell Owen were just a few Welsh people who climbed the naval career ladder to the very highest rungs. Having reached the crow's nest of naval employment, they assisted the ascent of other Welsh people. Each had a coterie of Welsh officers serving under them. People such as Captain John Lloyd of Brecon, Captain Walter Griffith (1727–79) and Captain Timothy Edwards, the infamous 'Hammer and Nails' of Nanhoron, had their careers steered upwards by the help of a Welsh patron.[207] They, in turn, assisted others. Captain Timothy Edwards supported many impoverished northerners in his service. Welshmen could be found throughout naval ranks, for the sea offered a natural career for many Welsh people. Between 1795 and 1815, thousands of Welsh people were active in the Royal Navy. Their life stories reveal in tragic detail the dangers that faced the simple sailor. James Davies of Pembroke was given a life pension on 3 June 1806, having lost his right leg at the Battle of Trafalgar. Ebenezer Jones of Carmarthen, who suffered 'a right acromion scapula fracture', received a pension of £5, while James Meyrick aged thirty of Cardigan, lost his right arm above the elbow and received a pension of £8 per annum.[208] They only survived, in all probability, because they had been wounded early in battle. Later, and the surgeon's knives would have been too blunt for effective amputation. Assisting the surgeons on Thomas Foley's ship, the *Goliath*, at the Battle of the Nile in 1798, were a large number of women whose names are actually recorded in the ship's log. It was reported that several women were wounded and that one, remarkably, gave birth in the heat of battle. Although it was rare, it was not unknown for women to choose a life at sea – one of the most celebrated was William Prothero, a private marine of the *Amazon*. This Amazon was discovered to have been a love-struck Welsh girl of eighteen who had followed her lover to sea.[209]

Within the wooden world of the British Navy, the Welsh made a significant contribution. Perhaps the most important contribution to the development of British naval supremacy was made by a man who only rarely ventured to sea. The prickly, pugnacious, stormy petrel Sir Edward James Reed (1830–1906) rose from lowly beginnings, as an apprentice shipwright, to become the chief constructor of the navy. His designs revolutionized warships in the 1860s. After a dispute with the Admiralty, he entered private practice, during which time he designed warships for several foreign navies, including those of Japan and Germany. Another arms dealer and fellow Liberal Member of Parliament, Stuart Rendel, described Reed as 'a self-seeking bully and impostor'. In 1875, Reed became MP for Pembroke Boroughs and later represented Cardiff. It was a very broad-based Liberal Party which could accommodate Edward Reed and the 'belligerent, uncompromising' 'Apostle of Peace' Henry Richard. Fitting monuments to Reed's memory are the Royal School of Naval Architecture and Marine Engineering, which he helped to establish in 1864, and the naval dockyards at Milford Haven.[210]

Reputations, whether appropriate or inappropriate, endure. The Georgian and Victorian navy was allegedly composed of 'rum-soaked sodomites goaded into battle by the lash', but the army was even worse. Their leader, the duke of Wellington, described the troops under his command as 'the scum of the earth – the mere scum of the earth'.[211] The memoirs of Thomas Williams, Capelulo (1784–1855), provide a fascinating insight into conditions as a 'day-labourer of death' within Wellington's army.[212] Williams was frequently punished with up to 300 lashes for indiscipline and an almost unbelievable incompetence. Awarded £10 in bounty money, rather than purchasing essential commodities and clothes, Williams spent it all on a wild spree of drunken debauchery. In Bombay he fought and fornicated. The money that was not stolen from him, he spent on drink and dark ladies. In later life Capelulo repented and became a tolerated, if not respected, figure in the temperance movement in the north. He confessed abundant past sins with the conviction of a convert, claiming at one meeting that he had squandered most of his money on wine and women, and that the rest, he had just wasted. His complexion became as scarlet as his uniform and he soon acquired a pungent animal tang about him. His jacket was not changed or cleaned for at least six months, so that he smelt of old sweat, vomit and urine laced with the stench of black powder. Capelulo and his brothers-in-arms used foul language, had the old soldier's talent for dodging and scrounging, associated with bad company, drank to excess and used the four letter expletive for the sexual act with monosyllabic monotony. In contrast, the journals written in the years 1807–16 by Captain Thomas Henry Browne, brother of Felicia Hemans, who penned some of the Empire's most famous images, reveal both the harshness of discipline and the hardness of military life. In contrast to Thomas Williams, Browne echoes the older, nobler Homeric face of war, where courage and camaraderie merged with the brutalities of the killing fields.[213] He also evokes the bedraggled caravanseri of children and wives, weeping and waving as they followed their men to war. The letters Lieutenant St John George of the Marines wrote home to his parents in the Blue Boar Inn, Haverfordwest, speak of the genteel poverty of a lonely, sensitive officer trapped in an insensitive militaristic world.[214]

Yet, this ill-disciplined scum provided vital support to the navy in maintaining British supremacy.[215] It also undertook a crucial role in the preservation of public order, all the more so because of a lack of an effective police force. It was also frequently engaged in support of the Revenue in the war against smuggling. There were times when a sense of real danger swung public opinion firmly behind its army. In 1795, such was the anxiety that the French were about to invade that the women of Neath petitioned the Prime Minister for the right to raise their own home-defence regiment, claiming:

> There are in this town about two hundred women who have been used to hard labour all the days of their lives, such as working in coal pits, on the high road, tilling the ground etc. If you would grant us arms, that is *light pikes* . . . we do assure you that we would in a short time learn our exercise . . . I assure you we are not trifling with you, but serious in our proposal.[216]

September 1803 was another period of paranoid invasion panic. A gentleman travelling through Radnor was apprehended by locals who mistook him for Napoleon. It was only after the extreme unlikelihood of the First Consul travelling unaccompanied through mid-Wales was pointed out to the rustics that the imprisoned traveller was released. In

Unknown artist, Thomas Williams, Capelulo. When 'he heard the sound of the undertaker preparing his grave', Capelulo converted to the temperance cause. In his earlier life, however, Capelulo was one of the most ill-disciplined soldiers in British ranks. In India, he fornicated more than he fought.

February 1797, the much anticipated invasion force arrived on the coast of Wales at Fishguard. Posterity seems to have bequeathed this landing an air of comedy and farce.[217] The French, wearied by the sea journey, were allegedly terrified by seeing ranks of soldiers in their red uniforms marching on the hills around the town. Unbeknown to the French, these were, in fact, local women in traditional costume, led by the redoubtable Jemima Nicholas, wielding pick-forks. The invaders were also met by the well-disciplined ranks of the Carmarthenshire militia and Pembrokeshire Fencibles and promises that further militia forces were on their way. In the face of such odds, surrender appeared the better part of valour.

Those experiences of shared danger, and the visceral fear of the enemy at the door, brought the Welsh deeper into the British fold.[218] Indeed, Wales, which had been written off as a potential hot-bed of sedition and possible revolt, proved itself in the moment of danger to be loyal and dependable. The initiatives to raise volunteers to provide a home guard against the threat of invasion from France, in the 1790s and early 1800s, met with a remarkable degree of support from Wales. Linda Colley has estimated that 7,914 volunteered to serve from Wales in 1804.[219] These official returns are however incomplete; figures in the Welsh press indicate that 15,862 in 1810 actually volunteered to serve.[220] Those who served included a wide cross-section of Welsh society. The hundred-man strong volunteer corps formed in the parish of Machen, in Monmouthshire in 1803, is perhaps typical. Its members included a gentleman, a lawyer's clerk, a bevy of farmers and agricultural labourers, a sprinkling of rural craftsmen, and ten men who worked in the local ironworks.[221] The Welsh peasant, for a variety of reasons, was rapidly becoming a Briton. In the heady, intoxicating atmosphere of the fair-day volunteer recruitment meeting, Welshmen bewitched by the 'romance of a warrior's life' and the prospect of a hero's death, strutted off in search of the 'universal pant for glory'. These men were not simply class-traitors or working men suffering from 'false-consciousness'.[222] They, too, were patriots.

Many also volunteered to serve in the militia regiments that existed in every Welsh county and strived to fight not just in Wales, but wherever there were enemies to destroy.[223] In 1798, in and around Newry, the Ancient British Fencibles led by Sir Watkin Williams Wynn were brutal agents in the suppression of the Irish Rebellion.[224] 'Brave Sir Watkin's' deeds were celebrated in Welsh broadsheets and ballads. The songs ignored the brutalities enacted by the brawny, brawling and brainless Welsh troops. Others were more critical and honest. One eyewitness spoke of the wholesale burning of homes and the slaughter of defenceless old men and boys. The corpses were disposed by the cartload into mass graves dug at several places along the southern

perimeter of the town. Others were thrown into the river in the expectation that they would float out to sea. Throughout the internment,
Welsh troops showed as much disrespect for the dead as they had the
living. Many bodies were dragged along the ground by the heels, or
pulled by ropes tied around their necks, into the open pits.[225]

The heroism and heroics of the Welsh in the Napoleonic Wars further
cemented the integration of Wales into a greater Britain. Above the
tumult of battle, the crashing of cannon, the screeching of men and
horses, bands played inspiring and inspirational tunes to maintain discipline and motivate the troops. In their midst was John Roberts, son of
Robert, an itinerant fair-singer, a fourteen-year-old drummer in the 21st
Welsh Fusiliers. To Sir Thomas Picton, the wars against France were an
opportunity to redeem his reputation after his controversial governorship of Trinidad. In 1808, he was promoted to the rank of
major-general. The following year, he took part in the siege of Flushing
and in 1810, he was appointed to command the 3rd Division in the
Peninsular War. At Busaco, Fuentes de Onoro and at Badajoz (where
he was badly wounded), he led from the front, on occasion in top hat
and tails rather than in the traditional red uniform. In 1810, he was
knighted. Shell-shocked and tired of battle, having had a premonition
of his own death, Picton reluctantly agreed to Wellington's request to
lead the 5th British Infantry Division at Waterloo. His premonition of
death proved prescient. On 18th June, at about 2 p.m., he was shot dead
through his top hat while leading his men forward to repulse Donzelot's
division. In death, Picton continued to be larger than life. He had the
privilege of three burials, at Waterloo, then at St George's London, and
finally at St Paul's Cathedral in 1859.[226] The ballads and songs penned
to mark his 'noble' death revealed that the fashionable virtues of sensibility, civility and *tendresse* had to accommodate the barbarous values
of militarism and male hauteur. For the next fifty years, it was uncertain
how heroism would be domesticated.

Another celebrated casualty on that fateful day was Henry Paget,
earl of Uxbridge, later marquis of Anglesey of Plas Newydd. Uxbridge
scandalized polite society when he, the father of eight children, ran
away with Lady Charlotte Wellesley, the wife of Wellington's younger
brother. Uxbridge was in charge of the 11,000–strong multinational
cavalry force at Waterloo. He lost his leg either to passing shrapnel or
to an exploding shell. Undoubtedly surprised, but clearly unperturbed,
Uxbridge turned to Wellington and exclaimed: 'By God Sir! I've just
lost my leg.' To which, the Iron Duke replied: 'By God Sir, so you

have'. The British tradition of heroic understatement, in the face of insurmountable odds and adverse circumstances, perhaps started at that moment. Although he lost his leg, Uxbridge's libido appeared unaffected, for he fathered a further ten children with his new wife. The distrust and dislike of Uxbridge continued, as is revealed in the anonymous epitaph written to his lost leg: 'Here lies the Marquis of Anglesey's limb; / The devil will have the rest of him'.[227]

The leaders were not the only ones to lose limbs at Waterloo. Robert Evans of Privy Street, Denbigh, also lost his leg. Such heroism at all levels reinforced the image that the Welsh were part of a broader British identity. This was further strengthened by the journeys which the heroes of the Napoleonic Wars took through Wales. Nelson's tour of 1802, through the south, was flanked by crowds of cheering spectators. So many former comrades-in-arms greeted the great hero that it is remarkable that the tour finished in time for Trafalgar. At Swansea, above the cheers of the crowd, Nelson allegedly recognized the whistle of his former bosun Tom Cleaves, and enjoyed an emotional reunion. Upon meeting the great man, the iron-hard Richard Crawshay burst into tears and ordered his workers to 'cheer you beggars'. They responded with a deafening roar that must have been heared on Dowlais Top.[228] Between 1806 and 1815, vicars reported that many boys were being christened 'Wellington', 'Nelson' and 'Thomas'. Wellington Nelson Lewis of Cwmbwrla, born in 1814, had a lot to live up to.

Cannon fodder and common heroes, Welsh soldiers were among the worker bees in the expansion of the British Empire, strengthening the thin red line as it spread around the world. In India, they won plenty of money, plenty of wounds, but no more taste than their betters. One of their 'betters' was Sir William Nott, the son of a tenant farmer from Neath and later owner of the Ivy Bush Hotel in Carmarthen.[229] His portraits by Thomas Brigstocke, of Carmarthen, which can still be seen in the Town Hall in Carmarthen, the Oriental Club in London, and the Town Hall in Calcutta, show a proud, almost haughty, self-reliant man.[230] When the opportunity arose, Nott proved that he possessed a genius for war. In Afghanistan, it was Nott's troops who were principally responsible for avenging the murder of Macnaughten at Kabul in 1841. Villages and markets were razed to the ground, civilians were displaced, and the symbolic gates to the temple of Somnát were stolen and carried to Britain. The Welsh press, in order to feed the self-esteem of public opinion, described these atrocities as the justified actions of a brave, heavily outnumbered underdog. In view of the overall disastrous record of the British in Afghanistan, it is remarkable that in each of his engagements Nott emerged victorious.[231] In appreciation of his service in guarding their opium profits, the East India Company granted him a pension of £1,000 until his death in 1845. Upon his death, they contributed £100 to erect a statue made of the guns captured by Nott's troops at the battle of Maharajpúr. To give the statue appropriate room, several Carmarthen houses were demolished, the owners compensated, the tenants displaced, and Nott Square created.[232]

Wales and war were again in accord in the 1850s, at the outbreak of the Crimean War.[233] This war for possession of the Holy Places had an ostensibly religious cause which gave it immense popularity in Wales. The new telegraph, which had been installed in Swansea in 1852 and Carmarthen in 1853, gave an immediacy that other wars had lacked.[234] The war has a peculiarly Welsh perspective for it sounds as if the Welsh landscape was in battle. Lords Cardigan, Raglan and the marquis of Anglesey all led forces. Among the cavalry who rode into the 'valley of death', in the celebrated 'Charge of the Light Brigade', were Frederick and Godfrey Morgan, sons of Lord Tredegar. Despite being surrounded by guns, as told in Tennyson's dramatic poetical reconstruction, they both rode out unscathed. Frederick died in 1909, Godfrey in 1913, both greatly mourned. One tenant expressed a sentiment that encapsulates the feelings of many Welsh people towards the gentry, 'If I could worship anyone but God, it would be Lord Tredegar.'[235] Others were not so fortunate in the Crimea. John Crosby Vaughan, of Brynog in the Vale of Aeron, fought valiantly, but ultimately in vain, for he was killed in battle and immortalized in a famous folk song.[236] As in all wars, women played their part. Many of the injured were comforted and nursed by Elizabeth Davies-Cadwaladr (1789–1860) of Bala, one of a regiment of nurses recruited by Florence Nightingale to care for the wounded.[237] Despite the gravity of the situation in 1855, not all Welsh fighters were welcome in the Crimea. The Monmouthshire militia volunteered for action, but such was their reputation that even the pugnacious Palmerston refused to allow them to travel. Undaunted, this Falstaffian militia went to camp at Pembroke Dock at their own expense and in their own time. There, in 1855, they mutinied and, the following year, enjoyed a savage battle with their mortal enemies, the Montgomery Rifles.[238]

The Jewel in the Crown

America was the gem which the British Empire lost in the late eighteenth century, India the jewel which replaced her. Both countries attracted emigrants of a peculiar and particular kind. America, the land of freedom and boundless opportunity, attracted many who were disenchanted with the curtailment of political and religious liberties in Britain, as a result of the repressive reaction to the French Revolution. India attracted many who were at ease with the ideals and ideology that was being forged in Britain in the late eighteenth century.[239] Many of the Welsh who emigrated to India did so for their own personal gain. India beckoned because it offered the prospect of a swift fortune. Go east young man, make your fortune, and return to retire in splendour, was the message of the lives of several Welsh role models. It was this lust which drove people to endure India's tropical climate, the chill nights followed by burning sunshine, devastating monsoons, millions of biting insects, man-eating tigers and persistent diseases.[240]

In several communities, the return of one got-rich-quick nabob served as an activator and motivator for others to take the passage to India. The return of Major Cornelius Grant, Henry Grant and John Grant to Lawrenny in Pembrokeshire served as the incentive for the Voyle family to decamp and seek fortune, if not fame, in India.[241] Lamphey in Pembrokeshire in the early nineteenth century was a virtual microcosm of British India. The Morgan family of Cleggars, the Parrys of Portclew and the Thomases of Lamphey Park had all prospered as they progressed in the service of the East India Company Army. But the strongest and richest thread of Indian interest in the parish was the vicar, Thomas Broff Byers. Born in Sumatra, in 1785, Thomas was the son of Major Isaac Byers of the Bengal Army. Like his father, he also served in the East India Company, rising to the rank of captain before he returned, in 1819, to enter Queen's College, Cambridge, to train for the ministry.[242] Castle Hall, Milford, was built between 1770 and 1775 by John Zephaniah Holwell, formerly a governor of Bengal. In landlocked Brecon, awareness of the success of the brothers Walter and Jeffrey Wilkins in the East India Company, and the patronage of the surgeon Thomas Evans of Merthyr Cynog were the incentive for John Lloyd to become a 'surgeon's servant' in the Company. John worked his way through the ranks until he became the first Welshman to become one of 'God Almighty's Captains', as captains of Indiamen were known in the eighteenth century. His life was an epic of survival. For almost forty years, he survived the rigours of long voyages, tropical diseases, shipwrecks, a naval battle in which he was wounded, a ship-to-ship battle, during which his ship was forced to surrender, and two years in prison in Bangalore. By his retirement, he had amassed a fortune of around £2 to £2.5 million in twenty-first-century terms.[243]

The relationship between conqueror and conquered was complex. The process of adjustment to the country, climate, customs and cultures to which people had never been exposed before was difficult. It was not simply a tale of imperial exploitation and extortion. In the early stages, it was often one of mutual respect and a genuine wish that both cultures would benefit from integration and interaction. The remarkable scholar, linguist and lawyer, Sir William Jones (1746–94), in a short but remarkably productive life, drew attention to the longevity of the ancient writings of India, the time-depth and character of the subcontinent's past, and the inner wisdom of its major beliefs. But despite all his achievements in the law and in publishing, perhaps his greatest was to survive the changing fashions of academic study with his reputation intact.[244] Many Welshmen 'went native' and had relationships with Indian women. George Elliot (1733–99), the son of a Laugharne surgeon, went to Calcutta in 1780 as a 'writer', a junior rank in the East India Company. There he lived with 'a native woman, a resident of Calcutta, named Marcimnissa, the mother of my three children'.[245]

Gradually, however, the relationship changed from one in which the cultures sought to coexist and collaborate to one in which they were antagonistic.[246] The career of Sir Henry Bartle Edward Frere (1815–84) is indicative and illustrates this change in attitude. Born in the Vale of Clydach, Bartle Frere was devoted to public service and entered the Bombay Civil Service in 1834. In the 1840s, he worked as resident with the rajah of Sattara and counselled the London government against annexing the territory. Yet in 1858 he was one of the key figures in the suppression of the Indian Mutiny. Benjamin Millingchamps (1756–1829), a chaplain in Madras, and Sir John Harford Jones Brydges (1764–1847) of the East India Company both learned that a dictatorship, however benevolent, would encounter bloodshed. Timothy Richards Lewis (1841–86), a surgeon major in the India Medical Service, had to deal at first hand with the bloody consequences of conquest.[247] Apart from the fortune that he appropriated and accumulated in India, the only evidence that Captain John Lloyd had a taste for anything Indian is a recipe for lamb curry and rice written on the last page of his logbook.[248] This deterioration in the relationships between the British and the Indians can be seen in the history of George Elliot Voyle (1824–83), one of the descendants of the previously mentioned George Elliot. This George also sought his fortune in India and was involved in a number of campaigns. He was present at the battles of Aliwal (28 January 1846) and Sobrahon (10 February 1846) during the Second Sikh War in the Punjab. He assisted in the conquest of Burma in 1852–3, experiencing action at the White House Stockade and the taking of Rangoon. During the Indian Mutiny in 1857, George, newly promoted to the rank of captain, was in charge of the Rangoon magazine. After the Mutiny, the East India Company Army was absorbed into the Indian Army and he was transferred to the Royal Artillery.[249] The portrayal of the Indian Mutiny in the Welsh press provides further evidence of the deterioration that had taken place in Cambro-Indian relationships. The Asian Indians were described in the same terms as were the American Indians, who 'treacherously' attacked wagon trains. They were oleaginous – 'slimy' in their person, 'slithering' in their demeanour. By contrast, 'The English', a term which included the Welsh, were 'heroic' and 'brave' in 'defence of their interests'. In January 1858, the *Monmouthshire Merlin* devoted its front page to the heroic British relief of Luknow, and that 'favourite son of Carmarthen', Thomas Brigstocke, painted a portrait in oils of the hero of the hour, General Sir J. Outram. The *Merlin* also recounted that 'much sensation' was occasioned by 'the sad return' of an unnamed, but well-known, clergyman's daughter from Newport, 'widowed and terribly mutilated. The Sepoys have cut her tongue out, and inflicted other horrible injuries.' Other Welsh families such as the Williamses and the Thomases suffered and died during the Cawnpore Massacres. Thomas Thomas was shot in the head, whilst a sepoy 'dashed Georgina Williams brains out with a club'.[250]

To keep her 'Jewel in the Crown', Britain had to build up her military power in India. By the time of the Indian Mutiny in the 1850s, the military forces had grown significantly. Among the unsung heroes was the 'honest, godly and generous' Griffith Davies (1788–1855) of Llandwrog, who never raised more than a pen in anger. But it was this mathematical genius, the author of *A Key to Bonnycastle's Trigonometry* and a FRS, who audited and organized the finances of the military funds of Bombay and Madras, making it possible for the military to be able to afford to fight. In the ranks of the 'Honourable

Company's Army' were 3,223 Welshmen, many of whom were enrolled in the 'Dirty Shirts' battalion, so-called because of their fighting prowess and power, not the quality of their laundry. They included men such as John Davies of Cardiff, an 'indifferent character' who, despite his 'broken condition', embarked for India on 27 July 1858, on the *Owen Glendower*.[251] With such poor-quality soldiers, it was only their technological advantages that enabled the British to retain their domination. These included information technology, for in the late eighteenth and early nineteenth centuries, knowledge was power. Power lay in maps. One of the greatest achievements of the East India Company was in accurately mapping the vast expanse of India, which included not just its present borders, but also large parts of modern Pakistan, Burma, Bangladesh, southern Persia and Nepal. The Great Trigonometrical Survey of India was established in 1800 to map the territory that Britain had conquered. From 1818, it was led by the irascible and irritable Sir George Everest of Crickhowell.[252] Working at night to protect their theodolites from the sun, the cartographers triangulated their way across the subcontinent to create the first definitive atlas of India. Along the way, they confirmed the location of the world's highest mountain and, with the conqueror's characteristic condescension, ignored local names by renaming the mountain after a Welshman. To name was to take, for this was imperialism masquerading as cartography.

Anxiety, Stress and Suicide

Indians were not the only people to encounter problems with technology. Technological changes wrought profound transformations in the lives of people in nineteenth-century Wales. By the 1850s, the pace of life seemed to have accelerated to a speed to which many individuals failed to adjust. Canals, roads, steam-powered engines, boats and railways brought a new awareness of speed. In 1815, a Welsh soldier rode for two days to bring the exciting news that Wellington had triumphed at Waterloo.[253] In 1854, news of the engagements of the Crimean War were telegraphed to Wales in a few minutes. The pace of life had quickened. One battered commentator commented, 'then you crawled and were overset gently; now you gallop and are bashed to atoms'. The newspapers were filled with advertisements warning against the dangers of such high octane living: 'in these days of worry and hurry, in the everlasting race to reach a goal of wealth and position, asthma is one of the symptoms'.[254] The description of those symptoms is close to a modern nosology of anxiety. Life was consumed at pace, pleasure at haste. People were convulsed with anxiety and they continuously felt under pressure. *Merched y gerddi*, the seasonal workers who migrated to the orchards and harvest fields of the English border counties, filled their time knitting en route.[255] 'Life to them was a continuous round of a lot of work and little sleep, with leisure a very scarce commodity.'[256] In a painting *The Welsh Curate*, the pressures of modern living were clear. Leaders of the Church in Wales have been portrayed as lazy and indolent, neglectful of their duties, but the painting reveals an individual traumatized by stress. His eyes, his hands and his feet, every limb of his body, and every faculty of his soul were fully employed. The painting shows him reading a folio that lay on a table to his right, whilst simultaneously listening to his little boy read, rocking the cradle with his foot and paring turnips.[257] Was this a caricature of an impoverished rustic cleric? Or was the stressed curate a thoroughly modern, Georgian new man?

Ambition added anxieties to the lives of people who were already deeply worried and concerned. An anonymous author warned: 'Pan fo waethaf arnoch, gobeithiwch; pan fo orau arnoch, ofnwch. Ym mhob cyflwr, gwyliwch' (When things are bad for you, hope; when it is best for you, fear. In every condition, watch). Anglican dogma warned against the danger of unbridled and unchecked ambition. *Yr Haul* advocated 'resignation in the face of hardship: all must accept their diverse stations and be silent under the powerful hand of Providence'.[258] The warning was not simply the diktat of a class frightened by the riotous behaviour and revolutionary rhetoric of the lower classes, for Nonconformists also warned against the melancholy and depression, which were too common in modern life. In 1872–3, the Revd Dr William Rees, Hiraethog, wrote lines which reveal a people tired of ceaseless, unrelenting pressure:

> I went searching through creation
> For my soul a place of rest –
> Disappointment and vexation
> Everywhere repaid my quest.[259]

A common theme in many hymns of the 1830s and 1840s is an expression of unease at the pace of change. They reveal a yearning for stability, some safe, sure and secure anchorage within a frighteningly fast-changing world. In contrast to their torment on earth, God and heaven were unchanged and unchanging 'o dragwyddoldeb i dragwydd-oldeb' (from everlasting to everlasting). Hiraethog also penned a superb hymn which has the anguished plea 'Arglwydd gad i'm dawel orffwys, yng nghysgodau'r palmwydd clud' (give me quiet resting-places, Lord, beneath the shade of palms). One minister reflected the pressures and problems of the era, when he remarked that: 'prosperity is the blessing of the Old Testament, adversity is the blessing of the New'. In the 1830s and 1840s, there was a gradual, subtle change in theology from an emphasis on the Old Testament to the New. Many warned that the pressure to progress had dangers: 'prosperity is not without many fears and disasters, and adversity is not without comfort and hopes'.[260]

In many respects, the demographic and economic transformation of Wales in the period 1776–1871 unhinged Welsh society. People were torn from their roots by immigration, emigration and migration. The old certainties no longer held. There were several profound battles for domination of Welsh mentalities in these years. Tension existed between rural and industrial communities, as competing worldviews clashed. The *joie de vivre* which had always been part of Welsh life was challenged by a powerful religion that argued forcefully that through temperance and teetotalism lay the road to salvation. Preachers preached that lamentation should replace laughter. Beneath such confusing and conflicting burdens, people's minds fractured. They suffered from a range of fears and phobias, worries about their moral value, their religious ideals and delusions and a host of other vexing problems that appeared to have been absent from earlier societies. Llew Llwyfo was convulsed with anxieties and worries which inten-sified when he competed in *eisteddfodau*. Twm o'r Nant ended one of his *anterliwtiau* with the worried warning 'a'r byd a'i holl dreiglad yn dwad i'r dim' (the world and all its turns is come to naught). One of the main characters in this gloomy outpouring was Mr Gofid (Mr Worry). In increasing numbers, people's identities went soft. Many of the more dangerous characters like Hyam Jacobs, the fraudulent Cardiff jeweller who tried to pawn his face, were bundled into jail. In the 1820s, it was estimated that one tenth of gaol inmates were 'mentally weak'. But custody was gradually replaced by an awareness that these victims deserved care.[261] To cater for them, society estab-lished 'mad houses'. The first such institution opened its doors in

Swansea in 1815 to cater for 'the melancholy effects of Mental Disease'. It was followed by a number of other similar institutions built by both private enterprise – Vernon House, Briton Ferry (1843) and Amroth Castle in Pembrokeshire (1853) – and by county authorities – the Pembrokeshire Asylum (1824), the North Wales Asylum at Denbigh (1848), the Monmouthshire County Asylum at Pen-y-Fal near Abergavenny (1851), the Glamorgan Asylum at Bridgend (1864) and the Joint Counties Lunatic Asylum at Carmarthen (1865).[262]

Initially, the asylums were conceived as curative institutions, designed to restore the mentally ill to health and society. For some, the sojourn in the asylum did lead to their successful return to society, but to many others the experience was brutalizing and damaging.[263] The human refuse of Welsh society, those people who suffered from distressing congenital conditions for which there could be no cure, were swept into the asylums. Cure changed into custody. The architecture of the asylums did not help. Forbidding and foreboding, the asylums resembled 'museums of madness'.[264] These asylums were not isolated from society, but an actual part of it, which reflected society's problems and phobias. Studying the tragic life stories of their inmates enables us to penetrate beneath the stereotypes of Welsh historiography and capture a different layer of reality. The pressures that bothered and broke the individual in Wales had been created by their society. In the tears of mentally ill, we can perceive the fears of their society.

One of the most remarkable stories in the history of psychiatry in the early nineteenth century is the painful tale of James Tilly Matthews, a Cardiff tea merchant. In the years of conspiracy, paranoia, war and revolution, Matthews assumed a shadowy role as an agent of the British government in Paris. Some of the incredible episodes in which he later claimed to have been involved undoubtedly happened, but others were the creation of his warped imagination. In 1796, he cut across a parliamentary sitting, claiming that a gang using 'The Air Loom' was seeking to control the government. The Air Loom, according to Matthews, worked by animal magnetism, sending invisible rays to control the minds of its victims, forcing thoughts into their heads and tormenting them with unbearable agonies if they resisted. Matthews's delusions were those of an age of machines, when people's bodies and minds were damaged by the depredations of science and technology. He was as much a political prisoner as a mental patient. Matthews was incarcerated in Bedlam at the behest of the Home Secretary, Lord Liverpool, whom he had apparently previously served as a negotiator, trying to stop war between Britain and France. Matthews's is one of the first recorded cases of paranoid schizophrenia, a modern disease of a modern age.[265] Matthews also suffered delusions that he was one of the most powerful people in Britain. In this he was representative of a large number of the mentally ill and unstable in Wales. Welsh asylums contained many men whose madness revolved around the very notions of heroism, of power and strength. At one time in the 1850s, Welsh asylums contained a Russian tsar, a prince of France, a king of Europe, and several kings of England. John Evans, Y Bardd Cocos (1827?–95), a simpleton who was celebrated for his metreless, senseless poetry, wrote to the widowed Queen Victoria seeking her hand in marriage. Victorian masculinity, it seems was far from an unassailable source of power. Patriarchal society was riven with insecurities and worries.

At least those incarcerated in the asylum received some comfort; a significant element of Welsh society was beyond care. The most intimate and impenetrable human act is suicide. Even when committed in public it remains the most private act.[266] Coroners' inquests into deaths by suicide reinforce the impression that contemporaries were suffering under ever-increasing burdens of stress. In 1830, a coroner remarked that 'the crime of suicide was never perhaps more prevalent than at present'.[267] Despite the melodramatic presentations of notes in Victorian poems and plays, in reality the participants usually left behind them no written records to explain their behaviour. Often, there was just a rippling pool of regrets and temporary sadness, gradually wiped away by time and forgetfulness, as if they had never existed, or perhaps remorse lingered longer in the conscience of a friend or relative. These tragic, tormented, truncated lives are tales without a denouement. The secrets of the heart remain hidden. But coroners' inquests, doctors' records and newspaper reports enable us to penetrate at least a little of the mystery.[268]

As with madness, suicide reveals the fears and phobias, the stresses and anxieties, which traumatized and tortured Welsh people. Powerful social and spiritual pressures and prohibitions were placed to try and prevent people from committing suicide. In 1833, *The Cambrian*, in a report on the death of 64-year-old William Harries of Llyswen, explained that

> self-murder is wisely and religiously considered by English law as the most
> heinous description of felonious homicide; for no man has the power to destroy
> life but by the Commission of God, the author of it. The suicide is guilty of a
> double offence; one spiritual, in invading the prerogative of the Almighty and

rushing into his presence uncalled for; and the other temporal against the King, who has an interest in the position of his subjects.[269]

As punishment, many who failed in their suicide bids were imprisoned for up to six months for their attempted offence against the king and God. Punishment reached even unto death. On 18 December 1787, the death-obsessed diarist William Thomas noted in his diary:

> As for the body of Thomas Jenkins Miles, it was risen the 22nd instant past out of the grave by order of the Coroner and buried on the highway, for the servant maid confessed it was hang himself he did and it was she did cut him down.[270]

Jeffrey Vallet, an eighty-year-old sailor of Swansea, hanged himself just before Christmas 1816. So determined was he on his own destruction that, to the horror of *The Cambrian*, 'this hoary wretch . . . actually greased the rope by which he suspended himself to a hook in the ceiling'. He was buried 'in a cross-roads at an early hour this morning'.[271] In March 1844, David Lewis, an impoverished tenant farmer of Llangadog, hanged himself in an outbuilding. He was buried the following night at 10 p.m. in the parish churchyard without any religious ceremony.[272]

Despite the prohibitions and phobias, people still sought to escape from the unbearable burdens of their disenchanted lives. Financial difficulties, problems at work, debt and insolvency were the triggers for many individuals to terminate their existence. In 1830, Nathaniel Richards of Cowbridge hanged himself in a small wood near the village. 'Melancholy and despondent in consequence of adverse circumstances', he left 'a widow and six children totally destitute'.[273] In 1815, an unnamed farmer, for many newspaper reports did not give the suicide even the comfort of an identity, drowned himself because 'of an apprehension that he had engaged a farm at too high a rent'.[274] In 1829, Charles Collins, the nearly bankrupt owner of the schooner *Gledw*, cut his throat with a razor in Swansea harbour.[275] Thomas Jones, a cabinet-maker of Jackson's Court, Carmarthen, was discovered hanging in the cellar. When he was cut down, it was found that his feet could reach the floor but that he had 'held himself in a bending position'. Thomas was despondent and desperate as the 'consequence of some unfortunate money transactions . . . he was buried privately last night, without the usual funeral rites being performed over his remains'.[276] In 1845, George Henry Guardian, master of the schooner *Mary*, which had suffered severe financial losses, committed 'self-destruction by discharging the contents of a small pocket-pistol through his head'.[277] Stress was the unbearable pressure that compelled a teacher at the British School in Llangollen to hang himself. He was preparing for a government inspection within the month.[278] In 1853, W. S. Harries, son of a former MP for Leicester, was found naked and dead in the Boar's Head in Carmarthen. 'Unable to face his creditors', he drank a bottle of prussic acid; leaving behind him a wife and six children, and £53 in one of his pockets.[279]

The wounds of love were the pains that forced many to take their own lives. On 1 August 1868, Jane Williams of Ty'n y Caeau, Cynwyd, near Corwen, drowned herself in the local river after a broken courtship. Against her wishes, 'na chodwch faen na chofnod' (raise no stone or epitaph), Jane was commemorated in a famous poem and a celebrated song, 'Yr Eneth Gadd ei Gwrthod', composed by John Jones, Llew o'r Wern.[280] The mournful, plangent song has been responsible for establishing the impression that the characteristic Welsh suicide was a young, pregnant girl, betrayed in love. Many Welsh girls shared Jane's Ophelian, watery end.[281] In May 1820, Miss Roberts of Broughton, Flintshire, 'drowned herself in a pit in consequence of an illicit connection being discovered'.[282] But men, too, felt the pains of love's labour's lost. In 1850, Ellis Williams, a farmer near Denbigh, hanged himself because he had seen his wife shake hands with a neighbour in Blossom Fair. Before he undertook his last, rash action, he burned his clothes and ripped open the bodies of two valuable mares, in colt, for which he had been offered £40 at the fateful fair.[283] Jacob Jenkins of Llanharan took poison to end his life because he was 'dan reolaeth nwydau aflywodraethus' (under the influence of unbridled lusts).[284]

Fear was a forceful, frightening emotion that many individuals could neither control nor conquer. John Williams, alias 'John Prussia', cut his jugular and windpipe following the death of his wife from cholera.[285] Having been missing for over a month, the decomposed body of William Edwards, the postmaster of Talywaun, was found hanging in a plantation owned by the Ebbw Vale Iron Company. William was convinced that he would suffer a brain haemorrhage.[286] William Brookman, a Bristol merchant, hanged himself in a Swansea guest house because of the onset of eryspelas. Ironically, he had moved to live in Swansea 'for the sea air's beneficial effects'.[287] William Jones, a collier of Newbridge, hanged himself because he thought, incorrectly, that he was diseased. Three children who saw him hanging himself in the woods ran home terrified, informing two men on the way. Sadly, they arrived too late to help William. Seventy-four-year-old

Gwenllian Thomas and her husband were admitted, in 'much distress', to Brecon New Poor House in the excruciating cold of November 1839. In accordance with the rules, males and females were separated. It was the first time Gwenllian had been parted from her husband during over fifty years of marriage. Gwenllian was 'much affected' and spent the night 'frequently calling for her husband'. She ended her misery when she jumped through a top-floor window.[288]

The palliatives and placebos that people took to soften life's pain often created more problems. In July 1843, an inquest in Carmarthen heard how a man suffering delirium tremens in Lammas Street begged passersby to 'drive off the persons who were then molesting him, and charging him with various crimes, although no person was near him at the time'.[289] Evan Prosser, a printer and bookseller of Pontypool, blew his brains out with a hand pistol. The sole reason given for his demise was his addiction to drink.[290] At an inquest into the death of Whitfield Evans, a carpenter who died in a public house in Swansea, the verdict was reached that 'the deceased had departed this life by excessive drinking'.[291] Jenkin Nicholas, St Dogmaels Arms, Newport, attempted suicide through drinking spirits and a bottle of laudanum.[292] William Walters, who lodged near the Iron Bridge in Merthyr Tydfil and 'dragged out a rather wretched existence selling nuts and bootlaces', attempted suicide through taking opium. The *Cardiff and Merthyr Guardian* noted unsympathetically that 'he should recover, unless he dies of cholera'.[293] Grace Woodcliffe of Pistyll, Llansadwrn, the wife of an old, pensioned soldier, who had been bedridden for twenty years, was found dead after she had taken two opium tablets – 'a lower dose than usual' according to the press report.[294] Religion, 'the opium of the people', was often a disruptive force in disjointed minds. In September 1848, *Seren Gomer* reported the death of Mrs Morgan, a 'responsible' woman and the wife of a minister in Machen. She believed that Heaven was ready to receive her, and had frequently remarked that she was tired of life on earth.[295] The captain of the barge *Golondrina*, which carried copper between South America and Swansea, tried to take the crew with him to the 'Glorious Place'. After a vicious fight, he jumped overboard, leaving the crew, none of whom had any navigational knowledge, helpless on the ocean for five days.[296]

The study of 1,700 cases of suicide committed in Wales between 1776 and 1871 reveals that there were as many motives and methods as there were people.[297] The picture these cases present is a vastly complex mosaic, in which there is no clearly discernible image. Very often, these people are left in the anonymity of death by the newspapers which reported the case but which gave no details of the individual's name, often one of the victim's few possessions. Servants in particular were often given no identity in the papers, except the identifying clue of their master's name. *The Cambrian*, in June 1832, reported that the 'sixteen year old footman to Richard Maliphant Esq. committed suicide by hanging himself from a coupling strap in the stable'.[298] Perversely, the paper added, 'it looked as if the corpse was smiling'. Gory facts were often etched lovingly in careful detail. In the same issue of *The Cambrian* was the report that a 'wretched creature terminated his existence at a lodging house near Pontypool by deliberately cutting off his tongue. He sat on the bed, until all his blood covered the floor'.[299] That rare character in Victorian Wales, the Tory poet Talhaiarn, gout-ridden and in constant pain, terminated his existence with a pistol shot to the brain in 1869.[300] After reading the tragic stories, it is hard not to feel deep sympathy with the children of the people who had taken their own lives. Unprepared, they stumbled upon the horrific discovery of a parent hanging in the barn, outhouse or tree, or dead in bloodstrewn bedrooms. Three of the seven children of Elizabeth Roberts of Llanfihangel-y-Creuddyn, Cardiganshire, found their mother hanging by a hay rick.[301] Often, the life stories reported in inquests and press reports reveal lives of unbelievable and unenviable misfortune in which woe swiftly followed woe. E. Jones, a farm servant of Llandrillo near Corwen, drowned himself in the river Dee. His mind had been unsettled after he lost his arm in a threshing machine eighteen months earlier.[302] Christmas 1850 was marked by the death of Evan Miles of Caerphilly. His 'proud spirit was greatly grieved that he had lost his leg and become dependant on others. The other day, he tied his sound leg to his crutch, and then drowned himself in a pool not more than five feet deep.'[303]

The history of suicide in Wales is full of examples of bizarre behaviour. The heartbreaking and horrifying details of what appear to be random, inexplicable acts were lavishly described and detailed in the press. These acts were not inexplicable; they were rooted in Welsh society. Because death was so common, it was viewed not with fear but with a morbid fascination. People were not afraid of death in the period 1776–1871, but rather accepted it as a constant companion. Death was an all-pervasive presence in nineteenth-century Wales. It had a density and an omnipresence in Victorian culture. Preachers dwelled on it, writers constantly returned to it. Death punctuated and permeated every aspect of life.[304]

3

Life and Death

Glyn Cysgod Angau: Life in the Shadow of Death

Divine scripture and debased superstition, by definition, are not often in accord, but in the period 1776–1871 they were in agreement in warning that 'in the midst of life, we are in death'. Death cast its dark shadow over the living. Accidents, affrays and industrial disasters combined to make the last agony and the livid corpse a familiar sight. The largest gatherings of Welsh people were the crowds who gathered to watch the twitching, swinging corpse of a criminal executed for his, and sometimes her, crimes.[1] In their homes and slums, the poor died as they had lived, huddled together. In the cholera epidemics of 1832, 1836, 1839, 1849 and 1866, coffin carts loaded with corpses creaked their way from houses to cemeteries with distressing frequency. Reminders of the crudeness of death were evident in the crudeness of living; dead animals littered gutters, and blood covered the pavements outside butchers' shops and slaughter-houses in most Welsh towns. In the bedrooms of the rich, the Grim Reaper weeded out fragile sons and daughters. In 1829, C. R. Leslie painted the touching and tragic scene of *The Dillwyn Family*, in which the immediate relatives are gathered around a deathbed.[2] The deaths of royalty, celebrities and heroes, such as Sir William Nott, drew countless hundreds onto the streets.[3] In rural Wales, black figures, drawn from remote farms by death's magnet, often covered the hills. Henry Clarence Whaite's *To the Cold Earth*, a remarkable painting completed in 1865, depicts a frozen cortege crossing an icy wasteland.[4] It was a scene of rustic remembrance that occurred frequently in the hard, harrowed hills. After autumnal gales, inhabitants of coastal villages scoured beaches and rocks searching for the bodies of seamen and travellers.

Travellers across the undulating hills of Montgomeryshire were warned against pausing to listen to the beautiful singing which could sometimes be heard on clear moonlit nights. This was the 'singing of angels', a portent of the enchanted listener's impending death.[5] In the south-west, religion and superstition combined. People believed that corpse candles, nightly ghostly lights which traced out the route which a forthcoming funeral would take, had been sent by St David to warn his countrymen of the approach of death.[6] In 1854, at Llandeilo, George Borrow during his intrepid journey through wild Wales met a toll gate keeper who complained:

> We were in the habit of seeing plenty of passengers going through the gate without paying toll; I mean such things as are called phantoms or illusions – sometimes they were horses and mourning coaches, sometimes a funeral procession on foot . . . once a traveller passing through the gate called out to me 'Look! Yonder is a corpse candle coming through the fields beside the highway'.[7]

Across Wales, *y cyhyraeth*, a ghostly spirit dog, the *aderyn corff*, a wingless phantom bird, and *gwrach y rhibyn*, a ghostly hag, terrified travellers.[8] At Llanfair Caereinion in Montgomeryshire, several people testified that, in workshops where coffins were made, 'knockings' were heard previous to a death taking place. The sleep of people who lived within earshot of Joseph Astley's workshop was often interrupted by these ominous noises which presaged death. Thomas Roberts, who combined the roles of verger and gravedigger at Llanfair, always heard the noise of a spirit in the churchyard previous to a death occurring in the parish.[9] Every region of Wales had tales of ghosts who troubled the gullible, poltergeists who tormented the credulous.[10]

Premonitions and portents of death were not just tall tales told to terrify children and alarm the aged. People placed great faith and belief in these traditions. In 1866, *The Cambrian* reported the homecoming of James Grant to Newport. James had emigrated from his home fifteen years previously and refused to return to visit his family because he had dreamt that he would drown at sea in view of his home. In February 1866, he relented and took passage home on the ship *Hannah Moore*. The ship floundered in a storm off the coast and, within sight of his home, James drowned.[11]

Religion, which placed hope in a resurrection which followed a brutal crucifixion, seized every opportunity to warn people to prepare for their end. Hell's horrors and heaven's harmony were evoked in countless sermons and prayers. Theologians had difficulty in explaining to the Welsh people what heaven was like. A place of unearthly bliss proved beyond the descriptive powers of many, but hell,

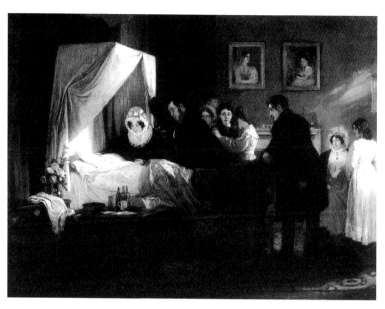

C. R. Leslie, *The Dillwyn Family*, 1829 (National Library of Wales). A touching depiction of death – the 'Great Leveller' at work. Such scenes struck a common chord among people who were anxious to emphasize that 'rich and poor were equal in the grave'.

Henry Clarence Whaite, *To the Cold Earth*, 1865 (City of Nottingham Museum, Castle Museum and Art Gallery). A funeral cortege makes slow and stately progress through a frozen wasteland, indicating the great loneliness of upland Wales.

a place of endless pain, fired fertile imaginations. A battalion of hell-fire preachers in thunderous sermons ensured that the fires of hell were well stoked throughout the nineteenth century. During the cholera revival of 1849, the temperature of hell increased substantially.[12]

Hope was not the monopoly of Christians. Few people in the early nineteenth century rejected the possibility of a future life. The main current of thought of the time was theistic, not atheistical or even agnostic.[13] Doubts were expressed about revelation, the Christian plan of salvation was questioned, but few seem to have doubted the goodness of God, or the existence of a life to come. People hoped for a life beyond the grave. Cemeteries, which were at the centre of villages and hamlets named after dead saints, were places of repose and meditation. The ballad singer Levi Gibbon was one of many who visited the cemetery to muse on the mystery and meaning of life:

Ar ei fedd yn awr eisteddaf,	On his grave I now sit,
A myfyriaf wrthyf fi fy hun;	Contemplating by myself;
Gan y meirw yma dysgaf	From the dead here I learn
Mor fyr a brau yw bywyd dyn.[14]	How short and fragile is man's life.

Others were more direct in their warnings that everyone should be ready to meet their maker. Edward Matthews, Matthews Ewenni (1813–92), uttered a terrifying truism: 'anadl sydd rhyngom a thragwyddoldeb yn wastad' (there is always only a breath between us and eternity). A popular couplet warned: 'Angau a biau bywyd, / Ac angau a bia'r byd'[15] (Death owns life, and Death owns the world). While Morgan Williams doubled the warning into *cynghanedd*:

Edau wan ydyw einioes – a diddim	Life is a weak cord – and as nothing
Yw dyddiau dy feroes:	Are the days of your short life:
Na haera y cei hiroes,	Do not think you will have a long life,
Cans dyma, ddyn, derfyn d'oes.[16]	For here, mankind, is your end.

This sentiment was echoed in the work of the Welsh American authoress Maria James:

> There's blight on earthly joys, my love;
> There's blight on earthly joys . . .
> The fairest flowers will soonest fade, –
> Will soonest fade and die . . .
> Time speeds us on towards the tomb, –
> Speeds on through weal and wo [*sic*].'[17]

Dic Dywyll, the blind ballad singer warned:

Yn dy i'cngtid hyfryd hafaidd,	In your lovely summer youth,
Cofia ddyn a gad dy ffoled;	Remember man's plight and leave your folly;
Pan êl dy gorff yn fwyd i bryfaid,	When your body becomes food for worms
Pa beth a ddaw o'th unig enaid?[18]	What will become of your only soul?

Many Welsh poets who accepted death as inescapable and inevitable faced it with a stoic submission to the will of God, but 'fervent souls' such as William Williams, Pantycelyn, and Ann Griffiths desired it: 'as the end of their exile and happy arrival in harbour after a long burdensome voyage'. Thomas Rowlands reveals the pessimistic tired-of-this-weary-life-on-earth thread that underlay much religious poetry and hymnology:

Ca'dd ei guro gan y gwyntoedd,	He was beaten by the winds,
Ca'dd ei faeddu gan y dôn,	He was defeated by the wave,
Ca'dd ei ddryllio gan y creigiau	He was battered on the rocks
Blinodd ar y ddaear hon.[19]	He tired of this earth.

The Revd John Roberts of Conwy, 'JR', brother of the more famous 'SR', sang of:

A weary traveller
Beside the river stood;
His lamp was in his hand,
And shone across the flood;
It brought the other shore in sight,
Where many angels walked in white.[20]

Death was almost joyously accepted by the Christian, especially in the mid nineteenth century. One mother who had lost seven children remarked with heartbreaking candour: 'God was so fond of my children that he kept taking them to be his angels. Oh, how happy it makes me feel – and how sad!' The poetry of Elen Egryn (1807–76) has the characteristic loneliness and hiraeth of the depressed emigrant, but also a gloomy, Gothic obsession with death. Her 'Cwynfan Mam: Ar ôl ei dwy ferch, a fuont farw yn ieuainc' has the remarkable concluding stanza which mixes heartbreak with hope:

Fy mlodau tlws!	My sweet flowers!
Paham yr wyf mor ffol,	Why am I so foolish,
A wylo'n drist	To sadly weep
O hiraeth ar eich ôl,	From grief after you,
A chwithau'n awr	For you are now
Yn seintiau yn y nef,	Saints in Heaven,

| Yn canu'n fwyn | Singing sweetly |
| Yr anthem 'Iddo ef!'[21] | The anthem 'Unto Him'. |

Her 'dear little angels, now before God in Heaven', had been taken away before the 'gold of their innocence had been tarnished by the soil of the world', and this was a subject for rejoicing, not remorse. Such powerful, unshakable faith was the support which anchored many through periods of intense loneliness. In May 1855, the daughter of Ebenezer Thomas, Eben Fardd (1802–63), died. Three years later, another of his three daughters died. In 1859, his nephew and his best friend, Siôn Wyn o Eifion, both died. The year 1860 saw the death of his wife, while in January 1861, his son 'canwyll ei lygaid' (candle of his eye) died. Despite these experiences, Eben's loneliness did not degenerate into despair. From the emotional turmoil, he fashioned the hymn 'O! Fy Iesu bendigedig, unig gwmni f'enaid gwan' (O! My glorious Jesus, only companion of my weak soul). Eben's was a survivor's tale, his last years of life ones of loneliness amongst strangers.[22] Loneliness was also the muse for the poet John Jones, Pyll Glan Conwy (1786–1865), who sang 'Fe ddarfu'n hen gyfoedion hael, fy ngadael braidd i gyd' (My dear old friends have left me one and all). Loss of his first wife Jessie in childbirth, and the serious illness of Caroline his second, prompted Henry Hussey Vivian to abandon his industrial enterprises in order to join the forces of Garibaldi as one of the 5,000 who marched over the Alps to liberate Italy in 1859.[23]

People who had beaten the odds and survived into old age were treated as novelties. Mary Davies of Llanfynydd, a centenarian, had eighty-six grandchildren but had never once left the village. In July 1817, one of the tenants of J. B. Bruce, Aberdare, an 87-year-old woman, died after ploughing with oxen for nine hours.[24] John Rees was another person obsessed with work at an advanced age. In 1810, the allegedly 110-year-old John fell off the roof of his hut while thatching it.[25] In 1821, the death of a 'Merioneth Methuselah' was reported in the Welsh press. The mild mountain air of this Celtic Shangri-La was not just efficacious of health, it also promoted a remarkable fertility, for the 105-year-old farmer: 'by his first wife he had 30 children, 10 by his second, 4 by his third, and 7 by two concubines. His youngest son was 81 years younger than his eldest, and 800 persons, descended from his body, attended his funeral.'[26] The celebrated centenarian's life story reveals one aspect of Welsh history which is often overlooked: the urgency and frequency with which people sought to remarry after the death of a partner. Marriages were not broken by divorce, but by death. People married at haste, but took little leisure to repent their actions. Even so, the story of a Swansea woman must have been exceptional. With her first husband she bought a farm, but he died. She married again and with her second husband she sowed the fields, after which he died. Undaunted, she married a third time and with this husband she reaped the harvest but then he died. With her fourth husband she threshed the crop, but he, too, died. Remarkably, in 1810 she married for a fifth time within eighteen months and with this husband she enjoyed the farm's produce. The poet Islwyn, author of 'Y Storm', one of the most powerful and passionate poems of Victorian Wales, married Martha soon after the death of his fiancée, Ann Bowen, of 'gastric fever'. After years of marriage, his final words to his long-suffering wife are either appalling or appealing, honest or horrible, according to taste: 'You have been a good wife to me Martha, but I'm going to Ann.'[27] Thomas Edwards, Caerfallwch (1779–1858), the word-coining, dictionary-compiling, hymn-writing auditor to the Rothschild financial dynasty married three times between 1800 and 1816. There was no religious sanction against remarriage in the years 1776–1871, for ministers regularly remarried upon the death of their partners. David Charles II (1803–80) and David Charles III (1812–78), ministers with the Calvinistic Methodists and hymn-writers, both married for the second time in the 1830s. The precociously gifted John Evans (1814–75), another Calvinistic Methodist minister, the sixteen-year-old author of *Hanes yr Iddewon*, also married twice. John Elias (1774–1841), the most famous Calvinistic Methodist of all, the staunchly conservative, Y Pab o Fôn, owner of one of the saddest faces in Welsh religious history, was keen on his personal comforts. In 1830, following the death of his first wife, he married Ann, widow of Sir John Bulkeley, of Presaddfed, Bodedern.[28]

The orphan is not just a character placed in sentimental Victorian ballads and poems to inspire sympathy. Many people were left to fend for themselves in a savage world. David Evans (1814–91), Dewi Dawel, was one of nine children left destitute when their father, a tailor, drowned in the river Cothi by Rhydodyn, on 9 December 1833. Richard Llwyd, Bard of Snowdon (1752–1835), was orphaned following the death of his father from smallpox and had to earn a living as a child labourer on Anglesey farms. Sally Jones, the wife of Thomas Charles, lost her father at six years of age. Charlotte Greville, Sir Watkin Williams Wynn's seventeen-year-old bride in 1771, was an orphan; Sir Watkin himself had been fatherless from the age of five months.[29] Ideal families were idealized in Victorian literature, principally because they existed so rarely in real life. Robert Rees, Eos Morlais (1841–92), lost his parents as an eight-year-old and began to work in a local mine. His prodigious natural musical abilities were nurtured through considerable efforts in burning the midnight candle. Owen Jones, Meudwy Môn (1806–89), was orphaned as a toddler and raised by his aunt Elizabeth. He was a carpenter's apprentice, a farm servant, a private tutor and a schoolteacher before entering the Calvinistic Methodist ministry. Few, however, were as unfortunate as this unlucky baby:

> 7 April – was buried in St George's the grandson of William Miles of Throp, of three or four weeks old. He was half Christned on the coffin of his father and full Christned on the coffin of his mother, who were both buried in Penlline within few days the one to the other. It was the 17th of December last they married.[30]

Demographically, Welsh society in the period 1776–1871 was a young society, but it was also a society whose people died young. In 1851, life expectancy in Merthyr Tydfil was seventeen-and-a-half years. Dr William Kay reported, with horrifying candour, that: 'more than half of the funerals which take place in Merthyr are those of children under five years of age; and more than one-fourth of infants under a year'. 'People did not live long in Merthyr', said one of the town's earliest historians, with an understatement uncharacteristic of Merthyr Tydfil historians.[31] Rees Arthur Rhys (1837–60), a promising poet, died after a long illness in 1860, and left 'am wlad lle nad oedd neb o'r preswylwyr yn dychwelyd mwy' (for a country, from which none of the inhabitants return). Posthumously, he won an *eisteddfod* prize for an eulogy to the Revd J. Vincent, of Llandudoch. Reuben Davies, *Reuben Brydydd y Coed* (1808–33), a schoolmaster and author of over fifty hymns, left only one poem 'Dydd Barn' (Judgement Day), but faced his much sooner than he thought.[32] An even more famous hymn-writer, Ann Griffiths (1776–1805), died bravely under the rain-hammered rafters after an agonizing two weeks' sickness, following the birth of her only child.[33]

One of the most dangerous places in Wales in the period 1776–1871 was in bed, especially when a woman was giving birth. The remarkable diary of William Thomas of Michaelston-super-Ely, near St Fagans, is a veritable Glamorgan Book of the Dead, daily chronicling the death of his neighbours. On 3 January 1787, he grimly records:

was buried in Llandaff with the Ruins of her child, Betty Jenkin alias David, wife of Evan David of Fairwater and sister to John Jenkin of Canton. Of 27 years of age, from child delivery, which was drawn from her in pieces, being alive a few days before, and in full time to be born. This was the third so drawn from her. She was a dwarfish sized woman.[34]

To relieve some of pain and trauma, Dr Richard Williams of Aberystwyth reported that women were given: 'large potations of gin and water and I can hear bear testimony to the impunity with which spirituous liquors may be administered during labour'. There was little comfort for mothers in the agony of childbirth, and there was often less after giving birth. In 1853, the *Caernarvon and Denbigh Herald* began including advertisements for Dr Townsend's 'American Atmospheric Breast Cup', which were brutally direct as to its purpose: 'this is an invention designed to draw milk from the breasts after the loss of the child'.[35]

The most dangerous period of life was the first month, then the first year. Afterwards, the odds on survival increased significantly. Some families were particularly unfortunate in the losses they suffered. Charles Kemble (1775–1854), the eleventh child of the celebrated actors Roger Kemble and Sarah David, lost five of his children. Thomas Makeig IV of the Vale of Aeron also lost five of his children in their teens, the others in their early twenties and was only survived by his son George.[36] It was as if his children entered a zone of autumn around the age of fifteen when they fell silently, like leaves. High above the azure sea in New Quay, Cardiganshire, the mute stones of the churchyard tell tragic tales. Thomas Nicholas, a sailor, and his wife Margaret lost six children between 1854 and 1865. The tombstone of Elizabeth and Griffith Davies sadly records the deaths of their eleven children who passed away between 1801 and 1829. It was not just the poor who suffered the great loss of children for death – 'the great leveller' – was no respector of persons. Jonathan Catherall (1761–1833), a wealthy Flintshire industrialist, and his wife Martha had eight children. Five died young and in 1818 both daughters died in their early twenties. Their sole surviving child, William, inherited the family's business interests.[37]

In cemeteries throughout Wales, 'talking stones' reveal the fact that little children named David, William and Ann died before they had learnt their names. Many historians have suggested that the Herodian experience of nineteenth-century societies hardened people to death. With infant mortality rates high, and the death of a child a probable, rather than a possible outcome, it is suggested that contemporaries did not make an emotional investment in their children.[38] Such a view is not supported by the evidence from Wales. Terms of endearment in the literature of mourning reveal that people had real bonds of emotional attachment with their children. One of the strangest aspects of Victorian literature is the stoic bravery with which children confronted death. But the deaths of children were devastating blows to many parents. Robert ap Gwilym Ddu penned a poignant epitaph to his daughter, Elizabeth, who died of tuberculosis at the age of seventeen:

Angau arfog, miniog, mawr,	Death sharply, armed and vicious,
Ar ei gadfarch ergydfawr,	On his powerful charger,
Wele yma carlamodd,	Here he rode,
A'i rym ar egni a rodd;	His power and energy he used;
Torodd i lawr, drwy fawr feth,	To spitefully cut down
Ein diddig, unig eneth.[39]	Our sweet, our only daughter.

Following the death of his much-loved daughter Mariamne, on 4 July 1811, Thomas Johnes instructed a friend: 'we must now do all the good we can to enable us to hope for a happy meeting when we shall follow her'.[40] The death scene was touchingly carved in marble by Francis Chantrey in 1811. The statue enshrined sentiment and sadness in stone.[41] William Thomas, although hardened to death, was devastated by the death of his son from 'the King's Evil', and considered it 'my greatest loss since my Birth on Earth'.[42] Another diarist obsessed with death, Thomas Jenkins of Llandeilo, an undertaker and inventor, painfully recorded the death of his son George in 1844. Despite considerable expenditure on the administrations of Dr Prothero:

who ordered his head to be shaved and bathed with cold salt water and leeches applied to his temples . . . it pleased God for some wise end to relieve my dear boy from his suffering at 11½ pm. I shall never see his like again. God grant that I may become rejoined.[43]

William Thomas and Thomas Jenkins were both subsequently troubled by visions and dreams of their dead sons. This was also the experience of the Revd Dr William Rees, Hiraethog, who lost his son in 1856. Hiraethog recorded his grief in a remarkable essay 'Fy Mab', published in *Y Traethodydd* in 1857.[44] In poem and prose, Hiraethog underwent a psychological catharsis. The appearance of his son in his dreams were explained to him in English by Dr Gee as: 'you may accept it as a message, direct from heaven . . . Heaven and earth have more intimate intercourse with each other than we ever imagined'.

Hiraethog's essay contrasts startlingly with that of David Owen, Brutus, who also lost a son and published his sorrow in an essay 'O Fy Mab'.[45] Brutus, a stalwart champion of the Church of England, shows less certainty that he would be reunited with his son in the next world. His is a more pessimistic, perhaps even more realistic, appraisal of death, for mankind was just 'bwyd i bryfed' (food for worms). John Evans, a minister from Amlwch, took his son on a preaching mission across the north in 1809. Although the father lived to be ninety-five, the son, also called John Evans, died from an illness contracted during the tour. Shortly before his death, to comfort his grieving father, John Evans the younger wrote a hymn that enshrines the Christian faith:

O! angau, pa le mae dy golyn?	O! death, where is thy victory?
O! uffern, ti a gollaist y dydd	O! hell, you have lost the day
Y baban a anwyd ym Methlem	The baby born in Bethlehem
Orchfygodd pob gelyn y sydd,	Has defeated all enemies,
Nid rhaid i blant Seion ddim ofni	Seion's children need not fear
Mynd adref, dan ganu, tua'r wlad;	They go home singing to Heaven;
Mae eu ffordd hwy yn rhydd tuag yno,	Their journey there is clear,
A honno agorwyd â gwaed.[46]	Opened and cleared by blood.

If the fate of mankind was just to be food for worms, some still appeared unfairly doomed. The regular rhythmic variations in the frequency of childbirth were marked with a grisly and ghastly 'massacre of the innocents'. Everywhere mothers, desperate to avoid the burden of a child, murdered their unwanted offspring. Servants were exceptionally vulnerable to the predations of sexual predators. In 1864, four servants were convicted and imprisoned at the Pembrokeshire Assizes for concealing the births of their children, whom they had concealed in boxes.[47] Jane Mathews was given seven days hard labour by Cardiff magistrates for placing her baby at the door of Mr Constantine, who 'has a single gentleman as a lodger'. Jane explained that 'she placed it there through starvation; one thought it better that the father should keep it than she be burdened with it'.[48] Fishermen often caught a ghoulish catch. George Davies, a boatman on the river Wye, recovered the body of a female child about six weeks old in 1862.[49] Four years later, the body of a three-week-old female child with its skull fractured, and a cord around its neck, was recovered from the Glamorganshire Canal.[50] In 1864, the appropriately named Mania Street, Cardiff, was shocked by the discovery of 'a male child found with its throat cut in a water closet'.[51]

The attitude of the authorities to these gruesome discoveries is sometimes puzzling. When a three-week-old child was abandoned in Little Bridge Street, Carmarthen, the discoverer took it to the workhouse. The workhouse master refused to take it in and insisted that the person 'put it back where you found it'.[52] At Pembroke Dock, boys playing in a field smashed a bottle and within it: 'found the body of an infant. The town's police superintendent refused to do anything as it was found outside his jurisdiction. The county police superintendent also refused to do anything as he insisted the body was now in the town.'[53] In 1826, the village of Bassaleg was shocked at the news of the discovery of the mutilated body of a baby. The mother, a single woman who lived with her parents, had 'destroyed the child by various lacerations to the throat'. The 'mangled remains' were kept in their house for three days until the 'miserable paramour of the girl – a young married man with two children of his own' – arrived to dispose of it. He

> deposited the bundle in the carrion cart, among the provisions collected for the dogs, under a shed near the kennels on the Tredegar estate! An unusual motive happening to take one of the upper-bailiffs into the shed in the ensuing morning, he was struck by the singularity of a piece of coloured cotton appearing among the carrion, and horrified when a further search disclosed its contents.[54]

Ann Williams was another unmarried girl who took drastic action to rid herself of her unwanted offspring. She placed her baby in a rabbit warren on the Crawshay estate in Merthyr Tydfil, because she had no means to support it. 'The baby had been placed there on the Tuesday morning and had survived until 7.00 p.m. on Wednesday night, when its cries brought the gamekeeper who thought it was a hare ensnared in a trap.' So common was infanticide in Flintshire that it is said that the cries of murdered children still echo from the water restlessly flowing beneath Holt Bridge.[55] The fate of these unhappy infants throws a harsh, cold light on the cruel underside of a period of intense religious devotion and spiritual rapture.

Death's Dark Warriors (1): Nature and Nurture

Mewn hyfryd fan ar ail y bryn	On a beautiful spot near the hilltop
Mi welwn fwthyn bychan,	We see a small cottage,
A'i furiau yn galchedig wyn	Whose walls are whitewashed white
Bob mymryn, mewn ac allan.[56]	Every inch, inside and outside.

Thus spake Samuel Roberts, in 'Y Teulu Dedwydd', one of the most popular poems published in Victorian Wales. Ieuan Gwynedd's 'Atgof o'r Brithdir', Mynyddog's 'Cartref' and Ceiriog's 'Nant y Mynydd' are comparable poems which attach powerful emotional associations to the Welsh countryside.[57] Rural Wales was the locale for 'y ffordd draddo-diadol Gymreig o fyw' (the traditional Welsh way of life). Life there was natural. It was a world of peace, innocence and tranquillity, a natural idyll. The rural family was considered to have all the virtues, and was praised as a pillar of society. Through rapturous images in poetry, the thatched, whitewashed cottage that looked so good in paintings and photographs was transformed into a shrine. In several paintings, white sugar-cube houses crouch on the hillside beneath gathering cumulus clouds, the white of their walls reflecting the magnificent light of the Welsh air. In Ceiriog's verses, the harshness of the lives of picturesque Welsh-speaking peasants living in beautiful surroundings was ignored. Since poverty could not be abolished, it was not only excused but extolled as a positive virtue. Dignified poverty had become the ideal. Ceiriog's shepherds lived simple, saintly lives. Like the whitewash on the cottage walls of 'Y Teulu Dedwydd', these pastoral paradises hid a darker reality which was unintentionally hinted at in Crych Elen's remarkable poem, 'Y Bwthyn Bach To Gwellt.' The poem, which became a much sung song, sought to evoke the cosy comforts of the 'nefoedd fach gu' (cosy little heaven), of her grandmother's thatched cottage. But it is an orphan's lament of loneliness and despair which marks the poem. For in an atmospheric storm that symbolized life, the author had lost both her parents. Crych Elen points towards the sorrows of life in a beautiful, but sorrowful, land.[58] Life on the land was hard and laborious. Winter days, coloured like dull silver, dragged on endlessly, and the atmosphere in people's homes was often oppressive and uneasy. Gethin, in his collected works, poignantly recorded the pessimistic outlook which endless rain inculcated:

> Peth arall sydd yn erbyn ein huchel-dir yw y mynych wlaw sydd yn disgyn arno oherwydd uchder y mynyddoedd sydd rhyngom a'r gorllewin. Mae mwy o lawer o leithder yn ein hawyr ni nag sydd wedi myned trosodd i Gapel Garmon, neu Pentrefoelas . . . Mae bywyd ac amaeth yn Dioddef oherwydd.[59]

> Another factor against our highlands is the frequent rain which falls on them because of the height of the mountains between us and the west. There is more rain in our area than in Capel Garmon or Pentrefoelas . . . Life and agriculture suffer accordingly.

The cottages which looked so picturesque in paintings and pictures were pungent in practice. Home-made homes, like 'y bwthyn bach to gwellt', only resembled dream cottages in dreams or through the distorting filters of nostalgia. The floors were of compacted mud to which generations of feet, mostly bare, regularly added new material. In 1864, while investigating the conditions in a cottage in the south-west, Dr Hunter found his feet sinking into the soft wet mud floor. To get some desperately needed ventilation into the 'habitation of death', he punched a hole in the mud walls. How the inhabitants reacted is not recorded.[60] Roofs leaked; that of the farmhouse of a Mr J. Williams of Abergwesyn was the location for a 'rabbit's nest'.[61] Walls were damp and cold. There was no running water. One of the first tasks for many children was to carry buckets of water from local fountains. Privies, when they existed at all, were located at the bottom of the garden. They were often clogged and overflowing, and the stench had an almost corporeal presence. But more terrifying were the early morning or late night winter visits, for garden bottom privies were the haunts of 'bwcis' and malicious spirits. As late as 1870, a visitor to Caernarfon-shire wrote that:

> the great blot upon this county is the condition of its cottages. The exteriors sometimes promise well, but are deceptive. There is an appearance of neatness in the thatched roof and whitewashed walls which creates at first a favourable impression . . . Nothing, however, can be conceived more wretched than the interior of most of these habitations . . . The windows have no apertures; ventilation is supplied by the chimney and the door; the floor is of clay, and in this close damp, dreary hovel are often housed a labourer, his wife, and six or eight children.[62]

In Radnorshire, the condition of the cottages had degenerated into 'fly-ridden, cock-roach infested, filthy hovels'. Above the central fireplace hung the only cooking pot, in which all the family's meals were cooked.[63] Vegetables were boiled until all the vitamin and nutritional content was dissipated. Walter Davies, as he roamed Cardiganshire in 1810, gathering information for his report for the Board of Agriculture, collected recipes. These included one for *cawl caws y tlawd* (the cheese broth of the poor), consisting of a little bread, hot water and salt – the name was a ghastly joke, for there was no cheese. *Twym Llaeth* was a mixture of oatmeal and sheep's milk cream, poured into boiling water and flavoured with herbs, leeks and barley. *Cawl Dail* (leaf broth) was made of just herbs and hot water. *Cawl*

Tato was a mixture of potatoes, hot water and salt.[64] Several sound more like recipes for edible glue than for a nutritious meal. In the north, the principal meal was either *swcan* or *llymru*, both of which were unsatisfying as was revealed in a popular couplet: 'Llymru lled amrwd / i lenwi bol, yn lle bwyd' (Raw *llymru* / to fill the stomach, instead of food). Those in the south were equally able to voice their culinary frustrations in verse: 'O Arglwydd, dyma fwyd / Cawl sur a bara llwyd'[65] (O Lord, what food, / Sour broth and mouldy bread).

Debilitated by a deficient diet, bereft of the basics of life, people were an easy and early prey to disease. In 1864, Dr Hunter reported that:

> The farmer in Wales as well as the labourer, must be taken to mean a person generally badly lodged, and insufficiently fed and clothed . . . In Cardiganshire district, a medical practitioner described the children as 'pining for want of food as soon as weaned', and thought that if the climate were cold the whole race would perish.[66]

Small farmers and labourers laboured for long hours to gather the meagre resources which placed a banknote's width between themselves and the glorified jail of the workhouse. In winter, they had no means of adequately drying their clothes. In summer, they were again at the mercy of the weather. In 1856, Gwen Elis of Ty'n Cerrig, Llangywer, 'fell down dead' after working in the intense heat of a hayfield.[67] The coroner passed a verdict of death by a stroke of the sun, 'coup de soleil'. On the same day, John Williams of Abererch, and Peter Evans and H. Pugh of Dolgellau also died from the effects of the sun, while a terrible explosion of thunder convinced people in Bethesda and Llandegai that Apocalypse was now.[68] Work in the fields and the timber and woollen mills of rural Wales involved bone-cracking labour in which the weight of harvests and timber ruptured the gut and twisted shoulders and spines into stooped attitudes of toil, as immutable as statues carved in stone. Wirt Sikes, during his journey through the Welsh fairs, noted that farmers' bodies were locked in supplicating postures.[69]

Despite their heroic efforts, horrific weather often prevented people from reaping the benefits of what they had sown. A series of wet and unproductive harvests between 1789 and 1802 brought such great distress that the ballad singers beseeched God for release and relief. In 1811, from 'blighted Cardiganshire', Thomas Johnes wrote to George Cumberland:

Our weather for these last eight weeks has been uncommonly wet, which has ruined our harvests; and I am sorry to say that much corn is now rotting on the ground. Our potatoes and herring fishery have failed, so that our prospect is very miserable and I dread the consequences, for a scarcity will come like Pandora's box, but without hope at the bottom.[70]

In 1815 Tambora, an Indonesian volcano, erupted. The trade winds carried the debris around the world, creating strange aerial shapes which produced lurid light shows above western Europe. The strange meteorological phenomenon provided an appropriate apocalyptic atmosphere for the troops trudging home from the European wars. But the brilliant Turnerian sunsets could not conceal that temperatures had plummeted by up to three degrees centigrade. 'The year without a summer', 1816, was a single season of constant rain and cold. As a result, harvests failed and, in the following year, Wales faced famine. On 7 June 1818, David Williams wrote a letter which eloquently described the distress of Cardiganshire:

the imagination cannot conceive the prevalent distress – none but those who witness it can conceive its extent and intensity . . . The overseers testify to their total inability to keep the poor alive . . . The poor are attempting to prolong life by swallowing barley meal and water – boiling nettles etc – and scores in agonies of famine have declared to me this last week that they have not made a meal for two days together . . . hundreds have therefore been in the habit of begging from door to door near the sea shore . . . I declare to God from what I see and hear, that I fear half the labouring population will perish as things are, before next harvest in this neighbourhood – nor did I ever conceive before that human nature could bear up amidst such Privations as these poor have endured and are suffering.[71]

Tremendous gales and floods in the Tywi valley and elsewhere reduced an already desperate people to destitution. Farmers sold their beasts to buy the necessities of life, and obtained only a fraction of their normal price because of depressed markets. For several years the land was understocked, to the prolonged detriment of Welsh agriculture. Scarcity of food led to rioting in all parts of Wales.[72] In July 1819, the Montgomeryshire Yeomanry had to suppress a riot at Abermule. In many of the popular protests women took a leading role, indicating that life had become desperate. In 1816, a mob comprised solely of women, and armed with dripping pans, came down upon John Hughes and the Cardiganshire enclosure officials 'like a rolling torrent . . . They directed his attention to a pit which had been dug for the internment of every surveyor who approached their rights.'[73] In 1839 and 1842–3, atrocious weather leading to scarcity and starvation drew the disenchanted and disadvantaged into the 'hosts of Rebecca'. In 1846, the potato crop upon which the poor mainly depended for subsistence failed and the high prices of all articles of food in local markets prevented people from obtaining the necessities of life. Labourers were forced to purchase more expensive barley to survive, and in consequence found themselves deeper in debt. In 1847, £75 was collected in Cardigan to purchase food at the cheapest possible price to distribute to the poor. Local gentry were said to have subscribed the sum of £3,000 to the Cardigan Corn Relief fund. But such generosity was too little, too late.[74]

Photographs of hamlets and small towns in the 1850s and the 1860s show places of great loneliness, poverty and neglect. Hens and dogs walked across the dung and dog-turd covered streets, while many shop windows displayed advertisements for sailings to America. The traveller Malkin provides valuable insights into the darker aspects of rural Wales. Llandovery he considered a 'dreadful place ... Its buildings are mean, irregular and unconnected; the streets filthy and disgusting.' Haverfordwest was so poor that it 'had no shews; nor any jugglers, except a recruiting party', but the people were at least 'gifted with a saucy wit and jaunty air of good humour'. Fishguard, or as he contemptuously called it 'Fiscard', was the only town in which he had met with 'literal and bona fide dunghills'. It was filthy, unpaved, unciv- ilized, a shambles.[75] The smell of these strongholds of rural Wales was the smell of decay and damp, of deep-rooted dust and poverty, and above all the stench of hopelessness, a sour compound of unwashed bodies spiked with the elderflower fragrance of urine. Peat fires added a musky scent to the concoction and covered everything with a grey dust. In this atmosphere, the old lived on their memories, while the young longed to leave and exchange their simple, laborious, tedious lives in that lovely corner of the earth for the high wages and debased pleasures, the bustle and excitement, of 'the works'.[76]

Poverty was the power that prised people from paradise. Poverty meant lives of desperation and deprivation, a tasteless, unsatisfying diet, freezing and damp living conditions, engagement in back- breaking toil for a pittance, and no future prospects except a continuation of suffering and shame. People therefore never looked before they leaped and moved in their thousands to work in industries in Wales, England, America and anywhere in the world which offered them the prospect of an end to their suffering. It is this which explains the docile equanimity and good cheer with which these simple people,

Comte Maudet de Penhouet, *Inhabitant of Ruins near Neath*, 1797 (National
Library of Wales). One of the few depictions of the tortuous poverty of many
of the people of Wales.

irrevocably uprooted, set out to encounter a strange and unknown destiny. They left the bounds of the land which composed the entire smell and substance and geography of their lives, the fields, meadows and shimmering woodland dwindling away behind them, remembered only in a person's darkest hours of *hiraeth*.[77]

Hope evaporated upon arrival. The industrial areas of Wales, which promised so much, were themselves tormented by savage social problems. Many emigrants left behind the miseries of a bottom-of-the-cottage-garden midden privy for the boisterous ten-hole privy which was shared by an entire street. The morning rush of a coarse, uncouth, rag-tag-mob to the clap-boarded ruin with its ripe, pungent, immediate odours must have been agonizing for any sensitive soul. In Carmarthen in 1864, Daniel Lewis fell from the communal privy in Dame Street which emptied over the river Tywi, and was drowned in 'night soil'.[78] Immigrants rapidly acquired the bewildered look of a people betrayed, whose certainties had turned into mist, their hopes a helpless threnody.

Cardiff, Swansea, Newport, Merthyr Tydfil and Wrexham, the coal and iron towns of the south-east and north-east, and coastal and quarrying towns, grew rapidly in population in the early to mid nineteenth century. The growth was unregulated and placed an insupportable burden on the sanitary and health infrastructure of the towns. So bad were the conditions that government agencies and private individuals undertook a series of inquiries into social conditions. By the 1850s, there were more fact-finding missions than facts.[79] Countless reports drew attention to the gross deficiencies of the social fabric of Welsh towns. At Merthyr Tydfil, more than 700 people shared the water from one standing pump. The water that trickled from the pump was brackish and 'evil-smelling'. Moralists condemned David Jones in 1849 for preferring to drink Merthyr Tydfil beer rather than its water. Jones might have been the wiser, because at least the brewing process killed some bacteria.[80] Milk was poison delivered to the doorstep, so contaminated was it with virulent bacteria. Even after the Adulteration of Food Acts, most food sold in Wales was adulterated; bread, for example, contained sawdust.

In Caernarfon, the courts and lanes were dreadfully overcrowded, unventilated and filthy. In Cross Keys Court:

> there are nine houses, several of them occupied by two families; here also there is no supply of water; only one privy, and that in a most disgusting state. There are six pigsties, with accumulations of dung, from which the smell is very offensive, there being none but surface drainage.[81]

Drs William Roberts and Robert Jones, the surgeons who prepared a report on the town's health, noted that: 'from the pig slaughter house near Bridge Street, the blood ran in an uncovered drain by the side of the street . . . the slaughter house and tallow-chandlers at Tanybont are in a very unsatisfactory state'.[82] It is little surprise that one street, perhaps with mock irony, but probably with accuracy, was named Cwrt-y-baw-ieir (Chicken Shit Court). Mill Lane, soon to become notorious for its brothels, was described as 'very ill-ventilated', and 'without any supply of water or privies'.[83] At Crown Street and Turkey Shore, there were more than sixty houses without privies. Most people used 'a hole in the town wall, near the archway as a privy, frequently exposing their person in the open street'. Despite the critical and caustic nature of the report, and the dire warnings of the dangers facing the town, nothing was done until after the cholera epidemic of 1866. The town of Denbigh had a street named Lôn Fudur (Dirty Street). The two words spoke volumes. Monmouth was awash with human and pig waste, mingled with the rubbish of butchers' shops. 'An abominable Styx meanders through Monow Street', while Overmonow was 'an ill drained, open, cesspit'. The town's drinking water was drawn from the Wye into which the upriver town of Hereford was dumping up to two million gallons of raw sewage every day in 1870.[84]

In 1854, *The Cambrian* boasted that:

> Swansea is still in the forefront of watering places. The influx of visitors this year has exceeded our wildest expectations . . . Those jolly sons of Neptune must be assured, as indeed we are, that the tide of industrialism, while rising and growing daily more irresistible, has not yet marred or detracted from the delights which Swansea affords the visitor in search of sand, sun, and sea.[85]

The alliteration could be extended by a fourth 's' word which is the one most people thought of, if and when they thought of Swansea – 'smoke'. The 'jolly sons of Neptune' lived in a town that was heavily besmirched by the grime and pollution of heavy industry. Clouds of acidic, carcinogenic smoke billowed over the town, despoiling the landscape and killing plants as far north as the upper Neath Valley. In 1791, James Baker visited Clasemont, a Palladian-style house unfortunately upwind of the Upper and Middle Bank works. He noted that the smoke was so destructive of vegetation that places where the 'infection fell with most force', were 'marked by absolute sterility'. In a reversal of the *tai unnos* tradition, it was rumoured that Clasemont was dismantled in 1805, and the materials moved, 'all in one night', by hundreds of carts to Sketty Park, and rebuilt downwind of the works. In the great copper smoke dispute that raged in the 1840s and 1850s, doctors sided with their class allies by arguing that the copper smoke was harmless. Some claimed that clouds the colour of burnt umber, which permanently hung low over the town, had protected people from the onset of cholera in 1839.[86] These doctors well remembered that they had salaries to collect, but forgot that they also had wider duties to discharge.

In 1845, Sir Henry T. de la Beche, in a report on the health of Swansea, showed conclusively that, in the 1840s, people were living in conditions which were not only a negation of civilized existence, but a menace to civilized society.[87] Houses were overcrowded and undrained. The contents of privies, unconnected to the public sewers, were allowed to percolate into the adjacent soil and into the shallow wells, from which much of the town's water was drawn. The Swansea Paving and Lighting Act of 1804 had made provision for a drainage scheme, but this was totally incapable of dealing with the torrent of excrement which descended upon the town. Swansea's population grew from 6,099 in 1801 to 20,152 in 1841. Many parts of the town, especially the new housing areas, were totally without drainage. Even if they had drains, there would have been no water to flush them, for this essential service was also grossly neglected. In 1845, the water supply provided by the Swansea Waterworks Company was connected to about 470 houses out of a total of 3,369. Nearly 3,000 householders had to depend on polluted wells and streams, or on the services of the water-vendors who hauled it noisily about the streets and sold it at a penny a pailful.[88]

The worst part of Swansea was the Greenhill district, or 'Little Ireland', as it was known.[89] This area presented a desolate scene of badly paved, ill-formed streets and alleys. Dilapidated, overcrowded houses had no sanitary conveniences. Rivulets of urine seeped out of homes, and Dyfatty Street was 'knee deep in dirt', while almost all the homes in Back Street and Mariner Street were without privies. The few privies which did exist defied the descriptive powers of the medical officers. Against intense competition, Morris Lane was described as 'the dirtiest alley in the town'. It had only ten houses, but not a single one of them had a lavatory, or drain, of any description. All refuse and household waste was thrown into the lane and there it remained, unless the rain washed it back again into the houses. Here, just before Christmas 1819, a coach crashed into a pile of dung dumped in the road, injuring several passengers and throwing the driver so fiercely that he broke his ribs.[90]

Swansea had pretensions to the sense and sensibility of a refined town, but Merthyr Tydfil had no such ambitions. It was the Augean stables of the sanitary history of Wales. Throughout the 1840s and 1850s, an endless series of reports drew attention to the gross deficiencies in the town's housing, health, sanitation and sewerage. In 1853, the Merthyr Tydfil Board of Health heard the latest litany of filth. Houses were 'overcrowded', 'undrained', 'dirty', 'disgusting', 'revolting', 'pestilential'. In Cae-pant-tywyll, Quarry Road, Irish Row, Newfoundland and Cinder Tip, conditions were universally bad. The cellar dwelling of Daniel McCrohen came in for particular condemnation. In fifteen homes in Penydarren Road, 137 Irish people were 'very, very filthy':

> In a court on the left-hand side is a privy which is full and is unfit to use. Human excrement is consequently thrown about in all directions, and urine streams down the steps leading to the court, and emits a most offensive smell. The homes are filthy and swarm with vermin . . . People refuse to use quick lime because of the expense . . . There are empty cottages in the area, which have been condemned, which have been broken into and used as privies.[91]

The report's author believed that the children who played barefoot in the streets stood little or no chance of reaching their teens. The flies, which swarmed like airborne black carpets on the dripping meat hanging outside butchers' shops and slaughterhouses, and the rats which infested the town would ensure that they died young. The back alleys and cul-de-sacs of Cardiff, Swansea, Merthyr Tydfil and Wrexham were no-go areas for the respectable. Their inhabitants were the sad people of the hock-shop world, broken old men with sacks of junk, and wispy, ugly old ladies hurrying bent-backed with their scant possessions. People were like living carrion, weak and wasted creatures. With their rice-paper skins and sparrow-claw wrists, these people were described as 'coffin bait'. The people of some courts sounded like troglodytes working in their caves, the places alive with the rasping of crones, the sibilance of gossip, the wailing of wasted children and the screams of voices raised in anger. These were the 'lazy', 'dissipated', 'vermin-covered', 'disease-breeding' and 'disease-carrying' people who so shocked the medical authorities. Scabies and postulating skin conditions marred and scarred complexions. In these courts, the *cwrwau bach* and the low dram shop polluted the Sabbath air, disturbed the sacred silence, and at closing time sent out crowds of inebriate wretches to howl, blaspheme, fight, puke or simply to lie prostrate on the sidewalks. They sold crude home-brewed produce that included a variety of ingredients to strengthen the potency of the brew – denatured alcohol, camphor and opium – so that many of the customers became permanent, if not eternal. In 1820 in Mountain Ash, a man died from drinking a pint of 'rot-gut' spiked with opium.

If living conditions were harsh, working conditions were even harder and harmful to health. The use of mercury by the hat makers of Tal-y-bont in Cardiganshire ensured that there was considerable truth in the saying 'as mad as a hatter'.[92] Boys of twelve were employed at the Hafod copper works in Swansea, but started at nine years of age at Taibach. Young boys were allocated to 'lighter tasks', but these could still be heinous – cleaning ash pits, greasing wheels and machinery, wheeling ore and coal to the furnaces breaking the slag for remelting. With only a ten-minute break for breakfast and fifteen minutes for dinner, Owen Jones, a twelve-year-old 'greaser' worked fourteen-hour shifts in 1842.[93] In 1822, it was said that one in five of Swansea workers were suffering from acute aggravated hernia. *The Cambrian* newspaper wished 'to congratulate the town of Swansea and its neighbourhood on the recent formation of a Truss Society', which provided 'The Patent Anatomical Self-Regulating Truss' to Swansea's sufferers.[94] Women and girls worked in sweltering, dusty environments and were often assigned the less savoury jobs. They broke ore into smaller lumps, separated the ore from the gangue, and wheeled ore and coal to the fires. In one nine-hour shift, Elizabeth Matthew wheeled more than twenty tons of copper in 150 separate loads. She confessed to the Commissioner into the condition of employment for women and children in the early 1840s 'that her shift left her far too tired to attend evensong'.[95] The hellish heat was the least of the hazards of working in the copper works; worse were the sulphurous vapours. 'The men suffer greatly . . .', wrote one visitor to a Swansea works, 'they cover the mouth and nostrils with a handker-chief, and occasionally rush to a distance to inhale a less impure air.' A pickler at the Morfa works, who looked like an emaciated early saint, confided: 'When I came here from the iron works six years ago, I suffered much from my stomach. The sulphur affected me. I spat blood for some time, but I became used to it.'[96]

Many who did not get used to it died. Injury was also 'accepted as an inevitable part of iron working'. Merthyr Tydfil and Ebbw Vale became notorious for their hideously deformed beggars and crippled or blind musicians.[97] Men had to be agile and swift to avoid splashes and spillages of molten metal, and many were burnt and deformed. In the mines, children were burnt by fire damp and scarred by sharp outcrops of stone and coal. Their pallid faces were veined with subcutaneous coal-dust and their blood-shot eyes blinked with nystagmus. At the best, working a narrow seam could lead to serious skin lesions to the knees and elbows; at worst, mining meant death by emphysema or silicosis. In between were a variety of distressing and debilitating ailments. William Isaac, aged eleven, an air-door keeper at Dinas Colliery in the Rhondda, was described by the Commissioners in 1842 as: 'neglected; the whole skin of his face was burned and he has a very disagreeable appearance; the eyes are much inflamed'.[98] The published report of 1842 commented on the physical effects on children working in the mines of the south:

> their strength diminishes and they may lose their robust appearance; that these then become pallid, stunted in growth, short of breath, sometimes thin and often burnt, crooked, crippled, and that in addition, they are peculiarly subject to certain mortal diseases, is the direct result of their employment and the state of the place in which they work.[99]

Death's Dark Warriors (2): Disasters and Misadventure

Work not only weakened the sinews and warped the bodies of men and women, it was a destructive general in death's arbitrary army. The workplace was one of the most dangerous places in nineteenth-century Wales. In ironworks, mines and quarries, on the land and at sea, death was the ultimate predator, patient, powerful, ever vigilant. Derelict and working coal shafts were left unguarded, a hazard to the unwary. In 1832, Thomas Davies, a carter of Hirwaun, was pushing his cart when he plummeted forty-six yards to his death down an abandoned mine shaft, the cart landing on his broken body.[100] He left a widow and four children. Defective winding gear took an annual toll of colliers' lives. In 1814, a man and two boys, descending a coal pit at Hawarden, fell fifty yards to their death when the rope broke: 'precipitating them to the bottom . . . killing the man and one boy instantly'; the other boy was taken up 'dreadfully mangled' and died later. The man left a wife and seven children destitute.[101] Perhaps the most dangerous task in mining in the early nineteenth century was that of the sinkers, the pioneers who began the coal cutting. In 1831, two sinkers fell to their death down the shaft at a mine in Landore, Swansea.[102] In 1831, another sinker, Morgan Rees at the Pentre colliery, was dragged down the pit when his clothes caught in winding gear. Pieces of his body were later recovered.[103] Reckless sinking had other dangers. In 1833, the new County Hall at Mold nearly collapsed from subsidence caused by underground workings.[104]

Flooding was a frightening possibility which terrified colliers. Workers at the Landshipping collieries had reason to be more fearful than many because their coal face lay beneath an underground river. Unsurprisingly, the inevitable happened and several lives were lost.[105] In 1852, twenty-seven men drowned at the Gwendraeth colliery in Pontyberem when water broke through to their level from older, abandoned coal seams.[106] Several families were devastated and thrown into destitution. In 1860, twenty-six men and boys drowned when the Bryn-coch colliery was flooded. Four putrid, decomposed bodies were not recovered until several months later.[107]

Fire damp had been a terrifying companion for many colliers since the seventeenth century, and retained a sinister pre-eminence as a cause of deaths. Sir Humphry Davy's safety lamp, which enclosed the flame but still indicated the presence of the dangerous and deadly gas, was only reluctantly and slowly introduced into Welsh mines. Expenditure was one reason, fear of innovation was another. The great inventor himself recorded how colliers' wives assembled on the banks of one of the Ruabon pits and tried, with 'noise and lamen-tation', to prevent their husbands from taking these new 'scientific horrors' down with them.[108] The lamps provided a safer alternative to the naked flames which many miners used to light their work. In 1829, nine men were killed at the Dee Green Colliery in Flint when a boy's candle ignited a pocket of fire damp: 'Dreadfully wounded, eleven men were so shockingly scorched that they won't survive'.[109] William Thomas, David Hughes, Thomas Jenkins, John Thomas, John Morris and Thomas Morgan were all 'blown to atoms' at the Broad Oak Colliery, when John Morris's candle ignited a pocket of 'hydrogen gas'. *The Cambrian* uttered a verdict that was typical of the times: 'No blame can attach to the Proprietors or their agents, for it was proven by an old collier that the working part of the colliery was better venti-lated than any he had ever worked in.'[110]

Ballad singers were clear as to the true price of coal:

| Ti sy'n llosgi glo y ddaear | You who burn the earth's coal |
| Ar dy aelwyd mewn mwynhad, | On your hearth with satisfaction, |

Cofia mae ei werth digymar   Remember that its purchase price
Ydyw gwaed y glowr mad.[111]   Is the innocent miner's blood.

Each disaster brought forth a ballad, which outlined the horrors of the
event, and the tragic trauma which was a constant part of life of
colliery communities. Dewi Santesau and an anonymous ballad-
monger sang ballads to the Llety Shenkin explosion of 1849, and
Eiddil o'r Nant and another anonymous ballad-writer to the Pwll y
Dyffryn, Aberdare, disaster in 1852. The Risca explosion of 1860
touched the muse of Deio Bach y Cantor, and several anonymous
ballad singers, into expressions of sympathy and sentiment for the
devastated community. Press reports were even more evocative of the
devastation and destruction inflicted on mining communities by terrifying explosions. As mining activities intensified, deaths multiplied.
The 1850s and 1860s saw the annual haemorrhage of a few lives lost
transformed by several major disasters. On 10 May 1852, sixty-four
were killed in the Duffryn disaster, 114 died at Cymmer on 13 July
1856 and 146 men, women and children were destroyed at Risca on
1 December 1860. But the capital of sorrow was Ferndale. There, on
8 November 1867, 178 souls were blasted away.

Bad news was good copy for the newspapers. In 1837, the
Monmouthshire Merlin reported the 'work of Mr Alexander Brewer,
surgeon to the Iron Works colliery', and the 'heroics of Messrs Davies
and Tuckett in rescuing bodies from the shattered mine'. Despite their
efforts, 'David Thomas died in less than an hour after being brought
out; he was very much burnt and received a severe fracture of the skull,
from which his brain protruded'.[112] In March 1862, the same paper
published a special issue featuring the explosion at Merthyr's Gethin
Colliery. In all, forty-eight men and boys were killed. The inquests
were a lengthy process: 'The jury then went to view the mangled and
scorched corpses of the victims; a proceeding which lasted from 10
o'clock till half past four, owing to the distance the bodies lay apart in
their respective dwellings.'[113]

In sympathy with the grieving communities, the local works were
allowed to close at midday on Saturday, so that the workers could pay
their last respects to the dead. The scenes were remarkable:

> A thick, drizzling rain, and masses of heavy clouds which overhung the vast
> range of mountains which environ 'the iron metropolis of Wales' tended to
> increase the solemnity of the occasion. A funeral procession, under any circum-
> stances, is a solemn spectacle, but when, as in this instance, nearly fifty human
> beings cut off in the health and vigour of manhood are being conveyed to their

last resting places under such circumstances, the sight is calculated to strike awe into the hearts of the most obdurate; especially when the misery and poverty of which it is the forerunner are presented to the mind in all their hideousness.

In Caraway roadside, four corpses were brought out, all within a few doors of each other, and some hundreds of persons followed them. The roads were literally covered with spectators; whilst every now and then the cries of distress and mournful sobs of the poor widows and orphans struck painfully in the ear. Four were carried six miles to Aberdare – people took turns to carry the biers; the crowds were in tears. Twelve corpses were carried to Cefn Cemetery, 800 men followed after each – everywhere there were massive crowds.[114]

For one boy, it had been his first and last day at work. The lessons were not learnt. On 20 December 1863, another thirty colliers lost their lives in the Gethin Merthyr mine.

Ironworks took a less dramatic but consistent toll of lives. On 1 July 1839, a large Chartist procession from Coalbrookdale to Risca was held up as the body of a man killed at Blaina was carried through on a plank.[115] The pressure in the early steam engines used in several of the Welsh ironworks was difficult to control, resulting in frequent explosions. In 1836, an engine exploded at the Dowlais works, throwing large pieces of debris weighing several tons into the grounds of Dowlais House, demolishing a 120 foot tower, and killing several people.[116] In 1860, despite improved pressure control valves, a steam boiler exploded at a Swansea works, causing several fatalities.[117] Men were frequently dragged into the machines, mangled and mashed. In 1824, William Phillips, a mill-worker at Dowlais, was dragged into the machinery when he attempted to rescue his hammer. His hand and right arm were torn off from his 'frightfully mutilated body'.[118] Another mill-worker at Llanelli, a 'poor blind man', was cut in half after becoming entangled in the machinery.[119] John Lewis, a worker in the steam-grist-mill of John Roberts, Llanelli, was 'literally crushed to atoms', while attempting to oil the machinery.[120]

The biggest danger in the copper and iron works was fire. Workers had to be constantly vigilant to ensure their safety. Evan Thomas was one of the many iron workers who was rendered incandescent by the forces he was meant to harness. Perhaps the drink he had consumed before starting work had made the experienced thirty-year-old furnace tapper clumsier than usual. Whatever the cause, he died in agony when he fell into the molten metal. Eventually, his remains were recovered from the furnace. Several others just melted. At the Landore Copper Works in 1811, four men disappeared when tapping a furnace.[121] Their families were left with nothing but memories. Lime-kilns were another source of incendiary danger. In 1837, the bodies of two men were discovered burning at the Strand lime-kiln in Swansea.[122]

Wherever people worked, death lay in wait for the unsuspecting. At the Cae-braich-y-cefn quarry, five men were killed by a fall of rock in 1836.[123] On Good Friday of that year, two men were crushed when a quarryman suspended by a rope high above the quarry unsettled a large boulder which crashed down.[124] It took rescuers two hours of tireless efforts to recover the bodies and rescue the mangled body of a third quarryman. In 1811 at Narberth, a labourer died when the mud walls of the cottage he was building fell on him and his wife and two children.[125] Bruised and battered, the wife and children survived. A farmer died sweating and tugging the hooves of a calf from its mother. The umbilical cord snapped, catapulting the farmer backward and fatally against a gatepost, fracturing his skull. Unperturbed, the calf peered from the membranes while its mother licked the afterbirth. To criminals, especially in the late eighteenth century, death became an occupational hazard which they faced with remarkable stoicism. At the Radnorshire Great Sessions in April 1827, William Williams was condemned to death for stealing horses, and Thomas Jones for stealing four bullocks. Though the sentences of many were commuted to a period in prison, or transportation, many offenders were hanged in public.[126]

In May 1817, *The Cambrian* reported the deaths of two men, three women and three children who had been drowned while picking cockles on Lafan Sands in Caernarfonshire. While they were at the beds, fog descended and the stranded people were drowned. 'The sea was so calm and the tide flowed so gently, that the men were found with their hats on.' The funerals of the eight in Aber church were dramatic: 'A more affecting sight can hardly be conceived – husbands lamenting the loss of wife and children, and wives lamenting the loss of husband and children.'[127] The sea was not always such a calm killer. When the sky changed colour from a deep episcopal purple to a sinister Bible black, and the wind changed pitch from a scream to a screech, people's fears turned into prayers to the God of Psalm 107. These became terrifying occasions. Simon Jones of Llangrannog, a sailor on the *Ann Catharine*, confided his terror to his log. Near Cuba, the sea was

> very fiery: all around being in a blaze like as it were floating in a sea of burning brimstone. Am I ready to die? O! No, O!! No, well then what will come of me?

> I have deserved an eternal punishment in Hell; and am no more worthy to be
> called the son of God: and O! what an unbearable calamity is to die in my sins
> . . .[128]

The terrified Simon survived to sail another day. Others were less
fortunate. The obituary notices and shipping news columns in Welsh
newspapers chronicle the devastation wreaked by storms. There was a
seasonal pattern: January, March, August, October and November
were months when winds of Wuthering Heights power pounded Welsh
shores and between ten and fifteen ships were lost in an average week.
The sea separated lovers more effectively than even the most tyrannical
of fictional Victorian patriarchs, and regularly drowned the best of the
young men, leaving villages comprising women, a few children, old
men and cripples. At New Quay, one street in 1841 was known as
'Widow Street'. The 1851 census revealed that thirty-eight widows
lived there in loneliness.[129]

The list of the ships and the lives lost in savage weather around the
coast of Wales is vast. In the great storm of December–January
1810–11, in 'tempestuous weather' which delayed the land-based
London–Swansea mail by sixteen hours, the *Theresa* from Trinidad,
carrying sugar, cotton and coconuts, sank near Nash Point in
Glamorgan, the *James* of Milford was battered on the rocks near
Llanstephan, the *Jane* and *Ann Prothero* of Milford, the *Linnen Hall*
of Dublin, and eighteen other ships were reported wrecked off the
south-west coast.[130] On Christmas Day, near Milford, an unknown
vessel was seen to founder and every soul on board perished.[131] In
1816, firkins of Irish butter, much to the delight of local inhabitants,
were washed ashore in Pembrokeshire from the wreck of the
Greyhound of Cork, which saw 124 soldiers drown before ever seeing
battle.[132] A year later, in late October 1817, the sloop *William and
Mary*, carrying passengers from Bristol to Waterford, hit the Wolves
rock near Flatholm and went down 'stern foremost'.[133] The correspondent of *The Cambrian* attempted to capture the drama:

> Here a scene of horror ensued of the most agonising description. Nearly seventy
> souls, including twenty five females and six or seven children, were floating in
> the water uttering the most piercing and heart-rendering shrieks for relief which
> would not be obtained, and sinking one after the other into eternity . . . Twenty
> were rescued . . . but others were consigned to their fate. The ballier refused
> permission to get into a rescue boat and stayed with his wife of three weeks . . .
> A poor sailor took his wife to the bow where they sat down and calmly awaited
> their fate; as the ship sank, they clung to each other, floated a moment on the
> surface, and then disappeared, clasped in each others' arms.[134]

For weeks, bodies were washed up along the Glamorgan coast. With such high drama and tragedy in real life, it was difficult for bards and ballad singers to capture the scene without lapsing into sentimentality. Although they have been disparaged by some literary critics for their excessive pathos, many Victorian poems and songs lamenting shipwrecks have the merit of at least attempting to depict the travails and trials of real life. Perhaps the most celebrated of these songs were those written to mark the loss of the *Rothesay Castle* in 1831, and the *Royal Charter* in 1853. The Revd William Williams, Caledfryn (1801–69), penned a notable poem 'Drylliad y Rothesay Castle', to mourn the loss of the ship off the Anglesey coast in the great storm of August 1831. With its Spielbergian catastrophic and epic effects, it remained a celebrated *awdl* until the late nineteenth century.[135]

Deep-blue-water sailing brought even greater dangers than the coastal trade. In August 1843, *The General Nott*, on her voyage from Cuba to Swansea, caught fire and sank, incurring a loss of £30,000.[136] Many of the ships of this trade were so poorly constructed that they were creaking, leaking assemblages of oak, pitch and nails seemingly kept together simply by faith. Voyages were month-long battles against the elements, shifting cargoes and the fear of fire. The harsh conditions were often even harsher, as was the case on the *Cornwall*, when the cook was a laudanum addict and an alcoholic, so the crew had to endure starvation rations. Many ships and sailors disappeared, leaving behind them for a few moments only a trail of bubbles, and then nothing, not even bubbles. George Laugharne, a Cardiff sailor of the *America*, bound for Shanghai, has not been heard of since 7 January 1861. The register of lost shipping 'presumes that he is lost at sea', as if he might still turn up one day.[137] It is no surprise that mariners became highly superstitious. Whistling or talking loudly aboard a ship at night was considered to tempt fate and call the wind. Men also kept clear of ships with an unlucky reputation or a fateful name. Few were willing to sail on the *Happy Return*. The sailors' reluctance proved wise, for the ship sank on her maiden voyage.[138]

Many people regarded a shipwreck as a windfall from which they were entitled to benefit. Several parts of Wales acquired an unsavoury reputation on account of the depredations of the local 'country people' on the goods and bodies washed up from shipwrecks. Legends were still current in the 1850s that the Dunraven family of Glamorgan and Dynion y Bwyelli Bach (the Men of the Little Axes) of Bury Port used lights to lure ships onto the treacherous rocks in their areas in order to wreck them. In 1818, when the *Despatch* sank near Cardiff, the Glamorgan militia had to be called out to attempt to prevent the theft of the cargo. It was reported that:

> A young man was drowned in attempting to obtain a cask that was floating in the water; and his father, who was in sight, could not afford time to give his son any assistance, being over zealous in carrying away anything he could get hold of belonging to the wreck – what an example from a parent![139]

Others possessed greater humanity and rendered considerable assistance to those in peril on the sea. Lifeboats were established in many Welsh coastal towns in the 1850s.[140] In 1860, a long-boat was launched from the treacherous Cefn Sidan sands to rescue the crew and the wife of the captain of the *Catherine*. Upon landing at Ferryside, the wife gave birth to a child who was christened Catherine Pottyer Cefn.[141]

Storms were not the only danger facing sailors. Incompetence in navigational techniques and sailing were responsible for the loss of many lives. In 1850, seven of the crew of the *Minerva* drowned at the entrance to Beaumaris when she hit another ship. Others were even more unlucky and unfortunate. The ship of Captain Skelle, an old sailor who looked like Coleridge's Ancient Mariner, hit a whale on his way into Milford harbour and sank. In 1875, the ship the *Minstrel King* was attacked for two hours by an angry whale.[142] Some were more fortunate and received a Piscean blessing. The *Endeavour* was damaged in a storm and had to call into Holyhead to check the damage. When placed in the dry dock, it was discovered that a small fish had been sucked into the hole, preventing water from entering the ship.[143] Having survived the dangers and drama of the sea, it was ironic that many sailors met their deaths in port. In 1830: 'an apprentice aboard the brig *Naome* of Aberystwyth, lying in the river at the port, fell from the mast of the vessel onto the deck, landing on his head, his skull was so dreadfully fractured as to cause death in a few hours afterwards'.[144]

The Welsh Victorian press seemed to revel in a good disaster. *The Cambrian*, the *North Wales Chronicle*, the *Monmouthshire Merlin* and the *Cardiff and Merthyr Guardian and Pontypridd Intelligence*, and denominational periodicals like *Yr Haul* and *Seren Gomer*, had regular columns entitled 'Accidents and Disasters'. These contained uninhibited revelations of the goriest details, almost as if the authors were savouring the degree of suffering inflicted on the victims. Perhaps this was due to the fact that the Victorians lived much closer to pain, disaster and death than did subsequent generations. Ghastly, nauseating sights were frequently seen in Victorian lives. It is clear that the

Victorians were not only conscious of the precariousness of their lives, but they seemed also to be endlessly fascinated by death.[145]

The dangers of travel were frequently recounted in reports of accidents in the Welsh press. An unnamed servant of John Daniel, farmer of Capel Iwan, Llangynwr, was drowned while trying to cross the river Tywi. Her body was recovered at White Mill.[146] John Evans, the landlord of the Plough and Harrow, drowned in Loughor in 1860, and his decomposed body was recovered from the river months later, though the four pigs he had purchased at Llandovery market were found safe and sound. The report in *The Cambrian* has harrowing descriptions of the extent of the decomposition – the head dropped off as the body was lifted from the water. Some families were exceptionally unfortunate. In 1831, an anonymous girl drowned attempting to cross the Taff. The paper reported that: 'it is but a short time since the father of this girl was killed at Dowlais, by a large mass of limestone rock, which had been blown up and, falling on his head, destroyed him in an instant'.[147] In June 1825, *The Cambrian* reported that: 'the body of a female drowned last November in a weir in the Wye was found this week. The body was in a state of utter decay, pieces flaked away and fell apart.'[148] In 1820, a freak wave swamped the Caernarfon ferry, drowning twenty women and the ferryman. A family of ten was left orphaned by the sad event.[149] Travel in winter had greater danger than swollen rivers. In 1839, a woman lost her way on the hills above Blaenavon and froze to death.[150] In early February 1814, a young man's body was found in the snow at Neath, a bargeman at Swansea died in the freezing water, and a woman 'with a child at her breast' was found frozen to death at Abergavenny.[151] John Morgan, a mason of Llangathen, was found frozen to death in deep snow within a hundred yards of his home.[152]

Many people were victims of misadventure and violence. In 1814, two children in Narberth died after washing themselves in arsenic.[153] William Blunt, 'a renowned Montgomeryshire fisherman', died after a 'delirious repast on a leg of mutton, a sack of potatoes, washed down with eight or ten pints of beer'.[154] An 'aged woman' of Swansea drowned when she fell into a vat of beer in the brewery.[155] Sudden, violent death came through many agencies. In 1860, *The Cambrian* published a remarkable report which recounted some of the violent deaths which had taken place in the previous twelve months:

> One was killed while 'somnumbulizing at night' ... there were hundreds of suicides – several took poisons including aconite, oil of vitriol and prussic acid

– the favourite means in this county of opening the door of escape from the evils of a troublesome world; a suicide burnt herself to death; one person was killed by lightning; one died of hydrophobia, three of starvation and neglect; and a child was killed by a turkey.[156]

Animals were unpredictable, undisciplined and dangerous. Thomas Edwards of Vaynor was enjoying himself watching a bull-baiting until the bull escaped and killed him.[157] Joseph Lodge, a twelve-year-old from Pontypool, was killed by his father's galloping horse. Joseph was exercising the horse when he became entangled in the stirrups, the horse bolted, dragging the unfortunate boy behind it on a wild gallop into the town. The first person who attempted to rescue the battered, bloody boy was his mother, who later collapsed. When the horse was eventually stopped, his father PC John Lodge also collapsed as he embraced his dead son.[158] In September 1817, two children of a farmer at Castell-Dreinog, Ystrad, near Lampeter, were killed by a boar. The girl whipped it: 'it flew at her, the brother whipped it while the mother dressed his sister's wounds, and it pulled out his entrails'.[159] Several babies were devoured by prowling porcines. In November 1821, the wife of David Lloyd, of Fountain-Hall, Carmarthen, had left her cottage to get a message from her neighbours, leaving her five-month-old baby in its cot:

In the meantime a sow belonging to one of the neighbours entered the room where the child lay. The mother returned after an absence of three minutes and shocking to relate, found that the sow had fast hold of the child's face! The poor woman, whose state can be better felt than described, immediately seized the animal, and with much difficulty forced its mouth open, and extricated her infant from its jaws; but the parts were so much lacerated as to preclude all hopes of recovery. The infant lingered until Monday morning and died in great agony! We cannot deprecate too much persons keeping a number of half-starved pigs, whilst in fact they can hardly keep themselves; when such animals are set loose, they devour every thing they meet with.[160]

Throughout most of the period 1776–1871, guns were freely available throughout Wales.[161] These added considerably to the danger of living in Welsh communities, especially when they fell into inexperienced hands. In 1817, a Machynlleth man returned home after shooting crows. He placed his gun on a table. His seven-year-old son picked it up and shot his father dead.[162] Lord Clive was shot by his son in a shooting accident in 1848. Remarkably, the son was afterwards known to other members of the family as 'Bag Dad'.[163] In jest, the nine-year-old son of Dr Phillips of Aberystwyth picked up a gun kept in the kitchen and told his three-month-old sister 'Lal, mi a'ch saethaf' (Lal, I will shoot you). He took aim, fired, and killed his sister.[164]

Fire was a greater danger than firearms, however deadly and destructive the latter could be. In 1827, the infant daughter of William Watkins, a glazier of Brecon, burnt to death in their cottage.[165] The wizard John Harries of Cwrt-y-Cadno allegedly foresaw the day of his death. To avoid fate he stayed in bed, but his home caught fire and Harries fell off a ladder while fighting the flames and died.[166] In 1835, ten men burnt in a tenement in Mynyddislwyn when the pitch of a Mari Lwyd they were constructing caught fire:

> Liquid fire splashed about the room setting everyone in a blaze from head to foot. They smashed a window and escaped . . . At this period the spectacle beggars all description; the unfortunate creatures running in all directions – some into pools of water, others stripping clothes and flesh off . . . a child was burnt to cinders . . .[167]

Without sympathy, or the decency of adding a name, *The Cambrian* reported that: 'A poor woman, occupying a miserable hut in one of the passages in Mill Street, Abergavenny, was burnt to death on Saturday.'[168] Many fires which were not caused by the incautious use of firing or combustible materials by people were started by lightning. In 1820, the cottage of a Llandrindod butcher was destroyed by fire. The butcher was 'struck dead' by the lightning, his wife and children died later of the horrific burns inflicted by the unexpected bolt.[169] Lightning destroyed the farmhouse, outbuildings and much of the stock of Edward Phillips, a farmer near Cardiff in 1826.[170] A boy from Little Pale, Kenffig, sitting by the fire in his cottage home, was killed instantly when lightning forked down the chimney. His brothers and sisters sitting around him were unharmed.[171] Such bizarre, inexplicable phenomena had an obvious explanation in the early nineteenth century. The victims, through their profligate, prodigal, sacrilegious behaviour, had done something to incur the wrath of God. Thomas Harries, a Denbigh farmer, had been rude to the harvesters who left his fields to attend Sunday worship. God's revenge, according to the ballad singer, was frightening:

> Pan ydoedd yr yd wedi ei gasglu, fe ddarfu Duw ei daro a mellt yn wenfflam i gyd, ynghyd a'r gŵr a'r wraig a chwech o blant, a thri gwas, a dwy forwyn, i gyd yn ulw.[172]

> When the corn was all gathered, God struck the farmer's fields with lightning, setting it all on fire, killing the husband and wife and six children, three servants, and two female servants, all burnt to a cinder.

Sometimes, God moved in mysterious ways his vengeance to perform. Thomas and Edward Hope, aged twenty-one and eighteen respectively, 'injudiciously taking shelter under an oak', near Knighton in 1778, were struck by lightning. The second part of Edward's epitaph on his tombstone in the churchyard dares to hint that God's judgement was misplaced, perhaps mistaken, but the author accepts it:

> At thy powerful voice, O Lord,
> Tremendous thunder roll,
> And pointed lightnings at thy word
> Dart swift from pole to pole.
> Reader think not thy judgement seized
> Two youths so honest could expire,
> Victorious to pure Heaven so well placed
> And snatched them in celestial fire.

In 1819, *Seren Gomer* decreed that the deaths of Hugh Thomas and his son of Trawsfynydd from lightning were attributed to God's judgement.[173] This savage vicious God, who interfered in temporal matters at the slightest provocation, had a wealth of instruments to torture Earth's brittle creatures. On his way home from harvest in 1839, Hugh Derfel Hughes (1816–90) imagined that: 'Tymhestloedd o dân ac o frwmstan / O'r Nefoedd ddylifant i lawr'[174] (Storms of fire and brimstone / From Heaven flood down). The weather in that year was frightful. Inexplicable red rain, tempestuous downpours, powerful thunderstorms, deep snowstorms and a dry period so intense that the ground became parched and scorched were all regarded as evidence of God's displeasure at mankind's wicked ways. David Davies provided several examples of God's summary punishments in *Dwy bregeth; yn gyntaf ar ragluniaeth Duw; a'r ail, ar gyfiawnder Duw yn Nghosbedigaeth yr annuwiol*, published in Cardiff in 1842. This vengeful, psychotic God had one unseen weapon in his armoury of retribution, which wreaked even greater havoc and horror amongst mankind than terrifying lightning. He had the microbe.

Death's Dark Warriors (3): Disease and Devastation

The *danse macabre* traditions of the ballad singers presented death as the 'great leveller', visiting high and low without regard to class, rank or social status. 'Nid edrych marwolaeth, pwy decaf ei dalcen' (Death does not look for the fairest forehead) was the stark warning of a popular proverb. Twm o'r Nant warned: 'Y tlawd a'r cyfoethog sydd gydradd yn y bedd' (Rich and poor are equal in the grave).[175] Literary portrayals of the death of sickly siblings of wealthy families reinforced the impression of equity in the face of death. The background noise to the correspondence of Thomas Johnes of Hafod is his family's cacophonous coughing from coughs, colds and sore throats.[176] A note of epic tragedy enters the correspondence when he writes of the death of his daughter, Mariamne, from consumption. In 1862, Golyddan, a medical apprentice, poet and son of Gweirydd ap Rhys, died of tuberculosis. The public expressions of sorrow at his premature demise further strengthened the notion that death was an even-handed enemy.[177] But if death weeded out some of the wilting weeds of the wealthier classes, he harvested the poor.

In the 1860s, tuberculosis took a toll of 300 lives per annum in Denbighshire where Golyddan died.[178] Other diseases were also devastating in their impact. Malaria was endemic in Wales in the late eighteenth and early nineteenth centuries, especially in the Cardiganshire bogs – Cors Caron and Cors Fochno – and the marshes of Anglesey. This tertian malaria, known as 'Y Deirton Dridiau', caused rigour and fever within minutes of each other. The victim's body suffered alternate bouts of polar cold and hellish, Saharan heat, so that he or she convulsed with terrifying tremors. In north Cardiganshire, the disease was personified as 'Yr Hen Wrach' (the old witch), who made periodic forays out of her marshy home to seize her victims with a fatal shaking sickness.[179] Typhoid and typhus, difficult to distinguish, created havoc in several Welsh communities. Typhus caused a vicious epidemic in Llanfair Talhaearn and Llangynhafal in 1831. In 1840, 140 died of typhus in Denbighshire, and 35 in Wrexham in 1860.[180] At Caernarfon in 1867, typhus savaged the inhabitants of the town's low lodging houses. In one house, a local medical officer found three people dying of the disease. The father lay in the only bed, the mother in filth on the floor. Next door, Anne Makin contracted the disease after attending a dying friend. For seven weeks, she lay across two chairs in a lower room covered by bits of carpet. Miraculously, she survived to suffer another day.[181] In Merthyr Tydfil, in the same year, thirty-three inhabitants of the workhouse were less fortunate and died.

The scant medical knowledge of the late eighteenth century meant that it was impossible for people to recognize or identify the afflictions which swept away the poor. On 11 August 1789, 27-year-old John Jenkins of St Fagans, when visiting his sick aunt, fell down dead without warning. 'He was bleeded', recorded the distraught William Thomas, 'but in vain'. The same death-obsessed diarist recorded the appearance of a fatal throat disease in Whitchurch which killed twenty-one people: 'The Parson denyed to have their bodies brought to church, for he fear'd their disease were infections, and several children have lately been buried there of the same disease.'[182] In 1795, the mystery disease had reached Llancarfan, where four children died in parched agony.[183] Influenza was probably the cause of the terrible suffering in Monmouth town and jail in January 1837 when forty succumbed.[184] Scarlet fever was rampant in 1840, claiming 224 deaths in Denbighshire alone.[185] In May 1836, the four children of Daniel Matthias, 'an industrious bookbinder' of Cardiff, all died within a few hours of the disease.[186] Another constant hazard was diphtheria, while measles frequently proved fatal. Three-year-old William Miller Jr of Wenvoe was one of the legions who died of this painful killer on 26 December 1791.[187] At Blaenafon in 1870, an outbreak of measles increased the mortality rate from 22 per 1,000 births to 166 per 1,000. In the 'massacre of the innocents', six or seven children died every day.

The intensifying trade between Swansea copper works and ore-rich South American countries heralded new dangers for the port's people. Endemic to South America, yellow fever or 'Yellow Jack' or 'black vomit' produced a tell-tale jaundice and killed by destroying the liver and the kidneys. It created a great fear because it was exceedingly deadly, killing most of its victims. So many Welsh sailors died in Santiago de Cuba that it was dubbed the 'Swansea Cemetery'.[188] More terrifying, in 1862–5, when the switch from sail to steam ships meant swifter passage and conditions on the return voyage allowed the survival of the bacilli-carrying mosquitoes, Yellow Jack made his ghastly appearance in Swansea. In 1865, the *Hecla*, flying the yellow flag to indicate that she was carrying disease, was allowed to dock and unload her cargo in the port rather than enter quarantine. The *Cambria Daily Leader* alleged that the only reason she was allowed in was because the *Hecla* was owned by a friend of the mayor and her cargo was destined for his brother's firm. One item of cargo had deadly effects. In all, twenty-nine people in the vicinity of the spot where the *Hecla* unloaded died of yellow fever.[189]

Rabies and 'hydrophobia' were terrifying diseases. In 1832, 'mad dogs' were reported to be 'on the rampage in Cardiff, Llandaff,

Cowbridge and Bridgend', biting several small dogs, horses and sheep, all of which were destroyed.[190] In 1836, many rabid dogs were shot near Llanfair, Anglesey.[191] The reason for the panic measure was clear. John Davies, a butcher of St Mary's, Cardiff, was one of many who died in frightful agony.[192] In June 1833, a twelve-year-old girl from Penallt, Monmouthshire, was bitten by two savage dogs roaming in a dilapidated ruin.[193] There was no cure. The gullible could try Rowed and Co.'s 'Imperial Composition' and the superstitious could try salt water bathing – a man from Brecon bitten by a cat in 1849 walked to Cardiff to bathe in the sea – but nothing could alleviate the suffering.[194] It might be a cynical observation, but one of the earliest examples of effective preventative medicine in Wales is the following: 'Was lately smothered to Death at Pencoed, Llangallo, being in great rage from the bite of a Mad Dog, a child, vizt a maid from five to six years of age. Had first bitten her mother and the other children.'[195]

Smallpox, highly contagious, frequently deadly, destroyed the beauty of many of those it did not slay. Traces of childhood infections could be seen on the adult faces of hymnist William Williams, Pant-ycelyn, the playwright Twm o'r Nant and Captain Cook's surgeon, David Samwell. The Registers of Criminals kept by nineteenth-century police forces contain frequent references to criminal visages which were 'pock-pitted', 'pock-faced', 'scarred'. Smallpox was a horrific way of dying – in misery and disfigurement, a terrible death, nothing like the pastoral metaphors of sentimental literature of flowers slowly wilting or autumnal leaves gently falling. The disease caused terror in several communities across Wales. In Myddfai and Cil-y-Cwm in 1792, 1793, 1796, 1838 and 1841, the depredations of smallpox precipitated a demographic crisis.[196] In 1812, the disease took a heavy toll on the inhabitants of Bangor. At Wrexham in 1837–8 over a hundred died. Llanrwst experienced a 'brisk visitation' in 1860. In 1867 a general epidemic struck hard, killing 161.

Wales never seemed further from paradise and closer to hell than it did in 1832. In that year, a new disease made its terrifying appearance. A virulent bacterial disease of the intestinal tract, asiatic cholera, caused intense diarrhoea and dehydration, and often took its victims in a matter of hours. Stools turned to a grey liquid, described as 'rice water', until nothing emerged from the sufferer but liquid and fragments of gut. Extreme cramps followed, with an insatiable desire for water. The patient soon displayed the classic cholera physiognomy – puckered blue lips in a shrivelled hollow face. In the sinking stage of the disease, the victim's life force simply drained away. The speed of cholera's spread was greatly increased by one of the early nineteenth century's most vaunted achievements, the increasing pace of ocean and overland transport between Britain and India. Cholera travelled the trade routes, tracing the pathways of the global economy with a finger of death. The Welsh had seen it coming. Reports appeared in newspapers of a terrifying new disease which was raging in India in 1831.[197] Then it marched across Asia to Europe, reaching Poland and then France; in November 1831, it reached Sunderland. Forewarned was not forearmed. Welsh health and medical authorities did nothing to prepare their communities for the devastation which ensued.

In May 1832, cholera reached Flintshire, spread rapidly to Bagillt and Flint, and was exceptionally virulent in Denbigh.[198] The disease appeared in the town on 9 June 1832, and in less than a month it had killed over forty people, the majority in the first few days.[199] Daniel Jones, Parc y Twll, son of Robert Jones of Rhos-lan, proved himself to be a Celtic chronicler of cholera to rival Boccaccio's account of the plague in Florence, giving a graphic eye-witness account:

> Torrwyd i lawr mewn ychydig ddyddiau tros bymtheg ar hugain o eneiniad i'r byd tragwyddol yn yr heol hon yn unig!! Pump o gyrff meirw yn mynd o'r un tŷ; sef gwr a gwraig a phlentyn a dau eraill oedd yn lletya yno. Pedwar o dy arall yn agos, sef y wraig a thri o'r plant . . . Pobol y wlad yn cyrchu i'w cartrefi am y cyntaf, yn ffoi megis rhag byddin o elynion arfog! Yr ieuenctyd wedi sobri, gwedd eu hwynebau wedi newid, yn ofni ergydion angau bob trawiad amrant! A phawb yn rhyfeddu a synnu pa'm ni wedi ein harbed, a chynifer wedi eu torri i lawr.[200]

> Within but a few days, thirty-five souls were sent into the eternal world from this street alone. Five bodies were taken out of the same house – husband, wife a child and two lodgers. Four from a neighbouring house – the wife and three of her children . . . Country people are escaping from their houses as if from an armed enemy! Youths have sobered, their faces terrified, for they fear death's unexpected assaults! Everyone wonders why we have been spared, when so many have been cut down.

The places of worship were full almost every day. Few people were seen on the streets except doctors visiting house after house, and hearses creaking to and fro. The dead were quickly buried in their clothes, in deep trenches in the churchyard. Later in July the cholera reached St Asaph, by August it was sweeping through Caernarfon, causing over thirty deaths. Cholera reached Beaumaris at about the same time as Princess Charlotte and her daughter, Victoria, duchess of

Kent, and the 'Royal *Eisteddfod*'.[201] On 17 August, the Revd Robert Humphreys, a Wesleyan minister, on his way to Beaumaris from Llanidloes with his family, was advised at Bangor not to proceed to his destination since cholera had broken out there. Bravely or rashly, he ignored the advice and proceeded to minister at prayer meetings which began at five in the morning. On 30 August, he contracted the disease and died the following morning.[202] By mid-August, cholera had spread throughout south Wales. Beginning at Newport on 24 June, it spread to Swansea, Llanelli, Briton Ferry, Neath, Carmarthen, Haverfordwest, Builth, Margam and Aberavon. The greatest suffering occurred in Merthyr Tydfil where at least 1,600 people died of the disease.[203]

The reasons for the spread of the disease were not mysterious. Welsh towns festered under layer upon layer of dirt, which were compounded by the fact that businesses which engaged in insanitary activities – slaughtering, butchery, bone-boiling – simply deposited their waste products onto the public thoroughfares. Added to this was the accumulation of offal and manure from the omnipresent animals and their carcasses, and the effluvia from the toilets which had no water to flush waste away. The story of cholera in Wales was the story of the Welsh marinating in their own filth. The minutes of the meetings of the health boards established in most Welsh towns reveal in nauseating detail the insanitary and insalubrious conditions in which people lived.[204] Public meetings and petitions in support of installing clean water, sewerage systems and scavenging of waste were held in several Welsh towns in the years between 1832 and 1849. Despite the complaints, the conditions, described by T. W. Rammell and Dr T. J. Dyke in 1849, were probably worse than those encountered in 1832.[205]

Then, before the anger turned to action, cholera once more roared into Wales. The contagion began in Cardiff on 13 May 1849. At the end of this year of fear and terror, the Registrar General reported that 4,564 people had died of cholera, the lucky ones quickly, the majority horribly. Putrefying corpses were buried in shallow graves, the prey of rats. At Ystalyfera and other towns, cemeteries overflowed with corpses.[206] The *Cardiff and Merthyr Guardian* reported that the grave dug for Margaret Clendenning was only eighteen inches deep. The next body buried in Tywyn graveyard was only interred fourteen and a half inches deep. The Revd E. Jenkins claimed that you can 'see coffins, bones and flesh in the Dowlais churchyard'.[207] Several communities were deeply scarred by their losses. In Holywell, 46 died, in Holyhead 42, in Carmarthen 102, in Swansea 262, in Neath 245, and in Cardiff 396. But the unrivalled leader in this grim table was the town of Merthyr Tydfil, where 1,682 people died between May and September 1849.[208] Eye-witness accounts related some of the horrors encountered in the town. Lady Charlotte Guest wrote in her diary:

> I am sorry to say the accounts of the cholera at Dowlais are fearfully bad. They are beyond anything I could have imagined, sometimes upwards of twenty people dying in one day, and eight men constantly employed in making coffins . . . one of our Infant School-Mistresses is dead. One of the medical assistants sent down from London is dying and the whole place seems in a most lamentable state.[209]

The historian of the town, William Edwards, a survivor of the epidemic, wrote:

> Nid oedd nemawr dŷ yn dianc heb brofi pwys y fflangell geryddol hon! . . . Cludid rhai ar gerti, tua'r gladdfa, o ganol gruddfanau ac ochneidiau torcalonus y gweddwon a'r amddifad . . . Dyma'r amser y gwnawd mynwent ar Bant-coed-Ifor; oherwydd nad oedd caniatad, na lle i'w claddu yn un o fynwentydd y dre!'[210]

> Hardly a house escaped without feeling the lash of this scourge! . . . Some were carried on carts to the burial grounds, from the midst of the heart-rending cries and sighs of the widows and orphans . . . This was the time when a cemetery was made on Pant-coed-Ifor; for there was neither permission, nor place to bury them in any of the cemeteries of the town.

Horrors were not without their heroes. In Merthyr Tydfil, the heroic rector of Dowlais, Evan Jenkins, collapsed as a result of his great services to his parishioners, but later recovered. At Swansea, the Roman Catholic priest Father Kavanagh worked tirelessly salving and saving the 'low, superstitious Irish' of 'Little Ireland'. In Caernarfon, the Revd Robert Ellis, Cynddelw, disagreed with the opinion of his fellow ministers and insisted that cholera was not a divine punishment but the consequence of dirt and disease, and so campaigned to clean the town.[211]

Protestations and promises that something needed to and would be done went unheeded and unhonoured. In 1854, the cholera returned to Wales, claiming over 1,000 lives. Again, mortality was heaviest in Merthyr Tydfil, where 455 people died, but there were also significant losses in Cardiff (225), Brecon (54), Haverfordwest (40), Neath (34) and Newtown (19).[212] Cholera broke out once more in 1866, killing over 2,400 people. This time, death moved his dark capital from Merthyr Tydfil, where 229 people died, to Swansea, where 521 people perished and Neath, which lost 520 people. The outbreak was also virulent in Pembrokeshire. In Narberth 18 died, 40 succumbed to the scourge in Haverfordwest and 42 were victims in Pembroke. In the north, 75 died in Caernarfon and 88 in Holywell.[213] In Holywell, nearly all the deaths could be linked to one particular well which was contaminated with sewage. The story of that well encapsulated the history of cholera in Wales. The custom of municipal laziness bred a culture of lethargy and ensured that the financial cost of improvements would always outweigh the human benefits. Everyone knew that dirty water was dangerous, and agreed that someone should do something about it, but nobody did anything.

Yet the dark clouds of cholera had a silver lining for some. In June 1849, the *Cardiff and Merthyr Guardian* reported that the cabinet-makers of the twin towns, who had for a long time suffered from a lack of orders, were now working long hours because 'coffins are in such great request'.[214] In September, Mr Bassett Jones, undertaker and funeral furnisher of 9 Smith Street, Cardiff, announced that he had recently considerably altered and enlarged his premises. To celebrate, he made a special offer of a 'good substantial Elm coffin, full trimmed' for £1. 8s. 0d.; 'inch oak coffins, full trimmed, covered with black cloth, nailed or laced in an unique finish' for £3. 16s. 0d. Jones also offered 'children's coffins corresponding with the above details at special prices'.[215] No winter, it seems, ever skips spring.

Defences Against Death

Welsh wit depicts the doctor as burying his mistakes and duping the survivors into gratitude by using incomprehensible jargon. Twm o'r Nant in his *anterliwtiau* portrayed medical people in rural Denbighshire unequivocally as humbugs, with an exaggerated affectation of speech and manner. In *Y Farddoneg Fabilonaidd* (1768), he followed Ellis Wynne's *Gweledigaetheu y Bardd Cwsc* in his satirical comments on apothecaries, and again in *Tri Chydymaith Dyn* (1769) and in *Pedair Colofn Gwladwriaeth*, he depicted them as bogus ineffectuals, mouthing an inglorious and incomprehensible mixture of Welsh and English. William Davies in *Casgliad o Ffraethebion Cymreig* relates an anecdote of a doctor pausing to watch the grass cutters at work in a cemetery in Aberdare in 1871. Recognizing shoddy workmanship, the doctor remarks 'Caleb, gwaith tlawd sydd gyda chwi yma' (Caleb, you have poor work here), 'O! Doctor', came the answer, 'y mae gyda chwithau waith tlawd yma hefyd' (Oh! Doctor, you too have poor work here).[216] Many satirists questioned whether the doctors deserved their exorbitant fees, claiming that they killed more than they cured. It would be tempting to give instances to justify the suspicions of the wits and satirists that medicine was almost useless to the individual patient. Tempting but misleading, for the foundations of modern medical practice were laid in the period 1776–1871. Against the background of religious fatalism, popular superstition and prejudice, filthy and festering living conditions and gross social inequalities, medicine acquired a recognizably modern, professional profile.[217]

Smallpox should have lost much of its power to terrify by the early nineteenth century since it was one of the very few diseases for which there was an effective preventive therapy. Since the early eighteenth century, Welsh people had been said to 'be buying the small-pox' – inoculating persons at risk from the disease with fluid from the blisters or pustules of a sufferer, the secondary infection being much less malign. From about 1777–82, William Woodville MD, one of the foremost advocates of inoculation in Britain, was a physician in Denbigh.[218] In 1796, he produced his two-volumed work *The History of the Inoculation of the Small-Pox in Great Britain*. David Pennant, son of the more famous traveller, Thomas, obtained some cowpox from a relative of Edward Jenner, and used it to inoculate his workers and their families in Downing during September 1800.[219] His dispensaries for this purpose were set up throughout Wales by 1810, but popular prejudice prevented the total eradication of the disease. At Narberth in July 1814, and Pembroke in June 1815, it was stated that opposition by the poor to inoculation was the cause of outbreaks of the disease.[220] Indeed, vaccination was not without its dangers. In 1829, fifteen cases of people suffering from smallpox, four of whom had been vaccinated, were reported in Swansea. Mr Powell, the house surgeon to Swansea Infirmary, complained at the

> prejudice against vaccination especially amongst the lowest class, in whose dirty and ill-ventilated houses, disease is the curse likely to be destructive. Though there have been two or three cases of vaccinated people catching small-pox, it has prevented it for many more.[221]

At Brecon, the same message was propounded by the medical authorities:

This dreadful disorder has lately manifested itself in the town of Brecon . . . in one cottage a woman and four children have been carried off by it . . . Surely parents will no longer neglect getting their children immediately vaccinated, and not let prejudice stand in the way when *life itself* is concerned.[222]

But people continued their neglect and suffered for their prejudices. In August 1833, two children of Richard Holder were laid to rest in the same grave in Penallt churchyard: 'While the funeral party were carrying them out, another child, an infant in arms, expired on the lap of the mother.' The trio of tiny victims all died of smallpox.[223]

Inoculation, however, had a profound effect. Some historians have argued that it arrested the increasingly virulent cycle of smallpox which attacked British communities from the late eighteenth century. But perhaps inoculation's greatest impact was psychological. It gave a new and unexpected glimpse of hope of the probability of medical progress, and a corresponding increase in the prestige of the medical profession.[224] In 1839, the Institute for the Gratuitous Vaccination of the Poor opened in Swansea.[225] Though disparaging satirists, such as William Davies, continued their sarcasm, doctors now had a magical recipe to secure the beauty of women and preserve the lives of men. Gradually over time, the medical profession acquired the upper hand in its battle against charlatans, mountebanks and quacks.

Inevitably, in these years of high mortality and harsh theology, ideas of death, hell and judgement were frequently present in people's minds. Religious fatalism – the view that disease was God's punishment for 'gwael, golledig, euog ddyn' (wicked, lost, guilty mankind) – was an even greater barrier than popular prejudice. It was futile to resist divine retribution. The gravestone of Thomas James, who died aged twenty of cholera in 1849, in the forlorn and forsaken Cefn-golau cemetery high on the mountain above Tredegar, reveals people's stoical acceptance of fate:

> One day and night I bore great pain
> To cry for cure was all in vain
> But God knew what to me was best
> Did ease my pain and give me rest.

Seren Gomer in 1842 was also certain that cholera was scripted in the scriptures:

Y mae diriwyad a darostyngiad y natur ddynol drwy bechod, wedi ein gadael yn agored i liaws o gosbau, barnedigaethau, a cheryddon . . . Y mae y Duw mawr yn awr a phryd arall yn arwyddaw ei anfodlonrwydd yn achos pechod, drwy geryddu y byd mewn amryw a gwahanol ddulliau o farnedigaethau . . . Tua y flwyddyn 1832 a 1833 y gwelwyd llaw Duw yn amlwg ar y maes, drwy y Geri heintus (*cholera morbus*).[226]

The decline and fall of human nature through sin, has left us open to several punishments, judgements, and warnings . . . God now and again indicates his displeasure at sin, through punishing this world in numerous and different ways of judgements . . . About the year 1832 and 1833, God's hand was busy in this work through the infectious disease *cholera morbus*.

The road to health lay along the path to salvation. A healthy soul was required before the body could be healthy. During the cholera visitations of 1832, and especially 1849, chapels and churches were packed with people confessing past sins, beseeching salvation.[227] The government gave sanction to this religious causation of cholera for it ordered *A special form of prayer to be used in all churches and chapels and to be continued during the prevalence of Cholera in this country; By H.M. Special Command:*

Most gracious Father in God . . . look down we beseech thee, from Heaven thy dwelling place, upon us thy unworthy servants, who under an awful apprehension of thy judgements, and a deep conviction of our own sinfulness, prostrate ourselves before thee. Have pity, o Lord. Have pity on thy people, and remove from us that grievous disease, against which our only security is thy compassion.[228]

In 1832 and 1849, days of fast were held in Swansea, Cardiff, Merthyr Tydfil, Pembroke, Carmarthen, Pontypool and Milford. When the scourge finally abated, 'days of thanksgiving for relief from cholera' were held throughout Wales. Shops closed, and chapels and churches were packed with grateful penitents. In 1849, the *Cardiff and Merthyr Guardian* reported that:

The prevalence of cholera still continues to generate fear and gloomy forebodings in the public mind . . . This is reflected in the thousands who attend chapels in Merthyr and watched the Baptists baptise people in the Taff every Sunday afternoon . . . At market square, hundreds of Latter Day Saints gathered to express penitence for the sins which have brought upon the town a divine judgement – the cholera.[229]

If sin was responsible for the scourge, then sinners deserved their fate. A spiteful moralistic tone entered the reporting of the deaths of cholera victims. Beer shop keepers, *cwrwau bach* purveyors, prostitutes and all degenerates deserved death. This spiteful, un-Christian attitude is one of the most repulsive features of religion in Victorian Wales. The sin of revenge was stronger than the virtue of charity. When Harriet Thomas, wife of Thomas, landlord of the Lame Chicken beer house of Whitmore Lane, Cardiff, died of cholera, it was reported that: 'The deceased's constitution had been broken by habits of intemperance in which she had long continued. Persons who are in the habit of drinking to excess are more likely to fall victims of cholera than persons whose habits are temperate.'[230]

The Revd M. H. Seymour reckoned that: 'there were two major causes of cholera – drunkenness and fear. Drunkenness seems to attract the disease as if it were a magnet for the cholera. The other predisposing cause is fear, which often acts on the bowels and stomach, and should be carefully guarded against.'[231] The daughters of Phillip Taylor of St Mary Street, Merthyr Tydfil, 'deserved their fearful retribution of dying of cholera because they drank all the brandy which the relieving officer had given the family to help relieve their parent's suffering'.[232]

Religious fatalism which ascribed cholera to supernatural causes gradually lost its grip on the Welsh people. In 1849, when the cholera epidemic was accompanied by a religious revival of seismic, psychic power, voices were raised that stated that it was dirt, not sin, which caused cholera. The editor of the *Cardiff and Merthyr Guardian* wrote with deep irony and bitter resentment:

> There was a general fast proclaimed for Monday and divine service was held in the numerous churches and chapels of the town . . . The cholera is supposed to be not the product of physical causes, but a divine judgement – but poverty is the prolific generator of cholera . . . It is cheap piety for the ironmasters to stop their works, and order their clerks to church in a body, as examples to the workmen; but it is misery, and in many cases death to the poor workmen, who are thus deprived of one-sixth of their earnings. We have no faith in compelling or compelled piety.[233]

The paper went on to question the justice of a God who could allow a young girl from Neath to die of cholera on the morning of her wedding. Did this 'sinless bride to be' deserve to spend eternity in the company of 'sinful beasts'? Such sceptical comments indicated that the medical authorities' sermon that cleanliness should be the path to godliness was at last finding a receptive audience. Doctors could still do little to save a patient who had been struck down by one of the major killing diseases; except for inoculation for smallpox, quinine for malaria and mercury for venereal diseases, they had no effective cures.

But their ministrations were not always useless. They knew the value of sound diet and cleanliness, the importance of clean water and effective disposal of animal and human waste. Doctors saved more lives in providing good advice for local health boards than they could do at bedsides. Prevention, they preached, was better than cure. Dr Dyke announced in 1860 that a 'brighter day had dawned for Merthyr Tydfil':

> The death rate has diminished from 36 to 24 per 1,000; infant mortality from 527 to 434 per 1,000 live births; the number of persons attaining the age of 70 has increased from 55 to 89 per 1,000 deaths and the average age at death has extended from 17½ to 24½.[234]

Dyke explained the improvement in terms of medical advances. An impartial observer might reasonably observe that 24-and-a-half was still a painfully young age to die.

When an epidemic struck, the doctors were at least temporarily heeded. Offal and manure dumps vanished from the streets, and bonfires blazed everywhere, burning rubbish. At Carmarthen in 1832, it was the local doctors who insisted that the entire town should be cleaned, for 'some seemed to believe that the cholera cannot enter their mansions but through the front doors'.[235] The Cardiff Sanitary Board in 1849 was thorough in its enforcement of the special by-laws recommended by local doctors. They prevented people using 'the new privy of Mr W. Vachell, in John Street', fined Mr Hemingway for 'using an improper cart for the conveyance of night soil . . . thereby committing a disgusting nuisance of the most offensive kind along Mary Ann Street', ordered the windows 'of the Skeleton House in Great Frederick Street be shut up', and demanded that 'Mr Kent did not let the Union hearse remain any time unnecessarily in the public street'.[236] In St Asaph, Wrexham, Bethesda, Caernarfon, Llanidloes, Aberystwyth, Cardigan, Pembroke, Carmarthen, Swansea, Neath, Aberavon, Margam, Cardiff, Newport and Abergavenny, local health boards were established to counter the worst abuses and sanitize the towns.[237]

This was often achieved against considerable opposition. At Brecon in 1832, a Board of Health was not established because it was considered: 'too heavy a burden on the taxpayer'.[238] Local Chartists and workers' leaders in Merthyr Tydfil were opposed to sanitary reform because the local board consisted of 'sinister figures' from the managerial and legal classes.[239] As late as 1866, a writer to the *Caernarvon and Denbigh Herald* complained that sanitary reforms in

Caernarfon had been blocked in the past because of the cost and asked simply: 'How many of those who had gone to Llanbeblig [the local cemetery] might have now been alive had that which should have long ago been done, not been thwarted by opposition?'[240] In the activities of the bureaucrats, administrators and medics, we can discern the germination of the idea that people should act in the public interest. Medicine began to acquire greater prestige, which would assist it in its eventual triumph as a profession and a scientific discipline.

The story of the progress of medicine, from the ridicule of the satirists to the respect of society, is not as simple as many historians have argued. Medicine and medics did not have a monopoly of effective cures and enlightenment. Some of their treatments were brutal. Suffering a painful bunion on his big toe, a Mr Dobbs of Monmouth went to a doctor who: 'with a large hammer and chisel took the toe off'. Mr Dobbs thought that the most painful part of the operation was paring the rough edges.[241] Many doctors were complex figures, whose contribution to the advancement of medical science is questionable. The mercurial Dr Thomas Williams of Swansea was undoubtedly a talented and gifted scientist. He was elevated to a fellowship of both the Linnean Society in 1855 and, for his work on the lungs and the blood, of the Royal Society in 1838. But his reputation suffered greatly for his myopic and misguided defence of the copper smoke which smothered Swansea and other towns. Williams portrayed the town as an Elysium of health, arguing that the clouds of copper smoke were largely responsible for this happy state of affairs, since they prevented the 'miasmic effects' of infectious diseases. In his *Report on the Copper Smoke and its Influence on the Public Health and Industrial Diseases of Coppermen*, Williams argued that, far from harming the inhabitants of the copper works, the smoke set up a *cordon sanitaire* which protected the inhabitants living beneath the sulphurous clouds. Williams even argued that the arsenic fumes which copper workers inhaled were not harmful to their health.[242]

Dr Thomas Williams was not the only local doctor to praise copper smoke as the shield protecting Swansea from disease. T. Wilkinson was even clearer:

> Swansea . . . at this time may be considered as fortunately protected by the smoke emanating from its numerous copper works. The gas which is evolved (principally sulphurous) although injurious to vegetable life does not produce any effects destructive to man . . . from the agency of this copper smoke, this watering place may be considered as insured from the terrible destructive disease the Asiatic cholera.[243]

But they would argue this, wouldn't they? Their positions were dependent upon the copper masters. Until the atmospheric theory of the spread of disease was disproved, it was extremely difficult for people to argue against Williams and Wilkinson. The dispute over the efficacious or poisonous effects of copper smoke rambled and rumbled on until it entered the courts in the 1860s. The experience of Swansea in 1849, when cholera swept through the town, showed that there was a fundamental flaw in Thomas Williams's arguments that Copperopolis was a healthy paradise.

Medical progress often resembles the sideways march of the crustacean rather than a progressive forward advance. Bleeding, blistering, purging and puking continued to be fixed treatments until well into the nineteenth century. Doctors could not cure so patients had to endure treatments which inflicted terrifying pain. At the onset of the first great cholera epidemic in 1832, *Seren Gomer* published, in English, the advice of a local doctor as to how to cure the disease. Calomel pills, castor oil and arrowroot and a diet of thin broth and rice were considered appropriate treatment for the diarrhoeal stages of the disease. If the patient worsened, the doctor advised:

1. The patient is to put on a flannel shirt or waistcoat with long sleeves and go to bed.
2. He is to be wrapped in a warm blanket.
3. Large stone ware bottles filled with hot water and wrapped in flannel, are to be laid at his feet and sides.

The fourth, fifth and sixth stages involved the patient drinking varying degrees of common salt dissolved in warm water. If he continued to worsen, then: 'the application of a few leeches to the pit of the stomach and behind the ears the following day may be necessary'.[244] Mr James Bird MRC, surgeon of Cardiff, advocated a similar treatment in February 1832, but advised 'avoid unnecessary exposure to the night air, and keep the bowels temperate'.[245] Sixteen years later, *Seren Gomer* reported that the certain cure for cholera was the administration of '12 dyferyn o ether mewn brandi a dŵr twym, un grein o calomel, ac un grein o opiwm' (12 drops of ether in brandy and hot water, one grain of calomel and one grain of opium). It was a recipe not so much for cure as for temporary, if not permanent, oblivion.[246]

The 1820s was a crucial decade in the public perception of the medical profession in Wales. The press reported several remarkable surgical successes. In January 1825:

> Captain Bird of the 5th Foot who had two ribs fractured at the battle of Albvera in 1811, was obliged last week to have one of them removed by a surgeon of Abergavenny. The gallant and meritorious officer, had occasionally suffered excruciating pain from the fracture.

The pain from the operation must also have been excruciating since it was performed without any anaesthetic. But Captain Bird was accustomed to pain: 'He lost the sight of his right eye at the battle of Vittoria, and had his left arm broken in two places in the battle of the Pyrenees.' This stoic survivor was 'likely to do well' after the operation.[247] Amelia Knight probably encountered severe pain for the first time in the surgery of Mr Felton in Caerphilly. Suffering from a cancerous growth on her breast, Amelia was told by her doctor that her only hope was to remove it. She consented to the ordeal and 'er mor fawr oedd y chlwyf a wnaed . . . dim ond un llais a wnaeth hi yn hyd yr amser'[248] (despite the size of the wound that was made . . . she only screamed once throughout the time). At General Warde's Llanelli Collieries, the surgeons to the works, Mr Howell and Dr Howell, were much praised for mending the dislocated shoulder of an injured worker. Praise was also heaped on Mr Rowlands, surgeon at Nant-y-glo ironworks, for curing Benjamin Williams of Yr Wrwst. The operation involved opening his stomach and reassembling his intestines. Benjamin had no anaesthetic, just a determination to survive.[249]

The achievements of the works' surgeons were closely linked to an older tradition of Welsh medicine, that of the bone-setter. Thomas Rocyn Jones (1822–77) began his medical work fixing the limbs of animals on his farm in Maenordeifi, Pembrokeshire. When he moved to Rhymney, Thomas began to work on humans and became noted for the splints he invented.[250] Evan Thomas (1735–1814) was the first of a dynasty of bone-setters in Anglesey. Local legend had it that the family were descendants of a Spanish boy washed ashore on the island's coast, the sole survivor of a shipwreck. The survivor carried the special knowledge of setting bones. The family's history, like that of the celebrated Meddygon Myddfai, reveals how folk knowledge could benefit conventional medicine. Evan Thomas's eldest son, Evan Thomas (1804–84), continued the family tradition and trade of setting bones, but with less success than his father. The son and grandson, Hugh Owen Thomas (1834–91), transformed family tradition into a professional medical career. Educated at Edinburgh and University College, London, he became an MRCS (England) in 1857, and established his own practice in Liverpool. In 1875, he published his book

Diseases of the Hip, Knee and Ankle Joints, which merged folk traditions into mainstream medicine. During the 1914–18 war, many
wounded soldiers had cause to thank the 'Thomas calliper' for saving
their limbs and lives.[251]

The mid nineteenth century saw a struggle between an increasingly
professional core of medical workers and experienced amateurs
administering tried and tested remedies. For a period, it was uncertain
which tradition would triumph. In midwifery, horror stories continued
to abound. Among the methods practised were placing grains of sugar
outside the birth canal to entice the baby out with something sweet,
cutting the umbilical cord too close or failing to tie it, forgetting the
placenta, and crippling babies through rough handling, so that generations of Welsh people were atrophied, deaf, one-eyed, hare-lipped,
lame or twisted. Yet, gradually, the profession gained respect and
status. Mary Morgans of Lledrod, Cardiganshire, during a thirty-five
year career to 1846, was said to have assisted over 1,230 children into
the world 'heb un anhap annisgwyl' (without one unexpected
happening).[252]

Well-publicized failures of doctors and surgeons undermined their
professional credibility. In 1846, the *North Wales Chronicle* reported
the death of Jane Jones of Oswestry, 'a miserable miser'. She died with
a bundle in her possession containing £69 in coins and £79 in notes,
but still demanded that a local doctor should return £5 to her because
he had failed to cure her.[253]

During the cholera epidemic, a bizarre panic ensued that, because of
the haste to bury bodies, people were being buried alive. In 1832, *Seren
Gomer* reported on the unease expressed in Swansea that people were
being buried before their 'bodily frame' had ceased to be:

> Cyhuddir y meddygon o roddi gormod o gysglyn i'r cleifion, trwy yr hyn y
> dywedir fod llawer wedi eu lladd. Mae llawer o anfodlonrwydd mewn perthynas
> a hyn yn Abertawe oherwydd y claddir y marw mewn ychydig oriau, y mae
> terfysg mawr wedi bod, gan y creda y bobol fod llawer wedi eu claddu yn fyw.
> Cyfeillion y rhai oeddynt wedi eu claddu a ymgasglasant, ac agorwyd llawer o
> feddau i gael gweled a oedd y cyfryw beth wedi digwydd . . .[254]

> Doctors are accused of giving too much sedative to patients, and through this it
> is claimed that many have died. There is considerable disquiet regarding this in
> Swansea because the dead are buried within a few hours. Protests have occurred
> because people believe that many have been buried alive. The friends of those
> who have been buried gathered, and many graves have been opened to see if this
> had occurred . . .

In August 1832, the *Carmathen Journal* reported:

> A narrow escape from being buried alive occurred last week at Llanelly. A man who it was supposed had died from the cholera morbus, and who exhibited almost unequivocal signs of death, was regularly laid out by his friends for internment, when suddenly the suspected deceased person arose from amidst his death like habiliments, coffin, etc. and after staring about at the oddity of his situation, he bolted out of the house stark naked, and made off as quick as he could exclaiming as loud as he was able 'I am not dead yet' to the no small terror of the people, who had assembled to pay their last duties to their friend.[255]

Urban myths gathered around this ghoulish obsession. It was claimed that one Welsh sailor, locked in a coma, was buried when his ship docked in an Irish port. The following day, children playing in the graveyard heard loud knocking coming from the newly dug grave. The locals opened the grave and rescued the entombed mariner.[256]

The process of establishing a medical profession, the transformation of apothecaries into pharmacists, crones into midwives, quacks into chemists, looks far tidier in hindsight than it did to contemporaries. Many of the unconventional medical movements of the years down to 1850 – homeopathy, hydropathy, phrenology, mesmerism – had their champions within the medical fraternity. Some people transposed into medicine the radical grass-roots anger which in politics fuelled radicalism and in religion generated the dissidence of Dissent. Heretics in faith and politics were also heretical in medicine. In Wales, the controversial and charismatic Dr William Price of Llantrisant best represents this phenomenon. This protean power of nature was unorthodox in every aspect of his life, but he remained an excellent doctor, qualifying as a surgeon after only twelve months of study, the only person ever to do so. A vegetarian, an advocate of free love, the rights of women, birth control, co-operative movements and cremation, Price championed causes and cures which, for several generations, appeared outlandish until they entered mainstream medicine. Price also had a taste for the better things in life. When offered cider on his deathbed, Price replied indignantly, 'No, give me champagne'.[257]

It is hard to differentiate the mainstream from the fringe. The world of 'internal medicine' reveals that orthodox and heterodox practices were far closer to each other than many historians have allowed. The major treatment available to doctors was the use of opium to relieve pain and suffering.[258] Since 1700, when the Welsh author John Jones had published his *Mysteries of Opium Revealed*, the palliative powers of this miracle drug had been widely recognized. Doctors injected their patients, a bee-sting of pain and then relief oozed through the patient, like crushed ice in a desert. Opium was widely available in various forms throughout Wales. Iolo Morganwg and David Samwell were both addicted to laudanum, the liquid form of the drug.[259] Iolo took 300 drops a day to relieve his pains and fuel his hyperactive imagination. The Revd Christmas Evans took large doses purchased from a local chemist in Anglesey. According to Brutus: 'Bu yn cymeryd digon o opiwm unwaith yn un llwnc a fuasai yn ddigon i roddi tri neu bedwar o ddynion mewn hun dragwyddol'[260] (He took enough opium once in one swig which would be enough to put three or four men in an eternal sleep). At a time when the average wage of a labourer in Anglesey was a shilling a day, Christmas Evans spent over £9 at a time on opium with local druggists. The minister relied on more than the scriptures for his sustenance.[261] For many Victorians, opium was the opium of the people. Dr Hunter reported that he saw agricultural workers popping pills as they worked in the fields. Dr Richard Williams noticed that opium addiction could be passed from mother to infant: 'Opium administered to the mother exerts its full power on the child and I have known an infant remain in a constant torpor for nearly a fortnight while the Parent who continued to suckle was taking a preparation of that Medicine.'[262]

At the coffee houses of Denbigh, old women met for coffee, gossip and opium. Mothers administered opium-based patent medicines such as Mother Bailey's Quieting Syrup, Mrs Winslow's Soothing Syrup and Batley's Sedative Solution, or just administered laudanum to ensure that children slept while they worked. Welsh chemists stocked opium pills, opium soup, opiate lozenges, opiate plasters, opium enema, opium liniment and the deadly lead and opium pills. Opium was also placed in pints of beer. According to one ballad, a man died in Aberdare 'o ganlyniad i yfed laudanum mewn cwrw' (as a result of drinking laudanum in beer). Mrs Beeton advised all householders to keep their kitchen cupboards well stocked with opium in both powder and liquid form. It was Britain's need to conquer pain which led to the conquering of India and conflicts with China.[263]

Diseases and ailments such as gout, asthma, consumption, worms, rheumatism, arthritis, the King's evil (scrofula), jaundice, colic, wind and all manners of gastro-intestinal infections, and surgical conditions such as fistula, stone, ruptures and carbuncles were the complaints which the 'advertising physicians' were confident they could cure.[264]

The development of the newspaper press, a central feature in the consumer revolution of the early nineteenth century, was made viable by the revenue generated by the advertising of patent medicines. Perhaps one of the most significant aspects of the capitalist innovations of the nineteenth century was the commercialization of healing. Every newspaper circulating in Wales from the late eighteenth century carried advertisements lauding the efficacious powers of patent medicinal products. Many sought to establish their unique selling-points in niche markets. Some claimed medical authenticity, such as Dr Fothergill's 'Tonic Female Pills' to aid digestion and cure debility. Others took supernatural inspiration, as did Crosswaite and Co.'s 'Occult Lozenges' which 'cured colds, coughs, asthma and shortness of breath'. Many were London-based companies, such as Holloways cure-all pills and ointments, which were often sold through Welsh chemists like F. W. Joy and William Evans in Cardiff.

Welsh entrepreneurs were also quick to prosper on the pain of the people. David Gravell (1787–1872), the conscientious, modest, pious farmer, book publisher and author of several Christian histories, made his money from *Eli Gravell Cwmfelin*, a cream of astounding properties.[265] Robert Oliver Rees (1819–81), author of the tear-jerking epic *Mary Jones, Y Gymraes fechan heb yr un beibl*, made his fortune by realizing the potential of the pill-rolling machine invented in the 1830s.[266] S. Tardrew, druggist of Carmarthen, and J. Williams of the Cambrian Office, Swansea, offered various tinctures of peppermint for sale, 'remedies which should be immediately resorted to in the first attack of *Cholera Morbus*'. The celebrated Cambrian Medicine, anti-bilious pills for stomach and liver complaints, produced by the Cambrian Pill Department of Tremadog, had a Welsh strap-line on its adverts 'Tra Môr, Tra Brython'.[267] Many of the major brand names of London companies translated their advertisements into Welsh. The problem to be cured was usually described in clear and direct terms in most advertisements, but some were couched in more delicate language. Dr Cullen offered his 'scarlet pill' to cure 'certain diseases . . . with safety and secrecy'.[268] In order to 'defeat quackery', Dr Thomson offered a book of advice on: 'Nervous and general debility, spermatorrhea, loss of memory, failing sight, epilepsy, consumption, indigestion, giddiness . . . and diseases known as nervous complaints, resulting from the errors of youth and manhood.'[269] The book outlined the only certain and safe cure for the affliction, Dr Thomson's creams and pills.

Until the Pharmacy Act of 1868, these and other harmful and

hazardous concoctions were sold widely in chemist and druggist shops, and openly by vendors on street carts throughout Wales. The fairs of Wales drew not only horseback evangelists, but also many patent-medicine salespeople, each peddling their rival forms of salvation. Twm o'r Nant, Brutus, Llew Llwyfo and many others were strong in their condemnation of the spurious claims of patent-medicine sellers and the false knowledge of urine gazers.[270] Despite the Apothecaries Act of 1815, such medieval mountebanks continued to prosper in the mid nineteenth century, offering their miraculous unguents to the gullible. Joseph Jones was only one of several whose health was undoubtedly undermined by the treatment he received at the hands of a 'quack' in 1838. Suffering from smallpox, but bled and treated for pleurisy, Joseph died on the morning of his wedding day in October 1838.[271] In 1850, following a dreadful accident in which several colliers of Aberdare were injured, police investigations were initiated into the activities of a quack doctor who 'is preying on these people by saying that he can cure their wounds by means of gasses to be inhaled from a lamp'.[272]

The police were also involved in the activities of the flash and flamboyant fraudster Baron Spolasco, who made his home in Swansea in the late 1830s. Spolasco was supposedly the lone survivor of the steamer *Killarney*, in which he lost not only his young son, but also his fortune of £25,000. The self-styled baron claimed to have done immense good in the area between Swansea and Merthyr Tydfil during his stay, by curing hundreds. T. W. Ball of Bryn Llanerch testified that his wife had suffered an ulcerated leg for seven years which doctors had failed to cure. 'All others had failed her, but Baron Spolasco, without delay, cured her'. 'Massive crowds' followed the Baron whenever he left his home at Adelaide Palace in Swansea. The Castle Inn, Neath, was besieged when he arrived to treat locals. The scenes at the Castle Inn resembled those when Jesus healed the sick in Nazareth. To celebrate his survival from the shipwreck, and his joy at being in the area, the Baron ordered that: 'a massive ox be cut up in chunks so that the poor could celebrate. So many paupers turned out that the Baron had to order more meat.' This was medicine as a theatrical and magical performance for, above all, Spolasco used spectacle to stir people's emotions.[273] This charming, Mephistophelean showman, dressed in a crimson, white, scarlet and gold uniform, with his over-the-top hyperbole, promised the impossible and more. He merged hard- and soft-sell, generated excitement and amusement, bathos, pathos,

surprise, even titillation. His career in Swansea almost came to an
abrupt end when he was arrested for manslaughter, after Elizabeth
Arnolt of Bridgend died, as a result of his treatment, but he was
released for lack of evidence. His medical career shuddered to a halt
when the Commissioner of Stamps and Taxes charged him with
'feloniously uttering forged medicine stamps'. Bail was set at the
extraordinary high level of £500, suggesting that it was alright to kill
your patients, but unforgivable to defraud the taxman. It was time for
the Baron to achieve the most remarkable feat contained in his
magician's box of tricks and wonders, and he duly disappeared.[274]

Other wizards claimed to be able to cure an even greater array of
afflictions than Baron Spolasco. Mrs Hopkins of Meifod, Mrs Evans
of Viggin, Maes-mawr, and the Lloyd family of Llanbadarn Fynydd
in Radnorshire, cured people of cancer and other malignant growths,
through herb medicine, manipulative treatment and magic. Dr John
Harries and Henry Harries of Cwrt-y-cadno served the people of a
large area of south Wales, with a whole range of magical and medical
services. In 1809, John Harries was visited by several people who
sought cures for plague, measles, malaria, fever, tetanus, colic, scrofula
or King's evil, jaundice, typhus, scarletina, puerperal fever, whooping
cough, palsy, apoplexy, epilepsy, dysentery, diabetes, piles, 'haemor-
rhaging' (*sic*), cancer of the uterus, smallpox, putrid fever and slow
nervous fever. Many of his recipes for cures included in his case-books
contained herbs and opium which, whilst harmless, at least had a
pleasant taste, though others appear to have been more harmful
concoctions utilizing mercury and arsenic.[275] Throughout the period
1776–1871, people in dire straits turned to the wise men and wizards
of Wales, for the relief of distressing symptoms. Desperate times called
for desperate remedies. The potions and spells of medicine men and
witch doctors were considered efficacious in combating a plethora of
debilitating and disturbing afflictions. People clung to the beliefs that
had sustained their communities for generations. Popular belief taught
that smallpox could be prevented if women wore red gowns. A doctor
in Vaynor, in the 1850s, was horrified that the mustard poultice which
he prescribed for a patient was replaced with a pat of cow's dung.[276]
The mustard poultice was used instead to cover a hole in the patient's
coat. When William Thomas died of cholera at Castletown, Merthyr
Tydfil, in 1849:

> Some of the country people affirmed that death was caused by a toad being in
> the tea-pot from which the family took their supply of tea! Another rumour was

that an adder was boiled in the tea-kettle. Another, that it was not an adder but an asp!! The bones of which had since been found.[277]

The history of disease and death provides graphic evidence of the tragic lives lived by many people in the years 1776–1871. Despite the establishment of a Poor Law system, the initiation of a public health movement, parliamentary legislation to alleviate laborious and poisonous work conditions, and the emergence of a modern medical profession, human life was often, because of the horrific conditions of daily life, and the constant presence of death, treated with scant respect. John Griffiths of Cardigan was refused permission to enter the workhouse and left by the authorities 'to die on a dung hill'.[278] Of all the thousands of sad stories scattered in the Welsh press, it is hard to find a more poignant story than that of Ellen Quinn.[279] Her ghastly odyssey, carrying the dead body of her child which she said had died near Cowbridge, was stopped by police outside Cardiff. Bony and haggard, Ellen gently rocked the fleshless body in her thin arms. She cradled it close to her breast with infinite and patient grief, as if to offer it the sustenance denied in life. Around them was the unmistakable rank, sweet and fetid stench of rotting flesh. Ellen told police that she was searching for her husband, and that she wished to bury the six-week-old infant in the same grave as her other child, whose dead body she had carried from Liverpool, but she no longer knew where it was buried. The magistrates ordered that she be held pending police enquiries. As the door of the police cell closed on Ellen, this weary sad soul disappears from history.

4

Fear and Anger

'Ofn sydd arnaf yn fy nghalon' – *My Heart is Fearful*

The refulgent refrain of Psalm 23, 'nid ofnaf niwed' (I will fear no evil), were probably the words uttered most often by the Welsh in the years 1776–1871. Many drew comfort from the mantra, but others in their lonely, lantern-lit darkness lived in fear. Evil forces lurked at every corner. The devil and his infernal legions were frequent visitors to Welsh communities. One dark midsummer's night in the 1850s, the devil participated in a card game in Mary Ann Street, Cardiff, which led to a brutal knife fight and left three men dead.[1] The devil was frequently blamed for tempting the Welsh people into rash suicidal acts and vicious murderous assaults. Spirits, ghosts and ghouls lived and lurked in the dark corners of the land. Fear of disease and disaster, misadventure and misfortune, penury and poverty sent many to obtain charms to ward off evil from local wise men, white witches and wizards. In place of charms others obtained 'cures' from quacks and mountebanks, and sought relief of their fears and afflictions from patent-medicine peddlers whose advertisements filled the Welsh press.

Fear followed the footsteps of many people in their journey through this vale of tears. William Williams, Pantycelyn, described his life journey as a *via dolorosa*:

> Cul yw'r llwybr imi gerdded,   The path I walk is narrow,
> Is fy llaw mae dyfnder mawr   To either side are massive depths,
> Ofn sydd arnaf yn fy nghalon.[2]   My heart is fearful.

His work is the threnody of a terrified man, in which the words *ofn* (fear) and *ofnau* (fears) frequently feature.[3] To Williams, God was the harbour in life's stormy oceans. But to others, the secure refuge was the font of fear. Angels, God's messengers to Earth, delivered messages, few of which were good news: 'God be with you' is not an unmixed blessing. Many people believed that God could, and did, punish a wicked world in physical ways. His angry laughter was heard in thunder and his bitter ire would flail with lightning and hail.[4] To many, the Book of Revelation was a better guide to the weather than the vacuous forecasts of Will Awst, an almanack or a wise man.[5] It forecast storms of thunder and lightning, and they were frequent. God's most terrifying punishment were the cholera epidemics which he, allegedly, sent into Wales in 1832, 1836, 1849 and 1866. The political development of Wales in the 1840s and 1850s, evocatively chronicled by Ieuan Gwynedd Jones, were not only a preparation for greater democratic participation, but were also tempered by people's fear. Thomas and Sally Charles, Christmas Evans and many devout Christians were forced into faith by their fear of death, especially of their dying 'mewn cyflwr annuwiol' (in an ungodly condition).[6] Although many feared God's anger, others were terrified by his absence. As geology undermined Genesis, and the evolutionary theories of Alfred Russel Wallace and Charles Darwin explained Creation, a new kind of fear swept over Wales from the 1850s. People had to contend with the severe emotional impact of cosmic isolation and the terror of absolute solitude.[7] Those who were uncertain hedged their bets, and prayed 'O God! – if there is a God – save my soul – if I have one'. Spiritual and supernatural terrors tortured many tender consciences, but the source of most slippery-gutted, adrenaline-in-the-mouth fear, was human. Mankind's greatest fear was of mankind.

Everywhere people listened and looked there were warnings that their lives were in danger. At fairs and markets, ballad singers sang, and narrators told, frightful and frightening tales of mayhem and murder. Details of vicious, violent acts were broadcast on many street corners. Every ballad singer had a murder ballad in his or her repertoire to celebrate and commemorate the evil deeds of local, national and international murderers. The scarlet thread of murder seemed to mark the years with greater significance for ordinary people than many of the great events of religion and politics. Every brutal murder brought forth its ballads. In 1813, Rebecca Williams and Richard Davies sang ballads to lament the murder of Mary Jones, Penrhyn. In 1822, Owen Kyffin and Ywain Meirion commemorated the death of Lewis Owen of Caernarfon. The red year 1829 saw the horrific death of Hannah Davies on Pencader mountain which inspired Thomas Harris, Stephen Jones and J. Richards to compose classic ballads.[8] Contrary to popular belief, ballad singers were still composing and oedd ganddynt; torodd ei wraig ei chalon, a bu farw yn lled fuan; marw un o'r plant yn ehrwydd wedi hyny, ac y mae y lleill yn wae ar y plwyf.—*Na wna odineb.*

Cynddaredd.—Lladdwyd ei cynddeiriog yn Abertawe pythefnos i'r Sadwrn diweddaf. Cyfarfu yr Ynadon yma ar y Mawrth canlynol, a chytunasant i annog pawb i gadw eu cŵn i mewn. Darllenwn fod amryw ddynion wedi marw yn druenus yn Lloegr o'r gynddaredd, y rhai a gnowyd gan gwn cynddeiriog.

Mellt.—Crybwyllasom yn ein rhifyn diweddaf fod cwmwl wedi tori, a'i gynhwysiad wedi disgyn ar fynydd Mânod, Meirion, ar amser ystorm o dyrfau. Rhuthrodd y dyfroedd i lawr o bob parth o hono, gan beri dychryn mawr i'r holl edrychwyr; chwyddodd yr afonydd yn ddisymwth dros eu glânau, gorchuddiasant y maesydd, rhuthrasant i lawer o dai, a dygasant amryw bontau o'u blaen yn fuddugol, a dystrywiasant rai melinau. Trwy drugaredd ni chollwyd neb bywydau. Torodd y cwmwl lliw dydd.

Syrthiodd mellten i fendŷ (*carthouse*) Mr. J. Philips, Caerlicen, Mynwy, a llosgodd yr holl adeilad, ynghyd â 30 o glwydau defaid, a rhyw gymaint o goed. Diffoddwyd y tan cyn gwneuthur o hono niwed ychwanegol.

Tanu tai—Gyrwyd dyn i garchar Caerfyrddin, dan y cyhuddiad o osod tŷ ar dân yn Llandeilo.

Terfysg.—Dirwywyd chwech o weithwyr Tredegar, wythnos i echdoe, am aflonyddu yr heddwch cyffredin, yn neilltuol am fod llaw ganddynt mewn ymryson a gymerodd le yno boreu y Sabath wythnos i'r diweddaf; a gyrwyd un i'r cospdŷ gwaith am gynyg rhwystro yr hedd-geidwad yn y cyflawniad o'i ddyledswydd. Ceryddwyd hwy yn llym gan yr Ynad: a rhybuddiwyd amryw o werthwyr cwrw yno i gadw gwell trefn yn eu tai o hyn allan.

Dedfrydwyd. T. Thomas, llech-dŵr (*tiler*), o Gaerdydd...yn y brawdlys trimisol diweddaf, i ddyoddef chwech mis o garchar, am ruthr ar Mr. Wm. Wynn, heddgeidwad o'r dref uchod, tra yr oedd yn cyflawni ei swydd.

Hir-hoedledd.—Ychydig amser yn ol, bu farw ynghymydogaeth Ffestiniog, (neu Ffestiniog) swydd Gaerfyrddin, hen ddyddynwr onest yn 105 mlwydd oed; yr hwn a gafodd 20 o blant o'i wraig gyntaf; 10 o'r ail, 4 o'r drydedd; a 7 o'i ddwy orddderchwraig; yr oedd ei fab hynaf yn 81 oed pan anwyd yr ieuangaf; ac yr oedd 800 o bersonau, a ddaethant o'i lwynau, ynghyd ar dydd ei angladd, yn ei hebrwng i dŷ ei hir artref!!!—*Allan o waith Arg. Lyttleton.*

Brawdlysoedd.—Trallwn.—(Trefaldwyn.) Dechreuodd wytnnos i'r Sadwrn diweddaf; cyhoeddwyd dedfryd marwolaeth ar T. Edwards, am ledrata caseg; a Watcin Watcins, am ledrata pedair aner;—Hugh Lear Dawson, am ledrata llogell-lyfr yn cynwys naw punt, i'w alltudio dros saith mlynedd;—Thomas Owen, am ledrata deg gwningen ddôf, tri mis o garchar a chaled-waith. Rhyddhawyd dau garcharor ereill.

Mynwy.—Dechreuwyd y brawdlys yma wythnos i heddyw: y mae yma 24ain o garcharorion i'w profi—dau am lofruddiaeth.

*Henffordd.—*Benj. Powel, am ledrata gwenith—*marwolaeth!!*—Ioan Drincwater, am gynyg ysgrifau ffugiol, ac yspeilio Wm. Brown—*alltudiaeth dros 14eg mlynedd.—*Elisabeth Efans, am dŷ-doriad, a Tomas Puw, am yspeilio ei feistr—*alltudiaeth dros 7 mlynedd.—*Wm. Liwcas, am ladd ei fam yn ddygwyddol, a Wm. Daw, am ladd D. Saunders yn ddygwyddol—y cyntaf 6 wythnos, a'r llall mis o garchar!!!

Y TRAED-FUANYDD.

(*Gwel y Darluniad o hôno yn tu dalen* 153).

A page from *Seren Gomer*, 25 August 1819 (Hugh Owen Library, The University of Wales, Aberystwyth). The illustration shows the latest fashionable means of transport, but the stories of murder, mayhem and misadventure suggest that the traveller should take great care.

singing songs to commemorate violent deaths in the 1860s. In 1861, the brutal death of Richard Williams of Llanfaethlu moved E. Griffiths, Levi Gibbon, D. Jones and R. Hughes to put pen to paper. Those who stopped to listen to the street-corner balladeers soon found themselves among a motley crew of the village's idlers, the rogues and dregs of the community, penniless drunks and cripples, scroungers, cretins, vagabonds from Ireland, hare-lipped roustabouts, squatters on common lands, incorrigible loafers, so-called 'labourers' who never laboured and 'washerwomen' who never washed, rapscallions so mean and reptilian in spirit that they heightened the respectable listener's visceral fear. These were people who had stepped out from the nightmare visions of Bosch and Bruegel. Listeners were also wise to be wary of the singers. In 1824, the violent robbery of Arthur Lawrence's home in Brecon was attributed to three men 'in sailor's dress' and 'a woman in a long red cloak and silk bonnet', who had been singing ballads in the town's streets the preceding Saturday. Not only could the ballad singers sing of brutal murders, but they also rhapsodized on the 'true confession' of the murderer and his or her subsequent summary execution. These ballads revealed the fear of 'the hideous beneath' that was present in Welsh society. Underneath the apparent innocence lay something unseen and horrible. The murderers wore the forms of the world; they pretended to follow the rules, but inside they had no moral thresholds, only a terrifying darkness.[9]

The Punch and Judy shows, which perambulated around the fairs and markets of Wales, further emphasized violence and death.[10] In the puppet show, the racist Mr Punch, convicted child-murderer and serial wife-beater, got the better of the hangman Jack Ketch. People appreciated and applauded Mr Punch's gallows humour, for many of them had witnessed horrifying executions. Above Dolgellau and at Tavarnspite for many years in the 1790s, gallows and gibbets were allowed to stand, a grim *memento mori*, sobering reminders of the violence inherent in Welsh society.[11] In 1800, there were over 200 offences punishable by death, but although judges donned the black cap and passed the dreaded and dreadful sentence of death, many were later reprieved, strengthening the arguments of many in the 1840s that Wales was a lawful land, free of serious crime.[12] Yet, when executions were carried out, newspapers often reminded their readers of previous hangings in their area. When John Roberts was executed before a crowd of 10,000 in Caernarfon in 1853, the *Caernarvon and Denbigh Herald* gave a roll call of the area's notable executions – 'Civil Will' in

1799, 'Hugh Sir Fôn' in 1802, Lewis Owen in 1822 and Jesse Robert's murderer in the 1820s.[13] In 1852, the *Monmouthshire Merlin* devoted a large section to the execution of Abel Ovans for the brutal murder of a child. The paper lamented that: 'Newport is attaining so unenviable a notoriety in the annals of murder, as the graves in the prison yard at Monmouth and the convict hulks, too truthfully attest'. In four years, there had been seven murders in the town. Ovans's execution was 'watched by 4,000 low, vagrant people and laughter and feasts were heard on all hands, chiefly amongst the females'.[14]

The law also dealt savagely with vagrants. Twenty-two-year-old James Reed, 'unable to give a good account of himself', was 'flogged out of Cardiff' in 1818.[15] In August 1792: 'Jo Joseph of Llantrisant a mighty one for the law, for perjury was to stand in the Pillory for three Saturdays and to be transported for seven years'.[16] Bob Robins, one of Caernarfon's habitual drunkards, frequently found himself in the stocks, where he was pelted with rubbish and rocks.[17] John Jones, a travelling hat maker and hat cleaner, was 'confined in the Parish stocks for six hours for disturbing the ministration of Divine Service in the Parish Church of Devynock, Brecknockshire'.[18] It was his fourth such offence. At Caernarfon, William Roberts was whipped in public for stealing a piece of rope. Mr Fletcher, 'a notorious vagabond', was publicly whipped at the tail of a cart in Swansea. When liberated on the Neath road, he 'laughed at the officers and told them the flagellation he had received was nothing to what he had before undergone, of which his back exhibited evident marks'.[19] Many Welshmen lost their liberty to the violent onslaughts of the press gangs. These bruisers hunted cannon fodder for the navy and militia regiments around the low lodging houses, *cwrwau bach* and brothels of seafront Wales. In Swansea in the 1790s, there was a riot at the theatre, when the press gang tried to impress members of the audience and one man was brutally stabbed to death.[20] This was violence with an official guise.

People's insecurities and uncertainties were intensified by the development of the newspaper press. The editors of *The Cambrian* (1804), the *Carmarthen Journal* (1810) and succeeding papers realized that blood-splattered stories sold newspapers. Bad news made good sales. They devoted increasing space to the salacious and sensational details of the crimes committed in their areas of distribution. Surprisingly, denominational periodicals and magazines like *Seren Gomer*, *Y Dysgedydd* and *Yr Haul* also established columns devoted to

'Newyddion o'r Brawd Lysoedd' (News from the Assizes). Horrific crimes were described in the loveliest Welsh. The Welsh language was alleged to be incapable of coping with the linguistic requirements of modern society and science, yet it had no difficulty in detailing the atrocious acts of the beast at the heart of Welsh men and women. Books also told tragic and terrible tales. The murder of poor Hannah Davies, Pencader, was once more detailed by 'the peripatetic philosopher', Jedediah Richards', in *Hanes Cywir am Lofruddiaeth Hannah Davies*, published in 1829, a classic of its kind and time. From the 1840s, 'penny dreadfuls' detailed spectacular brutalities. These popular novels, published as books, leaflets and pamphlets, have familiar, creaking plot-lines – jealous husbands killed their adulterous wives and their lovers; almost as many wives killed their adulterous husbands and their mistresses; desperate young lovers of both sexes killed the focus of their affections, or unrequited and abandoned, committed suicide. These books detailed a steady massacre inspired by love, which must have almost accounted for as many deaths as disease and disasters. Money, honour, prestige, the desperate struggle for power and survival and the world of vice also provided examples of the dangers that confronted ordinary people.[21]

Fear taught the Welsh that they should approach life with the hypersensitivity of a tracker in the forest – watch behind you, but look ahead, listen for those warning murmurings, be wary, be vigilant. Travel terrified Welsh people. The outskirts of many towns were the abode of danger and death. Gangs of robbers and thieves roamed across Wales, and until the 1850s, were virtually unhindered and unimpeded by the forces of law and order. Hymn-writers frequently warned of the perils of life's journey. People who had to travel often made their wills before departure and sought special blessings from chapel and church. Those who carried valuables found ingenious places of concealment. The father of the beautiful Ruth Watcyn of Abergwesyn, Lady Goodrich's maid in Regent Street, London, brought his daughter's wages home concealed in the soles of his shoes.[22] He either had big shoes, or his daughter a small wage. The Revd David Jones of Llangan, while on a preaching mission in London, sent a fish home to his wife with a message that she should read Matthew 17: 27. The wife read the verse 'Cymer y pysgodyn a ddal i fyny yn gyntaf; ac wedi i ti agoryd ei safn, ti a gei ddarn o arian: cymer hwnw, a dyro iddynt drosof fi a thithau' (take the fish which came up first, and after you have opened it you will find some money;

take this and share it with mine and yours). With a knife, she opened the fish and found a letter from her husband and five guineas.[23] In 1832, robbers entered a house in Milford while the family were in chapel and stole two chests and forty shillings in silver. The money concealed in the Bible was left untouched.[24] Prostitutes and female pickpockets had a variety of places to conceal their ill-gotten gains from their fellow miscreants. Ellen Reece explained some of them:

> The places for hiding money are pockets in the underside of the stays towards the lower part . . . Also wrapping it in a piece of rag or paper and putting it in the hair. Putting it in the shoes another way . . . Also pockets inside the stocking below the Garter. Also putting it where decency forbids to name – has known thirty Sovereigns hidden there at one time and secured.[25]

In desperation, they also swallowed money, later taking 'opening medicine' or laxatives to recover it.

Crime, Criminals and Criminality

Whether or not the Welsh were justified in their fears, that in order to safeguard their wealth they needed to conceal it cunningly, is difficult, if not impossible, for the historian to determine. The historian cannot take the criminal pulse of the past. English historians have encountered profound problems in interrogating and interpreting their criminal statistics.[26] One of the most obvious weaknesses of the statistics is that they only reveal failures. Successful criminals are not enumerated. There is thus a 'dark figure' of unrecorded crime which escaped the detection of contemporaries, and eludes the comprehension of historians. In Wales, the situation is even more problematic. Much to the delight of contemporary moralists, Welsh criminal statistics were often included in those for England, giving the impression that the English were much more sinful. In the mid nineteenth century, Wales experienced a bitter propaganda war between two opposing views of the Welsh and crime.[27] Edmund Head, an assistant Poor Law commissioner in the south, 'believed the evidence of his own eyes' and compared his region in 1839 to a 'penal colony', inhabited by 'bad characters, runaway criminals and vagrants'.[28] In 1847, several witnesses gave evidence to the Education Commissioners, published in their infamous report, that Wales was a lawless, perjured, law-breaking, immoral, violent, Godless land. The big guns of the Nonconformist pulpits and press launched a counter-barrage. Wales, they insisted, was a lawful, honest, law-abiding, moral, peaceful, God-fearing land. Their arguments became encapsulated and enshrined in the concepts that Wales was 'Hen Wlad y Menig Gwynion' (the old land of the white gloves) and 'Cymru Lân, Cymru Lonydd' (Pure Wales, Peaceful Wales). Henry Richard, Thomas Phillips, Ieuan Gwynedd and Thomas Rees used court statistics to 'prove' that the level of serious crime in Wales was exceptionally low. Nor did their praise of her inhabitants stop there, for immigrant miners, navvies, tramps, holiday-makers and 'strangers' were blamed for the little criminal behaviour that was recorded. External agitators were also credited with popular disturbances, even those which occurred in monolingual Welsh communities.[29] The Cymric Eden had been corrupted by the criminal English.

Nowhere perhaps is the true meaning of Lytton Strachey's characteristically glib remark, that 'the history of the Victorian Age will never be written; we know too much about it', more apparent than in the history of crime.[30] The execution of the due process of the law has bequeathed tons of documents about the criminal condition of Wales. Amongst these are some of the most remarkable documents that the historian is privileged to consult. In the Carmarthen Record Office is a terrifying ledger of human suffering, *The Felon's Register.* Its heavy pages, withered and yellowed with time, reveal the petty and pitiful nature of such crime. Virtually any moveable and mobile item moved from the rightful owner's possession to that of a thief – books, watches, cash boxes, tobacco, coal, iron, lead, oak, coats, smocks, money, shoes, clothes, stockings, shawls, vests, umbrellas, underclothes, corsets and American cloth. Edible materials were even more irresistible targets – mutton, bacon, bread, cheese, lamb, beef, cockles, apples and pears were frequently stolen. People stole milk by milking a farmer's cows late at night in a field. Thieving naturally had a seasonal aspect. At Christmas 1869, a Carmarthen gang of three – Thomas Sweeny, John Davies and John Cromwell – stole several geese and turkeys, while another miscreant diverted a donkey from a nativity play to a personal pilgrimage.[31]

The government, alarmed by the apparent rise in criminal activity in the nineteenth century, made it compulsory for local police authorities to count and categorize crimes within their areas of jurisdiction.[32] This evidence indicates that the highest levels of crimes were encountered in the early part of the Napoleonic Wars and the first years of peace, the years of the 'Reform Crisis' of 1830–2, and the economic depression of the late 1830s and early 1840s. By 1857, 16,529 persons were being prosecuted annually in the Welsh Petty Sessions. Only 655 of them were committed or bailed to appear at the Assizes and Quarter Sessions, where more serious crimes were tried.[33] Some insisted that this was firm evidence that Wales was relatively free of serious crime. Others argued that it was proof that too much criminal business was conducted at the lower courts. Certain towns were more criminal and threatening in their propensities than others. Sin-soaked Merthyr Tydfil was an infamous town which was frequently mentioned as 'Satan's stronghold', the undisputed capital of Welsh crime.[34] There, in 1858, 1 in every 113 people was apprehended and sentenced for serious offences. But people were in greater physical danger in Cardiff, Swansea and Newport because in each of the troublesome triplet, 1 in 63 people was the victim of violent crimes. 'People must have lived in real fear of being attacked' concludes the leading historian of crime in Wales.[35] The 1850s were the high point of crime, not just in the populous centres, but in rural areas as well. In the manufacturing towns of Welshpool, Llanidloes and Newtown, violent behaviour was a threat not just to victims, but to municipal pride and respectability.[36] It no longer appeared that the rural poor conformed to the ideal of being 'slow to anger', polite or lacking in envy. Crime rates did not reduce significantly until the 1870s. Historians have agreed that the fall in the number of recorded crimes reflected a genuine reduction in the amount of delinquency in society. 'Something extraordinary happened then' was the conclusion of one of the most perceptive historians of the crimes of the 1870s.[37]

Unlike victims, 'statistics', as Koestler reminds us, 'don't bleed'. Crime has been counted and quantified but much of the experience of people has been ignored and forgotten. People are left anonymous in a ghostly army of statistically summoned spirits. Beneath the tidy tables, human experience is concealed. The assertations of moralists that Wales was a land free of crime, and the arguments of historians that a person was in greater physical danger in Merthyr Tydfil than in Meifod, would be of little comfort to Thomas Williams of Henfaes, Llanrwst. Only a hundred yards from the relative safety of his home, he was beaten, robbed and murdered by a 'gang of ruffians'.[38] Thomas's painful and tragic experience indicates that, even in the 1830s, the medieval world of bandits and travelling fraternities of thieves and highway robbers had not completely disappeared. Some of the desperadoes captured and committed confirm the argument of the

Welsh that crime was endemic to the English in Wales. In 1829, a £400 reward was offered for a gang who robbed two banks of Messrs Walters and Co. Three men were later arrested in Bristol with 'flash notes' valued at over £8,000.[39] In 1827, one of a gang of 'bad characters' who stole £80 from a widow in Monmouth was apprehended 'before he took the steam-packet for Bristol'.[40] The thieves who stole thirty watches from a shop of John Edwards in Bassaleg also took the steam-packet to the freedom of Bristol.[41] Edward Bishop appeared before the Glamorgan Assizes in June 1835, charged with the theft of a bundle of crumbs from John Lewis of Merthyr Tydfil. Edward was one of those outsized henchmen – 'Evil's foot-soldier' – who relished every working day, so common in the history of Welsh criminality. He had only recently left Warwick jail, where he had been flogged. He was sentenced to be transported for seven years: 'On hearing his sentence the prisoner expressed great indignation that he (a Birmingham thief) should have met with his deserts in so unknown a country, and looking at the Jury exclaimed "to be found guilty by such a bl—y set of Nanny Goats".'[42]

The Welsh were equally capable of dishonesty, brutality and violence. John Hardy, a man of 'dissolute, idle, violent habits', was hanged at Hereford jail for theft at Cilgwyn, Llandovery. He was captured at Ross-on-Wye. He made several attempts to escape from jail – taking out the rivets from the cell bars, and trying to force his way past the guards. The twenty-year-old John had previously been convicted and sentenced to seven years' transportation, for robbery with violence and horse rustling, but he had escaped from Newgate. John refused to 'go gently into that good night'. At his execution, much to the disgust of the assembled multitude, he tried to fight his way free from the grasp of the constables and gaolers.[43] Owen Davies of Bodwrog, Anglesey, had his face 'beaten into a pulp' in 1849 by three local men who stole £15 in gold and silver from him.[44] In August 1829

the notorious David Davies or Dai Gam and Dick Parry were apprehended at Merthyr Tydfil, the last remnants of a numerous and atrocious gang who had infested Merthyr and its neighbourhood for the last twenty years, the successors of the gang that were broken up when John the Fox and Nehemiah Lee were transported.

Dai, allegedly, cut off his thumb in 1807 to avoid service in the Glamorgan Militia. Early in his career, Dai was: 'as celebrated in the hilly districts of the country, as ever Rob Roy was in Scotland'.[45] In

1850, 'a gang of desperadoes ... ill looking fellows ... depraved characters' terrorized travellers and householders in Bryn Mawr, in the north.[46] Whilst the forces of law and order had considerable difficulty apprehending the desperadoes, others were easy to trace. In December 1839, the home of Miss John of Hobby Bank, Haverfordwest, was robbed while she was in church. On that bitterly cold night, during the time Miss John was in the service, the snow had fallen deep and crisp and even. John Richards, James Lewis and Thomas Devereux were later apprehended in a local public house by a constable who had simply followed the footprints they had left in the snow.[47] Elias Jones, together with James Phillips, 'two men of bad character', were leaders of a vicious gang of thieves in Newport. Elias was described as 'a man of about forty years of age, about five foot eight inches high, marked with the small-pox, has sandy whiskers, and is rather deaf'. Police saw Elias, quickly and quietly sneaked up on him, and arrested him.

Certain people in certain situations were particularly vulnerable. Piety did not always pay. Miss John's fate was shared by a poor and infirm old couple from Monmouth who were robbed of 'what little money that they had' while they were in church.[48] While Mr Jones the jeweller and his family were worshipping in Carmarthen, his shop was broken into and ninety-eight watches and a large quantity of silver stolen.[49] A man broke into the Independent chapel in Milford during a service, and stole the missionary society subscription box. Although he was chased by the minister and the congregation, he was never apprehended. The description given to the police was of little help – 'he looked like the prophet Isaiah'. Robbers and thieves took note of the absences of people at markets and fairs.[50] In 1826, William Perkins of Porth-mawr, St David's, went with his three servants to the town's fair, but on their return discovered that four locks had been forced and £1,000, surely a suspiciously large sum of cash, stolen. In 1832, the aged Mrs Powell of Crickhowell died, and her body was laid out in readiness for a wake. While her relatives were absent, thieves broke in and stole the deceased's valuables and, 'cymaint oedd eu haerllug-rwydd, nes iddynt ddwyn y clustdlysau a'r modrwyon oddi wrth y corff' (such was their audacity that they stole earrings and rings from the corpse).[51] John Jones, a blacksmith from Hope, was hanged in Wrexham in 1810, for a brutal assault and robbery on John Wynne, when he was delivering wages to the lime works.[52] In 1826, Morgan Morgan, alias Morgan Mawr, was charged with assaulting and robbing Isaac Jones of Risca on his way home from Newport market.

Morgan, it seems, took on more than he could handle: 'Morgan it appears is a large and powerful man, and Jones rather diminutive, but not at all deficient in strength and courage'.[53] The battered Morgan Mawr was glad to reach the safety of jail. Although Isaac Jones had been drinking, he had not allowed himself to get into the condition of the 'jolly butcher of Bangor', who knew nothing of the fact that he had been robbed of £10 until he found himself sleeping in railway sheds.[54]

The elderly were exceptionally vulnerable. David Rees, the eighty-year-old servant of Lord Cawdor had been collecting the rent from local farmers around Newcastle Emlyn, when he was attacked by John Owen and robbed of his horse and saddlebags containing £2,000. Despite his age, the redoubtable David gave chase shouting 'stop thief', and gathering, as he ran, an increasing crowd of country people who joined in the chase and the chant. Despite having a pistol in his possession, John Owen was quickly apprehended.[55] Margaret Williams was 'put in bodily fear and danger' by William Evans upon the high road between Gwynfe and Llandeilo, and robbed of £19. 0s. 6d.[56] In 1825, three men with blackened faces broke into the Tavern-y-Trap public house, Loughor, kept by 82-year-old Margaret Matthews. 'After tying the harmless old creature and her two grand-daughters to their bed posts, they broke open a chest and stole sixty guineas, eighteen sovereigns, eleven one pound provincial notes, £5 in silver, £1. 10s. in copper, and three promissory notes in sums of £20, £1 and £5.' Whether this was the real or the insurance value was never revealed.[57]

The realization that they were not safe in their own houses gave rise to a debilitating fear, a hyper-vigilance, a wariness, and a tendency to jump at their own shadow amongst victims. After being robbed by two men of £25. 19s., David Walter, a pig-dealer of Carmarthen, explained that the worst part of the ordeal was not so much the physical punishment but the robber's capacity to wield the most powerful weapon of all, the ability to inspire terror.[58] Householders who encountered robbers and thieves in their homes late at night related similar terrifying encounters with evil incarnate – the heart of darkness. One Pembrokeshire family experienced the following, late one evening in the 1830s:

> I heard my wife making a melancholy noise. I saw the prisoner with a sword in his hand and a soldier jacket, black mask on his face and a cap on his head with a black fringe round the bill trimmed with red on top. I hallowed so much as I could to awake the girls . . . He said 'I am a Robber and I got sixty men at my

command' . . . My wife told me to take the candle from the powder or else it would blow the house up. I took the candle and put it on the table. Prisoner told 'Deliver the keys and all your money' . . . Before then he cried out and after 'My name is Rubroi [Rob Roy] the Chief of Robbers. I have robbed England, France and Scotchland and I now come to Wales I have heard that people got a great deal of money in Wales', and he asked me to tell him who had money that he might robb them, but I refused. He told me 'Tis death for me to break into your home and tis death for you' . . . My daughter came down the stairs and asked for her mother . . . and my daughter was crying about her mother and I told her she must be fainted or his men had killed her. And he wanted to kiss my daughter and I told him that I would risk my life before he should touch my daughter.[59]

The armed robber stole £112. 14s. from the terrified family. Such white-knuckled terror is frequently encountered in the criminal documents. These and other testimonies point us to a broader under-standing of the nature of criminality in Wales in the period 1776–1871. Wales, like all nations, had a significant core of habitual, hardened career criminals. In the 1870s, Llewelyn Price, a 'notorious character of Cardiff', commenced his Fagin-like career. John Jones of Tregaron, a bankrupt farmer, appeared for the thirty-first time before the petty sessions on a charge of arson.[60] 'Dick the Thief', 'Burglar Bill', 'Bob the Goose', 'John Wilkes' (named John Evans by his parents) all appeared more than ten times each for theft, robbery and assault.[61] T. Carew Phillips, an accomplished poacher, sheep-stealer and burglar, was, according to the *Carmarthen Journal*, a 'Rob Roy figure in south west Wales', until his enforced departure to Australia in 1845.[62] Some were exceptionally violent and dangerous. By 1842, James Evans of Newcastle Emlyn had committed a rape, four assaults and two vicious attacks on constables. Almost a year later, he nearly killed his wife with a knife.[63] Official estimates of the number of these malign miscreants vary from 8,700 to over 16,000 people annually.

Whichever estimate is true, people had just cause to fear for their safety not only in 'urban', but also in 'rural' Wales. In 1817, gangs forced young girls to buy overpriced 'gold' rings on the roads in the Monmouthshire countryside.[64] John Bond was transported to Botany Bay for the 'despicable trick – the Green Eyed Monster Con' – which he performed in the rural fairs of south Wales.[65] In 1820, 'a nefarious gang of swindlers' worked the markets and fairs in the neighbourhood of Brecon.[66] In January 1830, 'a man of colour calling himself Charles Cope and pretending to be dumb' was imprisoned in the Carmarthen house of correction. Since his commitment 'he has miraculously found the ability of his tongue, which he now uses fully'.[67] Often, the stories that these con artists told were so convincing that women wept as they heard them. Men would beseech them to take their last shilling. Sometimes their stories sounded so convincing that they would weep themselves. Born actors, the pavement was their theatre.

The Wales praised in pastoral poems and passionate prose for the simple, saintly, sinless lives led by inhabitants was not immune from crime. Fairs and market days were the occasions for brutal and bruising contests between rival gangs. At Beddgelert, rural youths and quarrymen frequently fought. The pugnacious youths of Llanwynno and the temperamental teenagers of Llantrisant had the sensitivities of Sicilians in matters of village pride and honour. Pitched battles between the bitter rivals were frequent.[68] In Cardiganshire it was alleged that the police in the 1860s exercised undue and unfair vigilance over people living in *tai unnos*. They, it was claimed, were arrested far more frequently than farmers or farm labourers, who engaged in the same rough rural pursuits. Others, however, insisted that the authorities had good cause for their vigilance. Richard Banks of Knighton informed the commissioners into commons enclosures in 1844 that:

> I could name a place in Brecknockshire named Mutton Street, where there were a great many squatters, it was a perfect den of sheep stealers . . . another in the parish of Beguildy . . . a place called the Scrubs . . . where there is a similar colony and several of the parties were tried at the last quarter sessions of the county, for stealing and driving the flocks of sheep off the common into a wood, getting the wool off their backs in any way that they could affect it, and slaughtering the sheep to prevent detection – burning some of the carcases, throwing others to the dogs, and eating some themselves; no less than thirty-one fleeces were found in one man's possession.[69]

The poet Robert Southey claimed that, 'if the Welsh are addicted to any offence, it is sheep stealing, because the sheep have ceased to be wild, and the people have not'. In 1831, Charlotte Williams, her three sons and two daughters of Llanddeusant were charged with sheep-stealing. The authorities discovered the carcasses of twenty-four sheep near the cow-house and another thirteen under a rock near the dwelling house. According to Charlotte, they had been 'brought down the mountain by strangers'. The jury declined to believe her, the judge sentenced two of her sons to transportation for life, and herself and her thirteen-year-old son to fourteen years in Van Diemen's Land. Despite the evidence of the mother's obvious involvement, the judge refused to believe that girls would be involved with such a trade and acquitted both daughters.[70] Llangelynin in Merionethshire in the 1790s was the focus for a celebrated gang of sheep rustlers. The brief biographical details of one of the ringleaders, Mary Lewis, provides graphic evidence that punishment did not lead to reform. Publicly whipped at fifteen, condemned to death but reprieved at twenty-two, Mary was transported at twenty-nine to Van Diemen's Land.[71] Thomas Thomas, sheep-stealer and highway robber of Llanfynydd, was hanged in 1845. Before his execution, the 24-year-old Thomas entertained the Brecon crowd with tales of his misdoings, and finished with a warning to the young people assembled that they should not emulate his wrongdoings. To the authorities who believed in the expiatory powers of execution, his was a good death. In 1824, Edward Jarman, William Sheen, Ezekiel Watkins and James Davies, 'infamous' horse thieves in Radnorshire and adjoining counties, were transported for life, after their attempts to diversify their criminal activities failed and they were caught in possession of over fifty sheep.[72] It is tempting to describe these parts of rural Wales as an underworld, but evidently they were ubiquitous, visible and vociferous.

Many of the crowd who gathered to watch Thomas Thomas hang in Brecon wondered how so much wickedness could have been compressed into that small span of years from his birth to the fatal act of violent robbery. Juvenile crime became an increasing problem for Welsh authorities as the nineteenth century wound its wicked way.[73] In 1853, Mary Williams, 'a little girl' wasting 'a life of profligacy', and Dennis Murray, 'a little dirty boy', were both given three months' hard labour for petty theft. It is impossible now to know the extent of such 'juvenile depravity'. In 1853, it was estimated that 200 children in Cardiff, 110 in Swansea and 180 in Merthyr Tydfil earned their living by 'dishonest practices'.[74] The Catholic priest at Merthyr Tydfil expressed his frustration and sorrow that: 'Whilst children of both sexes are allowed to drink, smoke, swear and talk obscene language before twelve years of age, they cannot be expected to come up to the morality even of Canadian savages'.[75]

In 1846, Swansea magistrates sat aghast, mouths agape, as the following gang of hardened criminals were brought before them:

> John Nash (alias 'Clap the Bellows') aged ten, John Davies ('Slip the Jacket' or 'Captain Bennett') aged nine, Daniel Sullivan ('Fire Skull') aged seven, John Sullivan ('Stallion') aged eight, Edward Williams ('Dick Turpin') aged seven, and William Davies ('Thunderbolt') aged seven. The police inspector who arrested the gang, stated that several parents of the children were almost entirely

dependent upon the vicious practices of their children. The mother of Nash was said to be a confirmed drunkard and was in the habit of ill using her son if he returned home at night without anything to enable her to indulge in her excesses.[76]

Nash himself claimed that his mother was a prostitute, the busiest in Swansea. Since the police were unable to find the owners of the stolen property, the youngsters were discharged but not before several newspapers engaged in vacuous moralizing, a nostalgic regret that things were no longer as they had been and a debate on the causes of crime. In that debate, the effect of nature and nurture as the causes of crime were voiced, but the most dominant voices implied that criminals produced crime 'like a snake produced venom'. People chose their lives of crime. Unfortunately for those who idealized Wales as a land free of crime, authors of letters admitted that women were also capable of choosing a life of crime. Mary Ann Cooney of Merthyr Tydfil, Jane Benson of Swansea and Catherine Brian of Cardiff all entered the official records in their teens. The official documents give detailed descriptions of these fiery, light-fingered females. Sarah Davies was born in Tre-lech a'r Betws in 1840 and by the age of forty-two had spent four long terms in prison. Life took a hard toll on Sarah, who was described as of 'fair complexion; grey hair; 5 foot 1 inch tall; terribly pockmarked; face very much scarred; lost all upper front teeth; scar right forearm; lost left arm; lame left leg'.[77] The circumstances which occasioned such physical damage are not recorded. Mary Howell, 'the wife of Howell Howell (allegedly), a woman of notorious character', escaped from the Cowbridge house of correction. She had 'previously been exercising herself on the treadmill in Haverfordwest'. She was believed to be travelling with a young man, John Davies, passing base coin in the villages around Carmarthen. Her husband Howell had been transported for life a year previously.[78] One who survived trans-portation was the 'Amazonian' Ann Thomas of Monmouth. The experience appeared to have done little to curtail her criminal activities for in 1831 she was charged with stealing wool. Ann survived in Australia through prostitution, and selling her sexual favours to the guards. She returned a relatively wealthy lady with sufficient funds to 'buy' a husband.[79]

While many female victims of crime sought redress of their griev-ances through law, others turned to traditional methods of settling disputes. A bellman was sent around Lampeter in 1810 to publicize a fight between the victim and the accused in a dispute over an alleged theft. The combatants, two pauper ladies, respectively aged eighty-six and eighty-eight, boxed for an hour, and then fought with cudgels. One of them was able to re-establish her honour before the constables arrived. The victor was one of 'Cochiai'd Pencarreg', 'a name given to a peculiarly obstinate race of fighters who never call for quarter'.[80] Such episodes of octogenarian obstreperousness indicates that violence was never far below the surface in rural and urban Wales. The guns carried by many robbers and thieves were frequently fired in anger. William Parry was shot and robbed in Holywell in December 1814.[81] The Revd Robert Wynter of Penderyn, a JP at Brecon, was shot and robbed outside Rhayader in 1825.[82] William Lewis, a carpenter from Merthyr Tydfil, was overtaken by two soldiers on his way home and bayoneted in his eye and throat. He eventually recovered, but his military assailants were never captured.[83] On their way home from Wrexham fair, a Mr Woodward and a Mr Urwick were attacked by at least five armed men and left 'barely conscious and helpless in their blood'. The appropriately named Mr Sturdy was attacked and robbed by a highwayman near Capel Curig. The assailant demanded money and held a pistol to Mr Sturdy's breast. He refused to stand or deliver. Instead he fought and was shot in his arm. Again he refused to give up his money, and so the assailant levelled a second pistol at him and fired: 'but Providence again interspersed, and the ball passed through his hat without further injury; upon which the ruffian then began a violent assault'. The assailant stole Sturdy's horse and money, leaving him for dead. But the horse was later recognized in Capel Curig and local people gave chase, eventually capturing the assailant, Lewis Owens, near the Swan Inn, at Denbigh.[84]

Robbers and thieves were not the only ones to use firearms. Gentlemen still settled disputes of honour by duelling in nineteenth-century Wales. The adventurer and surgeon David Samwell issued a challenge to Edward Jones, Ned Môn, the adjudicator at the Corwen Eisteddfod, for failing to award a prize to his friend, Twm o'r Nant. Had Ned accepted, the duel would have been one of the most remarkable in Welsh history, for Samwell would probably have been assisted by another opium addict, Iolo Morganwg.[85] At Carmarthen in 1822, two men, one of whom was a magistrate, fought a duel.[86] In 1805, Mr William Richards, the mayor of Tenby, exchanged shots with a Mr Mannicks following a dispute over the election of a guardian of the poor.[87] The decade following 1810 was probably the golden age of the Welsh duel. In 1811, duels were fought at Holyhead, Connah's Quay and Llandeilo, at Brecon, Swansea and Abergavenny in 1817,

and at Abergavenny and Cardiff in 1819. In the latter year, two Welsh
military officers, General Gwynn of Glanbrân and Colonel Holford,
fought a duel and were condemned by *Seren Gomer* for setting a bad
example to their tenants. Duels were also fought in 1821, 1822 and
1831.[88] In 1834, in a bid to settle a dispute over enclosed land, two men
duelled in Llanfachreth, Merionethshire. When one of them was shot
in the leg and arm, his brother was so enraged that he attacked the
successful duellist and beat him to death.

'Vicious Words' and Violence

Violent words and conduct permeated almost every aspect of Welsh
life. In the 1840s, schoolchildren in Anglesey were beaten across their
face with a rod for minor infringements of a draconian code of
conduct. More severe breaches merited and often received a
whipping.[89] Corporal punishment was praised for its beneficial effects.
Britwn penned a song praising 'Gwialen Fedw Fy Mam' (My mother's
cane), with which he was beaten when he 'sinned' as a child, and which
had kept him on 'llwybrau dyletswydd' (the paths of duty). Sarah Jane
Rees, Cranogwen (1839–1916), a dried spinster of ferocious irritability,
often clouted her navigational pupils so hard that they saw stars. The
Welsh did not spare the rod and did not spoil the man.[90] People traded
scabrous insults with scandalous frequency. The words leap out from
the court records: 'you fornicating old bugger', 'y Diawl bach cachlyd'
(you shitty little devil), 'you damned great fat beast', 'y wanton witch'
(you wanton witch), 'yr hwch ddiawl' (you hellish sow), 'yr hen hwren
aflan' (you dirty old whore), 'you bloody bitch from hell', 'you smelly
strumpet', 'you pox-faced whore of Babylon', 'ti yw'r pot a'r pisio'
(you are the pot and the piss), 'yr hen bitch boeth' (you hot old whore),
'yr hen ffwlcen' (you old fucker) and the timeless 'kiss my arse'. These
were words that could wound. Often they were accompanied by
gestures and actions that made them even worse. Trading in such terms
of enmity rapidly led to the exchange of blows. Mrs Wilkins, a
butcher's wife of Quarry Street, Swansea, had an unique conception of
customer care. She asked Mrs Priscilla Fewens: 'What do you want,
you nasty slut?' The question was followed by a beer mug in the face.
Mrs Wilkins was sentenced to three months in prison with hard
labour.[91] Ann Williams of Dafen promised Margaret Hopkins that she
'was going to wash her hands in her blood'.[92]

Ann Williams's promise was unhonoured, but many others were true to their wicked words, and thus blood flowed frequently. The year 1812 was described by the *Chester Chronicle* as the 'year of blood, the age of Welsh murders'. Among the most notable of murders that year was the brutal killing of Mary Jones by Thomas Edwards, Yr Hwntw Mawr, near Porthmadog.[93] The murder had two characteristics that conformed to the accepted view of murder in Wales – it involved a bungled robbery and it was committed by a stranger. Thomas Edwards, a casual labourer from the south, had been drawn to the area to work on the construction of the Cob across the mouth of the Glaslyn estuary. While he was robbing the farm where she worked as a servant, Mary Jones surprised Edwards. It proved to be her last act. He cut her throat with a pair of sheep shears. The same week, reapers in the harvest fields near Denbigh quarrelled and fought until separated by a rider on horseback. The assailants turned on the intruder and stabbed him to death.[94] A week earlier, James Waters, ferryman at Bolwell, Milford Haven, was robbed and murdered by an American, John Bruce.[95] John Jones was executed on the Flint marshes for the murder of John Wynne, the overseer of Nant-y-taith lime works.[96] In the same year, another lime works overseer from Wrexham was 'waylaid' and murdered by a local blacksmith. Suspicion fell on the blacksmith when he was seen buying a new hat and shoes on the following day with 'known notes'. At Abergwili in 1814, 'an elderly lady' was robbed and murdered.[97] John Vaughan, a shoemaker from Llangyfelach, was attacked and murdered when three intruders forced themselves into his house and beat him to death with a shovel. His wife escaped 'out of the window' to neighbours, 'quite naked'.[98] Robert Jones of St Asaph, while threshing wheat, was murdered by Thomas Williams who stole the wheat and his watch.[99] At Llanbedr, Jane Williams, an aged widow and shopkeeper: 'thought to have amassed a little wealth, was found murdered behind her shop-counter! Her little grandchild heard the screams, but was too scared to find out what was going on.' In Monmouth, 'a poor woman', Esther Stephens, had her throat cut by Edward Burrett, a wood-cutter from the Forest of Dean. Police offered a reward of forty guineas for Burrett, who escaped 'without either coat, hat or shoes'. Despite the reward and a detailed description: 'twenty-three years old, five foot ten inches tall, short build, rather stoops and shuffles as he walks, dark complexion, freckles, has a heavy swollen look', the stooping, shuffling, swollen murderer was never brought to justice.[100] Each year witnessed a similar grim human harvest fuelled by greed.[101]

Even more feared than the vicious English were the ferocious Irish. In 1848, a dispute between three Welshmen and five Irish navvies in a Swansea *cwrw bach* escalated into a pitched battle. The three Welshmen – John Williams, Jenkin Evan and Edward Morgan – were beaten to death with shovels. Four of the Irish were captured near Cowbridge and the fifth was later captured naked, hiding in a wood.[102] At Pant-y-bwlch, Thomas Morris, a shepherd, found the body of a twenty-year-old man. Near the body, which had been robbed, was the murder weapon, a razor with the letter 'V' on it and the name 'Meaghan' and 'a coat of the type worn by an Irishman'.[103] In 1826, the Irish robber and serial killer James Wallace, who was wanted for four murders in Ireland, was apprehended in Brecon after a bungled attempt at pickpocketing.[104] Several other Welsh people were murdered by Irish robbers, but many deaths were unmotivated, the alleged results of the tempestuous tempers of the Irish.[105] At Cardiff in 1848, a man and his wife were attacked for no apparent reason by an Irishman. The husband died of his stab wounds. The murder so incensed the local Welsh population that they attacked the town's Catholic church, smashing windows and assaulting the priest who was believed to be harbouring the murderer. The Irish were turned out from their jobs and 'mae yr elyniaeth fwyaf yn cael ei dangos rhyngddynt hwy a'r Cymry' (the greatest enmity is displayed between the Irish and Welsh). Other visitors to Wales also proved volatile. In 1826, the travelling caravans of a freak show, which included the star turns of an Indian Chief and the Waterloo Giant, trundled into Carmarthen:

> A poor man, an inhabitant of the place, felt rather curious to have a peep at one of them; and while in the act of climbing the wheel of one of the caravans, to gratify his curiosity, the Indian Chief feeling chagrined at being made a laughing stock by a Cambro plebeian, struck the poor man through a pane of glass with his lance in the eye, which was instantly severed from the socket.[106]

The man died, leaving a wife and 'a great many children' to mourn his death and to curse his curiosity.

Only the adventurous and the curious were victims of Indian outrages, but many more were victims of the outraged anger of a relative. It seems largely to have escaped notice that the most relentless, the most persistently brutal, embittered and the most continuous current of violence running through these years was not urban, rural or political, but domestic. The most dangerous place of all was 'home, sweet home'. Wives were the victims of a torrent of verbal abuse and physical assault, children were drenched by cascades of cruelty.[107] No year was exempt. In April 1843, the *Carmarthen Journal* reported the horrific murders of three wives by their husbands.[108] Drink was often cited as the cause. A man 'drinking in one of the temples of Bacchus', on Rhiw Syr David, Blackwood, was lectured by his wife on the effects of dissipation. 'He responded by kicking her mercilessly to death'.[109]

Many took a less violent, but no less effective, method of disposing of unloved and unwanted wives. James Griffith of Haverfordwest was an expert on poisoning techniques. By gradually adding arsenic to treacle and porridge, he managed to poison his first two wives. The suspicions of his lodgers saved his third wife.[110] In 1817, six of the children of William James of Genau'r Glyn, Aberystwyth, gave evidence that their father had poisoned their mother.[111] Thomas Bevan was acquitted by the Pembrokeshire Assizes in 1829 for poisoning his wife, when he claimed that he had given his wife poison because of her illness. This early pioneer of mercy killing had killed from kindness.[112]

Some men might have escaped conviction for murder had it not been for the timely intervention of the authorities. James Harry had prepared his dead wife's body for burial, and had made all the arrangements for a quick funeral.[113] Mr Parnell, the Monmouth coroner, forced him to open the coffin and discovered that the woman had been brutally beaten to death. Another James Harry had buried his wife in a secluded spot near Monmouth, explaining her disappearance to inquisitive neighbours by claiming that she had abandoned him. But 'avarice was his undoing', suspicion fell on him when he tried to sell his wife's clothes.[114] Dic Tanar murdered his mother and placed her corpse under his bed, where she remained for over a week until his wife complained at the smell.[115]

Sexual jealousy was the spark that fired many savage murders. At Letterston, Pembrokeshire, in 1827, David Owen in a fit of jealousy cut his wife's throat, as did Ishmael Jones in Llanfair Caereinion, in 1862.[116] One of the most vicious and brutal murders in nineteenth-century Wales was committed by Thomas Davies of Cefn-rhuddlan-isaf, Llanwenog, on his wife and daughter. Together, they had dug the farm out of unfruitful soil, simultaneously digging themselves into a cold, uncongenial marriage. Thomas's motives are lost in the black hole where madness and evil meet, but he was convinced, without foundation, that their third child was not his but the offspring of a local farmer. A slander case proved otherwise, but

Thomas marinaded in his misery and obsession. Early one morning he sent his two eldest children away from the farm on separate messages, before attacking his wife with a billhook, deeply gashing her neck, shoulders, head and arms:

> He then drew a razor across the lower part of her person, inflicting a very dreadful wound, through which her intestines intruded . . . He cut the infant's throat from ear to ear, almost severing the head from the body . . . He attempted to drown himself in the river Teifi, but the water was too shallow. He got out and then cut his own throat, several other parts of his body and inflicted a wound across the abdomen through which his intestines protruded. The screams of the woman attracted the attention of neighbours who helped her into the house. He was carried to the barn on a sheet, where he died. Although the wife received medical attention, she too died . . . They had been married for eighteen years.[117]

Wives were not always the victims. In 1835, the children of Rachel and William Williams gave evidence of the abuse that their father had suffered at their mother's hands. Terrified and traumatized by the defendant's 'hardened manner and stares', the daughters Priscilla and Margaros burst into tears in court when they reported how their mother had beaten their father until he had 'a hole in the back of his head, and blood came out of his eyes'.[118] John McCabe, a milliner of Market Lane, Cross Keys, threatened his wife that he would 'run her through with a sword'. His wife retaliated by throwing a stone, which killed him. Thomas Lewis of Aberdare threatened to hit his wife, Mary, with a stool. This prompted her to get a hammer and 'I struck him one heavy blow, and I then resolved to give him two or three thumps on the floor. I have no remorse for what I did.'[119] Mary was later declared insane. Another who was clearly unhinged was Mary Davies. In 1811, her suspicious behaviour led to the exhumation of the body of her husband, Benjamin, nine days after his funeral in New Quay. His corpse was found to contain substantial traces of arsenic. When asked to explain, Mary responded, pointing at the corpse, saying 'there he is, ask him'.[120]

'The Massacre of the Innocents'

Anger, abuse and hatred, rather than patience, care and love, characterized many Welsh families. Children were often at the mercy of the vicious behaviour of parents.[121] An inquest held at the Cyclops Inn, Nant-y-glo, in 1856 heard of the 'barbarous treatment' meted out to George Williams, the illegitimate ten-year-old son of Elizabeth Dram.

His body had 'severe excoriations and was covered in bruises'. Neighbours reported that George had frequently been in a state of starvation, 'picking up garbage and eating it and even going to the pig's trough for food'. Elizabeth was charged with wilful murder. William Jones of Nevern, Pembrokeshire, was a strange and unpopular character who knocked the life out of his six-year-old daughter in 1848. His transportation for life was greeted with celebrations in the area.[122]

Abandoned by their husbands, women were left in a state of utter desperation. Festering in misery, and often starving, they sought release in the murder of their children. Margaret Hughes of Llan-non in Carmarthenshire threw her twins down a deep mine shaft. Her husband had been transported to Van Diemen's Land for his involvement in the Scotch Cattle movement.[123] Depressed, but 'not desolate', Mary Hughes of Llanybydder, whose husband was away in the mines in Aberdare, hanged her three children aged five, two and one with silk handkerchiefs in an upstairs bedroom. In prison she confessed to a fellow inmate that 'my children are happy now', and told another that 'some people are born under good and bad planets'. She was eventually declared insane and confined for life.[124] Mary Bennett of Connah's Quay was also declared insane at the Flintshire Assizes in 1866 after murdering her child,[125] as was Griffith Roberts of Garndolbenmaen, after murdering his two-year-old son in 1817.[126]

Juries often returned verdicts of insanity in the cases of mothers who murdered their children. In other cases, however, the verdict reached by coroners' courts and juries appear bizarre. In 1832 an inquest at the New Inn, Ystradgynlais, reached a verdict 'died by the visitation of God' in the case of Jane Morgan, a two-year-old illegitimate daughter of Hopkin Morgan, of Cwm-twrch. At the inquest, it was reported that the mother, Elizabeth Morgan, had administered severe beatings to the child and had thrown her across a room, after which she collapsed. The child was forced to sleep in an old candle box under a bed. In 1859, Henry and Ellen Jayne were charged with the manslaughter of Ann White at Llangatock near Caerleon. The child, one of the couple's six illegitimate children, was kept in a state of starvation so that she would raise more money begging.[127] They were found not guilty of murder. Hannah Davies, a servant at the Mount Pleasant beer house, was found not guilty of the murder and concealment of birth of her new-born child. The jury maintained that it could not have been concealment for she had placed the body on top of a stable wall for all to see.[128]

Concealment of birth was the desperate, but frequent, resort of unmarried mothers. Many of the deaths were undoubtedly the result of the terrible circumstances in which the birth took place. Others were the innocent victims of wilful malice. Young girls, abandoned by their lovers, had to continue to work up until the moment of birth. Weakened by the confinement, debilitated by their diet, depressed by the prospect of an even bleaker future, mothers took the darkest option open to them. The newspapers of Victorian Wales named this grim harvest 'the massacre of the innocents'. Among the saddest and most distressing features of the Welsh press is the frequent reports of the discovery of the dead bodies of newly born babies. In 1836, Ann Ellis, a servant girl of Pennal, Merionethshire, was charged with the murder of her bastard child.[129] In 1836, while digging in his garden in Newtown, Richard Lowe discovered the body of a new-born female wrapped in rags. The mother, a married woman, was discovered and explained 'that being too poor to pay the burial fees, she had interred it herself'.[130] Although her dead baby was discovered under her bed with a 'black ribbon tied tightly around its neck', Anne Crutchly of Abergavenny was found not guilty of infanticide, because the two doctors at the inquest disagreed as to whether the baby was born alive or dead. Before a 'packed court', Crutchly was given two months hard labour for concealment of birth.[131] Ann James, a colliery worker of Hook, Pembrokeshire, was charged with the wilful murder of her child. Suspecting her odd behaviour, a fellow miner, a young boy, followed her and heard a baby's screams. The child was later found at the bottom of the mine shaft.[132] Mary Prout of Amroth also threw her new-born child down a mine shaft. In court, Dr Thomas Henry Newsam of Saundersfoot explained that the child had been poorly developed, 'because the milk in our area is not good'.[133] Anne Owens buried her twins in the sands at Swansea, and was imprisoned for a year, with hard labour, by the Glamorgan Assizes for concealment of birth. It was the second time she had committed the offence. In June 1838, Elizabeth Vaughan was given two months' hard labour, at the Pembrokeshire Assizes, having 'dropped and deserted her infant child on Trefgarne mountain, with intent that the child should perish for want of food'. The child was discovered by a stray cow, which attracted the attention of the farmer searching for the lost beast. Elizabeth gave a stark and simple explanation to the shocked court: 'I had no choice.'[134]

Infanticide was distressingly common in nineteenth-century Wales.

Justice George Hardinge, who condemned Mary Morgan to death for murdering her child at Presteigne in 1805, considered: 'in our part of Wales it is thought no crime to kill a bastard child. We had two cases, equally desperate.'[135] In 1815, Mary Howard of Churchstoke, charged with the wilful murder of her child, escaped from prison. Appeals for her arrest went unheeded, and the reward for her recapture remained unclaimed.[136] Juries in coroners' courts were forced to return verdicts of 'wilful murder against some person, or persons, unknown' in infanticide cases. Often, the desperate plight of the young, unmarried mother met with hearts of stone. In 1849, an inquest at Pentrefelin, Llandovery, heard that a servant girl on a farm in the remote mountain parish of Llandeilo'r-fân had given birth to a stillborn child at 4.00 a.m.: 'On being informed, the farmer ordered her off with the dead child in her arms, and she walked to a cottage in the hamlet of "Yscleidach" from which she was also ordered out ... Eventually a neighbour took her in.'[137]

Occasionally, children committed acts of shocking brutality against their parents. In 1813, in Abergavenny, Richard Glover and his wife were beaten to death by their son wielding a cart axle. Suspicion fell on the son when he cleared all his debts too swiftly following the murders.[138]

Love and Death

Love, one of the most powerful healing forces in Welsh society, also gave rise to hatred. Girls who spurned and scorned their former suitors placed themselves in great danger. John Insole of Merthyr Tydfil beat and kicked Mary Thomas to death when she ended their courtship in 1843.[139] In Welsh history, 1829 was the angry summer. Among reports of several ghastly murders is the death of Hannah Davies on Pencader mountain. The brief report given in the *Carmarthen Journal* does little to convey the sense of horror felt in the area:

> On Sunday last, on Pencader mountain, as some persons were going to a place of worship, they were horror-struck at finding, in a ravine in a small rill of water, the body of a young woman most frightfully mangled. The head was severed from the body, and was retained to the trunk by a small ligament – the chin had been detached from the upper part of the head, and rested in the chest – the right arm was nearly cut off, and various other wounds had been inflicted on the body, each of which of itself would have proved mortal. The water was crimson

with her blood for upwards of two miles. She appears to have made a desperate resistance, for her hands are covered with wounds.[140]

For his brutal crime of passion, David Jones was hanged in front of one of the largest crowds that ever gathered in Carmarthen.

Many murdered so that the result of their love would never be discovered. The strangled body of the heavily pregnant Margaret Williams was discovered in a marsh adjoining Cadoxton. The son of her master, a Neath farmer, was arrested.[141] Rees Thomas Rees, a lay preacher, was hanged for the murder of nineteen-year-old Elizabeth Jones of Llangadog. Rees had given Elizabeth a 'noxious drug' to terminate her pregnancy and save his good name.[142] John Evans of Glandulais, Breconshire, attempted the same course of action with the same tragic result for Margaret Williams in 1827.[143] Also at Brecon, David Edwards cut Gwenllian Morgan's throat in 1817, so that she could not give birth and shame him.[144] Not all murderers were caught; many lived with their guilt. In 1814, on his deathbed, James Jones of Monmouth confessed to the Revd Mr Sayer that he had murdered a girl carrying his unborn child twenty-seven years previously.[145]

Ménages à trois were frequently split asunder by all-consuming jealousy and greed. Thomas Evans, a highly respected shopkeeper of Castell Caereinion, Welshpool, was poisoned by his wife, Elizabeth, and their servant, Edward Rogers. The couple absconded with the profits of the mercer's shop to England. The dying Evans described Mrs Evans as 'well informed and well educated, respectable in appearance, with much of the manner and gait of a French woman', and Rogers as 'about five feet seven inches high, with black hair, deep frowning eyebrows, about twenty five years of age, and walks rather quick'. Despite the detailed descriptions, police never caught up with the fast-walking Rogers and his French-looking companion.[146] Similar cases occurred in Abergavenny in 1848, Holyhead in 1842 and Pembroke in 1863.[147] While 'in a jealous rage', William David murdered his wife's suspected lover at the Castle public house in Hirwaun in 1859. After a day's drinking, he became enraged when his wife declared that she planned to sleep with David and Ann Williams.[148]

Neighbours from Hell

People brought into households were also problematic. Several servants poisoned their master or mistress. Elizabeth Gibbs of Laugharne was charged with poisoning her mistress and a fellow servant in 1850.[149] An unnamed servant girl from Nantmel, Radnorshire, took such a strong dislike to her employer that she placed arsenic in her gin bottle. When she became ill, a doctor was summoned from Rhayader. After a tortuous and tiring ride from village to farm, the doctor asked for something to revive him. He was given gin and he too became ill. The servant girl absconded to Rhayader, where she finished the arsenic. Only the doctor survived.[150] Ann Jones, a widow of Gwnnwsmechan, Aberystwyth, was also poisoned by a servant in 1850.[151]

The frustrations and frictions of the workplace frequently boiled over into brutal, murderous assaults. Richard Jones (alias Dick of Forden) scythed through R. Gardner's head in a harvest field in Montgomeryshire, killing him instantly.[152] John Roberts of Llanddeiniolen, Caernarfonshire, also 'flew in a violent rage' in a harvest field. He killed a servant, severely wounded another and seriously injured a young girl.[153] At the Pembrokeshire Assizes in 1831, Captain Thomas Hewitt was charged with causing the brutal deaths of three men aboard the *Irene*. The three had been whipped to death with the 'cat o'nine tails' for breaches of ship discipline.[154] In 1818, Captain Rider was poisoned by his own crew on the journey from Manhattan to Britain. Both cases were sent from the Pembrokeshire Assizes to the Admiralty Court in London.[155] When a servant refused to carry out tasks on his new farm in 1831, at Llandeilo'r-fân, Breconshire, the outraged farmer kicked him to death.[156] Two years later, in Lampeter, Joseph Evans put a two-pronged manure drag through 'the tender part of David Jones's head'.[157] When farmer Josiah Evans of Llanboidy refused to give his labourer bread and cheese, John Hicks hit him with a hammer, instantly killing him.[158] Others were more subtle, but no less brutal, in their revenge. William Williams, a collier, fell fifteen fathoms to his death, after an unknown person cut through the rope of the lowering gear.[159] At Pembrey colliery, it was discovered that someone in November 1827 had cut away half the pillars supporting the coal face, in an attempt to endanger life.[160]

Welsh neighbourhoods endured vendettas of almost Sicilian proportions. George Harrison, a timber-valuer and surveyor, was shot in front of his wife in the Red Lion, Wrexham, by his mortal enemy George Thomas.[161] Evan Thomas of Llangynllo was dragged from his bed by Richard Brace, and beaten to death with a stone.[162] William Bevan threw a dog at Edward Thomas and eventually killed him in a fist fight.[163] William Owen murdered John Gunter, a poor shoemaker from Bryn Siriol, near Abergavenny, in revenge for a guinea paid by him two years previously in compensation for a stolen chicken.[164] Thomas Ebsworth, enraged that his daughter was courting his enemy James Davies, challenged him to a fight at Tinker's Hill, Amroth. Davies hit Ebsworth with a large stake, causing instant death.[165] Perhaps the worst Welsh feud was the age-long battle between the Lewis and Price families, of Llanafan Fawr, Breconshire, in which vengeance crossed generational divides with all the tragedy of the Montagues and Capulets. In 1784, following arguments over the suspected theft of sheep, Lewis Lewis junior strangled Thomas Price and his dog and threw the bodies into a local lake. Seven months later, Thomas Lewis, Lewis's brother, discovered Price's body under a foot of water. In a wild panic, he burnt the body and scattered the ashes over the garden. To save his own skin, Thomas gave evidence against his father and brother. Both Lewis Lewis senior and Lewis Lewis junior were hanged for the murder of Thomas Price. Over forty years later, in 1829, history repeated itself, not as farce but as tragedy. At almost exactly the same spot, Lewis Lewis, the grandson of the murderer, murdered John Price, the grandson of the murdered Thomas Price.[166]

Drink and Death

Drink played a prominent part in many brutal confrontations. Men and women drank with a desperate, addicted, quarrelsome single-mindedness. After a quarrel in the Ship Inn, Newport, Pembrokeshire, enraged locals broke in late at night, beat the landlord Jeremy Thomas and his wife to a pulp, and set fire to the pub.[167] In 1834, David Jonathan of Rhosmaen, Llandeilo, was beaten to death in broad daylight by four men, William Devereaux, William Hughes, James Richards and William Handoll, who had followed him from a local public house.[168] Somewhere in the argumentative small hours during a *cwrw bach* between Llanelli and Swansea, Thomas Martin stabbed John Williams to death, and Michael Leary beat Jenkin Evans to death with a shovel.[169] Three men who had been drinking with two others in the Navigation House, Crymlun, followed them home and literally beat their brains out.[170] A £20 reward was offered in 1837, for information leading to the capture of William John, a cooper. He was described as 'five feet seven inches tall with a dark complexion and forbidding countenance, but with an easy and plausible address'. John had allegedly beaten and stabbed a Bridgend publican, William Hopkins, so badly that his 'bowels protruded'.[171] On 28 October 1798, Richard Hodge, 'a fisherman of infamous bad character', went into the Beaufort Arms, Chester, quarrelled with Joseph Thomas, a sheriff's officer, and stabbed him to death.[172] Many of the Sabbath-black bars of Wales were the haunts of sawdust, spit, spilt liquor and blood. After a quarrel in the White Hart, Cilgerran, the publican John Bowen was mysteriously shot. John Thomas stabbed his fellow drinker Edmund Williams to death in the Castle Inn, Tredegar, in 1837.[173] In 1853, a constable, William Wines, was stabbed by John Davies, a Cardiff boatman. Davies was one of an estimated crowd of 100–200 boatmen and prostitutes trying to rescue a woman from PCs Taylor and Wines. The crowd had rushed out of the pubs and brothels of Whitmore Lane, reeking of beer, frustrated at the interruptions, and bent on beating someone senseless.[174] Welsh drinkers were often bored, bitter and pugnacious.[175] It was claimed that Wrexham beer was made from sheet music and boxing gloves, since it made people either sing or fight.

Violent People and Places

Manslaughter and murder were the most extreme and publicized acts of violence committed in Wales during these years. According to the traditional picture, Welsh society became more civil and civilized by the mid nineteenth century. Yet, the evidence from the police and coroners' courts opens a window on to a different, darker reality. Welsh society continued, until at least the late 1860s, to be brutish, and unsqueamish in its use of violence. Men and women alike turned naturally to assaulting those who in any way offended them. When the elderly Susannah Ryder of Llanymynach quarrelled with her daughter in 1846, she attacked her with a knife, stabbing her several times all over her body. Her daughter fainted. Susannah, believing her to be dead, dragged her into a nearby room, gave her a further beating and 'gwthiodd ysgybell i fyny i'w gwendid, er mwyn bod yn sicr ei bod wedi terfynu ei hoedl' (she pushed a broomstick up her vagina to ensure that she had terminated her life). Miraculously, the daughter survived the onslaught, and, even more incredibly, she forgave her mother.[176]

Certain areas acquired a fearful reputation for the ferocious behaviour of the inhabitants. The body of William Thomas was found on Swansea beach in 1826. The night before he had been very drunk and fighting with Robert Wood, alias Robin Hood, in a local pub.[177] In 1854, several cases of stabbing, theft and drunkenness occurred in Llanelli. Early that October, there 'were upwards of 150 sailing ships at anchor with crews of 800 or 900 at large and no body of police to exercise control'.[178] During his journey through the north, in the early nineteenth century, Edward Pugh noted the violent fighting between rival gangs, and the use of 'clubs, sticks and stones in a most ferocious manner' and recounted his own personal experience: 'I have even seen females enter the bout in defence of their brothers and even in the middle of rivers scuffle and contend with the robustest men'.[179] Amlwch, Blackwood, Caernarfon, Carmarthen, Haverfordwest, Llanelli, Newport, Milford, Swansea, Tremadog and Welshpool acquired a reputation for weekly bruising battles. In 1862, it was said that amongst 'wholescale warfare ... some questionable notoriety appears to be attaching itself to Blaenavon, from the variety and extent of its assault cases'.[180] From the late 1840s, Cardiff's Tiger Bay area became the Welsh capital of mayhem. On 23 August 1849, PC John Wilkes confided to a reporter the arrest of a prostitute, Jane Widdle, alias 'Lady Jane', and her pimp, John West, the arrest of 'two miserable looking wretches', John Morgan and John Harries, for theft, and the arrests of Nicholas Vipond of Albany, New York, and William Neville, also for theft. Towards the end of his shift, he encountered Thomas Alexander, 'a diminutive little fellow, about 3 foot 5 inches', engaged in riotous behaviour, at a local brothel. When PC Wilkes and fellow officers interfered, Alexander gave several of them a 'good thrashing' before being overpowered. The Welsh Napoleon, with his exaggerated machismo and extreme aggression, provided a fitting end to PC Wilkes's busy night.[181] Among the most vicious characters who trod the dark streets of Tiger Bay was John Ryan. One of his many appearances before the Cardiff Assizes was for a brutal assault on Susan Davies in 1852. He beat her in Betty Holliday's brothel in Charlotte Street, held her prisoner for two hours, followed her, beat and kicked her again, and finally tried to drown her in the canal. When he was eventually arrested, he attacked the police superintendent.[182] Border country villages were little better than the coastal towns, especially at fair time. Thomas Langelow, a prize fighter and a frequenter of fighting booths in fairs, was executed for beating, cutting and maiming John Green in an affray near Knighton.[183] Robert Jones, 'a notorious ruffian', of Bethesda, followed Rowland

Thomas out of the King's Arms and assaulted him. When police arrived to separate them, Jones attacked them. In court, it was reported that he had 'recently assaulted' Evan Thomas of Pant, Robert Ellis of Tregarth and 'very recently assaulted and abused a poor woman, the wife of a shoemaker at Pen-y-groes'.[184]

Wild ridings at weddings, old and new New Year's Day carousing and fighting, football on Shrove Tuesday and a host of other customs which often degenerated into open warfare survived until well into the 1860s. At Cardigan on the night of 31 December, a rabble from within and without the town, said goodbye to 1858 by throwing mud at houses, breaking windows, kicking in doors, lighting firecrackers and assaulting passers-by.[185] At Cefn fair, in Merthyr Tydfil in the late 1840s, workmen 'perambulated the streets, reeling, vomiting and quarrelling'. Three decades later, in 1872, at Twyn-y-Waun fair, near Dowlais, sons showed that they had inherited their fathers' bad behaviour.[186] The *Ceffyl Pren*, a crock horse used to punish society's enemies, still stalked the land.[187] In 1864 'unpleasant rumours about a married man' in the seaside area of Llanelli saw the horrific appearance of the *Ceffyl Pren*. The man was given a severe beating and, to the accompaniment of beating drums, firing guns and rockets, was paraded around the neighbourhood.[188] In Rhayader in 1839, the *Ceffyl Pren* punished a woman for her alleged unchastity and infidelity.[189]

Animal Maiming, Arson and Aliens

Welsh society often vented its anger at its enemies in vicious ways. In 1833, Evan Evans was imprisoned for six months with hard labour for wounding a mare of John Davies.[190] Four years later, John Harrby did the same to Thomas Williams's heifer.[191] In 1860, Evan Jones, a haulier, 'a brute in human form', was caught mutilating a valuable horse in the stable of a Merthyr Tydfil ironworks.[192] In 1812, 'some wicked and malicious person or persons, or rather monsters in human shape, entered the stable . . . and savagely cut out the tongues of two valuable animals, one of them a mare in foal'.[193] The painful removal of cows' teats and the poisoning of pigs, dogs and game were part of the general conflict of the Rebecca Riots. Even when there was not an element of vengeance involved, people's treatment of animals in the nineteenth century was cruel. In 1866, Sarah Cook of Mill Sands,

Neath, was fined 11s. 6d. for beating her cat, throwing it on to a pile of stones and killing it.[194] In 1850, the *North Wales Chronicle* reported a two-hour dolphin killing spree near Bangor.[195] For fun, people would tie two cats together by their tails and drape them over a stile, before provoking and torturing them.

When people could not exact revenge on an enemy's animals, they turned to their property. Alfred Adams and John Ogden were imprisoned for twelve months with hard labour for setting fire to a haystack at Newtown.[196] In 1862, Thomas Symington was imprisoned for seven years for a similar offence at Coity.[197] In 1810, John Gough lost £200 worth of farm buildings in Newtown at about the same time as a clothing factory was disappearing in flames nearby.[198] In 1819, the locality of Llanmilo was lit at night with the flickering lights of several burning hayricks.[199] Arson was the most dramatic, despised and dreaded method of destroying property. Others took a subtler, perhaps crueller form of inflicting harm on an enemy. Steven Davies of Llanfyrnach diverted the course of a stream so that water no longer flowed over the land of his neighbour John Davies.[200]

If the Welsh were violent towards their fellow countrymen, women and children, they were even more brutal to foreigners. The Irish were heartily loathed. In 1852, two labourers kicked an Irishman to death outside the Black Bull in Merthyr Tydfil. They claimed they were too drunk to remember anything, but showed no remorse. Riotous battles between the Irish and the Welsh occurred frequently in Cardiff, Newport and Swansea. At Ferryside and Bancynfelin in 1851, Irish navvies were driven from their homes. There were similar attacks on Irish and English communities in Amlwch, Aberystwyth, Pyle, Llantrisant, Nant-y-glo and Brynsiencyn.[201] The success of Swansea as a port drew a large contingent of Greek sailors to the town's waterfront. Assaults on Greeks became so common that the town's newspaper, *The Cambrian*, had a special column entitled 'Beating a Greek'. In 1853, Moses Williams seriously assaulted a Greek while his prostitute, Ann Jones, robbed the battered seaman.[202]

Brutality and violence were common throughout society. Because his sexual activities were disturbing the entire household, one man's ears were nailed to the boards of the kitchen table as a warning.[203] In 1839, in order to make a man 'dance home', guns were fired at his feet all the way from Cwmdwyfran to Carmarthen. In 1834, a writer to the *Cardiff and Merthyr Guardian* stated that:

> The way-faring traveller passes the scene of outrages of sin bordering on murder, in silence and fear; no sound escapes his pale lips, no gesture indicates the tragedy of which he is a witness; for all that he sees is a living proof that, from Dowlais to Abergavenny, to him there is no law.[204]

Similar voices were heard further west. Following a spate of arson attacks in the Ystradmeurig area, it was said that:

> the country is become so lawless, that no officer dare approach them without running the risk of losing his life, but if it were possible to get a troop of horse, I would undertake to unkennel every Caitiff of them and effectively end their future depredations.[205]

On several occasions in the period 1776–1871, 'society seemed to sink down to subconscious regions where it made contact with an older civilization that knew only the tribal law'.[206] People often justified their breach of unpopular criminal and civil laws, by claiming that they were obeying the dictates of an older customary or moral law. The game laws, like the enclosure Acts, were detested because they conferred on the gentry a monopoly on game which was considered both selfish and unfair. It was widely regarded as the birthright of the freeborn Welshman that he could hunt the lands and harvest the waters of Wales. Poaching was therefore undertaken with a free conscience, since both poachers and the wider community regarded shooting rabbits and pheasants, and the capture of salmon, sewin and trout, as a legitimate, customary right of the people.[207] Breaching the game laws is a consistent feature in the criminal history of Wales.[208] At certain times and in certain places, prosecutions under the Fisheries and Game Acts reached epidemic proportions. The Denbigh magistrates asked for powers of summary arrest in January 1862 in order to cope with the 'infernal poachers' who infested the area.[209] The banks of the Tywi and Teifi were frequently scenes of epic battles between gamekeepers and poachers during the heyday of the Rebecca troubles, 1839–43. In the 1860s, PC Evans of Pennal confided to his diary that he was powerless to act against a number of notorious poachers in his area. Unlike the poachers, he operated without the full support of the local inhabitants.

Perhaps the most troublesome area for the authorities was the Cwmdeuddwr–Rhayader region in 1839–43, 1856–8, 1866–8 and 1875–81.[210] In years of abundant salmon, the authorities tolerated the incursions of poachers into their harvest, but when stocks declined, tensions mounted and clashes between game stealer and gamekeeper intensified. The night of 22–3 December 1866 witnessed a famous, indeed infamous, clash which still registers in local legend. On that windy winter's night, the snow lay deep and crisp and uneven as ten water-bailiffs confronted twenty to thirty poachers, near a ford on the river Ithon.[211] The poachers fled into a neighbouring field where they formed a square, one side of which was armed with spears. All the poachers wore grotesque disguises; one had a large quantity of straw wrapped around his hat and on the front of it was a cock's head. Another had a false hump-back made of straw. Some were dressed in classic rural protestor's garb – a wife's petticoats, smocks and mackintoshes. Despite the arms and their ferocious cries – 'like a lot of Indians' – three were apprehended and were brought before the Penybont Petty Session Court. Although they were released on a technicality, such was the resentment of the authorities that they arranged a rigged retrial in 1876, following which the three were imprisoned.

Poaching often involved almost entire communities. In February 1782, George Reed wrote from Llanerfyl to complain that: 'Parson Worthington has been continually coursing in this neighbourhood since his Lordship left the hills in a very ungenteel poaching manner and has by all accounts killed a hundred and fifty hares'.[212] The major poacher in the Beaumaris area in the 1860s was the Revd Henry Harries Davies. Some people undoubtedly made a reasonable living from their depredations. Every night, until their capture in 1857, Jonah John, William Owen and William Watkins set almost a hundred snares on a rabbit warren at Laugharne and sold their catch in local markets.[213]

Smuggling and Wrecking

Smuggling was another activity which attracted widespread community support and sanction. Exorbitant 'English' duties were considered an unjustified, and unjustifiable, burden on the pleasures of the Welsh. In the late eighteenth century, virtually every Welsh coastal community was actively engaged in smuggling brandy, rum, lace, silk and tobacco. In the Cardiff area in the 1830s, female smugglers specialized in concealing dutiable goods under their clothing, and often disguised illicit cargoes of lace, silk and even stays as advanced pregnancy.[214] The gentry actively supported and participated in

smuggling activities. In 1795, a large quantity of wine intended for the
local gentry was confiscated by the Revenue, and impounded in the
great barn at Talacre. During the night, scores of Mostyn colliers
captured the Revenue officers and carried away the wine. The officers
observed that many of the supposed colliers had diamond rings on
their fingers and wore fine linen beneath their homespun.[215] In 1805,
the Pembrokeshire Sea Fencibles discovered a secret store of illicit rum
and vodka. Rather than complete the cumbersome reporting proced-
ures, the captain ordered that they should drink the evidence. For
hours, vodka flowed like the Don, though less quietly. In order to
prevent such behaviour, coastguards and excise officers were predominantly people from outside the area. At New Quay in 1851, the Excise
officers comprised Irish and English people but no locals.[216]

Smuggling was a highly professional and profitable enterprise and
was undertaken on a substantial scale. In 1821, the coal-carrying
schooner *William-Henry* from Swansea was seized on her way to
Ireland, on suspicion of being a smuggler. When examined, she was
discovered to have a false deck, keel and bottom, in the former of
which eight tons of tobacco had been artfully concealed. The captain
and crew escaped when they reached port.[217] Three years later, *The
Swallow*, a Revenue cutter, gave chase to a large smuggling lugger off
Cardigan. Although the chase lasted six hours, the lugger saw the
Revenue ship off by superior sailing.[218] Others were less skilful.
Captain William Morgan of the *Amelia* was caught in possession of
five gallons of brandy. His defence, that it was intended for his sick
wife, met with little sympathy.[219] Henry Bennett, who captained the
slave ships *Favourite* and *John* in the 1790s, supplemented his income,
with a profitable sideline in smuggling contraband tobacco and liquor
on the return journey from the West Indies.[220]

When the wind wuthered, Welsh people's thoughts were with those
in peril on the sea, not so much from a desire to offer assistance, but
rather to despoil and plunder wrecks. In November 1843, when a
packet got in difficulties in Cardigan Bay, the crew and travellers clung
to the rigging in an attempt to save themselves. Local people offered
no assistance, being too busy carrying off goods that were washed up
with the bones and driftwood of the wreckage.[221] During that terrible
storm, the wreck of the *Mary Hughes* was plundered at New Quay, the
Margaret and Ann pillaged at Cardigan and the *Margaretta* was picked
clean at Barmouth. The Revd W. Davies, a local minister, condemned
the brutes who carried off goods at Mwnt and Ferwig. In 1832, a

writer from Holyhead lamented the sad fate of a Captain Stainner
who had been washed overboard. A solid gold watch, a solid gold
chain and a considerable sum in sovereigns were stolen from his body.
The author concluded: 'it is hoped that the perpetrators of so
shameful a robbery will yet be discovered'.[222] In 1835, the authorities
were powerless to prevent the local country people from attacking the
wreck of the *Silas Richards*:

> They broke open some of the rum puncheons and drank to such an excess that
> one man died in consequence. A great deal of the property would have no doubt
> been pilfered, had it not been for the strenuous exertions of several respectable
> individuals.[223]

In 1829, there were no 'respectable individuals' to offer assistance to
the stricken ship, the *George*, in Swansea harbour:

> Seven or eight fellows . . . got into their possession a jar of whiskey of which
> they drank so freely, as to be totally incapable . . . and two of them were in such
> a shocking state of drunkenness, that they were obliged to be handed up from
> the hold by ropes. In this beastly condition, they were carried on ladders to their
> respective houses, where they became so alarmingly ill that medical advice was
> deemed necessary, and to save the fellows' lives, the gentleman who attended was
> obliged to eject the liquor they had drunk by means of a stomach pump.[224]

In 1816, *The Cambrian* regretted to report that the *Teresa*, a 'West
Indiaman', was wrecked on the Glamorgan coast on Christmas Day:

> It really is horrible to reflect that at the moment when distressed and
> shipwrecked mariners have every claim to the appropriate exertions and assist-
> ance of their fellow creatures on shore, the latter appear wholly animated by the
> desire of plunder and robbery.[225]

Compassionate people who offered assistance to distressed
mariners, and who sought to safeguard wreckages, found themselves in
bruising contests with the 'country people' and 'peasants', who
considered material washed from the sea 'their God-send'. In 1817,
John Brown, solicitor to Lord Cawdor, rode sabre-drawn to protect the
Norwegian brig *Bergetta*, which had been stranded all-hands-lost on
the treacherous Cefn Sidan sands. He was immediately surrounded by
crowds of wreckers who cried 'kill him, kill him'. Others beat him with
staves stripped from the crates that had washed upon the shore.[226] In
1820, it was only the 'soldierly conduct of the Swansea Cavalry' that
prevented the *Bounty Hall* from being despoiled by local people.[227]
The wreck of *The Eclipse* of Liverpool in 1817 was robbed even
though a number of special constables had been sworn in to protect

her.[228] In revenge against Colonel Jones of Llanina, Cardiganshire, a justice of the peace who had sworn in the specials, four men dressed in sailor's uniforms stolen from a wreck broke into his house late at night armed with pistols. They eventually escaped when the colonel's butler used his firearm. In Llan-non, Cardiganshire, in 1806, twenty-three excise officers were attacked by a baying mob of hundreds. In the same month, the Yeomanry Cavalry fought hard to protect the wreck of the *Resolution* at St David's.[229] At Beaumaris, in 1772, the authorities asked for the services of a man-of-war to protect shipping from smugglers and wreckers.

Wrecks were the scenes of wild, reckless abandon and the source of considerable profit for some. The people of Marloes were described as 'a determined set of villains'. One Pembrokeshire parson described his parish as a 'nest of smugglers, cattle-stealers, idlers, with every sort of immorality rife in it'.[230] In the 1840s, in the Kidwelly region, 'Dynion y Bwyelli Bach' (the men of the little axes) were alleged to still use lights to lure unsuspecting ships onto the rocks. The legend of the wreckers of Dunraven Castle was perpetuated by one of the most popular songs of Victorian Wales, 'Brad Dynrafon'. The song reaches a dramatic climax. The cruel wrecker, who had drawn a ship onto the rocks with his false lights, while robbing a body washed onto shore turned it over only to see his dead son's face. It was a moment of perdition, poetic justice in song.[231]

Disobedience towards Authority

The forces of law and order battled bravely in the early nineteenth century to control an ungovernable people but were often ineffective in their efforts. In 1833, when the Pembrokeshire police attempted to arrest Henry Gwyther, his wife Anne stabbed and wounded a constable.[232] Prendergast, on the outskirts of Haverfordwest, was a no-go area for the authorities until well into the nineteenth century. When the authorities tried to arrest William White, a butcher, for debt, local women threatened to murder the man who had brought the charges and promised the bailiffs 'that their bones should be carried home in bags'. A second attempt by six special bailiffs also ended in failure.[233] The inept and unprofessional police were supplemented by special constables drawn from trusted local people and professional bounty hunters. Daniel Evans and John Gayton of Newport, William Phillips,

Henry Crowe and Richard Lewis of Tredegar, and David Jones of Pontypool were a small, but dedicated, crew of professional bounty hunters who captured runaway Chartists after the 1839 rising, and received rewards totalling over £1,000.[234]

Even when the authorities succeeded in apprehending miscreants, prisons often proved incapable of containing them. Two prisoners in Swansea jail, Phillips and O'Connor, succeeded in freeing themselves from their leg irons and their cell door 'by means of a file and pick lock which had been given to them by another prisoner whilst in church. Although debtors raised the alarm, the pair escaped.'[235] In 1835, John Jones, alias Shoni Coal Tar, and William Jenkins, 'incorrigible and depraved characters', who were imprisoned for intimidating behaviour in a 'Scotch Cattle outrage' at Bedwellty, made a rope out of bedding, escaped onto the gallows and over the prison wall.[236] In 1832, a girl imprisoned for robbing Miss Rose of Swansea escaped down a ladder made from bedding.[237] On 26 May 1827, four prisoners simply walked out of Usk jail. Although one of them was later recaptured in Brecon, the other three never darkened the prison's doors again. Brecon jail in the 1820s was so poorly controlled that it was virtually an open prison. In 1829, five prisoners escaped. Four years later, William Salt and John Hart opened four locked doors and escaped.[238]

The authorities in remote rural areas had serious problems transporting prisoners to jail and court. At least twenty-three of the prisoners sentenced by the Radnorshire Assizes to transportation to Australia escaped during their transfer to the hulks and ports. In 1832, the *Carmarthen Journal* reported 'the happy march' of a warden and seven prisoners, all thieves, 'along the most wild and solitary road in the Principality' from Dolgellau jail to the Assizes at Bala. They arrived without irons or handcuffs, for the capable warden had provided 'copious drafts of *cwrw da* for the journey'.[239] Not all prisoners crawled so willingly, if drunkenly, to court. In 1832, the terrible trio with the unlikely surname, Smith – Henry, William and John – 'an unbelievably dissipated crew', were charged with 'a conspiracy to defeat the ends of public justice in getting a witness out of the way to prevent his giving evidence'.[240] At Wrexham, the trial of John Jones was abandoned when the main prosecution witness mysteriously fell out of a window and broke his jaw. Jones's friends were alleged to have assisted the witness's exit. Local people in Neath raised money to free the penniless William Davies, alias Slanton, 'this ornament of society', from jail for assaulting Matthew Whittington, a special constable. The 'local pot-houses celebrated his return to freedom into the early hours'.[241]

Cynicism towards the law was widespread. Welsh juries were notorious for the unconventional, perhaps illegal, verdicts that they reached.[242] In 1811, David Thomas of Llanelli was acquitted on charges of having murdered his wife because the jurors did not believe 'the blows he gave her would have killed her'.[243] Radnorshire juries were notorious for acquitting people, despite the evidence. At the Glamorgan Assizes in January 1866, seventy-six prisoners were due to appear: 'but to the astonishment of the chairman and others in the Court, the Grand Jury ignored about half the calendar'.[244] In 1843, John Davies wrote to a fellow lawyer that: 'In my opinion it is a complete mockery of Justice to place such a set of men in a Jury Box as there were at Brecon. I am sure one of those who tried your case was nearly drunk, and slept all the time the Chairman was summing up.'[245]

In 1843, Margaret Howells of Llanon, Carmarthenshire, who was obviously nastier than she looked, was convicted of murdering her two new-born bastard boys, by throwing them down a pit. The jury, however, acquitted her, and being asked afterwards to account for their verdict explained 'how could we do otherwise, when the new Poor Law acts so hardly against the poor woman?' A Pembrokeshire jury reached the remarkable verdict: 'not guilty, my Lord, but he must not do it again'.[246] A Caernarfonshire jury laughed at the judge's summing up and decided that an obviously guilty prisoner should walk free. In 1827, the judge at the Glamorgan Assizes expressed his disgust that the jury had reached the verdict of 'guilty of forgery and uttering base coin but not with an intent to defraud'. In 1877, a writer to the *Cornhill Magazine* recounted the story of an eminent Welsh judge remarking as his hounds overtook a hare: 'By God, even a Cardiganshire jury can't save her now'.[247]

Such attitudes showed that many Welsh people were resentful of, not respectful to, the law. There was a perception, popularized in Twm o'r Nant's *anterliwtiau*, that the law was framed and enforced by those with the power to cajole and coerce the people.[248] It was a common preconception that there was one law for the rich and another for the poor. In February 1864, a Chepstow publican complained to the magistrates that he was being victimized. Turning to the police in court, he said: 'If you went to the Beaufort Arms and found Squire Currie there, you would say nothing about it.'[249] The protection of property was one of the central aspects of the development of the law by the 1770s.[250] The game laws which restricted hunting to squires were the most hated aspect of this. Under an Act of 1770, nocturnal poachers were liable to six months' imprisonment. Another Act of 1803 prescribed death for poachers who resisted arrest with arms, while an Act in 1816 recommended transportation even for an unarmed man caught with a net. Crimes especially damaging to capitalism were punished with exemplary severity. Coiners and forgers were shown no mercy, for they endangered the system of credit from top to toe.[251] John Greenwood was hanged in Merionethshire in May 1812 for minting base coin.[252] In a desperate, but futile, attempt to save himself from the gallows, William Baines offered to share with the authorities the secrets of his printing press at St Clears which had produced superb-quality forgeries of Bank of England notes.[253] In order to safeguard the rapidly increasing industrial and commercial wealth, a whole new raft of legislation was passed. By the time of the general (anti-) Combination Acts of 1799 and 1800, over forty Acts were already on the statute book, forbidding combinations to raise wages. Thefts of coal and minor and major items from the works were increasingly punished by dismissal and imprisonment.

Riot, Rising and Revolt

Vicious, violent conduct was a constant and consistent feature in Welsh society in rural and urban areas. The people of Nefyn, in the strikingly beautiful Llŷn peninsula, according to the Revd William Jones in 1847: 'are in the most wretched condition that I have seen, for insubordination, disorder and ignorance – disorder in the most comprehensive sense of the word'.[254] At the other end of the country, in the more populous Pontypool, the people were described as being in the same condition. Dr Phillips, in the same report, stated that 'it is impossible to think of the social and political conduct of the people without alarm'.[255]

On occasion, that alarm was even greater, for the authorities of Wales were acutely aware that unsettled elements and propagandists could stoke the anger of the people into the open fires of riot, rebellion, revolt and rising.[256] Times of crisis were times of deep anxiety for the authorities who feared that their grip on society was being loosened. The 1790s were a decade of exceptional stress for officials. The legitimacy of the law was openly and violently contested.

People had long been opposed to enforced service in the militia. In 1779, mobilization in Merionethshire led to riots in which 300 to 400 people so abused the magistrates and deputy lieutenants that they were unwilling to raise the militia without the assistance of regular troops to pacify the baying crowds. The Navy Act of 5 March 1795 and the Act of 11 November 1796, for augmenting the militia, led to riots at Denbigh in April 1795,[257] and in Carmarthenshire, Merionethshire and Flintshire in November and December 1796. Heightening the sense of crisis were severe food shortages throughout Wales in this decade of pain, panic and paranoia.[258] Many people were incensed that profiteers were achieving considerable profits in times of scarcity. Between 1793 and 1795, there were riots in Swansea, Bangor, Aberystwyth, Dolgellau, Denbigh, Fishguard, Bridgend and Haverfordwest. In 1795–6, riots and protests at corn and food prices occurred in Barmouth and Machynlleth. In 1799–1800, there were other violent responses to grain shortages in Merthyr Tydfil, in many villages in Pembrokeshire, and several places in mid and north Wales.[259] In Merthyr Tydfil in September 1800, two rioters were hanged as a warning against further large-scale damage to property.[260] That women were often in the vanguard of protest during corn riots indicates that these were affairs of life and death, for without food no community can survive. At Haverfordwest on 18 August 1795, at Hay on 23 August 1795, at Swansea in February 1793 and at Beaufort in March 1800, women were prominent participants in food riots. The opinionated diarist John Bird noted at Swansea on Monday, 20 April 1801:

> About four o'clock in the afternoon a number of poor women with two Common Girls of the town at their head assembled and paraded the streets, and being joined by a number of poor children whom the women encouraged to Holler and Scream, the whole body proceeded to a Corn Warehouse, in which was a large quantity of Barley belonging to Messrs Grove and Co., and forced open the door.

The arrival of the Cardigan militia prevented the looting of Messrs Grove and Co.'s property, and the brawny, brawling women dispersed. After a brief period in the 'friendly custody' of the Swansea Independent Volunteers, the two prostitute ringleaders were permitted to escape.[261]

The authorities' alarm and fears were heightened by highly politicized and seditious outbursts across Wales.[262] In 1793, the copper workers of Llangyfelach, Swansea, warned in a petition protesting against their condition: 'Unless you seek our God we seek your own Destruction and put us all in the same state as France',[263] and in June 1800, John Phillips of Llangefni, Anglesey, declared: 'I am a Jacobin and a Republican and know a Republican Government will be a much better one than the present, and I'll lay a wager that there will not be a Crowned Head in Europe in three years time and that there will soon be a change in Government.'[264]

At a *cwrw bach* in Brechfa, Carmarthenshire, in March 1801, seditious songs against 'Vile George' were rousingly sung.[265] The small rural community of Llanbryn-mair, where Yr Hen Gapel was a forcing-house of Independent traditions and belief in the rights of the people, was a veritable hotbed of sedition.[266] In the mid-1790s, a local farmer, John Ellis, told his fellow farmers and labourers: 'The poor are oppressed by the Rich and we are determined to have another government, and it is not in the power of the gentlemen of the county to prevent it if they do, it shall be blood for blood'.[267]

Hugh Jones, in his *Hymnau Newyddion ac Ychydig Benhillion ar yr Amserau*, voiced the people's desires into song: 'O tyn y gorchudd yn y mynydd hyn; / Llewyrchied Haul Cyfiawnder Gwyn . . .'[268] ('O lift the covers from this mountain; / Let the sun of blessed justice shine . . .'). The message burst like bright sunlight onto the minds of its readers. William Jones of Llangadfan, Ezekiel Hughes, George Roberts and Edward Bebb of Llanbryn-mair also added to the millenarian attempts to raise the curtain onto a new order. When their ideals confronted the bitter reality of repression by authorities, their energies were transferred into the creation of a new Cambria in America.[269] William Jones was particularly active in organizing his fellow farmers on the harrowed hills of Montgomeryshire to seek a new future in Madog's land.[270] In Denbighshire, John Jones, Jac Glan-y-gors (1766–1821), was widely considered to be 'Tom Paine's Denbighshire Henchman'. Jones expounded and expanded the principles propounded by Tom Paine in *The Rights of Man*, in two remarkable works, *Seren Tan Gwmwl* (1795) and *Toriad y Dydd* (1797).[271] Like Hugh Hughes, Jones believed that a new dawn of religious and political freedom was about to break. The ordinary people were praised as honest toilers who worked the land, while the aristocracy were parasites – a 'seraglio of males', existing only for their lazy pleasure. Jones also derived great enjoyment from satirizing the Hanoverian kings of England, their German origin and the lunacy of George III.[272]

The outpourings of these 'organic intellectuals' were amplified by
the influential works of a remarkable group of London Welshmen.
Notable among them was Dr Richard Price, who published an agenda
for freedom, *Observations on Civil Liberty*. [273] Price argued that sover-
eignty was vested in the people, and that the king and ministers were
responsible to them. Even more radical was David Williams, a friend
of Benjamin Franklin and author of *Letters on Political Liberty*.
Written in support of the Americans, it argued on behalf of principles
such as universal manhood suffrage, a cause taken up later in the 1830s
by the Chartists. In this ferment, Dissenting ministers were influential.[274] Dissenters had a profound sense of aggrievement and
persecution. Even after the repeal of the Test Acts they continued to
suffer under disabilities which curtailed their freedoms and ability to
worship as they wished. Thomas Evans, Tomos Glyn Cothi, 'Priestley
bach', the impassioned freedom-fighting minister, was imprisoned in
Carmarthen jail, in 1803, for his alleged sedition.[275]

The 1830s were an even more troubled decade than the heady *fin de
siècle* of the 1790s. Serious economic crises which had caused the
disturbances of 1816, the Scotch Cattle activities in Glamorgan and
Monmouthshire, disorder amongst the unemployed weavers of
Glansevern and Newtown and rioting by the colliers of Ruabon
provided the background to the clarion calls for parliamentary reform.
Carmarthen, still one of Wales's largest towns and enchained in a
tradition of political violence, saw the first disturbances in April
1831.[276] But the most remarkable events were those which characterized 'The Merthyr Rising'. Since 1829, depression in the iron trade
had led to a decrease in iron production and a reduction in wages. As
debts grew, credit at local shops evaporated and people starved. The
Court of Requests, established in 1809 to deal with debtors, became
increasingly busy. Mass meetings of workers called for the abolition of
the hated trust Acts and greater rights for workers to enable them to
cooperate to defend wages. People's hopes were encompassed in the
magic term 'Reform'. A reformed parliament, it was widely believed,
would address the injustices suffered by workers. When bailiffs of the
Court of Requests tried to distrain on the property of Lewis Lewis,
Lewsyn yr Heliwr, in June, an insurrection began. Merthyr Tydfil was
held by the workers who went from house to house restoring goods
taken by the Court of Requests to their former owners. The magistrates sent for the Argyll and Sutherland Highlanders from Brecon. In
front of the Castle Hotel, troops and workers clashed. Troops opened

fire, killing twenty-six people. Of the sixteen soldiers injured, six were badly wounded. Although the government sent in further troops, the workers held the town for six days.

Reprisal was swift. Twenty-eight miners, colliers, artisans and labourers were brought to trial for raiding houses, violence or seizing arms. Two men, Lewis Lewis, Lewsyn yr Heliwr and Richard Lewis, Dic Penderyn, were sentenced to death. Lewis Lewis's sentence was commuted to transportation. Richard Lewis, despite his protestations and considerable evidence of his innocence, was hanged at Cardiff jail in August 1831. His last words: 'O Arglwydd! Dyma gamwedd!' (O Lord, this is iniquity) echoed out across the assembled crowd. By October, the men and women who had continued their strike were starved back to work. The Reform Act, when it came in 1832, brought only a slight extension to the franchise.[277] The people's hopes had turned into heartbreak.

Another occasion of high drama, one of those moments when history accelerates and expands, was experienced in November 1839 when thousands of Chartists marched on Newport. Their aim was an extension of political democracy for men, all of whom should be allowed to vote for annual parliaments. The movement commenced in 1836, at Carmarthen, under the influence of Hugh Williams, and gathered force in the cloth and flannel manufactures of mid-Wales. There, in 1838, between 3,000 and 5,000 people met in one of the first Chartist mass demonstrations.[278] When the Charter was refused by Parliament in 1839, moderate leaders who argued for moral persuasion were swept aside by those who advocated the use of physical force. In November, three groups of demonstrators arranged to converge on Newport – from Blackwood under the leadership of John Frost, from Ebbw Vale under Zephaniah Williams and from Pontypool under William Jones. Hysteria hung over the town like thunder. George Shell, a nineteen-year-old cabinet-maker, captured the drama and anticipation in a letter to his parents: 'I shall this night be engaged in a struggle for freedom, and should it please God to spare my life, I shall see you soon.' On this fateful, stormy night, William Jones's group failed to make the rendezvous at Risca. The other demonstrators reached Newport drenched and demoralized. It was a scene of damp and drizzly pathos. The Chartist force was not outnumbered, but was outpositioned and outgunned, in a lopsided downhill assault, and intimidated nightmarishly by soldiers who sent coolly aimed volleys of gunfire into their ranks from the Westgate

Hotel. The mob shot at the musketeers, but the musketeers shot at the
mob with deadly efficiency. Thomas Davies, a special constable
stationed in the hotel, described the scene as 'dreadful beyond
expression – the groans of the dying, the shrieks of the wounded, the
pallid ghostly countenances and the bloodshot eyes of the dead in
addition to the shattered windows, and passages knee-deep in gore'.[279]
After twenty-five minutes of battle the crowd fled, leaving at least
twenty-two dead. When the dust settled, the leaders were betrayed,
arrested, tried and transported to Australia.[280]

In 1839, all was disquiet on the western front, for the year was also
climacteric in the rebellious history of west Wales. Discontent dislocated the social history of the three western counties of
Carmarthenshire, Cardiganshire and Pembrokeshire for most of the
late eighteenth and early nineteenth centuries. The corn and food riots
of the 1790s were followed by bitter protests against the enclosure
Acts. In the Mynydd Bach area of Cardiganshire, the inhabitants
waged 'Rhyfel y Sais Bach' (the War of the Little Englishman) in the
1820s against an Englishman, Augustus Brackenbury, who had
purchased the previously common land after an enclosure sale. He was
warned three times. Twice he ignored the warnings. Three times his
property was burnt.[281] The three counties were the hunting ground of
the *Ceffyl Pren*, which meted out severe punishment to society's
enemies.[282] The Rebecca movement advanced this tradition of protest
into an astute political movement in which the Carmarthen Chartist
and solicitor, Hugh Williams, was influential. Rebecca, this
remarkable leader, voiced the frustrations of the poor and disadvantaged. Although west Wales had lost large numbers of people through
migration, the area still contained too many people for the available
resources. The area resembled 'bowlen o gawl wedi ei amgylchynu a
gormod o lwyau' (a bowl of broth surrounded by too many spoons).
The unholy trinity of Poor Laws, tithe and road tolls took most of the
little cash that farmers had. Denied a harvest of happiness, they
reaped the grapes of wrath. Squeezed on all sides, the community
exploded in January 1839, not in an attack on the tollgates, but by
burning Narberth workhouse. Destruction of the tollgates followed on
13 May, when the gate at Efailwen was destroyed. When it was re-
erected, Rebecca and her daughters destroyed it a second time.

During 1839 some forty incidents, ranging from assaulting bailiffs,
attacking police officers, burning workhouses, destroying gates, tearing
down hedges that enclosed fields, beating and intimidating witnesses,

burning and damaging farms, can be attributed to the Rebeccaites. Then, there was a lull, until the violence began again in 1842, with the destruction of several gates owned by the Whitland Trust. In 1842, fourteen incidents were attributed to Rebecca. The year 1843 was one of anarchy, with 263 reported acts of violence and vengeance. One of the most notable occurred in June 1842, at Carmarthen, when over 300 horsemen, augmented by rioters from the town, ransacked the workhouse. At Hendy, rioters shot the elderly female gate-keeper. Thereafter, much of the popular sympathy evaporated with the gunsmoke, and two men, John Jones, Shoni Sguborfawr, and David Davies, Dai'r Cantwr, were hunted down, convicted and transported. Despite, or because of the destruction, Rebecca gained a sympathetic hearing for rural grievances in *The Times*, and a reduction in tolls from the newly established county road authorities.[283]

Tradition claims that, with the ending of the Rebecca movement, the riotous and rebellious behaviour of the Welsh ended, and Wales entered a new era of quiescence and quietude.[284] People prepared themselves for participation in the political process through becoming involved in the work of the Liberation Society and other organizations. Sense and sensibility, rather than anger and vengeance, now characterized the Welsh people.[285] But the ideal was not always reflected in reality. Collective bargaining by riot continued to be a marked feature of Welsh society until well into the 1870s. In September 1854, Rebecca sent a bilingual proclamation from 'my mountain fastness to my daughters':

Ie, Fy Anwyliaid! . . . mae yn debyg y bydd galw am fy ngwasanaeth i eto; gan hyny, taclwch eich Bustles, codwch eich Peisiau mewn parodrwydd, a'ch Boneti wedi eu trwsio! Mae Gormesiaith Eglwysig yn gwasgu ar fy mhobl. Codant eu llef am gyfiawnder, a chyfiawnder a attelir. Ni allaf droi y glust fyddar at apeliadau taerion fy mhobl . . . GWAE, GWAE, GWAE a fydd i'r rhai hynny a feiddiant ameu fy Awdurdod Oruchel, neu a anteriant i dynu arnynt fy anfodlonrwydd; canys byddant fel ûs o flaen y corwynt, ac fel sofl i dân.

Yes, My Darlings! – From information received, it is probable my services will soon be wanted again, so rig on your *Bustles*, get your *Petticoats* ready, and *Bonnets* trimmed! The arm of Oppression and Ecclesiastical Tyranny has been laid on my people. They cry for justice and that's withheld. I cannot turn a deaf ear to the appeals of my people . . . WOE, WOE, WOE be to them who would dare to dispute my Imperial Power with a high hand, or venture to incur my Royal displeasure; for they shall be as chaff before the whirlwind and as stubble to the fire.[286]

For a time in 1854, Pembrokeshire appeared to be relapsing into the excesses of 1843. Communities along the banks of the river Wye, especially Cwmdeuddwr and Rhayader, had never been free of the excesses. The years 1856–8, 1866–8 and 1875–81 were those of 'the Second Rebecca Riots'.[287] The coalfield of the north-east was frequently disturbed by unrestrained communal violence. In 1850, the colliers of Brymbo and Holywell expressed their industrial discontent through the destruction of houses and colliery property. More rioting took place in Denbighshire between 1852 and 1854, in Wrexham, Llangwstenyn, Holyhead and Acrefair during 1856,[288] in Ruabon in 1859, Mold in 1863, Mostyn in 1864, Halkyn and Mold in 1865, at Halkyn again in 1867 and Ruabon throughout most of March 1868.[289] In 1869, the police and the army failed to control a large crowd of protesting colliers near Mold railway station. Panic-stricken, the soldiers fired into the crowd. Four people were killed, one of them nineteen-year-old Margaret Younghusband from Chester, an innocent bystander.[290] The *annus mirabilis* of Welsh politics, the 1868 election, is set against a backdrop of mob violence. Riots took place in November 1868 at Abersychan, Blaenafon, Newport, Pontypool and

Unknown artist, *The Riot at Mold Flintshire, 1869* (National Library of Wales). The Mold Riot of June 1869 resulted in the army shooting four people. One of them, Margaret Younghusband, was an innocent bystander. North-east Wales was a storm-centre for violent protest throughout the 1850s and 1860s.

Tredegar. The Royal Welsh Fusiliers and hundreds of special constables clashed with a large force of rioters in Pontypool and forty-four people were arrested.[291] Following the riotous behaviour of the north-east, Karl Marx informed the Communist International that the area was fertile ground for a people's rising.

The Curious Absence of a Welsh Revolution

Marx was being uncharacteristically optimistic. Although the years 1776–1871 experienced a remarkable series of riots, rebellions and risings, Wales never, except in the wildest opium-fuelled dreams of the Welsh Jacobins of the 1790s, witnessed a revolution. Despite the fears of anxious authorities, popular anger never led to more than a rising. The political fabric – frequently torn and tattered – was never ripped to pieces. Battered and bruised, the old order kept its grip on power. Historians, trapped in hindsight, have frequently emphasized the revolutionary potential of the troubles and turbulence that tortured Welsh society. But 'Revolutionary Britannia' never ruled. In an 'age of revolutions', Britain was spared the upheavals that overthrew governments in continental Europe. Wales, supposedly a land of disenchanted, disloyal and seditious people, was also immune from this contagion. Why?

The answer to this deceptively simple, monosyllabic child's question is difficult. Protest was only one aspect of Welsh society. There was also a deeper, perhaps more persistent and consistent element of loyalty to King and country in Wales. For the one William Jones of Llangadfan, who preached sedition and the rights of man, there were three namesakes – William Jones, Y Fenni (1755–1821), William Jones, Gresford (1762–1846) and William Jones, Cynwyd (1764–1822) – who preached a gospel of duty and obedience. As Jesus had suffered during his earthly existence, so, too, they argued, should men shoulder their burdens and suffer in silence. Not all Welsh workers welcomed Tom Paine's *Rights of Man*. In Merthyr Tydfil, loyalist workers insulted Paine's name, by arranging the hob-nails on their boots to form the initials 'T.P.', which they trampled underfoot.[292] His effigy was burnt in Cardiff, Carmarthen, Llandovery and several other places. The burning of Paine's house was celebrated in a popular song raucously sung throughout Wales.[293] In Wrexham and Neath, on 6 December 1792, branches of the Association for the Preservation of Liberty and

Property against Republicans and Levellers were established. Others followed within a few days at Swansea, Kidwelly, Cardiff, most of the parishes of Flintshire, Carmarthen and St Clears. Declarations expressing loyalty were also sent to Parliament from Talgarth, Radnor, Presteigne, Beaumaris, Laugharne, Caernarfon and Cardiff. Throughout their campaign to secure greater rights for worship, Dissenters stressed that they too, though bitterly opposed to the Church, were loyal to crown and country. At a Bala meeting in June 1793, the ministers of the Independents denied that they were enemies to the King and crown, and appealed in those 'terrible times' to be allowed to prove their loyalty. Forty years later, the favourable reports in the journals *Seren Gomer* and *Y Greal* showed that the Non-conformists were still loyally devoted to all things royal. The Welsh were sychophantic if not superstitious in their king worship.[294]

People proved in several ways that they possessed considerable loyalty to royalty. The all-too-rare royal visits to Wales were greeted by hip-hip-hurrahing, flag-waving, joyous and jubilant crowds. In 1821, Hugh Hughes painted *The landing of George IV at Pembroke*. It must have been a major achievement to have steered the portly king through the crowds who packed the harbour walls as tightly as sardines in a tin. His coronation on 28 July 1821 was celebrated with the ringing of bells at Bangor, Brecon, Caernarfon, Cardiff, Wrexham, Milford and Machynlleth. At Carmarthen, hundreds of children paraded behind massed bands, while the corporation of Monmouth left the strenuous marching to others and treated themselves to a special celebratory dinner. After the king's return from Hanover in 1821, several Welsh corporations sent 'An Address to his Majesty upon his return to his Native country'. In July 1830, the townspeople of Carmarthen proved that devotion could switch between rulers with the speed of the announcement that 'the King is dead, long live the King', and opted not to mourn George IV, but celebrate William IV. At the town hall, 'the King's Health was drunk with all the rapturous enthusiasm which the toast is ever want to inspire in the loyal breasts of our countrymen'.[295]

The 'sailor king' proved to be highly popular with the Welsh people, a sturdy buttress against reformers. Royal rites of passage were marked with the pealing of church bells, feasts and festivities in all areas of Wales. The births of Princess Victoria and princes Edward and Albert were occasions of exceptional celebration from Anglesey to Amroth, and from Prestatyn to Penarth. The fact that five Welshmen achieved positions as royal doctors was a source of particular pride. Indeed, the only time that the Welsh were actively hostile to the monarch was during the 'Trial of Queen Caroline', in 1820. As in England, the majority in Wales supported 'the scandalous' Caroline's right to be enthroned and crowned alongside her husband George. In her support, house lights were lit across the country, church bells rung, bands marched and played, ballads were sung and crowds chanted 'Caroline dros fyth' (Caroline forever) and 'Buddugoliaeth Diniweidrwydd' (Victory to Innocence).[296] Such loyalty suggests that the people resembled Edmund Burke's 'cattle contentedly chewing the cud', rather than his more celebrated 'swinish multitude' of revolutionaries. Revolutions are usually initiated by minorities, but at some point they need the willing acquiescence and compliance of majorities. Although they came close on occasion, especially at one giddy moment in the 1830s, this they failed to win, not for want of trying, but because the governing classes proved themselves better at winning mass public support.

The propaganda distributed by Welsh Jacobins, freethinkers, seditionists, Chartists and Rebeccaites was countered by a barrage of 'conservative' counter-propaganda which was much greater in variety and volume, and had a deeper geographic and social penetration. Bonds of deference and respect were stronger than has been supposed. Charitable bequests and donations, philanthropic benevolence and generosity, all cemented relationships of loyalty between people. It was hard for people who received money for food, land to build a chapel, or any other gift, to visualize the giver as their enemy. Although they tried, the radicals and revolutionaries never succeeded in persuading people that benefactors were evil. There were two other features of the popular mind which protesters could not eliminate – indifference and force of habit. Most people were more committed to the daily task of keeping body and soul together than to the demands of a political cause. Personal survival was more important than political liberty. Habit was a powerful force which kept people, sometimes unwillingly and unwittingly, always firmly in their places. People were fearful of change and disruption; they could not envisage the practical implications of radical ideals and ideas. They could only tolerate gradual, evolutionary change rather than sudden, revolutionary transformations.[297] The revolutionary crisis of the 1790s was a libertarian and egalitarian force, but its result was probably and paradoxically a strengthening of the traditional position of the elites.

People were deeply committed to their current political and legal

system in several profound and powerful ways. They used the courts of
the legal system to gain redress for their grievances. Many of the debts
reclaimed by the Court of Requests in Merthyr Tydfil from 1806
onwards were those owed to petty tradesmen and small shopkeepers.
Those who slandered with Swansea fish-market scurrility found
themselves in court to answer to charges brought by people in the same
rank of society as themselves.[298] In 1847, the Cardigan small debts
court heard fifty-eight cases, and that at Haverfordwest adjudicated on
214 plaints, 'many of which were simple cases of goods sold and
delivered'.[299] Although the 'Laws', as Goldsmith's laconic monosyl-
lables stated, 'grind the poor, and rich men rule the law', the
not-so-rich also used the law to redress grievances. More significant,
perhaps, than the radical movements among workers was the initiative
to establish friendly societies. Far more working men affiliated and
associated with this movement than conspired and colluded with the
seditionists. By the 1850s, thousands had joined Welsh friendly
societies. The historian of friendly societies in Wales noted that
'friendly societies were recruiting a large proportion of the population
even at the beginning of the nineteenth century', and concluded that
such societies were not 'an institution mainly for an elite or aristocracy
of workers, whether agricultural or industrial'.[300]

This is not to say that people did not feel aggrieved by the iniquities
and inequalities which surrounded them in their daily lives. Their fears
and frustrations burst forth in the violent outbursts that disrupted
Welsh society during the years 1776–1871. But the protestors' aims
were direct, defensive and limited: corn rioters wanted bread and food
at old prices, workers wanted the restoration of long-standing wage-
rates, tollgate rioters wanted the clearing of old rights of way. The
people appealed to a traditional order, to be restored by society's traditional leaders. They wanted the magistrates to enforce regulatory
statutes on food, not to control the grain market themselves.[301] Even
the Chartists had no programme of revolutionary socialism, or even
democracy. Theirs was only partially a manifesto for modernity. They
wanted an extension of the franchise to adult males, one half of
society would still be excluded from their charter for a brave new
world. The head of state would continue to be unelected. The fears of
the authorities at the extent of the Chartist threat should not be under-
estimated. James Brown's letters give the impression that fear was
omnipresent in the south-east. He never ventured out except when
armed, and told Thomas Phillips that his 'house inside has the

appearance of a little barracks'. The dream of freedom and reform awoke the fear of authorities as to how the frustrated rage of the disinherited and outcast army could be contained and controlled. But in the end, the march on Newport was a poor, unlikely project nourished by whispers and swollen by fantasies of violence. It was an ill-planned, badly co-ordinated failure. It was over in a few hours, but the vengeance of the authorities, as John Frost later testified, lasted for months. It was not simply a Chartist failure, but a victory for the united front of the governing classes.

Riots in the 1860s, as in the 1790s, were dramatic and, like the best theatre, cathartic and finite. Many of the leaders involved were astute, able and brave individuals, but they too had a stake in society. They wanted the harsher elements of the political structure softened, but they did not seek its total destruction. David Williams, though declared an honorary French citizen, turned critic when liberty transformed itself into the tyranny of the September massacres of 1792. John Frost, the Chartist leader, was a justice of the peace, a Poor Law guardian and a former mayor of Newport. Hugh Williams, legal defender of the Rebeccaites and a leading figure in Welsh Chartism, was a prosperous lawyer in Carmarthen with offices in London, and the inheritor of substantial lands in St Clears. His son, William Arthur Glanmor Williams, was educated at Sandhurst, won the DSO with the South Wales Borderers and died a hero's death in the Boer War. Hugh Williams was one of several shadowy figures in the Rebecca movement, who became uneasy when the initiative passed from relatively respectable farmers to specialists in mayhem for money like John Jones, Shoni Sguborfawr. Williams and his colleagues wanted the amendment of the system to accommodate their needs, not anarchy. One of the most obvious reasons for the lack of revolution in Wales was that there were no revolutionaries to achieve it. There were plenty of angry young and old men who articulated the grievances created by an unjust and iniquitous system, but few developed a revolutionary ideology for its complete overthrow.

The diffuse, amateur, local, part-time but numerous men who governed proved remarkably resilient and responsive to the pressures that a new commercial, market-orientated, industrial economy and society produced. Power and prestige was concentrated in an elite, which shared a common education in the public schools and at Oxford or Cambridge, which was reinforced and reinvigorated through intermarriage. But it was not totally insulated from the currents that transformed society. New commercial, mercantile and industrial wealth and interests were absorbed and accommodated. The challenges posed to this governing group were tackled, if not always solved, in novel and generally humane ways. The demographic explosion of Wales – the population increased from 587,245 in 1801 to 1,046,073 in 1841 and to 1,412,583 in 1871 – produced both a people problem and problem people. Malthus's pessimistic propositions were confounded by the fact that the majority of the expanding population was accommodated within the borders of Wales, while others, hearing the Pied Piper flutings on the winds, sought their future in other lands.

Problem people were placated and propitiated through a plethora of institutions and initiatives. To solve the problem of the criminal, the eighteenth-century legal system developed punishments of a draconian severity. By the early nineteenth century, the legal system was almost universally referred to by the terrifying title, 'the Bloody Code'.[302] Sentences were severe. Criminals were physically punished. Vagrants and vagabonds were whipped around, and out of, Welsh towns. Miscreants were pelted with missiles in stocks and pillories. Forgers, thieves and murderers were hanged in public. More terrifyingly, their dead bodies were handed over to dissectionists and their remains buried, not in consecrated ground, but within prison walls. Punishment reached beyond the grave. Prisoners were subjected to a terrifying form of spiritual and theological terror. How could the pieces of a dissected body rise to glory on Judgement Day? A murderer, William Griffith of Beaumaris, expressed his terror that such a fate awaited him. 'The idea of being interred within the precincts of the prison was a source of terror' for John Roberts of Caernarfon, in August 1853, 'and was present with him even to the last hour'.[303] But by the mid nineteenth century, mercy was shown as often as vengeance. When three were condemned to death by the Carmarthen Assizes in April 1835, the sentences of all were commuted to terms of imprisonment.[304] Influential voices voiced their opposition to the barbarity of public hanging. The editors of *The Cambrian*, the *Caernarvon and Denbigh Herald* and the *Monmouthshire Merlin* frequently vented their anger at the 'uncivilized' and degrading spectacle of the saturnalia of the baying crowds at public executions.[305] They argued that civilization would be better safeguarded by effective policing and prisons which would serve not just as custodial centres, but as curative institutions in which the refractory could be reformed. By the 1850s, most sizeable towns in Wales had established a prison, and most counties and urban authorities had a police force. This was one of the greatest weaknesses in the arguments of Thomas Phillips and Henry Richard that Wales in the mid nineteenth century was in a state of docility and civility. If it was in this condition, why were so many police forces established and prisons erected, enlarged and extended?

The Victorians placed considerable faith in the beneficial effects of 'total' institutions. The perennial problem of the poor could be solved in the workhouse, the sick saved in hospitals, the insane cured in mental asylums. All these institutions were built in the noble hope of achieving heavens below, earthly utopias. Despite the initial hopes, the intractable nature of intransigence, illness and insanity created a dystopia. However, the initial optimism of the founders of these institutions was evidence of a new enlightened, civilized view of society. Nurture could conquer nature. The harlot could be turned into a good housekeeper, the rogue made respectable, the imbecile cured, the child educated.[306] The career of the Newtown entrepreneur Robert Owen provides 'a consummate illustration of the application of enlightened ideas to the empire of industry'. His social journey from a mid-Wales errand boy to wealthy Clydeside mill-owner was the epic story of self-sacrifice and heroism, in the Smilesean self-help mould. At New Lanark, he sought to prove that character could be moulded by correct environmental influence. Industrialization held out the promise for Owen of untold human benefit, provided the competitive system was regulated with cooperation to redistribute the benefits throughout society, not simply to the rich. In his *A New View of Society*, published in 1813, Owen called for national social rebuilding on the basis of universal education. Ignorance was the enemy:

> On the experience of a life devoted to the subject I hesitate not to say, that the members of any community may by degrees be trained to live *without idleness, without poverty, without crime, and without punishment*; for each of these is the effect of error in the various systems prevalent throughout the world. *They are all the necessary consequences of ignorance.*[307]

Such ideals were also articulated in Wales. In 1845, the Revd W. H. Bellairs, alarmed at the behaviour of the 'ill-educated, undisciplined, dangerous' population of the south, claimed 'that a band of efficient schoolmasters is kept up at a much less expense than a body of police or soldiery'.[308] Considerable effort was put into establishing schools and moulding the pliant minds of the young into new patterns of thought and behaviour. It was a tragedy of major proportions that the dispute over the alleged immorality of Welsh women, scandalously included in the 1847 Education Report, deflected attention from the need to establish a national education system until the late 1860s. By that time, a new world could be discerned in Wales. The old world had not totally disappeared. The wrecker walked with the watchers of the lifeboats and lighthouses, the ingratiating warble of beggars was still to be heard, but they were no longer whipped out of villages and towns. Fear still stalked the land and anger would burst forth in violent protests. But 'civilizing influences' had softened some of the harsher, brutish characteristics of Welsh society. The Welsh, under the evolutionary influence of their rulers, had transformed themselves into what they insinuated and insisted was 'a respectable society'.[309]

5

Love, Lust and Loneliness

Love in a Cold Climate

The battle between love and lust was bitter and protracted, and had far-reaching consequences for Welsh society. Not the least of these was the portrayal of the moral character of the Welsh people. The popular perception of the period 1776–1871 is of two distinct eras of contrasting and contradicting characters. The nineteenth century began with happy and hedonistic Georgians, romping and revelling in 'an age of scandal', and concluded with holy and hypocritical Victorians, obsessed with the importance of being earnest. The turning point, according to many commentators who were influenced by Lytton Strachey's poison-pen letter to his parent's generation, *Eminent Victorians*, was the enthronement of Queen Victoria in 1837.[1] A new era dawned which frowned on humour and which adopted a rigid, frigid, puritanical attitude towards sex. 'Victorian' became synonymous with 'virtuous'. The Victorians, we are meant to believe, were a generation of pure women and passionless men, citizens of a solemn, glandless utopia where duty defeated desire. This chaste, brave new world experienced such a morbid decay of the libido that many foreigners wondered how the Welsh managed to reproduce themselves. For, although children were frequently born, they were never made.

Such views continue to have powerful associations today. Many historians seem to have accepted the argument of some contemporaries that pious saints defeated passionate sensualists.[2] Yet the adjective 'Victorian', when used to describe a particular set of attributes, is confusing because it encourages the assumption that 1837 and 1901 are crucial dates in the fortunes of prudery and passion, high-mindedness and hedonism. Contemporary evidence from the years 1776–1871 shows that a different picture of Welsh sexuality is possible. However often ministers and moralists belaboured the fact,

Victorians did not have a monopoly of virtue. 'Y Diwygiad Mawr' (The Great Revival) of the eighteenth century was also characterized by a passionate desire to reform the sexual waywardness and wantonness of Welsh people.[3] In 1811, the Revd John Elias delivered a sermon of apocalyptic power against the frolicking and fornicating which reputedly occurred in the fairs of Rhuthun. 'At once', according to one author, 'frivolity finished'. At Swansea in January 1820, the Society for the Suppression of Vice congratulated itself on having achieved eighty-five prosecutions which led to convictions: 'We have checked the sale of Toys and abominable devices, which were imported in large quantities from France and other countries. Obscene books have also been seized.'[4]

In the same issue of *The Cambrian* newspaper in which the Vice Society's report appeared is an advertisement for Swansea Theatre's latest production, 'A trip to Paris'. It is one of those curious coincidences which reveal the complexity of Welsh life. One of the most influential figures in the moral purification of Swansea in the 1810s and 1820s was Dr Thomas Bowdler. In 1818, the pure doctor completed his collaboration with the bard, by publishing a ten-volume, 'de-sexed' *Family Shakespeare.* 'It has been my study', explained Dr Bowdler, 'to exclude from this publication whatever is unfit to be read aloud by a gentleman to a company of ladies.' The prolific doctor further extended public reading material for gentlemen in 1822, with an edition of the Old Testament, devoid of 'irreligious and indelicate' sections, and in 1826, with a six-volume 'Bowdlerized' edition of Gibbon's *History of the Decline and Fall of the Roman Empire.*[5] Repressed, reticent and reserved, many Welsh ladies and gentlemen were 'Victorian' before the 'age of respectability' began. It would be equally misleading to suggest that people who lived in Wales after 1837 were not amoral, amorous or lustful. Those men in the 1850s and 1860s who exhibited 'lusts worthy of the Devil' before the pliant and compliant prostitutes of Caernarfon's Mill Lane, Cardiff's Bute Street and Merthyr Tydfil's 'China' were rakes long after the demise of the sinful 'Regency'.[6]

The concept that men and women moved in 'separate spheres' became increasingly powerful as the nineteenth century progressed. While the woman was in the house, busily working, the man was out in the world, bending it to his will.[7] In *Y Gymraes* in 1851, an author writing on 'Merched Brycheiniog' stated with certainty that a woman's place was in the home – 'yn y tŷ, dyna lle y dylai merched fod' (in the house, that is where women should be).[8] The writer went on to extol the virtues of the domestic goddesses of Breconshire, complain at the fact that some of the county's women drank alcohol and condemn the impurity of their spoken Welsh. A woman's place, according to this author, was also in the wrong. The idea and ideal of the woman as 'yr angel ar yr aelwyd' (the angel on the hearth) was fostered in dozens of conduct and advice manuals, and in magazine and periodical articles.[9] Man, according to this ideology, was the doer, the discoverer, the defender. Spiritual women even had to accept that man was the creator. His energies for adventure, war and conquest, provided it was just, should be given a free rein. In contrast, women's power was not for battle, but for sweet ordering, arrangement, domestic decisions and decoration. While man encountered peril and trials on the rough seas of work, woman was safeguarded in the secure harbour of her home.[10]

The fact that this message of separate spheres was propounded so frequently has been accepted as evidence that this was the universal reality of Welsh society. However, it could also be evidence of a crisis of masculinity.[11] The message was reiterated in pulpit and pamphlet because it went against the grain of the times. In many areas, despite the ideologies presented in works such as Coventry Patmore's *The Angel in the House*, and Ieuan Gwynedd's magazine *Y Gymraes*, women were making unparalleled advances, both socially and politically, throughout the nineteenth century.[12] By the 1810s, in the ironworks and coal mines, women represented a substantial element of the workforce. Agriculture was heavily dependent upon women's work. Domestic service was almost exclusively carried out by women. The commercial and retail trades, and the information technology industries which emerged in the nineteenth century, employed armies of women. By the mid nineteenth century women had acquired greater rights at law. The Infants and Child Custody Act of 1839 enabled women who had not been divorced or separated because of their adultery to sue for custody of children under seven. A more comprehensive Act in 1873 extended the right to children under sixteen. Wives subjected to severe cruelty, or desertion, could obtain a legal separation under the Matrimonial Causes Act of 1857, and gain court-enforced maintenance payments from their estranged husbands. Under the Married Women's Property Act of 1870, women could inherit property without ownership passing immediately to their husbands. In 1854, at a time when many were calling for greater educational opportunities for boys, Robert Jones, Derfel (1824–1905), published an influential article in *Y Traethodydd*, entitled 'Yr

Angenreidrwydd o roddi Addysg Gyffredinol i Ferched' (the importance of giving a general education to girls), an enlightened plea for the
education of girls. Another voice crying from the educational
wilderness for female education was the redoubtable Revd Hugh Evan
Thomas, Huwco Meirion (1830–89). By the early 1850s there were
thirty-six schools in Wales, providing an education for young girls. In
their midst were Mrs Hugh Jones's School for the Education of Young
Ladies at Red-Hill Mansion, Beaumaris, and Miss Amelia D'Austen's
Boarding and Day School at Swansea.[13] Such developments indicated
that women were not cocooned in a separate sphere but loose in the
world, living and enjoying rich and complex lives. Hidden in the
profusion of Dickens is a phrase which inspired Ibsen, and which
encapsulates the new optimism in fledgeling feminism: 'I want', said
Bella Rokesmith to her husband, 'to be something so much worthier
than the doll in the doll's house.'[14]

Contemporaneous with, and complementary to, the notion of
separate spheres were distinct conceptualizations of Welsh women.
Many authors considered that the 'Angel on the hearth', as portrayed
by Patmore, was more 'doll' than 'angel'. There was something
unacceptable, and alien, to the Welsh in the notions of leisure and
pleasure which characterized the idealization of womanhood by
English middle classes. Therefore the Welsh did not just adopt the
model, but adapted it to the particular and peculiar circumstances of
Wales. Augusta Waddington Hall, Lady Llanover, Gwenynen Gwent
(1802–96), characterized the ideal Welsh woman as possessing three
main characteristics – she was highly moral, spoke Welsh and wore the
national costume and hat. As the nineteenth century wore on, she
acquired one further characteristic: intense religiosity. She became 'Y
Fam Dduwies' (the Mother God) – pious, proper and as tirelessly
industrious as a bee.[15] This was the ideal of Welsh womanhood which
Sarah Jane Rees, Cranogwen (1839–1916), idolized and idealized in
her poem 'Gwraig Dda':

Caru beunydd, gwenu'n hyfryd,	Loving constantly, smiling lovely,
Caru, chwerthin, byth yn surllyd;	Loving, laughing, never morose;
Glân a diwyd, sobr, difrifol,	Clean and industrious, sober, serious,
I foddio'r gŵr yn wir egniol:	To energetically please her husband:
Coeth a moesgar a charedig	Wise and moral and kind
Ac o feddwl gwych puredig;	With a pure mind;
Mam grefyddol, priod wiw,	A religious mother, faithful wife,
Yn caru dyn, yn ofni Duw . . .	Loving men, fearing God . . .

| Nid caethferch hi, Nid morwyn chwaith, | She is not a slave, or a maid, |
| Ond ffrynd urddasol ar y daith.[16] | But a good friend on life's journey. |

Travellers in Wales, in the early nineteenth century, went in search of another type of Welsh woman. In the 1830s, Thomas Medwin came 'angling' for the 'Cambrian Amazon', and published his adventures in double entendres in *The Angler in Wales or Days and Nights of Sportsmen*.[17] The Revd Joseph Romilly, a fellow and registrar of Trinity College, Cambridge, made several forays into Wales between 1827 and 1854. During one visit, Miss Jones of Fonmon, the ideal of porcelain womanhood, five foot two and eyes of blue, with her light fairy figure, ringlets, spirited and informed conversation, caught his fancy.[18] In 1833, T. McLean painted *The Welsh Coquet* with her dark auburn ringlets tumbling over rosy cheeks, gazing sidelong at the artist through come-to-bed eyes, finger provocatively poised at luscious lips.[19] Such were the charms of Jane, daughter of the vicar of Maentwrog, that Thomas Love Peacock transferred his infatuation from sublime mountain scenery to her stunning contours. Percy Bysshe Shelley, a fine poet but a poor zoologist, described her as 'the white Snowdonian antelope'. In the fantasies of many males, Welsh women living in accord with nature were noble savages, sensual, sexually insatiable, an easy and willing prey. Edward Pugh met a 'beautiful brunette' near Aran Benllyn and considered the daughters of Merionethshire 'matchless maids'. Lord Lyttelton was obsessed with 'the lips of the fair maids of Bala', while another voyeuristic visitor was adamant 'that attractive Welsh girls had the finest ankles in the world'. In 1853, Mrs Gaskell, familiar with 'the extreme lengths of Welsh courtship', set her novel *Ruth*, a mould-breaking study of a fallen woman, in a Welsh village. It was a marked contrast to the much-voiced Welsh view that immorality was endemic to the English. This English rose said goodbye to England, and fell from grace in sinful Wales. Mrs Gaskell used the Welsh word for prostitute – 'y buten' – without translation, as if there were no English equivalent.[20] This was the notion of Welsh womanhood published in the infamous Education Report of 1847. This despised report notoriously claimed that Welsh women were 'universally unchaste'. No longer an 'angel', the wild woman of Wales was a whore – immorally wallowing in wantonness. Although many writers followed Ieuan Gwynedd and Thomas Rees by expressing their righteous indignation at this unfair presentation of Welsh women, many used the report as a warning of the wages of sin.[21] Throughout the nineteenth century, these contradictory caricatures of Welsh women remained, making it difficult for the historian to decide which was closer to the true spirit of the age.

There is one further feature of the characteristics of Welsh sexuality which deserves attention. The nineteenth century has often been portrayed as the golden age of the 'double standard' which tolerated men's indiscretions and immorality but was outraged by any misdemeanour committed by women. This inconsistent and immoral moral code enabled men to escape the obloquy heaped upon women.[22] While women were condemned and censured for their immorality, men behaved as if they had no part, even a modest one, to play in the sexual act. With a single jerk of his pelvis, a man could transform a woman from respectability into a pariah without detriment to his own moral standing. This phallocentric, hypocritical 'double standard' was seen at its worst in the Contagious Diseases Act of the 1860s. These Acts were introduced in an attempt to reduce the incidence of venereal disease in garrison towns such as Brecon, Wrexham and Pembroke, through the compulsory health inspection of women whom the authorities suspected of being prostitutes.[23] Men were exempt from the Acts, although they too suffered the ravages of sexually transmitted diseases. The Acts were undoubtedly unfair, and in all three towns were used as a pretext for cruelty and abuse. Despite the iniquity, many prostitutes welcomed the Acts as recognition of the legitimacy of their work. The government in 1886 followed the moral majority and repealed the Acts.

But the 'double standard' was not simply a Victorian phenomenon for its origins went back to the mists of time. Scriptures taught that, ever since Eve, women were wanton, and that sex was their want. They should therefore be controlled. The law, since the days of King Ethelbert, in order to safeguard inheritance and property, emphasized that female infidelity was a greater crime than male unfaithfulness. The double standard was therefore an aspect of a long established code of social conduct for women, based entirely upon their place in society in relation to men.[24] Throughout the ages, women were, broadly speaking, thought of as incomplete in themselves, and as existing primarily for the sake of men. Hence the contempt in Welsh society for unmarried women – old maids, who had failed to achieve the main purpose of their existence, marriage to a man. This was seen in a poignant and pitiful way in the advertisements for a husband which a woman placed in the Welsh press in 1822.[25] Wife sales might reflect the fact that divorce was too expensive, but many men regarded and treated their wives as chattels, to be disposed of how, and when, they pleased. In the eighteenth and nineteenth centuries, foreigners were firmly of the opinion that British people could sell their wives, provided they put a halter around their necks and led them into the open market.[26] In 1815, after only three weeks of married life, William Jones, a 79-year-old pauper of Llanrwst, sold his wife for three farthings in the town's fair.[27] In 1824, *The Cambrian* reported the sale of Lydia Jones (née Williams):

> the crier of the town proclaimed her to be sold, and she was produced with a halter round her waist, and was instantly purchased by one Aston of Coalbrookdale, for the sum of 10 shillings, a quart of ale, and paying the toll. The satisfied purchaser and seller went to a tavern to celebrate with great glee.[28]

In 1835, an unnamed wife was sold in Merthyr Tydfil for an undisclosed sum.[29] By 1863, inflation had obviously affected the prices asked and achieved for wives in Merthyr Tydfil market. In March that year, a worker from the Cyfarthfa ironworks sold his wife to one of his colleagues for £3. The bulk of the fee was paid in cash, together with ten shillings' worth of beer.[30] The beer was shared between the husband, the wife and her purchaser, all of whom declared themselves to be well satisfied with the deal. Such transactions provide an interesting if somewhat exaggerated illustration that the ownership of most women was vested in men.

The Power of Love

The search for love was one of the greatest objectives and obsessions of Welsh people in the years 1776–1871. Several simple stories show the power of love. When Jennie, the wife of Sam 'Waterloo', was informed that her husband had been killed in the Battle of Waterloo, she refused to believe the reports, walked to the battlefield and found him in the care of a French family. She stayed with Sam, nursed him back to health and carried him home to 'Waterloo' Cottage, Llanegryn.[31] Betsy Williams's remarkable love story is related in a ballad, with a title so long that it must have exhausted the singer even before he began to sing: *Cân o Hanes Miss Betsy Williams Yr Hon a Wisgodd Dillad Mab a Aeth ar Ffwrdd Llong y Brenin, ar ôl ei chariad. Cymerwyd hi yn garcharor gan long o Spain, ac wedi cael ei rhyddid a fu mewn perygl am ei bywyd ar y môr, a eisiau lluniaeth; yn nghyd a'r modd rhyfeddol yr adnabuasant eu gilydd.*[32] Betsy donned a sailor's uniform and went to sea in a man-of-war in search of her lover. Her ship was

captured by Spanish pirates, but Betsy and a number of sailors
escaped in an open boat. Adrift at sea, without food or water, the
desperate sailors resorted to cannibalism. When their larder of dead
bodies was exhausted, they drew lots to decide who would be killed to
feed the ravenous crew. Betsy lost. Only after they stripped her ready
for death did the inattentive sailors discover that their colleague was a
woman. The dramatic disclosure coincided with the sighting of a sail
in the distance. They signalled and were rescued by a London ship, on
which Betsy's lover was serving. Deliverance led to the happy ever after
of marriage.

Love was as much a source of pain as of pleasure. The poet Wil Ifan
was well aware of this in his poignant couplet: 'Wnaeth hi ond tynnu'r
ddraenen o'm llaw, a'i osod yn fy nghalon i'[33] (she only took the thorn
from my hand, and placed it in my heart). William Edwards of Kerry,
Montgomeryshire, also felt the powerful pains of love. He deserted
from the 43rd Regiment in Caernarfon, in 1832, and returned home to
his sweetheart. In order to stay in the bosom of love, and prevent any
further military service, he cut off some of his fingers.[34]

Love was a powerful, all-consuming and transforming force in the
lives of many Welsh people. Christians, of all denominations, were
probably the people most consumed with an obsessive search for love.
They sought love divine, excelling all love, in every waking and
worshipping moment. People's realization and response to the transforming power of God's love led to the 'moral earthquakes' of the
religious revivals of 1810, 1818, 1828 and 1859. The love of God was
above and beyond earthly human love. Ann Griffiths, the most fervent
of Welsh hymn-writers, expressed her experience of 'caru delw
sancteiddiaidd' (loving a heavenly image), adding: 'O fy enaid, gwêl
addasrwydd, Y person dwyfol hwn'[35] (O my soul, appreciate the worth
of this Godly person).

Yet the attempt to explain the nature of their love deposited many
layers of conflicting symbolism. By studying the songs of a diverse
group of hymn-writers such as William Williams, Pantycelyn, Ann
Griffiths, Mary Owen, Jane Roberts and Elizabeth Phillips, one
discovers evocations of a figure who is both paternal and maternal,
Oedipal and Electral, sexual and sado-masochistic. By the late
eighteenth century, Methodism had so totally immersed itself in
Christ's blood and wounds that, even allowing for the metaphoric
language and established religious symbolism, it is unsettling to the
modern mind.[36] The weeping wounds of Christ, the man of Sorrows,

promoted more empathy than his halo. There may be some deep symbolism in the fact that many of the blood-soaked hymns were written by women.[37] The scriptures, particularly the Old Testament, have many references to the dirty and debased nature of a menstruating woman. Was this obsession with Christ's blood sacrifice an attempt at redemption for their monthly blood-sheddings? Were the wounds caused in his body by the spear a link to the central wounds of women? What is certain is that there was an extraordinary assimilation of wounds and sexual imagery. Mankind, 'y pryfun pechadurus' (the sinful worm), must find 'cuddfan glud yng nghlwyfau'r oen' (a hiding place in the lamb's wounds). Such bathing in blood was not just a feature of Methodist imagery. In the 1860s, the Revd Daniel Evans compiled *Hymnau a Thonau er Gwasanaeth yr Eglwys yng Nghymru*. The services leading up to Easter were awash in blood:

Y gwaed, y gwaed a lifodd	The blood, the blood that flowed
Ar groesbren un prydnawn,	On a cross one afternoon,
Haeddiannau hwnw roddodd	His graciousness gave
I'r ddeddf foddlonrwydd llawn:	To the earth great pleasure:
Y gwaed, y gwaed a olcha	The blood, the blood that washes
Bechadur du yn wyn –	A black sinner white –
Dadseiniwn Haleliwia	We sing Hallelujah
Am waed Calfaria fryn.[38]	To the blood of Calvary.

And after washing whiter in the blood, the author wished: 'Gad im brofi ffrwyth ei glwyfau, / Gad im deimlo rhîn ei waed'[39] (Let me taste the fruit of his wounds, / Let me feel the flesh of his blood). The language is sacrificial, masochistic and erotically charged, indicating that one of the great tensions in Welsh religion in the nineteenth century was that between the needs of the soul and those of the body. It was ironic that people who placed such great importance on love put such strong prohibitions on its physical manifestation in sex. Energies and emotions which were dangerous in the social order were released in the safe forum of the *seiat*, the prayer meetings and the public meetings.[40] At such gatherings, preachers spoke in a raw emotional manner of their spiritual experiences, temptations, battles with sin (often sexual) and contests with the evil one. Public confessions of sin were greeted with the congregation's outbursts of prayer and praise. It was in this sense, as much as in the conservatism of its early leaders, that Methodism served as a brake on revolutionary impulses. The passion and sensualism of revivalist meetings became a matter of

considerable concern for many observers who complained at the
excesses. But these 'Sabbath orgasms of feeling' provided a constant
goading to the faithful to indulge in sober and industrious behaviour.
God was eternally vigilant. In one devout author's stark phrase, he was
'presennol ym mhobman' (omnipresent); all-seeing, ever-vigilant.[41]
People were taught not only to bravely bear their cross of poverty and
humiliation, but to behave and live sin-free lives. Sexual behaviour
could only be tolerated within the confines of marriage, without
pleasure, and never on a Sunday. This was the message propounded in
the first Welsh marriage guidance guidebook, published in 1777 by
William Williams, Pantycelyn. The book takes the form of a dialogue
between two women, Martha and Mary, one of whom has loved
wildly, the other wisely. Although the book is short, the title is long
and provides the crux of the story:

> *Ductor Nuptiarum: neu, Gyfarwyddwr Priodas, Mewn Dull o Ymddiddan rhwng*
> *Martha Pseudogam, a Mary Eugamus, ill dwy oedd ar y cyntaf yn proffesu*
> *Duwioldeb, ond y naill wedi gwrthgilio, yn priodi ar ôl y cnawd; a'r llall yn dal at*
> *Rym Duwioldeb, yn priodi yn Ofn yr Arglwydd. Yn dri Ymddiddan (Dialogue). Y*
> *Cyntaf Am Ddull Carwriaeth, a Phriodas lygredig Martha, a'i Bywyd anhapus ar*
> *ôl Llaw. Yr ail, Am Garwriaeth a Phriodas Nefol Mary, a'i Bywyd cariadus a*
> *chysurus hithau ar ôl Llaw. Yr olaf yn cynnwys Cyngor Mary i Martha i foddio ei*
> *gŵr, a thrwy hynny wneud ei Phriodas yn fwy dedwydd a chyttunol, ac o bosibl ei*
> *ennill ef i'r Ffydd. At ba un ychwanegwyd Ymddiddan rhwng Efangelus a*
> *Phamphila, Ynghylch y Perygl o briodi y rhai digred.*

In this remarkable work, William Williams showed that he was well
versed in the popular courtship customs of the people:

> ar welyau, mewn ysguboriau, a gwactai, gelltydd, ac ogofeydd y byddem yn
> treulio ein hamser wrth ein carwriaeth; lle gallem fod mor gnawdol ag y byddai
> chwant arnom . . . yn danllwyth o chwant . . . dau ddyn yn ymrwymo i
> ymgofleidio, ac ymfawrhau, ac yfed trachwantau natur, fel yr eliffant yn trachtio
> dwfr yr Iorddonen.[42]

> on beds, in barns, in ruins, woods, and caves we would spend time in our
> courting; we could be as sinful as our lusts dictated . . . a bonfire of lusts . . . two
> people devoted to grappling and worshipping the urges of nature, like an
> elephant drinking the waters of Jordan.

Yet, despite such colourful evocations of Welsh lovemaking, Williams
was more a pharisee than a pleasure hunter. Mankind, he warned,
should guard against the lusts of sinful flesh, and concentrate on
higher, nobler things. A good and godly life was a wise preparation for

inevitable, unavoidable death and a glorious reward in the glory of the hereafter. Many historians have insisted that the battle between lust and love led to an unhealthy obsession with death. The Victorians, in particular, have been ridiculed because they were not obsessed with sex, but with death. While people today are repressed and reticent about death, and celebratory about sex, the Victorians were repressed and reticent about sex, and celebrated death. In modern society, sex is public and death private. In Victorian Wales, death was public and sex private. Some authors have even gone so far to suggest that the Victorians were not very good at sex – historians, it seems, do it better.[43] But such a conclusion is not borne out by the enormously rich and diverse sexual lives led by Welsh people in this period. Moreover, perhaps people in these years realized that safeguarding sex within strict confines meant that it could be better savoured.

Love in the Time of Cholera

Loneliness was the enemy which taunted and tormented many Welsh people in the years 1776–1871. The denominational and secular press of Wales is littered with sad reports of the suicide of young boys and girls, forsaken by love. The popularity of the poignant song 'Yr Eneth Gadd ei Gwrthod' was testimony to the familiarity of the Welsh with the Ophelian, watery, wide-eyed death of abandoned lovers. The details of these tragic tales of the riverbank, and the histories of truncated lives, reveal the loneliness and losses which troubled and tortured the young. The poetry and the songs recited and sung in beerhouses, pubs, *cwrwau bach* and fairs warned against loneliness. The song 'Y Ferch o Blwyf Benderyn' has the tragic closing stanza:

Rwy'n myned heno, dyn a'm helpo,	I'm going tonight, man help me,
I ganu ffârwel i'r seren syw,	To sing farewell to my sweetheart,
A dyna waith y clochydd fory	And the gravedigger's work tomorrow
Fydd torri 'medd o dan yr yw	Will be to open my grave 'neath the yew.

Another ballader claimed that silence was golden:

Os yw'th galon bron â thorri, paid â deud,
Am fod serch dy fron yn oeri, paid â deud,
Ac os chwalu mae d'obeithion, paid â deud,
Ni ddaw neb i drwsio'th galon, paid â deud.[44]

If your heart is nearly broken, say nothing,
If the love in your heart grows cold, say nothing,

> And if your hope is in tatters, say nothing,
> No one will come to fix your heart, say nothing.

In the mid nineteenth century, the song 'Ar Lan y Môr' was popular in the Trefin and Fishguard areas of Pembrokeshire. The second verse warned:

Oer yw'r rhew ac oer yw'r eira,	Cold is frost and cold the snow,
Oer yw'r tŷ heb dân yn y gaea'	Cold is the house without a fire in winter,
Oer yw'r eglwys heb un ffeiriad,	Cold is the church without a vicar,
Oer wyf finnau heb fy nghariad.[45]	Cold am I without my loved one.

Popular proverbs encapsulated people's fears of loneliness in a nutshell of wisdom: 'Hir yw'r nos i goban unig' (every night is long for a lonely negligee). An unknown author in 1819 doubled the sentiment into the startling similies of: 'Trwm y plwm, a thrwm y cerrig, / Trom yw calon pob dyn unig'[46] (Heavy is lead, heavy are stones, / Heavier the heart of a lonely man).

During one of her many visits to the north, the novelist Mrs Gaskell noticed a sad old couple. He was blind. 'Both', she thought, were 'lonely'. In 'Bugail Cwmdyli', Ieuan Glan Geirionydd lyrically outlined the lonely sorrow of a shepherd, whose only love had left for 'dwndwr tre' (the town's clamour):

F'anwylyd wiw,	My fairest love,
Nac anghofia un a fydd	Do not forget one who will be
Ar dy ôl, yn wylo'n brudd	Weeping tears of sorrow over you
Yng Nghwmdyli nos a dydd.[47]	In Cwmdyli night and day.

The future he faced and feared was bleak, the private dereliction of being alone, of living with loss. At the fairs where these ballads and songs were sung, people could see all around them human evidence of the erosive and corrosive effects of loneliness – bent, dead-eyed, ancient bachelor brothers down from the farms, reeking of their isolation, of stale urine and lost chances, who worked together on their family's farm where nothing very much grew, except their sense of separation; virgin old donkey men with prune faces, suffering through life under the cross of loneliness; wizened old ladies from whom all the marrow and meaning had been sucked by years of lonely toil; and fat ladies who laughed a lot, but never jollied anyone's days. In the towns themselves, in the closed-curtained airless chamber of their rooms, in the thick, musty mists of perfume, spinsters suffocated with loneliness.

It is this search for companionship and comfort which explains the vitality and verve with which the Welsh, especially the young, approached fairs and markets, prayer meetings and most social gatherings. Fairs offered opportunities to escape the custody of mothers, fathers, masters and mistresses. Commissioners into the condition of labourers on the land in Wales, who eventually reported in 1893, uncovered evidence that

> the girls if so inclined may mislead their parents by suggesting that they intend returning to the farms, while they may also mislead their masters by intimating their intention of going home. The result is that there have been cases where girls have by this device been able to stay late in the town . . . Shame and disgrace are the almost inevitable consequences.[48]

Most authors could not resist the temptation of issuing stern warnings at the raw and raucous behaviour of youth. David Owen, Brutus, in an epistle against 'y bwystfil cnawdol' (the lustful Beast) who threatened Wales, complained in 1843:

> y merched yn heidiau ym mreichiau eu gilydd yn cerdded ar hyd yr heolydd; yn gwamalu, yn chwerthin, yn ynfydu megis pe byddent wedi ymwerthu i drythyllwch! . . . Yn y tafarnau y mae y meibion a'r merched brith draphlith, heb na moes na gweddeid-dra yn ganfyddedig ond pob halogrwydd ymddygiadau! Deuant adref gyda'u gilydd dan gysgodau y nos yn debycach i wallgofiaid nac i ddynion wedi eu gwareiddio.[49]

> the girls in gangs in each other's arms walking the streets; joking, laughing, behaving as if they had sold themselves to sin! . . . In the pubs, boys and girls are mixed without any visible morality or respectability but every brute behaviour! They come home under the cover of darkness more akin to animals than civilized people.

The self-righteous disgust of another author at such behaviour is obvious in the following outburst, but was insufficient for the writer to append his name, for he, or she, wrote under the pseudonym 'Llywelyn': 'yn y ffeiriau a'r tafarndai . . . gwelir merched a meibion yn cydyfed, ac yn eistedd ar linau eu gilydd, ac mewn agweddau mwy anweddus na hynny' (in the fairs and pubs . . . you can see girls and men drinking, sitting on each other's laps, and in more unrespectable behaviour). Another anonymous author, Pelagius, in the same issue of *Seren Gomer*, complained at the youth in a pub on fair day:

> yn tynu, yn ymwthio, ac yn llusgo eu gilydd ar draws cadeiriau, byrddau, gwelyau; yn colli cwrw, yn trystio â'u traed, ac yn sathru eu gilydd fel mintau o anifeiliaid heb reswm ynddynt . . . Y merched arosant yn y loddest annuwiol hon yn aml tan y diwedd, i ymddiffyn eu cariadau . . . ac i gadw gwyliadwriaeth rhag

i eraill eu dwyn oddi arnynt; oblegid y mae yn anghenrhaid deall mai ychydig o ffydd sydd mewn Carwriaeth Gymreig o'r dull hon – 'allan o olwg allan o feddwl'![50]

Pulling, poking, and dragging each other across chairs, tables and beds; spilling beer, falling over, and pushing each other like wild animals without reason in them . . . The girls stay in this ungodly environment until the end to defend their lovers . . . and to keep watch in case another steals them from them; for it is important to realize that there is little faithfulness in Welsh courtship – 'out of sight, out of mind'.

Ffair-y-Cefn at Cefncoed-y-cymer on Easter Monday, and the mid-May fair at Bala were celebrated, infamous social occasions, drawing the youths from miles around. At Sardis, Llandysul, the annual Ffair Cileth was famous as the starting-point for the courtships of local couples.[51] One of the few to observe the rowdy romping of Welsh fairs without a veneer of moral worry and warning was the American consul in Wales in the 1880s, the rumbustious Wirt Sikes. In his *Rambles and Studies in Old South Wales*, he recounted with obvious delight the fair at Llandaff:

roaring with bustle; Punch and Judy squeak; hawkers howl; exhibitors of curiosities bawl at the highest pitch of their voices. There are curiosities enough here, at least – fat women, living skeletons, waxworks, pigmies, giants, performing dogs and monkeys and an endless array of idle and profitless diversions. Merry-go-rounds whirl their laughing, shrieking freight through the air – 'warranted to make you sea-sick for a penny'. Shooting-galleries, and even perambulating photograph-galleries are there. 'Come and get your picture pulled Sally', is a favourite form of treat offered their sweethearts by lads of the labouring class . . .

By night fall, the scene becomes a sort of pandemonium . . . Deep darkness falls; but the diversions of the pleasure-fair abate no jot. On the contrary, they increase; for all the young folks of the village being now assembled on the green, they not only dance, but play kissing-games full of romping and boisterous merriment. A great circle is gathered in one part of the field, lads and lasses to the number of fifty joining hands in the fitful light of the torches, and amid much slapping of backs and frantic scampering, playing *cusan-yn-y-cylch*, or kiss-in-the-ring. They . . . are as full of fun as young colts; and the air echoes with shrieks of laughter mingling with the music of the band, and the rousing smack of rustic lips on rustic red cheeks rivals the popping of the air-guns, where the gaudy shooting-gallery glitters in the light of a dozen flaring flambeaux.[52]

Sikes added that the hiring fairs, horse shows, flower shows, Christmas shows, fat-cattle shows and poultry shows were also occasions for merriment and mirth and observed:

At these fairs there is undoubtedly a considerable consumption of *cwrw da*; a temperance or teetotal fair would hardly thrive . . . Beer is not a quarrelsome beverage, at least in Wales, it moves a Welshman's feet to dancing not his fist to mauling, and he grins instead of growls. The Cambrian proverb is *'Allwedd Calon Cwrw Da'* (good ale is the key of the heart) . . . The streets are so densely thronged with people that it is almost impossible to move among them. Vehicles cannot go about at all, and this is not attempted. Torches light up the scene; drums beat; hawkers and Cheap John's bawl; Punch and Judy add their squeaking to the din; and any Mairi or Cati whose waist is not encircled by the arms of a Twm or Siôn, is a reproach to the traditions of her race.[53]

In 1859, in a gross cartoon, *Y Punch Cymraeg* insinuated that the ladies of the Wesleyan *Offeren* or *Wylnos* were not a reproach to the traditions of their race. As the clock strikes the midnight hour, they parade in their tight-waisted, ample-busted, bustled finery, leading the men astray.

The joyful carousing and courting of the fairs was captured and chronicled in tuneful and mirthful folk songs and ballads. Almost every fair had a ballad to celebrate its characters, Llangyfelach fair had five ballads written to praise its amorous atmosphere. The ballad singers served as the gossip columnists of their regions. They were analysts, chroniclers, custodians of popular memory and petty biographers. In social groups where reading was almost unknown, the singers of ballads carried the local memory like walking books. In the ballads, individuals were identified by name, nickname, address or character trait. One of the most remarkable was *Cân Newydd yn rhoddi hanes ffair Aberhonddu, pan oedd Siôn Carwr Merched yn Faer arni* by the blind ballad-monger Richard Williams, Dic Dywyll. The facts probably did not match the song at every point, but that mattered little. People identified with this ballad because they knew many of the ballad's abundant cast of characters, and they could laugh at their misbehaviour and misalliances:

O'r golwg balch wnaeth Siani'r Wanc, pan gafodd lanc o fwynwr;
A Mari'r Bryn yn canu ei cant, ar Rolant y Chwarelwr;
Roedd Doli fain o Stryd y Glen, ar garu Jem y Gyrrwr;
A Dai Defynnog oedd yn dynn, yn dilyn merch Siôn Deiliwr,
Gan ddweud, 'mi fynnaf i fy ffrynd, pe costiai im bunt yn bentwr'.

Roedd Dai Llangynwyd yn dra ffond o Nani Fach Bont Newydd,
A Nel Llanwrda gerdda'n gwic, i ganlyn Dic y Celwydd,
Roedd Huwcyn Fawr o Dy'n-y-clwt, am Siani Bwt o'r Betws;
A Ben Llanabo, megis ffŵl, yn cethan ar ôl Catws;
A silver Tom roes gusan teg, debygaf ar geg Begws.

Ond yn y dafarn gyda'r nos, roedd Robin o dros yr Aber,
Yn sych gusan gyda'r serch, Siân Feddw, merch Siôn Fyddar;
Roedd Jac y crudd yng nghil y drws, yn dofi Cadws Dafydd,
Gan ddweud, 'Mae'th gusan fel y gwin, rwyt un o burion deunydd;
Ni chawn i ferch o gystal stamp, pe rhown i dramp hyd drenydd'.[54]

O the proud look of Siani'r Wanc, when she had a quarrying lad;
And Mari'r Bryn sang of her lust, for Rolant the quarryman;
Thin Doli from Glen Street, was set on loving Jem the driver;
And Dai Defynnog was the man, for Siôn the tailor's daughter,
Saying 'I'll have you for my friend, whatever the cost'.

Dai Llangynwyd was very fond of small Nani Bont Newydd,
And Nel Llanwrda walked quickly, to court Dic the liar,
Big Huwcyn from Ty'n-y-clwt, was set on small Siani from the Betws;
And Ben Llanabo, like a fool, was crying after Catws;
Whilst silver Tom gave the sweetest kiss on Begws's mouth.

But in the pub that night, Robin from across the estuary,
Was dryly and lovingly kissing drunken Siân, daughter of deaf Siôn;
Whilst in the doorway Jac the cobbler was taming Cadws Dafydd;
Saying 'Your kiss is like wine, you're made of rare stock;
I won't get as good a girl as you if I walked until the day after tomorrow'.

As Jac y Crydd recalled, the ballad singers had some wonderful
chat-up lines. The same author, Dic Dywyll, in *Cân Newydd, sef
ymddiddan rhwng mab a merch ieuanc ynghylch priodi*, offered this
sarcastic or sweet, depending on your taste, greeting:

Mae dy lais di feinir addfwyn,	Your voice sweet, tender maid,
Lliw gwyn rhosyn yr haf,	The colour of the summer rose,
Yn fy nghlust fel tannau telyn,	In my ear is like harp strings,
Lliw gwyn rhosyn yr haf.[55]	Sweet maid the colour of the summer rose.

Terms of endearment were also in prominent profusion in valentine
greetings, which had become a tradition in Wales by the 1840s. In the
valentine sent by Edward Edwards to Elizabeth Roberts in Merionethshire, however, the verse was more tortuous than tender, the fruit of a
muse whose first language was obviously Welsh:

As I leaid Musing on My Bead
Though of my Love came in my head I
Roas up and though it time to
Drow my Love a Valentine
The Roase is Read the Vialent is
Blew the Carnation is Sweet
And so are you.

Despite his best efforts, Edward had a rival. David Edwards also sent a valentine to Elizabeth in 1841. Alas, she was true to neither. As far as is known, Elizabeth only ever sent one valentine, to a John Jones in 1844.[56]

Other men resisted the temptation to versify their feelings, preferring to express their emotions in the finely carved lines of a love spoon.[57] Mothers and moralists were agreed that when men abandoned their usual monosyllabic mutterings, and expressed their feelings in verse and carved them in wood, they wanted only one thing. Meetings in the fairs, markets and religious societies often led to couples arranging to meet again. Because of the long hours of work of males and females in rural areas, and the lack of other social facilities, couples would arrange to court in the girl's house or bed-chamber. Thus developed the cosy and convivial custom of *caru yn y gwely* (courting in bed).[58] Often, people's behaviour was innocent for the entire duration of lengthy courtships. One couple chastely courted for thirty-nine years, gradually saving for their big day, only for the man to die a week before the long awaited, and eagerly anticipated, wedding day. Arrangements would be made for the young man to call at the house and throw sand or gravel at the girl's bedroom window to be let in for a night of bliss. Many desperate men were disappointed, as the song 'Y Gwydr Glas' made clear:

Os daw 'nghariad yma heno	If my lover calls here tonight,
I guro'r gwydr glas,	To knock the blue glass,
Rhowch ateb gweddus iddo	Give him a courteous reply
Na atebwch mono'n gas –	Answer him not severely –
'Nad ydyw'r ferch ddim gatre',	For his girl is not home,
Na'i h'wyllys da yn y tŷ,	Nor is her will in the house,
Llanc ifangc o'r plwyf arall,	A boy from another parish,
Sy wedi mynd a hi.[59]	Has taken her away.

Others must have been delayed in their arrival, for the young lover in the song 'Os daw 'nghariad i yma heno' was told:

Dewch yma nos yfori	Come here tomorrow night
Rhyw awr neu ddwy ynghynt,	An hour or two earlier,
Cewch ryddid i'm cofleudio,	You'll have freedom to grasp me,
Fel yn yr amser gynt'.[60]	As in the olden times.

Despite the promise of future grapplings and gropings, the young man took umbrage at the refusal and left for 'gwlad y negro du' (the black negro's country) – America. There were other disappointments, in addition to locked doors and windows, associated with *caru yn y gwely*. In June 1822, thieves broke in and stole £300 – surely an improbably large sum – from the Union Tavern in Caernarfon. The landlord, his brother and two servants had been too busily engaged 'in that disgraceful custom of the county . . . such a shameful practice called 'bundling', to notice any other noise'.[61] In 1815, a farmer assaulted his servant and her lover because the noise of their 'incessant and indecent' bundling had disturbed the household.[62] John Edwards, a Cardiff wheelwright, was seen by a landlord entering a window into a woman's bedroom. Assuming him to be a robber, the police were summoned. John was dragged from under the woman's bed, 'by men who are callous to such feelings of love and whose disregard of tears and entreaties, is only equalled by their regard for the public weal'.[63] An anonymous ballad singer explained that *caru yn y gwely* had undoubted advantages in terms of comfort and cosiness:

> Mae'r gwely'n llawer gwell i garu rwyf yn coelio . . .
> Bydd nwydau yn eu nerth, a'r cariad yn gwresogi,
> Mewn gwely gwelir gwerth yr amser i briodi'.

> Bed is the best place to court I believe . . .
> There lust can grow, and love warm,
> In bed you'll see the value of marriage.

But the custom also led to obvious problems. Twm o'r Nant was unchar-acteristically subtle in pointing this out:

> Er caffael munud digri, i bleso cnawd a ffansi,
> Ni wiw mo'r gwadu wedi, pan fyddo'r bol yn codi.[64]

> Although you have a funny moment to please body and fancy,
> You won't be able to deny it, when the stomach swells.

Dr Richard Williams, a Cardiganshire doctor, claimed in 1837 that

> In no Country in the World is Chastity so little valued as in Wales and the loss of virtue is to be ascribed more to the continuance of rude and barbarous customs, than to any innately bad or corrupt feelings in the female mind . . . More illegitimate children are born in Wales than in any other part of the kingdom.[65]

William Bingley and Samuel J. Pratt also observed the custom of courtship in action at the turn of the nineteenth century. Men walked up to ten miles to visit their 'favourite damsels', and though the behaviour of some was above reproach: 'it is a very common thing for the consequences of the intercourse to make its appearance in the world within two or three months of the marriage ceremony having taken place'.[66]

One who appeared promptly after his parents' marriage was the future rail and coal tycoon David Davies of Llandinam, the 'Top Sawyer'.[67] Pryse Pryse, heir to Gogerddan, was born on 1 June 1815, just one month after his father's marriage to Jane Cavallier. Masters used their positions of considerable power over female servants to obtain sexual favours. Maids sometimes had suspect morals, but their honour was always under fire. The 'lonely and friendless' Mira Turner, an upper house maid, committed suicide in 1851 at Llanelli House after being accused of having an affair with C. Howell, the butler. In a letter to her 'dearest aunt', Mira insisted on her innocence for 'my heart must burst, I am in agony. I am not guilty. Bury me by my brother.' The butler, when examined by the coroner, 'admitted that he had been guilty of some romping, and such familiarities, not proper for a married man'. His wife insisted that the butler did it, for she had watched them 'through the railings in the pantry with their arms around each other'. Robert ap Gwilym Ddu fathered a child on his servant, who later emigrated to America.[68] Walter Wilkins, the inheritor of the fortune that his father made in partnership with Lord Clive in India in the late eighteenth century, was alleged to be the father of his servant Mary Morgan's bastard child. Mary was hanged at Presteigne in 1805 for the child's murder.[69] Samuel Homfray, a Merthyr ironmaster, 'a bull-necked, snub-nosed bruiser, vengeful and abusive', had an engorged libido. In 1797, it was widely rumoured that he had been 'caught at close quarters with Crawshay's daughter', and at least three bastard children were attributed to him in Merthyr Tydfil parish registers.[70] Further north, masters were no less lustful. The libido of ironmaster John Wilkinson was insatiable. In addition to the children sired within wedlock, the 'father of the iron industry' was also parent to three love children who fought for a share of his inheritance, much of which was consequently frittered away in costly legal fees.[71] Sir Thomas Picton avoided such expensive posthumous litigation. When he died, unmarried, in 1815, the four children he had fathered with his lusty mulatto mistress, Rosette Smith, were each left legacies in his will, written nine days before his death at the Battle of Waterloo.

David Samwell, the amusing, affable and amorous surgeon on Captain James Cook's last voyage of exploration on the *Resolution*, 1776–80, was probably the most prolific Welsh progenitor of bastards. In Antarctica, Samwell, ever the lusty opportunist, conceived the idea of trading tobacco for the women, whom he found 'very comely'. At Hawaii and Tahiti, where sex could be traded for a single iron nail, 'the ardent women' satisfied even Samwell's insatiable lusts. He later bragged in verse:

> Where led by love's enchanting smile
> Among the tawny maids
> We peopled more than half the Isle
> With Welsh and Saxon blades.[72]

John Evans (1770–99) of Waunfawr, Caernarfon, was another lusty explorer who enjoyed sexual encounters with native people around the world. John was one of several ensnared by the fable that a tribe of Welsh-speaking Indians had survived Madog's medieval voyage to America. Irrefutable proof of their Welshness was the rumour that raven-haired Mandan girls were pretty and garrulous, talking incessantly even when they made love, a theory which John happily put to the test. When not engaged in such pleasurable encounters, John Evans charted much of the uncharted land of America, providing valuable cartographic plans for the later voyages of the Welsh-descended Meriweather Lewis. The lives of Lewis and Evans have an odd parallel. Both died of drink, disappointed and violently.

Several witnesses brought before the 1847 Education Commission testified that the Welsh saw nothing wrong with sex outside marriage and continued to court in bed. The publication of the report led to a war of words, supported by statistics, relating to the respective immorality of the Welsh and English and of different areas within Wales. When the dust eventually settled on the debate, the results were probably inconclusive. Wales in terms of illegitimacy was only marginally more immoral than England. One feature escaped the notice of the debaters. In Wales, illegitimacy was highest in the rural areas. Whilst in 1842, for example, the illegitimacy rates for those capitals of sin, Merthyr Tydfil, Cardiff and Swansea, stood at 4.7, 5.4 and 4.0 per 100 births respectively, the rates for Llanfyllin and Machynlleth were 7.00 per 100 births, and for Newtown and Montgomery 10.3 per 100 births. Radnorshire had the highest illegitimacy rate in Britain at 14.5 illegitimate births per 100 live births.[73] Thomas Rees, in his *Letters on Wales*, attributed this to the fact that the county was so Anglicized it might as well have been in England.[74] However, many counties in Wales acquired a reputation for the high levels of illegitimacy within their borders. Haverfordwest workhouse in

November 1843 contained eighty children, of which sixty were illegitimate, one woman having just delivered her ninth bastard child. One inmate commented wryly: 'it is a bad time for girls, sir, the boys have their own way'. *Profedigaethau Enoc Huws*, by Daniel Owen, commences with the slanderous quip at the inhabitants of Anglesey: 'Mab llwyn a pherth oedd Enoc Huws ond nid yn Sir Fôn y ganwyd ef' (Enoc Huws was an illegitimate child, although he was not born on Anglesey). Surely the fact that one of the first great novels in Welsh is the history of an illegitimate child indicates that Welsh society took a more tolerant attitude to illegitimacy than the attitude suggested by images of angry fathers turning their anguished, disgraced daughters out into the snow? This is perhaps the lesson to be drawn from the experience of Anne Williams, one of the ten children of George Williams of Swansea. This bushy-bearded patriarch was a respectable pillar of the town's society – a deacon at his local chapel, a Sunday school superintendent, and a multiple property owner. Yet he had a skeleton in his cupboard. The mother of his daughter Anne was not his wife, Anna, but George's sister-in-law, Amy. In his youth the behaviour of the amorous agricultural worker George was akin to that of Nogood Boyo, the lusty country boy who was 'up to no good in the wash-house with Lily Smalls' in his grandson Dylan Thomas's *Under Milk Wood*.[75]

The pattern of higher rural illegitimacy is not a Welsh pecularity. T. C. Smout and others have shown that it was also a feature elsewhere in Britain. However, the trend is in marked contrast to European patterns of higher urban illegitimacy. Historians have sought to explain this with the observation that, as the economy modernized and more women left their rural communities and the control of their kin to seek employment in the cities and towns, they left behind 'traditional values' which stressed that pre-marital sex was wrong. In urban environments, they encountered the values of the marketplace, which stressed personal independence and self-gratification, and consequently began to search for a sexual fulfilment, which they found in illicit sexual encounters. From this, argue historians, stemmed the rise in illegitimacy.[76] Yet Wales, obviously and awkwardly, does not, for a variety of reasons, conform to this picture. Rural Wales was well acquainted with pre- and post-marital sexual encounters. Urban Wales, as the 'toys and abominable devices' confiscated by the Swansea Vice Society in the 1820s indicate, might have found ways of indulging their sexual wants without causing a rise in the illegitimate birth rates.

Courtships which led to childbirth often, as the cases of the Davies and Pryses showed, ended in marriage, but others ended in tears. Young girls abandoned by families and former lovers had one final recourse. They could appeal to the Poor Law authorities, and, from 1850, to police courts, for affiliation orders to force fathers to pay for the maintenance of their child. These cases were heard in courtrooms packed with the curious and prurient, who longed to discover the personal secrets of young couples. The cases lay bare the aspirations, desires, hopes and feelings of the men and women involved in a broken dream. Despite his strenuous denials, Griffith Thomas was ordered to pay for the maintenance of Ann Thomas's child in January 1850. The restricted geographical confines of Bardsey Island, where they both lived, had given her witnesses too many opportunities to observe the lovers in action.[77] In 1860, Margaret Jones won an order against Richard Tillet of Llanbedr and Rhuthun, after a witness admitted that she had heard him promise her money 'if she'd keep it secret'.[78] Unbelievably, Catherine Hughes of Aberdaron won an affiliation order against William Roberts, an 'old bachelor 85-years-of-age', in 1872.[79] But in her rumour-rich, rural village, the breaking waters of her pregnancy released a surge of speculation. The court believed Catherine that the feisty William was the father and ordered him to pay 1s. 6d. a week for thirteen years to support the child.[80]

The majority of girls involved in affiliation order transactions claimed that they had been seduced after a promise of marriage. This is understandable when we remember that the girls had been raised in a society which placed great emphasis on the values and virtues of purity, chastity and marriage. In order to win a case, society demanded that the girl prove she was the innocent victim of a calculating seducer. Many applicants stated that it was the promise of marriage that led to their fall from virtue. It was as if the promise pulled back a curtain in the girl's mind and led to thoughts of marriage, of a house, of a family, and above all to visions of happiness and an end to loneliness. In the man's mind, after the promise was uttered, there was probably just one all-consuming thought. Remorse followed, then regret. John Carpenter was one such person. In 1851, he was ordered to pay two shillings a week for sixteen years by Merthyr Tydfil magistrates to support the illegitimate child of Louise Thomas, despite the fact 'that this is the third time that the lady has appeared in court in an interesting condition'.[81] Some men, however, sought strenuously to deny anything and everything. Frederick Osborne caused a sensation at the Pontypridd police court in

December 1857, during the affiliation case brought against him by Rachel Lewis, a servant at the Wern, Llanfabon. PC Price gave evidence that he had frequently seen the couple together, to which Osborne retorted: 'It's a set up job. She gives her favours to the police.'[82]

Many people took the breach of promise as a serious affront to dignity and honour, and sought compensation from the offending parties. Such action was costly in time and experience. In 1841, J. D. Morgan of Liverpool paid £19. 3s. 6d. to a Swansea solicitor (who would not get out of bed for less than seven shillings) to act on his behalf, in a case of breach of promise of marriage against his daughter's suitor, Mr Burn. The case was eventually settled for £20 and an annuity of £12.[83] Mr Romilly, whilst waiting for fresh horses at Carmarthen, went into the courthouse to listen to 'an absurd trial about sitting up and breach of promise' brought by an innkeeper's daughter at Llanfynydd. The court was packed with over 200 people in their holiday finery, the women in silk bonnets and tasselled shawls, the men in black morning suits. Stern, aggrieved and curious, they crowded together on the straight-backed benches like a gathering of owls, listening to the details of an obviously very public courtship. The young girl claimed damages of £500 and was awarded £15.[84] Another who claimed damages of £500 was the orphaned Jemima Kenwood, a dressmaker of Llangattock. Although she was 'a respectable young woman', she lost her case against farmer Herbert James because she could produce no witnesses to their 'clandestine courtship' and 'secret liaisons' which had taken place between 1854 and 1860.[85] In 1830, Anne Griffith won £200 damages from Thomas Williams at the Pembrokeshire Assizes. The case received considerable attention in the press because Williams was a minister with the Presbyterian connection at Pembroke Dock. Williams's sermon was 'do as I say, not as I do', for he was 'a character of the most disgraceful description'. The love letters which were read out in court from Thomas Williams to Anne Griffith, and which revealed in detail the lusts which tempted local ministers, must have kept the tongues of local gossips wagging for weeks. On 25 May 1826, he wrote to Anne:

> I had a letter from Jonathan Davies, in which it was stated that Jonathan Davies, Llanrhian (your friend), has a base child, and that one of the students at Neuadd Lwyd, who is now a minister at Kidwelly, has deceived a girl I know very well.

Together, Thomas and Anne bought a ring. When Anne became ill with a fever at Solva and was bed-bound for six months, he switched

his attention and affection and married another. Williams denied that
he was author of the love letters for they 'were written in bad English',
or that he had 'congress' with Anne for 'she was much too ugly to kiss',
and put the case down to 'malicious people: at large in society whose
object it is to bring into contempt Ministers of Religion'.[86]

Many ministers did not need assistance to win the contempt of
society. In 1846, the Revd William Williams, a clergyman with a
Gladstonian elasticity of conscience, had to pay £100 in compensation
to Margaret Owen of Troedyrhiw, Lampeter, for a breach of his
promise of marriage. *Seren Gomer* devoted two pages to the story,
headlined with the largest font which the compositors could access.
His love letters and poems were printed in full by the Baptist
newspaper, not with any malicious intent of course, but simply to show
'i'r byd gweithredoedd OFFEIRIAD O EGLWYS LOEGR!' (the
world the behaviour of a CHURCH OF ENGLAND VICAR).[87]

Marriage and Family

The family was the cornerstone of Welsh life throughout this period.
Few questioned its importance, fewer comprehended its kaleidoscopic
differences, and all were agreed that it should be nurtured within the
bounds of matrimony. Richard Williams, Dic Dywyll, set this out
clearly in his humorous and scandalous ballad: *Cân Newydd, sef
ymddiddan rhwng mab a merch ieuanc ynghylch priodi.* In the girl's
mind's eye she saw a house with a garden, roses above the porch, the
patter of tiny feet, domestic bliss. He foresaw continuous drudgery,
compensated for only by the possibility for the frequent satiation of his
lusts. William Williams, Pantycelyn, considered marriage as a 'rhodd
sanctaidd o Dduw' (a holy gift from God). Thomas Charles and Sally,
after only a few meetings, conducted their courtship through correspondence before their marriage on 20 August 1783. All possible
difficulties had been discussed in detail beforehand.[88] Others leapt into
marriage at the first opportunity. The portly Thomas Wynn, on one of
his grand tours, purchased the fourteen-year-old beauty Maria Stella
from her parents for £4,000 and brought her to Glynllifon as his
'trophy bride'.[89]

During 1850–2, out of every thousand females aged fifteen in Wales,
no fewer than 839 could expect to have been married at least once by
the time they were fifty, and, of those aged between 35 and 45, 762

were married and 82 widowed.[90] Even in the mid nineteenth century, the popular customs of 'broom weddings' continued. A couple simply jumped over a brush on the doorstep. The greatest expense in this marriage ceremony were the three mugs of ale which had to be purchased for witnesses. In one village in north Cardiganshire in the late eighteenth century, there were fifty families united by such 'little weddings'. The custom proved reluctant to die.[91]

People married for all sorts of reasons though some, as the story of these star-crossed lovers indicates, were hard to discern:

> Saturday last was married at Clyrow, in the county of Radnor, Mr Eynon Beynon, an eminent Methodist Preacher in that neighbourhood, aged *eighty-seven*, to an agreeable young lady of *nineteen*, with a *handsome fortune*. The motives to this union are not easily to be accounted for, as the above gentleman has ever been remarkably severe in preaching against covetousness, wordly desire, etc.[92]

Perhaps the notions of 'romantic love' which filled novels and magazines from the 1830s had run amok. Undoubtedly, the old man could not believe his good fortune. Whatever the reason, stories such as these, even in an extreme form, indicate the importance of marriage throughout Welsh society. The corroding effects of loneliness were set out in: *Cân o fidus sef hanes teimlad hen ferch weddw yn methu cael gŵr.* Print, the most public of media, entered into the most private rooms and in the impersonality and the anonymity of the typed fonts, promised real people real consolations. In 1853, the Matrimonial Institution commenced advertisements in the *Cardiff and Merthyr Guardian*. The adverts promised that customers could be treated 'with the strictest honour and secrecy', and offered 'for the receipt of 12 stamps . . . the work of Matrimonial Alliances by a Clergyman . . . which is of particular interest to the unmarried'.[93]

The size of families and households (which were not the same thing) varied greatly. Many families, even by Victorian standards, were large. David Evans, Dewi Dawel (1814–91), a peripatetic tailor, publican and bard, had ten children by his wife Mary. William Thomas Edwards, Gwilym Deudraeth (1863–1940), a stationmaster at Tanybwlch was one of twelve children. Thomas Taylor Griffith (1795–1876), a doctor and antiquary, was the eldest son of the eleven children of the Ruabon doctor Thomas Griffith. David Alfred Thomas (1856–1918), first Lord Rhondda, coal magnate, a multi-millionaire and Food Controller in the First World War, was the fifteenth of seventeen children.[94] One woman, a mother to twenty-three children, was greatly praised for hardly ever missing a meeting of her local Sunday school. It was no surprise; with so many children it was probably a rare opportunity for some peace and quiet.[95] A lady in Amlwch was even more fertile. In 1819, it was noted that she and her husband, over a period of twenty-three years, brought twenty-six children into the world, twenty of whom were still alive.[96] Such large families became increasingly exceptional as the nineteenth century wore on. The availability of contraception and a weakening in the economic and biological imperative for large families might have combined to create smaller families from the 1860s.[97] These families have traditionally been regarded as extending over three generations of mutually supportive people. The evidence of the Poor Law authorities, however, points to a different story. While the courts invariably tried to force parents to maintain children, the requirement of the original Poor Law of 1601 that grown-up children support elderly parents had become so moribund that the bulk of assistance came, not from kin at all, but from the widely detested new Poor Law system established in 1834. By the late 1840s, two of every three women aged seventy and above were supported by regular cash payments from this source.[98]

The family was the haven from life's storms, in which parents could nourish and nurture their young. At the end of the eighteenth century, stern Calvinist ideas about upbringing persisted in several social classes. The strength of belief in original sin stressed the innate depravity of children and from therein arose the need and the incentive to break the child's will and repress impulses to sin. Many children were drilled into strict obedience to parental instruction. The combination of physical force and moral manipulation needed to control these basic instincts varied from family to family. In many families, the culture of poverty dictated the treatment children received. People living on the economic margins of existence, at the mercy of chance, whose scant resources could disappear through a bad harvest, unemployment or sickness, might treat their children with a rough, even extravagant, affection in good times and with casual indifference, even brute brutality, in bad times.[99] This was a society which was generally horribly cruel to animals, and as the late Professor David J. V. Jones showed, children were often treated in a similar manner.[100]

How far the opposite and opposed notions of child rearing extended into society is impossible to gauge with any accuracy, for the evidence is elusive and inconclusive. The papers of Mrs Hester Lynch Piozzi (1741–1821), Dr Johnson's 'Mrs Thrale', provide an unique view of one mother's relations with her children. Mrs Thrale from Bodfach near Pwllheli, encouraged by her friend and confidant, Dr Johnson, sought to subdue totally the wills of her children through physical force. Yet she merged this with a strong maternal ambition to produce a series of intellectual child prodigies. Mrs Thrale's family history is tragic. Her failure to breastfeed her children, her harsh educational methods and her selfish ambition to make her children exceptional in learning and achievements alienated their affections, while her extraordinary fertility – between 1764 and 1778 she had two miscarriages and produced twelve children – produced a race of puny children, the majority of whom died young. Her eldest child, Hester or Queeney, was a child wonder in an age of child prodigies, but gradually rebelled at the obsessive, incessant educational regime imposed by her mother. This soured Mrs Thrale against child rearing. Most upsetting and unsettling of all was the death of seven of her children within a few years of each other. The heaviest blow was the death, through a ruptured appendix, of Henry, the 'talented, handsome and amiable only son and heir'. Mrs Thrale lamented: 'I was too proud of him, and provoked God's judgements by my folly. Let this sorrow expiate my offences, good Lord . . . suffer me no more to follow my offspring to the grave.'

Following these tragic events of 1776, Mrs Thrale abandoned her struggle to subdue her children's wills and to cram book-learning down their throats. She sent her surviving children away to school, and turned her energies to literary pursuits and the creation of an intellectual salon of her own. In 1781, her husband, the philandering brewer Henry Thrale died of apoplexy, leaving his widow with five surviving daughters (one of whom promptly died). The bitter truth then dawned on Mrs Thrale: 'They are fine lovely creatures to be sure, but they love me not. Is it my fault or theirs?' In 1784, she abandoned both her old friend Dr Johnson, and her four surviving children for the sake of a passionate romance with their Italian music teacher, Mr Piozzi. Fearing scandal, she fled to Italy. There, she discovered that passion and pleasure could be found in married life.[101]

From the 1830s, Wales experienced a remarkable transformation in the way in which children were regarded. Although many were still sent out to work as soon as possible, in many families there was a change in the way in which they were treated. There was a stronger emotional investment in children. The expanding consumer culture provided more toys and toy shops. These were not simply amusements and diversions, but devices intended to inculcate valuable lessons. Girls, dressed in miniature replicas of the previous decade's adult fashion, played with dolls which were learning tools for emotions such as love, compassion and care. In some families, the stern father so popular in Victorian fiction created an atmosphere of austere severity in which children were forced to sit and obey like eerie museum specimens not quite killed by taxidermy. These children were reared on folk tales (the nastier the better), and selected episodes from the Old Testament (the scarier the better). Yet, many of the family paintings of Victorian Wales depict groups where affection crossed gender and generational boundaries. Some parents also participated in their children's play. Welsh families continued to be diverse in their character.

Marriage was unquestionably a major institution in Welsh society. Those who had lost a partner, as we have seen from the history of the Calvinistic Methodists, David Charles II and David Charles III, longed to re-enter a married partnership. In 1845, 1,372 Welsh people remarried.[102] Some were so keen to do so that they entered into bigamous partnerships. In 1830, Thomas Evans of Bangor (alias Thomas Bevan) was jailed for bigamously marrying Margaret Hughes while his second wife, Catherine Frain, was still alive. In 1848, Evan Jones, a farmer, was imprisoned for six months with hard labour for bigamously marrying a 'putain' (prostitute) in Neath.[103] In August 1830, William Griffith appeared before Caernarfon magistrates charged with bigamy. A week later, he was charged at the Anglesey Assizes with burning his wife Mary to death and was executed a week later in Beaumaris. 'Before an immense multitude', reported the *North Wales Chronicle*, 'he died as he had lived, without any manifestation of Christian feeling or even of manly firmness'. His strong fear of death made him attempt several escapes.[104] In 1842, *Seren Gomer* reported every bride's nightmare. When the minister asked whether anyone knew of any just cause why the marriage should not proceed, a woman in the back of the church announced: 'Gwn i, mae'n briod yn barod i fi' (Yes, I know. He's already married to me).[105]

Despite the enormous popularity of marriage, others insisted that marriage was not a word but a sentence. Marriage was as much a theatre for tension as it was for tenderness. Twm o'r Nant, when told of a friend's forthcoming marriage, remarked: 'ni wn i pam rwy'n hapus fod fy ffrind yn priodi – wnaeth e rioed niwed i fi' (I don't know why I'm happy that my friend is getting married, he never caused me any offence'). In a churchyard in the Elan valley, a wife buried in the early nineteenth century lies under a spiteful epitaph. On limestone quarried near the spot, these words were cut:

> I plant these shrubs on your grave, dear wife,
> That something on this spot may boast of life.
> Shrubs may wither and all earth must rot,
> Shrubs may revive but you, thank God, can not.[106]

The popular folk song 'Bwmba' is a frolicsome tirade against a worthless first wife, providentially now departed, which concluded with the advice to all men: 'Gofalwch fod yn ben ar y wraig ar ôl i chwi briodi' (make sure that you dominate your wife, after you are married).[107] Some men completely failed to dominate their wives. Cuckoldry is a common theme in both folk songs and court cases of Wales. John Ceiriog Hughes, Ceiriog (1832–87), one of the greatest lyrical poets of Wales, penned the poignant ballad 'Bugail Aberdyfi'. The song is a lament for a lost wife, who abandoned her husband and children for love.[108] A popular folk song in the Mynytho area near Pwllheli was 'Cân y Cwcwallt' (the Cuckold's Song), in which a drunken husband arrives home to discover a series of mysterious objects. His wife explains them as gifts from her mother. The husband sees white horses, but she explains these as new hound dogs. He sees a coach and carriage; she claims it is a dung cart and that beer casks are butter pots. However inebriated this gullible husband was, even he recognized human feet on top of his wife's for what they were.[109] Marital incompatibilities were also fertile ground for Richard Williams, Bardd Gwagedd, who related one husband's discovery:

> Rhyw noswaith wedyn, pan ddeuthym i'r tŷ,
> Does neb yn fwy drwbwl rwy'n meddwl na mi;
> Roedd Wil yr hen deiliwr mewn ffwndwr mor ffast
> Gyda'm gwraig yn y gwely yn chwarae'r hen gast . . .[110]

> One night later, when I came into the house,
> No one I think was more surprised than me;
> For Wil the old tailor was in a fast frenzy
> With my wife in the bed acting the old bitch . . .

In the Hayes area of Cardiff in October 1849, a riot broke out after a husband arrived home unexpectedly to find Thomas Taylor, 'an amorous excavator', in bed with his wife.[111] In 1825, in the same neighbourhood, a man escaped through a bedroom window when the cuckolded husband arrived home unexpectedly. 'The lady made of more solid material, was not so fortunate, and got stuck in the window and received a severe beating.'[112]

With so many tensions simmering within the bounds of marriage, especially when two sets of furious spites clashed in recurring violence, it is surprising that society did not find more varied methods of separating warring partners. The biblical injunctions on the sanctity of marriage, and the fear that an abandoned partner and children might become expensive burdens on parishes, are undoubtedly major components in the explanation. Divorce was available, but it involved a complex legal process which was too expensive for most Welsh people to contemplate. Cases for compensation and *crim. con.* (criminal conversation) could be brought before the Lord Chief Justices in the King's Bench in London, usually by men aggrieved by their wife's infidelities and indiscretions. In the 1790s, those who dared air their dirty laundry in public also had to brave the wrath of Lord Kenyon. The moral panic of the *fin de siècle* led to concern amongst many that the fabric of society was not only unravelling, but being torn to shreds. Appointed Lord Chief Justice in 1788, Lord Kenyon inaugurated a reign of terror against adulterers. He was described as

> Irascible in his temper, like his countrymen the Welsh, destitute of all refinement in dress or external deportment, parsimonious even in a degree approaching to avarice, he never the less more than balanced the defects of deportment and character by strict morality, probity and integrity.[113]

Kenyon believed that the *crim. con.* cases brought before him were evidence of the sexual irregularity and moral turpitude which threatened the very fabric of society. To combat these, he decided that the damages should be set at a level which would be a lesson to sinners. In 1794, Kenyon awarded Lord Cadogan £2,000 damages for *crim. con.* against the Revd William Henry Cooper, who had absconded with Lady Cadogan and two bull-finches in a cage to Abergavenny. The impoverished cleric was imprisoned in Monmouth jail until Lady Cadogan paid his fine. Kenyon often delivered his verdicts with all the conviction and righteous rhetoric of a hellfire-and-brimstone preacher. In one summation, Kenyon described the seducer as 'that hoary, detestable, abandoned, and degraded lecher who had broken through every social and religious obligation'. Kenyon used the law as the weapon of his own vengeance and even on one occasion lamented of a defendant seducer: 'I wish the law could punish capitally'.[114]

Yet, despite Kenyon's thunderous declarations and his draconian damages, the number of cases of *crim. con.* and divorce increased as the raunchy eighteenth century turned into the 'respectable' nineteenth century. By the 1820s, cases of *crim. con.* were heard outside the London courts, so great had the business become. In 1822, at the Caernarfonshire Great Sessions, an action for *crim. con.* was brought by Mr Stevenson, a music and dancing master from Bangor, against Mr Jones, a surgeon, who had recently been released from the Caernarfon jail under the Insolvent Debtors Act.[115] The offended party claimed damages of £1,000 against Jones for the seduction of his wife. After the full details were heard before a packed courtroom, the jury awarded damages of £20. The weakness of these cases for the aggrieved parties was that the award of damages was not accompanied with a legal separation. The 1850s witnessed a loosening in the divorce laws, which made it easier for people to obtain a separation. One of the most sensational cases in Wales was the case of Marsden v Marsden of 1860. The aged couple relived the traumas of all their yesteryears before the laughing court. Andrew Marsden, a draper in Merthyr Tydfil and Swansea in 1833, wanted a dissolution of his marriage to Elizabeth on grounds of her adultery with Mr William Meyrick. Mr Meyrick, the family solicitor, obviously had a strong grasp on another meaning of soliciting for he had 'adulterous intimacies' with Mrs Marsden. In court

> It was proposed that when Mr Marsden was absent on business, Mr Meyrick was in the habit of going to the house and that acts of adultery were frequently committed both there and at Mr Meyrick's house. In 1847, when Mr Meyrick discovered the improper-intimacy, he separated from his wife, and Mr Meyrick then took a house for her at Tenby, and co-habited with her until 1852 when he died.

In court the crowds revelled in the tales of the exploits of the coastal concubine, while Mr Marsden revealed that time does not heal all wounds. The marriage was dissolved.[116]

Sex and Sexuality

The Victorians were the people who allegedly and imprudently allowed prudery to conquer passion. Yet the evidence from a host of individuals suggests that the conquest was not complete. In the 1820s, machines were introduced at Swansea and several other Welsh bathing towns to enable people to change sedately before going to bathe. Many people ignored the 'wheeled monstrosities', took their clothes off on the beach and bathed in the nude.[117] In 1872, the Revd Francis Kilvert, the young vicar of Clyro, wrote lyrically in his diary about the delights of plunging nakedly into the sea:

> I was out early bathing from the sands. There was a delicious feeling of freedom in stripping in the open air and running down naked to the sands where the waves were curling white with foam and the red morning sunshine glowing upon the naked limbs of the bathers.

He was particularly indignant when recording attempts to deny him this freedom:

> To-day I had a pair of drawers given me which I could not keep on. The rough waves stripped them off and tore them down my ankles. While thus faltered I was seized and flung by a heavy sea which retreating suddenly left me lying naked on the sharp shingle from which I rose streaming with blood. After this, I took the wretched and dangerous rag off and of course there were some ladies looking at me as I came up out of the water.[118]

The ladies, it seems, had been looking for a considerable part of the nineteenth century. In the 1830s, there were complaints at Swansea, and in the 1840s at Llandudno, of 'ill disposed' women who watched boys and men bathe without costumes. An author at Neath in the 1870s complained about the lack of bathing facilities for colliers:

> the presence of young girls, crouching round naked boys and full grown men, certainly ought to be checked and the little hussies sent homewards . . . This utter want of decency as regards nudity in the presence of the opposite sex, of course, arises out of the 'wash all over' which is imperatively necessary when men engaged in the collieries and works have finished their duties . . . Montaigne argues, from the practice of Greek and other ancient nations, that the continual exhibition of a nude figure [leads to] nothing further than a cold admiration for the beauty of nature's handiwork . . . but . . . inasmuch as the English and Welsh people are not artists or highly educated, one comes to the conclusion that . . . it is best for the interests of society at large that we should call in the tailor.[119]

The presence of these female voyeurs suggests that the traditional view of women as sexually inert and uninterested requires reconsideration. The evidence of the ballads, folk songs and court cases indicates that Welsh women played a prominent and passionate part in sexual liaisons. Mary Morgan, the young girl hanged for the murder of her illegitimate child at Presteigne in 1805, had two lovers, either of whom could have been the child's father. The upper classes were also no strangers to feminine lusts. Edith Williams, a descendant of Thomas Williams 'the Copper King', spent her youth in much seduced circumstances. Later her soignée sophistication caught the roving eye of the future King Edward VII. Their affair prompted the jealous, syphilitic Lord Randolph Churchill to issue a challenge to a duel. To some of her assignations with the portly prince, Edith travelled in her favourite carriage drawn by four ostriches. The tradition of 'Canu Llofft Stabal' (Stable Loft Songs) suggests that girls were as active as boys in arranging liaisons:

Mae morwyn yn y Wernas,	There's a maid in the Wernas,
Ac un yn Ninas Moch,	And one in Dinas Moch,
Ond rhyfedd yw dywedyd,	And strange it is to say,
Mae ganddynt walltau coch,	That they both have ginger hair,
Mae 'pob merch goch yn gythral'	'All red heads are devils'
– ac felly mae y ddwy,	– and so are both of these,
Ond Dic a Guto benwan	But mad Dic and Guto
Sy am eu mentro hwy![120]	Are going to try them out!

According to one of Dic Dywyll's dark ballads, a girl hiding in a haystack awaiting for her lover was killed by her father's pitchfork.[121] In Radnorshire, a farmer suspicious of his wife's loyalty and fidelity went to a conjurer who put a spell on the lady's chamber pot. Anyone who touched its china would become stuck fast to the pot. According to the scurrilous song 'The Enchanted Piss Pot', the charmed pot caught not only the wife and her lover, but when it spilled onto the streets it captivated two dogs and a passerby.[122] The works of the poetess Ann Julia Hatton, Ann of Swansea, the 'troublesome sister' of actress Sarah Siddons, reveals that women were no strangers to lusts and passions. Many of her poems describe the temptation of sexual passion in graphically physical terms:

> I confess, dear seducer, afraid of the bliss,
> I scarce dare allow to thy pleading a kiss;
> For so warm are thy pressures, so sweet is thy breath,
> I fear 'twill to reason and virtue be death.[123]

Hatton drew on considerable personal experience for her risqué verses. In 1783, abandoned by her bigamous husband, she turned to the desperate measure of working in a brothel. Later, as one of the lightly clad 'goddesses of health', she operated 'the Grand Celestial Bed', and delivered lectures 'on the most unbecoming subjects' at Dr James Graham's 'Temple of Health and Hymen' in the Strand, London.[124]

Welshmen were also not just the lascivious and licentious brutes, brutally satisfying their animal lusts, that they are often portrayed to be. Some were sensitive and sensual, gifted lovers. Dr William Price, a Chartist, an unconventional doctor and a promoter of cremation, and one who used long words to describe 'dirty things' in his advocacy of free love, was a masterly lover. On 14 June 1868 Price, described simply in *Y Bywgraffiadur Cymreig* as 'dyn od' (an odd man), received this letter from his lover Vanessa:

> My dearest, most extraordinary, most loveable Welshman . . . I still tingle to the memory of your hands caressing my body, of the thrill of your possessing me, so different from the clumsy attentions of my husband, a man whose emotions are in a permanent ice age. He knows little of the needs of a woman. But you, my Druid lover, you do not just *use* a woman, you seem to know my needs. You make love so I share your pleasure.
>   Vanessa[125]

The tall, blonde, good-looking Vanessa and her Celtic Casanova possessed and pleasured each other for two years.

Sex, like most aspects of nineteenth-century life, was not immune from the pressures of commercialization, professionalization and specialization. In the 1780s, the morbid and moralistic diarist William Thomas noted with distaste:

> Did fall down dead in Cardiff's street since the beginning of this month, one of the common maids that frequented the Road and Cardiff while the Militia there, of about 20 years of age . . . Also another maid of about 16 years of age, about the same, that followed the Road with the above, had the foul disease and came to St Faggans in a pittyfull condition, where she was some days till they had an Order, and then in a court they Removed her to Bassaleg in Monmouthshire, her Parish, where she dy'd in few days.[126]

Anywhere, it seemed, that the militia went, the whores were sure to go. By the 1830s, the solitary, lonely whores had organized themselves into platoons of prostitutes who paraded the towns of Wales. At Carmarthen, the local theatre was the venue for local prostitutes to ply their trade. Robert Dyer recalled his performance in *George Barnwell*: 'I played "George Barnwell" at the Carmarthen Theatre and my speaking the line: 'Avoid lewd women, false as they are fair' offended the ladies of the pavé so highly that they hissed me heartily and not one of them came to my benefit.'[127]

The authorities tried to quell the rising problem of prostitution with draconian punishments. The Radnorshire Assizes in August 1835 sentenced Mary Jones to fourteen years' transportation for the theft of a purse from Thomas Evans, with whom 'she had been very familiar and sat on his lap'. But the 'great social evil' became so widespread that the mid-Victorian years appear not so much the gilded age of prudery and purity, as the golden age of prostitution and promiscuity. Girls went into prostitution for a host of reasons. The cycle of poverty, pregnancy and survival by theft or prostitution formed the plot for a thousand melodramas and ballads because it was one of the most common things that could happen to a girl. Poverty and abandonment by a lover were powerful factors which pushed girls into prostitution. Many girls discovered that they could earn more in twenty minutes on their back without breaking sweat than they could in a week in one of the sweated trades. Unlike dressmakers and laundresses who worked fourteen hours a day, prostitutes tended to avoid consumption. The 'slaves of the needle' could also escape to an easier life by satisfying men's needs. Prostitution seemed to offer enjoyment, freedom and titillation which no other trade could match. As prostitutes paraded in fine clothes and fripperies, local girls could only conclude that the wages of sin were higher than those based on sweat. Yet prostitution was not without its dangers. If the girl worked the street, she would find herself progressively devalued, carrion to vultures who would pimp her and beat her, a prey to the police, who would rob her and demand favours, and periodically arrest her in any case, a slave to bad liquor, drugs, disease, malnutrition and the elements. Very soon she became tarnished and backdated merchandise.[128]

Brothels were the workshops of the whores, commercial centres where madams operated as entrepreneurs of sex. The quality of Welsh brothels varied enormously over the years and across social divides. Unfortunately, the records fail us because the chroniclers of the age were too blinded by moral outrage to note physical details. The low lodging houses and base, bare beerhouses which doubled as brothels were devoid of decor and had only a few chairs and tables, and a bed in which young men performed athletic feats with youthful limbs and organs. The descriptions of squalor in the medical officer's reports make it almost impossible to believe that there was anything sensual in this trade. Rather it appears sordid, more animalistic than arousing, brutes satiating their basic instincts. The Lame Chicken in Whitmore Lane, Cardiff, the Omar Pasha in Abergavenny and the appropriately named Spread Eagle in Cardiff offered their customers no diversions as they satisfied their lusts. But brothels did provide a refuge, however brief and depersonalized, for the acutely lonely, a reminder of intimacy and warmth. To the police, their only redeeming feature was that 'at least they kept the sluts off the streets'.

Other establishments, like Carey's and the Nova Scotia in St Mary's Street, Cardiff, were celebrated brothels, famous throughout the town for the beauty, skills and lascivious charms of their girls, well-worn in moonlight ecstasies.[129] George Evans of the Dynas Arms, Cardiff, 'a notoriously bad character', had a speciality of offering two-girl specials in 1858, as did Elizabeth Pritchard's house of ill fame in Mill Lane, Caernarfon, in 1872.[130] In 1865, Merthyr Tydfil brothels offered games of 'Strip Jack Naked' to their customers, one of whom, Michael Mae, 'a simple-looking young man' who 'didn't know how, when or where he lost his clothes'.[131] At Newport, Margaret Morgan hired out a variety of clothes – silk dresses, silk skirts, silk jackets, magenta dresses, cloaks, chemise, stockings and corsets – to the girls, according to the customer's fantasies and desires. Margaret was given two months' hard labour by Newport magistrates in 1862 for operating 'a house of ill repute'.[132] Some girls were not only famous but infamous for the high quality of their services. Hannah Jones left her Welsh brothel to work with Miss Ring, Sally Taylor, One-eyed Peg, Bauld-cunted Poll and Ebony Bet in Mrs Bertley's London harem. Here you could be 'birched, whipped, fustigated, scoured, needle-picked, half-hung, holly-bushed, furse-brushed, butcher-brushed, stinging nettled, curry-combed or phlebotomized'[133] by the skilful Hannah. Ask nicely, or pay enough, and she would even whisper sweet nothings in your ear in Welsh. It was in such an establishment that the Welsh temperance lecturer Robert Parry, Robin Ddu Eryri (1804–92), was robbed by two prostitutes in 1841. Robin was obviously not temperate in all matters. In celebration of the celebrated Independent's fall, Brutus, the controversial and caustic editor of the Church of England's magazine *Yr Haul*, published a play explaining the whole sorry, sensational story.[134]

The activities of Hannah and her sisters were often described in language as formal and figurative as that of the communion service. They were members of the 'frail sisterhood'. Mary Williams 'an unfortunate little girl', Elizabeth Jones 'a woman of no great repute', Elizabeth Farmer 'a woman of improper character', Ann Williams 'a discreet looking woman, but an old offender', the veteran Mary Ann Evans 'a very bad character', a 'nymph of the pave'.[135] Such language hints that many contemporaries regarded these women, if not exactly as good for nothing, as certainly not good for much. All were well known to the police and frequently passed through the doors of police stations and jails. Theft from the person was one of the commonest crimes committed by prostitutes. In February 1864, 'the very deaf' Nicholas Blackmore was surrounded by a 'group of women who kept caressing him' in the Butcher's Arms, Monmouth. When his excitement subsided, he noticed that Ann Morgan had stolen £1. 10s. from him.[136] Elizabeth Ford robbed a Portuguese sailor of 19s. 6d. in 'a house of ill fame' in Charlotte Street, Cardiff. A gang of three women robbed David Llewelyn in the same street earlier that evening. For her part in the assault, Margaret Allen was given three months' hard labour.[137] Margaret John, 'a shameful woman', was arrested after giving counterfeit coins to a butcher. When the police arrived, she swallowed the coins and was released because of the lack of evidence.[138] Language was often lewd. Jane Roberts, 'a disorderly prostitute', was given a month's hard labour for obscene language in Whitmore Lane, Cardiff, as was Margaret Ann Phillips, 'a flashily dressed girl', at Swansea in 1866.[139] Many girls found that departure from their traditional haunts could lead to arrest. Eleanor Jones, Mary Davies, Margaret Jones and Ann Davies were arrested for 'street-walking and soliciting, vile language, assaulting people and annoying the police' at Crockherbtown and near the Cardiff Arms Hotel in 1853.[140] Asked to explain why they had migrated from their usual hunting grounds, an outraged Mary explained: 'What do you expect? Times are hard, business is terrible.' Prostitutes were no strangers to violence from the public, pimps and the police. Catherine Williams, alias Kitty Pen Bont, clad from head to hem in scarlet, 'a nineteen year old lady of the pave', fought with William Evans, a customer, in 1833 and was given twelve months with hard labour, with a week at the end of each month in solitary confinement.[141] Julia Cock (surely an alias?), was severely beaten by her pimp, Charles Diamond, and was too terrified to testify against him.[142] PC Neale was suspended from duty for fourteen days by the Swansea Borough Police for the severity of his treatment towards Margaret Thomas. The crimson-complexioned, drunken Margaret had been beaten and carried by three officers on a stretcher to the police station screaming: 'O you barbarians'.[143]

Some of the prostitutes became notorious characters in their areas. Elizabeth Jones, alias 'Neathy', and 'Big Jane' Thomas worked for the 'bully' Thomas David alias Tom Tit and Tom Robbins 'the Navvy' in the Neath and Merthyr Tydfil areas. The ample-breasted Julia Carrol of Merthyr Tydfil was described in the press as 'the heroine of a

hundred brawls', while Sarah Banner, 'The Great Western' of
Carmarthen, Elisabeth Edwards alias Garibaldi and Elizabeth Davies
alias Betsy Ty'n-y-coed of Merthyr Tydfil had formidable reputations
as fighters. These glandular women, hard-boiled and loaded with sin,
terrified many men in their neighbourhoods. Many spent almost as
much time in front of the magistrates as they did satisfying their
clients.[144] Elizabeth Davies's approach was often signalled by runners
who warned publicans – 'Betsy's coming'. Bars would clear on her
arrival, and the bartender would greet her with a truncheon and
knuckledusters. Betsy would sail into an ecstasy of foulness, urinate on
the floor, and then leave. In 1866, Rhoda Rees made her thirty-sixth
appearance at the Cardiff Police Court alongside Dinah Sims,
'another notorious woman', who was there for the thirtieth time and
the relatively inexperienced Emma Davies, a pot-bellied stove of a
woman, who was making her twenty-first appearance.[145] At about this
time, the remarkable Ellen Sweeney of Swansea began her appearances before Glamorgan magistrates which totalled 255 by 1895.[146]
Some of these were mountainous women who wore skirts so tight that
it seemed they would burst; they were bigger even than many of their
biggest customers, who were themselves gigantic. Margaret Evans of
Merthyr was called Buffalo, 'a name conferred from the taurine
appearance of the young lady's frontispiece'. She appeared as one of
the enormous cast of characters in one of Dic Dywyll's ballads:

A Buffalo yn rhegi	And Buffalo swore
Rhyw golier bach o Rymni	At a little collier from Rhymney
Am biso yn y gwely	Who pissed in the bed
A chwedyn dechrau chwydu'.[147]	And then started to vomit.

Her death was reported with little sympathy, but much sarcasm, in the
Cardiff and Merthyr Guardian in September 1849. The cause of death
was either 'the domestic correction of John Wilde, the pugilist, or
Asiatic Cholera'. Despite the hardship and hardness of their society,
these characters lived in heart-warming female communities where sex
was often secondary to companionship and where relationships
developed, not only among the women, but also with some of their
regular clients. Life settled into a dull routine when the girls were not
with a client – an eternal round of cards and lotto, alcohol and a pipe,
or cigarettes by the 1860s, a visit to or from the hairdresser, the same
old jokes, more alcohol and tobacco, or a little lesbianism, which was
resorted to rather as men turned to homosexuality in prison.

Prostitution was far more widespread across Wales than has perhaps been realized: the geography of immorality was extensive. In 1862, the chief constable of Anglesey complained of the activities of the prostitutes of Amlwch.[148] The life of 'sin and dissipation' of Ann Daniel, alias Nanny Boy, came to an end at Bangor in October 1872. Falling ill during a drinking spree, she collapsed and died after being carried to the police station in a wheelbarrow. Although she had lived for only twenty-eight years, her face had a colour that could only be described in shades of grey, like someone long deprived of sunlight – which was the case, for she had spent long periods on her back in the dark and in jail.[149] Mill Lane in Caernarfon became notorious for its brothels in the 1870s. Elizabeth Morgan, all silk and satin, was one of several celebrated prostitutes in the town.[150] Evan Jones kept an illegal lodging house which served as a brothel in Pwllheli.[151] In 1849, the Superintendent of Police at Wrexham complained that 'there are in the town of Wrexham 41 lodging houses . . . of the very worst description . . . prostitution is also to be complained of; scarcely a lodging house in the town refuses to harbour for this purpose'.[152]

At Rhuthun, Elizabeth Jones alias Beti Llygad-y-Geiniog was the most famous of the town's prostitutes.[153] Thomas Williams, Capelulo, in his autobiography, recalled his drunken, public coupling with a prostitute in the town:

cyfarfyddais â dynes ddrwg ar y dref, ac ymddygais yn bur warthus gyda hi ganol dydd golau; a yr oedd tyrfa fawr o blant, ac eraill, oedd yn digwydd mynd heibio ar y pryd, yn gylch o'm deutu yn edrych arnaf. Cymerodd Mr Williams yr Exciseman chwip a chwipiodd ni, nes ein gwahanu oddi wrth ein gilydd.[154]

I met a wicked woman on the town, and I behaved disgracefully with her in broad daylight, in front of a large crowd of children and idle people which had gathered to watch us. Mr Williams the Exciseman got a whip and whipped us, until we separated from each other.

In 1867, the *Caernarvon and Denbigh Herald* reported on the scandalous behaviour of the Holyhead Board of Guardians: 'who appear incapable of discharging the most elementary of their functions'. Among their failings was the fact that they supplied young girls and orphans to Caddy Owens at 51 Baker Street, Holyhead: 'This house of Caddy Owens is a brothel, and to it the Guardians do not scruple to send children of tender years.' When Dr Buchanan visited the house, he found several twelve- and fifteen-year-old girls there. Mr Jones, a guardian, later admitted: 'it was true that Mrs Owen's house was known to be a brothel, and that sick people and orphan girls had been sent there by the Guardians . . . it was a matter of common notoriety'.[155]

When not at the theatre, the prostitutes of Carmarthen were often to be found fighting in the streets. Margaret Jones and Mary Protheroe, 'drunk and riotous', were arrested by PC William John before a large crowd. Respectively, it was their sixteenth and sixth unrespectful arrest.[156] At Llanelli, the growth and development of the docks attracted droves of whores. Elizabeth Richards was one of several who appeared before the police courts.[157] At Swansea, prostitution was even more prolific. One local moralist complained that there were 'more Magdalens than Methodists in the town'.[158] When police intervened in a pitched battle between prostitutes and pimps in the town, Lucy Hunt 'then raised her clothes in a very indecent and offensive manner'. She spent Christmas in the cells.[159] The inquest into the death of Annie Watts, 'a young unfortunate residing in William Street who had been found drowned in the South Dock', heard details of the entertainment offered to sea captains in the 'lovely ugly town'. Henry Adams, a tailor in the town, testified that he met Captain Washington at Mr Steele's public house, The Scotch Hero, at the bottom of Wind Street. Invited by the captain to 'show him the town', they proceeded to Mr Hunt's Salubrious Passage, for a glass of brandy, then for supper to the faggot shop in Rickland Street, then on for some 'girls of the town' at Annie's in 27 William Street, where she was 'in the habit of having men and women there'. Adams thought that he and the captain had 'a pint of brandy between us, I think I paid for it. I left the Captain at Annie's and heard next day that she had fallen off the bridge.'[160]

Cardiff, like Swansea, had abundant facilities to satisfy a sailor's lusts for liquor and ladies. John Willett, the Secretary of the Cardiff Associate Institute for Improving and Enforcing the Laws for the Protection of Women, estimated that 1,500 women and children gained a living from prostitution in Cardiff in 1860.[161] The railway embankment divided the town as effectively as the Taff. As one crossed it, the whole temper of the town changed. Rents dropped. Streets darkened and narrowed. The architecture shrank in size and houses and pubs were of bare, smoke-stained brick. The dancing houses and drinking dens of the lanes leading off Bute Street – Whitmore Lane, Charlotte Street, Adam Street – doubled as brothels. Their fetid bars were the working premises of local prostitutes. Crews of Austrian,

Chilean, Dutch, English, French, Greek, Lascars, Malayan, Portuguese, Scottish, Spanish and Welsh ships cavorted with poverty-stricken, squalid and wicked whores every night. Transients who lived a furtive and persecuted existence were regarded as the flotsam and jetsam of Cardiff, carried in on the tide, which many people hoped would carry them straight back to sea. The most evident type of transience amongst the clientele of the beer shops and brothels was the transience of failure – shady goods dealers, inept con men, tramps, vagrants and vagabonds, and podgy, balding lodgers who absconded on rent day. These were people who drank alone, close to the bar, where the action was in most pubs. By the late 1840s, this area of Cardiff revelled under the name of Tiger Bay, a society of people driven to a dark place by greed and pain. Do-gooders failed to do good in this area, but were sent on their well-wishing way with excrement on their shoes and execrations in their ears. Bute Street was 'the street of a thousand whores'. Members of the 'frail sisterhood', like Mary Ann Williams, despite the 'cow like gentleness of her eyes', were violent and vicious. Elizabeth Evans, 'a diminutive nymph of the pave', specialized in drugging her clients before robbing them. Captain Robert Stapledon, master of the *Endeavour*, had no recollection of where or when he had been with Elizabeth when he was found penniless, naked and sleeping outside the National Schoolroom at 3.15 a.m.[162]

Brothel owners were entrepreneurs of vice, who controlled their vicious empires with a savage severity. Edward Llewelyn was the notorious owner of a beer shop and brothel in Charlotte Street, famous for its bosomy serving women in their frilly finery, and the rubato hurly-burly of the piano.[163] Joseph Colburn, landlord of the New Crown beerhouse on Bute Street, was charged with: 'keeping a disorderly house and fighting with a musician which was most disgraceful'. The police superintendent noticed upon entry that: 'all were drunk, none were sober, several were fighting including the landlord and the musician and the landlord's wife and the musician's wife, none were singing . . . the house is a notorious brothel'.[164] One of the most infamous brothel-keepers in Cardiff's history was Jack Matthews. 'Highly individualistic, totally unamenable to discipline with an ungovernable temper and prodigious strength', Matthews was twice flogged before being dishonourably discharged from the militia. He became a familiar figure on Cardiff's streets, his hoarse voice shouting out 'Razors to grind, scissors to grind'. In 1849, he began his career of vice at the Forresters Arms, 21 Adam Street. Soon he owned three adjoining properties and had them ingeniously interconnected, so that the girls could reach their rooms and escape from the clutches of the law. In 1851, he married the Rubenesque Elizabeth Davies, 'whose beauty and air of innocence, belied a savage and undisciplined nature'. She often fought side by side with Jack in their brothel, but more often they fought face to face. Elizabeth was charged with the assault and murder of Mary Sullivan in 1859, but escaped punishment after Jack allegedly blackmailed, or bribed, the judge. In that year, Jack took over the Flying Eagle in Charlotte Street, a tough street in a tough area. Once again he purchased neighbouring properties to create a complex, interlocking maze. Jack frequently appeared before Cardiff magistrates, and on one occasion, so aggrieved was he at a perceived miscarriage of justice, that he paid his fine in a wheelbarrow full of 4,800 farthings, which he poured before the clerk of the court, with the words: 'There's your bloody fine'. During 1869, he appeared before the magistrates six times, yet he still had the effrontery to stand in the municipal authority election. He was defeated by Pat Carey, whom, Jack claimed, kept a high-class brothel in Queen Street. In contrast to Carey's sumptuous palace, Jack's Eagles were down-at-heel and quite literally downhill and downtown. In 1875, Jack Matthews retired to a plush villa in Severn Road, living off the income of the businesses which he rented to others. His children were educated in London boarding schools and 'finished' in Lyon. Yet, his hopes for them were dashed when his favourite daughter ran off with a man she had met at a circus. Matthews died in 1888 and was the subject of an obituary in the *Cardiff Argus*. Jack Matthews lies under a large sandstone memorial stone in Cathays Cemetery, with the hopeful inscription – 'God is Mercy'.[165]

In 1860, the Cardiff branch of the Society for the Suppression of Vice and Immorality led a concerted campaign against the town's 'houses of ill fame'. In all, twenty-one cases were brought before the Glamorgan Quarter Sessions in February 1860. The atmosphere in the crowded courtroom was carnivalesque: 'To hear these cases the Court was crowded with the wretched occupants of both sexes, of the dens of infamy which abound in this town, and who gave vent to their feelings in loud applause.' Almost all the inhabitants of Charlotte Street, Whitmore Lane, Alfred Street, Francis Street, Nelson Street, Christina Street and Mount Stuart Square had decamped for the duration of the cases to the court, which resounded with raucous laughter. Mr Evan Davies, who lived opposite Robert Dolbeer's 'infamous house' in Christina Street, bravely, or foolishly, gave evidence that 'twelve men at a time, whole ship crews would visit, disturbances were frequent and girls appeared at the windows partly undressed'. When the prosecuting solicitor uttered the phrase 'such were the ups and downs of life', the courtroom exploded in laughter and the hearing adjourned for a respite.[166] At Cardiff in the early 1860s, Swansea in the late 1870s, and Caernarfon in the early 1870s, anti-vice campaigners filled police cells with a gibbering and jabbering company of prostitutes. Once it became clear that they were to be arrested, girls would beg to be allowed to slip home to feed their cat, dog or leave a child in the care of neighbours. The atmosphere in the cells was oppressive, for the girls smelt pungently of unwashed clothes, tobacco smoke, alcohol, sweat and sex. Voices, hoarse from screaming or drunkenness, would insist that they were not wicked women like those dissipated women who had been arrested in the company of ragmen and tramps. Once one began crying, an entire cell would be flooded with tears. The excuses trotted out in court had a weary familiarity: 'the police were mistaken', 'it wasn't me', 'they have a grudge against me', 'I'm being persecuted'.

The only serious rival to Tiger Bay, in the long and complex annals of Welsh prostitution, was the Pont-y-storehouse district of Merthyr Tydfil. Like the characters who lived there, the area was better known by its nickname, 'China'. From a thousand pulpits, it was condemned as Wales's very own Sodom and Gomorrah. To the pious, it conjured up the abominations of the book of Prophets and the stews of Babylon and Corinth, or a narthex to hell. During the day, it was a somewhat silent place but it grew much noisier after dark, when the shadows brought confidence, and the alcohol began to bite. The first prostitutes worked in the area from 1825, and from the opium wars of 1840–3 it acquired its infamous title.[167] In the 1830s, the Empress was the hot-headed redhead Elizabeth James, Betsy Bengoch. This desperate and gigantic virago was every Merthyr boy's Saturday night delight – passionate, rosy-cheeked, big-bosomed, with piston rods for legs.[168] The world of China is revealed in a remarkable document, 'A Journal Kept by a Scripture Reader' deposited in the National Library of Wales.[169] The journal was written by a young Anglican who had the courage to turn his creed into deed and embark on a mission to China to rescue the fallen women from the 'dens of misery', and bring them back to decency and respect. In contrast to the claims of many Welsh moralists that prostitution was an English vice, the 'Scripture Reader' revealed that, of the thirty-six prostitutes interviewed on his first visit, six were English, five Irish and twenty-five Welsh. Ann Jenkins ran a specialist Welsh-medium brothel. Many co-habited with men: 'James Jones with Sarah Davies, Juno Daley with Ann Sullivan, Jonah Davies with Hannah Lloyd, Benjamin Phillips with Catherine Jones, James Phillips with Catherine Sullivan, William Jones with Sarah Boilum, William Michael with Caroline Keith . . .'.[170] These were girls of easy leisure, and boys of roaring pleasure. According to the 'Scripture Reader', the men were unemployed, choosing instead to live off their 'paramour's earnings'.

One of the most noteworthy aspects of the Scripture Reader's Journal is the respect which was accorded to every girl. This remarkable document was the product of a true Christian. The motives of the girls for entering the trade are frequently recorded: 'Ellen Lewis – went to prostitution to keep her five children . . . she had been led astray by a man after being in China for eight months . . . Elizabeth Williams ran away from home . . .'. Some were out for fun and a quick fortune, while others were escaping from some private hell at home. Their stories had a central theme – work long enough to make a stake and then try to enter respectable life. When young, they had been adventurers and runaways with gleaming hair and fresh faces, confident of their ability to control their lives. When the 'Scripture Reader' met them they were less certain of their futures. Many had realized that they were high up on the rungs of a ladder of degeneration and desperation, with no means of escape, except by falling.

Like these girls, China itself by the early 1860s had passed its heroic days:

> There are no men going to China now but the vilest of the vile . . . some of the clerks of the town and well dressed men who used to go there are no longer going. Prices are coming down from 1/- to 6d and from 3/- per night to 1/6 . . . their companions in wickedness used to vary from ten years of age to eighty but the youngest and oldest are keeping off now . . . customers are mostly idle boatmen.[171]

Catherine Spence, whose 'paramour' was at Cardiff, lamented: 'China is not what it was a few months ago – one half of the unfortunate girls are gone from there – some to their houses, some to work to different places, some are married, and some are returning to religion.'[172] Other places of work included the Omar Pasha beerhouse in Monk Street,

Abergavenny, the Tredegar Public House, Llan, Tredegar, Hill's Terrace *cwrw bach* in Newport or the Llanfaes alehouse, Brecon.[173] From the 1840s, Wales witnessed several brave attempts to 'reclaim poor, erring, sinful, unfortunate women from paths of misery and vice'. In 1849, the good ladies of the Cardiff Female Refuge Society, all God's deputies in bonnets, under the patronage of the marchioness of Bute, began trying to save girls.[174] At Swansea a decade later, a house for fallen women was established to save women from an 'untimely grave',[175] but much of their work was too little, too late.

Diversity and Perversity

While respectable women furiously but fruitlessly battled the sex trades, they bravely held their own in another arena, control of their own fertility. The average number of children born to Welsh families fell from seven or eight in 1800 to five in 1860. One of the leading weapons in women's birth control arsenal was abortion. Although a woman who practised abortion was condemned as 'the butcher of her own bowels', the practice was probably widespread across Wales.[176] The denominational and secular press of Wales contains many advertisements for 'female medicines'. Although some were targeted at women who wished to conceive and be fruitful, the majority appear to have been intended for those who wished to terminate pregnancy. Dr Locock's Female Wafers, Frampton's Pill of Health, Dr Kent's Female Medicine, Keersley's Original Pills and Widow Welch's Female Pills were all 'valuable medicine effectively removing obstruction and relieving all the other inconveniences to which the female frame is liable'.[177] By 1849, Dr Locock was even claiming that his 'Female Wafers', which 'have no taste of medicine', were under 'Royal Patronage'. His wafers, which 'act like a charm' and 'remove all obstructions', could be purchased from Evans and Sons, Wholesale Agents, Cardiff, Mr Griffith Phillips druggist, Merthyr Tydfil, Mr White bookseller, High Street, Newport, Mr E. J. Phillips and Messrs Rogers and Co., druggists, Tredegar, and Mr Crewe's Medical Hall.[178] Robert Isaac Jones, Alltud Eifion (1815–1905), the publisher of *Y Brython* newspaper, included abortificants in the pharmacopoeia produced by his Cambrian Pill Depot at Tremadog.[179]

Evidence given at criminal and coroners' courts suggests that abortion was widespread in Welsh society. In 1813, an itinerant female miniature painter collapsed and died in Matilda Street, Carmarthen, after taking a cocktail of alcohol, opium and other drugs obtained at Mr Goulstone's druggist shop in Lower Market Street.[180] In 1836, in a sensational court case at Dolgellau, Richard Jones was charged with '[g]weinyddu rhyw gyffuriau meddygol i ferch ieuanc o'r enw Catherine Edwards, yr hon oedd yn feichiog ohono ef, gyda bwriad i beri erthyliad' (administering drugs to a young girl named Catherine Edwards, who was carrying his child, with the intention of procuring an abortion). The fact that Jones was an Independent minister at Bala drew crowds to listen to the details of the couple's secret liaisons. Catherine claimed that they had sexual intercourse in the parlour of the Eagles Hotel in Llangollen, and that afterwards Jones attempted to force her to take drugs to abort herself.[181] Rees Thomas Rees, an occasional 'preacher of the Presbyterian persuasion', was hanged before a crowd of 10,000 in Carmarthen, and his body dissected, for murdering Elizabeth Jones of Llangadog. When Rees learnt that Elizabeth was carrying his child, he forced her to drink liquid

> from a grey bottle . . . which according to her sister Gwenllian, burned her like liquid fire so that she screamed. Her throat was completely ulcerated, gums and cheeks so swollen as to adhere to each other . . . her teeth were black and so loose, that she took them out with her fingers to show her mother . . . in a few hours she died.[182]

The involvement of ministers in these well-publicized cases suggests that knowledge of birth control methods was fairly widespread in Wales by the mid nineteenth century. In the 1850s, Robert Dale Owen (1801–77), son of the Newtown social reformer Robert Owen, extended people's awareness of practices and techniques for birth control. In his magazine *The Free Enquirer*, Owen advocated free secular education, birth control and changes to both the marriage and divorce laws. His *Moral Philosophy* of 1850 recommended *coitus interruptus* as a practical, pleasurable and sensible method of birth control.[183] One miner later recalled how he had read the literature as a young man and opted for Owen's approach. The economist Richard Jones argued that the practice should be taken further to include complete sexual restraint and abstinence. By the time of his moralistic economic epistles, however, barrier methods of birth control had become widely available in Wales.[184] Condoms were sold in barbers' shops and surgeons and itinerant chemists and charlatans sold them at pubs, taverns, fairs and markets.

One forgotten aspect of the information technology revolution which swept over Wales in the nineteenth century is the sexual element. Alongside the torrent of books on religious topics came a trickle of books which sought to instruct and inspire the Welsh in their love-life. In 1842–3, John Jones of Llanrwst published *Gwaith Aristotle*. This was not the work of the ancient philosopher, rather a Welsh edition of the much printed and widely read sex manual, *Aristotle's Work*.[185] The work was one of the best-sellers in the backpack of the itinerant bookseller, Thomas Williams, Capelulo, whose raunchy behaviour we have already encountered.[186] Other advice books included Mrs Cockle's *Book for Instruction and Amusement*, which contained 'important studies for the female sex', and the *Handbook for Everyman* – 'worth a thousand prescriptions'.[187] The advice books included practical advice such as that people should 'use your right hand to eat, and your left hand for toiletry purposes' – wise counsel in an age of few toilets and no toilet paper.[188] A common theme in this literature was the danger to the Welsh people from the excitements and excesses of youth. *A Lecture to Young Men*, a tattered copy of which exists in the Carmarthenshire Record Office, explained the danger: 'The evil to which I refer, is in plain language, masturbation, a practice which consists of irritation of the organs of generation with the hand'. The author added a sentence whose pun must surely have been intentional: 'many a young man has gone to ship wreck on the sands of ignorance through want of a helping hand'.[189]

In 1811, the *Carmarthen Journal* began advertising for a 'four shilling book sold by J. Daniel, printer of this paper; North and Co., Brecon; Griffiths, Tenby; Wilmot, Pembroke; Thomas, Haverfordwest; and all the other good booksellers in the Principality' which warned against: 'Juvenile Debauchery, with the humble hope that the author's remarks, founded on long experience, may give a check to that progressive degeneracy in the Human Race, which appears to be making rapid strides to its total extinction'.[190]

The loss of vital fluids from *onaniaeth*, 'solitary vices and habits', or 'youthful delusive excess', was leading to the creation of a race of puny, tired, debased and debauched men.[191] 'To restore manly vigour', a whole range of medicinal cures and literary correctives to behaviour were offered by Welsh charlatans and mountebanks. These quacks in their all-pervading publicity – the *Carmarthen Journal* offered over 200 patent-medicine products on its front page – created a climate of fear in people's minds.[192] By 1860, the Welsh press had given this condition a name, whose suspicious medical title must have led many to believe in its authenticity – spermatorrhoea.[193] Dr Lambert offered a book of advice or consultations in his surgery to sufferers, and Dr Curtis a book of advice on *Manhood*. Dr Roper offered his Royal Bath Plasters, while Dr Roos claimed that his Concentrated Guttae Vitae, or vegetable life drops, 'effectively relieve those who have injured themselves by solitary habits or excesses, and brought the dreadful disease known as spermatorrhoea or nocturnal emissions'.[194] Lloyd and Co. offered the Cordial Balm of Angelica as 'hope for nervous invalids'. Dr Thompson presented his *Friend in Need* – 'a medical work on marriage' – while Dr Curtis offered *A Medical Essay on Nervous and Generative Diseases* and a lotion to prevent 'premature decline whether arising from youthful abuse or the follies of maturity, the effect of climate or infection'. In direct competition, and contradiction to Dr Curtis, Dr Charles Watson offered 'the newly discovered American invention which supersedes poisonous drugs':

> A truly extraordinary discovery for the treatment and self cure of spermator-rhoea, seminal weakness, debility, nervousness, lassitude, depression of spirits, loss of energy and appetite, pains in the back and limbs, timidity, self-distrust, dizziness, want of energy, love of solitude and involuntary discharges.

The cure was elementary. To those in need, Dr Watson also promised 'ruptures cured without a Truss'.[195] Most famous of all was Solomon's *Guide to Health*, a 200-page book printed in over sixty editions, adver-tisements for which could be seen in every secular and denominational newspaper in Wales. In a confidential, doctor-to-patient tone, Solomon warned his readers that they were suffering from almost unmentionable sexual disorders, involving shocking symptoms such as 'involuntary emissions, back pains, weak memory, dejection, depression, anxiety, chronic weakness, and poor eyesight' – the association between bad eyesight and solitary vices has a surprisingly long history. To cure such a distressing and debilitating condition, there was only one option – Solomon's Balm of Gilead – efficacious in every way.[196]

Sex provided good business for patent-medicine peddlers and quacks because sexual diseases were widespread, secret and shameful. Quacks are usually regarded as the mercenaries of the medical world, their cures cons, their remedies rip-offs, their unguents useless. Yet, if they fostered fear, they also fermented hope in the hearts of desperate people that they were not beyond rescue. Moreover, their advertise-ments and work encouraged a discussion of sexual matters and

problems in ways which are not often appreciated. The history of
venereal disease in Wales illustrates this point in a practical way.
Syphilis and gonorrhoea were far more common in Welsh society than
has traditionally been appreciated. In 1776, Mr Thrale showed his wife
a greatly enlarged testicle, caused, he claimed with little conviction, as
a result of bruising when he jumped out of a carriage some months
previously. Mrs Thrale refused to believe this improbable story,
recalling her father's warning when she announced her engagement to
the bawdy brewer: 'If you marry that scoundrel he will catch the pox,
and for his amusement set you to make his poultices.' Mrs Thrale
lamented: 'this is now literally made out, and I am preparing poultices
like he said and fermenting this elegant ailment every night and
morning for an hour together on my knees.' The famous actress, Mrs
Siddons, born in the Shoulder of Mutton public house in Brecon, was
outraged when her husband gave her the pox in 1792. After her
recovery, 'an indignant melancholy sits on her fine face . . . ; she is all
resentment'.[197] Syphilis was undoubtedly the cause of the industrialist
Robert Thompson Crawshay's erratic and eccentric behaviour and,
rather than arthritis or 'y gymalwst', was probably the factor which
brought about the suicide of the poet Talhaiarn in 1869. In 1857, a
physician at the Usk house of correction complained in his annual
report that during the year he had to deal with 'one death, one very
refractory patient pretending to be insane, one case of small-pox,
injuries of all kinds and a great deal of venereal disease'.[198]

Many Welsh people had cause to regret the fact that, for one night
of bliss with Venus, they spent a lifetime of regret with Mercury. Men
who consorted with prostitutes were exceptionally vulnerable for many
girls were ingenious in using gold leaf and chocolate to hide lesions,
sores and other symptoms of these diseases. Syphilis could be treated
fairly successfully by regular practitioners through mercury, but it was
a protracted, painful and unpleasant process. The treatment would
'flux' the patient: powerful evacuations, perspiration, and copious
salivation (often a couple of quarts of saliva a day) would be
produced, designed to force out the fever. The patient would be
incapacitated for a period through unpleasant side-effects, which
included swollen gums, aching joints and a fetid smell. Those who
offered cures which were not based on mercury therefore found an
anxious audience. The Welsh newspaper press abounds with advertisements for their products. Some sought to veil the purpose in coy
language. Dr Cullen offered his 'Celebrated Scarlet Pills . . . for the

prevention and cure of a certain disease', giving the added reassurance that they 'cured in safety and secrecy',[199] while Dr Boerhaave promised that his Red Pills were 'famous throughout Europe for the cure of every stage and symptom of a certain complaint'. But others could not have been more explicit as to what distressing affliction their drugs were intended to cure. From the front page of *The Cambrian* in 1810, Dr Hunter proclaimed that his 'Alternative Pills' were 'an infallible medicine of well-established reputation for years which effectively cures the VENEREAL DISEASES, in all its stages'.[200] Even in 1850, at the supposed height of the mid-Victorian period of sexual repression, Wray's 'Balsamic Pills' offered 'a certain cure for gonorrhoea, pains in the loins, irritation of the bladder or urethra and other diseases of the urinary passage'.[201] To give themselves credibility, these purveyors of cures for venereal diseases adopted medical terminology in their literature and stole the name of famous doctors for their products. But their discourse was often a blatant appeal by the quacks to the anxieties of their readers behind the backs of their legitimate medical counterparts, and was often of the most crudely manipulative sort. One who traded on the fringe of legitimacy was Dr Shadrach Jones.[202] He left the financial deficits of traditional medicine for the affluence of patent-medicine selling. Jones realized the profitability of selling secret remedies for secret diseases.

Although many people wished to keep their sufferings and shames secret, certain aspects of popular sexuality, like the adverts for venereal diseases, departed the private world and intruded into the public. A dark shadow lay over early nineteenth-century radicalism, which according to Thomas Williams involved 'alcoholic clubs combining intoxication, sexual promiscuity and blasphemous rituals'.[203] Following the loss of the market for radical pamphlets and prints, many publishers and booksellers dabbled in the obscene publications trade during the 1820s.[204] John Jones began as an occasional agent in the trade before publishing obscenity in his own right, thereby profiting greatly from human weaknesses. William Dugdale utilized the printing experience and contacts he had gained during his Chartist and radical campaigning, and became one of the nineteenth century's leading purveyors of pornography. Some of his publications were ancestors of the muck-raking Sunday newspapers, offering: 'fun and frolic . . . Police intelligence, murders, rapes, suicides, burnings, maimings, theatricals, races, pugilism!' The intention was to drag the upper classes down by revealing the true extent of their depravity. In practice, it proved to be a protracted, but profitable process. In addition to bawdy books and ballads, the pornographers soon adopted the latest technology to perfect their art.[205] Woodcuts were replaced by prints, and then were themselves made obsolete by photographs. These were not just tame pictures of gartered ladies in front of cheese plants, with the leaves delicately dangling before strategic body parts, but photographs of the varied perversions, peccadilloes and physical permutations in the mind of man. The plump women of the sensual underworld revealed pendulous Raphael breasts and much, much more.[206] It was in this pornographic tradition that the young Arthur Machen began his writing career, by translating the *Heptameron* of Margaret of Navarre, a fashionable mixture of religious fervour and voluptuousness, and Casanova's *Memoirs*. The translation was ordered by a man named Redway, who ran an indecent lending library.[207]

The redeeming appeal of antiquity was that it added respectability; no writer dead for over 400 years could possibly be deemed to be indecent. This tradition can also be discerned in art. The Conwy born royal sculptor John Gibson (1790–1866), in addition to sculptures of Queens Alexandra and Victoria and Robert Peel, produced a number of works which would have familiarized their viewers with the naked female body. *Hylas and the Nymphs*, the unfinished *Wounded Warrior Tended by Female Figure*, *Cupid Tormenting the Soul*, *Cupid Pursuing Psyche*, *Marriage of Psyche and Celestial Love* and two works titled *Nymphs Kissing Cupid* are all characterized by nudity of the classical period. Depending on Gibson's allegorical needs, dewy, spiritualized and idealized Welsh virgins lay demurely naked or slouched, clad in filmy muslin barely concealing their pudenda. The work *Preparing for the Bath* was described as 'one of very high character. The upper part is finely modelled, the pose being easy and graceful. It is in the Greek style. There is a vase containing oil with which bathers used to anoint themselves.'[208] A less intellectually elevated viewer might just have seen a group of naked women cavorting and oiling themselves in a group bath. The gentle curate Kilvert confided to his diary on 6 January 1872 his experience of viewing a painting at a London art gallery:

> The beautiful girl stripped naked of her blue robe and stabbed in the side under the left breast is sailing through the air and reclines half standing, half lying back, supported tenderly in the arms of her lover who has been stabbed in the same place. The naked girl is writhing and drawing up one of her legs in agony – but her arms are thrown back and clasped passionately round her lover's neck.[209]

Her bravery was well beyond the call of beauty, for here was passion entwined in pain. The recumbent, naked, or scantily clad figures of art created an imagery of vulnerability and availability which revealed, above all, the obsession of the Victorians with the perfect female shape. Already, by the 1840s, the ideal female figure was established as curvaceous, well breasted, slim-waisted and amply hipped. In the 1840s, the girls who modelled the traditional costumes of their areas in C. H. Marking's and Lady Llanover's parade of Welsh costumes – Miss Carmarthenshire, Miss Cardiganshire – had the ideal Welsh figure.[210] The secret of such chaste slenderness was the foundation of fashion – the corset. For, even in deepest rural Wales, Venus wore stays. Those women who were too portly to conform to the ideal were painfully laced into the requisite shape. By the 1860s, several newspapers, to the delight of the prurient, carried advertisements for corsets, which had line drawings of ladies dressed only in their lower garments. Though moralists complained at the indecency, doctors voiced concern that tight-lacing a voluptuous lady into a tight corset represented a long-term danger to the woman's health. One sensationally claimed in *The Lancet* that a woman had cut her liver in half through the practice. In life, as in art, the price of beauty was pain.[211]

Ballad singers were no less coy than artists in their descriptions of the female form and the sexual act. Although some printers insisted on the partial spelling of swear words – 'd—l', 'd—lio' and 't—n', others were far more open. Richard Williams had several terms for the sexual act, derived from the rich vernacular vocabulary of the Welsh: 'jig bol joggan', 'difyrrwch Jones o Lundain', 'ffit ffiri', 'taro bob a diri', 'jig my fando', 'pleser Dic Siôn Dafydd', 'dawnsio mownt y dinpan', 'yr hen lawenydd', 'jeri wo ji', 'jig yr hen bechod', 'sowndio'r machine', 'chwarae step Wil Gasseg', 'chwarae'r hen diri mewn llwyn' and 'diri rhwng dau'.[212] In the collection of ballads gathered by J. D. Lewis in the National Library of Wales is one dedicated to 'Y Golomen Wen'. It recounts the seduction of a lusty young man in the back room of a Welsh pub. One of the three girls invites the youth into another room 'i saethu'r g'lomen wen' (to shoot the white dove). He naively replies that he is unarmed, only to be instructed:

Wel gyda ti mae'r bwa	Well you have the bow,
A gyda fi mae'r saeth,	And I the arrow,
Pan elom i'r tywyllwch,	When we go into the dark,
Mi welwn fel y gath;	We'll see like a cat;
A dal y saeth yn gymhwys,	If you hold the bow properly

A llanw hyd y pen   And fill to the head
A saetha hi dan ei haden,   And shoot her under her wing,
Tydi bia'r g'lomen wen.   You'll own the white dove.

By the end of the final verse, the naive young man has been transformed into a sexual athlete.[213]

In 1827, Henry Owen found himself before the Caernarfon magistrates for selling and singing obscene ballads on the town's streets. The
offensive ballad was 'Cân Newydd o Hanes Dwy Ferch Ieuangc a
Gneifodd Gedor Llangc Tra yr oedd yn cysgu' (A new song relating
the history of two young girls who shaved a boy's pubic hair while he
was sleeping). The ballad relates how two girls decided to play a trick
on a young man sleeping soundly, by shaving his pubic hair. The ballad
relates their adventure, 'yn cneifio gyda scil – o gwmpas Wil un llygad!'
(shearing with skill around one-eyed Wil). Appropriately, it was sung
to the tune *Poor Jack*.[214] The metaphor used in this ballad – 'lladd
gwair' (killing grass) – is also present in the work of Jac Glan-y-gors,
together with other metaphors for the sexual act. In 'Miss Morgans
Fawr, o Blas y Coed' he remarks:

Roedd Siôn o Lun yn eithaf dyn,   Siôn of Lun was quite a man,
Ac wedi tyfu'n llencyn lysti,   A strong and lusty lad,
A chanddo fo 'roedd hynod ffordd   And he had a powerful way
I yrru'r ordd i gorddi.   Of sending the paddle to stir.

Similarly 'Priodas Siencyn Morgan', indicates the stamina of the
Welsh in love:

Ac wrth gusanu ei boch   Whilst kissing her cheek,
Aeth Siencyn i gynhyrfu,   Siencyn began to excite,
A chwarter cyn pedwar o'r gloch   And just before four o'clock
Fe dorodd gwaelod y gwely.[215]   He broke the bottom of the bed.

In 1871, *Baner ac Amserau Cymru* ran a serial on the nocturnal
courting adventures of 'Wil Dafydd, neu Helbulon y Noson-Garwr'.
The pieces are permeated by the bragging of a young man whose
obvious, and only, delight is in raunchy behaviour. The tales of nightly
courtship are told with self-glorification and glee, despite the fact that
they proved fatal to at least one of the female victims. In the Coedmor
papers in the Carmarthen Record Office is a scurrilous report from the
'Imperial Parliament' on 'Last Night's Debate' in which: 'Mr Lowe
asked the Secretary from the Home Department for some information
respecting the new Shagging machine; how many horse power and
how many women it would roger in an hour?' The great and the good

of Parliament all used unparliamentary language in this filthy, fictitious debate.[216]

Folk songs also resounded to the impassioned tempo of love-making. In the Mathri area of Pembrokeshire, the song, 'Hen Ladi Fowr Benfelin' (A buxom blonde lady), recounted the courtship of a youth with an intimidating lady:

'Roedd tonnen ar ei chanol,	She had a wave around her middle,
Digon o le i shinco llong;	Big enough to sink a ship;
Roedd gofyn cael bachgen teidi	You needed a powerful man
Cyn mentro mewn i hon.[217]	To enter into this one.

Another version of the song, 'Shacki Newi Ddwad' (Jackie Just Came), substituted the metaphors of the mines for those of a coastal and agricultural workplace. The popular song, still sung in Wales, 'Twll Bach y Clo', a version of an American Civil War song written by Henry Clay Work (1832–84), is often treated as a piece of fun. But carefully read the metaphors:

Clywch y gân ferched, clywch, clywch clywch,
Mae'r cathod yn mewian yn uwch ac yn uwch,
Mae cŵn y drws nesa' yn myned o'u co'
A Huwcyn bach yn sbeican trwy dwll bach y clo.[218]

Hear the song girls, hear, hear, hear,
The cats are miaowing higher and higher,
The dogs from next door are going wild,
And little Huwcyn is watching through the keyhole.

The song is sung to a throbbing tempo which reaches a glorious climax. This could be a voyeuristic celebration of the sexual act.

A notable aspect of this popular pornography was the youth of the participants. Some of those involved were as young as twelve. The 'Scripture Reader' met girls of ten who, if not quite yet involved, were already on the threshold of the world of prostitution. In an age of early death, it was not surprising perhaps that the age of consent, for most of our period, was twelve. Yet an unsettling paedophilic obsession existed among some writers. Kilvert's diary offers a window into this dark world. In his entry for 3 May 1870, he recounts a visit to the village school of Newchurch:

Janet was doing simple division and said she had done five sums, where upon I kissed her and she was nothing loth. Moreover I offered to give her a kiss for every sum, at which she laughed. As I stood by the window making notes of things in general in my pocket book Janet kept interrupting her work to glance round at me shyly but saucily with her mischievous beautiful grey eyes. Shall I

confess that I travelled ten miles today over the hills for a kiss, to kiss that child's
sweet face? Ten miles for a kiss.

Victorian clergy were always prone to sentimentality, but Kilvert seems
to have moved into a more suspect area. Here he describes, on 11 July
1870, the early morning sun entering a girl's bedroom:

and has kissed the white bosom that heaves uncovered after the restlessness of
the sultry night, and has kissed her mouth whose scarlet lips, just parting in a
smile and pouting like rosebuds to be kissed . . . she has risen and unfastened the
casement and stood awhile breathing the fresh fragrant mountain air as it blows
cool upon her flushed cheek and her half veiled bosom . . .[219]

Other men, with few literary pretensions, were more brutal. In 1858,
Robert Finch, a Cardiff bookmaker, was sentenced to three years hard
labour for indecently assaulting Sarah Jones, Mary Ann Stacey,
Elizabeth Haynes and Mary Abraham in a field at Cathays. 'All were
given a penny and told to come back next day and he'd give them 2d
each.' The girls were fortunate in that they braved the court together
and gave evidence in unison, but others had no support.[220] In 1862,
Ann Evans, aged six, who slept in the same bed as the family's lodger,
Richard Lloyd, at their home in Nant-y-glo, testified: 'He hurt me, and
then told me to stretch my legs out and go to sleep. When he hurt me
I cried out.' Terrified, it took her days to inform her parents. In court,
Ann received little sympathy. Her crippled brother's evidence was
discounted, her attacker acquitted on a technicality.[221]

Among the most dangerous places for women in nineteenth-century
Wales were the roads over the hills above the southern industrial
valleys.[222] James Thomas, a collier, raped and 'ravished' Janet Morris,
a girl under fourteen years of age, on the mountain on her way home
to Llanwonno.[223] Henry Perk, a 34-year-old collier, was charged on six
counts of rape on the mountains above Blaina. He was sentenced to
life imprisonment, as was Thomas Davies of Llandeilo, for rape and
robbery in 1830.[224] The experience itself was traumatic, but additional
indignities were also heaped upon women in the courtroom. Many
suffered severe character assassinations during cross-examination. In
some cases, women were actually convicted for defamation of the
alleged rapist's character.[225] Yet, in a few cases, the legal agents
followed the public indignation and popular anger:

John Thomas, am dreisio un Grace Rowlands, o blwyf Carregeinwen a gafodd
ei alltudio dros ei fywyd. Yr oedd Grace Rowlands yn hen wraig, dros drigain
mlwydd oed; a'r carcharor yn ŵr priod, ac yn byw o fewn i ychydig ffordd i dŷ
Grace Rowlands. Aeth y carcharor yno yn y nos, torodd y drws yn agored ac yna

treisiodd yr hen wraig. Yr oedd wedi cael ei brofi o'r blaen am drosedd cyffelyb, ond cafodd ei ryddhau y tro hwnnw.[226]

John Thomas, for raping Grace Rowlands, from Carregeinwen parish, was transported for life. Grace Rowlands was an old woman, over sixty years of age; the prisoner was a married man, who lived close to Grace Rowlands's house. The prisoner went there late one night, he broke the door down, and raped the old woman. He had been charged once before with a similar act, but had been freed on that occasion.

From 1788 to 1790, a Welshman Rhynwick Williams, nicknamed 'the London monster', carried out a series of random acts of violence on women in the city's streets. The attacks created such an atmosphere of fear that women took to wearing copper petticoats underneath their clothes. The monster's method was to approach a single woman, sexually harass her and, without warning, slit her clothing and stab her. The weapon would be concealed beneath his trouser leg, in a nosegay or up his sleeve and was seemingly intended to maim rather than kill.[227]

Rape and 'carnal ravishment' of women and children created considerable anger and anguish within Welsh society which was aired in courts, but other cases of sexual perversion engendered considerable regret which was quickly repressed. Incestuous relationships were one example. Despite jocular allegations that some areas, such as Trawsfynydd in the 1790s, were legendary for their inbreeding, few cases came before Welsh courts.[228] In Rhosllanerchrugog in 1847, the Education Commissioners claimed that local people accepted with apparent equanimity a father and daughter living together as man and wife and other unspecified 'bestialities'.[229] At Llanwonno in 1848 a 28-year-old man and his sister and in 1866 a widowed collier and his sixteen-year-old daughter were some of the few people who appeared in court charged with incest.[230] The collier, John Kerby, was sentenced to be imprisoned for life. Such behaviour was often hidden in impenetrable language – 'rhuddhawyd, Thomas Jenkins, o yn agos i Aberystwyth yr hwn a gyhuddwyd o gyflawni gweithred rhy annynol ac anweddaidd i'w henwi' (Thomas Jenkins, charged with an offence too unnatural and immoral to name, was released).[231]

Although some cases thus described involved incest, others were charges of bestiality. The remarkable document *The Felons' Register* reveals the difference in treating these cases which occurred between the relatively private world of the police office and the public world of the criminal court. Allegations of men's sexual involvement with animals were discovered and detailed by the police. In 1857, David Davies, a 53-year-old, was sent for trial charged with 'bestiality with a bitch' and 29-year-old James Watkins of Tivyside charged with bestiality with an unnamed animal.[232] In 1865, the 'cadaverous' Thomas Davies of Cynwil Gaio was charged with having committed 'bestiality with a donkey', and a year later Thomas Thomas, a 38-year-old 'fresh faced' labourer from Llandeilo'r-fân, was sent to trial at the Assizes, charged with 'bestiality with a donkey'.[233] A few years later, Daniel Griffiths, a 74-year-old labourer, of 'healthy complexion', from Laugharne, was sent for trial to answer charges of committing 'buggery with an ass'.[234] All the cases were dismissed by the court, despite the fact that there was considerable evidence and eye-witness accounts which would have led to prosecution in cases of theft or assault. The newspapers occasionally enable us to peer behind the solid wall of silence which society erected in such cases. The *Carmarthen Journal* in 1866 gave details of the opening address of Mr Justice Blackburn's remarks at the Assizes, during the case of the 'fresh faced' Thomas Thomas. Having expressed concern at the large number of cases, 'in two of which the charge was of an unnatural offence', the judge questioned whether any good could come from discussing these cases in court for

> public enquiries into offences of this disgusting character were in themselves great social evils, and produced real harm. Having regard to this, he had been in the habit, in common with most other judges of recommending the grand jury not look upon the case in the same manner as they would at other cases . . . Thus they avoided the evil consequences of a public enquiry. They should be certain, as far as they could, that the case brought under their notice ought to be justifiably brought before the court. In one case, indeed the chances of proving the case rested almost upon the evidence of a solitary witness. They must look at the manner in which he gave his testimony, and watching his conduct, see whether he might be considered as a respectable witness.[235]

Like people in all ages, the Welsh were no strangers to sexual perversion, and their sexual lives reveal a rich diversity of experience. Single-sex unions and partnerships, which in today's permissive society would be labelled lesbian and gay, were tolerated, even celebrated. Lady Eleanor Butler (1739–1829), and Sarah Ponsonby (1755–1831) – to the horror of their families – eloped in 1778, and settled at Plas-Newydd, Llangollen. Here they lived, 'charmingly together despite them all', enjoying 'pleasures unknown to vulgar minds'.[236] Their romantic love and civilized style of life attracted famous visitors from far and wide and was celebrated in commemorative earthenware produced by the Glamorgan Pottery.[237] Sarah Jane Rees, Cranogwen, lived openly with her life's soul-mate, Jane Thomas, in Llangrannog. Cranogwen described their relationship as a romantic friendship, rather than a courtship, in a poem to 'Fy ffrind' (My Friend), but the feelings ran much deeper:

Ah! annwyl chwaer, 'r wyt ti i mi,	Oh! my dear sister, you to me
Fel lloer i'r lli, yn gyson;	Are like the stars to the sea, constantly;
Dy ddilyn heb orphwyso wna	Following you without rest
Serchiadau pura'm calon.[238]	Do the truest feelings of my heart.

Mary Lloyd, a pupil in John Gibson's studio in Rome, met the anti-vivisection, women's rights and sexual freedom campaigner Frances Power Cobbe in 1860. As a result she abandoned art for love, living with Cobbe in London and then at Hengwrt, near Dolgellau. They are buried in the same grave in Llanelltyd churchyard, testimony to enduring friendship and fellowship.[239] Perhaps this was one of the bravest acts of nineteenth-century Wales – two unconventional lovers prepared and preparing to face Judgement Day together.

Homosexuality was infamously the 'love that dare not speak its name' in Victorian times. Yet it was far more common than contemporaries were willing to accept. All-male institutions were noted centres of homosexual affairs, liaison and predations. The Chartist leader, John Frost, transported for his part in the Newport rising, believed that the government maintained the probation gangs in all their turpitude in order to crush the spirit of class resistance. In his *The Horrors of Convict Life*, he recalled that 'the authorities at Van Diemen's Land were indifferent to this great offence, smoking was deemed a greater offence than that of Gomorrah, and punished with greater severity'.[240] Buggery, it has been said, 'is to prisons what money is to middle class society'.[241] It was as utterly pervasive in the world of the Georgian jail and Victorian prisons, as it is in modern penitentiaries. The 'crime of Sodom' was the 'nameless evil' of the 'citadels of sodomy'.

Schools were another citadel. School life was a round of beating, boredom and buggery. Love between boy and boy was sanctioned by reference to the Bible – the love of Jonathan for David – and in the homoerotic imagery of the classics. In *Coningsby*, Disraeli insisted that 'at school friendship is a passion. It entrances the being; it tears the soul.' Many parents considered that it was a good thing to send a son

to public school, as it would assuredly make the rest of his life
reasonably happy – no horror could overtake the cruelties, humili-
ations and curious sexual practices that their boy encountered at
Harrow, Eton, Brecon or Llandovery.[242] Indeed, in an age when male
bonding was universal, and all-male gatherings the norm, a little
buggery between friends might well have been taken as an extension of
existing norms rather than a flagrant transgression of them.

It was rare for the headmaster to be caught out. That, however, as
we have already noted, was the fate of Dr Vaughan, headmaster of
Harrow from 1844 to 1859. In 1858, Vaughan had selected as his love
toy, a boy, Alfred Proctor, who did not have the headmaster's capac-
ities for reticence. Proctor wrote to John Addington Symonds that he
was having an affair with the headmaster. Young Symonds, no angel
himself, told his father, who pressurized Vaughan to resign. Tastes
acquired at school were continued into later life.[243] One of the
homosexuals involved in the notorious Boulton and Park case of 1871
was 'Thomas' who plied his trade in the celebrated Evans's molly shop
in Covent Garden. Flagellation was considered the English vice par
excellence in the nineteenth century. Many men acquired their
penchant and predilection for flogging at school. Even after forty
years, Sir Charles Bruce, Governor of Mauritius, still trembled when
he recalled Dr Vaughan's castigation 'Cast forth that evil person from
among you' swiftly followed by the swish of his cane.[244]

George Powell (1842–82), 'the aesthete of Nanteos', acquired his
interest in flagellation and homosexuality at Eton, rather than at
Harrow. The obsession continued throughout his life. Powell was close
friends with the homosexual painter Simeon Solomon and closer
friends with the profligate poet, Algernon Charles Swinburne. They
visited each other in London and Aberystwyth, and both stayed at
Powell's cottage near Etretat, Normandy, in 1868. They shared a fascination with corporal punishment and its literary exegesis in the works
of the marquis de Sade. Powell named his cottage Chaumière
Dolmancé, after a character in de Sade's *La Philosophie dans le
Boudoir* and their adventures there are related in the Goncourt
brothers' *Journal* and by Guy de Maupassant in his story 'L'anglais
d'Etretat'.[245] Maupassant met Powell and Swinburne in the summer of
1868, when he attempted to rescue Swinburne from the sea. In
Maupassant's account, Powell initially appears gentle and kind to his
visitors, but his behaviour soon degenerates, living with a monkey yet
rumoured to eat only monkey flesh, sucking on the fingers of a severed

mummified hand and so on, to the outrage of the locals. Maupassant recalled: 'After lunch the two friends brought out gigantic portfolios of obscene photographs, taken in Germany, life-sized and all of masculine subjects. Amongst others, I recall an English soldier masturbating himself at a window.'[246] Maupassant later described Powell's character: 'he loved the supernatural, the macabre, the tortured, the intricate and every form of derangement'.

Some men who appear not to have enjoyed the disadvantages of a public school education were also not averse to their pleasures or sins. In July 1858, Anthony Jenkins, a 26-year-old haulier, was found not guilty by Cardiff magistrates of 'an assault with an intent to commit sodomy' on George Smith and on James Doel. 'There was no doubt that the prisoner had been guilty of a beastly assault, which might be punished by law, but the offence charged in the indictment was incorrect.'[247] But William Hood found no escape through legal technicalities. In 1827, he was sentenced by the Pembrokeshire Assizes to two years in prison for 'an unnatural crime'.[248]

Role reversals and cross-dressing brought forth mixed reactions from Welsh society. The unsettling thing about cross-dressing was that it transgressed the frontier between gender domains, which same-sex displays reinforced. In 1860, Catherine Owen, alias Punch was sentenced by Swansea magistrates to twenty-one days in jail for 'fighting with another riotous character of Regent Court'. The opponent, a woman by the name of Bird, 'took flight, wing and fled'. Catherine was described as 'a female sailor': 'She was attired as a true British tar – a man-o-war's man. Her "trousers" (forgive the expression, gentle reader, as it relates to a "lady"), were of large dimensions . . . Miss Owen appeared as brazened, weather-beaten a jack-tar as ever trod a plank.'[249] Many Welsh men sought the freedom of London before they indulged their taste for wearing women's apparel. One who indulged most freely was the dangerously violent 'Fat Phillis', alias 'Charley Jones, alias Vaughan, [who] is known to the officers of this police. He continually frequents Masquerades, and always goes in a Female Habit. He, as well as his companion, are extremely effeminate, and Vaughan was much painted.'[250] In 1852, at Cardiff, Edward Groffenberg, a foreign seaman, was:

> charged with the novel offence of being dressed up in a female's apparel and soliciting money from passers-by. His hair had been combed back, his face was destitute of whiskers and moustaches, and a straw bonnet surmounted all his charms. He wore a blue shawl and a plaid gown from underneath of which two large seaboots protruded.

When stopped by police, who had been attracted by the large crowd that followed him down Bute Street, Groffenberg replied that 'it was a lark'. Asked by the magistrates whether he had something to say: 'the prisoner replied (in a deep bass voice) "I have nothing to say . . . I was with my countrymen and we had been drinking"'. The magistrates decided to dismiss the case with a severe reprimand and warning: 'The prisoner then, without making a courtesy to the Bench, left the court amidst the laughter of all present, and even their worships themselves could not preserve their usual gravity'.[251] The ringing laughter of the court, and the frayed gravitas of the magistrates, revealed that the Welsh enjoyed the rich diversity of their lives. Victorians were often aroused, and sometimes they were even amused.

6

Worship and Wizards

'Joy Unspeakable and Full of Glory': Religion and Welsh Society

Reality was bent into shape by means of one of the Welsh people's favourite sedatives, religion. The years 1776–1871 witnessed a remarkable awakening in the spiritual life of Wales which penetrated and permeated almost every fibre of the fabric of life. Christian names were derived from the Bible to such an extent that the Chartist rising of 1839 might well have been a battle from the Book of Kings or Deuteronomy. Joshua Davies fought the battle of Newport, aided and abetted by Aaron Brain, Mary Brewer, Solomon Briton, Joseph Brown, Barnabus Brough, John Daniel, Daniel Evans, John Herford, James Hedge, Israel Firman, Esther Pugh, Job Tovey, Abraham Thomas, Matthew Williams, Zephaniah Williams and, not to be confused with each other, Samuel James and James Samuel. Thomas Phillips and the magistrates who prosecuted John Frost and the Chartist leaders received astounding missives, proclaiming and promising biblical vengeance: 'Ye serpents and generations of vipers, why seek ye the life of Frost? You may succeed but what think ye of the mighty millions. If ye can escape the bullet, who can escape the match?'[1]

The Rebecca riots reveal that country people also appreciated the punishments promised in the rougher pages of the scriptures. Rebecca took her name from Genesis and her letters used apocalyptic, millenarian language to warn the enemies of her hosts that revenge was nigh. She gorged herself on the grapes of wrath and promised to take an eye for an eye, irrespective of how many would be blinded.[2] Familiarity with the scriptures was evident in all walks of life. In October 1864, James Cadwallader, chaplain to the Usk house of correction, noted a rather remarkable 'male prisoner, who within a few months, committed

26 chapters of the New Testament, 28 psalms and 8 other chapters of the Old Testament' to memory. Although he was in the house of correction, this memory man needed little, for the scriptures were 'revisited with verbal correctness and much intelligence'.[3]

Like the people, the names of hamlets, villages and towns reflected religious influence and inspiration. Samuel Lewis's *A Topographical Dictionary of Wales* (1842) includes a congress of places beginning with the prefix 'Llan' followed with the name of a long dead, but still remembered, saint. Welsh geography in the nineteenth century came to resemble that of Israel as Bethania, Bethlehem, Bethesda, Bethel, Carmel, Casarea, Golan, Hermon, Joppa, Moriah, Nasareth and Nebo grew from chapel settlements to villages. 'Namyn Duw, nid oes dewin' (there is no magician other than God) was the reminder of a cautionary proverb, wisdom that was doubled into a warning rhyme – 'Y sawl a dynno nyth y dryw, ni chaiff weled wyneb Duw' (whoever destroys the wren's nest, will never see God's face).[4] Even their favourite expletives usually referred to God or hell. Despite the profound economic and social problems confronting Wales, politicians devoted considerable energy and effort to religious issues such as disestablishment, tithe and the right for Dissenters to bury their faithful followers in their graveyards according to their own order of service. In print, from pulpit and in practice, impassioned men and inspired and inspirational women sought to create an image of Wales as one of the most decent, moral and religious countries on the face of the earth.[5] They nearly succeeded.

Few areas of Welsh life have been subject to so much misinterpretation and misunderstanding as the religious history of Wales. In the interests of denominational loyalty, the complex truth of Welsh religion has been simplified into simple stereotypes. In the late eighteenth century, religion, it was once long agreed, was almost exclusively associated with the Methodist revival.[6] In contrast to their effervescent enthusiasm – for Methodists metaphorically and literally jumped for joy – older immobile Dissenters (Independents and Baptists) slumbered apathetically, while static church-goers somnambulated in musty and mildewed crumbling buildings. The clergy were frequently portrayed as gentry in vestments, Anglicized, antagonistic to the Welsh people, more interested in the cellar, the hunt and the table than in the church, salvation or the sacraments. The 'unnourished', 'tinder-dry' souls of the Welsh people were set aflame by the spiritual energy and enthusiasm of the Methodists. Methodism, it has been argued,

provided the dynamic driving force in the transformation of Wales
from a heathen haven to a religious heaven. Like all stereotypes, there
is a kernel of truth in this perception, but it only captures a portion of
the complexity of Welsh religious life. The overemphasis on the role of
the Methodists does a disservice both to Anglican efforts to reform
and revive their church, and the attempts of Independents and
Baptists to conquer and convert Welsh society. Evangelical enthusiasm
was not the exclusive preserve of the Methodists. Baptists and
Independents were equally engaged in the battle to save Welsh souls
from sin and win Wales for God.[7]

Such was their success that, by 1870, 'Welsh' and 'Nonconformist',
were regarded by many as almost synonymous terms. According to the
'Apostle of Peace', Henry Richard, 'the real people of Wales' were the
Nonconformists.[8] The Church, he argued passionately and powerfully,
had lost the hearts and the hopes of the Welsh people. It was attended
only by a small, exclusive coterie of gentry and their fawning acolytes.
This again is a distortion of the truth. Many devoted Welsh speakers
were devout Church attendees, genuflective in her services, vigilant of
her vigils and vespers. Indeed, it is irrefutable that the Church, through
the work of 'Yr Hen Bersoniaid Llengar' (the old literary parsons), did
more for Welsh culture and literature in the nineteenth century than
God-crazed Nonconformists who frowned on such fripperies.[9] Henry
Richard and several other commentators could not disguise the deep
divisions within Nonconformity. Emnity to 'Yr Hen Fradwres' (the
old traitoress), as they described the Church, could not cover over
denominational demarcations and divides. Like the core of their faith,
Nonconformity in Wales was a trinity, but this trio did not always act
as one. Baptists, Independents and Methodists had their own administrative and theological organizations and were riven with subsects.
The term 'Baptist' included General Baptists, Particular Baptists,
General Baptists – New Connexion, Scotch Baptists and Undefined
Baptists. The career of the charismatic Christmas Evans, 'llosgfynydd
o bregethwr' (a volcano of a preacher), is characteristic of a divisive
divinity. He left many scorched by his fire, for he possessed a thick-
skinned insensitivity that encased him like the armour of proof. His
pachydermous nature made him as invulnerable as a rhinoceros, and
his wit made him a formidable opponent in theological arguments.
The 'bishop of Anglesey' left the island in 1826, under a cloud, after
bitter and bruising disputes over baptism, and the heretical ideas of
Sandemanianism. His subsequent ministries in Caerphilly (1826–8),

REV.ᴰ CHRISTMAS·EVANS,

William Roos, *Revd Christmas Evans*, *c*.1835 (National Library of Wales). One of the most charismatic preachers in Welsh religious history, Christmas Evans lost his eye in a fight at a fair in Llandysul and was addicted to opium and patent medicines.

Cardiff (1828–32) and Caernarfon (1832–8) were also marred by controversy and conflict.[10] Methodists split into Calvinists and Wesleyans. The latter proved particularly disputatious and divisive, for the restrictive structure of the Wesleyans led to the establishment of subgroups like the Original Connexion, New Connexion, Primitive Methodists, Bible Christians, Wesleyan Methodist Association and Wesleyan Reformers. In contrast, the Calvinists were more united, allowing only Lady Huntingdon's Connexion to diverge from the central core. Theological differences between subsects like General

Baptists and General Baptists – New Connexion were slight, but they
were genuinely appreciated and observed by genuine people who
believed that, in their father's house, there were many mansions.
Nonconformity was not uniformity. Unity was more pronounced on
paper and in polemic than it was in religious practice. Despite the
intense contemporary propaganda, pew for pew, and prayer for prayer,
the Church of England could compete individually with any one of
the Nonconformist denominations.[11]

Religion in Wales was riven with tensions. One virtue the religious
community in Wales conspicuously lacked was tolerance in religious
matters. Denominations disputed definitions and interpretations of
divine scriptures. Men and women, young and old, debated and
disputed. The Revd Evan Davies, Eta Delta (1794–1855), took contro-
versies to new heights with his cantankerous views that men not trained
in theological seminaries, illegitimate children, cripples or disabled men
should not be allowed into the ministry. The thought that women might
wish to preach did not dawn on him.[12] But perhaps the most constant
division was that which existed between the enthusiast and the establishment. Welsh religion developed and expanded through revivals of
great emotional power and passion. Thousands of people were shaken
to the very sinews of their souls by all-embracing spiritual awakenings.
Almost every decade between 1776 and 1871 witnessed an awakening in
the religious life of Wales. Yet, though ministers prayed and yearned for
the renewal of religious life through revival, they were often embar-
rassed at the excesses of the enthusiasts. Leaders sought to control and
channel the spiritual energy of people into the paths of order and
respectability, but people were not always willing to be led. Private
realization of personal redemption often led to excessive public revel
that threatened reputations. Opponents of Nonconformity were quick
to castigate and caricature excessive behaviour. In 1846, in an article on
'Crefydd yr Oes' (the age's religion), the editor of *Yr Haul*, the irascible
David Owen, Brutus, condemned:

> Y 'diwygiad mawr a nerthol', fel ei gelwyd, a fu ymhlith yr Independiad, a
> ystyrid fel rhodd neilltuol i'r enwad gan y nefoedd; dim yn y byd ond crits a
> chrotesi yn gwaeddi, yn ysgermain, ac yn ymwallgofi, gan ymgofleidio a gwau
> drwy eu gilydd fel gwallgofiaid; ac yn gyrru eu gilydd i hysterics, fel y byddai
> bechgyn yn dihattru merched, ac yn tynnu cyllhell noethion allan i dorri
> llinynnau eu stayses, ac yn eu cario allan o'r synagogau. Ystyrid y gwallgof-
> rwydd alaethus hwn yn grefyddol, er na chynnyrchoedd ond cannoedd o
> fastarddiaid draw ac yma ar hyd y wlad.[13]

> The so-called 'great revival', which is amongst the Independents, is regarded as a special gift from heaven to the sect; it is nothing but boys and girls screaming in their madness, clutching and moving about each other like lunatics; they send each other into such hysteria that the boys undress the girls, use sharp knives to cut their stays, and carry them out from the synagogues. This madness is considered religion, although all it ever produced is hundreds of bastards across the country.

From the 1770s excessive zeal was both a blessing and a curse for Welsh religious elders. They were naturally delighted that more people were following them down the paths to salvation, but they wanted orderly progressions, not riotous processions. Within the Non-conformist denominations in general, and Methodism in particular, the behaviour of some groups was a matter for concern and conflict. 'Jumpers' who screamed, shouted, sweated and jumped in services were particularly worrying. Their behaviour seemed to push Welsh religion beyond the bounds of respectability and into ridicule. Increasing numbers of tourists who travelled through Wales during the years of the wars against France drew attention to the bizarre behaviour of Welsh Methodists. The campsite meetings of the Methodist *Sasiwn* drew thousands of people over the bleak and barren countryside to experience intense pleasure and spiritual sustenance. At the fringes of these meetings, enthusiasm ran wild. Bala, the storm-centre of Welsh Nonconformity in the nineteenth century, much to the disgust of travellers, was often the venue for remarkable scenes. Sir Richard Colt Hoare, artist and scholar, visited the town in 1801, during a fishing expedition, and discovered 'hundreds of Methodists' returning from their meeting, to which

> thousands are attracted, some from devotion, others from curiosity. The man who keeps the turnpike at Bala counted one year about three thousand who passed his gate and amongst them were nine hundred horses. Preachers came down from London who relieve each other, so that there is someone officiating almost every hour of the day. The town during this time affords a fine scene of noise, bustle and confusion . . .[14]

By 1819, the annual *Sasiwn* was even bigger business for toll gate keepers and innkeepers. At Bala in that year, a local landlord estimated that between 8,000 and 10,000 people attended and that over 3,000 horses had to be provided for. Yet, more noteworthy than the crowds of humans and horses was the behaviour. In 1818, John Elias attended and addressed an annual meeting in Llanrwst and the crowd 'scarcely suffered the service to conclude, but commenced waving their hats, jumping, shouting like enthusiastic fanatics'.[15] Two years later in Bala, the travellers Walmsley and Lathom, on their pedestrian tour of Wales, while enjoying a meal in the inn

> were disturbed with the confused clamour of some thousands of voices and looking out of our window, observed an immense concourse of people who were returning from the ground we had first seen them on. They passed in review, under our window, a motley group of all ages, some carrying chairs and others stools. Presently we observed a group at some distance using the most ridiculous gestures and throwing themselves into all sorts of attitudes. As they approached near we heard them screaming and shouting, using a kind of cant in which there was general similarity. Presently they halted and began to jump, clasping and shaking each other by the hands and throwing their arms about. The first impressions made on our minds, on their arriving opposite us, was that they were either idiots or under the influence of liquor. Their countenances were dreadfully distorted and they frothed and foamed at the mouth as if in fits. On enquiry we found that these were a sect denominated Jumpers and in curiosity led us to remark more closely upon their proceedings.
>
> ... The females were more violent than the males and worked themselves up to such a pitch of frenzy and delirium as to be obliged to be supported by others. Their eyes appeared to start out of their sockets and some were almost inaudible from excess of their passion.[16]

Enthusiasm was the engine which enabled religious leaders, from the late eighteenth century, to extend and expand the community of the devout in Wales. Welsh religion was revivalistic in its character; leaders had to harness excesses and extreme behaviour into the denominational halter. Thomas Charles, the founding father of Welsh Calvinistic Methodism, when it finally split from the Church of England in 1811, was often deeply upset by the behaviour of his listeners. At a *Sasiwn* at Aberystwyth in 1809, Charles continued observers' obsession with the equine, noting proudly that amongst the 7,500 people present, there were also over 1,000 horses – symbolic perhaps of the prosperity of the Methodists – but complained passionately that 'the jumping and horrid yells and screams, made at the end of the service, exceeds anything of the kind ever witnessed'.[17] John Elias was also troubled by the excessive behaviour of his followers. In a remarkable letter to F. Carmichael on 25 October 1822, he sought to explain 'the great noise that our congregations make':

> our Lord in his mercy called many wild, and presumptuous sinners from darkness to light, and, I hope, from the powers of Satan unto God ... we may look at it in the main as a work of the spirit of God, and an effect of the effusion

of the Spirit of Grace . . . Most of them who cry out in the congregations are under great concerns about their Souls, and the bodies of some are seized with trembling, fainting, and convulsive motions . . . They have a fear of the wrath of God's vengeance . . . and the dreadfulness of that wrath . . . so that when the revelation of salvation comes . . . they rejoice with joy unspeakable and full of Glory . . . and who can blame them for praising the Redeemer and sing his praises out loud.[18]

The authorities were highly suspicious of the vociferous joyfulness and glorious effusions of Welsh Methodists. In the 1790s, a decade of paranoia and panic, Welsh Nonconformity was closely scrutinized by magistrates and justices. The dissent in Dissent was declared a danger to government, law and order. *The Gentleman's Magazine*, in September 1799, claimed that

the preachers are in general instruments of Jacobinism, sent into this country to disseminate their doctrines; and I assure you, that Paine's work, and other books of a like tendency have been translated into Welsh and secretly distributed about by the leader of this sect. These are facts that can be depended on . . .[19]

Nonconformity undoubtedly had links with seditious and secret movements within Wales. Richard Price (1723–91), one of the most powerful thinkers of his generation and author of *A Discourse on the Love of our Country* (1789), was a graduate of Vavasor Griffiths's Academy at Tenter Alley, London, and a Nonconformist minister.[20] David Williams (1738–1816), philosopher, friend of Benjamin Franklin and author of *Letters on Political Liberty* (1786), was an acquaintance of Howell Harris and an Independent minister until 1773.[21] Morgan John Rhys (1760–1804), who campaigned for parliamentary reform in his *Cylch-grawn Cymraeg*, was a former Baptist minister at Pen-y-garn near Pontypool.[22] Such well-known, indeed infamous, links made it hard for Nonconformists to avoid charges that their faith was a threat to the established order. Accordingly, as the authorities intensified their persecution and prosecutions from the 1790s, increasing numbers of Dissenters left Wales in search of religious freedom. Those who stayed strove hard to prove that the forces which would evolve into Baptists, Independents and Methodists were not seditious or dangerous, but loyal and faithful. As far and for as long as possible, they sought to work within the confines of the Church of England. They also placed an emphasis on individual salvation. Christmas Evans, the Baptist leader, expressed the tendency most clearly when he declared: 'It is not the province of Christians to debate and discuss politics – but to behave humbly towards our superiors.'[23] Joseph Harris, Gomer (1773–1825), Baptist minister, a hymn-writer and 'the father of the Welsh periodical press', was bitterly opposed to Joseph Priestley and his branch of radicalism. By the 1810s, Baptists, Independents and Methodists were singing from the same hymn sheet; theirs was a religion for the salvation of souls not for the solution of society's problems. Twenty years later, the monotonous motto of David Rees, Y Cynhyrfwr, 'Cynhyrfer! Cynhyrfer! Cynhyrfer!' (Agitate! Agitate! Agitate!) turned into Condemn! Condemn! Condemn! when confronted with the 'cowardly' violence of the Rebecca rioters.

Religion, however, was not insulated from the world and its woes. Ministers were remarkably successful in persuading the Welsh people that the apocalypse which was central to their vision was at hand. Time after time, their anger was transformed into prophetic wrath, which brought people to the revelation and realization that the time to repent was not tomorrow, but today. These were portentous times when people sensed that 'mae'r Ysbryd Glan yn marchogaeth yn yr awyr' (the Holy Ghost is riding in the air) and 'cawson ein cludo ar adenydd angylion' (we were carried away on the wings of angels). The publication of *Caniadau y Rhai Sydd ar y Môr o Wydr* by William Williams, Pantycelyn, in 1762, perhaps marks the beginning of the modern Welsh revivalist tradition. Thereafter, religious revivals which awakened an acute spiritual awareness were a characteristic trait of Welsh religious life. Almost every year in the 1790s witnessed religious revivals in Wales. In 1795 at Bala, there was 'a powerful outpouring of the spirit', predominantly among people aged between eight and thirty years of age. The year 1805 was welcomed with the sounds of the hallelujas and hosannas of the Aberystwyth revival which again affected the very young. In 1817, 1818, and 1819 there was intense religious fervour in Beddgelert and Bala. Between 1820 and 1822, a powerful revival swept over Anglesey, leading John Elias to remark: 'The tenderness of the Lord towards us is wonderful. His visits and convictions under the word are truly powerful.'[24]

In 1828, the secluded village of Caeo in Carmarthenshire experienced an intense revival which saw 1,800 join the Calvinistic Methodists, 1,450 the Independents and 445 the Baptists. By 1829, it had reached Neath, Swansea and their environs and was spreading throughout the south, causing one commentator in *The Cambrian* to remark that the revival spread 'like a disease in which the people evidently catch the sympathy from each other'.[25] Disease was the cause of the next revival in Wales. In 1832, the 'fearful terror' of cholera swept hundreds into the chapels and churches. Within a few weeks of the outbreak of the disease, over 700 attended a church meeting in Denbigh as a strange atmosphere of psychological anxiety swept over the town. Amid the uncertainty and fear, religious revival offered stability, strength and salvation but, above all, it offered hope. At Caernarfon, over 2,000 people were saved by the Calvinistic Methodists. In 1839, 1849, 1859, 1862 and 1866, cholera visited Wales, each time sweeping thousands to painful deaths. The ghastly evidence of God trampling out the vintage panicked thousands more into Welsh chapels and churches.

Revivals marked the ebb and flow of religious currents in Wales and this points to one central truth. Good times were hard times for the religious causes and communities in Wales. Once the anxieties, fears and phobias lessened their grip, people fell away from chapel and church membership. For many faith followed pain. Piety followed panic. The years of the great revivals were deeply riven by profound economic and social problems. The 1790s was a decade of deep depression across Wales. In 1805, 1817, 1818 and 1819, temperate Wales witnessed catastrophic weather conditions more appropriate to the tempestuous prophecies of the Old Testament. Harvests were bad. People starved. The year 1828 was a hard one in a harsh decade of financial collapse and catastrophe. In 1832 cholera arrived, one of the most horrifying diseases that Wales had ever experienced. In 1839, 1849, 1859, 1862 and 1866, the shocking and shockingly powerful scourge struck again and again. This link between woe and worship was noted by many contemporaries. The Revd John Griffith of Aberdare thought that times of social distress

> were religiously speaking the best times the working man ever had. He turned the tide of prosperity not into the good of his soul, but into the ruin of his soul and body. The good times God gave him became the devil's own time: he it was who reaped a good harvest from them. Ah! who does not remember when wages poured into the workman's lap like a stream flowing from the horn of plenty, the drinking, the debauchery, the spending there was . . . it is only by tethering us with afflictions and trials that he prevents us from straying.[26]

Revival meetings served as clinics for souls. At times of deep crisis, people willingly endured the polar cold of the meeting houses to listen to sermons of great endurance. It seemed as if no prayer was long enough to express all that congregations would like to say about the need for mercy for their souls. Meetings were characterized by public confession of sin, intense and impromptu praying and weeping. Above all, they sang hymns. In all the services by the 1830s, there would be sweet music by and by. In these spiritual services, songs of love and lamentation gave rise to feelings of glorious, anarchic release:

A'r maglau wedi eu torri,	The chains have been broken,
A'm traed yn gwbl rhydd,	And the saints are now free,
Os gwelir fi bryd hynny,	If I'm seen at that time,
Tragwyddol ganu a fydd.[27]	What eternal singing there'll be.

Their singing caused people to believe in the presence of the Lord; indeed, it was not a question of belief, because the hymns made that presence appear real. Churches and chapels seemed to swell with the power they contained on these occasions, as people found orgiastic freedom from all their earthly problems. Guilt, sin and want fled. Some chapels appeared to be caught in a permanent Armageddon.

However much Baptists, Independents and Methodists might proclaim that they were 'yn y byd ond nid ohono' (in the world, but not of it), they benefited greatly from the demographic, economic and social forces that swept over Wales from 1776 onwards. The industrial development of Wales presented profound problems for religion. Thousands of ungodly people were drawn into new communities, challenging the goodly and godly Welsh to save their souls. New communities were created where no religious provision existed. Nonconformists adapted well to this challenge by building new chapels whenever and wherever there was demand. But the Church of England, ensnared in its parochial system of parishes, found the challenge of the redistribution of people far harder. One commentator noted, with considerable bias, that industrialization abandoned the Church 'where the new day that dawned on Calvary left them standing, stubbornly refusing to see the light'. The parochial system might have made sense administratively, historically and organizationally, but by the early nineteenth century, demographically and geographically, it was inefficient and ineffective. Across Wales, churches were like leviathans stranded on unpeopled, forlorn shores. In Llanwrin, the vicar Isaac Bonsall complained in 1851:

This parish is mountainous and entirely agricultural with extensive farms near the Church, which is situated at the southern extremity – consequently only a few of the inhabitants without inconvenience from the distance of their residences assemble in the Church or Church School on Sundays regularly.[28]

Further north, in Llanddeiniolen, the vicar T. N. Williams explained: 'the bulk of the present population, which has during the last forty years, been drawn together by the working of Mr Assheton Smith's slate quarries, lies at a distance from the Church of from 3 to 5 miles. There are, in the Parish, 13 dissenting Meeting Houses.'[29]

In Gower, P. Evans, one of the wardens of Llanrhidian asked: 'This Parish being about 11 miles long, how is it possible for a Clergyman to attend the spiritual requirements of such a Parish?'[30] John Williams, vicar of Cil-y-cwm, in the wilderness of deepest Carmarthenshire, voiced a similar complaint: 'This parish is unfortunately about 17 miles in length and the parishioners from the extreme points cannot be expected to attend the parish church'.[31] Llanfleiddan church near Cowbridge was in an 'extreme corner', while Capel Coelbren was in an 'outlandish part of the country'. At Llanfor, the parish covered over 32,812 acres, with the church being located '8 or 10 miles distant from the majority of the Population'. Attendance was often dependent on the weather, as William Jones of Carngiuwch explained: 'The Chapelry is in a mountainous district amidst a thinly scattered population. When the weather is inclement there is no attendance, or but very scant one at Church. It is impossible to give exact information. The people follow dissent.'[32] 'Impossible' or embarrassing? A hundred years later, R. S. Thomas, the most doubting Welsh church leader since the original Thomas, was less coy: 'people undertook the weekly journey to market to unlearn the lesson of Sunday. The rain never kept them from the packed town, though it kept them from chapel.'[33] The few people who attended often worshipped in buildings which smelt of dereliction, with streaks of birdlime down their aisles, bats in their belfries, and the Bible left on the lectern gone prematurely antique with the damp. The dank smell of must, mildew and old bones which clung to its buildings also worked its way into the antique and desiccated finery of its clergy – surpluses, stoles, capes and chasubles stank of decay. Llandeloy church was roofless, West Walton 'in a very dilapidated and dangerous state', not fit for 'Divine Service'. Saddest of all was Eglwys Dinas, where 'the chancel was washed away by an encroachment of the sea in November last and it has not been rebuilt'.[34]

Many churches in Wales were as poor as their mice. Lay impropriation had diverted funds out of the Church since before the Reformation. In the 1830s, almost a quarter of church income went into lay hands – £67,457 from a total tithe revenue of £304,563.[35] The churches of Pembrokeshire, Carmarthenshire and Cardiganshire suffered most since only 13, 16 and 33 per cent respectively of tithe payments found their way into Church hands. Laymen often had the right to appoint clergy. In the diocese of Llandaff, the bishop could appoint directly only to one parish. Some parish priests were the younger sons of the gentry, sad people too unadventurous or cowardly for a military career, and equally unsuited for a clerical life. Tithe-rich laymen sought to spend as little as possible on clerical stipends and salaries. Although landowners, industrialists and clergy are often portrayed as a devoted trinity, there were in reality deep tensions between them. In 1831, 'Constant Churchman' complained in a letter to *The Cambrian*, that the anti-truck shop meetings in Merthyr Tydfil were being held in the parish church.[36] George Phillips, the brave curate of Llanfachreth and Llanelltyd, was an unlikely class hero, but he was scathing of Sir R. W. Vaughan for keeping the majority of the £400 which he obtained from tithes for himself, 'out of which he pays his poor Curate the paltry sum above specified [£62] – at which sum his scullery girl would turn up her nose'. This was a grievance he aired again in a report on Llanelltyd: 'he pays the munificent sum specified – 4d a day to his unfortunate Curate – the average weekly allowance given to a pauper in this union'.[37] Such pious poverty forced many vicars to hold onto the livings of several parishes. Pluralism of offices frequently led to spiritual starvation in parishes where the priest was not resident.

The deep-rooted problems of the Church led many to look jealously at the perceived advantages of Baptists, Independents and Methodists. Their chapels did not need an Act of Parliament to be established; they were organic parts of their communities, edifices thrown up from stones torn from the fields. Ministers were also representative of their communities, horny-handed sons of toil, who understood workers, speaking to their souls in the rich and colourful idioms of the workplace. The Revd Thomas Aubrey began his working life as a worker at the Merthyr and Nant-y-glo furnaces, before entering the ministry for the Calvinistic Methodists, while the Revd Daniel Price worked as a collier in the Neath valley in the 1830s. The Revd William Lewis was a buildings foreman at the Dowlais works, before joining the ministry of the Baptists in the 1830s. His architectural skills were much used by his denomination in designing new chapels, though some, rather unkindly, insinuated that these chapels looked 'like a bank designed by a manic depressive'.[38] By the 1830s, theological seminaries and colleges were being established, to mould the innate wit and wisdom of such unlettered people into more formal and formalistic religious leaders more appropriate to an increasingly professional age. The pessimistic prophet John Elias warned of the dangers of 'gweinidogion colegol' (college ministers):

> If some preachers are more gifted and fluent speakers, yet they are not equal to their predecessors in speaking to their conscience. Their harangues do not alarm or terrify the ungodly, neither do they convey spiritual consolations and joy to the Christian . . . they walk in darkness.[39]

The college-groomed, bookish, unworldly minister was the butt of many a satirist's humour.[40] But the doom-obsessed Elias pointed to one long-term challenge to Welsh Nonconformity. As his generation of fire-and-brimstone preachers began to die away, there was a profound change of emphasis in the power and passion of Welsh preaching. Without these stokers, the heat from the fires of hell began to cool. Fear left theology and the spiritual terror which preachers had wielded declined. The emphasis switched from God as temperamental avenger to an elderly, temperate friend. Hence the crisis at the core of the 1859 revival, the last great outpouring of religious fervour and fever in the nineteenth century. Its emphasis was directed to the Word, to theological belief and definitions, as much as to effusions of enthusiasm. Preachers turned the pages from the gloomy prophecies of the Old Testament to the gospel of love in the New. This did, however, have one advantage, for it prevented the feelings of resentment which many converts felt when their fears at the terrors of eternity subsided and they saw through the belief that had converted them. The formalization of training for Nonconformity assisted the development of a remarkable coterie of new leaders. Many of the stars of the Nonconformist pulpit, 'y gynnau mawrion' (the big guns), from the mid nineteenth century were almost all college- and seminary-trained. The Baptists Thomas Thomas, John Jones and Robert Ellis, the Independents W. Rees and E. Herber Evans, the Calvinist Methodist Lewis Edwards and the Wesleyans John Hugh Evans and John Evans all came through theological nurseries.[41] But some still protested that, with the professionals, came the end of passion.

When they looked at Nonconformity, many Church leaders could be forgiven the envious feeling that the grass is always greener in the other cemetery. Yet, once the initial inertia was overcome, the Church also reacted to the challenges of a new society. The Revd Joshua Hughes (vicar of Llandovery 1846–70), later bishop of St Asaph, the

Very Reverend Henry Thomas Edwards (dean of Bangor 1837–84), the Venerable John Griffiths (archdeacon of Llandaff) and Dean Howell represented a new breed of clergy, who were more dynamic, enthusiastic and evangelical.[42] The establishment of St David's College, Lampeter, in 1822 was instrumental in training a new breed of minister for the Church in Wales.[43] An extensive programme of church building commenced in the 1840s, to rectify the demographic and geographical deficiencies. Some were grand and grandiose edifices, others were more basic and modest, which proved that the Church too could adapt to local needs. As Professor Ieuan Gwynedd Jones remarked: 'If the Baptists of Llangynwyd were glad to make use of an old storehouse belonging to the Llynfi Iron Company, so too, the Anglicans were not slow to adapt an old engine house.'[44]

The Pluralities Act of 1818 led to a reduction in a number of the grosser instances of clerical abuse. Although it suffered increasing polemical and political criticism from people who campaigned for the disestablishment of the spiritual arm of the state, reform in personnel, training and administration led to a resurgence in the Anglican Church. When the first in a seemingly unending series of disestablishment bills was introduced in May 1870 into the House of Commons by Denbigh's Anglican MP, Watkin Williams, the Church ironically might well have been in a stronger position than Nonconformity.[45]

Devotion and Denominations

In 1851, the government attempted the impossible by seeking to measure the religiosity of England and Wales.[46] A special census of that year attempted to ascertain how many people attended places of worship on 30 March 1851, Census Sunday. The interpretation of the statistics is difficult, for their collection was fraught with problems. They are reliant on the abilities and honesty of the ministers to whom the forms were sent. Not all were as conscientious and careful as the appropriately and prophetically named Elijah Jacob, minister of Ebenezer Chapel, Swansea, who remarked: 'most people would suppose we had 800 people last evening by viewing the assembly, but when numbered they were found short of 500'.[47] The majority followed the policy of the Independents at Henllan, and made 'a judicious estimate' of the number present. In those judicious estimates, many people were counted twice, or even three times, for the enumerators made no attempt to establish how many services an individual had attended. This was important in the mid nineteenth century since people would visit two, or even three, different services and denominations to enjoy spellbinding sermons and stirring singing.[48] Griffith Jones, warden of Llanfihangel Ysgeifiog, Anglesey, made a similar point when he claimed 'it is well known that in Wales those who attend church at one point of the day generally attend dissenting places of worship at another'.[49]

Elsewhere there was less accord across denominational divides. Many Churchmen expressed suspicion at the 'exaggerated' and 'inflated' claims of Nonconformist congregations, while Dissenting ministers zealously questioned the calculations of attendance at Anglican services. A curate, J. D. Palmer, was bitter in his condemnation of the Methodist chapel in his parish which claimed that there were fifty present at their service, stating that: 'the truth is the congregation seldom exceeds 15 and there are only 3 persons in the parish who call themselves Primitive Methodists'.[50] Such alternative views pointed to the hardship of life in these grim and pious little hamlets and villages of rural Wales. Many rural ministers complained that poverty, like the weather, kept people away from chapel and church. In urban areas, industrial depression, 'the ebbing of the sea of faith' after the cholera revival of 1849, illness and the 'craze for going to America' were given as reasons for diminished congregations.[51] Such explanations sound more like excuses and it is difficult not to conclude from the census evidence that the Welsh nation, like the disciples in the New Testament, were conscious that they, too, were deficient in faith.

Horace Mann, the officer at the Registrar General Offices charged with the unenviable task of overseeing the census, worked out a formula to ascertain actual attendance. To judge from his calculations, it is possible that around 50 per cent of the Welsh population attended some form of religious worship on 30 March 1851. Much to the delight of contemporaries, this figure was substantially higher than in England. Many commentators argued that this was incontrovertible evidence that the Welsh were a more devout people than the English. Other authors were sceptical. John Jones, vicar of Nevern, remarked that many people 'were living the lives of heathens'. Bleakest of all was the portrait the vicar painted of Kidwelly:

> Lord's Day in this Town is but very little regarded as a day for spiritual worship publick houses are allowed to be open, and frequented during Divine Services.

Publick houses are very numerous in this place, and even the Town Clerk keeps a publick house. Often times on the Lord's day we not only hear cursing and ... swearing in our streets, but frequently we see most brutal fighting and no notice taken thereof by the authority of the Town. This is the cause why places of worship are so little frequented and religion so little appreciated and professed at Kidwelly.[52]

Owing to the deficiencies in the statistics, many historians have focused on the proportion of the population which could be accommodated in religious buildings.[53] It was proudly proclaimed that the chapels and churches of Wales could have accommodated seventy-six per cent of the population. Even the most densely populated counties, Glamorgan and Monmouthshire, were near this figure, while in Merionethshire and Breconshire there were more seats than people. But, it must be stressed that abundant accommodation did not necessarily correspond to high attendance. Although this was a remarkably religious society, many vicars, curates and ministers often despaired that they were ministering to 'empty pine'.

The census points at broad patterns in the distribution of religion in Wales.[54] Of the people worshipping in religious services, the majority attended Nonconformist chapels. The greatest number of these, 120,734, attended the services of the Calvinistic Methodists, followed by the Independents with 96,527, and the Baptists with 65,290. The Church of England attracted an estimated 100,953 to its most popular morning services. The census also reveals the strength of the respective and rival denominations in Welsh communities. The Church of England was strongest in the more Anglicized areas such as Chepstow, Hay and Presteigne. In the north, the Calvinistic Methodists were supreme, while in an area from Pembrokeshire towards Bridgend, the Independents dominated. From Bridgend eastwards as well as in Llanelli and Merthyr Tydfil, Baptists predominated. The census also reveals the individual idiosyncrasies in the Welsh religious character. Unitarians were strong in the Merthyr area and in the 'Smotyn du' (black spot) of the Cardiganshire–Carmarthenshire borderlands. There were sizeable groupings of Quakers in many industrial communities in south Wales. Twenty-one Roman Catholic churches testified to the high numbers of Irish people who had forded the Irish Sea to escape the terrors of the famine. There were thirty-two congregations of the Mormons or Latter-Day Saints who, if popular propaganda was to be believed, spent their time persuading the Welsh that they, too, should emigrate. Moravians were influential in Haverfordwest; Jews had synagogues in Merthyr Tydfil and Swansea, Chepstow had a branch of the Catholic and Apostolic Christians, while Tenby could boast a congregation of Brethren in Christ and, rarest of all, the salt-stained town had an ecumenical chapel organized by all denominations as 'an united effort to benefit all the sailors and fishermen'.[55]

The Word and the World

In the early nineteenth century, religious leaders stressed that people of the Word should not intrude into the world. Yet such pious hopes were impossible to put into practice. To maintain their fingernail grip on life, people had to participate in the world of work. Success at work created profound problems for many religious people. In rural areas, prosperity was a sign of divine favour. The owners of the larger farms, with bigger and fuller hay lofts, and fatter cattle, were the people who sat in the *set fawr* of the chapels. These might appear slight, superficial differences, but to a people perched on the abyss of poverty, the successful breeding and sale of a single pig or cow could mean the difference between survival and starvation. In years of failure, a person's behaviour was closely scrutinized for evidence of where he or she had erred from divine favour – working on a Sunday, not contributing to a harvest thanksgiving, anything that could be interpreted as confirmation of impending doom. Creed and capitalism were closely tied. Religion had to have the money of the world in order to survive. It was a simple fact of life that buildings, even those erected from stones wrenched from moorland wastes, cost money to maintain. Between 1839 and 1840, the Revd William Williams set out on a dual mission. His ostensible purpose was to save souls on a rousing, revivalistic tour of Flintshire and Denbighshire. At times, his obsession with the number of souls he saved sounds like a score keeper in a billiard game, but Williams's real statistical obsession was with figures of another kind. In his remarkable three-month tour, he raised over £18,000 to try and clear debts of £34,000 accrued by his denomination.[56]

Inevitably as religion intensified its hold on the Welsh people, chapels and churches began to increase in architectural pretension, physical size and grandeur. Religious buildings, particularly in towns, grew in size as the nineteenth century progressed. Simple places of worship, constructed from plain materials and erected by faith, grew into grand and grandiose edifices, designed and built by architects.[57] These

buildings stood for a creed that everyone was supposed to believe in –
progress, self-improvement, a faith in the great metaphysical abstraction
of capitalism. Several of the Welsh captains of industry were also
leaders in church and chapel. Many of the pioneers of the Welsh
coalfield were also pathfinders in religion. The Quaker Harfords
showed the same 'qualities of industriousness, integrity, highmind-
edness'[58] in their devotional lives as they did in their daily toil. Across
the generations, devotion to duty paid dividends. In the late eighteenth
century, William Lewis led packs of coal-laden mules from Dowlais
down to Cardiff. A century later, his great-great-grandson, Lord
Merthyr, organized shipments valued in millions of pounds. David
Davies, the 'Top Sawyer', a devoted and devout Calvinistic Methodist,
considered his 'life's work a glorification of God'. As with many who
shared his faith, he believed that he was predestined by God for
salvation, and that the elect would succeed. Davies was a capital
Calvinist with a low, malicious view of mankind. He had a profoundly
gloomy view of predestination, believing that men could shape their
destiny through the same disciplined efforts that ensured success in their
business lives. His theological readings never ventured close to those
awkward pages of the scriptures in which Jesus expelled the money-
lenders from the temple; indeed, he seems to have had little sympathy for
the unworldly son of God.[59] The Calvinistic Methodists' *Cyffes Ffydd*
which, among other instructions, told followers that they should not
shorten the Sabbath by indulging in too much sleep, provided a
theological basis for David Davies's most vigorous prejudices.[60] He
approached business in a hard-headed, unsentimental manner, refusing
to look after his workers during winter lay-offs unless it could be
economically justified. Such attitudes created problems for religion. In
times of social breakdown and tension, it was difficult for many to avoid
charges that theirs was a creed for greed. The industrial unrest of the late
1850s and 1860s aroused resentment and regret that many of the more
prominent religious leaders were not supportive of the workers' cause.[61]
Shopkeepers and industrialists were criticized for praying on their knees
on Sundays, and preying on their neighbours for the rest of the week.

Industrialists and employers gave their support to religion because it
represented one of the most powerful mechanisms of social control.
Devout and moral people were often devoted and loyal workers.
Attacks on churchmen and churches during the Rebecca and Scotch
Cattle disputes suggest that working people resented the oppressive and
repressive side of religion. In such a religious age, it is a remarkable fact

that Welsh newspapers contain several reports of 'digwyddiadau gwaradwyddus' and 'sacrilegious outrages'. In 1819, the church at Llansamlet was broken into and surplices, money and wine stolen.[62] The following year saw a spate of attacks on Welsh chapels and churches, with damage inflicted and property stolen from St Arvan's, St Maughan's (Monmouthshire), Llanfihangel (Cowbridge), and Newcastle (Bridgend). Anglicans were not the only victims. The Baptist meeting house at Pen-y-garn (Glamorgan) was broken into and sacramental cups, cloths and books stolen. Outrageously, 'the depredators also drank a bottle of port wine, leaving the bottle upon a tomb-stone of the church-yard'.[63] In 1832, a loaded gun was discharged through the back windows of the Calvinistic Methodist chapel at Bontfechan, Llanystumdwy.[64] Many of these outrages were the work of opportunists, like Thomas Howells, who stole the offering cup from the church at Walwin's Castle, Milford Haven, and offered it for sale at Merthyr Tydfil market in 1825.[65] The activities of these 'hell-bound' reprobates were not necessarily a sign of anticlericalism or irreligion. Yet they helped to convince chapel and church elders that they could not hide ostrich-like from the woes of the world.[66]

The reformation of manners and morals became a central tenet of religious teaching and thought. Since the eighteenth century, the Society for the Suppression of Vice had been actively seeking to prevent the Welsh from enacting their lewd and lustful urges. In Swansea, in the early nineteenth century, the Society was exceptionally active. From the 1830s, Welsh religious leaders sought to transform their followers into gatherings of moral athletes – proud and pure in morals and in souls. Religion had become obsessed with the reformation of behaviour and manners, which is perhaps what made the reaction to the scurrilous remarks of the 1847 Education Commissioners so virulent. In delivering their charges of immorality and unchastity, the Commissioners touched a raw nerve. Chapel and church leaders had laboured long and hard to reform the Welsh people. Usually it was by persuasion, but occasionally it would be done by force. In October 1850, a Roman Catholic clergyman in Flintshire received a message that his parishioners were playing cards on the Sabbath. He burst in on them and beat them with a whip until he secured a promise that they would give up the practice.[67] The Revd William Rowlands, Gwilym Lleyn (1802–65), presided over parts of the north like a spiritual despot, an uncompromising and unflinching guardian of the manners and morals of the people, a rough little village pope. The latter comparison would have kindled his burning wrath for he, like most Methodists, abhorred the Holy Father.[68]

The reformation of manners found many targets. In the 1840s, many ministers began to preach against the 'weithred ffiaidd ac amharchus' (the disgusting and discourteous habit) of spitting on chapel floors. Tobacco chewers became a persecuted group within Welsh religion. To the general danger of health, the floors of many Welsh chapels were covered in the brown-stained mucus of tobacco chewers.[69] From the 1830s, spittoons were provided in many chapels to catch salivous discharges. In 1848, *Tywysydd yr Ieuainc* gave guidance to the young on the importance of avoiding this foul custom, or at least abstaining from it while at worship.[70] In 1858 David Rees of Llanelli complained in *Y Diwygiwr* that closing a chapel with its spit-covered floors for a week provided 'digon o dawch a lleithder i greu pla yn yr ardal' (enough cold and damp to cause a plague in the area).[71]

Welsh religion, by the mid nineteenth century, had acquired an irresistible conscience and a highly aggressive sense of duty which made many people intolerable meddlers in the affairs of others. Some took the moral and behavioural messages of the pulpit out into the world with unusual results. In 1862, Job Hamilton, the parish clerk at Monmouth, charged the 'very elderly' Sarah Jane Hayward with assault. It had been agreed in a service that the clerk should follow the members around the town and, to remind them of their Christian duties, he should shout 'Amen!'. Sarah tired of the chanting clerk and hit him with her umbrella. She was fined eight shillings. 'and requested not to take the law into her own hands; albeit, people did cry 'Amen!' after her'.[72]

Chastity and cleanliness were two of the pillars of the religious reformation of manners which was attempted in Wales from the turn of the nineteenth century. But there was a third member of this trinity of virtues who stood above the other two – temperance. Time after time from pulpit, in press and in print, the social danger and disloca-tion caused by drink was denounced. In 1834 the editor of *Seren Gomer* declared:

> Mae meddwdod yn bechod sicr, gwarthus a gwaradwyddus; mae'n agor y drws i bob pechod a ffueidd-dra . . . bob celwydd a trallod. Mae'n dinistrio pob cysur daearol . . . Mae meddwdod yn bechod . . . ac o'r herwydd yn anuwiol.[73]

> Drunkenness is a sure sin, very repugnant and atrocious; it opens the door to every sin and filth . . . to every lie and pain. It destroys every earthly comfort . . . Drunkenness is a sin . . . as a result it is ungodly.

In 1838, *The Cambrian* reported the stark but memorable warning of a teetotal campaigner in Swansea:

Intoxicating drink is nothing else my friends, but liquid hellfire, which was first compounded in the sulphurous laboratory of the infernal regions and there invented by that most diabolical of all chymists, the Devil. Stick then to water my friends . . . for you have no more occasion to swallow liquid hellfire than a duck has for an umbrella on a rainy day.[74]

But some ducks were addicted to their umbrellas. A witness to the 1847 Education Report remarked of Breconshire that: 'the morals of this part of the country are certainly very defective, owing to the system of drinking cider, so prevalent here; drunkenness is the common sin of both farmer and servants . . . In harvest time this practice is still more prevalent'.[75]

Drink destroyed the whole of man's higher nature; it caused his fall, and consequently temperance and teetotal campaigners had a moral compulsion to 'save'. *Yr Eurgrawn Wesleaidd* warned in 1836 'dim ond y cyfiawn, sobor gerdd gyda Duw' (only the just and sober walk with God).[76] These ancient Elijahs of the Welsh pulpit and press exploded in bearded and bitter anger that the sin was amongst them. The Spirit was against spirits. From the late 1830s, temperance and teetotal campaigners increased their hold on many Welsh communities. These moral militants campaigned so tirelessly that by 1860, temperance was regarded as one of the defining characteristics of the Welsh people. During times of economic depression and psychological chaos which marked religious revivals, temperance ranks were swollen further with the recently converted. The Revd Owen Jones claimed that the 1859 revival created 12,000 new teetotallers.[77] Children, men and women proudly marched after temperance bands around Welsh villages. Uniforms and regalia, banners and badges, music and songs, bands and processions gave magic and merriment to temperance societies. Mysterious and imperious titles, such as the High Chief Ruler of a Rechabite Tent, made the movement appear exotic and exclusive. At Bala in the 1850s, it was boasted that 5,000 out of the area's 6,000 people had signed the pledge not to drink alcoholic beverages.[78] Caernarfon Teetotal Society reported in 1838 that only 134 members out of a total of 2,433 had broken their pledges during the two years of the society's existence. The Aberystwyth Auxiliary Temperance Society kept a strict watch over its members between 1846 and 1855, such that a member of a Rechabite Tent was expelled for drinking peppermint.[79]

Welsh literature abounded with images of the destructive power of drink. Audiences failed the tear-test and wept openly as orators and singers told Mynyddog's tragic tale, *Dewch Adref Fy Nhad* (Come

Home My Father).[80] The song related the sad history of the death of a young boy and the suffering of his mother and sister while the father kept to his dissipation. *Yr Eurgrawn Wesleaidd, Seren Gomer* and *Y Drysorfa* provided detailed biographies of temperate and teetotal people, to serve as inspiring role models. Many of these, like Mrs Roose Williams of Bodwyn, Anglesey, and Mrs Elizabeth Jones of Cardigan, were women.[81] These papers also included many reports of the lonely and lousy deaths of derelict drunkards. These stories of dissolution and dissipation were spitefully detailed without any expression of human sympathy, and figure among some of the most nauseating aspects of the Welsh religious press. The temperance campaign in Wales reached its zenith in 1881, when Parliament passed the Welsh Sunday Closing Act.

The torrent of propaganda which poured forth from the temperance presses gave rise to the view that the religious leaders of Wales, as H. L. Mencken said of the Puritans, were miserable people tortured by the haunting fear that someone, somewhere, might be happy. Temperance and especially teetotal campaigners, despite the colour and pageantry of the movements, often provide the Welsh with a wintry character of laughterless misery. Their voices are often suspicious, full of cold November winds. One cannot help but reach the conclusion that many people, uncomfortable and unhappy with the transformation of Welsh life in the nineteenth century, found solace in the harsher messages of religion. Many seemed to have been at their happiest masochistically marinating in misery. As early as 1802, Edward Jones, Bardd y Brenin of Merionethshire, collector of traditional Welsh music and poetry, complained:

> The sudden decline of the national Minstrelsy and Customs of Wales, is in a great degree to be attributed to the fanatic impostors or illiterate plebeian preachers who have . . . over-run the country . . . dissuading the common people from their innocent amusements . . . The consequence is, Wales, which was formerly one of the merriest and happiest countries in the World, is now become one of the dullest.[82]

Despite the bitterness, it is important not to allow one view to represent the whole of Welsh society. Temperance was undoubtedly strong in Wales, and Christian soldiers marched onwards to fight the vices of the Welsh people. Yet they did not wholly represent the diverse complexity of Welsh society. Many influential individuals came out strongly against temperance in general, teetotalism in particular. The diaries of the Revd David Davies, 'Davies y Binder', lovingly detailed by

Professor Brinley F. Roberts, revealed that the minister was probably more at home in Swansea's Powell's Arms, in the company of 'Chili boys' – sailors who plied the copper trade to South America – than he was in his chapel's temperance meetings. Davies had wanted temperance, as St Augustine had wished for chastity – not yet. The Revd Benjamin Jones, P. A. Môn, argued that the teetotal movement attacked God as creator, for if teetotallers condemned alcohol they also, of necessity, attacked God, because he had created it.[83] Eben Fardd of Clynnog and the Revd William Williams, Caledfryn, of Caernarfon, considered the ceremonial pledges of alcoholic abstinence as an admission of humanity's weakness and a gross violation of the individual's potential for self-control.[84] Between March 1838 and February 1839, William Williams edited *Yr Adolygydd*, an anti-teetotal periodical advocating moderation as opposed to total abstinence. These people were as much the disciples of John Barleycorn as of John the Baptist. *The Cardiff and Merthyr Guardian* in 1839 reported that Ebenezer Thomas of Caerphilly had won a prize at the Cardiff Cymreigyddion Society for a song 'ridiculing teetotallers and tee-totalism, imputing it to their weakness and ignorance; and showing particularly the benefits, privileges and comforts that arise from drinking beer and wine in moderation'.[85]

Caught between conflicting religious imperatives, and sometimes between the Bible and the bottle, many placed stress on 'cymedroldeb' (moderation). In doing so, Caledfryn, P. A. Môn and Eben Fardd risked putting themselves on the side of the devil. Many Welsh people went further than moderation. In Cardiff in 1852, over 80 per cent of the Borough Police Court's cases were the result of drunkenness.[86] At Swansea, convictions for drunkenness almost trebled between 1869 and 1873.[87] In that quiet Bethel town of Pwllheli, convictions for drunkenness more than trebled between 1869 and 1870, and the average number of convictions for each year of the 1870s was twice that of every year of the 1860s.[88] It is impossible to decide which factor – the efficiency of the police, or the increasing thirst of Welsh drinkers – is most responsible for the increased convictions. Much evidence suggests that, despite the bands and the songs, the processions and the pledges, temperance and teetotal campaigners never fully conquered or captured the thirsts and thoughts of the Welsh people.

Welsh religion in this period enriched and enhanced the literary life of the nation through the creation of a rich heritage of hymns. This was undoubtedly the golden age of Welsh hymn-writing, during which

William Williams, Pantycelyn, Ann Griffiths, Dafydd Jones, Eben
Fardd and many others put their spiritual fears, neuroses and obsessions into song. These songs of praise put both the most pathetic
sentiments into rapturous tones and the most rapturous sentiments
into the most pathetic tones. But, above all, these hymns breathed the
prayer and complaint of souls boiling over with the bitterest anguished
cry to God for deliverance from their earthly confines. It is this
tradition which, despite all that has ever been written about it, makes
it so hard to understand Welsh religion. One needs to have heard a
congregation in rapture to grasp the power of the glory. Elsewhere one
looks in vain for the evidence of a great literary heritage bequeathed
by Welsh religion. The most perceptive Welsh literary and cultural
historian, who has spent a lifetime searching, concludes that

> In a country impregnated with religion one looks in vain for religious poetry of
> the first order and there is scant evidence in the numerous eisteddfod poems
> written on biblical subjects that the poets were burdened by a crisis of faith.
> Theirs was not a muse, as R.S. Thomas would put it for 'agonising over immens-
> ities that will not return'.[89]

What Wales experienced in the nineteenth century was 'a series of
religious revivals which had sanitized its literature, without enriching
the literary life of the country in a broad sense'. There were few Welsh
novels apart from those published in monthly instalments in
magazines, drama was neglected, and there were even fewer satirical
poems or prose works, as religion cast a dark shadow over literature.[90]

In contrast, the relationship between religion and education has
been traditionally regarded as flourishing. Before 1871, there was
hardly any state provision for primary education. One vital aspect of
the education of the Welsh people was the Sunday school. In the early
nineteenth century, Sunday schools, as organized by Edward Williams,
an Independent minister, and the radical Baptist Morgan John Rhys,
flourished. Pre-eminent in this popular movement was the work of the
Revd Thomas Charles of Bala. It was not until the 1840s that this
Nonconformist educational tradition, through the influence of Hugh
Owen, was channelled into support of the non-sectarian British and
Foreign Schools Society. In contrast to the Nonconformists, the
Church of England rapidly grasped Jesuit notions that the child is
father of the man. By the 1830s, on some estimates, there were nearly
1,400 schools in Wales linked to the Church of England, supplying
most of the country's elementary education. The British Society had
to subsequently work hard to redress this disparity in provision.[91]

Although the schools taught basic reading, and occasionally the '3 Rs' to people, their primary purpose was to support the efforts of Anglicans, Baptists, Independents and Methodists to capture the minds of the Welsh people. In Sunday schools, teachers were unpaid and required little more than the ability to read, since this was the simple, staple transferable skill. Catechizing – tortuous question and answer sessions on denominational texts – then took precedence. Pupils achieved prodigious feats of memory. But educationally the value was suspect.[92] One cannot escape the conclusion that much of the education provided in these Sunday schools was little short of 'religious terrorism'. The central tenets of Methodism stressed the aboriginal sinfulness of children, and the Sunday schools sought effectively to eradicate it. Emphasis on sin and sinfulness were terrifyingly real to children.[93] *Rhodd Mam* and other religious primers gave anecdotes of God's righteous punishment of the unrighteous which could traumatize and terrify children.[94] The purpose of the Sunday schools was to indoctrinate, not educate the Welsh people. The hated 1847 Education Reports revealed that educational standards were little better in the National and British schools.[95] Denominational bitterness and rivalries penetrated and permeated the schoolroom. In the National schools of Caernarfon, Nonconformist children were habitual onlookers when their Anglican counterparts were fed by their wealthy patrons, a factor which fuelled a powerful and understandable resentment.[96] In some parishes, rivalry between the Anglicans and Nonconformists led to the situation where two schools would be established, even though there were insufficient pupils to support one. At Llangefni and Llangaffo on Anglesey, the 1847 Education Commissioners complained that there were two bad schools, rather than one adequate school.[97] Even after the introduction of a new educational system in 1871, it took profound social changes before the potential of education was finally firmly grasped by the Welsh people.

Religion and the Individual

In addition to spiritual sustenance, chapels and churches offered a host of amenities for their members. Though some Puritan diehards condemned music and play acting within consecrated walls, chapels and churches became multi-media entertainment centres. Choirs performed cantatas, oratorios and a repertoire of biblically inspired musical works. By the 1860s, many children were baptized with the names Haydn and Handel, permanent reminders of their parents' favourite composers. Religion was not just a one-day-a-week chore. Chapels and churches reverberated throughout the week to the cheery noise of reading classes, Bible discussion groups, missionary society talks and lectures, singing practices and performances, penny readings, theatrical productions and the magical moving images of magic lanterns. Religion used entertainment to reinvigorate its central messages.[98]

The three significant events of an individual's life – birth, marriage and death – were marked by specific religious services. Personal rites of passage were celebrated in public ceremonies. But despite the religious monopolization of these events, there is evidence that the Welsh moved increasingly towards secular services. The Baptists had always insisted that baptism should only follow a person's understanding of the implications of leading a religious life. Consequently they baptized adolescents in the rivers of Wales. The baptism of ten people in the river Taff, near the Pentyrch works in 1830, was questioned by one sceptical and frozen observer, for the 'temperature was eight degrees below freezing'.[99] Anecdotal evidence suggests that Welsh people, having registered a birth with the local registry office, then ignored the need for a Christian christening. Increasing numbers also moved away from Christian marriages to civil services. In both urban and rural areas of Wales, civil marriage rates were among the highest in Britain. Almost inexplicably, Bala and Newcastle Emlyn, strong centres of Nonconformity, had civil marriage rates which were over four times the British rate. Welsh people preferred a civil, secular ceremony to a Christian, religious service, perhaps indicating that the old traditions of popular besom weddings were more persistent and pernicious than historians have assumed. It was only in death that many returned to chapel and church. However, by the 1880s, as a result of the campaigning of the charismatic William Price in support of cremation, this too was under threat.[100]

Religion aroused feelings of intense happiness and joy, inspired a deep sense of love, eased fears and often ended a person's loneliness.[101] People found companionship in congregations but, above all, comfort could be obtained from the knowledge that one had a friend in Jesus and, through him, God. The promise of future entry into paradise was sufficient reward for many people to endure sermons of Wagnerian duration. In the middle of all the religious drama was the soul, a fragile and timorous thing, always described as a pale, dull-like copy of a person, which gave a profoundly individualistic aspect to religion. Religion, as it developed in Wales, was remarkably self-centred. Piety was often fuelled by self-interest. Denominations which preached individual salvation gave rise to an egotistical gospel. Some people had the same easy familiarity in their prayers as they did in their private lives. One man simply prayed 'Hello Good God. Dai here – you know what I need I'm off now'. Hymns provide a graphic illustration as to how obsessed Welsh religion was with personal spiritual welfare and well-being.[102] The singular abounds and dominates the words of Welsh hymns. A brief glance through a Victorian hymn book reveals the individual crises which gave rise to religious coercion and conviction:[103]

Graig yr oesoedd gad i mi.[104]	Rock of ages cleft for me.
Arglwydd grasol, clyw fy nghri.[105]	Gracious Lord, hear my cry.
Pwy wrendy gwyn fy enaid gwan.[106]	Who will hear the cry of my weak soul.
Yn Eden, cofiaf hynny byth, Collais fendithion rif y gwlith,[107]	In Eden, I will remember, I lost blessings like the dew,
Iesu, fy Nuw, fy Ngheidwad cu Clyw fi pan lefwyf arnat Ti.[108]	Jesus, my God, my dear Saviour Hear me when I cry to Thee.
Pechadur wyf, y dua'n fyw Trugaredd yw fy nghri.[109]	I'm a sinner, the blackest living Forgiveness is my cry.

People gathered, sang and prayed in public groups, but their motives were private and personal. Welsh religion was underpinned by the deep pessimism of people tired of life on earth. One author asked:

Beth dâl im' roi fy serch a mryd	What good is it for me to give my all
Ar ddim a welais yn y byd?	On anything I've seen in the world?
Da, daear, dyn, pa gysur yw	The good things of earth, what good are they
Y dydd y del digofaint Duw.[110]	On the day of God's judgement.

In another hymn, the author complained that he was but a grain of sand in a desert of oblivion and that his only hope of salvation lay in his ability to take the leap into faith. Even the Revd Thomas Charles had difficulty in making that jump, for he was frequently cast down into a morbid depression of soul and spirit. Yet, once the step was taken, individuals derived immense conviction and courage from their faith. In 1811, the Revd David Williams captured 'the Devil instigated', murderous Thomas Edwards, Yr Hwntw Mawr, in a David and Goliath confrontation on Traeth Bach sands near Porthmadog.

Despite the promise of the taller, stronger, more powerful Edwards that he would make the minister 'yn fwyd i adar y traeth' (food for seagulls), Williams confronted him 'yn enw fy Nuw' (in my God's name). Others, however, found that their faith was irretrievably undermined by 'unfairness' in the world. Evan Powell Meredith, a lapsed ex-Baptist preacher of Monmouth, distilled his disillusionment into his atheistic book, *The Prophet of Nazareth*, published in 1864. Meredith's 'infidel book' was an early and eloquent testimony that the sea of faith was ebbing in Wales.

Many congregations included substantial numbers of elderly women, carried to the services on juddering legs wilted in varicose veins, their gnarled hands could barely close over prayer and hymn books. They sought salvation, forgiveness and love. Their presence indicated an idea central to Welsh Nonconformity, that suffering would flower into purity. Their belief made sense of tedium, suffering and sorrow. Religion warmed the tundra of their days and even seemed to heal the hurt of time. They had survived so much: deprivation, poverty, widowhood, loneliness. In the services, their aching, weary flesh at last found absolution. Out of the anguish and frustrations of their personal histories, a new world would be born. For years they had endured the wilderness and now they were ready to enter the Promised Land. Preacher after preacher, hymn after hymn, promised them that they would rise to wear 'y gynau gwynion' (the white gowns), for they had conquered 'gwae a gofid' (pain and suffering), had been washed in 'gwaed yr oen' (the lamb's blood) and would rise to join the heavenly angelic hosts.[111] Their entire lives had been a vigil, a long waiting for the last trumpet to sound, when they would be carried away on the wings of angels.

Angels, Heaven and Hell

Religion was the custodian of transcendence. Ceremonies and services offered glimpses of eternity which, like an opiate, created irresistible illusions. Religious and superstitious fables and fantasies produced a supernatural bestiary which exceeded the natural fauna of Wales. Of all the extra-terrestrial beings observed in Wales, it is probable that the ones seen most frequently were angels. People had no doubt of their existence, for the Bible told them so – 108 times in the Old Testament, and on 165 occasions in the New Testament, according to one statistically minded minister in *Yr Eurgrawn Wesleaidd*. The hymn-writers obsessively recorded their observations of these low-flying intermediaries between earth and heaven:

Angylion nef yn gysson,	Heavenly angels constantly,
Rifedi gwlith y wawr	Numbered like the dew
Ro'nt eu coronau euraidd	They place their golden crowns
O flaen y faingc i lawr;	Before his Throne;
Chwareuant eu telynau,	They play their harps,
Y'nghyd â'r saint yn un,	With the heavenly saints,
Byth, byth ni chanant ddigon	Never, never can they sing enough
Am Dduwdod yn y dyn'.[112]	About Godliness in the man.

Another author reported that, in addition to their musical work, the major task of angels was as God's white, little helpers:

Cerubiaid a Seraphiaid sydd,	Cherubs, Seraphs and,
Angylion disglair llon,	Angels bright and golden,
Yn fil o filoedd, nos a dydd,	A thousand thousand, night and day,
Yn gweini ger ei fron.[113]	Serve before Him.

Iago ab Dewi insisted that angels were ordered by God in an angelic hierarchy that reflected earthly social structures, with the archangel at the top.[114] Another hymn writer asked:

Pwy yw'r rhai'n fel ser y nefoedd,	Who are these like the heaven's stars,
Sydd ger bron gorsedd-faingc Duw,	At the side of God's throne,
Mewn ardderchog euraidd wisgoedd,	In splendid celestial dress,
Yn cydseinio clodydd gwiw?	Singing united in his praise?
Aleluiah	Hallelujah
Yw eu gorfoleddus gân.	Is their joyous song.

And answered his own question with certainty:

Dyma'r rhai a ddaethant allan	They are the ones who came out
Trwy'r byd hwn o gystudd mawr;	From this world's great pains;
Gwae a gofid fu eu cyfran,	Fear and worry were their lot,
Cyn cael gwynfyd uwch y llawr;	Before reaching heaven above the earth;
Ond fe'u golchwyd	For they were all washed
Oll yn lân y'ngwaed yr Oen.[115]	Clean in the Lamb's blood.

Belief in the cleansing power of blood that washed sins clean would enable the long-suffering Welsh to reach the heavenly spheres above and beyond the clouds. The hymns of Wales, in particular, seem to suggest that believers would be beamed directly up into heaven. The trials and tribulations of their earthly lives were considered sufficient for them to gain direct entry into the ranks of the heavenly hosts. Descriptions of what would meet them there were vague and impressionistic. This abode of unearthly bliss proved beyond even the immense imaginative powers of William Williams, Pantycelyn. He knew only too well that nothing he said could convey 'a thousandth part of the majesty and the splendour within this city'.[116] Many descriptions evoke a white, blissful, peaceful land where the saved would live, sinlessly, in the love of Christ and God. In contrast, John Thomas portrayed heaven as a rowdier place, full of 'loving, singing, and marvelling'.[117]

Judged and forever deprived of hope, the incorrigibly wicked were despatched straight to hell. The physiognomy of hell was more consistent – it was the fiery pit where the wicked were tortured and tormented. But its location varied. Its position at the centre of the earth was undermined by the discoveries of geological science. Many thought that it was located on the sun, others that it existed in an allegorical world. Hell had at least seven levels: 'uffern, dystryw, pwll llygreidigaeth, pwll terfysg, clai tomlyd, cysgod angau', and the 'ddaear isaf'. This infernal region was preceded by 'dyffryn wylofain', an area of Dantesque desolation shrouded in mist, a place of terrible torment: 'lle o boenfa i eneidiad drygionus i'r gele, yr hon a sugna y gwaed, yr hwn ydyw y bywyd' (a place where souls are tortured by leeches, who suck the blood, which is life). All authors were consistent in asserting that hell was ruled over by Satan and his hosts. Satan was huge and deformed, with lopsided wings because Michael had clipped them.[118] He too, according to Dr Henry Harries, had his helpers ordered in a hellish hierarchy – Belial, Muloch and Belzebub were generals in the armies of darkness. Denominational periodicals like *Seren Gomer* and *Yr Eurgrawn Wesleaidd* abound with detailed theological and philosophical discussions of the nature of the Prince of Darkness. The children's primer *Rhodd Mam* emphasized fear of the devil to instil terror into young minds. Each had no doubt in describing the devil as a physical presence in the life of Wales.[119]

Religion proved central to the delusions of many people. Thomas Price of Fishguard, much to the chagrin of his son, sold his lands because they were 'so full of brimstone'. Even after moving to a new farm, he continued to believe that 'sulphur and poisonous gasses were setting his brain on fire' and would only give instructions to the servants from behind locked doors or closed windows, because they too were infected with brimstone.[120] It was estimated that twenty-seven per cent of all admissions to the Monmouth asylum suffered delusions triggered by religious fears and guilt. One inmate believed that, as a saint, he did not need to work, while Alfred C. claimed that 'going down Capel Street he saw the Almighty, who told him to go and have a gin and water which he did'. Sarah Ann H. was admitted suffering 'gradually increasing melancholia. Charges herself with theft and lying years ago, says she stole half a crown as a child for which she is in continual dread of hell.'[121] In the early nineteenth century, many believed that God and the devil still fought for people's souls in a world of providences, prophecies, wizardry and wonders. So powerful were these perceptions on occasion that individuals were willing to follow enthusiastic and experimental religious leaders. In the 1780s, Mary Evans, Mari'r Fantell Wen (1739–89), dressed in a blood-red cloak, led a 'multitude' to her wedding with Jesus at Ffestiniog church. Despite her claims that she was immortal, Mary died in 1789. Her white and multi-coloured cloaks were kept by her followers because they believed that the clothes possessed magical curative properties. Martha'r Mynydd persuaded many of the inhabitants of Llanllyfni that she had magical powers, bestowed by an invisible people whom she called the *Anweledigion* (Invisibles). Although Mari and Martha were depicted as devout but deluded, even depraved, their messages were not simply the rantings and ravings of wild and weird women. To people ravaged and savaged by fear, Mari and Martha above all else offered hope. Their careers as religious leaders offers a corrective to the traditional view of women as impassive and uneloquent – the cigar-store Indians of Welsh religion.[122]

Superstition was even more graphic than scriptures in describing Satan. In Llanddewibrefi, Cardiganshire, and the Preselau area of Pembrokeshire, it was claimed that local girls sold their souls to the devil in special ceremonies. They would retain communion bread in their mouths, walk around the church nine times and give it to the first creature – cat, dog, frog or hog – they encountered. The folk tales and traditions gathered by the Museum of Welsh Life, Cardiff, testify to the frequency of the devil's Welsh visits. He appears to have been particularly drawn to card players and drinkers, for several tales relate his participation in games in Bangor, Pentrefoelas, Rhuddlan and the Tywi valley. Two late-night revellers from Risca (Monmouthshire) and Cyfarthfa (Glamorgan) met the devil on their return home. Many Welsh people, like John Roberts and Morgan Jones, frequently got the better of the devil in their night-time meetings. But the majority of Welsh people were less astute victims of the Prince of Darkness. Robert Llwyd Harri of Denbighshire allegedly died after falling from a great height while flying with the devil.[123] From the gallows, several Welsh murderers confessed that they had acted under the devil's influence.

In the 1850s, when Mr and Mrs S. C. Hall undertook a tour around Wales, they were both shocked that 'the visible appearance of his satanic majesty we have found rather prevalent in Wales'.[124] So prevalent, in fact, that any suspicious circumstances could be attributed to his malign influence and presence.[125] In 1848, two workmen at Lampeter Velfrey in Pembrokeshire discovered what they took to be the devil, sleeping on their coats. Terrified, they fell on their knees and prayed for deliverance. The noise of their prayers woke the creature, which ran away to a nearby farm, Castellheli, where it traumatized a servant girl who screamed 'The devil is in the dairy!' Unable to stand this threat to his business, the farmer turned the dogs onto the creature. It was later discovered that the mangled remains were those of a monkey, which had escaped from a circus at Narberth.[126]

Such gullibility aroused the supercilious smiles of some, but the anecdote highlights the fact that many did not just believe but were afraid, and fear follows no logic. Strange, inexplicable phenomena inspired terror in the Welsh people. June and July 1819 were permeated with a sinister atmosphere, in which the sun was a wafer of light barely visible, wanly tracing the hours across a threatening sky, coloured 'mor ddu a breuddwyd Jeremiah' (as black as the dream of Jeremiah). Powerful storms of thunder and lightning caused widespread flooding across south Wales, which carried away people and livestock. But most terrifying was the following:

> a shower of rain as red as blood, fell near the village of Bonvilston and extended from thence in a westerly direction over Llantrithydd, Flemingston and towards Llantwit-major . . . Several country people who witnessed it were dreadfully alarmed, imagining it to be an omen of coming misfortune.[127]

In June 1832, between two severe rainstorms in the Llyn Gwynant area of Caernarfonshire, there occurred a bizarre downpour of fish which resembled small herrings.[128] In the sun-soaked summer of 1844, a shortage of water tormented people, motivating many to pray to God for rain. To help its parched readers, *Seren Gomer* published several *Gweddi am Wlaw* (prayers for rain). Four years later, an earthquake shook Cardiff, Llandaff, Newport-on-Usk, Risca, Tredegar and Rupera. Workmen repairing the church at Radyr fled for their lives,

believing that there was a *Tolaeth* in the house of God.[129] Strange
lights were frequently seen in the skies above 'the wild region of
Barmouth'.[130] About six months before the outbreak of the Crimean
War in 1853, John Meyler and James Morris of Cilciffeth,
Pembrokeshire, spent two hours watching the apparition of a ghostly
bloody battle between two armies in the skies.[131] In the 1830s, the Revd
Griffiths, a Baptist minister from Pontfaen in Pembrokeshire, beheld a
great light above the church. His terrifying experience was said to have
changed his face in a moment, in the twinkling of an eye, into the
traumatized visage of a man who had walked with angels, wrestled
with demons and looked on the face of God.[132] The Revd Griffiths's
experience indicates that the worlds of religion and superstition were
far closer than many commentators have admitted. If sober religious
leaders emphasized the physical reality of unearthly angels, demons
and devils, why should simple, untutored people not believe in the
earthly presence of beings and beasts which did not have a theological
pedigree?[133]

Magic and the Pursuit of Happiness

The traditional view of historians and theologians has been that the
growth of religion led to a decline in magic.[134] This was the message
propounded and propagated by the Baptist minister William Roberts
in his *Crefydd yr Oesoedd Tywyll*, published in 1852, a coruscating
condemnation of popish celebrations and pagan customs.[135] In his
Illustration of the Dissent and Morality of Wales, published in 1849,
Evan Jones, Ieuan Gwynedd (1820–52), made a spirited proclamation:
'We now walk in the light. Fairies and ghosts have vanished. The
mighty fabric of superstition, reared by the industry of ages, lies
scattered in dismal and ignominious ruin.'[136]

Yet closer examination of the evidence indicates that the Welsh
people still walked in darkness. The old beliefs were still living and
thriving. In the 1780s, the Revd. Edmund Jones published *A Relation
of Apparitions of Spirits, in the County of Monmouth and the
Principality of Wales*, which documented the oral testimony of several
Welsh people who had been tormented by ghostly apparitions.[137] The
passionate and powerful preaching of Rhys Davies, Y Glun Bren
(1772–1847), was permeated with warnings of the dangers posed to
people by evil forces and powers. Both Jones and Davies were devout

believers in the physical presence of ghosts, ghouls, phantoms and spirits. Robert Roberts, the wondering 'Wandering Scholar' (1834–85) from Llangernyw, was also familiar with the close relationship between magic and religion, and offered this explanation:

> Methodist books ... swarmed with marvels, supernatural appearances, warnings, singing in the air, sudden judgements on rulers and persecutors; God's miracles and the Devil's miracles abounded everywhere. And for people who read the Old Testament histories so much, what was more natural than to expect miracles everywhere?[138]

In order to determine the best site to build a chapel, the people of the Pentrellyncymer area of the Hiraethog Mountain consulted the local *dyn hysbys* (wise man). He decreed that the chapel should be erected where a particular black sow was grazing and that, according to local tradition, was where Hermon chapel was built in 1868.[139] A complex symbiotic relationship existed between religion and magic. They were not simply competing forces, but complementary and collaborative. Religion offered solution to people's problems in the next world, but magic provided answers and solutions to the trials and tribulations of life on earth. Despite the considerable emphasis that has been placed on the high levels of religiosity of the Welsh people in the period 1776–1871, there is considerable evidence to suggest that this was the golden age of the Welsh wizard, wiseman and witch. The legions of light and darkness walked together.

Perhaps most frustrating to a historian intent on penetrating the darker corners of the human psyche are the terms 'once upon a time', 'unwaiths' lawer dydd' and 'long ago', which frequently precede folk tales and traditions. This chronological inexactitude makes it impossible to ascertain the period in which a story is set with any clarity or certainty. Memory is often hazy, as the stories curl back into the mists of time. Thankfully, there are a remarkable number of tales of Welsh wizards, wisemen and witches which provide the certainty and comfort of an actual date on which the events allegedly took place. Indeed, some stories indicate that the vague threats of times past created real dangers in the present. In August 1824, the *Carmarthen Journal* related the following:

> Carmarthen fair, on Thursday last, was but poorly attended, owing, we understand, to a most absurd alarm, founded upon an ancient prophecy of Merlin, that on that day, the town was to be utterly destroyed by inundation. Hundreds of people absolutely retired from the town to the neighbouring villages, to avoid

the threatened danger, and indeed so great was the terror of some of those poor deluded creatures, that they even set off on the preceding day for Swansea, and other towns. In all times false prophecies have abounded, but that in the present age of almost universal information and intelligence we should find persons so credulous, excites astonishment.[140]

The astonished editor noted the fact that the lack of floods did not lessen belief in the prophecies of the long dead magus. It should be little surprise, therefore, that people fervently believed in the efficacy of real live wizards.

Wisemen, Witches and Wizards

Certain areas were celebrated and famous for their *dynion hysbys* (wise men). In the early nineteenth century, Llandybïe in Carmarthenshire was home to Lodwick William, the famous bonesetter and infamous medical astrologer, the multi-talented and much named Anthony William Rhys Dafydd and John Evans of Piode.[141] The wild, mountainous area between Llangurig and Rhayader was home to Evan Griffiths, William Savage and his brother-in-law and brother-in-magic John Morgan.[142] Beddgelert, as befitted a village which prospered on a fiction, was home to several magicians.[143] Mysterious and mystical Pembrokeshire, in the early nineteenth century, reverberated to the spells and incantations of several wizards and witches. At Millin Dingle near Picton Castle, Abe (or Aby) Bidle practised his magic. At Nevern, the school master John Jenkin, Ioan Siencyn, was not only a gifted poet, but a conjuror or *consuriwr*, capable of calling and controlling evil spirits. Newport was the locale of the medical magician Levi Salmon, Dr Cwac. Jekky Arter of Williamston was a charmer who specialized in 'stopping the blood'. William Howells, Wil Tiriet or Wiliet of Caerfarchell, was a *dyn hysbys* and soothsayer who flourished in the years 1820–50.[144] His powers of hocus-pocus were legendary. When the Baptist chapel at Middle Hill was so flourishing as to require the services of two ministers, Will outraged the people by predicting that the younger of the two, William Jones, would soon die and that, at his funeral, a minister with a long white beard would preach. No one could think of a white-bearded minister in the area, and so the anger turned to mockery. But when the young minister died, many were traumatized. Several remained sceptical until the cortege arrived at the chapel to be greeted by a reverend gentleman with a long flowing white beard. He was Dr Thomas Davies, the principal of the Haverfordwest Baptist College, who had rushed on horseback to the funeral. For a long time people were terrified of Will's powers and predictions.[145] Even more powerful was Dr Joseph Harries of Werndew, near Dinas. He helped local people to recover their stolen property, cured the sick and organized ghostly aerial transport to speed people on their mercy missions to save the dying.[146] Pembrokeshire people who did not wish to consult the conjurers but were intent on harnessing or resisting the powers of darkness could enlist the services of witches such as Hannah of Walton West (fl. 1800), Maggie of Pontfaen (fl. 1820), Old Moll of Redberth (fl. 1840), Dolly Llewellin of Carew, Newtown (fl. 1850), Betty Foggy of Pembroke Dock (fl. 1850) and the male witches Tom Eynon of Lamphey (fl. 1840) and Ben Volke of Canaston Bridge (fl. 1810–20).[147]

Throughout the nineteenth century, wizards and their wonders were sources of considerable interest and fascination. In 1840, Monmouth Theatre was packed with people watching Barnardo Eagle, the Royal and Original Wizard of the South and his 'Cabalistic phenomena and conjurations, automatic wonders, Mephistophelian Transmutations along with Electrical, Magnetic and Hydraulic Magic and the Black Arts'. The same venue was crowded for the performances of Professor Buek, 'Wizard of Wizards', in 1863, the illusionist Professor du Cann in 1867, Signor Bosco with his Enchanted Palace in 1870, Herr Dobler with Eastern Wonders of the Wizard Art in 1871, and the Great Duprez with his dark and light seances in 1872.[148]

People believed in the supernatural powers of these people. Many of life's inexplicable misfortunes and mysteries were attributed to malignant forces. At Llanidloes in 1839 a mob attacked an ugly, wrinkled and wizened old woman who, they claimed, was a witch who had cursed a local child. The baying mob were calling on the men assaulting the woman to 'draw blood from the old witch to make her harmless'. Although one woman sought to prevent the outrage, the mob continued their assault and attempted to force the battered woman to bless the child and withdraw her curse. The old woman, realizing it was futile to resist, uttered a prayer. Instantly the child wriggled in its mother's arms, gave a happy little gurgle and appeared fully recovered. Whether or not she was a witch, the old woman certainly left the crowd bewitched, bothered and bewildered, contemplating a dilemma that demanded a Solomonic solution. If the old woman was a witch and had recognized any of them, would she curse them? On the other hand, if she was not a witch and had performed a miracle, would God punish them for assaulting his agent?[149]

In this galaxy of Welsh wizards and witches, the brightest stars were the father and son double act in the dark arts, John Harries (c.1785–1839) and Henry Gwynne Harries (1821–49) of Pant-cou, Cwrt-y-cadno, Carmarthenshire.[150] Although the irascible David Owen, Brutus, was inveterate in his condemnation of these 'charlatans', their mumbo-jumbo skills were widely sought by the people of a large area of the south.[151] Both were astrologers, qualified doctors and wisemen who provided a plethora of services for the anxious and the afflicted. Lost people and stolen property could be recovered by the Harrieses, through consulting their extensive collection of magical books for spells to summon benign and friendly spirits. One recorded case relates how Dr John Harries treated a man who was convinced that he was bewitched. Several doctors had prescribed bleedings, drugs and purgings to no avail. Desperate, the man turned to Dr John Harries who informed him that he had swallowed an evil spirit – a tadpole which had grown into a frog. After studying his texts and summoning the spirits, Dr Harries made the patient vomit. Unsurprisingly, in the vomit was a frog, and the man was cured.[152] In the Harries papers in the National Library of Wales are several instructions and details of how to invoke spirits and perform exorcisms. The well-stocked library at Pant-cou was considered the finest occult library belonging to cunning folk in nineteenth-century Britain.[153] Owning a library was a suspicious habit which ran counter to the practice of most Welsh householders, who possessed few books, and usually only a Bible. In the early nineteenth century, book learning was often a matter of suspicion, even in a religious context. The Revd Daniel Evans (1792–1846) was given the nom de plume Daniel Ddu (Black Daniel) because of his learning. He had studied at Oxford, where the natives of Daniel's home village of Llanfihangel-Ystrad believed the ancient colleges were the favourite haunts of a motley crew of ghosts of a very doubtful character. Daniel was allegedly an expert in raising spirits and, as to his familiarity with the black arts, they had no doubt, for could he not speak 'Latin as well as Mephistopheles himself?'[154]

On one occasion in November 1807, the inhabitants of Llandeilo, baffled by the disappearance of a young girl, consulted Dr John Harries. He informed them that they would discover her body near a certain tree at Maesyronnen for, Dr Harries claimed, she had been murdered by her boyfriend. The discovery of her body led to Dr

Harries being charged as an accessory to the crime. The case was transferred to Lloyd, Glansevin and Gwyn, Glanbrân, two Llandovery
magistrates who ordered Harries to appear before them. In his own
defence, Harries offered to demonstrate his talent for second sight,
asking the magistrates: 'Dywedwch chwi yr awr yr daethoch chwi i'r
byd, a mi a ddywedaf finnau yr awr yr ewch chwi allan ohono' (you
tell me which hour you came into the world, and I will tell you the hour
you will depart from it). Unnerved by this line of questioning, and
perhaps unwilling to discover their fate, the magistrates dismissed the
case.[155] Other cunning men were less fortunate before Welsh courts.
William Jenkin of Cadoxton-Juxta Barry in Glamorgan was punished
several times by the Llandaff Consistory Court in the late eighteenth
century.[156] In November 1807, a 'Dr' William Jones, 'an antiquated
impostor' and 'notorious offender', was committed to Cardiff jail by
the Glamorgan Assizes for witchcraft and conjuration.[157] Daniel Jones
of Llanafan Fawr was also prosecuted for such activities at the Brecon
Assizes in 1789. John Jones, a late eighteenth-century magician from
the Vale of Neath, was imprisoned in Cardiff jail for occult practices,
as was John Edwards of Llaneilian, 'the most evil place in Wales', at
the Flintshire Assizes in 1815.[158]

In addition to recovering lost property, Dr John Harries could mark
thieves so that victims would know who had stolen their property.[159]
Tregaron people fervently believed that a farmer who had bewitched a
neighbour's daughter had been marked by Dr Harries in a counter
spell. The farmer had to wear a scarf on his head to hide the horn.[160]
On another occasion, Dr Harries informed a farmer that he would
'know the thief who had stolen his horse by a big mark on his
forehead, like a horn'. The farmer returned home and discovered that
one of his nephews had developed a large cyst in the middle of his
head.[161] An old drover who had lost the £80 he obtained for selling
cattle was told by Dr Harries that he would soon recover the money,
and that the thief would be punished by being bedridden. Delight at
the news turned to dismay, when the drover returned home to his
newly bedridden wife who confessed her crime. Forgiveness did not
extend as far a second visit to Dr Harries for a remedial spell. The wife
remained bedridden for eighteen years.[162]

Among the astrological charts, abracadabras, charms and cabalas in
the Harries Cwrt-y-cadno papers are a host of cures for a plethora of
medical and mental ailments.[163] Although both father and son had
trained as surgeons in London and were Fellows of the Royal College

of Surgeons at Edinburgh, their interests in the occult took them to the boundaries of mainstream medicine.[164] Above all else, the Harrieses were magical medics tapping into a rich seam of medical folklore and folk tradition, inheritors of a tradition that stretched back to 'Meddygon Myddfai'.[165] In their agonies and afflictions, people were at their most vulnerable and sought relief and restitution from any quarter. Ebenezer Thomas, Eben Fardd (1802–63), hymn-writer, map-maker, historian, genealogist, school teacher and Methodist elder, suffered a variety of illnesses. His diaries reveal the tortured musings of a hypochondriac and dipsomaniac, and lay bare the poignant details of his family's health problems. As befitted a man who appears theologically confused, he was willing to turn to any source for relief. When his daughter Ellen was ill, he sought a cure from a wise woman at Bontllyfni. In 1844, his father-in-law became ill and Eben sought the help of a quack doctor. Later the same year, he sought the help of a bonesetter to fix the dislocated shoulder of his son James.[166]

There was a general feeling in the nineteenth century that God was not only omnipresent and omnipotent, but very practical. As well as interfering in the affairs of people, dispensing summary justice and punishment to sinners, he signposted various plants which he had created for the benefit of folk medicine. Kidney-shaped leaves were considered to offer certain cures for kidney complaints.[167] Herbs such as rosemary, groundsel, rue, parsley, wormwood and tansy were the basis for many cures. Timothy Lewis, in his *A Welsh Leech Book*, recommended the following cure for equine worms: 'Take rue and crush, then temper with thy own urine and give it to the patient to drink, and it will kill the worms and bring them out'.[168] One Caernarfonshire remedy for equine worms was brutal: 'take a small chicken and pluck it, push it down the horse's throat – the worms will loosen their grip on the lining of the stomach and feed on the chicken, which will eventually pass out of the horse'.[169] Extensive use was also made of various common weeds and flowers such as ivy, pennywort, horseleek, stonecrop, dandelion, dock and daisies. Ivy was chewed and crushed and used as a cure for cataract, while in Merionethshire it was used as a poultice for the removal of corns. Wild plants such as wood-sage, buckbean, plantain, colts-foot, cinquefoil and gorse were also utilized, as was the bark of many trees. In the Aberystwyth area, an infusion of wood-sage was used as a diuretic and stomachic, but in south Caernarfonshire its use was confined to making an ointment for sore udders.

Animal and human products were also greatly valued. Cow's milk was widely used for its cosmetic properties. Goose grease was kept in many households to ease sore throats and swollen joints, and given as an appetizer for croup sufferers.[170] The water of Welsh holy wells were believed to effect magical cures. Wales had nearly 400 such wells, and, of these, 78 were believed to offer cures for the eyes, 52 cured rheumatism, 47 cured skin diseases, 26 got rid of warts, while a dozen cured lameness and fractures respectively.[171] In this natural pharmacopoeia, no product was allowed to go to waste. Cow and horse dung were used as poultices. Urine was an unguent of universal value: an eggcupful of the sufferer's urine poured into the ear was a remedy for earache; washing one's face with one's own urine was considered to have great cosmetic value, and a similar treatment would be carried out for chilblains or sore feet. Even vermin and reptiles had their value. A remedy for incontinence was to roast a rat and to place the ashes secretly in the sufferer's bed. *Glain y Nadroedd* (adder beads) were regarded as being good for all afflictions of the eye and possessed many virtues.[172] Snails were greatly valued for their curative properties. One recipe advised, almost reverentially: 'Take the black slugs, having collected them from the dew on May Day, and roast them on a spit by a stone fire and collect the fat, and guard it dearly; then anoint the eyes with it, and they will be made clean and bright and healthy.'[173]

The same anxiety to document and detail as occurred in mainstream medicine can be seen in popular pharmacopoeia. Published editions of the remedies of the legendary Meddygon Myddfai were widely available. In 1813, Hugh Davies published his *Welsh Botanology*, which detailed the medicinal value and virtues of a large number of plants.[174] Davies had gathered the information when he was the incumbent of the parishes of Llandegfan in Anglesey and Aber in Caernarfonshire. Griffith Jones, Llanddowror, an unhappy hypochondriac, was described as 'a great a Quack in Physick as in Divinity' and many Methodist leaders followed his lead into magical medicine. William Williams, Pantycelyn, used the recipes of William Buchan's *Domestic Medicine*, and his pestle and mortar, to crush out cures for his family's ailments. The tradition of doctoring and divinity was not confined to Anglican Wales. Nathaniel Williams, a prominent eighteenth-century Carmarthenshire Baptist, produced in 1785 his *Darllen Dwfr a Meddyginiaeth*, a treatise on the medieval practice of uroscopy which became a stock-in-trade for many a folk practitioner.[175] A contemporary Scotch Baptist, J. R. Jones of Ramoth, Llanfrothen, in Merionethshire, also practised a traditional form of medicine. His library included manuscripts of herbal remedies, books on domestic medicine and, significantly, astrological tables.[176] Christmas Evans carefully collected recipes for cures to a variety of ailments and afflictions, many of which relied on their application at the correct astrological moment for their efficacy. Many people consulted popular almanacs, such as those published by the weather prophet Will Awst, or Robert Roberts's *Almanac Caergybi*.[177] The oral testimony gathered by the Museum of Welsh Life, Cardiff, reveals that this traditional folk medicine survived into the twentieth century. The worlds of the supernatural and the natural, magic and religion, doctoring and divinity, were not separate worlds of black and white, but were interrelated and interdependent through innumerable shades of grey. Pain was more powerful than rational behaviour.

Alongside religion, magic marked the great stages of the life-cycle. Despite the attempts of some religious leaders to ridicule them, the barnacles of old beliefs still attached powerfully to birth, marriage and death throughout the nineteenth century. Children's and infants' shoes were often preserved under floorboards and hearth stones and behind chimney places to serve as good luck charms.[178] In an age of high infant mortality, those who had just survived the Herodian years were considered particularly fortunate. The birth of many babies was believed to have been blessed by the appearance of a shooting star. A mother who gave birth to an illegitimate child with a hare-lip was told that 'it was the mark of Cain for my shame'.[179] The desire and anxiety that a person, especially a girl, should live content in love and marriage, and not in cold loneliness, gave rise to many charms to foresee a future partner. Many had a phallic aspect to them. Young girls in Cardiganshire, in order to see their future husbands, would walk around the house nine times with a glove in the hand, saying 'Dyma'r faneg, lle mae'r llaw?' (here is the glove, where is the hand?). In Carmarthenshire, they would circumnavigate the dung-heap, holding a shoe in the left hand, saying 'here is the shoe, where is the foot?'; or holding a sheath they would ask 'Here is the sheath, where is the knife?'[180] Sufficiently dizzy, they would see their future intended. Such charms were more effective if performed on certain saints' days, or on one of the three 'Spirits Nights', or at a certain phase of the moon. One girl from the Ystradmeurig area in 1800 walked around the church nine times in an attempt to see her lover. Instead, she saw what she believed to be a malign spirit, and assumed that, instead of being destined to marry, she was doomed to die. Although it was explained to her that a young minister had played a trick on her by wearing a dark cloak, she was said to be so terrified and traumatized that she wasted away and died.[181]

Death drew to it a plethora of simple and sinister beliefs and customs. To ensure the safe passage of a deceased person's soul to heaven, relations would call in the services of a 'Bwytawr Pechod' (Sin Eater). The person so called would silently go into the room where the dead lay and, repeating the Lord's Prayer very slowly, would eat bread and salt placed on the breast of the dead and then go away, carrying with him the sins of the deceased.[182] In his biography of Christmas Evans, published in 1881, Paxton Hood claimed that 'the superstition of the sin-eater is said to linger even now in the secluded vale of Cwmaman in Carmarthenshire'.[183] In 1852 Matthew Moggeridge of Swansea, at a meeting of the Cambridge Archaeological Association, reported that 'the custom of sin-eating has survived in the neighbourhood of Llandybïe, a few miles from Swansea'.[184] The practice could also be found in the mid nineteenth century in certain parts of Denbighshire and Flintshire.[185] In Caernarfonshire the custom was adapted into a 'sin-cake' which was fed to unworthy characters. These people were so hungry that they would greedily eat the cake and thereby acquire the dead person's sins.[186] In virtually all areas of Wales, the living stood in vigil over their dearly departed in order to safeguard their souls from evil.

Portents of death abounded. *Toili* or phantom funerals were seen frequently. Wil Canaan, a Pembrokeshire gravedigger, always insisted that he was informed at least two weeks in advance of a death in his area, so that he could prepare the coffin.[187] On his journey through 'wild Wales' in 1851, George Borrow heard the complaint of a Llandeilo toll gate keeper that many phantom funerals were passing through his gate without paying.[188] Spiritual black dogs were often taken to be forewarnings of woe, as was the inexplicable night-time howling of domestic dogs. The *aderyn corff* (corpse bird) was often seen. The presence of doves, pigeons, barn owls and even robins near the house of a sick person was interpreted as a sign of imminent death. Nature also warned of death by cockerels crowing in the night, bats entering a house, a swarm of bees leaving a house, or rats attacking a house. Perhaps the most famous and frightening premonition of death was *y cannwyll corff* (the corpse candle). It was still believed in the nineteenth century that God had granted St David his deathbed wish that his people would be warned of their death. Forewarned was forearmed.

People could amend their lives and get ready to face their Maker. Accordingly, ghostly nightly lights would appear before a death took place in south-west Wales. The light would float in the air and trace out the route which the funeral cortege would later follow. A small, barely discernible light indicated the death of a child, brighter lights forewarned the deaths of adults, and pale flickering lights foretold the deaths of the old. At Llandeilo in the 1820s, observers were baffled to see three or four lights floating above the river Tywi. A few weeks later a coach crashed into the river in full flood, drowning all the passengers. Three bodies were later recovered and carried along the same route as the phantom lights had taken. On 1 April 1833, Dafydd Williams of Pembrokeshire died. Late one evening four months previously he had seen his own corpse candle. Believing his fate was sealed, Dafydd declined and died.[189]

The ability to foretell the future was a skill widely sought in Wales in these years. At the time of the 1828 *eisteddfod*, Miss Lloyd, a fortune-teller of Park Street, Denbigh, was said to have a flourishing business with a wide custom base.[190] Edward Pugh, on his tour through north Wales in the early nineteenth century, met many remarkable characters – including a diminutive dwarf witch, Shâne Bwt, an 86-year-old bedridden fasting lady and a 'infant Hercules' of Aberogwen – but perhaps the most remarkable was 'Bella' the fortune-teller of Denbigh. 'The awful divineress' exploited the cupidity and curiosity of considerable numbers of people. She told Pugh that he would fall in love with a very pretty girl and advised him as to how he could win and secure her love. Pugh noted that Bella, and her mother, were exceptionally well-dressed and appeared to be 'living well off the credulous peasants'.[191] At Llangurig, Mary Evans – Mary Pen-y-geiniog (Mary Head of the Penny) made a fine living reading the futures of local people in her tea-leaves. She was also frequently consulted by persons who wished to enter into trading ventures, make purchases, or undertake long journeys. Often, on sunny Sunday afternoons, there would be queues of people outside her home, on the appropriately named Rhos-y-Wrach (Hag's Moor), waiting their turn to have their fortunes told. Mary charged according to a customer's ability to pay – a penny for the poor, half a crown for the 'upper classes'.[192] Others were less egalitarian and more dishonest. In 1825, a gypsy fortune-teller was arrested after extracting over £20 from the gullible people of Brecon. Timothy Stanley and Martha Cooper 'did pretend and profess to tell fortunes' and were each given one month

Edward Pugh, *Shâne Bwt*, from *Cambria Depicta*, 1816 (Hugh Owen Library, The University of Wales, Aberystwyth). Pugh was warned not to underestimate the danger posed to him by the dimunitive Shâne, the famous witch of the north, for she could be much nastier than she looked.

hard labour in Usk jail in February 1826 for their deceptions and deceits.[193] Twm o'r Nant insinuated that southerners were more credulous than northerners. One of his characters, familiar with the 'hocus pocus and wheel of fortune', was 'Anti Sal o'r South', a fortune-teller.[194] In the south, those who wished to foresee their own future

Edward Pugh, *Bella, The Fortune Teller*, from *Cambria Depicta*, 1816 (Hugh Owen Library, The University of Wales, Aberystwyth). Another of the characters encountered by Edward Pugh on his remarkable journey through north Wales. Almost every Welsh community had characters like Bella.

fortunes only had to obtain copies of Dr Parrins's *New Fortune Telling Book*, or Crosby's *Ladies Fortune Telling Pocket Book*, both of which could be obtained from John Daniel, proprietor of the *Carmarthen Journal*.[195]

Agriculture, totally at the mercy of the elements, acquired a wide and wonderful folklore and legend which foretold weather. A person well versed in such lore could always find a venerable maxim to fortify the view he or she happened to take. Yet for every optimistic proverb there were more pessimistic ones that warned that mortal providence was fallible, that life was short and that only the present was real. A new moon rising on a Saturday or Sunday was a portent of bad weather. Pessimism predominated in Welsh proverbs: 'Os y borfa dyf yn Ionor, Gwaeth y tyf trwy'r flwyddyn rhagor'; 'Braf yn Ionor, dial ym Mai'; 'Mawrth a ladd, Ebrill a fling'; 'Fel bo Mawrth y bydd yr haf' (If the grass grows in January, it will not grow in the rest of the year; Fine in January, revenge in May; March kills, April flails; As is March so will the summer be) and the horribly pessimistic and fatalistic 'Gwell yw gweled mam ar elor, na gweld hinon deg yn Ionor' (It is better to see a mother in a coffin, than fine weather in January).[196] Only a few Welsh proverbs have the warm air of summer; the majority were forged in the arctic chill of winter.

Those in peril on the sea were even more superstitious than their farming neighbours. In Pembrokeshire, the cunning man of Pentregethin made a living selling winds to harbour-trapped sailors. Those who braved winds which could make believers out of the most irresolute sinners carried with them a cargo-hold full of superstitions. Women were unlucky at the best of times. At sea they were positively dangerous. The albatross was a bird of ill omen, the storm petrel even more hated for it was believed that it was a physical manifestation of the unrestful souls of drowned sailors. In the mid nineteenth century, it was said that the entrance to Tremadog bay had a black post. It was black, not because it had been so painted, but because local sailors would throw imaginary coats representing their respectability over it as they sailed out to enjoy the ladies, liquor and pleasures of the world's ports. Upon their return they would ceremoniously recover their imaginary coats before returning to wives, families, friends and respectability.[197] Mining acquired so many portents of death which insisted that the miners should leave the pit, that it is a wonder that any coal was raised in Wales in the years 1776–1871. If a cap fell, or one met a woman on the way to work, miners would return home, for it foretold bad fortune. Miners were especially vigilant at times when broad beans were in flower, for that was the season of danger and disaster. When rats left the pit, it was considered an ill omen, as was an encounter with a white rat underground. At Morfa mine in Aberafan in the mid nineteenth century, miners were terrified at the pungent smell which they believed was produced by an invisible corpse flower. Many refused to return to work because death was hunting for victims in their mine. In the lead mines of Cardiganshire, miners believed that friendly spirits knocked out warnings of imminent danger so that men could escape. The Cardiganshire miners' 'drinking song' advised: 'Clap your ear to the ground and you'll hear ye sound of the Fairies and small picaninnies'.[198]

'Y Tylwyth Teg': Fairies and Fables

These helpful spirits were fearfully and fondly referred to as 'Y Tylwyth Teg' (the fairy folk). These fairies were usually invisible, and were so much smaller than humans that a grazing cow could blow hundreds of them away with every breath. They had their origin when the rebellious angel Lucifer and his followers were expelled from heaven, and God the Son warned God the Father that heaven would soon be empty. Like figures in a film that is suddenly stopped, the expelled angels falling towards hell halted where they were – some in mid-air, others in the earth, some at sea, and there they remained. They were jealous of humans and often did them harm, but were not totally malevolent since they had not given up hope of getting back into heaven one day.[199]

Tales of Welsh people's encounters with these beings abound. The effect of the strength of belief in the danger presented to humans by fairies can be seen in Welsh geography. Ordnance Survey maps show roads all over Wales which abruptly detour in a semi-circle to avoid a hill or dingle which fairies were supposed to inhabit. Fear that unhoused fairies would seek and wreak revenge forced the progressive, linear optimism of nineteenth-century engineering to take a sideways course. In 1841, the wife of Mr William Owen Stanley (1802–84), MP for Anglesey, visited an old friend, Beti Gruffydd at Holyhead. Unable to get a response, Mrs Stanley entered the house to find the old woman in bed, barricaded behind a mass of heather. Beti explained that she had undertaken this course of action to save herself from the torment of the fairies who were scornful towards her, turning her milk sour and breaking the crockery. In south-west Wales, *y pren criafol* was used to keep the fairies away.[200] Fairies would also steal good-looking and placid babies and place cantankerous changelings in their place.[201] Welsh mothers and midwives had to be exceptionally vigilant. One Radnorshire midwife had to resort to complicated intrigues on her journeys to attend pregnant mothers to prevent the local fairies from following her. One woebegone and woeful Welsh poet lamented:

Llawer plentyn teg aeth ganddynt,	Many a lovely child they've taken,
Pan y cym'rant helynt hir:	When long and bitter was the pain:
Oddiar annwyl dda rieni,	From their parents, loving dear,
I drigfanau difri dir.	To the fairies' dread domain.

T. H. Thomas, *Shui Rhys and the Tylwyth Teg*, 1879, illustration from Wirt Sikes, *British Goblins* (London, 1880) (Hugh Owen Library, The University of Wales, Aberystwyth). The *Tylwyth Teg* (The Fair People or fairies) could confer great blessings, but they could equally blight people's lives. There are many reports of people being carried away by the fairies.

In an age of high infant mortality and infanticide, the actions of a malevolent agency must often have been used as a convenient, perhaps convincing explanation, for a sudden death.[202]

Good fairies would provide money for certain favoured people on the strict proviso that they should not reveal its source. In 1891–2, P. H. Emerson collected the testimony of several people who knew someone who had benefited in this way. A saddler from Betws Gwerful

Goch in Merionethshire obtained a fortune from a fairy circle. When he told his wife, the money ceased. In 1816, on Anglesey, a young girl obtained money through sleeping with the fairies. Although she told her outraged father that she would die if she revealed the source of her income, he forced her to do so, and so the curse was fulfilled and the girl died.[203] Those who helped the fairies were helped in return. A shepherd at Glaslyn near Snowdon, seeing a fairy and her child in rags, gave them some clothes. Thereafter, he always discovered a gold sovereign in his shoes late at night. The shepherd prospered and became a prosperous farmer at Hafod Lwyddog. Such stories were perhaps the result of the jealous musings on the respective fortunes of people. There had to be some unearthly and unnatural explanation as to why certain people prospered on their arid acres whilst others perished. In the early twentieth century, Jonathan Ceredig Davies was informed by 95-year-old John Jones of Pontrhydfendigaid that, during his boyhood, a clergyman in the area had been educated by the fairies. With such magical assistance, the future minister could easily pass all his examinations.[204]

It is probable that the tradition of mermaids had the same origin as that of fairies. Mermaids were numerous on the long sea coast of Cardiganshire. A mermaid was supposed to have frequented the rock known as Carreg Ina, near New Quay. On one occasion when she was far out at sea, she became entangled in the net of some fishermen. She begged them to free her, which they duly did. In gratitude she told them that a great storm was blowing in towards them. They only just reached the shore in time.[205] In June 1823, at Llanllwchaearn, a farmer and his family watched a mermaid bathing in a pool near their farm. They left her be and prospered.[206] In the 1820s, a farmer at Treseissyllt captured a mermaid on cliffs near Aber-bach in Pembrokeshire. She placed a curse that no children would be born on his farm. This he interpreted as a terrible fate until a neighbour explained that he could now do as he wished with the servant girls.[207] In February 1821, *Seren Gomer* excitedly reported the discovery of a mermaid from Borneo who was due to tour Wales.[208]

Blithe Spirits and Fantasies

Those travellers who were not bothered by the fairies or mermaids were frequently terrorized by ghosts. Almost every village had its own spectre and spirit. Some of them, like the headless horseman of Pant, and the headless horse of Tregortha, were terrifying visions that struck fear into the hearts of everyone who met them.[209] Other blithe spirits were helpful. A tenant farmer named Edwards, who farmed on the Trawsgoed estate in the nineteenth century, was frequently bothered by a ghost. Tiring of this, he confronted the ghost and asked: 'Yn enw Duw, paham yr wyt ti yn fy aflonyddu i o hyd?' (In the Name of God, why do you always trouble me?). The ghost led him to a wall where the farmer found a lost cask containing treasure. Near Abbey Cwm Hir in Radnorshire, a ghost revealed the location of treasure buried at the time of Cromwell to a Baptist minister from Nevern. A white lady performed the same favour to a young man in Brogynin, Cardiganshire.[210]

In the 1860s, strenuous efforts were undertaken by Welsh people to make contact with departed spirits. In Merthyr Tydfil it was claimed that there were fifty spiritualist circles active: 'table-turning and spirit rapping have taken possession of a large portion of the people of the town, young, old and middle aged, and circles are formed and "investigations performed" in all parts of town'.[211] A reporter from the *Monmouthshire Merlin* had great fun in relating his experiences at one

Hugh Hughes, *Drychiolaeth*, from *Yr Hynafion Cymreig*, 1823. In the nineteenth century, the graveyard became a central feature in the lives of many people. Yet, as this cartoon showed, not everything one encountered there was placid.

of these seances. The first spirit mis-spelt the message, which was
explained by local people's lack of education. The final spirit's message
baffled everyone – it was believed to have been in German.[212]

Welsh folklore had by the mid nineteenth century acquired a
remarkably rich and multi-layered range of fables and fairy stories,
which are difficult to interpret.[213] Were they simply empty and false
fantasies, or do they reveal something about the nature of Welsh
society in the years 1776–1871? In many of these stories, the poor man
or girl is the hero or heroine who manages, against all the odds, to
attain wealth and happiness. But this is only possible when he or she
has been helped to break through the limitations of time, place and
position which initially inhibit them. The midwife of Nant Gwynen,
who rode with a well-dressed phantom to deliver his pregnant wife's
child, was rewarded with a bag of gold: 'and she lived happily on these
gains until she died'.[214] The invocation of magical rather than social or
economic power as a means of liberation was a commentary on the
means of advancement open to the poor. The ultimate success of the
hero or heroine of the fairy story or fable reveals aspirations for well-
being which were often unattainable in reality. Stories of inversion and
reversals provided an inverted image of reality, and satisfied dreams
and desires which people knew would never be managed under the
normal order of things. In the 1870s, as a legion of folklore collectors
affirmed, magic and mystery began to reaffirm themselves, partly
because science had not kept the overweening promises made on its
behalf, and partly because men and women are seldom content with
merely material explanations. Fairy stories, tall tales and the galli-
maufry of fables were condemned by Welsh religious leaders for their
sacrilegious nature. Educated observers criticized them as evidence of
the gross materialism and gullibility of the common people.[215] Yet this
rich tradition afforded its devotees temporary liberation from the
constraints of reality. Fiction and fantasies though they perhaps were,
to many listeners these tales of terror and treasure gave hope and
happiness.[216]

Happiness and Humour

The Pursuit of Happiness

'We are not amused': those words, uttered at the end of her long life by the woman who gave her name to the age, have been accepted as the motto of the Victorians.[1] Queen Victoria's ascent to the throne in 1837 is often regarded as a turning-point in British history. The rousing *joie de vivre* of the Georgians was supposedly quashed by killjoy royal declarations, ably assisted by a joyless religion and the work demon of industrialization. Fun and frivolity fled, gaiety turned into gloom, humour was transformed into humbug, laughter and levity left the land. It was this sombre tradition which prompted the novelist Gwyn Thomas to lament the apparent absence of a Welsh tradition of humour, and to remark: 'our only concession to gaiety was a striped shroud'.[2]

Portrayals of joyful Georgians and joyless Victorians continue to have their advocates. But the years down to 1837 were not as optimistic as has often been believed, and they bequeathed doubts as well as hopes. The legacy of the religious revivals of the late eighteenth century, and those of 1818 and 1821, was the reinforcement of the view that happiness should not be sought in this world, and could not be enjoyed here – except perhaps by those who were certain of their destiny in paradise. Queen Victoria is most often presented as the grieving widow, her reign one protracted and painful mourning. But the 'cult of sorrow' was not Victoria's creation. Georgians were also familiar with genuine melancholy at its darkest. In 1871, as in 1776, the Welsh were no strangers to leisure or pleasure. Contemporary observers and subsequent historians are agreed that the inculcation of a work discipline which was central to the complex process of industrialization eroded traditional pursuits and pastimes. But agricultural work, and country crafts, also constrained leisure activities, through the incessant demands of winning a living from the land. In the 1860s, rural work was still ruled by the cyclical demands of the agricultural calendar and the weather. Every generation of farming families laboured from before dawn to after dark, throughout the year, with barely any time for leisure. This is why there is such an air of skimble-skamble desperation about the fairs of Wales. Rather than curtailing play, industrialization created more opportunities for leisure. The Factory Act (1845) prescribed statutory holidays, giving precise delineation to the boundary between work and leisure time. Management might allocate the time of play, but it was the workers who played long and hard in the hours of their freedom. Industrialization increased industriousness but also created the idea that idleness should be enjoyed by the many, not just the few. Peel away the respectable veneer and it becomes clear that people in Victorian Wales, as had their forebears, put considerable vim and verve into their pursuit of happiness.

Travellers told tales of Wales as the land of lost contentment, in which the people lived happy, joyous lives. The adolescent Isabella Aldam, travelling with her family in 1830, to Machynlleth, felt confident enough to put her observations of the Welsh onto paper:

> as this was the third day after our arrival in Wales, we had had time to make a few observations. The Welsh pigs are white with large black spots. Poor people's hats are really very miserable. (Of cottages) a room (if it deserves that name) serving for pigs, fowls, eating, and in some places manufacturing. The beds are put on planks in the roof of the house. However they are as happy as the day is long.[3]

Thirty-eight years later, and forty-eight miles further north, at Betws-y-coed, Isobel Adderley, daughter of the secretary for the colonies, encountered the same contentment: 'in front of us was a pretty little cottage with a girl busy working about. She looks so happy and independent with her cows and her chickens around her. I must say that the Welsh are a very independent set.'[4]

Samuel Rogers (1763–1855), a poet best remembered for *Pleasures of Memory* (1792), recalled after a visit to Llantrisant in 1791 that 'the Welsh are a very joyous, social people'.[5] The Revd William Bushell, rector of Tibberton, sought a deeper explanation for the happiness of the Welsh. On a visit to a shepherd's cottage in Pumlumon in 1829, he

> found that the shepherd was a reported literary character . . . I had time only to examine two of his books the one was a good quarto Bible, the other a

geographical work, thus in this dreary spot, amidst filth and apparent wretchedness was an humble individual happier than many of the greatest of the earth cheering himself with the consolation of religion and the charms of literature.[6]

To other observers, the major consolation for Bushell's literary shepherd was the opportunity to live in accord with nature. The Romantic movement sought happiness in the Arcadian landscapes and bucolic beauty of rural Wales. Free from the hustle and bustle, the stress and the strains of modern life, Welsh people lived contented, happy lives. The diaries of Francis Kilvert, in the 1870s, perfectly evoke this rural idyll. In marvellous detail and with a poetic eye, he chronicled the changing seasons – snowy winters, the lark rising and singing springs, heavy blossomed summers, and colourful autumns:

This afternoon I walked over to Lanhill. As I came down from the hill into the valley across the golden meadows and along the flower-scented hedges a great wave of emotion and happiness stirred and rose up in me. I know not why I was so happy, nor what I was expecting, but I was in a delirium of joy, it was one of those supreme few moments of existence, a deep delirious draught from the strong sweet cup of life.[7]

No one probably ever enjoyed the simple pleasures of the country more than Kilvert, for life was a wonderful and curious thing. Not the least of his pleasures was the company of country girls – young girls to 'romp' with, older girls 'with sweet blue eyes', 'pearly teeth', 'tossing curls', 'mischievous glances', 'rounded arms as creamy as the milk', and 'white bosoms heaving tenderly'. Life in the countryside appealed to many. Thomas Johnes of Hafod discovered 'a very uncommon share of happiness' in shaping 'a miracle of a garden' from the 'picturesquely horrid hills' of Cardiganshire. His pleasure, however, was tempered by the realization that he would not live to see its 'full glory'.[8]

Yet to others the fun and frolic of the countryside represented loneliness, boredom and unhappiness. From the 1790s, newer voices could be heard advocating that happiness could best be secured in breezy and bracing coastal towns.[9] Swansea had already, immodestly, christened itself as the 'Brighton of Wales' and offered a plethora of bathing facilities and other entertainment. Aberystwyth became 'a capital for gay fashionables', Llandudno 'the Queen of Resorts' and Tenby's 'golden sands' were the destination of many pursuers of pleasure. Gradually, each resort evolved its own character of promenades, gardens, quiet gentility or donkey rides, Punch and Judy shows

and pierrots. By the 1850s, they offered all the reserve of the fastidious
and all the frivolity of the fun-fair. The hydrotherapy provided by the
sea could help sterility or coughs, consumption, even constipation, and
discourage the pernicious solitary practices which too many adolescents allegedly indulged in. Others argued that tourists and curists
should travel not to salt water but to the efficacious waters of the spa
towns of Builth, Holywell and Llandrindod Wells.

The increasingly new consumer culture of Wales from the 1830s
associated the assimilation of goods and material wealth with greater
happiness. People probably worked harder in the early stages of industrialization than they had ever done before, and they sought their
rewards in the therapy of retail. As standards of living rose, there was
a chain effect of greater expectation and greater desire for material
goods. Despite the pauperism suffered by many, and by a majority
at times of depression, more people were clawing themselves above
the poverty line and certainly above the zones of starvation, and
became capable of having priorities and choosing between alterna-
tives. Purchasing consumer goods could make one vicariously feel
happy, nostalgic, or loving. Interpersonal relationships were characterized by sentiment and intricate discussions of acquisitions and
purchases which were unimaginable in earlier generations. Many individuals, in *cofiannau* and diaries, confided that the achievement of an
ambition, in career, work or play, created contentment, happiness and
enjoyment.[10]

Although the Victorians were understandably pleased with their
material progress, a shadow of anxiety and doubt, accompanied by
fears of some impending catastrophe or revolutionary upheaval,
appears in many of their writings. Many authors warned that fortune
was notoriously fickle and history restless. Behind much of the religion
of the period are considerations of such questions as whether
mankind should expect happiness or damnation or perdition. In so
many aspects of their lives, people were torn between opposing views
of life and happiness. Love was universally sought, but many warned
against holding out too much hope of finding it. The lustier ballad
singers and Dr William Price eulogized its physical expression. Twm
o'r Nant's character 'Arglwyddes Chwantai Natur' (Goddess of
Natural Urges), as befitted 'merch i'r angel gwrthryfelgar' (daughter of
the rebellious angel), rousingly explained the secrets of love and lust.[11]

Marriage was looked forward to, especially by young girls, as an
Eden full of delirious joys, or at least something which gave them

Hugh Hughes, *Self-portrait with Sarah Hughes and Sarah Phillips Hughes*, *c*.1830 (National Library of Wales). Though the family was the centrepiece of the nineteenth century domestic ideology, one could perhaps conclude that Hugh Hughes's patience is wearing thin at the hyperactive child.

greater freedom. Yet the humorists and satirists warned that wedlock was a padlock. Christians of all denominations also warned that marriage was not a bed of roses. To succeed, personal priorities and pleasures should be sacrificed for the common good, for marriage was simply a sharing of suffering. Artists produced conflicting portrayals of marriage. The works of James Flewitt Mullock, *The Children of William Evans of 'The Fields' Newport, 1855*, and Joshua Reynolds's earlier masterpiece, *Charlotte Grenville, Lady Williams Wynn, with her three children* (*c*.1780), seemed to suggest that happiness and joy could be obtained in the company of your children. But countless others, such as Hugh Hughes's grim-faced *Self-portrait with Sarah Hughes and Sarah Phillips Hughes*, seemed to suggest that every minute spent before the mirror to draw a self-portrait, in the company of wife and hyperactive child, was a torture.[12] Respectability was only maintained with considerable hypocrisy – prostitution helped marital bliss, prudery depended on secret pornography. Religion, politics and science, which promised so much, did not completely dissolve the fears and frustrations of the people. Making money, education, improved hygiene and medicine were supposed to provide short cuts to well-being, but many found that their panaceas did not come soon enough and were incomplete.

Throughout the voluminous literature bequeathed us by the people who lived in this period there is no consistent or clear view of how one could cope with the conflicts of the heart and the head, of selfishness and generosity, of natural urges and the search for virtue, of the desire for repose and the fear of boredom, of the pursuit and possession of happiness. Some argued starkly that happiness existed only in the future, or in the past, where imagination and memory alone seemed capable of grasping it. Many sought it on their Grand Tours of Europe or in their studies of the ancient worlds. Men of the 'age of reform' and 'the railway age' sought escape into the mentality of a medieval monk. Probably the greatest escape into the 'foreign country' of the past was the phantasmagoric medieval fantasies of the third marquess of Bute, who commenced his refurbishment and remodelling of Cardiff Castle in 1865 at the age of eighteen. Sir Watkin Williams Wynn came closest to happiness by the use he made of his eyes, and his devotion to his art collection, and he almost despaired of it in his emotional life. Art transported Wynn to Wonderland. Field Marshal Lord Grenfell (1841–1925), who 'taught the Blacks how to fight, and taught England how the Blacks can fight when led by good officers' in the Battle of Omdurman, found happiness in his off-duty hours as an Egyptologist of considerable attainment. His excavation at Aswan led to the presentation of a number of Egyptian antiquities to the museum of the Royal Institution of South Wales at Swansea, including the mummy of the priest Tem-Hor.[13] The lawyer Sir William Robert Grove (1811–96), the copper magnate Henry Hussey Vivian, First Baron Swansea (1821–94), and the soldier Sir Charles Warren (1840–1927) sought happiness in the mysteries of science and became scientists of considerable distinction. The Swansea copper and railway baronet and landowner, Sir John Talbot Dillwyn-Llewelyn (1836–1927) became a Fellow of the Royal Society, and continued the family's experiments in photography.[14] Trebor Aled warned that 'gyda phleser daw poen' (with pleasure comes pain), and David Charles II that 'virtue was happiness in its highest form'.[15] Yet to all of them happiness appeared almost like a spirit; once you mentioned its name it was prone to disappear.[16]

The Welsh apparently were never happier than when in work. An author in the *Gentleman's Magazine* in 1785 described Wales as a land of happy people with Arcadian landscapes of deep valleys and 'melodious rivers . . . whilst from their upper regions are heard the songs and whistlings of genuine shepherds'. Those who did not whistle while they worked sang. But such contented workers created unexpected problems. In December 1802, Iolo Morganwg wrote to his colleague, William Owen Pughe:

> The Gloucestershire farmers and dairymen, who are fond of the Glamorgan Cattle, often curse the Ploughboys and Milkmaids of Glamorgan, for Oxen will, frequently, neither work, nor Cows stand to be milked, without their accustomed Music; and, there is but little music in Gloucestershire farmers.[17]

One unmusical Carmarthenshire farmer also complained at the oxen he purchased from Glamorgan for: 'I had to sing to them all day long, and was so hoarse when night came that I could hardly speak . . . They would not work if you did not sing for them.'[18] *Canu i'r Ychen* (Singing to the Oxen) was a notable feature of Welsh folk music.[19] Many writers have interpreted this as evidence that the Welsh were at heart a happy people. Yet, this singing might well have been a defence against drudgery. Perhaps the Welsh peasants sang most passionately and powerfully when they were unhappy. Many of the *tribannau* – popular three-part songs of Glamorgan – are chants to ease the confines of labour. They represent the heartbreak in Welsh hearts. Welsh workers often sang to exorcize their sorrows, not to express their happiness.

'Gwlad y Gân': The Land of Song

Whether they sang from woe or for worship, it appears that the Welsh by the early nineteenth century were already praising their Creator for making them a musical nation. Carnivals, fairs, markets, revels and wakes were often a razzle-dazzle cacophony of accordions, barrel-organs, harps, fiddles, pipes, drums – all mixed together in a brisk, discordant barrage. As events progressed the tempo would quicken, the volume rise and the sedate tunes turned into wilder songs and jigs, revealing both desperate happiness and deepest heartache. In 1797, an anonymous painter produced a remarkable painting of joyous rusticity, *Ffair Aberystwyth*, in which a tumble of acrobats performed to the accompaniment of a harpist and a fiddler. By the end of such events, the noise sounded 'like an awakened graveyard of souls in torment'.

Music crossed social barriers more effectively than many Welsh pastimes. John Roberts, Telynor Cymru (1816–1894), played his harp in rowdy pubs like the Eagles Inn at Llanfyllin and in the refined Aberhafesp Hall, Newtown. Both audiences were happiest when he plucked out the lonesome strains of sad tunes. The blind harpist John Parry enjoyed the patronage of Sir Watkin Williams Wynn of Wynnstay, who provided him with a house on the estate and possibly one in London.[20] Many of his most sombre phrases were attributed to the heightened sensitivity Parry possessed for being a man forever in darkness. In 1819, Carmarthen people flocked to St Peter's Church and the town hall to enjoy two concerts by the Bath Harmonic Society, the one for the descendants of poor deceased clerics and the other for 'decayed harpists'.[21] Harps provided the background both to hyper-active revels and the gentler *penillion* singing. The singing of verses to the accompaniment of a harp or fiddle was a popular form of Welsh musicality, which developed in the eighteenth century and entered the cultural mainstream in the mid nineteenth through the *eisteddfod*. Not all visitors appreciated the art of singing poetry in counterpoint to a traditional tune on the harp. Romilly considered it to be 'awful howlings', 'irresistibly absurd' and an 'untunable bellow' after hearing 'two howlers' with Lady Charlotte Guest in 1827.[22] But *penillion* singing remained a popular and prominent part of the *eisteddfod*. Like all other aspects of the cultural life of Wales, this plebeian cultural festival was transformed by the powerful forces of commercialization and professionalization. By the 1850s, the *eisteddfod* was a major event, attracting hundreds of participants and thousands of spectators, many brought from all over Wales in the first, second and third class carriages of the railways. This traditional cultural activity, like all Welsh music, benefited greatly from the development of printing in Wales. Edward Jones, Bardd y Brenin (1752–1824), published his extensive research into Welsh airs in *Musical and Poetical Relicks of the Welsh Bards* in 1784. John Parry, Bardd Alaw (1776–1851), gathered and printed collections of *cerdd dant* (Welsh harp music) in 1804, 1807 and in 1839 published *The Welsh Harper*. Publishing enabled a new professionalism to penetrate Welsh music. The commercialization of Welsh society was also witnessed in the marketing and sale of sheet music.[23]

Musical ability enabled talented individuals to escape lives of drudgery. Thomas Howells, Hywel Cynon (1839–1905), began working underground as a seven-year-old at Aberaman. In the 1850s, through the influence of John Roberts, Ieuan Gwyllt (1822–77), he purchased a press and ventured into music printing and publishing, supplementing his income as an assistant minister. Among the most famous of his printed works are *Awelon yr Haf* and *Cerddi Hywel Cynon*, which contained his most popular work, *Gwnewch bopeth yn Gymraeg* (do everything in Welsh). Another talented musician, also influenced by Ieuan Gwyllt, was David Emlyn Evans (1843–1913), editor of Y Gerddorfa (1872) and *Y Cerddor* (1880–1913). David had been apprenticed to a draper in Newcastle Emlyn, but swapped scissors for a baton and made his name as the editor of over 500 Welsh tunes, a dedicated adjudicator at *eisteddfodau*, and as a tireless campaigner for the improvement of Welsh music.[24]

These published songs and airs became a marked feature of Welsh life. Music was a refinement much praised and valued among almost all sections of Welsh society. The ability to play the piano was a mark of considerable accomplishment among ambitious and aspiring people. Mid nineteenth century Wales, in Gwenallt's memorable phrase, was 'parlwr o wlad ac ynddi biano' (a parlour of a country, and in it, a piano). The upright piano, with its fretted or inlaid front, and twisted candelabra was the focus of many drawing rooms, or for those with less cachet and cash, the parlour. In the mornings, young ladies practised tortuously and even the most unmusical were attributed with 'a lovely touch', in the same way that those who scratched at harps were 'angelic'. A slight tremolo in the voice added charm to the songs of Mendelssohn and sweetness to the popular

English and Welsh ballads that were published in their hundreds every year. The Welsh went into the garden with Maud, listened to the long farewells (but not goodbyes) of star-struck lovers and the plaints of enraptured romantic dreamers who looked towards Eternity. What young man could resist such enticement? Join in a trio, or even better a duet, sing terms of endearment, and get closer to the girl he reckoned would make him a wife, and live, as in the songs, harmoniously ever after.[25]

Sacred and sentimental songs were sung in drawing rooms, parlours and vestries, but also in the brothels, *cwrwau bach*, gaming houses, pubs and taverns. Audiences wept as sopranos warbled and tenors trilled out the pellucid notes of sad laments like Ceiriog's 'Ti Wyddost Beth Ddywed Fy Nghalon', Glan Padarn's 'Cân y Fam i'w Phlentyn' and Cymro Bach's 'Cân y Fam wrth ei Mab'. Many soloists like Eos Morlais, Edith Wynne, Mary Davies, Marian Williams and Bessie Waugh, with voices like nightingales or spring rain, became celebrated celebrities. Elsewhere, one-note singers droned loud and long. Some tunes were infectious, striking the heart and arousing a strange sensation of melancholy and uneasiness. All the world's sadness seemed compressed into one plangent phrase. The music made people feel sorry for themselves and everyone else – grown-ups became like wondrous children, sitting and standing motionless, lost in silence. In the low, lewd pubs sentimental songs must have performed some sort of expiatory function. The mind boggles at the spectacle of gamblers weeping at songs about shame, pimps and bullies sobbing at the tribu- lations of fallen girls, ear-chewers remembering their white-haired mothers. Pub and saloon singers soon discovered that the songs which went over best with thieves, extortionists, con artists and their assorted muscle were sad ballads. These were hard people with hearts of marsh- mallow. Apart from the sentiment, these songs about drunkenness, dereliction and death provided audiences with an opportunity for reflection, an embodiment of their own hideous lives, a chance to stare into the abyss. The wasp-waisted Elizabeth Jones was one of several who began singing in Welsh pubs. In that smoky and dirty environment, she was a genius heart-melter.[26]

Music was not a solitary virtue. Welsh chapels and churches, well versed in the public singing of hymns, established choirs and even orchestras from the 1830s onwards which performed an extensive repertoire of cantatas and oratorios.[27] By the 1850s, thanks to the influence of Ieuan Gwyllt's *Caniadau y Cyssegr* (1839), and *Llyfr Tonau*

Cynulleidfaol (1859), there emerged *Y Gymanfa Ganu* (singing festival) a remarkable and highly popular cultural phenomenon in which congregations sang in praise. Months of practice with the published hymn-books culminated in a harmonious climax. Highly popular at these *cymanfaoedd* were Ieuan Gwyllt's own hymn tunes, especially *Llanfair* named after the home village of the author of the words, Robert Williams (1782–1818) from Llanfairpwllgwyngyllgogerychwyrndrobwllllantysiliogogogoch, but wisely abbreviated, and *Liverpool*, which became one of the great disaster songs when it was played on the deck of the sinking *Titanic* in 1913, and in the film of the San Francisco earthquake, as 'Nearer my God to Thee'.[28]

Throughout Wales, during coming of age and other celebrations, members of rustic brass bands in brass-buttoned uniforms, glowing with pleasure, beer and exertion, played pompous and portentous music. During Christmas 1846, at Monmouth, the Original Moonstone Rock Band, a Steel Band, Hoffman's Organophonic Band and the Human Voice Orchestra all bowed, banged and blew their tidings of comfort and joy around the town.[29] By the 1830s, both the Cyfarthfa and the Llanelli Brass Band were widely celebrated. Many parts of Wales also throbbed to the beat of military bands. Music and the militia were close allies. By the 1870s, bands had been formed as part of the 2nd and 3rd Glamorgan Rifle Corps, all four battalions of the South Wales Borderers, 1st Battalion Welch Fusiliers, 1st Glamorgan Artillery, 1st Flint Artillery, 2nd Pembrokeshire Artillery, 1st Monmouthshire Artillery, 1st Breconshire Artillery and the 1st Denbighshire Artillery.[30]

The Lords of the Dance

The rhythm and tempo of many Welsh musicians proved so irresistible that a strong tradition of folk dancing emerged in Wales. The Revd Richard Warner attended 'a genuine Welsh Ball' in the long room of a public house at Pontneddfechan in the Vale of Neath in August 1798, and was captivated by the dancers but confused by the complexity of their dances.[31] According to John Thomas, father of the harpist John Thomas, Pencerdd Gwalia (1826–1913), some male dancers were so skilful that they jigged 'to the breadth of a hair'.[32] The Lords of the Dance, said he, were Welsh. Dancing was a notable feature of the feasts in Breconshire, the revels of Glamorgan and the *mabsant* of the north. Itinerant musicians travelled from one festival to the next to accompany the dancing, including one Glamorgan harpist who allegedly followed the same route for sixty years. On the heels of summer came the harvest festivals, when dances were held to celebrate the culmination of hard work in the fields. These events reinvigorated wholly exhausted people who had worked in harvests as half-mules, half-men. Christmas and the New Year saw the re-enactment of the *Mari Lwyd* ritual.[33] In Glamorgan, wassailing groups often included characters from the Punch and Judy, who danced their merry jigs alongside the *Mari* and *Cadi Ha* to the accompaniment of harp and fiddle.[34] Welsh religious leaders of all denominations were bitter in their condemnation of dancing. 'The father of Welsh history', the Revd Thomas Price, Carnhuanawc (1787–1848), recalled that his own parents knew 'an old man, I think about Llangamarch or Abergwesin, who play'd the Harp, but who joined the Methodists or Dissenters and then gave up the Harp and threw it under the bed, where it lay till it got unglewed and worm-eaten and fell to pieces'.[35] Yet, despite the condemnation, dancing continued long enough for it to be revived from the 1870s.

Balls and dances were a notable feature of the country house life of the gentry. Carriages criss-crossed south Wales, carrying dancers to the balls of the season that lasted a hundred days. In September 1815, the balls at Abermarlais, Edwinsford and Taliaris in Carmarthenshire were said to be 'more than usually gay this year'. In the same month, at Glansevin, the band of the Royal Carmarthen Fusiliers played in a marquee, and ten harps and violins summoned people to dinner. After partaking of 'a profusion of everything that was excellent', only a few could have danced. 'The company did not separate until long after daylight', when the guests, at last, wearily departed to prepare themselves to be wearied at the next ball.[36] It was not only their homes that the great landowners and industrialists utilized for balls and dances. Robert Thompson Crawshay's marriage to Rose Mary Yates in 1846 was celebrated by a ball and feast for the 'Ladies of Merthyr', organized in the huge wagon shed at Cyfarthfa ironworks.[37]

Plays and Players

The same pressures of commercialization and professionalization which transformed popular musicality were also at work in the theatre.

Late eighteenth-century Wales was the golden age of the *anterliwt*. Strolling players performed plays in the open air and markets, presented storming performances in barns, or set up 'their Temples of Thespis' in public houses like the Golden Lion in Brecon. Playwrights, such as Elis y Cowper, Jonathan Hughes and Hugh Jones, penned one and two act plays for their rustic thespian companies. Most famous of all was the one, the only Thomas Edwards Twm o'r Nant, proudly proclaimed as 'the Cambrian Shakespeare'. Twm took the *anterliwt* to a new level with his scathing satire and robust humour.[38] His plays portray the sorrows of the common man, but above all they lay bare the hypocrisy endemic in Welsh society. The interludes were usually divided into dialogues between personified virtues and vices and the more uproarious adventures of crude Chaucerian characters like the farmer and the tinker, the simple, sun-reddened drover and the scheming, stealing whore. The social purpose was plain in the condemnation of the steward's exactions, the Methodist's humbug, the clergyman's refusal to speak Welsh, the landlord's greed in enclosing the commons and the lawyer's rapacity. By his twentieth birthday, Twm had penned his first *anterliwt* – *Cain and Abel* – prompting Gwallter Mechain to comment: 'I cannot think Burns superior, if equal, to our Twm o'r Nant'. Twm reserved his bitterest ire for those Welsh people – gentry, parsons, doctors and justices – who enthusiastically packed the English-medium performances of Dublin and London players, but never darkened the barn door of the *anterliwt*. Women, claimed Twm in *Y Ddau Ben Ymdrechgar*, were even worse, for both lady and housewife hero-worshipped the *hommes fatales* of these companies: 'Ac ambell un y gode'n llon / Ei Dibleu i Chw'ryddion Dublin' (And a few happily raised / Their skirts for Dublin players). Disappointingly, they only turned up their noses at Twm.[39] Twm's envious criticism of these players was understandable, for it became increasingly difficult to win a living from his theatricals. He had to supplement his income as a lumberjack and as a publican at Llandeilo. But the biggest threat to Twm, and the peripatetic thespians of the *anterliwt*, came in the solid form of the bricks and mortar of Welsh theatres.

Between 1789 and 1836, theatres had been established in permanent buildings at Bangor, Beaumaris, Brecon, Caernarfon, Cardiff, Carmarthen, Chepstow, Denbigh, Haverfordwest, Holyhead, Milford, Newport, Pembroke, Swansea, Tenby, Usk and Wrexham. Theatres provided a range of performances to satisfy the theatrical tastes of the

Welsh. Much of the fare involved Shakespearian tragedies and comedies as well as *She Stoops to Conquer*, *The Deaf Lover*, *The Clandestine Marriage*, and pantomimes like *Cinderella* and *Whittington and His Cat*. They also adapted and wrote plays that were rooted in Welsh places and characters. Thomas Dibdin so enjoyed his sojourn in 'the Devil' ('a tavern so called in Carmarthen') that he wrote *St David's Day* dedicated to 'the inhabitants of Carmarthen and Haverfordwest and every native of the Principality who practices hospitality with the characteristic warmth experienced by the author in the above-named towns'.[40] His *Comic Songs*, published at Carmarthen in 1794, had a Welsh setting, as did Mrs Siddon's *London and Monmouth* and anonymous works like *Twm John Catty*, *The Heiress of Cardigan*, *Gwyneth Vaughan*, *The Welsh Sailor Boy* and *Coquette of the Bwlch*. Comedies like *The Wonder: A Woman Keeps a Secret!* drew large, curious crowds. Skits and comic sketches were ribald and physical, and were principally geared to a male and working-class audience. Performers set their topical gags and routines in Welsh saloons, streets and shipyards. Most popular of all by the 1820s was melodrama. This provided blood-and-thunder action, spectacular mechanical enhancements and starkly moralistic plots. Melodramatic heroes and villains – their characters written all over their faces – battled to an invariably happy ending, in which the forces of evil were defeated.

In order to fill the theatres, marketing professionals were employed to utilize the image-making apparatus of the nineteenth century graphic revolution. They produced flyers, playbills, posters, placed newspaper advertisements to publicize their productions and wrote press articles to promote and praise their performances. They also organized processions and parades to draw in the crowds. Performers at the Wynnstay Theatre, accompanied by pipers and drummers, toured the area in the early 1790s, dressed as characters from *The Merry Wives of Windsor*. Theatrical advertising revenue provided a welcome boost to the finances of newspapers like *The Cambrian* and the *Carmarthen Journal*, whose journalists soon acquired the cattiness of theatre critics. In 1829, one anonymous author in the latter newspaper opined:

> We must remind Miss Morse that when she is advertised for a part, the audience expects her to perform it; at present, she and the prompter play it between them. Decency of appearance is also looked for by the genteel audience and when she dances again, we would advise her to show regard for the one and respect for the other by lengthening her petticoats![41]

Despite the outrage of this author, performers continued with performances that were mildly risqué, and often lusty. Although some strove to make thespians as well as the theatre more respectable, even in the 1850s there was nothing like the whiff of forbidden sensuality to sell tickets. Miss Morse and her successors, corseted into the requisite hourglass figure, became the most lusted-after women in Wales.

Publicity people marketed not just theatres but also personalities. By the late eighteenth century, the cult of the star, pasteboard heroes and heroines, had been born. Lee Lewes, with his heart-throb good looks, inaugurated the age of the theatrical star on Welsh stages and was quickly followed by Keen, McReady, Roger Kemble and the Welsh-born Sarah Siddons, and Drinkwater Meadows, a famous actor of eccentric parts. The daily doings of famous actresses were chronicled in the newspapers and women's magazines, and their choice of clothes, jewellery and millinery began to set national trends. Make-up moved out of theatrical dressing rooms into respectable and unrespectable boudoirs. The portraits of young actresses – half women, half Bambi – graced soap packet covers and enticed the ugly to purchase the useless.

The press eagerly reported humorous and curious happenings on the Welsh stages. At Bangor, when *Hamlet* declared that 'everyone in England was mad' the whole house cheered. James Booth, increasingly a drunk, was greeted with hilarious approval for his insistence on really fighting the staged duels with stiff-legged swordplay.[42] At Caernarfon, an actor impersonating Grimdolf in *The Miller and his Men* was shot, much to the excitement of the crowd. In 1806, a local butcher (who was also a drum major in the Wrexham volunteers) was so drunk in the part of Romeo that he could not utter a single word, while Banquo refused to go on the stage to be murdered in Act III, scene 3, of Macbeth, unless he received an extra £2. The newspaper report of the occurrence suggests that he reckoned that too many murders had been committed already.[43] In many Welsh theatres the crowd was as much of a performer as the actors. At Tenby, hecklers refused to allow a popular actor to continue until he had explained, at length, that he was merely playing the part of an unworthy character.[44] The performance by Samuel Ryley 'The Itinerant' of *The Clandestine Marriage* at Swansea in 1786 was brought to an end just as it reached a climax, when a butcher's dog set up such a piteous howl that the audience went into convulsions of laughter.[45] In 1805, George Stanton was thrown violently downstairs in the Wrexham theatre and had his leg broken, as he endeavoured to prevent some disorderly persons from getting into the theatre without paying. Unsurprisingly, a Wrexham playbill of 1856 promised that there would be 'officers in attendance to preserve order'.[46]

Theatres faced many challenges. Traditionally their decline and demise has been attributed to steadfast and staunch opposition of Anglicans, Baptists, Independents and especially Methodists. In 1841, the proprietor of the only press in Aberystwyth refused to print notices for a production in the town's Assembly Rooms because he was convinced that 'the theatre was the home of the Devil and refused to assist Him in any way'.[47] This message thundered out from many pulpits across Wales. In these condemnations of sinful theatricals, one cannot but conclude that there existed an element of rivalry. Many of the great preachers of the early nineteenth century produced histrionic thespian displays worthy of any theatre. The supercharged and sensational pulpit perorations of Edward Matthews, Matthews Ewenni – 'the Dickens of Wales' – were amongst the greatest theatrical performances of nineteenth-century Wales. Dewi Hugh's sermons on 'Elias' and 'Haelioni Duw yn ei Ragluniaeth' were powerful dramatic events. Thomas John, Cilgerran, dramatically waved a red handkerchief at the start of his sermon on the sin of vanity in which a girl, in order to be fashionable at a dance, was forced by her mother to wear a scarlet dress. At the end she cried out on her death-bed: 'O mam! O mam! y gŵn sidan hwn yw achos fy namnedigaeth; bydd yn fflamio amdanaf yn uffern yn fuan' (O mother! O mother! this satin dress is the cause of my damnation; it will soon be burning on me in hell'). In this rivalry between pulpit and platform, there was considerable jealousy. The Revd J. W. Pugh, vicar of Llandeilo, published an *Address to his Parishoners on the Pernicious Effects of Theatrical Amusements*, at the famous press of Llandovery in 1842, in which he condemned 'the drinking at public houses which took place after the play is over', 'the vain conversation' during plays and expressed his frustration that the audiences at the plays were 'usually double ours'.[48]

The greatest problems, however, derived from the theatre's success. In order to attract crowds, performances needed a star name and stars were expensive to keep. Audiences also wanted action played out against stupendous and spectacular scenery.[49] In April 1790, Watson's company proudly presented *Captain Cook*. 'The scenery in this tropical tragedy was altogether too numerous to use and remove in one night, causing many unpleasant delays', so the performance was spread over two nights and those who attended the second witnessed: 'a truly affecting and awful picture of the assassination and funeral ceremony of our celebrated countryman' (those who attended one night presumably only saw half a play). By 1828, machines had taken over the work of scenery shifting, and the audience at Haverfordwest theatre was spellbound by the 'complicated and ingenious machinery' used in *The Flying Dutchmen*. One unkind critic commented that the machines performed more fluently than the actors. Twenty years later, Welsh audiences sat amazed as ships and balloons were brought on stage, forts were consumed by fire, and entire casts became flying Indians.[50] By the 1860s, Welsh theatres were spending considerable sums on quick lime (calcium oxide). Heated to incandescence, this emitted a dazzling light – limelight. The effect of such light on glass – twinkling, reflecting, bejewelling – was fascinating to a public starved of light and hungry for vicarious lavishness. Ostentatious show was box-office attraction. Tinsel, gilt, foil, sequins, spangles, plate glass and crystal mirrors to reflect and refract light added to the illuminated magic of the Welsh stage. In order to perform other people's dreams, theatres had to live beyond their means.

Theatres were also subjected to increasing competition from other entertainment entrepreneurs. The tradition of peripatetic theatres had not entirely vanished; indeed, it experienced a revival from the 1840s.[51] The Cambrian Theatre, under Hoare and Manges, visited Merthyr Tydfil, Aberafon, Aberkenfig, Neath and Aberdare in the 1850s. Peter Warren's 'The Welsh Model Theatre' travelled from Pembroke to Pontypridd to perform *The Maid of Cefn Ydfa* and *Llewelyn, the Last Prince of Wales*. At Llanelli, such was the public demand that Warren had to put on additional performances. *A Mother's Dying Child* and *Ten Nights in a Bar Room* were also popular with the brawling, bawling crowds, and the company's benefit nights were said to be 'a furore'. Competition for the attention, and wallets, of audiences also came from circuses – 'the show that smells' – and freak shows which travelled around Wales in creaking, painted wagons and clattering rail carriages. In 1826, Earl James and Sons brought their Royal Collection of Wild Beasts to Swansea:

> Including the Newly Discovered Royal Bonassus ... the Bonassus stands at 6 feet high and his consumption exceeds that of an elephant ... Ladies of distinction come in parties, with your families to view the stupendous and interesting Bonassus ... There are also Royal Ostrich, Male Lion, The Lilliputian Ox, Tigress, the Ring-Tailed Leopards, the Real Wapeti, the Bactaranus (9 foot

tall with a docile nature), Zebu, Laughing Hyena, Polar Baboons, Eagles of the Sun and the Wolverine or Glutton.[52]

Alongside the animals, acrobats tumbled, jugglers juggled, conjurers pulled strings of squawking doves from their mouths, automata and living statutory performed, and the ventriloquists baffled the gullible – at Tenby, one ventriloquist was assaulted because 'the little man on his lap was insulting the town's people'. Wrestling and boxing booths were frequent where, every hour, on the hour, for the reasonable sum of two shillings, the bold and the brave, or the very foolish, could pit their skills against 'the greatest conqueror that Wales has ever seen'. Visitors could play with lung testers, throw rings at cane stubble, shoot clay ducks, have their pictures taken, their fortunes read, their strength tested, their weight guessed. In 1829, the people of Swansea, Brecon, Carmarthen, Tenby and Haverfordwest were amazed at the tattooed faces of the New Zealand warriors. The editor of the *Carmarthen Journal* proudly related that: 'these reclaimed cannibals visited our offices and we explained to them the printing process'.[53]

'Roll-up, Roll-up', and roll up they did, particularly to the freak shows in which the Welsh could see Miss Wynn, 'the celebrated infant', Master Sewell, the Lincolnshire Gigantic Youth, Miss Anne Wheeler, 'Queen of the Dwarfs', the Cardiff Giant, the shorter Yarmouth Giant, Mr Richer and the 'far-famed Dog of Montargis', the Welsh Fairy (a five-year-old harpist), the Living Skeleton, the Baboon Woman, the Dog-Faced Boy, Hassan Ali the Egyptian Giant, Julia Pastrana the Nondescript, Henio Nono the celebrated legless acrobat, and the Fejee Mermaid. The professional world of the freak has come to exemplify the worst excesses of the Victorians for it offers a thumbnail sketch of their brutality, their credulity and their willingness to exploit the unfortunate. But, despite the pathos, not all freaks were the hapless victims of cruel employers. Many demanded considerable fees and, in their own unique way, became celebrated stars. Surely amongst the eminent Victorians there should be a little room for Tom Thumb.[54]

By the mid nineteenth century, towns like Cardiff, Merthyr Tydfil, Swansea and Wrexham had developed recognizable recreational quarters, for the world of Welsh entertainment was far-flung and fast-flowing.[55] Like moths pleasure-lovers and sensation-seekers headed to the lamp-lit sidewalks of the entertainment zones. The theatres, taverns, brothels, porter-houses, oyster-houses, dance halls, and gambling dens filled up with the rodomontade of sailors, young butchers, day labourers, brewers, colliers, quarrymen and iron workers. Harum-scarum gangs swaggered about, staking out territories, picking fights, defending the honour of their street, or village, or trade, or just kicking rubbish up and down the street as they wrangled over metaphysics. Gangs of butchers' boys were particularly obstreperous, hardened as they were by the bloody work of dispatching cattle and pigs, but colliers and iron men brawled as well, taking on builders and navvies. Hours were long, especially on weekends. On the Sabbath, saints on their way to worship would watch the lusty, muddy-eyed and ruddy-faced sinners, in their Saturday night best shirt and bright dresses, laugh, fight, copulate or just lie in their vomit-covered gutters of sin.

The entertainment market place also welcomed women, for they drew men and money. Women watched melodramas, laughed at the comedy sketches and listened at lecture halls. They also drank and sang in the beerhouses and pubs. But women were most in evidence in venues devoted to music, especially dance halls. Amidst 'the thunderous sounds of sinners' on Bute Street, Cardiff, girls could enjoy a pleasurable evening away from the prying eyes of neighbours, keeping an eye out for a permanent partner, in a much wider constituency of eligible men than was available to them through family and neighbourhood networks. Single men and women sought companionship, friendship and love. Everything was deferrable for a price – boredom, poverty, thirst, hunger, loneliness, disappointment. Healing, salvation, love – an unforgettable experience might be yours. Deliverance was for sale and certainly obtainable if you only had the gumption to buy a ticket for the draw or the show. Evenings opened at an adagio rhythm and built through accelerando into a climactic fortissimo.

Even in the depths of depression – especially in the depths of depression, much to the bafflement of contemporaries – crowds still flocked to the circuses, theatres and freak shows. The organizers and managers had grasped the essential, elemental connection between Hard Times and High Times. During the cholera epidemic of 1849, the *Cardiff and Merthyr Guardian* announced a 'Grand Balloon Ascent' by Mr Green the celebrated Aeronaut in his new balloon 'The Rainbow', to be followed by a grand display of fireworks.[56] At the theatre, the comedian 'Mr Angel, as the Mock Duke, made our sides ache with his intimate drollery. He is certainly a most amusing fellow. We laughed heartily at his jokes and we are indebted to him for so much pleasurable excitement and innocent gratification.'[57] Despised for their mediocrity by the discerning, these entertainments appealed to something more universal than fashion, more primitive than taste. The antics of the clowns, the wit and witticisms of the comedians, the theatrical magic of the actors remained in the memory of audiences when other earthly pleasures had faded. They were creatures of the lighted stage and symbols of that world of the imagination, which offered entertainment, comfort, but, above all, they gave escape into laughter and happiness.

Drugs, Drink and Dissolution

Others found more desperate means of escape. David Samwell, Iolo Morganwg, Christmas Evans and the Revd George Arthur Evors MP, of Newtown Hall, all sought oblivion from their worldly woes in the pleasure and pain of opium use and abuse. To them, happiness could be bought for a penny and carried away in the waistcoat pocket. Even more people found solace in snuff – *Llwch Mân Llanerchymedd* became famous for its nasal and head-clearing properties, and was 'generally snuffed by connoisseurs throughout the three kingdoms'.[58] Tobacco was also highly prized and praised in all social groups. The clay pipe became almost a permanent attachment to Welsh mouths. In the 1790s, conversation had been a much valued aspect of some social circles. Mrs Thale and Dr Johnson's table talk was famous. Even a cat, Johnson pointed out to his beloved 'mistress', Mrs Thrale, at one of the 'happiest moments' of his life, 'never purrs when it is quite alone'.[59] The 'Terrestrial Paradise', Mrs Thrale argued in *British Synonymy or an attempt at regulating the choice of words in familiar conversation* (1794), could be found in fine conversation and good companionship. Fenton, on his perambulations through Wales, was impressed by the quality of both the beverage and the conversation in a Denbigh coffee house. It was there that he heard news of Junot's surrender. Yet, by the 1860s, conversations took place behind thick grey cumulus of tobacco smoke and were frequently interrupted by the cacophonous catarrh-clearing coughing of smokers. Thomas Williams, Brynfab, once boasted: 'bûm yn cyd-ysmygu ag Islwyn nes oedd y lle fel anadl coelcerth' (I once co-smoked with Islwyn until the room was like the breath of a bonfire).[60]

In the 1860s, the habit, or vice, intensified its grip on the Welsh people as rolled cigarettes became widely available. Tobacco processing and snuff making were very important industries in nineteenth-century

Anglesey. At Amlwch, D. Lleufer Thomas, collecting evidence for the Royal Commission on Labour, was appalled: 'Practically everyone smokes or chews or does both. By the end of each meeting I held, the floor of the room was covered with tobacco spittle.'

But the real opiate of the Welsh was alcohol. In an age when water was dangerous to drink, milk an adulterated poison, and tea and coffee expensive, drinking beer, cider, spirits or wine was a sensible course of action. Alcohol was a thirst-quencher, a reliever of physical pain and psychological strain, a symbol of human interdependence, a morale-booster, a sleeping draught and a medicine. It was an essential calorific food, it provided 'Dutch courage' and offered an escape for those who found the reality around them too harsh to bear. Alcohol was an essential social lubricant.[61] People in all social classes drank alcohol, many to excess. Fenton at Llanwrda, on his tour of Wales 'met the Parson in a place where I ought not to have met him, in the Alehouse, near the Churchyard'.[62] Hugh Reverly (1772–1851) lived in an age in which 'drinking was a fashionable vice in all from the prince to the peasant'.[63] At the Monmouth workhouse, £60 was regularly spent on gin, which the master explained as 'mainly medicinal to invigorate our feebler charges'. Disgruntled temperance advocates pointed out that the lucky 167 inmates at the Monmouth workhouse must have consumed as much wine and spirits as 20,542 less fortunate inmates elsewhere. At the other end of the town's social circle, thirsts were just as unquenchable. At the mayor's luncheon in 1861, '21 men, the so called elite of the town', managed to drink forty-eight quart bottles of champagne, as well as a selection of other wines and spirits.[64]

Alcohol supplied much of the energy expended on hard arduous tasks. In rural areas special, often very potent, brews were prepared by farmers for harvest time. Certain periods of intense agricultural activity such as shearing, threshing, and the hay and corn harvests were noted for the prodigious quantities of beer and cider consumed. Drunkenness, accidents and brawls were common. In the 1810s, Monmouthshire farmers even had to curtail harvesting operations for the safety of all concerned. Cider was liberally dispensed at farm sales, in order to persuade people to part with their money more freely.[65] In the west, *cwrw ocshon* performed the same function and it was not unknown for an auctioneer to postpone the start of a sale until the general level of noise and merriment was judged to be sufficient. Special brews were prepared at Christmas and to celebrate New Year's Day. The completion of important tasks, such as the timbering of the roof of a building (*cwrw cwple*), was celebrated with the tapping of a barrel. Farmers produced beer for blacksmith and carpenter (*cwrw bando*) and to toast the arduous task of repairing a wheel at the local smithy. In Pembrokeshire and west Carmarthenshire, a special brew was usually prepared for the day on which pig slaughtering occurred, known as *cwrw bwtchwr*. The brew usually consisted of additives like whisky, and would be given to the butcher and his assistants before and after the killing.[66]

At the fairs and markets of Wales, thousands of little deals were sealed with a glass or two of beer. The Coity Revel was described as an 'annual custom in which the young of both sexes assemble in large numbers in various public houses for the celebration of a general holiday or fair – an orgy of dissolution'.[67] Swansea fair – 'this nursery of vice' – consisted 'mostly of booths selling alcohol'. From these jolly events, people would reel home under the stars, or through rain, sometimes, as in the case of David Davies in 1839, having indulged too freely, falling into ditches which some malicious fellows 'must have dug since I passed that way in the morning'.[68] The *cwrw bach* was a primitive form of hire purchase, in which parents would sell a cask of home-brewed beer to raise funds for a betrothed couple. Beer was also distributed to mourners and neighbours at funerals. At Llanfechain, Montgomeryshire, mourners spent three or four hours in the home, smoking shag tobacco and drinking spiced beer before forming the cortege.[69] At Ferryside in Carmarthenshire in the 1860s, the vicar received the tithes of the parish at a public house, and distributed tickets to his parishioners which entitled them to beer, depending on the amount of tithe paid.[70]

Workers in the forges and furnaces of Wales drank copiously to replenish body fluids lost by the heat. Drink was believed to impart physical stamina and was closely associated with strenuous trades. Others drank to forget the stresses and strains of living and working in some of the most unhealthy areas of Britain. Intemperance was a cause of poverty, but poverty was also a cause of intemperance, as the hopelessness of destitution demanded a short-cut to oblivion. People took the shortest route out of Merthyr Tydfil or Swansea or Cardiff or Blackwood or Amlwch.[71] The Blue Bell Inn at Gwalchmai was open from breakfast time, and had a clientele who sat and drank solidly throughout the entire day. A regular in this bar claimed that he had never seen a sober person in there. Often, by mid-afternoon, the owner and customers were comatose. A farmer from Holyhead, celebrating a successful sale, a labourer at a house-warming party and three navvies once all drank to the point when they could not get to their own beds – one slept on a bench, another on the road between the pub and his own house. These were the people who worshipped at the altar of 'St Monday', with the more devout also paying their respects to 'St Tuesday'. Industrialists adopted varying strategies to combat excessive drinking, such as long gaps between wage payments, or payment in tokens for company shops, but none were effective. At Newport, weekends and pay days were one long drunken spree 'with people immersed in habits of sensuality and improvidence . . . wasting nearly one (working) week out of five'.[72] The army was even more brutal than industrialists in trying to enforce and ensure sobriety in its ranks. At Brecon in 1839, a private in the 12th Regiment was given 150 lashes for drunken and riotous behaviour.[73]

The Welsh people certainly had plenty of opportunities to drink. Public houses and inns were a marked feature of all towns, providing a significant part of commerce and trade. In the Duke Town area of Newport there were five public houses and twenty-eight beerhouses higgledy-piggledy amongst 151 domestic buildings.[74] Pwllheli in the 1860s had twenty-one public houses on the short but appropriately named 'High Street', to cater for thirsty mariners, resident topers and visiting drinkers. In the town's alcohol trade, women played a prominent part, running ten of the establishments, including the pub of the notorious Magdalen Roberts.[75] Aberystwyth was 'a small, friendly, sea-washed town with a pub on every corner'.[76] Bangor in 1829 had seven inns and hotels, two maltsters, seventeen taverns and public houses, and two wine and spirit merchants.[77] Caernarfon possessed two inns and hotels, seven maltsters, five spirit dealers and twenty-nine taverns and public houses. No wonder that one visitor declared in the 1840s: 'I have travelled through many towns in England, but I have never seen so many drunkards in proportion to the number of the population as in Caernarvon . . . neglected children are like Arabs in the desert'.[78]

The shocked visitor had obviously not visited Carmarthen. The wild west town in 1822 could boast four inns, nine liquor dealers, nine maltsters, eighty-three taverns and public houses, and for the more refined, two wine and spirit dealers. Among the town's pubs were a bestiary of mythical animals – mermaids, unicorns and dragons, a menagerie of bears, buffalo, greyhounds, lambs and elephants, a stable full of black and white horses, a pride of golden, red and white lions, and an aquarium with three salmons, three trouts, and three sewins. Yet despite the profusion of drinking places in this wild, western market town, the place which claimed the title as the most drunken town in Wales was Monmouth. With over sixty licensed houses in 1871, it topped the British league table for the most pubs per person. While the British average was of one public house for every 242 people, at Monmouth people wobbled with a ratio of one public house for every 83 people. In order to counteract the pernicious effects of these 'palaces of vice' the vicar opened The Reformers Tavern to provide tea, coffee, food, dominoes, billiards and 'well aired beds' for the townspeople and visitors. Despite the attractions, the venture was soon declared bankrupt.[79]

Many of the pubs offered entertainment to attract customers. The Britannia Inn in Llannerch-y-medd, Anglesey, was known as 'the home of the harp'. Many poets, story-tellers, musicians and local people visited the inn to delight in the liquid sound of a choir of harps played by John Jones, Telynor Môn, and his family.[80] In addition to music, the Cow and Snuffers at Llandaff boasted that 'Disraeli slept here'. The Goat at Penymorfa, according to Mrs Gaskell, provided harpists to accompany the singing and dancing, and cheer the prosti- tutes who gathered there to await the roving drovers. Tafarn y Garreg at Abercrave was famous for the ballads sung in its bar.[81] Certain pubs catered to certain social classes. The Aleppo Merchant in Carno was home to farmers and rail workers. The latter so enjoyed its conviviality that the first train to run along the 'Dovey–Severn' railway began late 'because the engine got drunk'.[82] In the 1840s, the 'better sorts of people' in Chepstow gathered together in the Tippling Philosopher.[83] In Swansea, captains gathered in the George, bosuns and mates in the Cameroon Hotel, and crews in the Cuba, the Cape Horner and the Mexico Fountain. The Old Cuba, near the Strand, a gloomy hole, filled with tobacco smoke, its only natural illumination a rarely opened window, was the 'first drink' ashore and the 'last drink' before sailing.[84]

In addition to the licensed premises, there were thousands more unlicensed premises. At these unlicensed 'jerries' or *cwrwau bach*, the landlord was often at the mercy of his customers who could report him to the Excise, and a heavy fine could be exacted. In the west, people resented the restrictions on brewing, and stills were to be found every- where. Officer Rowlands at Narberth boasted that he had initiated forty prosecutions in 1844–5, but perhaps the most numerous and notorious

cases came from the Teifi valley.[85] Such places often became favourite
resorts for criminals, and halfway houses for the disposal of stolen
property. There were several such 'receiving houses' for goods stolen in
Merthyr Tydfil, north of the town, on the border of Glamorgan and
Breconshire. One such place was kept by the Italian immigrant Dominic
Mafia. When police raided his place on Christmas Day 1836, the floor
was mired with mud and liquor, and the drinkers were crowded and
stinking like wet dogs. In order to entice customers, the entrepreneurial
Mafia offered an early morning three-drinks-for-the-price-of-one
special. The low price was the attraction, oblivion the aim.[86] The
authorities were wise to be wary of some premises. The landlord of the
Three Horse Shoes in Merthyr Tydfil was 'a sound Chartist', as were
James Horner of the Queen Adelaide in Newport, William Williams,
landlord of the Prince of Wales in Newbridge, and Abraham Evans of
the Rolling Mill in Merthyr Tydfil.[87] Many of the worst outrages of the
Rebecca movement were planned in Carmarthenshire's most notorious
pub – the Stag and Pheasant, Five Roads.

Public houses were not just centres of dissipation and dissolution.
In the late 1830s, the Dowlais English Wesleyan Methodist Sunday
School met at the Swan Inn. Until the erection of a church in 1857, the
congregation at Hirwaun met in a public house. Vestry meetings were
held in both the Greyhound Inn, Llanfabon, and the Cooper's Arms
at Ystrad Mynach. The Calvinistic Methodist *seiat* met in 1802 at the
appropriately named The Virgin public house at Bangor. The Eagles,
in the same town, saw both the establishment of a branch of the
British and Foreign Bible Society in 1813, and the foundation of the
town's first literary society in 1810. The earliest *eisteddfodau* were held
in pubs, where the quality of the performances decreased as the noise
increased. Elections were often debauched occasions when the Welsh
encountered their favourite words – 'free bar'. At the Caernarfon
Boroughs elections of 1832, a huge total of 833 barrels, 7 gallons and
3 pints of beer, 2,469 gallons, 3 quarts and 1 pint of spirits, and 2,204
bottles of wine were consumed. The barrel was well and truly rolled
out at the Pembrokeshire election of 1831. By the count, the Whig
candidate owed one publican over £13,000 for drink, meal tickets and
lodgings.[88]

Brewing became big business. In 1792, the only significant brewer in
Wales was the Cambrian Porter Brewery of Messrs Phillips and Co.,
on the Strand in Swansea. By the early 1820s, they had been joined by
two other companies, one of whom had developed a significant

Unknown artist, publicity sign for Buckley's Brewery, Llanelli, *c*.1883. As the nineteenth century progressed, brewing, despite the activities of temperance campaigners, became big business. Small brewing houses were transformed into large-scale factories with complex distribution systems.

factory enterprise near the docks. Throughout Wales by 1830, over fifty breweries had sprung up. Giles and Harrap's Merthyr Brewery had the wisdom not to put all its beer into one barrel. They diversified into an extensive range of wines and spirits, with bonded stores in Bristol, London, Cork, Belfast and Greenock. Even more famous, and just a steady dray-ride away, was the Pontycapel Brewery at Cefncoed, whose Starbright brew was 'a beverage celebrated for its strength and flavour'. Cardiff by the 1830s also had two breweries, which were based on factory systems with complex distribution services. They were joined in 1863 by the much loved Samuel Brain, who soon invested £50,000 in new premises near the town centre. The transformation from domestic and small-scale ventures into a factory-based industry with larger companies greedily swallowing smaller enterprises, that characterized many Welsh industries, was particularly evident in the history of brewing.[89]

In the north-west, thirsts were mainly slaked by maltsters, although Bala had two brewers. The produce of one of them was lavishly praised by the original campaigner for real ale, George Borrow, on a visit to the town in the 1850s:

> I tested it and then took a copious draught. The ale was indeed admirable, equal to the best I had ever before drunk – rich and mellow with scarcely any smack of the hop in it, and though so pale and delicate to the eye nearly as strong as brandy. I commend it highly.[90]

Even stronger was the Royal Welsh Whisky produced by Richard Price of Rhiwlas, which was said to be 'the most wonderful whisky that ever drove the skeleton from the feast or painted landscapes in the brain of man'.[91] Another northern whisky was even stronger:

> Bydd i un llwnc demtio dyn i ladrata ei ddillad ei hun; dau lwnc a wna iddo frathu ei glust ei hun, tra y bydd i dri llwnc ei demtio i achub ei fam-yng-nghyfraith rhag boddi.[92]

> One sip will make a man steal his own clothes; two sips will make him bite his own ear; whilst three sips will tempt him to rescue his mother-in-law from drowning.

The north-east was well endowed with breweries. As early as 1844, Holywell had five breweries, one of which claimed to have efficacious, if not magical, properties in its brews, for the water was drawn from St Winifred's Well. The Llangollen brewery of the Walters Brothers in the 1850s used the rail network to sell its brews as far away as Manchester and Liverpool. The boozing George Borrow considered their ales nearly as fine as those of Bala. But the Welsh capital of brewing was the army garrison town of Wrexham. The town had long been a centre for the brewing industry. It was alleged that the disciplined puritanism of Cromwell's New Model Army collapsed in the town, for many deserted to taste the high quality of Wrexham's brews.[93] In 1835, *Piggot's Directory* considered that 'the malting trade is of consequence, and there are several respectable breweries'. By the 1860s, there were nineteen commercial breweries in operation, with *Worrall's Directory* of 1874 remarking: 'Wrexham has always been celebrated for the quality of its ale, and consequently the brewing trade has flourished here, within the last few years, however, this trade has enormously increased, and several very spacious and handsome breweries have been built at great cost.'[94] Malt permeated every aspect of the town. The corporation was dominated by brewers. Temperance and teetotal ministers were run out of town for, as William George claimed, 'Beer and Baccy are the creed of Wrexham'.[95]

The development in brewing was mirrored in increased business for police courts. Every year down to 1896 saw an increase in the incidence of drunkenness. The rate of such proceedings, about one per 116 of the population in 1896, has rarely been equalled since. The rate in the mid nineteenth century was exceptionally high. Hidden within the anonymity of statistics is the human reality. Some individuals acquired a remarkable record of convictions for being drunk and disorderly. Daniel Jenkins of Pontypridd, 'Peggy Clarach' of Aberystwyth, John 'Angel' Jones of Tywyn and Daniel Jones of Carmarthen became notorious characters in their communities.[96] Drinking them all under the table was the one-woman party, Ellen Sweeny of Swansea, whose appearances in the local courts began in the 1860s. By 1880, Ellen had been convicted 156 times for drunkenness.[97] The newspapers derived enormous fun in recounting the adventures of these dissipated characters. In 1871, John Jones, a collier from Wrexham Street, Mold, was found by police rolling in a gutter pleading: 'let me be so I can swim home'.[98] Complex categories of the stages of intoxication were developed. People were 'feddw chils', 'feddw gaib', 'feddw rhacs jibbaders', 'feddw gachu', 'yn feddw twll', 'yn feddw garlale', they were 'joyously and seraphically drunk', 'beastly drunk', 'insensibly drunk', 'helplessly and speechlessly drunk'. Towns had 'lurching drunks', 'singing drunks', 'crying drunks' 'fighting drunks', 'important drunks',

Unknown artist, *Y Mesurydd Diodyddol*, from *Y Punch Cymraeg*, 2 April 1859 (National Library of Wales). People spent considerable time chronicling and calculating the various stages and conditions of drunkenness. There is a bleak starkness about the final category – *yn farw feddw* (dead drunk).

'amorous drunks', 'mischievous drunks' and 'sleeping drunks'. Last and worst of all was the finality of the final category – 'dead drunk'.[99]

Sport and Society

Taverns were often the venues for traditional rough village sports, such as bull-baiting, cock-fighting and dog-fighting. In 1800, the Bull public house in Chepstow was a noted venue for bull-baiting and the Bear adjoining the Town Gate was rumoured to be the location for bear-baiting.[100] In the Bristol at Swansea in 1816, it was claimed that a bull had been baited.[101] In the north, the Eagles Inn at Wrexham was the main venue for these taurine deaths in the afternoon. A bull was tethered to a stake and dogs trained for the purpose were set on it one by one. Gentlemen brought their dogs for the baiting and paid a fee to the bull-baiter. After the baiting, the bull was killed, and it was believed that the baiting made the flesh more tender.[102]

Cock-fighting had an even longer history, being patronized by royalty and widely practised in several Welsh towns. Cock-fighting rings, the famous *talwrn*, could be found in Abergavenny, Cardiff, Carew, Carmarthen, Pembroke, Tywyn, Denbigh and Wrexham.[103] Cock-fights were occasions of great excitement, when two armed entries battled to see who would be dinner. In the steaming cauldrons of the *talwrn* feathers flew, spectators hollered, and the bookies often got into the ring with the pugilistic poultry. Pembrokeshire became famous for its 'black fighting cocks'. These were reputedly so vicious that English cockers refused to fight the ferocious 'black devils'. A verse from the Bible was uttered into the bird's ear before battle by a highly superstitious people. Charms were also utilized, and people believed that, to be successful, the cock should match the colour of the day: on cloudy days, a blue cock was the best bet; when skies were dark and lowering, a black cock seemed portentous; but on sunny days, the wise money went on red or golden cockerels.[104] Though the practice had been outlawed by the Act to Prevent Cruelty to Animals in 1835, it continued until the late nineteenth century. In September 1849, the *Cardiff and Merthyr Guardian* urged police in the twin towns to prosecute those engaged in the 'barbarous practice of cock-fighting'.[105] Dog-fighting, because it needed no theatre, post or props, was even more widespread. Gangs roamed the south stealing dogs for the sport. In 1853, the case against the notorious dog-fighter Owen

Sullivan of Newport Road, Cardiff, collapsed because witnesses had been so intimidated that they were terrified to testify.[106] Ten years later, although hundreds had watched the dogs of Henry Thomas and Thomas Hopkins fight in Bute Street, Cardiff, the authorities could not get anyone to give evidence.[107]

Hunting was highly popular in Wales throughout these years. Many of the poorer people, as Hugh Hughes's painting of the *Welsh Salmon Fishermen* of 1840 reveals, hunted to survive.[108] But others chased badgers, hares, foxes, rabbits, squirrels and otters for pleasure. All over Wales, the unmentionable pursued both the inedible and the barely edible. At the turn of the eighteenth century, Nanney-Wynn of Maesyneuadd, Merionethshire, confided to his diary his tiring week of hunting: on Monday he had hunted with the harriers; Tuesday he had fished for salmon in a lake; Wednesday he had gone fishing in a river; Thursday he had fished in a lake and spent time shooting rabbits; Friday he had gone fox hunting, chasing hares, fishing for trout and shot two teal which he had to swim out to reclaim; Saturday, with the typical boastfulness of the fisherman, he caught 'great numbers' while spearing salmon. Sunday was a deserved day of rest and repast when he ate some of the butchered meat.[109] Richard John Lloyd Price (1843–1923), squire of Rhiwlas, became famous as a breeder and judge of pointers and was an originator of 'Field Trails with the Gun'. He wrote a number of books on subjects as characteristic as *Rabbits for Profit and Rabbits for Powder, Practical Pheasant Rearing, with an Appendix on Grouse Driving* and *Dogs Ancient and Modern and Walks in Wales*.[110] The rational approach of Price and many Welsh squires transformed what had previously been almost solitary pursuits into scientific slaughter on a professional basis. Whole swathes of the mid-Wales countryside were laid down as grouse moors and pheasant coverts. Birds were increasingly bred and protected by gamekeepers and flushed out by beaters for the amassed shoot, with glory for the biggest 'bags'.

Scientific principles also entered fox hunting. Horses were bred specially for speed and jumping, and packs of hounds for scent and stamina. Celebrated packs of hounds were to be found all over Wales. Although the gentry and large farmers were the principal participants, many poorer people were employed in the upkeep of the dogs and horses. In 1830, W. J. Chapman painted *The Cyfarthfa Hunt*. Proudly the hunters sit on chairs giving chase to glasses of claret, toasting their health and their hunting, for this was a remarkable gathering. In their

W. J. Chapman, *The Cyfarthfa Hunt*, *c*.1830 (Cyfarthfa Castle Museum and Art Gallery). Toasting their health and their hunting, this remarkable group contained many of the great and the good of the town. They represented the middle class which social explorers had much difficulty in discovering in darkest Merthyr Tydfil in the nineteenth century.

ranks were shopkeepers, merchants, solicitors and publicans – representatives of the very middle class which the health and education reports claimed did not exist in the wild iron town of Merthyr Tydfil.[111] The Welsh gentry greatly prized the quality of the horses they bred. Grismond Phillips of Cwmgwili commissioned the busy W. J. Chapman to paint three oil paintings of his horses. Pride of place went to his hunter, Isaac. The proud owner inscribed on the back of the painting 'who won a match against A. S. Davies Grey Horse. For £20 a ride. Owned up . . . I shall never have such a horse again.'[112] The gentry speculated widely but not always wisely. Many families were as proud of their equine pedigree as they were of their genealogy.

By the late nineteenth century, the turf had become big business. Almost every town of any size had its races. Aberystwyth, Machynlleth, Bangor, Newport, Monmouth, Pembroke Dock and Swansea all had significant events lasting three or four days. In some, stands were built to protect the snobs from the mobs.[113] Some races were classics. Wrexham had its 'Gold Cup' and noble patrons. The vicar of Gresford, whom no one could accuse of aversion to the sport, told his young sons who wanted to ride over to the Wrexham races: 'There will be plenty of blackguards there without you.'[114] Sandown racetrack was built by Hwfa Williams, one of the heirs to the fortune accumulated by Thomas Williams of Llanidan, the 'Copper King'.[115] The prize at the Brecon races in 1838 was 50 sovereigns. All the smart money had been placed on Mr Gough's Dandina, the 2–1 favourite, but with a few furlongs left Captain Elmslie's Talisman came from nowhere, and 'won a fortune' for its ecstatic owner.[116] One of the many Welsh who was less fortunate was the 'hunting obsessed' sporting gentleman, John Mytton (1796–1834), an officer in the 7th Hussars, owner of estates with rentals of £18,000 per annum in Monmouthshire. Although an MP for two years, he only spent half an hour in the Commons, preferring to spend his time and money on horses, betting and drinking. He died in the pauper's prison of the King's Bench, London, in 1834, greatly mourned by his cronies, and cursed by his debtors. Charles James Apperley (1779–1843) of Plas Gronow and Wrexham, veteran of the bloody 1798 campaign in Ireland, was another on whom lady luck rarely smiled. He spent the years 1830–42 in debt-enforced exile in Calais, where he had sufficient time to pen two notable works – *The Chase, the Road and the Turf* (1837) and *The Life of a Sportsman* (1843) – and make several contributions to the *Sporting Times*. The jockey Reginald Herbert (1841–1929) of Abergavenny was more fortunate. Master of the Monmouthshire Fox Hounds for seventeen years, he set a record for the highest number of winning rides, including victory at the Cheltenham Grand Annual. He is still celebrated in sport's hall of fame as the first person to introduce polo to Britain.[117]

Archery was another sport which crossed social divides. Archers had been a vital aspect of the British militaristic tradition for centuries. Although it had declined from its medieval popularity, the sport continued to attract a significant following. In 1787, Sir Foster and Lady Cunliffe of Acton Hall near Wrexham established the Society of Royal British Bowmen, whose members were entitled to wear outlandish foppish hats ornamented with the Prince of Wales's plume of feathers. Rich money prizes were offered, and by the 1830s, the society was highly popular, meeting at many venues in the north. The participants followed the rules and regulations set out in the archery manual *Toxophilus*, edited by John Walters at Wrexham, in 1788.[118] Another sport which was organized on a more rational basis and was highly popular throughout Wales was cricket. Wickets were laid with loving care on estates and village greens. In 1802, the tradition of epic

Unknown artist (after Townsend), *Archery competition at Erddig, c.*1822.
The painting shows a meeting of the Royal British Bowmen at Erddig on
13 September 1822. Archery remained popular with a wide cross-section of
the Welsh people until well into the nineteenth century.

underachievement was established when England snatched defeat
from the jaws of victory by losing an epic three-day match to
Chepstow.[119] Such results prompted the editor of *The Cambrian* to
predict: 'we are happy to say, this manly exercise is likely to become a
national game with the Welsh'.[120] Boxing also began to be regulated as
the scientific sport of pugilism developed. But many bouts continued
to be brutal encounters. In 1831, at Swansea, a massive crowd gathered
to watch two butchers, Brown and Hollister, fight for £20 a round.
Surprisingly, rather than prolong the bout and earnings Brown, as
befitted his trade, went for the kill and Hollister 'was carried off the
ground insensible and is considered past recovery'.[121]

Football was also popular with the Welsh. Just as *Bando* was a
forerunner of hockey, so was *Cnapan* a rougher precursor of football.
Hundreds of youths from two rival parishes often, quite literally,
fought to get a wooden ball to their opponent's church door. To many,
the fun was not in the playing, but in the taking apart. These sports

were still tied to the days when holidays remained holy days and played on dates of significance in the Church calendar – Shrove Tuesday saw the brutal encounter between Nevern and Newport, while on Easter Monday and Ascension Day, the pride of Llandysul and Llanwenog played and fought. Many inter-village games quickly deteriorated into mass brawls. In 1843, the outraged editor of the *Caernarvon and Denbigh Herald* complained that rather than attempt to save two shipwrecked sailors, one of whom drowned:

> on the morning of Saturday, scores of young men from the neighbourhood (Llanbedr, Dyffryn Ardudwy and Talybont) congregated along the beach, and in bitter absence of all sympathy towards a fellow being . . . in the bitter pangs of death, amused themselves by playing at football. Will not the teachers of Merioneth cry aloud in their various circles against the barbarities of the 'wrecking system' and its resulting adjuncts.[122]

The response of many of those 'teachers' was to help to organize football on more rational lines. By the 1860s, crowds followed village and town teams who played on regulation-sized pitches. Chirk was particularly successful and many of the players were 'poached' by Wrexham Football Club founded in 1870.[123]

To some people, the attraction of sport was the opportunity it offered to gamble. At the turn of the eighteenth century, Wales was locked by gambling fever. People bet on the outcome of battles in the Napoleonic Wars, on the outcome of elections – or any future happening. Cards were the opium of the polite. In 1790, Jeremiah Humfrey of Cardiff lost £250 in a single hand to Dr Richard Griffiths of Pontypridd, a result he later challenged in court at Hereford, because he claimed the cards were marked.[124] By the 1820s, at least three Welsh estates had been lost in their entirety on the card tables. The poor played with a passion born of the possibility of a prodigious jackpot just out of reach – the golden future. To these gamblers, everything was 'next' – the next roll, the next card, the next hour, the next lucky break – the thrill of time standing still as a black ace descended like a spaceship on the smiling face of a red queen. Even if the bet was only a shilling, it was the excitement that mattered, the pursuit of happy endings. Most public houses in Wales, despite the attempts of police and moralists to crush the practice, had their card schools with a set cast of characters – a widow on a spree, the shaky loser whose face showed every good hand, a tattooed sailor and one flint-faced professional. Bets on foot races were particularly popular. Riots nearly occurred in Aberdare, in August 1845, when the people's favourite,

Howell Powell, was 'tripped by a little urchin who crossed the road just as he was coming up to him, it is supposed by accident'. Had he not moved so fast, the urchin would have been lynched by the outraged crowd who had lost their bets through his action.[125] A Cardigan solicitor, Mr Lucas, lost a £50 bet that he could race Thomas Lloyd of Coedmor from the town to Haverfordwest. To celebrate the event, bonfires were lit and church bells rung. The people of Cilgerran were so ecstatic that they broke the church bells. Until 1824, gambling was nationalized, for the state itself ran a lottery which was eventually brought to an end because of ruinous speculation. At Swansea, in 1814, anticipation was feverish as the £30,000 winning ticket no. 10,775 had allegedly been sold in the town – 'it could be you!'[126]

Indoor Indulgences

In 1812, Henry Murton, a native of Merthyr Tydfil, bemoaned the transformation which had taken place in Welsh recreation during his lifetime. 'Invigorating and manly exercises' such as gardening, tennis, fishing and badger-baiting had been abandoned for 'indoor indulgences' such as drinking and gambling, and to religious services and Sunday school activities, as the public house and chapel emerged as the major centres of social intercourse and enjoyment.[127] Yet perhaps the most widespread solitary and sedentary activity was not drinking or praying, but reading. During the eighteenth century, an estimated 2,500 Welsh books had been published by Welsh presses. By the 1760s, the roots of a professional printing industry had been established in Wales through the efforts of people like John Ross of Carmarthen and Rhys Thomas at Llandovery. These were able printers, capable of competing with their counterparts in England, the first of a generation of professionals whose advent would soon eclipse the amateur. In 1772, Richard Marsh, a bookseller in Wrexham, set himself up as a printer. At Trefriw in 1776, Dafydd Jones, author and bookseller, set up a printing business which his grandson transferred to Llanrwst in 1825, and expanded successfully. Bala and Bangor also became important book-publishing centres. By the end of the eighteenth century, professional printers could reasonably expect to make a decent living from the book trade. They bequeathed flourishing concerns to their families and established dynasties of printers. Titus Evans of Machynlleth was the father of John Evans, the Carmarthen printer, whose four sons in due course became printers. Printers' widows also showed considerable business acumen, two of the most successful being Mary, widow of Thomas Roberts of Caernarfon, and Esther, widow of Samuel Williams of Aberystwyth.[128]

The market for Welsh books grew considerably during the early nineteenth century and the cultural and information industries expanded dramatically. Sunday schools and the National and British Schools created increasing numbers of literate people. The gradual rise in wages and improvements in living conditions enabled more people to purchase more books, newspapers, pamphlets and periodicals. It is important not to exaggerate the spread of literacy in Wales, for the statistics gathered by the Registrar General indicate that literacy rates in Wales were among the lowest in Britain. Whether this was also the case in Welsh is problematic. Undoubtedly, a substantial number of publications were produced in the Welsh language, but this might not be evidence of greater literacy, for many continued to sign their wedding certificates with a mark. But the growth in population, together with enhanced educational provision, created an increased demand for reading material. By 1860, over 9,500 Welsh books had been published. Many of them discussed abstruse theological topics but there were also cookery books, general knowledge compendia, geographical and scientific works. Many of the books found their way on to the shelves of voracious collectors and readers, such as 'the Philosopher' John Lloyd LLD, Fellow of the Royal, Antiquarian and Linnean Societies and MP for Flint 1796–9. When Fenton visited his home at Cefn House in the 1800s, Lloyd had over 10,000 books.

Slaking the thirst for print and news, journals, newspapers and periodicals flooded onto the market. The first newspaper in Wales, *The Cambrian*, appeared in Swansea in 1804, and in 1807 the Chester firm of Borster extended its operations into north Wales and began to publish the *North Wales Gazette* at Bangor in January 1808. In 1810, the *Carmarthen Journal* appeared in the town.[129] The year 1814 saw the foundation of the first Welsh-language weekly, *Seren Gomer*, by a group of Swansea businessmen. The Chester printer and Calvinistic Methodist minister, John Parry (1775–1846) launched *Goleuad Cymru* as its northern counterpart. All the religious denominations came to establish periodicals to inculcate their values and indoctrinate their readers.[130] Relationships between some were bitter and protracted. From 1835 onwards, a monthly battle raged between *Yr Haul*, a Church and Tory magazine edited by the brilliant satirist and polemicist, David Owen, Brutus, and *Y Diwygiwr*, edited, printed and published by the Independent minister David Rees (1801–69), Y Cynhyrfwr of Llanelli. In 1845, the Welsh periodical press came of age with the commencement of *Y Traethodydd* – 'the highest court in the realm of Welsh literature'. Printed by Thomas Gee and edited by Lewis Edwards, principal of the Calvinistic Methodist Theological College at Bala, *Y Traethodydd* set new standards for Welsh journalism. As a young man, Edwards accidentally came across some issues of *Blackwood's Magazine* and felt a new world open up before him as he was introduced for the first time to the literature of England and Germany. His ambitions for a similar Welsh publication to broaden the intellectual horizons of his fellow countrymen and create a learned ministry were achieved by this highly influential and able character through this journal. Although the majority of Welsh periodicals were edited by ministers of religion, some ventured into the secular field of satire and humour. Between 1858 and 1864, *Y Punch Cymraeg* set out to satirize everyone and everything and blame anyone and anything for the condition of Wales.[131]

Alongside the Welsh-language books, periodicals and newspapers were the entertaining products of the presses of England.[132] During one of the golden ages of English literature, the Welsh were transfixed. They, too, wandered lonely as clouds, were amazed at Kubla Khan's measureless caverns, wept at the adventures of the *Heir of Radclyffe*, sympathized with Mrs Bennett's problem, were shocked at *Lady Audley's Secret*, scandalized by Ouida's *Held in Bondage*, angered at the disparity between the Two Nations, swooned on *Wuthering Heights*, and were traumatized at the death of Little Nell. An army of the culturally deprived – housemaids, weavers, coal miners, ironworkers, shoemakers, dressmakers – rapturously acclaimed the moment when they first picked up a book and commenced on their odysseys of self-education. The embrace of literature opened up wider perspectives and made people more articulate and critical. The literature available in Victorian Wales has been derided and denounced because of its sentimentality and its alleged tendency to reinforce conservative values, but a literate culture did represent a social revolution in which the oppressed gained control over their own minds.[133] People like David Christopher Davies (1827–85), a geologist and mineralogist, William Daniel Davies (1838–1900), a Methodist minister and journal editor in America, Joseph Jones (1787–1856), litterateur, writer and lead-works manager and countless others who struggled to educate themselves, testified that only through reading did they come to think of themselves as individuals.[134] Penny dreadfuls and sensation fiction were relished, along with the classics, and the Bible was valued, not just as a repository of truth, but as an anthology of adventure stories and bloody battles.[135]

Authors of Welsh extraction and connection appeared in the 'best-sellers' lists of their age. Anne Beale (1816–1900), Ann Julia Hatton (Ann of Swansea, 1764–1838), Felicia Dorothea Hemans (1793–1835), Hester Lynch Piozzi (Mrs Thrale, 1741–1821) and Mary Robinson (Perdita, 1756–1800) all sold significant numbers. But although Anne Beale's *The Vale of the Towey* (1844), and Felicia Hemans's *Casabianca*, with its celebrated opening line 'The boy stood on the burning deck', were very popular, few of these authors could support themselves solely by their literary outpourings.[136] Publishing was profitable, but it was useful to have the support of a wealthy husband, as in the case of Mrs Thrale, or for Ann of Swansea, the financial hand-outs of her more famous brother and sister. A whiff of scandal could provide a welcome boost to book sales. Sex sold. Mary Robinson's dangerous liaisons with the Prince of Wales from 1775, which filled the whispering columns of the London press, undoubtedly increased the sale of her published works. Notoriety helped her novels to sell, while immorality helped her memoirs to leave bookshop shelves. The influx of English-language publications into Wales had profound implications for the long-term health and survival of the Welsh language. In their reading material and in their daily lives, more and more people were becoming familiar with the use of English.[137]

The pace of artistic life in Wales also began to quicken. Increasing standards of living through agricultural improvements and greater job opportunities created groups of people who had surplus income, some of which would be spent on beautifying the home. By the 1830s, more painters could support themselves by their art. Patrons and purchasers of artistic work now came from all walks of life, not just from the gentry. In the early nineteenth century, craftsmen had produced to order, but from the 1850s many paintings were being valued as expressions of an individual and independent personality. William Watkeys established himself at Swansea from 1831 and James Flewitt Mullock at Newport in the 1840s. Caernarfon became a notable centre for art artisans to practise. Hugh Hughes, William Roose, Hugh Jones and William Griffith were all based in the town in the 1840s.[138] The increasing importance of the middle and working classes as purchasers of art naturally influenced the content of paintings. Cultural consumers could influence culture creators. Popular tastes dictated new brushstrokes, and fostered a domestic realism in painting which was perhaps best captured by Hugh Hughes. But it also encouraged, almost recreated, a love for meticulous still-life painting derisively known as the 'bird's nest school of painters'. Religious iconography also featured strongly in Welsh artistic works. Many images of Welsh religious leaders were produced in ceramics and in oils from the 1820s. Ironically, people who preached against vanity fashioned graven images of themselves – 'Gwagedd o wagedd'; 'Vanity of vanities, said the preacher, vanity of vanities, everything is vanity'.[139] Some ceramic workshops must have resembled spiritual souvenir shops.

Those who could not afford original works of art were not excluded from the artistic world. New printing techniques created a new market for the artistic print. The explosion in the purchase of prints was fuelled by a comparatively broad section of the Welsh people who were able to afford prints and so affect the character of artistic production.[140] The most popular works of many English and Welsh artists were mass-produced as prints. By the 1860s, influential Welsh people sought to professionalize and propagate the creative artistic abilities of the Welsh people. The sculptor William Davies, Mynorydd, was one of several artists who publicized Welsh artistic work under the aegis of Hugh Owen's 'Social Science Section' at the *eisteddfod*.[141]

Welsh Wit and Wisdom

Art provides a valuable mirror of the pastimes and pleasures of the people. Yet, despite the subject matter, few paintings showed people smiling – perhaps the long, laborious and tedious process of sitting for a painting wiped away the smile from Welsh faces. Perhaps people did not wish posterity to regard them as imbeciles, smiling at long-forgotten humour. For humour there certainly was. Many of the publications that were published in these years, in English and in Welsh, contain many humorous anecdotes and jokes. Some were incidental stories hidden in the corners of the denominational and secular papers, their humour accidental. The obituary of a woman washed into the sea, whose body recovered thirty miles up coast from Aberystwyth, was buried to the tune 'Ar fôr tymhestlog teithio rwyf' (on a stormy sea-journey); or the report of the Methodist teetotalist campaigner who thundered against the devilish effects of drinking and concluded his service with the opinion 'dylid taflu'r holl ddiod gadarn i'r môr' (all alcohol should be thrown into the sea) and then went on to announce the next hymn 'O arwain fy enaid i'r dyfroedd' (O lead my soul to the waters) are comedies of coincidence. Yet many others deliberately sought to make their fellow people smile. Despite the claims of some historians that a joke in Welsh was unthinkable, at least twenty compendia of jokes were published between 1840 and 1871. In all, this author has collected over 4,500 anecdotes or jokes that were written in the years 1776 and 1871. Add to these the wit and witticisms of the Welsh music halls, the rowdy reviews of the *anterliwt* players, the well-honed humour of the touring comedians, and it becomes clear that the Welsh people were not all solemn and serious, but were at heart humorous, outward-going, serene and serendipitous.

Amusing anecdotes were also published in the 'materion diddorol' columns of *Seren Gomer* and *Yr Haul*. The *Monmouthshire Merlin* ran a weekly column which gave examples of local witticisms:

'Are you short sighted miss?'
'Yes, I can hardly tell whether you're a pig or a puppy.'

'Aren't you cold?' (a pretty girl asked a match seller)
'I was, until you smiled.'

'Why are women extravagant in clothes?'
'Because when they buy a new dress they wear it out on the first day.'[142]

Y Punch Cymraeg, modelled on the more famous *Punch*, was scabrous in its satire on the hypocrisy of Welsh religion. Many religious figures such as Evan Harries, Stephen Jenkins and David Evans sought to lead their people on a happier trip to salvation.[143] Although horrible things had happened to Welsh people, many could not sustain a sombre mood for long and burst out in a magnificence of laughter. The dry humour of perfect despair was a familiar aspect of people's lives. Jokes would even be cracked at death. When a lazy woman died, her epitaph claimed: 'Os car hi'r bedd, fel y carai'r gwely / Hi fydd yr olaf yn Adgyfodi'.[144] (If she loves the grave as she loved the bed / She'll be the last at the Resurrection).

Seren Gomer also showed that the secret source of humour was not joy, but sorrow. In September 1848, it reported:

Mae nifer mawr o bobl wedi ymadael yn ddiweddar a Morgannwg a Mynwy i fyned tuag America. Mae yn llawn bryd i bawb ymadael â'r deyrnas hon, canys nid oes yma ond y gorthrymder a'r caledi mwyaf.[145]

A large number of people have recently left Glamorgan and Monmouth for America. It is high time everyone left this kingdom, for there is nothing here but oppression and hardship.

It is very difficult for a historian not to read the newspaper report of the death of a tenant of Mr Lewis, owner of Llanerchaeron, Cardiganshire, without concluding that the reporter was laughing while recollecting the details. The tenant had been shooting all day and had fired his gun thirty-four times consecutively before he misfired. To check it, he turned the gun and stared down the barrel – it worked.[146]

Many historians have laconically lamented several lacunae in Welsh history, but surely one of the saddest is that the laughter of the past has been silenced. Historians have been unwilling, or unable, to consider the historical importance of humour. This has been a general trend in Britain and many western countries, for it is only relatively recently that historians have grasped that humour is a key to the cultural codes and sensibilities of the past. Ironically, much of the best work in this field has been done in a country which, according to the British stereotype, is not renowned for its humour – Germany. Perhaps such research was more needed there. Studying apophthegms and anecdotes, spoonerisms and satire, practical jokes and puns, farce and foolery, tall stories and tales, reveals much about the inner realities of societies. Humour defies convention. It hastens the inevitable in social change. It fights taboos. Humour can also be studied in the context which conforms to the historian's favoured questions – who transmits what humour in which way to whom, where and when?[147]

The answer to the 'who' is, undoubtedly, the people. Names and nicknames are evidence of the people's natural wit. A father of thirteen children was known as 'Wil Population'. 'Dai Good Sort' was mean, 'Jack Sebon' dirty. An unsuccessful boxer went to his death as 'Horizontal Harry'. The unimaginatively christened Thomas Thomas became 'Twm Twice'. A preacher whose sermon droned on in a single monotonous tone was known as 'Jones Pregeth Hir' (Jones long sermon). Another, who flitted and fluttered around, with the fussy self-importance of a wagtail, became 'Fe Sigl-i gwt'. So popular was the name David that many schools resorted to a numbering system to differentiate between the children. The record was seven – Dai 1, Dai 2, Dai 3, Dai 4, Dai 5, Dai 6 and Dai 7. In contrast, Jonathan was a relatively new name to many Welsh people in the 1840s, and so people 'Welshified' it to 'John a Thân', which evolved to 'John a Thân, A Sigaret a Mwg a Matsien'. A boy whose mother married twice was referred to as 'John Dau Dad' (John Two Fathers). The parents of twins were known as 'Mrs Dai Eggs' and 'Twm Double Yolk'. Not all nicknames were bestowed with kindness, as 'Mari Slei' (Sly Mary) would testify. Two inhabitants of Privy Lane, Denbigh, carried nicknames that echoed the street's dirt and squalor – 'Dai Carthion' (Dai Shit) and 'Twm Cart Carthion' (Twm Shit Cart). The miserable and morose Glyn Jones was referred to under the biblical sobriquet 'Glyn Cysgod Angau' (Valley of the Shadow of Death), fondly abbreviated to the Miltonic 'Cysgod Angau'. He had a compatriot in misery in Dyffryn Nantlle – 'Guto Pryder' (Worried Guto). Two pious men were named 'John Amen' and 'Jones Hallelujah'. In contrast some who swore, like 'Dai Rhegi' (Dai Swearer), had to live with their favourite word for far longer than they hoped, as did 'Harry Bugger', 'Twm Bloody', 'Wil Mynuffarn i' and 'Dai Williams Drachrynllyd'. A man who refused to utter such crudities, but who uttered the phrase 'man alive' became better known as 'Harry Man Alive'. Others known for their favourite sayings were 'Jo Wir Dduw' (Jo True to God) of Rhosllanerchrugog, 'Twm Weda i Ddim' (Twm I'll Say Nothing) of Ystalyfera and 'Ianto Shw Mai' (Ianto Hello) of Cwm Rhymni. Nicknames showed far greater imagination and inventiveness than surnames. In 1839, four sisters from Garthbeibio, Montgomeryshire, were reported to have each married men with the name Evan Evans.[148]

Some Welsh people were uncomfortable with laughter. Many religious leaders, who modelled themselves on the gloom-and-doom prophets of the Old Testament, preached against the 'donkey faces' of the drunkards and fools who laughed uncontrollably. The conduct manuals advising aspiring gentlemen on social behaviour, mores and morals also warned that uncontrollable laughter was indecorous and ugly. To cover this ugliness, people should put their hands over their mouths when they laughed. Laughter was also the result of malice, envy and rivalry.[149] The laughter of the crowds at the freak shows was given as one example of laughter resulting from such vices. Yet this perhaps was as much evidence of people's relief that they had been spared the fate of the limbless acrobat or the bearded woman.[150] Laughter could be cynical, cold and aggressive, and destructive on those occasions when society was deemed to be under threat. The evening visits of Rebecca and her daughters to the houses of her enemies, the Scotch Cattle assaults on blacklegs, and the *Ceffyl Pren*'s corrective action against philandering husbands and wayward wives were often accompanied by rough music and laughter. In their raucous

laughter, the group reinforced its solidarity. This was a harshly intoler-
ant popular culture, hostile to privacy and eccentricity, and reliant on
the sanction not of reason but of ridicule. Laughter was often a crude
form of moral censorship. Thus, many voices in nineteenth-century
Wales spoke out against unruly and unregulated laughter.[151] They
sought to repress laughter in the same way as they sought to restrain
sex. There were several forms within Welsh humour which functioned
on social, cultural, linguistic and moral lines.

We have already encountered some of the fun of Welsh fairs. Ballad
singers sang countless songs to the 'rhialtwch' of these jolly plebeian
events, in which colliers and carpenters, maids and manservants,
mistresses and masters, publicans and pugilists laughed alongside each
other. An anonymous author in the J. D. Lewis collection of ballads in
the National Library of Wales in Aberystwyth penned a ballad to
'Dull Ffair Llanbedr Pont Steffan' which had a happy hilarity from the
very start: 'Fel 'rown yn rhodio Llanbed, ar forau ffair y ffri, / Fe
d'rawodd pwl o chwerthin Ryfeddol arnaf fi . . .'[152] (As I was roaming
Lampeter, on the fair's morn, / A burst of laughter broke over me . . .).

The ballads told amusing stories of misfortune and misadventure –
animals shot by accident in place of amorous youths; a drunken wife
who, seeing a white sow at the foot of her bed, believed it to be the
devil and confessed all her indiscretions to her husband and an eaves-
dropper, who passed the salacious details on to the community. Ellis
Roberts derived considerable fun from the frustrations caused by the
lack of tobacco during the American Civil War. Ellis also told of the
drunken dissipation and riotous events at Llangernyw. The almost
anonymous 'H.O.' of Llanllyfni sang a bawdy ballad about *Hanes gŵr
ifanc a gollodd ei glos wrth garu merch o Lanrwst oedd yn Nhreffynnon*
(The history of a young man who lost his trousers courting a girl
from Llanrwst in Treffynnon).[153] A similar tale was told by Yr Hen
Gowper, of a cuckolded husband who arrived home to discover his
wife with her lover hidden in her bed. The gullible husband was sent
for medicine for his wife's stomach pains. Panicking, he hurriedly
dressed and ran out wearing the wrong trousers, which proved too big
and clown-like, they fell down, tripping him up. Realizing the
deception, the husband put his hand in his pocket and discovered a
watch and a large sum of money, which he pawned and spent in the
local pub.

When they met at night to share the burden of completing repetitive
indoor tasks, the women spinning or sewing, the men making or

mending tools, country people would tell their favourite fables and fictions from folk-lore. Repartee consisted of the swift utilization of the appropriate proverb for the right situation. At Llanegryn, all members of the community for miles around were allegedly masters at talking in rhymes and riddles, which became rowdier as the proceedings progressed.[154] Scatological humour was highly popular, since it exploited 'the great primal joke' of the human body – the constant threat to dignity and formality levied by the rebellious pressure of bodily needs, particularly those associated with the digestive system. The most popular jokes were often practical ones, and brutality was not always absent from them.[155] Even the *Gwylnos*, in which mourners guarded a dead body to safeguard the soul, was not exempt from trickery and foolery. On one occasion in Anglesey, a young man hid under the table on which the coffin was laid, and in the stillness of the night, as the assembled mourners fell silent, put his arms over the body so that it appeared that the dead man was coming back to life, frightening half of the people halfway to the corpse's condition.[156] Wealthier people were not averse to practical jokes. A Pontypridd mine owner arranged a mock funeral for himself, with short bearers on one side of the coffin and much taller ones on the other, taking great delight in watching them negotiating narrow bridges, bends in the road and hills.

The tall story was also a speciality of certain areas. In 1846, a major advertising campaign was undertaken by a company selling guano. So effective was this product that a farmer claimed that his son, who had slept on bags of guano to shelter from a storm, had grown three feet in height overnight.[157] A master of the tall story was James Wade, Shemi Wâd (1816–97), of Pembrokeshire. Shemi was a sailor 'na hwyliodd erioed o olwg y tir, ond mewn niwl' (who never sailed from sight of land, except in fog) yet he waxed lyrical and long on his encounters with the Red Indians in Fiji, and the Eskimos of South America. He swore that his stories were 'yn wir bob gair' (true every word) and promised to 'dweud y gwir yn onest' (tell the truth honestly). If anyone was unwise enough to show that they had difficulty in believing his stories, Shemi would spit a nauseous red globule of shag tobacco into their eye. Shemi apparently spent hours refining this art in his much stained and filthy cottage. Only a fool or a stranger would stand within four to five yards of Shemi's mouth. His favourite and most famous story related the dynamiting of a gigantic potato.[158] A related trend was the ill-rhyming and poorly structured verses of the 'cocosfardd'. These inept 'poets' would pen atrocious verses with much rhyme, but little reason, to celebrate all sorts of significant local events. Caernarfon seemed to have produced more than its share of them. One of the most prolific was John Rowlands, Bro Gwalia, who published his verses in *Y Blwch Cuddiedig* in 1860. The publisher was Lewis Jones, establisher of 'Y Wladfa', the Welsh homeland in Patagonia. Jones was no stranger to humour for he also published, with Evan Jones, *Y Punch Cymraeg*. Bro Gwalia's verses oddly cross the threshold from the excruciating, to the entertaining, and his verses would be read aloud in the pubs and processions of Pen-Cei, Caernarfon. His eulogy to the spider is typical:

Dirwyn mae'r pryf copyn	The spider swiftly returns
Yn fuan i fyny i'w fwthyn.	Up to his cottage.
Os aiff un pwytyn i'w fwthyn	If one fly goes to his cottage
Y mae o yn sicr o fod yn gorffyn.[159]	He's certain to be a corpse.

People who were considered a *cymeriad* (character) were greatly valued in nineteenth-century Wales. A unique figure was Thomas Williams, Capelulo (1781–1855), whom we have already met as the fornicating and fighting soldier in India. He waited, in Elfyn's poetic phrase, 'nes clywed sŵn torri ei fedd' (until he heard the sound of the gravedigger opening his grave) before converting to religion. Even afterwards it was impossible to discipline the old soldier. One night, on his way to the *seiat*, he encountered a self-righteous saint, who asked if Thomas believed in predestination. 'Yes', replied Capelulo. 'Well, how do you know you've been chosen?' was the second question. 'How do you know I have not been' was Capelulo's prompt reposte, resulting, as they said in higher social circles at the time, in 'collapse of stout party'.[160] Such ready humour also found itself in the pulpit, for not all ministers were stern zealots. Dafydd Evans (1789–1866) of Ffynnonhenri described the Bible's bloodier battles with all the rich idioms and colloquialisms of his poor upbringing in Carmarthenshire. When Pharaoh refused to let his people go, according to Evans, God remarked: 'Rho fflipen iddo, Moses' (Give him a clout, Moses). On another occasion, he described the slaying of Goliath with such realism that an old man in the audience responded from the loft: 'D. . . dyna fe ar lawr' (D. . . that's him down). His sermons on Jonah and Noah were awash with the levity of the Baptist pulpit's master of wit and wisdom.[161] His lecture on temperance had so much not-in-front-of-the-ladies fun that the deacons banned it.

These home-made amusements were supplemented by those of

travelling entertainers. *Anterliwt* performers did not just perform moralistic or sentimental playlets, but also comedies and sketches. Magicians, acrobats and fortune-tellers had a ready line in wit and repartee with which they attracted customers. Clowns and comedians were warmly welcomed in hamlets, villages and towns all over Wales. In 1812, it was announced 'that rapidly improving town, and popular watering place, Aberystwyth, will shortly be enlivened by the arrival of Mr Dunn's very excellent company of comedians'.[162] In 1870, J. E. Noakes, 'the hard working comedian', left peripatetic comedy and set up a permanent home in the Star Theatre at Carmarthen. To relieve him of some of the burden of winning laugher from the townsfolk, Gardiner Coyne, an Irish comedian, became the chief attraction. His speciality was Irish jokes about Welsh people.[163]

'Collapse of Stout Party': Puns, Jokes and Witticisms

People who attended balls, dances, dinner parties and soirees and had access to the world of exquisite politeness, enjoyed an altogether different and allegedly more elevated form of humour. The Victorian age in particular was the great age of puns. They often lack the spontaneity of popular humour, for puns and wit were thought out in advance – some obviously slowly in advance. Disgusted at the import of large quantities of foreign eggs, Captain Gronow complained 'How much longer shall we endure this foreign yolk?' With others to carry out the tiresome chores – cooks, butlers, maids, boys to fetch and carry, housekeepers to control the privy purse – many people could afford the time to think and ponder puns. Wit was much cherished and nurtured, but to many it was a fragile flower that could soon wither. Behavioural advice manuals warned that there was a fine line between being regarded as a 'droll fellow', and being considered a bore who constantly attempted vain jokes.[164] *The Art of Conversation* advised that 'conversation is like lawn tennis, and requires alacrity in return at least as much as vigour in service'.[165] The Victorians were easily amused, but they were just as easily bored. Fools and snobs were as much resented in higher social circles as they were among the low:

| Mr Snookson: | 'A-yass- Jones is a very good fellow -a- I don't know that I quite call him a *gentleman,* you know'. |
| Miss Sharp: | 'Don't you really? Oh – but perhaps you are not a very good judge!' |

Hostess: 'What? Haven't you brought your sisters, Mr Jones?'
Jones: 'No; they couldn't come, Mrs Smith. The fact is, they're saving
                themselves for Mrs Brown's dance tomorrow, you know!'

Similar encounters were retold in Welsh newspapers. A banker visited
a highwayman in jail and told him:

Banker: 'I'm glad to see you here in jail'.
Highwayman: 'What ingratitude. When all the rest of the country refused your
                notes, I took them!'[166]

The most popular puns and conundrums were straightforward
questions and answers:

Q: 'Where is it that all women are equally beautiful?'
A: 'In the dark'.

Q: 'When is a blow from a lady welcome?'
A: 'When she strikes you agreeably!'

Q: 'What is the difference between an accepted and a rejected lover?'
A: 'One kisses his misses, the other misses his kisses'.

Q: 'What smells most in a chemist's shop?'
A: 'The nose'.

Y Punch Cymraeg offered a comparable series of questions and
answers to its readers:

'Pa bryd y mae hi yn beryglus sefyll yn ymyl cloc?'
– 'pan fo'r cloc ar fin taro'.
When is it dangerous to stand by a clock?
When the clock is about to strike.

'Pa dref yw y galetaf yn y byd'?
– 'Tref y Fflint'.
Which is the hardest town in the world?
Flint.

'Pa dref sydd a phopeth yn fawr?'
– 'Dim-bach'.
Which town has everything large?
'Dim-bach' – Denbigh.

'Pwy yw'r dyn mwyaf lloerig?'
– 'y dyn yn y lleuad'.[167]
Who is the biggest lunatic?
The man in the moon.

One of the strangest tastes in mid-Victorian Wales was people's ability to laugh at death. A woman looking at her husband's corpse remarked 'He looks so healthy – that weekend at Llandrindod did him a world of good'. But fictional deaths, in contrast, brought forth vales full of tears from the Victorians. The death of the Dickensian hero, Paul Dombey, so upset Walter Savage Landor that he threw his cook out of the window.[168]

The gentle art of parody was also a much praised and practised art among the upper classes. Malapropisms derived from Mrs Malaprop, a character in Sheridan's play *The Rivals* who was based on an eighteenth-century Swansea hostess, were highly popular. Satire abounds in the pages of *Y Punch Cymraeg*, with the cartoons of Owen Ellis of Bryn Coch, Abererch, a powerful weapon in bursting the balloons of social pomp and pretence. His satirical pen drew caricatures outlining the hypocrisy at the heart of many Welsh people. Religious leaders were not spared his ire.[169] Satire was also present in some unexpected places. The Revd Richard Williams of Fron penned two highly scurrilous parodies of sycophantic proclamations. The first, in 1786, was to King George III, at the time of an attempted assassination attempt, which commenced 'Dread Sire!' and went on to warn:

> The greatest of the Sons of Men,
> Should be reminded, now and then,
> By way of Caution that they must
> Like their Inferiors, turn to Dust.

The second, also in 1786, was aimed at Dr Jonathan Shipley (1714–88), bishop of St Asaph, and his son William. Perhaps this one was more deserved for Shipley took nepotism to new heights. In March 1770, he ordained his son William and then went on to give him the livings of no fewer than eight parishes with a combined annual income of over £2,000.[170] Although many rich and prosperous people showed an appreciation for the ruder and cruder elements of popular humour, many sought to distance themselves and smiled politely at ironic jokes and puns laden with double meanings, which they assumed the common people could not penetrate. George Eliot came at the end of a long tradition of such self-deception, when she remarked that 'the last thing in which the cultivated man can have community with the vulgar is their jocularity'.[171]

Yet there was far more community than the great novelist appreciated. The jokes published in D. L. Jones's *Y Ffraethebydd*, William

Davies's *Casgliad o Ffraethebion Cymraeg*, E. Cartwright's *Cymorth i Chwerthin*, Thomas Phillips's *Humours of the Iron Road*, *Ffraethebion y Glowr Cymreig* and *Y Punch Cymraeg* enable the historian to penetrate people's innermost assumptions. Jokes also provide a pointer to joking situations, areas of structural ambiguity in society itself, and their subject matter, which provides a revealing guide to past tensions and anxieties. The social tensions of the years 1776–1871 can be clearly discerned in the jokes of the time, particularly those arising from the meeting of divergent customs and unequal knowledge, as town-dweller collided with peasant, noble with plebeian, clergyman with layman. The following are only a few of several such examples:

> 'Wel, John' ebe y meistr, 'faint o gyflog sydd arnat ti eisiau am y tymhor dyfodol?' 'Wel' ebe John 'yr wyf wedi gwrthod deg punt gan Mr Jones Wernddu.' 'Yn wir, ti wnest yn onest; nid wyt yn werth mo hanner hynny', atebai y meistr.[172]

> 'Well, John' said the master, 'what wage do you want for the next term?' 'Well' said John 'I have refused ten pounds from Mr Jones Wernddu.' 'You were honest then; you're not worth half that' replied the master.

In another anecdote in *Ffraethebion Cymreig*, a master asked his gardener if he had ever seen a snail. Receiving a positive answer, the master retorted that it must have been coming to meet the indolent gardener because 'fyddet ti byth yn medru ei gorddiwedyd' (you could never overtake one).[173] Yet the winner was not always the master or mistress in these encounters:

> 'Mari', ebai boneddiges wrth ei morwyn, 'deffrowch fi chwech o'r gloch boreu fory, y mae gennyf rhyw orchwyl arbennig i'w wneud yr adeg hono.' 'Byddaf yn siwr o wneyd, Ma'm' ebai Mari, 'raid i chwi ddim ond canu'r gloch, a byddaf i fyny i'ch deffro mewn mynyd.'[174]

> 'Mari', said a mistress to her maid, 'wake me at six o'clock tomorrow morning, for I have a special task at that time.' 'I will surely do so, Ma'm' said Mari, 'you only need to ring the bell, and I'll come up to wake you at once.'

> 'Melldith ar ben y dyn a ddyfeisiodd weithio wrth oleuni canwyll' meddai saer. 'Ie, ac wrth oleuni dydd hefyd,' meddai ei brentis a safai wrth ei ochr.[175]

> 'A curse on the head of the person who invented working by candle-light' said the carpenter. 'Yes, and by daylight too,' answered the apprentice at his side.

Certain trades and professions were singled out for particular attention. Doctors were treated with justified derision, for it was notorious that they killed more patients than they cured. Doctors were believed to visit just before death so that they could present their bill. In another anecdote, a doctor asks a simpleton whether he knew that a man after a certain age was either a doctor or a fool, and received the answer 'wrth edrych arnoch chwi, yr wyf yn credu y gall fod yn bob un o'r ddau' (looking at you, I believe it's possible to be both).[176]

So hated were solicitors as avaricious cheats that the sharks who stalked the Swansea copper ships were described as 'sea lawyers'. Some insisted that lawyers were like the cheaper whores, not because they solicited, but for the fact that they charged by the minute. A barber once asked a lawyer for advice as to whether a half-crown was genuine or forged. The lawyer pocketed the coin as his fee and told the man that his servant would bring him four pence change the following day. The lawyer's obsession with money was evident in several anecdotes:

> 'A rhoddasoch chwi fil i'r dyledwyr?' gofynnai cyfreithiwr i'w glient. 'Do syr.' 'A pha beth a ddywedodd wrthych?' 'Efe a ddywedodd wrthyf am fyned at y d—l.' 'A pha beth a wnaethoch chi wedi hyny?' 'Wel, y pryd hwnnw y deuthum atoch chwi!'[177]

> 'Did you give the customer a bill?' a lawyer asked a client. 'Yes sir.' 'And what did he tell you?' 'He told me to go to the d—l.' 'And what did you do then?' 'That's when I came to you!'

Book-learning was also highly suspicious to the common people of Wales. Often the common sense and spontaneous wit of the unlearned deflated the pretences of the learned. A professor asked a simpleton how long a man could live without a brain. The simpleton responded with a sharp question: 'Pa beth yw eich oed chwi eich hun?' (What's your age?).[178] In another anecdote, a minister made a great fuss of the letters 'DD' after his name, only to receive the explanation that they stood for 'Dyn Dwl' (simpleton).[179]

Cheating tradespeople were also disliked and distrusted:

> 'Mae eich llaeth yn ymddangos yn denau iawn, heddyw,' meddai gwraig wrth y llaethwr wrth dderbyn ceiniogwerth o laeth o flaen y drws. 'Ydyw yn wir, ma'm; y rheswm am hyny yw, i'r gwartheg gael cawod drom o wlaw wrth ddyfod tua'r tŷ.'[180]

> 'Your milk looks very thin today,' a housewife told the milkman on the doorstep. 'Yes ma'm. The reason is that the cows had a heavy downpour of rain as they came in to be milked.'

Fashion also gave rise to considerable amusement. The craze for wide skirts and hoops was widely condemned, with claims that several chapels needed wider seats to accommodate broad-skirted women. Rapidly changing fashion, as we have seen, caused considerable problems for men intent on purchasing the latest fad for their lovers and wives as gifts.

Welsh jokes have a certain set of identifiable stock characters. The Irish were rowdy, garrulous, coarse eaters, heavy drinkers, dirty and slow-witted: on one occasion, 'Paddy' asked his friend 'Pat' why he was going after a rabbit with a broken gun, only to be told to be quiet – 'the rabbit doesn't know the gun is broken'. A researcher into living conditions in Ireland was shocked to discover a pig living in the house with a man and asked why: 'Mae gan yr hen fochyn yna bob hawl i fod yn y tŷ, y fo sy'n talu'r rhent!' (The old pig has every right to be in the house, he pays the rent!).[181] Irish poverty was legendary as was the love of strong drink:

> Gofynai plant rhyw Wyddel tlawd i'w tad paham yr oedd yn gwerthu y crochan? 'Er mwyn cael rhywbeth i'w roddi ynddo' oedd yr ateb.[182]

> The children of a poor Irishman asked why he was selling the cooking pot. 'To have something to put in it' was the reply.

> 'Pat, wyt ti yn caru dy wlad?' 'Ydwyf, yn sicr, eich anrhydedd.' 'Wel, beth yw'r peth goreu sydd yn Iwerddon, Pat?' 'Y Whisci, eich anrhydedd.'[183]

> 'Pat, do you love your country?' 'Truly, your honour.' 'Well what's the best thing in Ireland, Pat?' 'The whiskey, your honour.'

Not all Welsh jokes were hostile to their Celtic cousins. Others reveal that, though Paddy was given to drink and disorder, he was also witty, generous and hard-working. Anti-English humour, however, reveals that there was considerable tension between the Welsh and their more powerful neighbours. The English were supercilious, snobbish, but basically stupid:

> 'Sais yn gweld Cymro a'i bwys ar bost lamp yn edrych ar angladd yn dyfod allan o dŷ, a aeth ato, a chymerodd yr ymddidan a ganlyn le rhyngddynt':- 'Ai angladd yw hwn yna?' 'Ie, yr wyf yn meddwl.' 'Rhywun neillduol?' 'Yr wyf yn credi ei fod, syr.' 'Pwy sydd wedi marw?' 'Y gwr boneddig sydd yn yr arch, syr.'

> An Englishman, seeing a Welshman leaning on a post watching a funeral leave a house, went to him and asked:- 'Is that a funeral?' 'Yes, I think so.' 'Anyone special?' 'I think so.' 'Who's died?' 'The gentleman in the coffin, sir.'

> 'A wyddoch chwi,' ebai corach o Sais wrth Gymro, 'eu bod yn arfer crogi Cymry ac asynod gyda'u gilydd yn China?' 'Os felly,' atebai'r Cymro, 'mae yn dda i ti a minau nad ydym yno.'[184]

'Do you know,' an English dwarf told a Welshman, 'that they hang Welshmen and asses together in China?' 'If so,' said the Welshman, 'it is good for you and me that we are not there.'

Humour provided a superb opportunity for the Welsh to gain revenge on the English. Even more hated than the English, and reckoned as stupider than the Irish, were coloured people, who were seen as primitive.

'Sambo, a fyddi di yn chwyrnu pan y byddi yn cysgu?' 'Na fyddaf byth; canys arosais yn effro un noson er mwyn i mi gael gwybod hynny.'

'Sambo, do you snore when you sleep?' 'No, never; I stayed awake one night to make certain.'

Gypsies, giants and dwarfs were also suspect and suspicious characters often mocked and ridiculed. Gypsies were condemned as members of the 'giwaid felynddu gelwyddog' (the lying yellow-black brood).[185]

Some members of society were considered to have a special gift for humour and a rapier-like wit. Simpletons, often paraded around villages at times of carnivals, were in jokes frequently the brightest people in their neighbourhood. On one occasion, a tradesman asked a man from the Vale of Glamorgan 'yr hwn na chyfrifid fel pobl eraill' (who was not considered to be as other people), which he would prefer – a large penny or a small sixpence? The simpleton replied: 'nid wyf yn drachwantus, mi gymeraf y lleiaf' (I'm not greedy, I'll take the smaller).[186]

Children were shown laying bare the idiocy and hypocrisy of the adult world. After a chapel service, a small lad asked his mother whether God read the newspapers:

'Paham y gofyni y fath gwestiwn?' gofynnodd ei fam. 'Dim, ond fy mod yn meddwl nad oedd, oherwydd fod y pregethwr mor hir yn dweud popeth wrtho heddyw' oedd atebiad y bachgen.[187]

'Why do you ask such a question?' asked the mother. 'I was thinking that perhaps he did not, because the minister took so long telling him everything today' was the boy's answer.

Teachers, too, faced the wit of children:

Yr oedd athrawes yn holi twr o blant, a gofynnai 'Paham yr ydym yn gofyn ein bara bob dydd, ac nid gofyn digon am dri neu bedwar diwrnod ar unwaith?' Atebodd geneth fechan, 'Am fod eisiau cael bara "fresh" bob dydd.'[188]

A teacher questioning the class asked 'Why do we ask for our daily bread, and do not ask for three or four days together?' One little girl replied, 'Because we want our bread fresh every day.'

Surprisingly, drunkards were as often the source of wit as of stupidity. One drinker in the Lion complained that the beer did nothing for his head, but always succeeded in getting his legs drunk. Twm o'r Nant, while living in Carmarthen, went on a mission to Llandovery, drank too much and was later discovered in a ditch. When asked how he got there, he replied: 'Y brandy coch godymodd gant, / Rhoes godwm teg i Dwm o'r Nant'[189] (The red brandy that felled hundreds, / Gave a fair fall to Twm o'r Nant).

Love was one of the great subjects for Welsh humour. The different attitudes of men and women are immediately noticeable. Males shied away from talk of love, or sought to reduce it to its lowest form in lust or sex:

Aeth gŵr ieuanc yn ddiweddar i fasnachdy llyfrwerthwr, a dywedodd fod arno eisiau 'Cydymaith gŵr ieuanc'. 'Wel, syr, dyma fy merch i chwi,' ebai y llyfrwerthwr.[190]

A young man recently went into a bookshop and asked for 'a young man's Companion'. 'Well, sir, here's my daughter,' said the bookseller.

One author went into great detail outlining the opportunities for situational sex which the railways offered. The longer the tunnel the better: 'Y tren yn nghesail mynydd, / A Gwen yn nghesail John'[191] (The train in the lap of the hill, / And Gwen in John's lap). Different-sized lovers could also be a source for fun:

Aeth carwriaeth rhwng dyn o faintioli bychan â dynes o daldra rhyfeddol, a dywedodd rhywun ei fod wedi syrthio mewn cariad. 'A ydych yn ei alw "syrthio mewn cariad"?', atebai hen lanc, 'y mae'n llawer tebycach i ddringo ato.'[192]

There was recently a courtship between a very small man and a remarkably tall woman, and it was said that he had fallen in love. 'Do you call it "falling in love"?' asked an old man, 'it's more akin to climbing to it.'

Women, especially young females, seemed to be willing to endure anything in a desperate search for elusive love:

Dywedodd gwraig briod un tro wrth foneddiges ieuanc, y byddai yn well iddi daflu ei hunan dros raeadr yn Niagara, i'r dyfnder is law na phriodi. Atebodd y foneddiges hi – 'Mi a wnawn hyny pe gwyddwn y deuwn o hyd i ŵr yn y gwaelod.'[193]

A married woman recently told a young girl that she would rather throw herself off Niagara Falls to the waters below than marry. The girl replied – 'I'd do that if I knew for sure I'd come across a husband at the bottom.'

Cyfarfyddodd boneddwr ieuanc a llaeth–ferch brydferth yn y wlad, a dywedodd, 'Pa beth a gymerwch am danoch eich hunan a'ch llaeth' fy anwylyd?' Atebodd yr eneth ef yn uniongyrchol. 'Eich llaw, a modrwy aur, syr.'[194]

A gentleman recently met a pretty milkmaid in the countryside and asked, 'What will you take for your milk and yourself, my dear?' The girl replied at once. 'Your hand, and a gold ring, sir.'

There was a strong anti-woman and sexist element in Welsh humour, which warned of the vituperative vitriol of the female tongue. *Y Punch Cymraeg* asked what was the definition of 'perpetual motion' and answered its own question – 'tafod merch' (a girl's tongue). In another anecdote, three men argued as to which material lasted longest. The durability of iron and steel were mentioned, but universal agreement was reached on 'darn o dafod menyw' (a piece of a woman's tongue).[195] *Y Ffraethebydd* asked:

Pa beth yw y wers anhawddaf mewn atal nodi? Atal nodi tafod benyw. Pwy bynnag a ddarlleno hyn yn nghlyw benyw, gofaled fod y drws yn agored, a'r ffordd drwyddo yn glir![196]

What is the hardest lesson in punctuation? Stopping a woman's tongue. Who-ever reads this in the company of a woman had better make certain the door is open, and the way through is clear!

Some stories indicated suspicion about the fidelity of women:

'Wel, mae o'n debyg i'w dad,' ebai 'nurse' ar yr achlysur o fedyddiad plentyn, ac yr oedd ei dad yn 70 oed, ac wedi priodi gwraig ieuanc. 'Ydyw, yn debyg iawn,' ebai hen ferch sychlyd, 'does ganddo yr un dant yn ei ben.'[197]

'Well, he's like his father,' said a nurse at the birth of a child whose father was 70 years of age, and married to a young girl. 'Yes, very similar,' said a miserable old woman, 'he doesn't have a single tooth in his head.'

Of all the topics in Welsh humour, one of the most frequent was the perils and pitfalls of marriage. It was put with brevity in an anecdote which had a typically contemporary biblical theme to it:

'Pa hyd yr arosodd Adda ym Mharadwys cyn iddo bechu?' ebai gwraig wrth ei phriod mwynaidd y dydd o'r blaen. 'Hyd nes y cafodd wraig' oedd yr ateb.[198]

'How long did Adam remain in Paradise without committing a sin?' a woman asked her dearest husband recently. 'Until he had a wife' was the reply.

'Y mae dyn yn arwain y wraig at yr allor' (a man leads a wife to the altar) stated *Cymhorth i Chwerthin*, 'ond yn y weithred hono y mae ei arweinyddiaeth yn dechrae ac yn diweddu yn aml' (but in that act his leadership starts and finishes).[199] Edward Matthews (1813–92), in a lecture on Luther, noted that the Pope claimed infallibility and explained: 'Dyw e ddim wedi priodi, gwelwch chi' (He never married, you see).[200] *Y Punch Cymraeg* offered even more succinct advice to young men about to marry – 'Paid' (Don't). *Y Ffraethebydd* offered more detailed but similar advice:

Cyn myned i ryfel, gweddia unwaith; cyn mynd i'r môr, gweddia ddwy-waith; a chyn myned i dy briodi, gweddia dair gwaith.[201]

Before going to war, pray once; before going to the sea, pray twice; but before going to your wedding, pray three times.

Hwcin Morris, Pont-y-meibion, watched the clerk of Llansilin pay a few pennies to a vagrant girl and her young family and voiced an *englyn* which encapsulates the tragic reality of marriage for many:

Tylodi, priodi cyn pryd, – i fythu   Poverty, marriage too soon – to fail
Ac i fethu mewn adfyd;   And flounder in a harsh world;
Plant gan blant methiantlyd,   Children of the children of failure,
Dyna'r bai sy'n diwyno'r byd.[202]   That's the fault of that breaks this world.

The wife was often the butt of simple jokes:

'Rhys, paham yr ydych yn gwisgo yr hen het salw yna?' 'Am fod fy ngwraig yn dweyd na ddaw gyda mi nes y ceisiaf het newydd' oedd yr ateb.

'Rhys, why are you wearing that silly hat?' 'Because my wife said that she won't come with me until I get a new one' was the reply.

But the wife often had both the upper hand and the final say:

'Nid oes gennyf un gair i'w ddywedyd, fy ngwraig, nid wyf byth yn dadleu ag ynfydion.' 'Na fyddwch fy ngwr, yr ydych bob amser yn sicr o gytuno a hwynt.'[203]

'I have nothing to say, my wife, I never argue with imbeciles.' 'No you never, my husband, I know, you always agree with them.'

Gofynnwyd i foneddiges gan ei chyfeillion a oedd hi mewn gwirionedd yn bwriadu priodi Mr E. yr hwn oedd yn meddu ar ffordd od iawn. 'Wel,' meddai hi, 'os ydyw yn anhebyg i ddynion eraill, y mae yn fwy tebyg o wneyd gŵr da.'[204]

A lady was asked by a friend if she really intended marrying Mr E. because he had a very odd way about him. 'Well,' she replied, 'if he's unlike other men, he's more likely to make a good husband.'

In another story, a man on his way to market complained to his wife that their horse was not available and asked how he would come home. 'Sober' was the brief and direct reply.[205]

Although some sought to foster a cult of godly sorrow, which made their religious beliefs appear gloomy, their attempt to keep laughter out of religion was futile. The most numerous jokes were on religious topics. As we have seen, many ministers filled their sermons with witticisms and humorous anecdotes. Stephen Jenkins, Dafydd Evans Llwynffortun, Rhys Glun Bren, and Evan Harries of Merthyr Tydfil ministered to their flocks on the basis that 'a merry heart doeth good like a medicine'. These jokesters of the cloth provided a happy and humane religious leadership. There are several anecdotes which reveal the simple and saintly wit of Evan Harries. Walking past an accident on a building site, his companion was shocked by the language of the unfortunate man, only to be told by Harries: 'Beth sydd yn fwy naturiol iddo, druan, na galw ar ei dad?' (What's more natural for the poor man than to call on his father?). The cheerful creed of many Welsh religious elders and ministers was recounted in *Hynodion Hen Bregethwyr Cymru, gydag Hanesion Difyrus am Danynt.*[206] Welsh religion could laugh at itself:

> Nesaodd gweinidog at fachgenyn direidus, yn nghylch deuddeg oed ac ymaflodd yn ei ysgwydd, gan ddyweyd, 'Fy machgen i, yr wyf yn credi fod y cythraul wedi cymeryd gafael arnoch.' 'Yr ydwyf finnau yn credu hyny hefyd,' ebai y bachgen yn awgrymiadol.[207]

> A minister sneaked up on a mischievous twelve-year-old boy and grabbed him by the shoulder, saying, 'I believe that a devil has got a firm grip on you.' The boy replied 'I think so too.'

Anecdotes also occasionally show a bitter side to religion. Several reveal depths of hypocrisy:

> Hen ŵr o Fethodist selog a aeth yn bur sal ar hyd yr wythnos, ac yn myned yn waeth waeth. Ei wraig yn ei gynghori nos Sadwrn i gymryd 'salts a senna'. 'Gwarchod pawb Lowri bach!' ebai'r hen ŵr cydwybodol, 'na wnaf; pe cymerwn hwynt yn awr, hwy a fyddant yn sicr o weithio ar y Sabbath.'[208]

> An old faithful Methodist had been ill all week and was continually worsening. His wife on the Saturday night advised him to take salts and senna. 'Surely Lowri bach!' said the old man, 'no I won't; if I take them now, they're sure to work on the Sabbath.'

Some stories from the late nineteenth century reveal that denominational rivalry was still active. Two ministers conversed, as they made their slow way back home, black against a blacker black, into the shadows of the night:

Gofynai'r cyfaill i'r diweddar Barch. James Richards, Pontypridd, gweinidog gyda'r Bedyddwyr, 'A ydych chwi yn adwaun Dafydd —?' 'Ydwyf,' oedd ei ateb: 'Methodist yw ef. Nid oes gennyf lawer o olwg ar Fethodist, na dim mwy o olwg ar Faptist; ond yr wyf yn caru Cristion.'[209]

A friend asked the late Revd James Richards, Pontypridd, a minister with the Baptists, 'Do you know Dafydd —?' 'Yes,' was the reply: 'he's a Methodist. I don't have much of an opinion of Methodists, and even less of Baptists; but I love Christians.'

Y Punch Cymraeg derived great fun from exposing the foibles, follies and fripperies of religious people. The hypocrites who sneaked to the back doors of pubs so that they would not be seen, and the courting couples who turned Capel Mawr, Bangor, into 'cyfnewidfa i Venus' (Venus's exchange) were all condemned by 'Mr P.'. According to 'Mr P.' the lobby of Capel Mawr was a sensual, lustful place of rustling taffetas and unlaced bodices. Some chapels and churches were more like fashion shows than religious meeting places, as the bright and the beautiful, all fur and feathers, sought to out-bonnet and out-bustle one another in the eternal fashion rivalries of one-up-woman-ship.[210] *Y Punch Cymraeg* even had the audacity to satirize the Welsh conception of heaven, which would be almost uninhabited because so few could reach the ethereal entry standards, and uninhabitable, due to the harsh conditions that prevailed there.[211] Ministers were not spared the barbs of the critics and the humorists. Some jokes were gentle reminders to ministers that humility and humanity were noble virtues which should not be forgotten. But others were stronger rebukes:

Dododd pregethwr yn y wlad ei holl gynulleidfa i gysgu ond un dyn gwirion, Sabbath, yn ddiweddar, gydai bregeth ddwl, undonol. Cynddeirigodd hyn y pregethwr yn dost, a dechreuodd ddyrnu y pwlpud yn arswydus, gan waeddi, 'Beth, y cwbl wedi cysgu ond y dyn gwirion yma?' 'Ie,' ebai y dyn gwirion, 'a buaswn inau hefyd wedi cysgu, oni buasai fy mod yn un gwirion.'[212]

On Sunday the monotonous sermon of a minister in the country sent his whole congregation to sleep, except for an idiot. This angered the minister, who struck the pulpit and shouted 'What, everyone is asleep except this idiot?' 'Yes,' said the idiot, 'and I'd be sleeping as well, but I'm an idiot.'

Cwynai y gwrandawyr wrth eu gweinidog ei fod yn darllen ei bregethau, a gofynent paham y llusgai ddarnau o bapyrau gydag ef i'r pulpud. Atebai yntai fod rhaid iddo – nas gallai gofio'r bregeth. 'Wel, wel, os ydych chwi yn methu cofio eich pregeth, pa fodd y disgwyliwch i ni ei chofio?'[213]

The listeners complained to their minister that he read his sermons, and asked why he carried so much paper with him into the pulpit. He replied that he couldn't remember his sermon. 'Well, well, if you can't remember your sermon, how do you expect us to?'

Such jocular scepticism was not uttered by people who wished to overthrow religion, but it did have an effect and was an aid to correct behaviour. Even the most respectable and respected values of Welsh life could be mocked. The history of humour reveals that the burdens imposed by beliefs and institutions were borne only because they were not always taken seriously. Laughter gave relief from the burdens of religion and respectability. The Welsh, it seems, could draw humour out of the most unlikely subjects. In the Denbigh mental hospital it was said that 200 patients were enjoying themselves at a dance:

Dywed y gohebydd fod dau gant o wallgofiaid yn mwynhau eu hunain. Dyn an helpo! Y mae'n amheus gennym a oes gynifer a hyny o bobl gall yn holl Gymru yn mwynhau eu hunain, ond gwyddom fod miloedd o ynfydion a gwallgofiaid yn cael eu gwala.[214]

A reporter said that two hundred mad people were enjoying themselves. Heaven help us! It is doubtful to us if there are that many sane people in the whole of Wales enjoying themselves, but we know that there are thousands of imbeciles and mad people enjoying themselves.

The modern world, wits and satirists observed with weary wisdom, offered the Welsh an immense variety of diversions, but none seemed to provide the escape that people so desperately needed in their lives of quiet desperation. Hope sprung eternal, heartbreak haunted many, but the fugitive happiness was almost as elusive as fairy-gold.

Conclusion

At last the curtain must fall on the diverse cast of decent and desperate characters who have featured in this work. Who do you wish to call back for the curtain call? Which characters still rattle in the sounding shell of your mind? Henry Richard, Thomas Phillips and the portly and priestly men who, for so long in historical studies of the period 1776–1871, have been allowed to speak for Wales? Or Sir Thomas Picton, tyrant and hero, whose reputation was rescued by the Napoleonic Wars? Or John Wilkinson – 'Iron John' – the libidinous, hard-faced man who looked as if he had done even better out of the wars? Or Eben Fardd, the lonely hymn-writer, who hopefully regained fellowship and friendship in his afterlife? Or the chairman of the Pembrokeshire jury who found the accused not guilty but warned him not to do it again? Or Twm o'r Nant, lumberjack, publican and playwright? Or Evan Harries, the jovial and jesting minister? Or Caddy Owens, the immoral, insatiable and inscrutable brothel madam of Holyhead? Or Elen Egryn and Ellen Quinn, who suffered unimaginable and unendurable loss and loneliness? Or Mari'r Fantell Wen, who persuaded her followers that God and the devil were still battling for souls in an age of providences, prophecies and portents?

A few of these characters may have been new to some readers, many of whom may justifiably wonder why a historian of Wales should have given so much attention to such marginal phenomena. The honest answer would be the pleasure derived in encountering historical actors like those whom we have met, and the delight that comes from remarkable stories. A more serious answer would advance the claim that the margins illuminate the centre, and that the social history of Wales is incomplete without hearing from people on the edge. 'The most intense and productive life of culture', wrote Mikhail Bakhtin, 'takes place on the boundaries.'[1] Fresh insights and new information can be found about a complex and fascinating society not just by traversing the main historical thoroughfares, but by detouring along paths less travelled. Like the giant in the fairy tale, the historian needs to realize that whenever he, or she, scents human flesh, then that is where the quarry lies. The archives are full of surprises, it is a pity that so many are left at the margins of Welsh history. They need to be incorporated into the narrative, to enrich and enliven the world that we have lost.

That lost world of Wales possessed a more complex and contradictory character than is often appreciated. It is clear that there was no one universal ambition. Glory, money, happiness, security, influence were rival attractions. It was a deeply religious society, but many were lascivious and mendacious, living their lives according to the dictates of the seven deadly sins. Contrary to the arguments of the devout, religion did not lead to a decline in magic, for superstitious practices retained their grip on minds and habits. Confronted by strange stories of spirits and the wonders of the world, many people sought an explanation in the authoritative texts of the Bible, which explained the existence of an 'invisible world' of mystical beings: God, the devil, angels and demons.[2] Religion and magic rose and fell together. Contemporaries insisted that the Welsh were a moral, pious and respectable people. But many individuals were immoral, promiscuous and raunchy. Modernity coexisted with conditions of medieval simplicity and rusticity. Some people excitedly travelled on the clanking carriages of that most novel phenomenon – the railway – while others still walked the well-trodden paths of their forefathers. Though these were hard times for many, technological change, in the years between 1776 and 1871, brought the prospect of happiness within the reach of more people, because it provided a promise of being able to control the environment, of enjoying pleasure and mitigating pain. People's fears of the agonizing pain in the jaw, and the dread of rotting teeth being butchered by itinerant tooth pullers, which was a notable feature of the late eighteenth century, began to be alleviated by improving standards of dentistry. Medical advances, vaccination, public hygiene and contraception also added the hope that the future would be more hedonic and less painful.[3] There were many noble people who campaigned for the enhancement of democracy and human rights, but others ignobly profited from slaves and slavery. Missionaries sought to Christianize and civilize native people around the world, but Welsh marauders and merchants sought to conquer and exploit them. The rule of the stern, grim-faced men in public life was only tolerated because people built defence mechanisms around themselves, one of the most important of which was humour. In order to appreciate the rich diversity of our past, the jester needs to be readmitted to Clio's court. Despite the heartbreaks which they so stoically endured, the Welsh were at heart a humorous people who actively pursued happiness.

Happiness and heartbreak, ambition and anxiety, life and death, faith and folly, sex and violence, and the other themes that we have considered in this book, are powerful themes which encompass all human life. Though they are timeless themes at the heart of the tragedy of the human condition, they are also deeply rooted within a particular time and place. The stories that we have studied reflect the strains and stresses of their age and society. We have considered evidence from people who were considered to be reasonable and rational, but also from some who were confused and distressed, anxious and alarmed. Some of their tales were told in fantasies and fables in which curious things happened, or may have happened, or did not happen at all. Historians are justifiably suspicious of using such evidence, preferring to adhere to the apparent objectivity and judiciousness of official documents. But these sources, too, need to be treated with care. The evidence given to royal commissioners and government enquiries was first filtered by the memory of the witness, who reshaped it for political or personal purposes, and then was further rendered into a writing style which had to conform to legal conventions by the official clerk. The process of recording imposed order on events and recollections that were originally much more chaotic. The significance of specific events varied enormously for each individual. Many of the individuals who marched on Newport behind the Chartist banners in the damp night of 3–4 November 1839 were true believers, who sincerely thought that they were creating a better world. But others got caught up in the adventure as a result of accident, boredom or bull-headed folly. In contrast to all such motives, Myfanwy Evans, a luckless servant girl, remembered the evening and its excitement as the date of her seduction, abandonment and descent into loneliness.[4]

Dependence on official sources perpetuates an injustice that was inherent in contemporary Welsh society. Those higher up the social scale in terms of their gender, reputation and status, because they were literate, have been allowed to control the description of contemporary events and their subsequent interpretation by posterity. Should the testimony of a gentleman, a minister or one of the *parchusion* (worthy citizens) be allowed to count for more than that of an ignorant Rebecca rioter? Should men's testimony count for more than women's? Feminist historians rightly point out that the historical record has been controlled by male professional clerical, legal and journalistic processes. More problematically, many of our witnesses, while insisting on their trustworthiness and veracity, were actually, deliberately, spinning tales of deceit. Many were as economical with the truth as the Cardi was with money. We are justifiably suspicious of a murderer's 'true confession', as we would also be of one of Shemi Wâd's tall stories. But we must also be careful in using the evidence of those people who claimed that Wales was a pure and placid land. Their evidence needs to be set against the testimony of other individuals who saw events and life from another perspective. The conflicting views that clashed, so alarmingly and damagingly, in the rumpus over the 1847 Education Report is perhaps the most dramatic example of how differently different people viewed Wales. In approaching the evidence, the historian needs to adopt the suspicion and cynicism enshrined in the letter sent by socialist idealist Robert Owen to his former partner: 'all the world is queer save thee and me, and even thou are a little queer'.[5]

Historical situations are immensely complex. There can be almost as many interpretations of events as there were participants. Social situations cannot be analysed in simplistic terms of black and white. Temperance campaigners penned spiteful pen-portraits of hard-drinking, profane, quarrelsome, cynical and dissolute people whom they considered irredeemable. The temperance press rejoiced in spiteful tales which revealed that God possessed a maliciously macabre sense of humour – blasphemers were struck down and drunkards choked to death on their beer. But these anti-heroes were heroic figures to some, who admired and aped their exploits and eccentricities. This makes historical study immensely difficult. Professor Ieuan Gwynedd Jones in a memorable seminar, delivered on yet another forgettable, rain-washed grey day in Aberystwyth, compared the social historian's task to the process of unravelling an onion. The historian patiently peels away layer after layer, eventually arriving, tearfully, at an empty core. As D. H. Lawrence said of the English novel: 'whenever you try and nail something down in the novel, the novel gets up and walks away with the nail'.[6] History is equally elusive, so that many historians no longer argue that they are engaged in a science which will yield historical truth. After a century, Lord Acton's confident declaration, when writing of the French Revolution, 'that in a few years, all will be known that ever can be known', appears to be overly optimistic, confirmation that historians, aware of the perils of hindsight, should also resist the temptations of foresight.[7] Yet, although the past might ultimately prove to be intractable, its pursuit is always instructive.

Notes

Introduction

[1] Amongst the signatories are such Welsh sounding names as William Williams, Robert Morris, Francis Lewis, Lewis Morris, John Adams, Samuel Adams, William Lloyd and Stephen Hopkins. One of them, Francis Lewis, a self-made man, the 'delegate for New York', was born in Newport (Mon.). David Williams, *Wales and America* (Cardiff, 1946), p. 49; idem, 'The contribution of Wales to the development of the "United States"', *National Library of Wales Journal*, 11, 3–4 (1942), 99–108. See also *www.co.conialhall.com/lewis/* (accessed 20 Sept. 2001) and Eben Edwards, *Welshmen as Factors* (Utica, 1899).

[2] Henry Morton Stanley, *How I Found Livingstone: Travels, Adventures and Discoveries in Central Africa* (London, 1872), pp. 411–12. See also *www.kirgasto.sci.fi/hstanley.htm* (accessed 20 Sept. 2001).

[3] I am indebted to E. G. Millward for information on Dafydd Evans, Ffynonhenri. For biographies of these characters see Benjamin Thomas (Myfyr Emlyn), *Dafydd Evans, Ffynonhenri* (Carmarthen, 1893); Henry Hughes, *Cofiant Owen Owens, Cors-y-Wlad* (Dolgellau, 1898); and J. R. Hughes, *Humour Sanctified: The Memoir of Stephen Jenkins* (Tonypandy, 1902). For an introduction to the humour of Victorian Wales see E. G. Millward, 'Y Fictoriaid yn gwenu', *Y Casglwr* (10 March 1980). Amongst the first guidebooks to humour in Welsh are: Wil Digrif, *Yr ail rhan o cymorth i chwerthin: Yn cynnwys casgliad o hanesion difyrgar, dywediadau synhwyrol, anghyffredin anarferol, a rhesymau chwerthingar* (Swansea, 182?). Sadly the first part is not available – perhaps that is part of the joke? Wil Digrif, *Cymorth i Chwerthin: Gan Gynnwys Casgliad o Hanesion Difyrgar . . . Wedi eu Gasglu gan Twm Digrif ac Ychwanegu Ato Gan ei Fab Wil Digrif* (Carmarthen, 182?); W. M. Evans, *Y Ffraethebwr: Yn Cynnwys Casgliad o Ffraethebion, Ffraith – Ddywediadau, Byr-chwedleuon . . .* (Caerfyrddin, 1908).

[4] John Elias wrote to F. Carmichael of Llysdulas, Amlwch, on 25 October 1822, to explain the effects of revivals upon the behaviour of Welsh Nonconformist congregations. Though most congregations Elias explained were quiet, many 'made a great noise' because:

> our Lord in his mercy called many wild, and presumptuous sinners from darkness to light . . . Most of them who cry out in the congregations are

> under great concern about their souls, and the bodies of some are seized
> with trembling, fainting and convulsive motions . . . when the revelation of
> salvation comes they rejoice with joy unspeakable and full of Glory . . . and
> who can blame them for praising the Redeemer and sing his praises out
> loud?

National Library of Wales (NLW) MS 11,721C. See below, Chap. 6.

5   I am indebted to Robin Gwyndaf for his kindness in allowing me access to his
     collection of nineteenth- and twentieth-century joke books. These are discussed
     in Chap. 7 below.

6   There are several excellent biographies of Henry Morton Stanley, see Richard
     Hall, *Stanley: An Adventurer Explained* (London, 1974); Emyr Wyn Jones, *Sir
     Henry M. Stanley: The Enigma, Review of the Early Years* (Denbigh, 1989); and
     Frank McLyn, *Stanley: Sorcerer's Apprentice* (Oxford, 1992). Stanley's personal
     papers are in the Swansea Archive and Records Office, City Hall, Swansea.

7   K. O. Morgan, *Wales in British Politics, 1868–1922* (Cardiff, 1970), p. 92; idem,
     'Gladstone and Wales', *Welsh History Review*, 1, 1 (1960); idem, 'Liberals,
     Nationalists and Mr Gladstone', *Transactions of the Honourable Society of
     Cymmrodorion* (1960), 36–52.

8   Thomas Williams has received some biographical attention; see for example,
     J. R. Harries, *The Copper King: A Biography of Thomas Williams* (Liverpool,
     1964).

9   See, for example, G. E. Owen, 'Welsh anti-slavery sentiment: a survey of public
     opinion' (Unpublished MA thesis, University of Wales, Aberystwyth, 1964).

10   Nathaniel Phillips's papers are catalogued in the National Library of Wales.
     There are valuable studies of Phillips by Clare Taylor, 'The journal of an
     absentee proprietor, Nathaniel Phillips of Slebech', *Journal of Caribbean
     History*, 18, 2 (1982); eadem, 'Last days at Phillipsfield and Pleasant Hill',
     Bulletin of the Jamaican Historical Society, 7, 9 (March 1979); eadem, 'The
     perils of a West Indian heiress: case studies of the heiresses of Nathaniel
     Phillips of Slebach', *Welsh History Review*, 12, 4 (1985), 495–513; and eadem,
     'An absentee planter returns to his family: Dr John Gray's travels', *Bulletin of
     the Jamaican Historical Society*, 8, 12 (December 1982).

11   Some examples are the Pennants, see Alistair Hennesy, 'Penrhyn Castle',
     History Today, 45 (January 1995), 40–6; and Jean Lindsay, 'The Pennants and
     Jamaica 1665–1808', *Transactions of the Caernarfonshire Historical Society*,
     part 1, 43 (1982), 37–83, and part 2, 44 (1983), 59–96. For the Glynnes' and
     Gladstone's links to slavery, see Philip Magnus, *Gladstone* (London, 1970 edn),
     pp. 2–3; and Roy Jenkins, *Gladstone* (London, 1996 edn), pp. 6–7.

12   At least four of the largest slave plantations in the West Indies had strong links
     to Wales. These were 'Wales', 'Pennant', 'Denbigh' and 'Williams', see J. R.
     Ward, *British West Indian Slavery, 1750–1834* (Oxford, 1988), pp. 73, 154–8, 200
     and 228. See also Kenneth Morgan, *Slavery, Atlantic Trade and the British
     Economy, 1660–1800* (Cambridge, 2000).

13   Ben Bowen Thomas, *Drych y Baledwr* (Aberystwyth, 1958), pp. 50–1.

14   A remarkably biased approach is given by the anonymous author of

Gwrthrhyfel yn yr Iwerddon yn 1798 yn narostyngiad yr hwn y cymerwyd rhan gan Syr Watkin Williams Wynn, Barwniad o Wynnstay (Caernarfon, *c.*18??). In this version of events, Sir Watkin and his troops, outnumbered, bravely fought against insurmountable odds. For a more balanced view, see A. T. Q. Stewart, *The Summer Soldiers: The 1798 Rebellion in Antrim and Down* (Belfast, 1997), p. 37; Daniel Gahan, *The People's Rising: Wexford, 1798* (Dublin, 1995), p. 162; and Dáire Keogh and Nicholas Furlong, *The Mighty Wave: The 1798 Rebellion in Wexford* (Dublin, 1996), pp. 21, 124.

15 V. S. Naipaul, *The Loss of El Dorado: A Colonial History* (London, 2001 edn) gives several descriptions of the punishments inflicted during Thomas Picton's governorship, for example:

> after hanging the Negro the executioner took Bouqui's body down and cut off the head. The headless body was tied to a stake. The head was taken away and spiked on a pole on the mountain road to St Joseph . . . Pierre François was chained to the stake with the headless body. He was made to put on a shirt. The shirt was filled with sulphur. The jail Negroes built up the faggots. The executioner lit the fire. (p. 192)

For a less sensationalist but critical appraisal, see Alan Burns, *History of the British West Indies* (London, 1954) and Hugh Thomas, *The Slave Trade: The History of the Atlantic Slave Trade 1440–1870* (London, 1997). For Sir Thomas Picton, see Robert Havard, *Wellington's Welsh General: A Life of Sir Thomas Picton* (London, 1996) and Frederick Myatt, *Peninsular General: Sir Thomas Picton* (Newton Abbot, 1980).

16 On Sir William Nott see J. H. Stocqueler, *Memoirs and Correspondence of Major-General Sir William Nott* (London, 1854).

17 For John Thomas see T. Mardy Rees, *Noteable Welshmen* (Caernarvon, 1908), p. 127. For Captain Thomas Foley see Francis Jones, *A Treasury of Historic Pembrokeshire* (Brawdy Books, 1999), p. 179 and *www.stvincent.ac.uk/Heritage1797/people/foley.html* (accessed 19 Feb. 2003).

18 For John Corbett from Pontypool, see Jackie Dunn, 'John Corbett, A Peninsular Veteran', *Gwent Family History Society Journal*, 34 (1993), 15–17 and 36 (1994), 28–9.

19 On the debate over the dates of the eighteenth and nineteenth centuries see Linda Colley, 'The politics of eighteenth century British history', *Journal of British Studies,* 25 (1986), 359–79; and Mark Bevir, 'The long nineteenth century in intellectual history', *Journal of Victorian Culture*, 62 (Autumn 2001), 313–35.

20 On these themes see Prys Morgan, *Dyma'r Wyddfa a'i Chriw: Y Cymry a'u Mynyddoedd, 1700–1860* (Aberystwyth, 2002); Robert M. Morris, *Gweled Gwlad: Cymru Trwy Lygaid Arlunwyr* (Aberystwyth, 1991); and Malcolm Andrews, *The Search for the Picturesque: Landscape Aesthetics and Tourism in Britain, 1760–1800* (Aldershot, 1990).

21 See, for example, *Y Gwladgarwr*, 3, 29 (May 1835) for the behaviour of 'Y Behemoth neu'r Afon-Farch' (hippopotamus); or 3, 30 (June 1835) for the discovery of 'Y Lysard' (the chameleon); or 3, 33, for details of an expedition to the Eskimos.

22 *Seren Gomer*, passim, 1824–53. The edition of February 1853, p. 449, has a superb line-drawing of a missionary baptizing natives in Haiti.

23 For a general discussion of the development of Swansea see Glanmor Williams (ed.), *Swansea: An Illustrated History* (Llandybïe, 1990). For the development of the global economy see C. A. Bayley, *The Birth of the Modern World 1780–1914: Global Connections and Comparisons* (London, 2003).

24 W. J. Lewis, 'Lead mining in Cardiganshire', in Geraint H. Jenkins and Ieuan Gwynedd Jones (eds), *Cardiganshire County History*, vol. 3, *Cardiganshire in Modern Times* (Cardiff, 1998), p. 168.

25 For Richard Trevethick's experiments with stream see *www.spartacus. schoolnet.co.uk/ratrevithic.hlm* (accessed 1 Jan. 2002).

26 The longevity of superstitious practices and beliefs is discussed in Chap. 6.

27 Peter Lord, *Clarence Whaite and the Welsh Art World: The Betws-y-Coed Artist's Colony 1844–1914* (Aberystwyth, 1998), p. 131.

28 Eric Hobsbawm and Terence Ranger, *The Invention of Tradition* (Cambridge, 1982), especially the chapter by Prys Morgan, 'From death to a view: the hunt for the Welsh past in the romantic period', pp. 43–100.

29 Gwyn A. Williams, *Excalibur: The Search for Arthur* (London, 1994); see also Maurice Keen, *Chivalry* (London, 1984).

30 *The Cambrian* (18 October 1824).

31 Many of the nobility who journeyed to the continent kept journals or sent letters during their tours. See, for example, NLW MSS 17, 133A, Journal of a Continental Tour made in 1824 by Phillip Davies; NLW Glansevern 6,485–90, letters of William Earle from Rome, Florence and Piza to Anne Warburton Owen of Glansevern, Montgomeryshire 1829–36; NLW Glynne of Hawarden Nos 58–61, Journal of a Continental Tour; and NLW Harpton Court 2749, Journal of a Continental Tour of Mrs Harriet Lewis, 1832–3.

32 T. Mardy Rees, *Welsh Painters, Engravers and Sculptors* (Caernarfon, n.d.), p. 150.

33 Amongst the most notable are John Davies, *A History of Wales* (London 1993); Gwyn A. Williams, *When was Wales? A History of the Welsh* (London, 1985); K. O. Morgan, *Wales: Rebirth of a Nation: 1880–1980* (Cardiff and Oxford, 1982); and Geraint H. Jenkins, *The Foundations of Modern Wales: Wales 1642–1780* (Cardiff and Oxford, 1987); and David J. V. Jones, *Rebecca's Children: A Study of Rural Society, Crime and Protest* (Oxford, 1989).

34 Two well structured works on the period 1776–1871 are Neil Evans, '"As rich as California": opening and closing the frontier, Wales 1780–1870', in Gareth Elwyn Jones and Dai Smith (eds), *The People of Wales* (Cardiff, 1999); and D. Gareth Evans, *A History of Wales, 1815–1906* (Cardiff, 1989).

35 Authors of works on the history of 'primitive' or less developed societies have been particularly inventive in showing the non-linear development of time, see, for example, Jay Grififths, *Pip Pip: A Sideways Look at Time* (London, 2000); and Tim Flannery, *Throwim Way Leg: Adventures in the Jungles of New Guinea* (London, 1998).

36 For an attempt to study some of these themes in a Welsh context see Russell Davies, *Secret Sins: Sex, Violence and Society in Carmarthenshire 1870–1920* (Cardiff, 1996).

[37] Quoted in Geraint H. Jenkins, *Facts, Fantasy and Fiction: The Historical Vision of Iolo Morganwg* (Aberystwyth, 1997), p. 17, f. 4.

[38] A superb example of the Nonconformist school of historiography is the work of R. Tudur Jones, *Ffydd ac Argyfwng Cenedl*, 2 vols (Swansea, 1981 and 1982). For an English translation see Robert Pope (ed.), *Faith and the Crisis of a Nation* (Cardiff, 2004). For the 'labour' school see Gwyn A. Williams, *When was Wales?* For an interesting criticism of the traditional labour interpretation of Welsh history see Julie Light, 'Manufacturing the past: the representation of mining communities in history, literature and heritage . . . Fantasies of a world that never was', *Llafur*, 3, 1 (2000), 5–18.

[39] The best example of this view of Welsh history is Gwynfor Evans, *Aros Mae* (Swansea, 1971), translated as *Land of my Fathers;* and idem, *The Fight for Welsh Freedom* (Talybont, 2000).

[40] *The Cambrian* (4, 11 and 18 June 1831). The report of 11 June gives a vivid account of the Coffin family's fears that they would be killed by the mob, or burnt to death in their 'room of refuge'.

[41] Ieuan Gwynedd Jones and David Williams, *The Religious Census of 1851: A Calendar of the Returns Relating to Wales*, vol. 1, *South Wales* (Cardiff, 1976); and Ieuan Gwynedd Jones (ed.), vol. 2, *North Wales* (Cardiff, 1981).

[42] Anthony Jones, *Welsh Chapels* (Cardiff, 1996 edn) provides an excellent introduction and overview of the architectural history of Welsh chapels. Ieuan Gwynedd Jones provides a number of insightful discussions of the building of churches in Wales in *Communities: Essays in the Social History of Victorian Wales* (Llandysul, 1987), pp. 3–104.

[43] Jan Morris, *Venice* (London, 1993 edn), p. 71.

[44] The review appeared in *Llais Llyfrau: Books from Wales* (Autumn 1996), p. 14.

[45] For example, in Hywel Teifi Edwards (ed.), *Cwm Rhondda* (Llandysul, 1995); idem, *Cwm Aman* (Llandysul, 1996); idem, *Cwm Tawe* (Llandysul, 1993); idem, *Llyfni ac Afan, Garw ac Ogwr* (Llandysul, 1998); idem, *Cwm Gwendraeth* (Llandysul, 2000); and Geraint H. Jenkins (ed.), *Language and Community in the Nineteenth Century* (Cardiff, 1998).

[46] *Rape of the Fair Country* is the title of a very popular novel by Alexander Cordell (London, 1959).

[47] On Robert Owen see *The Life of Robert Owen By Himself* (London, 1857); and G. D. H. Cole, *Robert Owen* (London, 1925).

[48] Two biographies of David Davies have been published, the hagiographic Ivor Thomas, *Top Sawyer: A Biography of David Davies Llandinam* (London, 1938); and the more reliable Herbert Williams, *Davies the Ocean: Railway King and Coal Tycoon* (Cardiff, 1991).

[49] There is an extensive literature on Alfred Russel Wallace. His reputation has recently undergone a welcome revival, particularly amongst American scholars. See Alfred Russel Wallace, *My Life: A Record of Events and Opinions*, 2 vols (London, 1905); John R. Brooks, *Just Before the Origin: Alfred Russel Wallace's Theory of Evolution* (New York, 1984); Charles H. Smith, *Alfred Russel Wallace: An Anthology of his Shorter Writings* (Oxford, 1991); James A. Second, *Victorian Sensation: The Extraordinary Publication, Reception and*

Secret Authorship of the Natural History of Creation (Chicago, 2001); and Peter
Ruby, *Alfred Russel Wallace: A Life* (London, 2001). The quotations are from
Jane R. Camerini, *The Alfred Russel Wallace Reader: A Selection of Writings
from the Field* (London, 2002), p. 31.

[50] William Llewelyn Davies (ed.), *Y Bywgraffiadur Cymreig Hyd 1940* (London,
1953), pp. 105, 603, 900 and 991. Hereafter all references are to the English-
language equivalent, *Dictionary of Welsh Biography down to 1940* (*DWB*).

[51] *www.multiweb.ruralwales.net/~history.powys.org.uk* (accessed 9 Nov. 2003).

[52] A statue of Henry Richard stands on the square in Tregaron, waiting for his
modern biographer. Eleanor Roberts, *Bywyd a Gwaith Henry Richard A.S.*
(Wrexham, 1902); and Charles S. Miall, *Henry Richard M.P.: A Biography*
(London, 1889) are the only full-scale biographies to appear so far.

[53] Published in Machynlleth in 1854. For a discussion of the reaction of the Welsh
press to the Crimean War see P. H. Jones, 'Yr amserau a rhyfel y Crimea', *Y
Casglwr*, 43 (March 1991), 19. For many the Tsar was the enemy, see David
William Pughe, *Hanes bywyd Nicholas y Cyntaf, ymerawdwr holl Rwsia, etc yn
cynnwys ei ymddygiadau personol . . . a'i ymryfaelion estronol, yn nghyd a
crynhoad o hanes cenedl y Rwsiaid o amser ei chynflaenor, Ruric, hyd y rhyfel
presenol* (Caernarfon, 1855).

[54] A. J. P. Taylor, *The Struggle for Mastery in Europe, 1848–1918* (Oxford, 1973).

[55] For the action of the Royal Carmarthenshire Militia see *The Cambrian*
(2 December 1814); for the Swansea Volunteer Cavalry see *The Cambrian*
(26 October 1816), and for the Mold Yeomany and Royal Maylor Cavalry see
the *North Wales Gazette* (6 April 1826). The military tradition of Wales still
awaits substantial historical attention.

[56] Quoted in Roy Palmer, *The Folklore of Radnorshire* (Little Logaston, 2001),
p. 154.

[57] Douglas Porch, *War and Society* (London, 2001) has a useful chronology of
nineteenth-century wars. For the obscure wars of Empire see Byron Farwell,
Queen Victoria's Little Wars (London, 1973).

[58] *DWB*.

[59] Thomas Williams wrote his autobiography. See Gerald Morgan's highly enter-
taining *Lle Diogel i Sobri: Hunangofiant Capelulo* (Llanrwst, 1982). One of Jack
Matthews's descendants has gathered material in an interesting memoir which
is available in Cardiff Central Library; see E. O'Neil, 'The notorious Jack
Matthews'. For a highly sensational report on 'Betsy' Gibbs see *North Wales
Chronicle* (7 December 1850). For John Roberts see *Caernarvon and Denbigh
Herald* (13 August 1853); a graphic account of Susannah Rider's assault on her
22-year-old daughter (she thrust a broom inside her vagina – 'gwthiodd
ysgubell i fynny ei gwendid') is described in *Seren Gomer* (January 1846). The
murderous career of the psychopathic Isaac Davies is given in Dafydd Meirion,
Cymry Gwyllt y Gorllewin (Talybont, 2002).

[60] For the *Annales* methodology see Peter Burke (ed.), *A New Kind of History from
the Writings of Febvre* (London, 1973); Michelle Vovelle, *Ideologies and
Mentalities*, trans. Eamon O'Flaherty (London, 1990); and Paul Ricoeur, *The
Contribution of French Historiography to the Theory of History* (Oxford, 1980).

A similar multi-biographical approach is Luigi Barzini, *The Italians* (Harmondsworth, 1968).

[61] Sir Lewis Namier, *Skyscrapers and Other Essays* (London, 1931), p. 46.

[62] L. J. Williams, *Was Wales Industrialised? Essays in Modern Welsh History* (Llandysul, 1995).

[63] Chris Evans, *'The Labyrinth of Flames': Work and Social Conflict in Early Industrial Merthyr Tydfil* (Cardiff, 1993).

[64] The assertion was originally made by David Jenkins in 'Aberporth', in Alwyn D. Rees and Elwyn Davies (eds), *Welsh Rural Communities* (Cardiff, 1960), p. 53. For a discussion see C. Barber and David Howell, 'Wales', in F. M. L. Thompson (ed.), *The Cambridge Social History of Britain 1750–1950*, vol. 1 (Cambridge, 1990), pp. 281–354, especially p. 331.

[65] An excellent introduction to the contentious and confusing issue of class is David Cannadine, *Class in Britain* (London, 1997).

[66] *The Cambrian* (29 January 1820).

[67] The couples were Lady Eleanor Butler and Sarah Ponsonby (the Ladies of Llangollen), see Elizabeth Mavor, *The Ladies of Llangollen: A Study in Romantic Friendship* (Harmondsworth, 2001 edn); and Mary Lloyd and Frances Cobbe who were buried in the same grave in Llanelltud churchyard near Dolgellau, see T. Mardy Rees, *Notable Welshmen*, p. 103.

[68] There is a wealth of material on the sexual lives of the Victorians. Amongst the most insightful and informative are Frazer Harrison, *The Dark Angel: Aspects of Victorian Sexuality* (London, 1979); Cyril Pearl, *The Girl with the Swansdown Seat* (London, 1980); Ronald Pearsall, *The Worm in the Bud: The World of Victorian Sexuality* (London, 1983); Michael Mason, *The Making of Victorian Sexuality* (Oxford, 1994); Jeffrey Weeks, *Sex, Politics and Society: The Regulation of Sexuality since 1800* (London, 1981); and Françoise Barret-Ducroco, *Love in the Time of Victoria* (London, 1991).

[69] For a discussion see S. Minwel Tibbott, *Domestic Life in Wales* (Cardiff, 2002), pp. 129–39.

[70] For an interesting appraisal of Thomas and Sally Charles's relationship see Gwen Emyr, *Sally Jones: Rhodd Duw i Charles* (Bridgend, 1996).

[71] The painting of the weavers can be seen in the National Library of Wales (NLW, PE4899, slide no. 2323).

[72] For the two watercolours of coal mines in the south see Peter Lord, *The Visual Culture of Wales: Industrial Society* (Cardiff, 1998), p. 28.

[73] Martha Vicunus (ed.), *Suffer and Be Still: Women in the Victorian Age* (London, 1972); Brian Harrison, *'Separate Spheres': The Opposition to Women's Suffrage in Britain* (London, 1978); and Robert B. Shoemaker, *Gender in English Society, 1650–1850: The Emergence of Separate Spheres* (London, 1998).

[74] See J. Williams-Davies, ' "Merched y Gerddi": a seasonal migration of female labour from rural Wales', *Folk Life*, 15 (1977), 12–26; and the *Royal Commission on Women and Children in Agriculture*, PP1870, appendix O, p. 40.

[75] On Jemima Nicholas, see Stuart Jones, *The Last Invasion of Britain* (Cardiff, 1950), pp. 104–5; whilst for 'Betsy Cadwaladr' see Jane Williams (ed.), *The Autobiography of Elizabeth Davies (Betsy Cadwaladyr): A Balaclava Nurse* (Cardiff, 1987).

76 *www.hms.or.uk/nelsonsnavywomen.htm* (accessed 9 Nov. 2002). The role of the
Welsh in the naval history of Britain has been much neglected. John Cresswell's
British Admirals of the Eighteenth Century (London, 1972) does not include a
single Welshman, although Edwards, Foley and Gill were highly influential
figures in the late eighteenth-century navy.

77 See below, Chap. 3.

78 Two poets whose muse was suffused in death were O. Gethin Jones and Elin
Egryn. See E. Humphreys (ed.), *Gweithiau Gethin* (Llanrwst, 1884); and
W. Rees (ed.), *Telyn Egryn: Neu Gyfansoddiadau Awenyddol Miss Ellin Evans*
(Elin Egrin) (Dolgellau, 1850). This has recently been reprinted: *Telyn Egryn*,
ed. Kathryn Hughes and Ceridwen Lloyd-Morgan (Aberystwyth, 2001).

79 Declan Kiberd, *Inventing Ireland: The Literature of the Modern Nation*
(London, 1996), p. 38.

80 E. Wyn James, *Dechrau Canu: Rhai Emynau Mawr a'u Cefndir* (Bridgend,
1993).

81 The most famous female hymn-writer was Ann Griffiths. Useful collections of
her life and career are Dyfnallt Morgan (ed.), *Y Ferch o Ddolwar Fach*
(Caernarfon, 1977); and Siân Megan, *Gwaith Ann Griffiths* (Llandybïe, 1982).
An older but still interesting work is W. Caledfryn Williams, *Cofiant Ann
Griffiths . . . ynghyd â'i Llythyron a'i Hymnau* (Denbigh, 1865). Another notable
female hymn-writer was Margaret Davies of Llangeitho, Cardiganshire. NLW
MS 12,284 A.

82 On the history of the press in Wales see Aled Gruffydd Jones, *Press, Politics and
Society: A History of Journalism in Wales* (Cardiff, 1993); and Huw Walters's
monumental and magisterial *Llyfryddiaeth Cylchgronau Cymreig 1735–1850: A
Bibliography of Welsh Periodicals 1735–1850* (Aberystwyth, 1993) and
*Llyfryddiaeth Cylchgronau Cymreig 1851–1900: A Bibliography of Welsh
Periodicals 1851–1900* (Aberystwyth, 2003).

83 I am grateful to Peter Goodall of Swansea prison for copies of documents later
published in his *For Whom the Bell Tolls: A Century of Executions* (Llandysul,
2001). For Abel Ovans see the *Monmouthshire Merlin* (16 April 1852).

84 On these themes see Richard Cobb, *Reactions to the French Revolution* (Oxford,
1971); idem, *The Police and the People: French Popular Protest, 1789–1820*
(Oxford, 1970); David Smith, 'What does history know of nailbiting?', *Llafur*,
1, 2 (1970), 34–41; and Theodore Zeldin, 'Personal history and the history of
the emotions', *Journal of Social History*, 15, 3 (1982), 339–47.

85 Bethan Phillips, *Dihirod Dyfed* (Cardiff, 1988); Peter Fuller and Brian Knapp,
Welsh Murders, Vol. 1, *1770–1918* (Llandybïe, 1986), pp. 149–61.

86 The mysterious murderer's escape was reported in the *Caernarvon and Denbigh
Herald* (13 August 1853).

87 David J. V. Jones, *Crime in Nineteenth Century Wales* (Cardiff, 1992) provides a
valuable overview of the history of crime in Wales.

88 Two books which engage with these themes are Herbert Asbury, *Gangs of New
York: An Informal History of the Underworld* (London, 2002); and Luc Sante,
*Low Life: Drinking, Drugging, Whoring, Murder, Corruption, Vice and
Miscellaneous Mayhem in Old New York* (London, 1998).

89 This theme of violence against a background of bucolic tranquillity is discussed in John Cornwell, *Earth to Earth* (Harmondsworth, 1984); and Brendan Quayle, 'A village apart', *New Society* (19 April 1984).

90 David J. V. Jones, *Before Rebecca: Popular Protests in Wales 1793–1835* (London, 1973); idem, *The Last Rising: The Newport Chartist Insurrection of 1839* (Cardiff, 1999); idem, *Rebecca's Children: A Study of Rural Society, Crime and Protest* (Oxford, 1989); Trevor Herbert and Gareth Elwyn Jones, *People and Protest: Wales 1815–1880* (Cardiff, 1988); David Williams, *The Rebecca Riots* (Cardiff, 1971); Gwyn A. Williams, *The Merthyr Rising* (London, 1978); Ivor Wilkes, *South Wales and the Rising of 1839* (Llandysul, 1989).

91 Neil Evans 'The urbanization of Welsh society', in Gareth Elwyn Jones and Trevor Herbert (eds), *People and Protest: Wales 1815–1880* (Cardiff, 1988), pp. 7–38.

92 For a succinct discussion of riots in north Wales see Tim Jones, *Rioting in North East Wales 1536–1918* (Wrexham, 1997).

93 Jenny and Mike Griffiths, *The Mold Tragedy of 1869* (Llanrwst, 2001).

94 For riots linked to the 1868 election see the *Monmouthshire Merlin* (23 November 1868).

95 Peter Goodall, *For Whom the Bell Tolls*. For a contemporary report see *The Cambrian* (20 March 1858).

96 For the execution of Thomas Thomas see the *Carmarthen Journal* (11 April 1845); for Robert Coe see *The Cambrian* (12 April 1866); for 'Yr Hwntw Mawr' see Hugh J. Owen, 'The common gaols of Merionethshire during the eighteenth and nineteenth centuries', *Journal of the Merioneth Historical and Records Society*, 11, 1 (1957), 15–17. A useful survey of punishment in Wales is given in Glyn Parry, *Naid i Dragwyddoldeb: Trosedd a Chosb 1700–1900* (Aberystwyth, 2001), p. 34.

97 For details of the mass meetings held throughout Wales in support of the Elementary Education Act see the *Monmouthshire Merlin* (16 December 1870).

98 V. A. C. Gatrell, *The Hanging Tree: Execution and the English People 1770–1868* (Oxford, 1994) is a superb account. Chap. 1 assesses the importance of the event for the crowd.

99 Quoted in Carlo Ginzberg, *The Cheese and the Worms: The Cosmos of a Sixteenth-century Miller* (London, 1980), p. xxvi.

1: The Reshaping of Everyday Life

1 For a general survey of tourism in Wales, see Peter Howel Williams, 'The causes and effects of tourism in north Wales 1750–1850' (Unpublished Ph.D. thesis, University of Wales, Aberystwyth, 2000).

2 T. Medwin, *An Angler in Wales*, 2 vols (1834), preface, p. xii.

3 Richard Ayton and William Daniel, *A Voyage Around Great Britain, undertaken in the summer of the year 1813 and commencing from Land's End Cornwall*, 8 vols (London, 1813–25), vol. 1, p. 230.

4 Peter Humphreys, *On the Trail of Turner in North and South Wales* (Cardiff, 2001), p. 11.

5   Roger Thomas, *The Welsh Quotation Book* (London, 1998), p. 51.
6   Malcolm Andrews, *The Search for the Picturesque: Landscape and Aesthetics and Tourism in Britain, 1760–1800* (Aldershot, 1989), p. 112.
7   Paul Joyner (ed.), *Dolbadarn: Studies on a Theme* (Aberystwyth, 1990).
8   William Gilpin, *Observations on the River Wye, and several parts of South Wales* . . . (London, 1782), pp. 7–8.
9   Revd Richard Warner, *A Walk Through Wales in August 1797* (Bath, 1798), p. 28.
10 W. Wigstead, *Remarks on a Tour to North and South Wales in the Year 1797* (London, 1800), p. 32.
11 Samuel Jackson Pratt, *Gleanings through Wales, Holland and Westphalia* (London, 1795), p. 109.
12 On these themes, see Chap. 5 below.
13 Peter Lord, *The Visual Culture of Wales: Industrial Society* (Cardiff, 1998), p. 32.
14 Mr and Mrs S. C. Hall, *The Book of South Wales, the Wye and the Coast* (London, 1861), p. 292.
15 John Williams, *A Digest of Welsh Historical Statistics*, vol. 1 (Pontypool, 1985), passim. David Williams, 'A note on the population of Wales, 1536–1801', *Bulletin of the Board of Celtic Studies*, 8 (1937), 359–63.
16 David Williams, 'Note on population'; Gwyn A Williams, *When was Wales? A History of the Welsh* (London, 1985), pp. 173–81.
17 *Annual Reports of the Registrar General, 1837–71* (copies available in the National Library of Wales, Aberystwyth). For a graphic evocation of the death rate in Wales in the nineteenth century, see Gareth Jones, 'The grim reaper', *Dyfed Family History Journal*, 6, 6 (1993), 224–7; and R. U. Sayce, 'Need years and need foods', *Montgomery Collections*, 53 (1953), 55–80.
18 Brinley Thomas, *Migration and Economic Growth* (Cambridge, 1954); idem, *The Welsh Economy* (Cardiff, 1962).
19 J. D. Chambers and G. E. Mingay, *The Agricultural Revolution* (London, 1967); A. W. Ashby and I. L. Evans, *The Agriculture of Wales and Monmouthshire* (Cardiff, 1944); A. Martin, 'Agriculture', in B. Thomas (ed.), *The Welsh Economy* (Cardiff, 1962), pp. 76–83. There is an useful survey of the agricultural and industrial development of Wales by D. W. Howell and C. Baber in F. M. L. Thompson (ed.), *The Cambridge Social History of Britain, 1750–1950*, Vol. 1, *Regions and Communities* (Cambridge, 1990), pp. 281–354.
20 These themes are discussed in a European context by Martin Daunton, 'The wealth of the nation', in Paul Langford (ed.), *The Eighteenth Century* (Oxford, 2002), pp. 141–82; idem, 'Society and economic life', in Colin Matthew (ed.), *The Nineteenth Century* (Oxford, 2000), pp. 41–84; and Sheilagh Ogilvie, 'The European economy in the eighteenth century', in T. C. W. Blanning (ed.), *The Eighteenth Century* (Oxford, 2000), pp. 91–130.
21 'Enclosing common land', in Jane R. Camerini (ed.), *The Alfred Russel Wallace Reader* (London, 2002), pp. 28–9. For a general introduction, see M. Williams, 'The enclosure and reclamation of waste land in England and Wales in the eighteenth and nineteenth centuries', *Transactions of the Institute of British*

Geographers, 51 (1970), passim; and G. E. Mingay, *Parliamentary Enclosure in England: An Introduction to its Causes, Incidence and Impact, 1750–1850* (London, 1997).

[22] R. J. Colyer, 'The enclosure and drainage of Cors Fochno', *Ceredigion*, 8 (1977), 182; Alun Eurig Davies, 'Enclosures in Cardiganshire', *Ceredigion*, 8 (1976), 100–40; and Richard Phillips, 'Amgau tir ar Fynydd Bach', *Ceredigion*, 6, 4 (1971), 350–63.

[23] Ieuan E. Jones, 'The Arwystli enclosures 1816–1828', *Montgomery Collections*, 71 (1983), 61–70, and idem, 'The enclosure of the Llanidloes and Caersws Commons', *Montgomery Collections*, 73 (1985), 54–69.

[24] Gwenfair Parry, 'Queen of the Welsh resorts: tourism and the Welsh language in Llandudno in the nineteenth century', *Welsh History Review*, 21, 1 (2002), 120.

[25] John Davies, *The Making of Wales* (Cardiff, 1996), p. 95.

[26] Alun Eurig Davies, 'Enclosures', 104.

[27] NLW Llidiardau MS (unnumbered).

[28] Alun Eurig Davies, 'Enclosures', 103.

[29] David Williams, ' "Rhyfel y Sais Bach", an enclosure riot on Mynydd Bach', *Ceredigion*, 11 (1952), 39–52.

[30] David J. V. Jones, *Before Rebecca: Popular Protests in Wales 1793–1835* (London, 1973).

[31] *Report and Minutes of Evidence of the Select Committee on Common Inclosure*, BPP 7, p. 219.

[32] See Chap. 4 below.

[33] Quoted in David J. V. Jones, *Rebecca's Children: A Study of Rural Society, Crime and Protest* (Oxford, 1989), p. 285.

[34] Glyn Tegai Hughes (ed.), *Gregynog* (Cardiff, 1977), p. 70.

[35] *North Wales Gazette* (6 October 1814).

[36] *North Wales Gazette* (26 January and 18 February 1808).

[37] Albinia Lucy Cust, *Chronicles of Erthig*, vol. 2 (London, 1914), pp. 40–1.

[38] *Monmouthshire Merlin* (23 December 1837).

[39] Richard J. Moore-Colyer (ed.), *A Land of Pure Delight: Selections from the Letters of Thomas Johnes of Hafod, Cardiganshire (1748–1816)* (Llandysul, 1992), p. 252. His correspondence reveals that Johnes was obsessed with progress and seemed determined to make agriculture pay, irrespective of the cost.

[40] M. H. Jones, *Trevecka Letters* (Caernarfon, 1932), p. 185.

[41] *Bye-gones* (1888), p. 21. Richard Colyer, 'Early agricultural societies in south Wales', *Welsh History Review*, 12, 4 (1985), 567–81.

[42] *North Wales Gazette* (1 September 1814).

[43] Robert Clutterbuck, 'Journal of a Tour, from Cardiff, Glamorganshire, through South and North Wales in the summer of 1794', Cardiff Central Library MS 3,277.

[44] William Plomer (ed.), *Kilvert's Diary* (London, 1964), p. 47.

[45] J. Geraint Jenkins, *Life and Tradition in Rural Wales* (London, 1976), p. 57.

[46] T. C. Evans (Cadrawd), 'Ploughing with oxen in Glamorgan', *Canu Gwerin*, 14 (1991), 30–9; Ffrancis Payne, *Yr Aradr Gymreig* (Cardiff, 1954), pp. 110–11.

[47] W. Davies, *A General View of the Agriculture and Domestic Economy of North Wales* (London, 1810), chap. 5.

[48] Ibid.

[49] J. Geraint Jenkins, *Life and Tradition*, p. 59.

[50] Ibid., p. 87.

[51] On the early origins of money in the Welsh economy and the transfer away from a subsistence economy, see R. T. Jenkins, *Canrif o Hanes Banc Gogledd a Deheudir Cymru* (Cardiff, 1936); J. Ingman, 'Early Bangor banks', *Transactions of the Caernarfonshire Historical Society*, 5 (1944), 88–100. See also note 56 below for recent studies.

[52] John Davies, 'Agriculture in an industrial environment', in Glanmor Williams (ed.), *Glamorgan County History*, vol. 5, *Industrial Glamorgan 1700–1970* (Cardiff, 1980), p. 293.

[53] Ibid.

[54] O. Glynne Roberts, 'The Britannia bridge', *Transactions of the Anglesey Antiquarian Society* (1946), 92–112.

[55] Emlyn Richards, *Porthmyn Môn* (Caernarfon, 1998); Philip Gwyn Hughes, *Wales and the Drovers* (London, 1943).

[56] R. O. Roberts, 'Financial developments in early modern Wales and the emergence of the first banks', *Welsh History Review*, 16 (1992–3), 304–7. (I am grateful to Dr John Davies for drawing this article to my attention.) A. H. John, *The Industrial Development of South Wales 1750–1850* (Cardiff, 1950), pp. 33–53; and R. O. Roberts, 'Banks and the economic development of south Wales before 1914', in Colin Baber and L. J. Williams (eds), *Modern South Wales: Essays in Economic History* (Cardiff, 1986), pp. 65–80.

[57] Richard Colyer, *Roads and Trackways of Wales* (Ashbourne, 1984), p. 115.

[58] E. P. Williams, 'Early Victorian Denbigh', *Denbighshire Historical Society Transactions*, 22 (1973), 248.

[59] J. Geraint Jenkins, 'Rural industry in Anglesey', *Transactions of the Anglesey Antiquarian Society* (1967), 41–63,

[60] Thomas Pennant, *A Tour in Wales,* vol. 3 (London, 1783), p. 364.

[61] Richard Colyer, *Roads.*

[62] The painting is discussed in Peter Lord, *The Visual Culture of Wales: Imaging the Nation* (Cardiff, 2000), p. 196.

[63] Wirt Sikes, *Rambles and Studies in Old South Wales* (London, 1881), especially pp. 171–209. This section is drawn from this source.

[64] M. J. Baylis, 'A portrait of Thomas Makeig IV (1772–1838) of Little Scotland and Park y Pratt', *Ceredigion*, 5 (1965), 218.

[65] Lewis Lloyd, *Pwllheli: The Port and Mart of Llŷn* (Caernarfon, 1991), p. 74.

[66] There is a vast and growing literature on the industrial history of Britain in the period 1776–1871. Good general overviews are provided in M. J. Daunton, *Progress and Poverty: An Economic and Social History of Britain 1700–1850* (Oxford, 1995); Richard Price, *British Society 1680–1880: Dynamism, Entertainment and Change* (Cambridge, 1995); John Rule, *The Vital Century: England's Developing Economy, 1714–1815* (London, 1992); and E. A. Wrigley, *Continuity Change and Chance* (Cambridge, 1988). For the Welsh

context, see David Howell and C. Baber in Thompson (ed.), *Cambridge Social History*; the essays edited by W. E. Minchinton, *Industrial South Wales 1750–1914: Essays in Welsh Economic History* (London, 1969); and John Williams, *Was Wales Industrialised? Essays in Modern Welsh History* (Llandysul, 1995).

[67] Neil McKendrick, John Brewer and J. H. Plumb, *The Birth of a Consumer Society: The Commercialisation of Eighteenth-Century England* (Bloomington, 1982); John Brewer and Roy Porter (eds), *Consumption and the World of Goods* (London, 1993).

[68] The county historical society journals contain several interesting and instructive contributions to this discussion. See, for example, R. Ivor Parry, 'Aberdare and the industrial revolution', *Glamorgan Historian*, 4 (1967), 190–203; W. M. Richards, 'Some aspects of the industrial revolution in south-east Caernarvonshire', *Transactions of the Caernarfonshire Historical Society*, 5 (1944), 71–87; Stewart Williams, 'Cardiff Before 1890', *Glamorgan Historian*, 1 (1963), 104–7; A. H. Dodd, *A History of Wrexham* (Wrexham, 1957); Lewis Lloyd, *The Port of Caernarfon 1793–1900* (Caernarfon, 1989); and David Boorman, 'The port and its worldwide trade', in Glanmor Williams (ed.), *Swansea: An Illustrated History* (Llandybïe, 1990);

[69] Thomas Pennant, *Tour in Wales*, p. 281.

[70] Owen Griffith, *Mynydd Parys* (Caernarfon, 1897); John Evans, *Descriptions of Anglesey Or Mona* (London, 1810); Angharad Llwyd, *A History of the Island of Mona, or Anglesey* (Rhuthun, 1833), p. 31.

[71] J. R. Harris, *The Copper King: A Biography of Thomas Williams* (Liverpool, 1964), passim.

[72] Ronald Rees, *King Copper: South Wales and the Copper Trade 1584–1895* (Cardiff, 2000), pp. 3–23; Stephen Hughes, *Copperopolis: Landscapes of the Early Industrial Period in Swansea* (Aberystwyth, 2000), passim.

[73] Peter Lord, *Visual Culture: Industrial Society*, p. 81.

[74] Jean Lindsay, *A History of the North Wales Slate Industry* (Newton Abbot, 1974), passim; and J. Gordon Jones, 'The Ffestiniog slate industry: the industrial patterns 1831–1913', *Journal of the Merioneth Historical Society*, 5, 2 (1970), 193.

[75] T. A. Morrison, 'Gold mining in western Merioneth', *Journal of the Merioneth Historical Record Society*, 7, 1 (1973), 28–71, and 2 (1974), 140–87.

[76] There is an evocative and poignant history in Cyril Jones's *Calon Blwm: Portread o Hen Ardal Dylife ym Maldwyn* (Llandysul, 1994). The items referred to here are on pp. 11 and 17.

[77] Geraint H. Jenkins, *The Foundations of Modern Wales: Wales 1642–1780* (Cardiff and Oxford, 1987), p. 295.

[78] W. J. Lewis, 'Lead mining in Cardiganshire', in Geraint H. Jenkins and Ieuan Gwynedd Jones (eds), *Cardiganshire County History*, vol. 3, *Cardiganshire in Modern Times* (Cardiff, 1998), p. 168.

[79] On the lead industry, see also Mary Tucker, 'The system of watercourses to the lead mines from the River Leri', *Ceredigion*, 8, 2 (1977), 217–23; George Hall, 'A note on the decline of mining in Cardiganshire', *Ceredigion*, 7, 1 (1972),

85–7; W. J. Lewis, *Lead Mining in Wales* (Cardiff, 1967); and Marilyn Palmer, *The Richest in All Wales: The Welsh Potosi or Esgair Hir and Esgair Fraith Lead and Copper Mines of Cardiganshire* (Sheffield, 1983). For other non-ferrous minerals, see D. M. Rees, *Mines, Mills and Furnaces* (London, 1969).

[80] Chris Evans, *'The Labyrinth of Flames': Work and Social Conflict in Early Industrial Merthyr Tydfil* (Cardiff, 1993), p. 20.

[81] Harold Carter and Sandra Wheatley, *Merthyr Tydfil in 1851* (Cardiff, 1982), p. 17.

[82] A. H. Dodd, *History of Wrexham*, pp. 131–52.

[83] Arthur Young, *Travels in France* (London, 1973 edn), pp. 109, 183.

[84] On the general history of the iron industry in Wales, see A. Birch, *The Economic History of the British Iron and Steel Industry 1784–1879* (London, 1867); Madeleine Elsas (ed.), *Iron in the Making: Dowlais Company Letters 1782–1860* (Cardiff, 1960); John Lloyd, *The Early History of the Old South Wales Iron Works* (London, 1906); M. Atkinson and C. Barber, *The Rise and Decline of the South Wales Iron Industry* (Cardiff, 1987); and Ifor Edwards, 'Iron production in north Wales: the canal era: 1795–1850', *Denbighshire Historical Society Transactions*, 14 (1965), 141–84.

[85] A. H. Dodd, *History of Wrexham*, p. 137.

[86] John Davies, *The Making of Wales*, p. 105.

[87] Elizabeth Phillips, *A History of Pioneers of the Welsh Coalfield* (Cardiff, 1925), passim. For the general history of manufacturing, see Maxine Berg, *The Age of Manufactures 1700–1820: Industry, Innovation and Work in Britain* (London, 1994).

[88] A. H. Dodd, *History of Wrexham*, pp. 190–203.

[89] J. P. Addis, *The Crawshay Dynasty: A Study in Industrial Organisation and Development 1765–1867* (Cardiff, 1957), p. 71.

[90] J. H. Morris and L. J. Williams, *The South Wales Coal Industry, 1841–1875* (Cardiff, 1958).

[91] E. D. Lewis, *The Rhondda Valleys* (London, 1957), passim.

[92] A. H. Dodd, *History of Wrexham*, p. 192.

[93] In all there were three major potteries established in Llanelli and Swansea: the Cambrian Pottery, Swansea (1764–1870), the Glamorgan Pottery, Swansea (1813–39) and the South Wales Pottery, Llanelli (1839–1922). See Robert Pugh, *Welsh Pottery: A Towy Guide* (Bath, n.d.); Helen L. Hallesy, *The Glamorgan Pottery, Swansea* (Llandysul, 1995); and Dilys Jenkins, *Llanelly Pottery* (Swansea, 1968).

[94] A. H. Dodd, *History of Wrexham*, p. 194.

[95] *North Wales Chronicle* (30 August 1836).

[96] There is an excellent study of the attitudes of visitors to Wales in Ieuan Gwynedd Jones, *Mid-Victorian Wales: The Observers and the Observed* (Cardiff, 1992), especially the title essay, pp. 1–23.

[97] *Report of the Commission of Inquiry into the State of Education in Wales . . . In Three Parts, Part I, Carmarthen, Glamorgan and Pembroke. Part II, Brecknock, Cardigan, Radnor and Monmouth. Part III, North Wales* (London, 1847). Part I, p. 3.

[98] The following section is based on close reading of Elizabeth Phillips, *History of Pioneers*; A. H. John, *The Industrial Development of South Wales* (Cardiff, 1950); A. H. Dodd, *History of Wrexham*; Charles Wilkins, *The History of Merthyr Tydfil* (Merthyr, 1908); Glanmor Williams (ed.), *Glamorgan County History*; Ivor Thomas, *Top Sawyer: A Biography of David Davies Llandinam* (London, 1938); the *DWB*; J. P. Addis, *The Crawshay Dynasty*; M. Atkinson and C. Baber, *The Growth and Decline of the South Wales Iron Industry 1760–1880: An Industrial History* (Cardiff, 1987); M. J. Daunton, 'The Dowlais Iron Company in the iron industry, 1800–1850', *Welsh History Review*, 6 (1972), 16–48; M. C. S. Evans, 'Cwmdwyfran forge, 1697–1839', *Carmarthenshire Antiquary*, 11 (1975), 146–76; J. R. Harris, *The British Iron Industry, 1700–1850* (London, 1988); J. H. Morris and L. J. Williams, *The South Wales Coal Industry, 1841–75* (Cardiff, 1958); and L. J. Williams, 'A Carmarthenshire ironmaster and the Seven Years War', *Business History*, 2 (1959), 32–43.

[99] For Evan Evans, see Brian Glover, *Prince of Ales: The History of Brewing in Wales* (Stroud, 1993), p. 149.

[100] Elizabeth Phillips, *History of Pioneers*, pp. 33–5.

[101] On John Vaughan, see H. G. Reid (ed.), *Middlesbrough and its Jubilee: A History of the Iron and Steel Industries, with Biographies of Pioneeers* (Middlesbrough, 1881), pp. 130–41. A full biography of Edward Williams is available in *South Wales Institute of Engineers Centenary Brochure, 1857–1957* (Cardiff, 1957), pp. 41–3. For the Welsh community on Teeside, see David Ward, 'Culture, politics and assimilation: the Welsh on Teeside, c.1850–1940', *Welsh History Review*, 17 (1995), 550–70. I am grateful to Dr Huw Walters for these references; for a discussion, see his *Cynnwrf Canrif: Agweddau ar Ddiwylliant Gwerin* (Swansea, 2004).

[102] *DWB.*

[103] Glanmor Williams (ed.), *Glamorgan County History*, vol. 5, pp. 43–5.

[104] Lewis Lloyd, *Pwllheli*, pp. 40–1.

[105] Aled Eames, 'Slates, emigrants, timber and guano', *Cymru a'r Môr/Maritime Wales*, 1 (1976), 63–82; Lewis Lloyd, 'Aberdyfi, its shipping and seamen, 1565–1907', *Cymru a'r Môr/Maritime Wales*, 1 (1976), 22–46; idem, 'Early nineteenth-century ships and shareholders of the "Barmouth River"', *Journal of the Merioneth Historical Society*, 41 (1990–3), 207–29, 284–302, and 'The ports and shipping of Cardigan Bay', *Journal of the Merioneth Historical Society*, 4 (1979), 33–61; Susan Campbell-Jones, 'Shipbuilding at New Quay', *Ceredigion*, 7, 3–4 (1974–5), 273–306; G. Ivor Thomas, 'Captain John Richards (1813–1903) and the "Eagle Eyed" (1858–1897)', *Ceredigion*, 4, 4 (1987), 373–82; and J. Geraint Jenkins, *Maritime Heritage: The Ships and Seamen of Southern Ceredigion* (Llandysul, 1982).

[106] *Carmarthen Journal* (30 October 1835).

[107] Richard J. Moore-Colyer, *Land of Pure Delight*, p. 107.

[108] *The Cambrian* (21 August 1817).

[109] Herbert Williams, *Stage Coaches in Wales* (Barry, 1977), p. 88.

[110] W. K. Parker, 'The visits of Walter Davies to Radnorshire', *Transactions of the Radnorshire Society*, 47 (1977), 61. Walter Davies described the journey to

Llandrindod as 'a most disagreeable ride along bad roads meandering to every point of the compass except North', p. 54.

[111] Philip Gwyn Hughes, *Wales and Drovers*, p. 58.

[112] Keith Kissack, *Victorian Monmouth* (Monmouth, 1988), p. 31.

[113] E. Wyn James, *Dechrau Canu: Rhai Emynau Mawr a'u Cefndir* (Bridgend, 1987), p. 52. The travails of weary travellers are constant themes in the hymns of Dafydd Jones, Caeo, and William Williams, Pantycelyn.

[114] David Williams, *The Rebecca Riots* (Cardiff, 1971), pp. 158–84; Dewi Davies, 'The early years of the turnpike trusts in Cardiganshire', *Ceredigion*, 14, 3 (2003), 7–20.

[115] *North Wales Chronicle* (9 August 1836).

[116] Walter Davies, on a visit to the town in 1811, noted: 'dined at the Bethesdian Hospital, Llandrindod, with a motley group of such as either fancied themselves unwell or were really so, for no person in his health and senses would stop two days in such a place'. NLW MS 1,756,f. The efficacious powers of Llandrindod's waters had been praised in D. W. Linden's *Treatise on the Medicinal Waters of Llandrindod* (London, 1756).

[117] Reg Chambers Jones, *Bridges and Ferries* (Swansea, 1975), passim.

[118] Peter Lord, *Visual Culture: Imaging the Nation*, p. 143.

[119] David Williams, *Rebecca*, p. 183.

[120] Reg Chambers Jones, *Bridges*, p. 55.

[121] Charles Hadfield, *The Canals of South Wales and the Border* (Cardiff, 1960), pp. 18–19.

[122] Ibid., p. 81.

[123] Ibid., p. 18.

[124] Ibid., p. 99.

[125] Ibid., pp. 60–1.

[126] *The Cambrian* (30 June 1830).

[127] *North Wales Chronicle* (24 April 1836).

[128] D. S. M. Barrie, *A Regional History of the Railways of Great Britain: South Wales* (Nairn, 1994); and Peter E. Baughan, *A Regional History of the Railways of Great Britain: North and Mid Wales* (Nairn, 1991), passim.

[129] On the importance of Bristol for south Wales throughout the eighteenth and nineteenth centuries, see W. E. Minchinton, 'Bristol, the metropolis of the west', *Transactions of the Royal Historical Society*, 4 (1954), 69–79.

[130] *The Cambrian* (28 January 1804).

[131] Paul Joyner, *Artists in Wales c.1740–1851* (Aberystwyth, 1997), p. 81.

[132] Richard Phillips, 'Oes aur y ceffylau', *Ceredigion*, 5, 2 (1965), 125–42.

[133] For an interesting treatment of the tradesmen linked to horses, see Colin A. Lewis, 'Travelling stallions in and adjacent to Brycheiniog', *Brycheiniog*, 23 (1988), 75–85.

[134] Elwyn Bowen, *Vaynor: A Study of the Welsh Countryside* (Merthyr Tydfil, 1992), pp. 214–17.

[135] *Carmarthen Journal* (31 July 1835).

[136] Norman Lewis Thomas, *The Story of Swansea's Markets* (Swansea, n.d.); Mark Matthews, 'In pursuit of profit: local enterprise in south west Wales in the

eighteenth century' (Unpublished Ph.D. thesis, University of Wales, 1998). For the general history of consumerism and shopping, see Dorothy Davies, *A History of Shopping* (London, 1966); A. Adburgham, *Shops and Shopping 1800–1914: Where, and in What Manner the Well-Dressed English Woman Bought her Clothes* (London, 1981); Colin Campbell, *The Romantic Ethic and the Spirit of Modern Consumerism* (London, 1989); Neil McKendrick, Colin Brewer and J. H. Plumb, *The Birth of a Consumer Society: The Commercialisation of Eighteenth Century England* (Bloomington, IN, 1982); Lorna Weatherhill, *Consumer Behaviour and Material Culture in England 1600–1760* (London, 1988); and T. H. Breen, 'Baubles of Britain: the American and consumer revolutions of the eighteenth century', *Past and Present*, 119 (1988), 73–104.

[137] *The Morning Chronicle*, quoted in H. Carter and S. Wheatley, *Merthyr Tydfil*. See also M. B. and Helen Clifford (eds), *Consumers and Luxury: Consumer Culture in Europe 1650–1850* (Manchester, 1992); and Nick Rowley, *Commodities: How the World was Taken to Market* (London, 1987).

[138] H. Carter and S. Wheatley, *Merthyr Tydfil*, p. 19. See also Harold Carter, 'The growth and decline of Welsh towns', in D. Moore (ed.), *Wales in the Eighteenth Century* (Swansea, 1976), pp. 48–51; idem, *The Towns of Wales* (Cardiff, 1966).

[139] Peter Lord, *Visual Culture: Imaging the Nation*, p. 238.

[140] H. Carter and S. Wheatley, *Merthyr Tydfil*, p. 18.

[141] L. Twiston-Davies and H. Lloyd-Jones, *Welsh Furniture: An Introduction* (Cardiff, 1950), p. 9.

[142] Norman Lewis Thomas, *Swansea's Markets*, p. 42. For a general discussion on these themes, see Pamela Horn, *Children's Work and Welfare 1780–1880s* (Basingstoke, 1994); and Carl Gardner and Julia Sheppard, *Consuming Passion: The Rise of Retail Culture* (London, 1989). See also R. Tudur Jones, 'Darganfod plant bach: sylwadau ar lenyddiaeth plant yn oes Fictoria', in J. E. Caerwyn Williams (ed.), *Ysgrifau Beirniadol VIII* (Denbigh, 1974), pp. 160–204.

[143] *DWB*. John Griffith, *Y Gohebydd*, Sir Hugh Owen's assistant at the Cymdeithas Addysg Gymreig, spent most of his working life in Welsh and London shops before turning to journalism with *Y Faner* as a special reporter. For a general discussion, see David Alexander, *Retailing in Britain during the Industrial Revolution* (London, 1970).

[144] Glover, *Prince of Ales*, p. 56.

[145] Aubrey Neil Morgan, *David Morgan 1813–1919: The Life and Times of a Master Draper in South Wales* (Risca, 1977). (Sadly, the shop closed in 2005 and is due for redevelopment.)

[146] *Oswestry Advertiser* (12 December 1855). Savin invested the profits in the rail and coal ventures of his partner, David Davies.

[147] *The Cambrian* (6 January 1860).

[148] *Cardiff and Merthyr Guardian* (25 August 1849). For a general overview of these themes, see Vincent Vinikas, *Soft Soap, Hard Sell: American Hygiene in an Age of Advertisements* (Ames, IA, 1992); and T. J. Jackson Lears, *Fables of Abundance: A Cultural History of Advertising in America* (New York, 1994). (See also the discussion on patent medicines below, Chap. 3.)

[149] *The Cambrian* (29 December 1832).

[150] For the development of the press in Wales, see Aled Gruffydd Jones, *Press, Politics and Society: A History of Journalism in Wales* (Cardiff, 1993).

[151] *North Wales Chronicle* (1 November 1838).

[152] Dafydd Owen, *I Fyd y Faled* (Denbigh, 1986), p. 201.

[153] D. L. Jones (Cynalaw), *Y Ffraethebydd neu Cymhorth i Chwerthin* (Wrexham, n.d.), p. 34.

[154] Beverley Lemire, 'Consumerism in preindustrial and early industrial England: the trade in secondhand clothes', *Journal of British Studies*, 27 (1988), 1–24. See also Margaret Spufford, *The Great Reclothing of Rural England* (London, 1983).

[155] *Caernarvon and Denbigh Herald* (11 January 1862). For a discussion of the development of shoplifting, see Elaine Abelson, *When Ladies Go A-Thievin': Middle Class Shoplifters in the Department Store* (New York, 1989).

[156] *www.multiweb.ruralwales.net/~history/historypowys.org.uk/* (accessed 20 Aug. 2002).

[157] Neil McKendrick, 'Home demand and economic growth: a new view of the role of women and children in the industrial revolution', in McKendrick (ed.), *Historical Perspectives* (London, 1974); and Lorna Weatherill, ' "A possession of one's own": women and consumer behaviour in England, 1660–1740', *Journal of British Studies*, 25 (1986), 131–56.

[158] D. L. Jones, *Ffraethebydd*, p. 23.

[159] *Carmarthen Journal* (6 October 1843); W. P. Williams, *Tourism*, p. 393.

[160] Wirt Sikes, *Rambles*, p. 12; D. J. V. Jones, *The Last Rising: The Newport Insurrection of 1839* (Oxford, 1985), p. 13; *Merthyr Guardian* (29 March 1856). Care should be taken with these descriptions for the towns of Wales could attract both complimentary and caustic comment. Swansea was both 'the Brighton of Wales' and 'a miserable, muddy settlement'. One of the few places to be universally praised for its tone and elegance was Brecon. E. I. Spence considered: 'The society here is more select than in any other town in South Wales, from its chief inhabitants consisting of very old and respectable families who have retired on their fortunes' – *Summer Excursions . . .*, vol. 1 (London, 1809), p. 52. Malkin thought Brecon a 'very desirable residence'. For Brecon, see R. L. Grant, 'The townscape and economy of Brecon 1800–1860', *Brycheiniog*, 16 (1972), 102–25.

[161] Harold Carter, 'Growth and decline'; John Williams, *Digest of Welsh Historical Statistics*, passim.

[162] B. G. Owens, 'Benjamin Williams ("Gwynionydd") 1821–1891', *Ceredigion*, 5, 2 (1965), 368. In the 1860s, Aberaeron was sufficiently enterprising to publish its own paper for visitors, *The Aeron Visitor*, see Huw Walters, *A Bibliography of Welsh Periodicals, 1857–1900*, pp. 14–15.

[163] J. F. Rees, *The Story of Milford* (Cardiff, 1957), p. 24.

[164] Harold Carter, 'Growth and decline'.

[165] John Davies, *Making of Wales*, p. 111. See also F. J. Ball, 'Housing in an industrial colony: Ebbw Vale, 1778–1914', in S. D. Chapman (ed.), *The History of Working Class Housing: A Symposium* (Newton Abbot, 1971); J. B. Lowe, *Welsh Industrial Workers Housing, 1775–1875* (Cardiff, 1977); and D. N.

Anderson and J. B. Lowe, *Catslide Roofed Outshot Houses in Merthyr Tydfil and Related Areas* (Cardiff, 1973).

[166] John Williams, *Digest of Welsh Historical Statistics*, passim.

[167] E. Powell, *History of Tredegar* (Tredegar, 1885), pp. 15–21.

[168] Owen Griffith, *Mynydd Parys* (Caernarfon, 1897), p. 88.

[169] Alan Conway, *The Welsh in America: Letters from Immigrants* (Cardiff, 1961), p. 318.

2: Ambition and Anxiety

[1] This section is drawn from a reading of *The Cambrian* and *Seren Gomer* for July and August 1839.

[2] For Catherine Williams's colourful career, see *The Cambrian* (19 October 1833). For W. M. Jones's effectiveness in court, see the case of breach of promise of marriage brought by Margaret Howell against Daniel Stephens reported in *The Cambrian* (21 July 1838).

[3] National Library of Wales, Great Sessions Records, Montgomeryshire 1797, Gaol Files 4/1961. *Chester Chronicle* (1797).

[4] Walter Davies, *The Agriculture and Domestic Economy of South Wales* (London, 1815), vol. 2, p. 473.

[5] *Employment of Children in Mines* PP 1842, appendix, part ii, p. 550.

[6] T. W. Rammell, *Report to the General Board of Health . . . into . . . the sanitary condition of Merthyr Tydfil* (Merthyr Tydfil, 1850), p. 15.

[7] William Kay, *Report on the Sanitary Condition of Merthyr Tydfil* (Merthyr Tydfil, 1854), p. 23.

[8] An overview is provided in David Cannadine, *Class in Britain* (London, 1998). The most influential views have been E. J. Hobsbawm, *The Age of Revolution 1789–1848* (London, 1962); H. J. Perkin, *The Origin of Modern English Society 1780–1880* (London, 1969); A. Briggs, *The Age of Improvement, 1783–1867* (London, 1959); E. P. Thompson, *The Making of the English Working Class* (Harmondsworth, 1968); J. Foster, *Class Struggle and the Industrial Revolution: Early Industrial Capitalism in Three English Towns* (London, 1974); and R. S. Neale, 'Class and class consciousness in early nineteenth-century England: three classes or five?', in idem, *Class and Ideology in the Nineteenth Century* (London, 1972), pp. 15–40.

[9] The classic account in the Welsh context is Gwyn A. Williams' brilliantly committed *The Merthyr Rising* (London, 1978). The argument is also set out in his 'Locating a Welsh working class: the frontier years', in his *The Welsh in their History* (London, 1982), pp. 65–94.

[10] D. Wahrman, *Imagining the Middle Class: The Political Representation of Class in Britain c.1780–1840* (Cambridge, 1995); P. Mandler, *Aristocratic Government in the Age of Reform: Whigs and Liberals, 1830–1852* (Oxford, 1990); D. Eastwood, *Governing Rural England: Tradition and Transformation in Local Government, 1780–1840* (Oxford, 1994); A. Briggs, 'Middle-class consciousness in English politics, 1780–1846', *Past and Present*, 9 (1956), 65–74.

[11] Most famously in Eric Hobsbawm, *Primitive Rebels* (London, 1959).

[12] Hefin Jones, *Dic Dywyll y Baledwr* (Llanrwst, 1995), p. 21.

[13] Rhiannon Ifans, *'Cân Di Bennill': Themâu Anterliwtiau Twm o'r Nant* (Aberystwyth, 1997), p. 248.

[14] Quoted in D. Wahrman, *Imagining*, pp. 158–9.

[15] F. M. L. Thompson, *The Rise of Respectable Society: A Social History of Britain, 1830–1900* (London, 1988); for gentility and respectability see Philip Mason, *The English Gentleman: The Rise and Fall of an Ideal* (London, 1993); Christopher Hollis, *Death of a Gentleman* (London, 1943); and John Harvey, *Men in Black* (London, 1997).

[16] Chris Evans, *'The Labyrinth of Flames': Work and Social Conflict in Early Industrial Merthyr Tydfil* (Cardiff, 1993), pp. 65–7, 69, 71–3 and 79–81.

[17] L. J. Williams, 'The discharge note in the south Wales coal industry, 1841–98', in his *Was Wales Industrialised? Essays in Modern Welsh History* (Llandysul, 1995), pp. 150–64.

[18] Jean Lindsay, *A History of the North Wales Slate Industry* (Newton Abbot, 1974).

[19] Aled Eames, *Ventures in Sail* (Caernarfon, 1987); and R. S. Fenton, *Cambrian Coasters: Steam and Motor Coasters of North and West Wales* (Kendal, 1989).

[20] David Jenkins, *The Agricultural Community in South-West Wales at the Turn of the Twentieth Century* (Cardiff, 1971), and idem, 'Trefn ffarm a llafar gwlad', *Ceredigion*, 4, 3 (1962), 244–54.

[21] Herbert Williams, *Davies the Ocean: Railway King and Coal Tycoon* (Cardiff, 1991), p. 12.

[22] S. Minwel Tibbott, *Domestic Life in Wales* (Cardiff, 2002), p. 42.

[23] J. Geraint Jenkins, *Life and Tradition in Rural Wales* (London, 1976), p. 112. For Iolo Morganwg see Geraint H. Jenkins, *Facts, Fantasy and Fiction: The Historical Vision of Iolo Morganwg* (Aberystwyth, 1997), p. 12.

[24] David J. V. Jones, *Crime in Nineteenth Century Wales* (Cardiff, 1992).

[25] Keith Strange, 'In search of the celestial empire: crime in Merthyr, 1830–60', *Llafur*, 3, 1 (1980), 44–86.

[26] H. Mayhew, *London Labour and the London Poor* (Harmondsworth, 1985), passim.

[27] John Williams, *A Digest of Welsh Historical Statistics*, vol. 1 (Cardiff, 1985), pp. 88–99 provides a valuable overview of the census data.

[28] *DWB*.

[29] Ivor J. Bromham, 'Ann of Swansea (Ann Julia Hatton) 1764–1838', in Stewart Williams (ed.) *Glamorgan Historian*, vol. 7 (Cowbridge, n.d.), pp. 173–86.

[30] Froom Tyler, 'Thomas Bowdler: censor of Shakespeare', in Stewart Williams (ed.), *Glamorgan Historian*, vol. 8 (Barry, n.d.), pp. 194–204. From 1811 Bowdler lived in a house called Rhyddings, enjoying a wide view over the bay which his contemporary, Walter Savage Landor, regarded as finer than the bay of Naples.

[31] A discussion of similar developments in Scotland is provided in T. C. Smout, *A History of the Scottish People, 1560–1830* (London, 1969), pp. 338–40.

[32] *DWB*.

[33] Hywel Teifi Edwards, 'The eisteddfod poet: an embattled figure', in idem (ed.), *A Guide to Welsh Literature, c.1800–1900* (Cardiff, 2000), pp. 33–4.

[34] Ruth Evans, *John Williams 1860–1926* (Cardiff, 1952).

[35] Henry Jones, *Old Memories* (London, 1923).

[36] *DWB.*

[37] The Richard Morris Lewis papers are in the National Library with a brief biography. NLW MS 2249–50.

[38] R. C. B. Oliver, 'Holidays at Aberystwyth: 1798–1823', *Ceredigion*, 10, 3 (1986), 271.

[39] D. Spring (ed.), *The Great Landowners of Great Britain and Ireland* (London, 1971 edn). This has been well analysed by B. Ll. James, 'The great landowners of Wales', *National Library of Wales Journal*, 14 (1965–6), 301–20.

[40] B. Ll. James, 'Great landowners'.

[41] This section is based on an analysis of B. Ll. James, 'Great landowners'.

[42] David Cannadine, 'The theory and practice of the English leisure classes', *Historical Journal*, 30 (1978), 445–8.

[43] David Cannadine, *The Decline and Fall of the British Aristocracy* (London, 1992), passim.

[44] M. McCahill, 'Peerage creations and the changing character of the British nobility, 1750–1830', *English Historical Review*, 96 (1981), 259–84; J. V. Beckett, *The Aristocracy in England: A Comparative Synthesis* (London, 1984).

[45] This section is based on a close reading of D. Spring (ed.), *Great Landowners*.

[46] David Dykes, *Wales in Vanity Fair: A Show of Cartoons by 'Ape', 'Spy' and Other Artists of Welsh Personalities of the Victorian Age* (Cardiff, 1993), p. 33.

[47] *DWB.*

[48] For an excellent discussion of these themes, see Philip Jenkins, 'The creation of an "ancient gentry": Glamorgan 1760–1940', *Welsh History Review*, 12, 1 (1984), 29–49.

[49] T. Lloyd, *The Lost Houses of Wales* (London, 1986).

[50] Elizabeth Whittle, *The Historic Gardens of Wales* (London, 1992), p. 67.

[51] Peter R. Roberts, 'The social history of the Merioneth gentry *c.*1660–1840', *Journal of the Merioneth Historical and Record Society*, 4 (1961–4), 219.

[52] R. J. Colyer, 'The gentry and the county in nineteenth-century Cardiganshire', *Welsh History Review*, 10 (1980–1), 522. For Roderick Richards see R. J. Colyer, 'Roderick Eardly Richards and Plas Penglais, Aberystwyth', *Ceredigion*, 10, 1 (1984), 97–103.

[53] R. J. Colyer, 'The gentry', p. 523.

[54] Elizabeth Whittle, *Historic Gardens*, p. 56.

[55] *The Cambrian* (20 January 1816). The report added 'it is said that he actually did complete a machine which moved in strict uniformity with the rules laid down, but by then his funds had all dissolved'.

[56] Elizabeth Whittle, *Historic Gardens*, p. 41.

[57] Elizabeth Inglis Jones, *Peacocks in Paradise* (Aberystwyth, 1971).

[58] Elizabeth Mavor, *The Ladies of Llangollen* (Harmondsworth, 2001 edn), p. 67.

[59] Elizabeth Whittle, *Historic Gardens*, p. 49.

[60] Gerald Morgan, *Nanteos: A Welsh Home and its Families* (Llandysul, 2001), p. 188.

[61] It was still there when the author last visited.

[62] The landlord dominance of the post of justice of the peace continued into the

twentieth century. K. O. Morgan, 'Cardiganshire politics: the Liberal ascendancy 1885–1923', *Ceredigion*, 5 (1967), 320–1; E. Moir, *The Justices of the Peace* (London, 1969); C. H. E. Zangeril, 'The social composition of the county magistracy in England and Wales, 1831–1887', *Journal of British Studies*, 11 (1971); Matthew Cragoe, *An Anglican Aristocracy: The Rural Economy of the Landed Estate in Carmarthenshire, 1832–1895* (Oxford, 1996), passim.

[63] For example, in the Nanteos papers for the 1830s and the Cawdor papers for the early 1840s. Available in the Cardiganshire and Carmarthenshire Record Offices.

[64] Charlotte Williams-Wynn, *Memorials of Charlotte Williams-Wynn: edited by her sister with a portrait* (London, 1877); Miles Kikby Wynn Cato, *A Perfect Patriarch: William Nanney-Wynn, A Life in Georgian Merioneth* (Andover, private press, 1993); Anonymous, *Wynnstay and the Wynns: A Volume of Varieties* (Oswestry, 1876).

[65] There are excellent studies of Welsh political developments in Ieuan Gwynedd Jones, *Explorations and Explanations: Essays in the Social History of Wales* (Llandysul, 1981), especially chaps 3 (Merioneth), 4 (Cardiganshire) and 5 (Merthyr Tydfil).

[66] Arnold J. James and John E. Thomas, *Wales at Westminster* (Llandysul, 1981), pp. 46–8.

[67] Ibid., pp. 40–6.

[68] Philip Jenkins, 'Glamorgan politics 1781–1868', in P. Morgan (ed.), *Glamorgan County History*, vol. 6, *Glamorgan Society 1780–1980* (Cardiff, 1988), pp. 1–18.

[69] K. O. Morgan, *Wales in British Politics 1868–1922* (Cardiff, 1970), passim.

[70] *Carmarthen Journal* (16 September 1816).

[71] Peter Lord, *The Visual Culture of Wales: Industrial Society* (Cardiff, 1998), p. 79.

[72] Gerald Morgan, *Nanteos*, pp. 91–117.

[73] Peter Lord, *Visual Culture*, pp. 182, 183 and 232.

[74] On photographs see Iwan Meical Jones, 'Datgelu'r Cymry: portreadau ffotograffig yn oes Fictoria', in Geraint H. Jenkins (ed.), *Cof Cenedl*, xiv (Llandysul, 1999), pp. 133–62; Hilary Woollen and Alistair Crawford, *John Thomas, Photographer 1838–1900* (Llandysul, 1977); Emyr Wyn Jones, 'John Thomas of the Cambrian Gallery', *National Library of Wales Journal*, 9 (1955–6), 385–91; idem, 'John Thomas, Cambrian Gallery; ei atgofion a'i deithiau', *Journal of the Monmouthshire Historical and Records Society*, 4, 3 (1963), 242–73 and 14, 4 (1956), 385–92; and Elizabeth A. Darlington, 'High street photographers in Aberystwyth, 1857–c.1900', *National Library of Wales Journal*, 25, 4 (1988), 445–65. For paintings as a source of evidence on social life see M. Dorothy George, *Hogarth to Cruikshank: Social Change in Graphic Satire* (London, 1967); Hilary and Mary Evans, *The Man Who Drew the Drunkard's Daughter: The Life and Art of George Cruikshank 1792–1878* (London, 1978); John Hayes, *Rowlandson: Watercolours and Drawings* (London, 1972); Peter Lord, *Hugh Hughes: Arlunydd Gwlad* (Llandysul, 1995); idem, *The Francis Crawshay Worker Portraits: Portreadau Gweithwyr Francis Crawshay* (Aberystwyth, 1996); idem, *Words with Pictures: Welsh Images and*

Images of Wales in the Popular Press, 1640–1860 (Aberystwyth, 1995); F. G. Payne, 'Welsh peasant costume', *Folk Life*, 2 (1964), 42–57; and Jacqueline Lewis, 'Passing judgements: Welsh dress and the English tourist', *Folk Life*, 33 (1994–5), 59–47.

75 For women's fashions see Lady Violet Greville, *Faiths and Fashions: Short Essays Republished* (London, 1880); and A. Gernsheim, *Victorian and Edwardian Fashion* (London, 1981), p. 36.

76 *Y Punch Cymraeg* (3 March 1860).

77 C. Ehrlich, *The Piano: A History* (Oxford, 1990), pp. 100–4; and Gareth Williams, *Valleys of Song: Music and Society in Wales 1840–1914* (Cardiff, 1998).

78 Leonard Twiston-Davies, *Welsh Furniture* (Cardiff, 1950).

79 P. Johnson, 'Conspicuous consumption and working-class culture in late Victorian and Edwardian Britain', *Transactions of the Royal Historical Society*, 5th ser., 38 (1988), passim; and A. Palmer, *Moveable Feasts: A Reconnaissance of the Origins and Consequences of Fluctuations in Meal-Times* (Oxford, 1984), pp. 8, 37, 91; D. J. Oddy, 'Working-class diets in late nineteenth century Britain', *Economic History Review*, 23 (1970), 319.

80 Lady Llanover, *The First Principles of Good Cookery* (Llanddewi Brefi, reprinted facsimilie edn, 1991); Catherine Brennan, *Angers, Fantasies and Ghostly Fears: Nineteenth Century Women from Wales and English-Language Poetry* (Cardiff, 2003), pp. 63–86.

81 *Cardiff and Merthyr Guardian* (21 July 1849).

82 Walter Davies, *Agriculture*, pp. 74–136; idem, *A General View of the Agriculture and Domestic Economy of North Wales* (London, 1810), p. 82. J. Burnett, *A Social History of Housing 1815–1985* (London, 1986); E. Gauldie, *Cruel Habitations: A History of Working-Class Housing 1780–1918* (London, 1974), pp. 164–5.

83 Compare P. Smith, *Houses of the Welsh Countryside* (London, 1988) with J. B. Lowe, *Welsh Industrial Workers Housing 1775–1875* (Cardiff, 1977) and Eurwyn Wiliam, *Home Made Homes: Dwellings of the Rural Poor in Wales* (Cardiff, 1988). For the urine freezing under David Davies's bed, see Herbert Williams, *Davies the Ocean: Railway King and Coal Tycoon* (Cardiff, 1991), p. 22. For the Hook miner see *Where the River Bends* (Menter Preseli, n.d.), p. 12.

84 F. K. Prochaska, *Women and Philanthropy in Nineteenth-Century England* (Oxford, 1980), p. 224.

85 *The Cambrian* (19 January 1822).

86 *The Cambrian* (9 February 1822).

87 *The Cambrian* (13 January 1827).

88 *The Cambrian* (7 January 1832).

89 *The Cambrian* (13 February 1830).

90 Ibid.

91 For Swansea dentistry see *The Cambrian* (26 June 1824); Gwyn A. Williams, *Madoc: The Making of a Myth* (London, 1979).

92 S. Pennington and B. Westhover, *A Hidden Workforce: Homeworkers in England, 1850–1985* (London, 1989); J. Bowke, 'Housewifery in working-class

England 1860–1914', *Past and Present*, 143 (1994), 167–97; Project 'Grace' has also uncovered a vast array of valuable evidence on women's work.

93 W. J. Lewis, 'Lead mining in Cardiganshire', in Geraint H. Jenkins and Ieuan Gwynedd Jones (eds), *Cardiganshire County History*, vol. 3, *Cardiganshire in Modern Times* (Cardiff, 1998), p. 331.

94 S. Minwel Tibbott, 'Cheese-making in Glamorgan', in idem, *Domestic Life in Wales*, pp. 59–78. For general studies of women's work see Caroline A. Davidson, *A Woman's Work is Never Done: A History of Housework in the British Isles, 1650–1950* (London, 1982).

95 S. Minwel Tibbott, 'Cheese-making in Glamorgan', p. 26.

96 Robert M. Morris, *Gweled Gwlad: Cymru Trwy Lygaid Arlunwyr* (Aberystwyth, 1991), p. 26.

97 S. Minwel Tibbott, *Domestic Life in Wales*, pp. 22–45; C. Hardyment, *From Mangle to Microwave: The Mechanization of Household Work* (Oxford, 1990).

98 For the Ann Griffiths quotation see W. Caledfryn Williams, *Cofiant Ann Griffiths . . . ynghyd a'i llythyrau ai' Hymnnau* (Denbigh, 1865), p. 39. PP 1842 XVII, *Children's Employment*, appendix, part 11, pp. 625, 514. Angela V. John, *By the Sweat of their Brow: Women Workers in Victorian Coalmines* (London, 1984), passim.

99 James Walvin, *A Child's World: A Social History of English Childhood 1800–1914* (Harmondsworth, 1982); H. Cunningham, *The Children of the Poor* (Oxford, 1991); P. E. Hair, 'Children in society 1850–1980', in T. Barker and M. Drake (eds), *Population and Society in Britain 1850–1980* (London, 1982).

100 David J. V. Jones, *The Last Rising: The Newport Chartist Insurrection of 1839* (Oxford, 1985), p. 27.

101 Ibid., p. 29.

102 R. M. Evans, *Children in the Iron Industry 1840–42* (Cardiff, 1972).

103 Ibid., p. 34.

104 Ibid., p. 36.

105 *DWB*.

106 Ibid.

107 E. Jones, 'A Welsh wizard', *Carmarthenshire Antiquary* (1945–6), 47–8.

108 *DWB*.

109 Ibid.

110 E. Theodore Hoppen, *The Mid-Victorian Generation 1846–1886* (Oxford, 1998), p. 97; J. T. Ward, *The Factory Movement 1830–55* (London, 1962), p. 425.

111 Deirdre Beddoe, *Welsh Convict Women* (Barry, 1979); M. Vicinus, *Suffer and be Still: Women in the Victorian Age* (Bloomington, IN, 1972); J. Walkowitz, 'The making of an outcast group: prostitutes and working women in nineteenth-century Plymouth and Southampton', in M. Vicinus (ed.), *A Widening Sphere: Changing Roles of Victorian Women* (Bloomington, IN, 1979).

112 *Merthyr Telegraph* (10 September 1864).

113 *Cardiff and Merthyr Guardian* (5 August 1853).

114 *The Cambrian* (13 January 1860).

115 *The Cambrian* (7 February, 17 April 1824).

[116] S. C. Ellis, 'Observations of Anglesey life through the quarter sessions papers', *Anglesey Antiquarian and Field Club Transactions* (1986), 142–3.

[117] David J. V. Jones, *Crime in Wales*, p. 194.

[118] Dafydd Ifans, *The Diary of Francis Kilvert* (Aberystwyth, 1989), p. xx.

[119] *The Cambrian* (24 February 1817).

[120] *Cardiff and Merthyr Guardian* (13 January 1849).

[121] *Carmarthen Journal* (20 April 1832).

[122] David J. V. Jones, *Crime in Wales*, p. 194.

[123] Jack Larkin, *The Reshaping of Everyday Life 1790–1840* (New York, 1988), p. 101.

[124] Eldra and A. O. H. Jarman, *Y Sipsiwn Cymreig: Teulu Abram Wood* (Cardiff, 1979).

[125] *DWB*.

[126] Robert Hughes, *The Fatal Shore* (London, 1987), p. 235.

[127] Ibid., p. 236.

[128] Deirdre Beddoe, *Welsh Convict Women*, p. 39.

[129] R. Hughes, *Fatal Shore*, pp. 125–227.

[130] The most entertaining account remains Jan Morris's magisterial and memorable trilogy: *Heaven's Command: An Imperial Progress* (London, 1973), *Pax Britannia: The Climax of an Empire* (London, 1968) and *Farewell the Trumpets: An Imperial Retreat* (London, 1979). The most authoritative study is *The Oxford History of the British Empire*, especially vol. 2, ed. P. J. Marshall, *The Eighteenth Century*, and vol. 3, ed. Andrew N. Porter, *The Nineteenth Century*.

[131] E. A. Cruickshank, *The Life of Sir Henry Morgan, with an Account of the English Settlement of the Island of Jamaica 1655–1688* (London, 1935). The role of the Welshman Henry Morgan as one of the founders of empire is discussed in Niall Ferguson, *Empire* (London, 2003), p. 13.

[132] Emrys Jones, *The Welsh in London 1500–2000* (Cardiff, 2001).

[133] *DWB*.

[134] Gwyn A. Williams, *When was Wales? A History of the Welsh* (London, 1985), pp. 159–72.

[135] Roland Thomas, *Richard Price* (London, 1924); Walford Gealy, 'Richard Price, F. R. S. (1723–91)', *Y Traethodydd*, 146 (1991), 135–45; Martin Fitzpatrick, 'Reflections on a footnote: Richard Price and love of country', *Enlightenment and Dissent*, 6 (1987), 41–58; idem, 'Richard Price and the London Revolution Society', *Enlightenment and Dissent*, 10 (1991), 35–50; D. O. Thomas, 'Gwleidyddiaeth Richard Price', *Y Meddwl Cymreig* (Cardiff, 1995), pp. 142–153; Chris Williams, *Richard Price and the Atlantic Revolution* (Cardiff, 1991). I am grateful to Dr Huw Walters for drawing several of these sources to my attention.

[136] Simon Schama, *A History of Britain*, vol. 3, *The Fate of Empire 1776–2000* (London, 2002), p. 49.

[137] NLW MS SA/RD/21, p. 29.

[138] Cecil Price, 'The Merionethshire Macaroni', *National Library of Wales Journal*,

6 (1949–50), 107; idem, 'The unpublished letters of Evan Lloyd', *National Library of Wales Journal*, 8 (1953–4), 437.

[139] Cecil Price, 'Polite society in eighteenth century Wales', *The Welsh Anvil*, 5 (1952), 92.

[140] Joseph Grego (ed.), *The Reminiscences and Recollections of Captain Gronow*, 2 vols (London, 1892).

[141] *Vanity Fair* (24 August 1872), has a caricature of Vaughan looking like a rather podgy cherub. David Dykes, *Wales in Vanity Fair*, p. 71; for an evaluation of Vaughan's career see Angus Wilson, *The Victorians* (London, 2002), pp. 290–1. See also Matthew Parris, *The Great Unfrocked: Two Thousand Years of Church Scandal* (London, 1998).

[142] David Dykes, *Wales in Vanity Fair*, pp. 47,73.

[143] Hywel M. Davies, *Transatlantic Bretheren: Rev Samuel Jones (1735–1814) and his Friends: Baptists in Wales, Pennsylvania and Beyond* (Bethlehem, Lehigh, 1995), passim.

[144] Gwyn A. Williams, 'Morgan John Rhys and his Beula', *Welsh History Review*, 3, 4 (1967), 441–72.

[145] Robert Owen, *The Life of Robert Owen by Himself* (London, 1857); G. D. H. Cole, *Robert Owen* (London, 1925).

[146] *The Cambrian* (24 October 1818).

[147] A. H. Dodd, 'Letters from Cambria County, 1800–1823', *Pennsylvania History*, 22 (1955).

[148] *Cardiff and Merthyr Guardian* (10 March 1849). This issue of the paper contained several advertisements for opportunities to join the Gold Rush in California.

[149] *Cardiff and Merthyr Guardian* (21 July 1849).

[150] Ibid.

[151] *North Wales Chronicle* (15 June 1850).

[152] *The Cambrian* (6 April 1866).

[153] *http://historytogo.utah.gov/danjones.html* (accessed 20 Oct. 2003). Ronald D. Dennis, *Truth will Prevail: The Rise of the Church of Jesus Christ of Latter-Day Saints in the British Isles, 1873–1987* (Cambridge, 1987); idem, *The Call of Zion: The Story of the First Welsh Mormon Emigration* (Provo, Utah, 1987); idem, 'The Welsh Mormon exodus', *Planet*, 73 (1989), 39–45. I am grateful to Dr Huw Walters for drawing several of these sources to my attention.

[154] Dee Brown, *The American West* (New York, 1994), pp. 29–30.

[155] On the 'reality' of the Indian threat to settlers, see Frank McLynn, *Waggons West: The Epic Story of America's Overland Trails* (London, 2003), pp. 31–2.

[156] *Caernarvon and Denbigh Herald* (15 November 1862).

[157] Dafydd Meirion, *Cymry Gwyllt y Gorllewin* (Talybont, 2002), pp. 77–9.

[158] William D. Jones, *Wales in America: Scranton and the Welsh 1860–1920* (Cardiff, 1993), p. xvii.

[159] *DWB*.

[160] Edwin G. Burrows and Mike Wallace, *Gotham: A History of New York City to 1898* (Oxford, 1999), pp. 396–413.

[161] Eirug Davies, *Y Cymry ac Aur Colorado* (Llanrwst, 2001), pp. 29–43.

[162] Ibid., p. 31; Dafydd Meirion, *Cymry Gwyllt*, p. 32.

[163] Herbert Asbury, *The Gangs of New York* (London, 2002), p. 162, 217–219.

[164] Dafydd Meirion, *Cymry Gwyllt*, p. 10.

[165] T. J. Stiles, *Jesse James: Last Rebel of the Civil War* (London, 2003), p. 404.

[166] The author met a descendant of John Porter in the West Glamorgan Archive Office in Swansea in October 2001.

[167] T. M. Bassett, *The Baptists of Wales and the Baptist Missionary Society* (Swansea, 1991); E. Lewis Evans, *Cymru a'r Gymdeithas Genhadol* (London, 1945); Ioan W. Gruffydd (ed.), *Cludoedd Moroedd: Cofio Dwy Ganrif o Genhadaeth 1795–1995* (Swansea, 1995); G. Pennar Griffith, *Hanes Bywgraffiadol o Genhadon Cymreig i Wledydd Paganaidd* (Swansea, 1897); Jane Aaron, 'Slaughter and salvation', *New Welsh Review*, 38 (1997), 38–46.

[168] Noel Gibbard, *Cymwynaswyr Madagascar 1818–1920* (Bridgend, 1999), pp. 15–17.

[169] *http://www.annibynwyr.org/saesneg/rgthomas.htm* (accessed 21 June 2002).

[170] *DWB*.

[171] *Y Cronicl*, 3, 32 (December 1845).

[172] *http://library.victu.utoronto.ca/exhibitions/baxter/baxter.htm* (accessed 21 June 2002).

[173] Ednyfed Thomas, *Bryniau'r Glaw: Hanes Cenhadaeth Dramor Eglwys Bresbyteraidd Cymru, Y Gyfrol Gyntaf, Cenhadaeth Casia* (Caernarfon, 1988), pp. 25–71. Nigel Jenkins, *Gwalia in Khasia* (Llandysul, 1995), pp. 12–16.

[174] *DWB*.

[175] Ibid.

[176] Ibid.

[177] Noel Gibbard, *Griffith John: Apostle to Central China* (Bridgend, 1998), p. 47.

[178] G. Pennar Griffith, *Hanes*, pp. 19–20.

[179] G. E. Owen, 'Welsh anti-slavery sentiment: a survey of public opinion' (Unpublished MA thesis, University of Wales, Aberystwyth, 1964).

[180] *The Cambrian* (19 October and 26 October 1805).

[181] *The Cambrian* (14 June 1826).

[182] *Seren Gomer* (16 December 1818).

[183] G. E. Owen, 'Anti-slavery sentiment', p. 20. For similar complaints about gentry influence in the same area see Ieuan Gwynedd Jones, 'The anti Corn Law letters of Walter Griffith', *Bulletin of the Board of Celtic Studies*, 38, 1 (1978), 109.

[184] Hugh Thomas, *The Slave Trade: The History of the Slave Trade 1440–1870* (London, 1997), pp. 289–312.

[185] R. O. Roberts, 'Penclawdd brass and copper works: a link with the slave trade', *Gower* (1961), 36.

[186] Ibid., 42.

[187] NLW Slebech Papers 8925.

[188] Jean Lindsay, 'The Pennants and Jamaica: part 1, the growth and organisation of the Pennant estates', *Caernarfonshire Historical Society Transactions*, 43 (1982), 77.

[189] *DWB*.

[190] I am grateful to my former tutor in the Department of History at Aberystwyth, Dr Clare Taylor, for drawing these papers to my attention. The Slebech Papers

in the National Library of Wales are a substantial collection which reveal Nathaniel Phillips's obsession with money. For the significance of the papers see B. G. Charles, 'The records of Slebech', *National Library of Wales Journal*, 5 (1947–8), 188–9.

[191] Clare Taylor, 'The perks of a West Indian heiress: case studies of the heiresses of Nathaniel Phillips of Slebech', *Welsh History Review*, 12, 4 (1985), 512. Other valuable articles by Dr Taylor on Phillips are: 'Last days at Phillipsfield and Pleasant Hill', *Bulletin of the Jamaican Historical Society*, 7, 9 (1979); 'The journal of an absentee proprietor Nathaniel Phillips of Slebech', *Journal of Caribbean History*, 18, 2 (1982); 'An absentee planter returns to his family: Dr John Gray's travels', *Bulletin of the Jamaican Historical Society*, 8, 12 (1983); and 'Aspects of planter society in the British West Indies', *National Library of Wales Journal*, 20 (1977–8), 361–72.

[192] See, for example, his letterbook for 16 March 1777 (Slebech MS 11,485) and the scribbled notes in his journal for 1787 when he purchases 210 Negroes (Slebech, 9,417).

[193] For a damning account of Thomas Picton's leadership in Trinidad, see V. S. Naipaul, *The Loss of El Dorado: A Colonial History* (London, 2001), pp. 139–97.

[194] Robert Havard, *Wellington's Welsh General: A Life of Sir Thomas Picton* (London, 1996); and John William Cole, *Memoirs of British Generals Distinguished During the Peninsular War*, 2 vols (London, 1856); for a sensational account of battle with Picton see Captain MacCarthy, *Recollections of the Storming of the Castle of Badajos* (London, 1916).

[195] Full details of the case against Picton can be obtained in *Howell's State Trials*, vol. 30 (London, 1822).

[196] Eric Williams, *History of the People of Trinidad and Tobago* (London, n.d.), p. 82.

[197] Alistair Hennessy, 'Penrhyn Castle', *History Today* (January 1995), 42.

[198] For Stanley see Richard Hall, *Stanley: An Adventurer Explored* (London, 1974).

[199] Frederic Bancroft, *Slave-Trading in the Old South* (Baltimore, MD, 1931), pp. 51–8, 274. Another shadowy figure with links to Wales was the sinister Moncure D. Conway.

[200] J. A. H. Evans, 'Nathaniel Wells of Piercefield and St Kitts: from slave to sheriff', *Monmouthshire Antiquary*, 18 (2002), 91–106.

[201] For a superb study of the Georgian navy see N. A. M. Rodger, *The Wooden World: An Anatomy of the Georgian Navy* (London, 1988).

[202] *DWB.*

[203] *The Concise Dictionary of National Biography* (London, 1993).

[204] Ibid.

[205] Ludovic Kennedy, *Nelson and his Captains* (London, 2001 edn), pp. 43–4, 210–11, 274, 280, 339–40.

[206] *Concise Dictionary of National Biography.*

[207] David Beaumont Ellison, *Hammer and Nails: Capt. Timothy Edwards Nanhoron* (Caernarfon, 1997), pp. 118–19, 137.

[208] Reginald Davies, 'Welshmen at the Battle of Trafalgar: was your ancestor a one-

legged survivor of the Battle?', *Dyfed Family History Journal*, 5, 5 (1995), 198–200.

[209] David Cordingly, *Heroines and Harlots: Women at Sea in the Great Age of Sail* (London, 2001), pp. 64, 114–15.

[210] David Dykes, *Wales in Vanity Fair*, p. 37.

[211] Richard Holmes, *Redcoat: The British Soldier in the Age of Horse and Musket* (London, 2001), p. 148.

[212] Gerald Morgan (ed.), *Lle Diogel i Sobri: Hunangofiant Capelulo* (Llanrwst, 1982).

[213] Roger Norman Buckley (ed.), *The Napoleonic War Journal of Captain Thomas Henry Browne* (London, 1987).

[214] Dillwyn Miles, 'The letters of St John George of the Marines, 1799–1808', 2 parts, *Pembrokeshire Historical Society Transactions*, 10 (2001) and 11 (2002). Another interesting account is provided in Allan Fletcher, 'Edwin Griffith at Corunna', *Denbighshire Historical Society Transactions*, 50 (2001), 98–115 and 51 (2002), 61–79.

[215] The story of Wales's military exploits has yet to be written. There are some accounts of the main Welsh regiments, for example: Major Rowland Broughton-Mainwaring, *Historical Records of the Royal Welch Fusiliers* (London, 1889); A. D. L. Cary and Stouppe McCance, *Regimental Records of the Royal Welch Fusiliers*, 2 vols (London, 1921, 1923): interestingly, more attention is given to the death of the regimental mascot – a goat – and its replacement through Queen Victoria's generosity, than to the deaths of hundreds of soldiers in several campaigns); D. A. N. Lomax, *A History of the Services of the 31st (the Welch) Regiment* (Devonport, 1899); and H. Avray Tipping, *The Story of the Royal Welch Fusiliers* (London, 1915). For a valuable social study see Edward M. Spiers, *The Army and Society 1815–1914* (London, 1980).

[216] Roger Norman Buckley (ed.), *War Journal*, p. 5.

[217] David Salmon, 'The French invasion of Pembrokeshire in 1797', *West Wales Historical Records*, 14 (1929), 202; idem, *The Descent of the French on Pembrokeshire* (Carmarthen, 1934); E. H. Stuart Jones, *The Last Invasion of Britain* (Cardiff, 1950); J. Kinross, *Fishguard Fiasco: An Account of the Last Invasion of Britain* (Tenby, 1974); T. Llew Jones, *Berw Gwyllt yn Abergwaun* (Llanrwst, 1986); Richard Rose, 'The French at Fishguard: fact, fiction and folklore', *Transactions of the Honourable Society of Cymmrodorion*, 9 (2003) 74–105.

[218] Linda Colley, *Britons: Forging the Nation 1707–1837* (London, 1992).

[219] Ibid., p. 379.

[220] *The Cambrian* (5 May 1810).

[221] NLW, Tredegar MS 405.

[222] E. P. Thompson, *The Making of the English Working Class* (Harmondsworth, 1979), p. 511.

[223] Bryn Owen has written several interesting histories of the militia companies of Wales in his series *The History of the Welsh Militia and Volunteer Corps 1757–1908, Carmarthenshire, Pembrokeshire and Cardiganshire* (Wrexham,

1995); *Denbighshire and Flintshire* (Wrexham, 1997); *Glamorgan* (Wrexham, 1994); *Anglesey and Caernarfonshire* (Wrexham, 1993); and idem, *Glamorgan: Its Gentlemen and Yeomanry 1797–1980* (Newport, 1983); see also Hugh J. Owen, *Merioneth Volunteers and Local Militia During the Napoleonic Wars (1795–1816)* (Dolgellau, n.d.); Lionel V. Evans, 'The Royal Glamorgan Militia', in Stewart Williams (ed.), *Glamorgan Historian*, vol. 8 (Barry, n.d.), pp. 146–59. For the expenditure by one family on civil defence see Michael K. Stammers, *A Maritime Fortress: The Collections of the Wynn Family at Belan Fort, c. 1750–1930* (Cardiff, 2001). The records of the Glynllifon Militia Company (1778–1825) provide graphic evidence how a small community dealt with war. NLW MS 2374.

224 For a pro Sir Watkin report see J. E. Vincent (ed.), *The Memories of Sir Llewelyn Turner* (London, 1903), pp. 1–24.

225 For scathing accounts of the Welsh barbarities see A. T. Q. Stewart, *The Summer Soldiers: The 1798 Rebellion in Antrim and Down* (Belfast, 1997), pp. 36–7; Dáire Keogh and Nicholas Furlong (eds), *The Mighty Wave: The 1798 Rebellion in Wexford* (Dublin, 1998), pp. 21, 124–9; and Daniel Gahan, *The People's Rising: Wexford, 1798* (Dublin, 1995), pp. 162–3, 222–3, 258–65.

226 Mark Adkin, *The Waterloo Companion* (London, 2001), pp. 104–5. The extent of the rehabilitation of Sir Thomas Picton's reputation can be seen in the ballads and poems which were penned to mourn his death. See, for example, *Marwnad yr Ardderchog Lywydd hwnnw, Syr Thomas Picton, Marchog Milwraidd o Swydd Benfro*; and J. Evan's ballad which must have left every singer breathless after the title – *Marwnadau er coffadwriaeth am y Milwriad anrhydeddus ac ardderchog hwnnw Syr Thomas Picton: Yr hwn a drôdd Dafol y Fuddugoliaeth gyntaf o ochr y Brytaniaid ym mrwydyr waedlyd Waterloo, ac a Gollodd ei fywyd yn y Funud yr oedd yn enill y Dydd, ac yn sicrhau Llwyddiant a Heddwch i'w Wlâd, Mehefin 18ed, 1815* (Carmarthen, 1815).

227 Adkin, *Waterloo Companion*, pp. 106, 154. Uxbridge's artificial leg is now a central feature in an excellent exhibition on his life and wars in Plas Newydd, Anglesey. See National Trust, *Plas Newydd, Isle of Anglesey* (London, 2001).

228 Edward Gill, *Nelson and the Hamiltons on Tour* (Monmouth, 1987), p. 42.

229 Nott still awaits his modern biographer as do so many of Wales's military heroes. There is a lengthy entry on him in the *Dictionary of National Biography*. See also J. H. Stocqueler, *Memoirs and Correspondence of Major General Sir William Nott, G. C. B.*, 2 vols (London, 1854).

230 For Thomas Brigstocke see T. Mardy Rees, *Welsh Painters, Engravers and Sculptors (1527–1911)* (Caernarfon, n.d.), pp. 16–18.

231 Sir John Kaye, *History of the War in Afghanistan* (London, 1851).

232 Pat Molloy, *Four Cheers for Carmarthen: The Other Side of the Coin* (Llandysul, 1981), pp. 26–8.

233 Trevor Royle, *The Great Crimean War, 1854–56* (London, 1999).

234 Aled Gruffydd Jones, *Press, Politics and Society: A History of Journalism in Wales* (Cardiff, 1993), p. 29; Huw Walters, *Llyfryddiaeth Cylchgronau Cymreig: A Bibliography of Welsh Periodicals 1735–1850* (Aberystwyth, 1993); and idem, *Llyfryddiaeth Cylchgronau Cymreig: A Bibliography of Welsh Periodicals 1850–1900* (Aberystwyth, 2003).

[235] Keith Kissack, *Victorian Monmouth* (Monmouth, 1988), p. 84.

[236] Roy Saer, *Caneuon Llafar Gwlad*, vol. 2 (Cardiff, 1994), p. 34; and idem, 'Marwnad Capten Vaughan, Brynog 1855: ei chefndir a rhai o'i chysylltiadau', *Ceredigion*, 6, 4 (1971), 423–37.

[237] Jane Williams (ed.), *The Autobiography of Elizabeth Davis (Betsy Cadwaladyr): A Balaclava Nurse* (Cardiff, 1987).

[238] Keith Kissack, *Victorian Monmouth*, p. 84. One who took part in the 'battle' was the talented musician James Conway Brown (1838–86), son of the owner of the Blaina Ironworks.

[239] On the 'alternative' type of emigrants to India see William Dalrymple, *White Mughals: Love and Betrayal in Eighteenth Century India* (London, 2002); and Linda Colley, *Captives: Britain, Empire and the World 1600–1850* (London, 2003).

[240] Steve van Dalken, 'The Voyle family of Pembrokeshire and India', *Journal of the Pembrokeshire Historical Society*, 6 (1994–5), 47.

[241] Ibid.

[242] Idem, 'Lamphey and India', *Journal of the Pembrokeshire Historical Society*, 5 (1992–3), 52.

[243] Ken Jones, 'John Lloyd 1748–1818: an adventurous Welshman', *Brycheiniog*, 33 (2001) and 34 (2002), 67–118.

[244] S. N. Mukherjee, *Sir William Jones: A Study in Eighteenth-Century British Attitudes to India* (Cambridge, 1969); David J. Ibbetson, 'Sir William Jones 1746–1794', in Thomas Glyn Watkin (ed.), *Legal Wales: Its Past, its Future* (Cardiff, 2001); and *http://www.picatype.com/dig/da2/da2aa06.htm* (accessed 12 July 2003).

[245] Steve van Dalken, 'Voyle family', 48. For the general relationships between Europeans and native people see Urs Bitterli, *Cultures in Conflict: Encounters between European and Non-European Cultures, 1492–1800* (Oxford, 1989), trans. Ritchie Robertson.

[246] John William Kay, *A History of the Sepoy Wars*, 4 vols (London 1864–80); Christopher Hibbert, *The Great Mutiny, India 1857* (London, 1978); H. H. Bodwell (ed.), *The Cambridge History of India*, vols 5 and 8, *British India* (London, 1929); and Penderel Moon, *The British Conquest and Domination of India* (London, 1929), which provides damning evidence of atrocities carried out by William Nott's troops.

[247] On Bartle-Frere see David Dykes, *Wales in Vanity Fair*, p. 83; Benjamin Millingchamps NLW MS 4,391–4,412; Sir John Harfod Jones Brydges NLW MS 4,901–12; Timothy Richards Lewis NLW MS 14,381–14,407.

[248] Ken Jones, 'John Lloyd', p. 74.

[249] Steve van Dalken, 'Voyle family', 52–3.

[250] *Monmouthshire Merlin* (2 January 1858). For similar racist language see *The Cambrian* (6 April 1861) on the murders in the well at Cawnpore. For the Williams and Thomas families see Andrew Ward, *Our Bones are Scattered: The Cawnpore Massacre and the Indian Mutiny of 1857* (New York, 1996), pp. 328, 360, 366 and 164.

[251] For Griffith Davies see *DWB*. Reg Davies (ed.), *The Welsh Family History Societies in London Index of Welshmen in the East India Company Army* (London, 1997).

[252] John Kay, *The Great Arc: The Dramatic Tale of How India was Mapped and Everest was Named* (London, 2000); idem, *The Explorers of the Western Himalyas* (London, 1996); Matthew Edney, *Mapping an Empire: The Geography of India* (London, 1997).

[253] The event was commemorated in a notable painting by Sir David Wilkie, *Chelsea Pensioners Reading the Gazette of the Battle of Waterloo* (1822). Why the soldier rode first to the pensioners not the government is never explained. For a detailed analysis of the painting's role in the symbolism of Britain see Linda Colley, *Britons*, pp. 364–8.

[254] R. J. Colyer, *Roads and Trackways of Wales* (Ashbourne, 1984), p. 142. For the general feeling of being lost in time see Jerome Hamilton Buckley, *The Triumph of Time: A Study of the Victorian Concepts of Time, History, Progress and Decadence* (Cambridge, MA, 1966).

[255] Elwyn Bowen, *Vaynor: A Study of the Welsh Countryside* (Merthyr Tydfil, 1982), p. 385.

[256] John Williams-Davies, 'Merched y gerddi: a seasonal migration of female labour from rural Wales', *Folk Life*, 15 (1977), 16.

[257] Peter Lord, *Words with Pictures*, p. 70.

[258] Trans. Ieuan Gwynedd Jones, *Mid-Victorian Wales: The Observers and the Observed* (Cardiff, 1992), p. 76.

[259] H. Elvet Lewis, *Sweet Singers of Wales: A Story of Welsh Hymns and their Authors, with Original Translations* (London, n.d.), pp. 100, 115.

[260] For a thought-provoking study of Victorian mentalities see W. E. Houghton, *The Victorian Frame of Mind 1830–70* (New Haven, CT, 1957), especially pp. 1–14, for an awareness of a world which is 'all acceleration'. David Newsome, *The Victorian World Picture* (London, 1997), pp. 13–38, also makes a number of interesting points. See also Elaine Showalter, *The Female Malady: Women, Madness and English Culture 1830–1980* (London, 1987); and Janet Oppenheim, *'Shattered Nerves': Doctors, Patients, and Depression in Victorian England* (Oxford, 1991). I am grateful to Dr Huw Walters for these references.

[261] David J. V. Jones, *Crime in Wales*, p. 83. Rhiannon Ifans, *Twm o'r Nant*, pp. 66, 91; Eryl Wyn Rowlands, *Y Llew oedd ar y Llwyfan* (Caernarfon, 2001), p. 52.

[262] Pamela Michael, *Care and Treatment of the Mentally Ill in North Wales 1800–2000* (Cardiff, 2003), p. 3; see also T. G. Davies, 'An asylum for Glamorgan', *Morgannwg*, 37 (1993), 40–53; and idem, *A History of Cefn Coed Hospital* (Swansea, 1982).

[263] Russell Davies, 'Inside the "house of the mad": the social context of mental illness, suicide and the pressure of rural life in south-west Wales, c.1860–1920', *Llafur*, 4, 2 (1985), 20–35; T. G. Davies, 'Bedlam yng Nghymru: datblygiad seiciatrig yn y bedwaredd ganrif ar bymtheg', *Transactions of the Honourable Society of Cymmrodorion* (1980), 105–22; idem, 'Of all the maladies', *Journal of the Pembrokeshire Historical Society*, 5 (1992–3), 75–90; idem, ' "Shrouded in mystery": events in the history of psychiatry in Carmarthenshire', *Carmarthenshire Antiquary*, 39 (2003), 105–17; idem, 'Mental mischief: aspects of nineteenth-century psychiatric practice in parts of Wales', in Colin Baber

and John Lancaster (eds), *Healthcare in Wales: An Historical Miscellany* (Cardiff, 2003), pp. 81–103.

[264] Andrew T. Scull, *Museums of Madness: The Social Organisation of Insanity in Nineteenth Century England* (Harmondsworth, 1982); idem, *Madhouses, Mad-Doctors and Madmen* (Philadelphia, 1981); idem, *Masters of Bedlam: The Transformation of the Mad-Doctoring Trade* (Princeton, 1996); idem, *The Most Solitary of Afflictions: Madness and Society in Britain 1700–1900* (London, 1993); William Llywelyn Parry-Jones, *The Trade in Lunacy: A Study of Private Madhouses in England in the Eighteenth and Nineteenth Centuries* (London, 1971); Michael Foucault, *Madness and Civilization: A History of Insanity in the Age of Reason* (London, 2001); Roy Porter, W. F. Bynum and Michael Shepherd (eds), *The Anatomy of Madness: Essays in the History of Psychiatry*, vol. 3, *The Asylum and its Psychiatry* (London, 1988); S. E. D. Shortt, *Victorian Lunacy: Richard M. Bucke and the Practice of Late Nineteenth-Century Psychiatry* (Cambridge, 1986). I am grateful to Dr Huw Walters for drawing several of these sources to my attention.

[265] Mike Jay, *The Air Loom Gang: The Strange and True Story of James Tilly Matthews and his Visionary Madness* (London, 2003). For the pressures of a new age on people see Humphrey Jennings, *Pandemonium 1660–1886: The Coming of the Machine as Seen by Contemporary Observers* (London, 1985).

[266] Superb accounts of suicide are Olive Anderson, *Suicide in Victorian and Edwardian England* (Oxford, 1987); Barbara T. Gates, *Victorian Suicide: Mad Crimes and Sad Histories* (Princeton, NJ, 1988); Richard Cobb, *Death in Paris: The Records of the Basse-Geôle de la Seine* (Oxford, 1978); Victor Bailey, 'This Rash Act': Suicide across the Life Cycle in the Victorian City* (Stanford, CA, 1998); Henry Romilly Fedden, *Suicide: A Social and Historical Study* (London, 1938); and Michael MacDonald, *Sleepless Souls: Suicide in Early Modern England* (Oxford, 1990). I am grateful to Dr Huw Walters for drawing several of these sources to my attention.

[267] *The Cambrian* (16 February 1830).

[268] Russell Davies, 'Do not go gentle into that good night: women and suicide in Carmarthenshire, *c.*1860–1920', in Angela V. John (ed.), *Our Mother's Land: Chapters in Welsh Women's History 1830–1939* (Cardiff, 1991), p. 98.

[269] *The Cambrian* (8 June 1833).

[270] R. T. W. Denning (ed.), *The Diary of William Thomas of Michaelston-super-Ely near St Fagans, Glamorgan: 1762–1795* (Cardiff, 1995), p. 361.

[271] *The Cambrian* (13 December 1816).

[272] *Seren Gomer* (March 1844), 122.

[273] *The Cambrian* (13 March 1830).

[274] *Carmarthen Journal* (24 November 1815).

[275] *The Cambrian* (7 June 1829).

[276] *Carmarthen Journal* (16 March 1849).

[277] *Carmarthen Journal* (22 August 1845).

[278] *Caernarvon and Denbigh Herald* (13 October 1866).

[279] *Cardiff and Merthyr Guardian* (6 August 1853).

[280] The song was published by H. Humphreys in Caernarfon in 1870. Huw Williams, *Canu'r Bobol* (Denbigh, 1978), p. 313.

[281] Russell Davies, 'Do not go'.

[282] *The Cambrian* (30 May 1820). Other suicides by drowning of young unmarried mothers can be found in the *North Wales Chronicle* (19 January 1836) and *The Cambrian* (7 June 1817), and two cases in the *Monmouthshire Merlin* (16 August 1862).

[283] *Monmouthshire Merlin* (23 April 1850).

[284] *Seren Gomer* (October 1835), 311.

[285] *The Cambrian* (16 February 1833).

[286] *The Cambrian* (13 April 1860).

[287] *The Cambrian* (15 June 1839).

[288] *The Cambrian* (1 June, 9 November 1839).

[289] *Carmarthen Journal* (14 July 1843).

[290] *Seren Gomer* (November 1842), 326.

[291] *The Cambrian* (12 June 1824).

[292] *Monmouthshire Merlin* (6 February 1864).

[293] *Cardiff and Merthyr Guardian* (7 July 1849).

[294] *The Cambrian* (29 July 1833).

[295] *Seren Gomer* (September 1848), 396.

[296] *The Cambrian* (9 November 1866).

[297] The author has collected 1,700 cases of suicide from the *North Wales Chronicle*, *The Cambrian*, *Carmarthen Journal*, *Monmouthshire Merlin*, *The Welshman*, *Seren Gomer* and *Y Cronicl* and from the coroner's records for Glamorganshire and Carmarthenshire. It is hoped that a detailed study can be published at a later date.

[298] *The Cambrian* (2 June 1832).

[299] Ibid. For gory reporting in the Victorian era see Thomas Boyle, *Black Swine in the Sewers of Hampstead: Beneath the Surface of Victorian Sensationalism* (London, 1990), pp. 84–92, 103–18; Robert Lee Wolff, *Strange Stories* (Boston, 1971); and Lucy Brown, *Victorian News and Newspapers* (Oxford, 1985).

[300] Hywel Teifi Edwards, *Guide to Welsh Literature*, p. 26. See also Dewi M. Lloyd, *Talhaiarn* (Cardiff, 1999).

[301] *The Cambrian* (4 March 1815).

[302] *North Wales Chronicle* (2 February 1856).

[303] *North Wales Chronicle* (28 December 1850).

[304] On death's dominance of Victorian lives see James Stevens Curl, *The Victorian Celebration of Death* (Stroud, 2000); Regina Barreca, *Sex and Death in Victorian Literature* (Basingstoke, 1990); and Ian Crichton, *The Art of Dying* (London, 1976).

3: Life and Death

[1] The largest crowd which gathered in the period 1776–1871 was the 25,000 assembled in Swansea in 1858, to watch two Greek sailors hang for murder.

[2] Peter Lord, *The Visual Culture of Wales: Industrial Society* (Cardiff, 1998), p. 85.

3 Pat Molloy, *Four Cheers for Carmarthen: The Other Side of the Coin* (Llandysul, 1981), p. 26.

4 Peter Lord, *The Visual Culture of Wales: Imaging the Nation* (Cardiff, 2000), p. 291.

5 For portents of death and their superstitions, see Chap. 6 below.

6 Russell Davies, *Secret Sins: Sex, Violence and Society in Carmarthenshire 1870–1920* (Cardiff, 1996), p. 212; and R. C. Bosanquet, 'Corpse candles in Carmarthenshire', *Carmarthenshire Antiquary*, 66, 25 (1934), 72–4.

7 George Borrow, *Wild Wales: Its People, Language and Scenery* (London, 1856), p. 301.

8 For these and other beliefs see P. H. Emerson, *Welsh Fairy Tales and Other Stories* (London, 1894); idem, *Tales from Welsh Wales, Founded on Past and Current Tradition* (London, 1894); Jonathan Ceredig Davies, *Folk-Lore of West and Mid-Wales* (Aberystwyth, 1911); and W. Howells, *Cambrian Superstitions: Comprising Ghosts, Omens, Witchcraft, Traditions etc.* (London, 1831).

9 *Bye-Gones* (18 February 1903); A. Bailey Williams, 'Customs and traditions connected with sickness, death and burial in Montgomeryshire in the late nineteenth century', *Montgomery Collections*, 52 (1951–2), 56.

10 Evan Isaac, *Coelion Cymru* (Aberystwyth, 1938); John Rhŷs, *Welsh Fairy Tales* (London, 1881–3); Edmund Jones, *A Relation of Apparitions of Spirits in the County of Monmouth and the Principality of Wales* (Newport, 1813). (A new edn, ed. John Harvey, was published in 2003 by the University of Wales Press, Cardiff.)

11 *The Cambrian* (2 March 1866).

12 George Williams (ed.), *Pregethau William Morris* (Denbigh, 1873); Anonymous, *Gwelediad y Palas Arian* (Wrexham, 1820); *Gwaith Barddonol Islwyn* (Wrexham, 1897); R. Tudur Jones, 'Hapus dyrfa: nefoedd oes Victoria' *Llên Cymru*, 13 (1980), 236–77; and Michael Wheeler, *Heaven, Hell and the Victorians* (Cambridge, 1994).

13 Ieuan Gwynedd Jones, 'Religion and society in the first half of the nineteenth century', in idem, *Explorations and Explanations: Essays in the Social History of Victorian Wales* (Llandysul, 1987), pp. 217–35; K. S. Inglis, *Churches and the Working Classes in Victorian England* (London, 1963).

14 M. Lilian Parry-Jones, 'Baledi Levi Gibbon, Thomas Harris, Stephen Jones, Ac Eraill', *Llên Cymru*, 19 (1996), 92.

15 Alan Llwyd, *Y Flodeugerdd o Ddyfyniadau Cymraeg* (Llandysul, 1988), p. 27.

16 Ibid., p. 7. Owen Williams, Owain Gwyrfai (1790–1874), was equally pessimistic: 'Rhodiais ddoe mewn anrhydedd, – / a heddiw / Fe'n huddwyd i'r dyfn fedd; / Ddoe yn gawr, heddiw'n gorwedd, / Ddoe'n y byd, heddiw'n y bedd,' (ibid., p. 297).

17 Catherine Brenan, *Angers, Fantasies and Ghostly Fears: Nineteenth Century Women from Wales and English Language Poetry* (Cardiff, 2003), p. 115.

18 Hefin Jones, *Dic Dywyll y Baledwr* (Llanrwst, 1995), p. 19.

19 H. Elvet Lewis, *Sweet Singers of Wales* (London, 1889), p. 118.

20 Ibid., p. 121.

21 Kathryn Hughes and Ceridwen Llwyd Morgan facsimile reprint of Ellen Evans *Telyn Egryn* (Dolgellau, 1850), p. 69.

[22] E. Wyn James, *Dechrau Canu, Rhai Emynau Mawr a'i Cefndir* (Bridgend, 1993), p. 31.

[23] For H. H. Vivian see Robert R. Toonney, *Vivian and Sons 1809–1924: A Study of a Firm in the Copper and Related Industries* (London, 1985).

[24] David J. V. Jones, *Rebecca's Children: A Study of Rural Society, Crime and Protest* (Oxford, 1989), p. 39; *The Cambrian* (17 July 1817).

[25] *The Cambrian* (5 May 1810).

[26] *The Cambrian* (11 August 1821). On 26 February 1850 the *North Wales Chronicle* reported the death of Catherine Parry of Llanerchymedd, Anglesey, at the great age of 106. Catherine put her longevity down to the beneficial effects of 'llwch mân Llanerchymedd' (snuff). The paper also reported the death of a 106-year-old man who fought with Nelson at Trafalgar.

[27] Glyn Tegai Hughes, 'Islwyn and *Y Storm*', in Hywel Teifi Edwards (ed.), *A Guide to Welsh Literature c.1800–1900* (Cardiff, 2000), p. 70. See also idem, *Islwyn* (Cardiff, 2003).

[28] *DWB.*

[29] T. W. Pritchard, 'Sir Watkin Williams Wynn: fourth baronet (1749–1789)', *Transactions of the Denbighshire Historical Society*, 28 (1979), 60. Gwen Emyr, *Sally Jones: Rhodd Duw i Charles* (Bridgend, 1996), p. 7.

[30] R. T. W. Denning (ed.), *The Diary of William Thomas of Michaelston-super-Ely near St Fagans, Glamorgan: 1762–1795* (Cardiff, 1995), p. 312. For orphans in society see P. E. Hair, 'Children in society 1850–1890', in T. Barker and M. Drake (eds), *Population and Society in Britain 1850–1980* (London, 1982), p. 52; and R. Tudur Jones, 'Darganfod plant bach', in J. E. Caerwyn Williams (ed.), *Ysgrifau Beirniadol VIII* (Denbigh, 1974), pp. 198–204.

[31] Ieuan Gwynedd Jones, 'Merthyr Tydfil: the politics of survival', *Llafur*, 2, 1 (1976), 22; William Kay, *Report on the Sanitary Condition of Merthyr Tydfil* (Merthyr Tydfil, 1854), p. 16.

[32] *DWB.*

[33] Siân Megan, *Ann Griffiths* (Llandybïe, 1982).

[34] R. W. Denning (ed.), *Diary of William Thomas*, p. 403.

[35] *Caernarvon and Denbigh Herald* (25 June 1853). For Richard Williams see NLW MS 12,165D.

[36] *DWB.*

[37] The tombstone of Elizabeth and Griffith Davies can be found just inside the church gate at the eastern side of the church in New Quay. *DWB.*

[38] For example, by Edward Shorter, *The Making of the Modern Family* (London, 1976), p. 169.

[39] Alan Llwyd, *Y Flodeugerdd o Ddyfyniadau Cymraeg*, p. 298.

[40] Richard J. Moore-Colyer (ed.), *A Land of Pure Delight: Selections from the Letters of Thomas Johnes of Hafod, Cardiganshire (1748–1816)* (Llandysul, 1992), p. 267.

[41] Peter Lord, *Visual Culture: Imaging the Nation*, p. 164.

[42] R. T. W. Denning (ed.), *Diary of William Thomas*.

[43] D. C. Jenkins (ed.), *The Diary of Thomas Jenkins of Llandeilo 1826–1870* (Bala, 1976), pp. 48–9.

44 William Rees, 'Fy Mab', *Y Traethodydd*, 13 (1857), 64–87, the sighting of his son's ghost is on p. 79.
45 David Owen, *Brutusiana: Sef Casgliad Detholedig o'i Cyfansoddiadau* (Llandovery, 1855), p. 363.
46 E. Wyn James, *Dechrau Canu*, p. 82.
47 J. R. Gillis, 'Servants, sexual relations, and the risk of illegitimacy in London 1801–1900', *Feminist Studies*, 5 (1979), 153–5; Russell Davies, 'In a broken dream: some aspects of sexual behavior and the dilemmas of the unmarried mother in south west Wales', *Llafur*, 3, 4 (1983), 24–33. Pembrokeshire Assizes, Spring 1864.
48 *Cardiff and Merthyr Guardian* (19 March 1853).
49 *Monmouthshire Merlin* (1 March 1862).
50 *The Cambrian* (26 October 1866).
51 *Monmouthshire Merlin* (3 February 1864). Other reported cases of infanticide are *Seren Gomer* (July 1849, in Capel Curig); *North Wales Chronicle* (14 December 1850, in Cerrig-y-Drudion).
52 *Carmarthen Journal* (1 May 1846).
53 *Carmarthen Journal* (14 January 1864).
54 *The Cambrian* (18 November 1826).
55 *Cardiff and Merthyr Guardian* (27 October 1849); Richard Holland, *Supernatural Clwyd: Folk Tales of North Wales* (Llanrwst, 1989), p. 179.
56 E. G. Millward, *Ceinion y Gân: Detholiad o Ganeuon Poblogaidd Oes Victoria* (Llandysul, 1983), p. 3.
57 Idem, 'Canu'r Byd i'w Le', in idem, *Cenedl o Bobl Ddewrion: Agweddau ar Lenyddiaeth Oes Victoria* (Llandysul, 1991), pp. 22–5.
58 E. G. Millward, *Ceinion y Gân*, p. 6.
59 T. Roberts, Scorpion (ed.), *Gweithiau Gethin* (Llanrwst, 1884), p. 259.
60 *Seventh Annual Report of the Medical Officer of Health for the Privy Council for 1864*, PP XX VI (1865), Appendix IX 'Dr Hunter on the death rate of the population of south Wales', p. 499.
61 *Carmarthen Journal* (8 June 1832).
62 Eurwyn Wiliam, *Homemade Homes* (Cardiff, 1993), p. 35.
63 R. U. Sayce, 'Food through the ages', *Montgomeryshire Collections*, 49 (1946), 275.
64 Walter Davies, *General View of the Agriculture and Domestic Economy of South Wales 11* (London, 1815), pp. 229–31.
65 S. Minwel Tibbott, *Domestic Life in Wales* (Cardiff, 2002), p. 56. For a general history of food see Peter Brears (ed.), *A Taste of History: 10,000 Years of Food in Britain* (London, 1993).
66 Dr Hunter, *Seventh Annual Report*, 1864. I am grateful to Emeritus Professor Ieuan Gwynedd Jones for a typescript of this report.
67 *North Wales Chronicle* (9 August 1856).
68 Ibid.
69 Wirt Sikes, *Rambles and Studies in Old South Wales* (London, 1881), p. 195.
70 Richard J. Moore-Colyer, *Land of Pure Delight*, p. 273.
71 NLW Nanteos 3,589. This is quoted at length in Alun Eurig Davies, 'The

condition of labour in mid-Cardiganshire in the early nineteenth century', *Ceredigion*, 4, 4 (1963), 328–30.

[72] David J. V. Jones, 'Corn riots in Wales', in idem, *Before Rebecca: Popular Protests in Wales 1793–1835* (London, 1973), pp. 13–34.

[73] Idem, 'The resistance of small farmers and squatters, 1793–1830', in ibid., pp. 35–68.

[74] Alun Eirug Davies, 'Wages, prices, and social improvement in Cardiganshire, 1750–1850', *Ceredigion*, 10, 1 (1984), 43.

[75] Quoted in Christopher Cobbe-Webbe, *Haverfordwest and its Story* (London, 1882), passim.

[76] For two treatments of the miseries of life in rural Wales see David J. V. Jones, 'Distress and discontent in Cardiganshire, 1814–1819', *Ceredigion*, 5, 3 (1966), 280–9; and M. J. Baylis, 'A portrait of Thomas Makeig IV (1772–1838) of Little Scotland and Park y Pratt', *Ceredigion*, 5, 2 (1965), 209–28.

[77] The emotions, experiences and feelings of Welsh emigrants are powerfully captured in A. Conway (ed.), *The Welsh in America* (Cardiff, 1961), passim.

[78] *Carmarthen Journal* (18 March 1864).

[79] Ieuan Gwynedd Jones, 'The observers and the observed', in idem, *Mid-Victorian Wales: The Observers and the Observed* (Cardiff, 1992), pp. 1–23.

[80] *Morning Chronicle*, letter (1 March 1850). The *Morning Chronicle* published a remarkable series of letters on the social condition of Britain between 1849 and 1851. These have been gathered by Jules Ginswick, *Labour and the Poor in England and Wales 1849–51*, vol. 3, *South Wales* (London, 1983).

[81] *Caernarvon and Denbigh Herald* (12 December 1846).

[82] Ibid.

[83] Lewis Lloyd, *Port of Caernarfon* (Harlech, 1989), p. 149.

[84] Keith Kissack, *Victorian Monmouth* (Monmouth, 1988), p. 44.

[85] *The Cambrian* (10 October 1854).

[86] For Clasemont and the 'Copper Smoke Dispute' see R. Rees, *King Copper: South Wales and the Copper Trade 1584–1895* (Cardiff, 2000), pp. 60 and 92–5. For two contrasting views of Swansea in terms of its health, compare R. T. Price, *Little Ireland: Aspects of the Irish and Greenhill, Swansea* (Swansea, 1992); and with David Boorman, *The Brighton of Wales: Swansea as a Fashionable Seaside Resort, c.1780–1830* (Swansea, 1986).

[87] Tom Ridd, 'The health of a town: Swansea in the 1840s', in Stewart Williams (ed.), *Glamorgan Historian*, vol. 1 (1963), p. 174.

[88] Ibid.

[89] R. T. Price, *Little Ireland*, p. 31.

[90] *The Cambrian* (25 December 1819).

[91] *Cardiff and Merthyr Guardian* (1 October 1853).

[92] Gwyn Jenkins, 'Hetwyr Llangynfelin', *Ceredigion*, 10, 1 (1984), 24.

[93] R. W. Jones, 'On the Employment of children and young persons in the Copper Works at Llanelly and Swansea', *Reports to the Commissioners on the Employment of Children* (London, 1842), pp. 679–90.

[94] *The Cambrian* (21 June 1817, 14 September 1822).

[95] Tom Ridd, 'Swansea's barrow boys and girls', *Gower*, 17 (1967), 51–3.

[96] W. R. Lambert, 'Swansea and its copperworks', in Stewart Williams (ed.), *Glamorgan Historian*, vol. 5 (Barry, 1969), pp. 206–12.

[97] Chris Evans, *'The Labyrinth of Flames': Work and Social Conflict in Early Industrial Merthyr Tydfil* (Cardiff, 1993), p. 45.

[98] *First Report of the Commission of Inquiry into the Employment of Children and Young persons in Mines* (1842) XVII, p. 256.

[99] Ibid., p. 194.

[100] *Seren Gomer*, 218 (1832), 350; Roger Williams and David Jones, *The Cruel Inheritance: Life and Death in the Coalfields of Glamorgan* (Pontypool, 1990); idem, *The Bitter Harvest: The Tragic History of Coalmining in Gwent* (Pontypool, 1988).

[101] *The Cambrian* (25 November 1814).

[102] *The Cambrian* (29 January 1831).

[103] *Seren Gomer* (August 1831), 227.

[104] A. H. Dodd, *The Industrial Revolution in North Wales* (Wrexham, 1971), p. 196.

[105] St Fagans MS 2130, poster to commemorate mining disasters.

[106] *Monmouthshire Merlin* (14 May 1852).

[107] *The Cambrian* (13 January 1860).

[108] A. H. Dodd, *Industrial Revolution*, p. 197.

[109] *The Cambrian* (31 May 1829).

[110] *The Cambrian* (20 February 1830).

[111] Ben Bowen Thomas, *Drych y Baledwr* (Aberystwyth, 1958), p. 107. For other ballads relating to disasters and the workplace see Owen Griffith, *Baledi Ywain Meirion* (Y Bala, 1980); Tegwyn Jones, *Abel Jones, Bardd Crwst* (Capel Garmon, 1989); idem, 'Brasolwg ar y faled newyddiadurol', *Canu Gwerin* (Folk Song), 25 (2002), 3–25; and idem, 'Y baledi a damweiniau glofaol', *Canu Gwerin*, 21 (1998), 3–21. I am grateful to Dr Huw Walters for these references.

[112] *Monmouthshire Merlin* (24 June 1837).

[113] *Monmouthshire Merlin* (1 March 1862).

[114] Ibid.

[115] *Monmouthshire Merlin* (13 July 1839).

[116] *North Wales Chronicle* (22 November 1836).

[117] *The Cambrian* (20 January 1860).

[118] *The Cambrian* (14 August 1824).

[119] *The Cambrian* (8 March 1817).

[120] *The Cambrian* (13 April 1838).

[121] *The Cambrian* (15 February 1811).

[122] *Monmouthshire Merlin* (31 March and 23 December 1837).

[123] *North Wales Chronicle* (29 November 1836).

[124] *North Wales Chronicle* (12 April 1836).

[125] *Carmarthen Journal* (9 February 1811).

[126] *The Cambrian* (14 April 1827). For the significance of public execution see V. A. C. Gatrell, *The Hanging Tree: Execution and the English People 1770–1868* (Oxford, 1996), pp. 29–99.

[127] *The Cambrian* (3 May 1817).

[128] J. Geraint Jenkins, *Maritime Heritage of Dyfed* (Llandysul, 1982), p. 249.

[129] S. C. Passmore, 'New Quay at the time of the 1851 census', *Ceredigion*, 10, 3

(1986), 307. The valuable journal *Cymru a'r Môr/Maritime Wales* has brought a number of Welsh shipwrecks to historical attention, see for example Philip O. Butler, 'Beddargraffiadau morwrol ardal Bangor', 10 (1986), 146–52; W. Carol Hughes and Tomos Williams, 'Crynodeb o hanes llongddrylliadau a ddigwyddodd ar arfordir Llŷn', 4 (1979), 106–11; Lewis Lloyd, 'The wreck of the ship *Lancaster* on Sarn Badrig', 4 (1979), 116–17; idem, 'The wreck of the barque *Wapella* in January 1868 at Dyffryn, Merioneth', 7 (1983), 123–5; and Iona Roberts, 'Llongddrylliad yn y Borthwen 1863', 12 (1989), 85–9.

[130] *The Cambrian* (28 December 1810, 4 January 1811).

[131] Ibid.

[132] *The Cambrian* (27 January 1816).

[133] *The Cambrian* (1 November 1817).

[134] Ibid.; a report in *The Cambrian* on 5 January 1822 dramatically recounted the loss of several ships on the coast of south Wales. When the Milford brig *Helena* was dismasted, all hands had to work the pumps. Several men were washed overboard when the bulwark went, leaving one man at the pumps who later died of exhaustion after the *Helena* was pulled into port by the sloop *Mary* of Weymouth.

[135] For the poetry see Hywel Teifi Edwards, *Guide*, p. 30; and Dafydd Owen, *I Fyd y Faled* (Denbigh, 1986), pp. 211, 213. Dramatic reports of the *Rothsay Castle* are in *Seren Gomer* (1831), 205 and *The Cambrian* (27 August 1831). The story of the *Royal Charter* and a subsequent salvage operation has been well told in Alexander McFee, *The Golden Wreck: The Tragedy of the 'Royal Charter'* (London, 1968) but the most dramatic account remains Charles Dickens, 'The shipwreck', *The Uncommercial Traveller* (Boston, 1871), pp. 2–10. For a superb evocation of humans dwarfed by the immense power of the sea see R. G. Howell, *Under Sail, Swansea Cutters, Tallships and Seascapes 1830–1880* (Swansea, 1987).

[136] *Seren Gomer* (August 1843), 256.

[137] *www.welshmariners.org.uk/search* (accessed 20 May 2004).

[138] *The Cambrian* (10 November 1825).

[139] *The Cambrian* (21 March 1818).

[140] Grahame Farr, 'The first Welsh lifeboats', *Cymru a'r Môr/Maritime Wales*, 2 (1977), 59–66.

[141] *The Cambrian* (6 January 1860); *North Wales Chronicle* (24 August 1860).

[142] *The Cambrian* (1875) quoted in R. Rees, *King Copper*, p. 36.

[143] *Seren Gomer* (June 1835), 191.

[144] *The Cambrian* (20 February 1830).

[145] R. Brown, *Victorian News and Newspapers* (Oxford, 1985), pp. 52–3; Louis James, *Print and the People 1819–1851* (Harmondsworth, 1978), pp. 83–7; Christopher Hibbert, *The Illustrated London News Social History of Victorian Britain* (London, 1977).

[146] *The Cambrian* (26 October 1816).

[147] *The Cambrian* (5 October 1860, 19 February 1831).

[148] *The Cambrian* (6 June 1825).

[149] *The Cambrian* (9 August 1820).

[150] *The Cambrian* (28 December 1839).
[151] *Carmarthen Journal* (7 February 1814).
[152] *The Cambrian* (28 December 1816).
[153] *Carmarthen Journal* (15 April 1814).
[154] *Carmarthen Journal* (8 February 1812).
[155] *The Cambrian* (5 July 1817).
[156] *The Cambrian* (20 January 1860).
[157] Elwyn Bowen, *Vaynor: A Study of the Welsh Countryside* (Merthyr Tydfil, 1992), p. 435.
[158] *Seren Gomer* (July 1836), 216.
[159] *The Cambrian* (27 September 1817).
[160] *The Cambrian* (17 November 1821).
[161] On the widespread use of guns in British society see G. W. B. Allen, *Pistols, Rifles and Machine Guns* (London, 1953); and Harry Hopkins, *The Long Affray: The Poaching Wars in Britain 1760–1914* (London, 1986), pp. 161, 213, 246–9.
[162] *The Cambrian* (27 December 1817).
[163] *http://history.powys.org.uk/history/newt/clife.html* (accessed 1 March 2002).
[164] *Seren Gomer* (October 1841), 316.
[165] *The Cambrian* (3 February 1827).
[166] *DWB.*
[167] *Carmarthen Journal* (9 January 1835).
[168] *The Cambrian* (16 October 1830).
[169] *The Cambrian* (8 July 1820).
[170] *The Cambrian* (18 November 1826).
[171] *Carmarthen Journal* (1 May 1866).
[172] M. Lilian Parry-Jones, *Baledi*, p. 104.
[173] *Seren Gomer* (February 1819), 62.
[174] E. Wyn James, *Dechrau Canu.*
[175] *Gweithiau Twm o'r Nant* (Cyfres y Fil), p. 18.
[176] Richard J. Moore-Colyer, *Land of Pure Delight*, pp. 95, 102 and 215.
[177] *DWB.*
[178] G. Penrhyn Jones, 'Some aspects of the medical history of Denbighshire', *Denbighshire Historical Society Transactions*, 8 (1959), 66.
[179] R. Morgan, *Cymru* (1909), 198.
[180] G. Penrhyn Jones, 'Aspects'.
[181] *Caernarvon and Denbigh Herald* (16 March 1867).
[182] R. T. W. Denning (ed.), *Diary of William Thomas* (12 August 1792).
[183] Ibid. (17 February 1792).
[184] *Monmouthshire Merlin* (4 February, 28 June 1837).
[185] G. Penrhyn Jones, 'Aspects'.
[186] *North Wales Chronicle* (17 May 1836).
[187] R. T. W. Denning (ed.), *Diary of William Thomas* (26 December 1791).
[188] R. Rees, *King Copper*, p. 39. For yellow fever in Swansea see C. E. Gordon Smith and Mary E. Gibson, 'Yellow fever in south Wales, 1865', *Medical History*, 30, 3 (1986), 322–40; and G. Buchanan, *Report . . . on the Outbreak of*

Yellow Fever at Swansea, appendix No. 15 to the Eighth Report of the Medical Officer to the Privy Council 1865 (London, 1866), pp. 440–1.

[189] *Cambria Daily Leader* (29 September 1865). On 2 October, a letter to the mayor was published, denying all the claims of 'Constant Reader'.

[190] *The Cambrian* (31 March 1832).

[191] *North Wales Chronicle* (2 August 1836).

[192] *The Cambrian* (27 April 1839).

[193] *The Cambrian* (1 June 1833).

[194] *Cardiff and Merthyr Guardian* (13 January 1849). *Carmarthen Journal* (28 December 1838).

[195] R. T. W. Denning (ed.), *Diary of William Thomas* (29 August 1785).

[196] Gareth Jones, 'The grim reaper', *Dyfed Family History Journal*, 6, 6 (April 1999), 224–7.

[197] *The Cambrian* (11 June, 19 November 1831).

[198] Alan Fletcher, 'Cholera in north-east Wales', *Denbighshire Historical Society Transactions*, 44 (1995), 25–44.

[199] NLW, 2,581.

[200] Daniel Jones, *Llef yr Arglwydd ar Gymru yn yr haint erchyslawn Y Cholera Morbus: Yn cynnwys ymddaeniad yr haint drwy'r byd; ac yn neilltuol yn Ninbych, ynghyd â'r effeithiau ar y trigolion; y pechodau a alwodd am y farn arnom; a galwad ar y bawb i edifeirwch* (Carmarthen, n.d.), p. 7.

[201] G. Penrhyn Jones, 'Cholera in Wales', *National Library of Wales Journal*, 10 (1957–8), 285; R. J. Morris, *Cholera 1832: The Social Response to an Epidemic* (New York, 1976).

[202] *DWB*.

[203] *The Cambrian* (24 November 1832).

[204] Particularly detailed minute books are available in the Glamorgan Records Office in Cardiff. U/C 3 Cardiff Union Sanitary Committee Minute Book, Daily Meetings August–September 1849.

[205] G. T. Clark, *Report to the General Board of Health on a Preliminary Inquiry into the Sewerage, Drainage . . . of the town of Swansea* (Swansea, 1849); T. W. Rammell, *Report to the General Board of Health on a Preliminary Inquiry into the Sewerage, Drainage . . . of the Town of Merthyr Tydfil* (Merthyr Tydfil, 1850); Thomas Jones Dyke, 'The sanitary history of Merthyr Tydfil', *British Medical Journal* (1885), 192.

[206] James Rogers, *A Sketch of the Cholera Epidemic in the Autumn of 1866* (Swansea, 1867), p. 5. See also *Report to the General Board of Health on the Epidemic of Cholera of 1848 and 1849*, appendix A, 1850 (1274), vol. XXI.

[207] *Cardiff and Merthyr Guardian* (19 May, 30 June 1849).

[208] G. Penrhyn Jones, 'Aspects', p. 295.

[209] Lady Charlotte Guest, *Extracts from her Journal* (Cardiff, 1950), 31 July 1849.

[210] W. Edwards, *Traethawd ar Hanes Plwyf Merthyr* (Merthyr Tydfil, 1864), p. 62.

[211] D. Williams, *Cofiant y Parch R. Ellis (Cynddelw)* (Caernarfon, 1935), p. 281. R. T. Price, *Little Ireland*, p. 25.

[212] G. Penrhyn Jones, 'Aspects', p. 296.

[213] *Report on the Cholera Epidemic of 1866 in England*, pp. 1867–8 (4072), vol.

XXXVII (London, 1868). Despite the title, pp. xlix–li, 241–51 give details of the visitation in Wales.

214 *Cardiff and Merthyr Guardian* (16 June 1849).

215 *Cardiff and Merthyr Guardian* (22 September 1849).

216 William Davies, *Casgliad o Ffraethebion Cymreig* (Treherbert, 1876), p. 50.

217 E. Clarke (ed.), *Modern Methods in the History of Medicine* (London, 1971); N. Longmate, *Alive and Well: Medicine and Public Health, 1830 to the Present Day* (London, 1970); Roy Porter, *Blood and Guts: A Short History of Medicine* (London, 2003), passim.

218 G. Penrhyn Jones, 'Aspects', p. 63.

219 Ibid.

220 *Carmarthen Journal* (24 July 1814, 24 June 1815).

221 *The Cambrian* (22 November, 6 December 1829).

222 *The Cambrian* (2 February 1829).

223 *The Cambrian* (25 August 1833).

224 Anthony S. Wohl, *Endangered Lives: Public Health in Victorian Britain* (London, 1983), pp. 132–5. B. Lucklin, 'The decline of smallpox and the demographic revolution of the eighteenth century', *Journal of Social History* (1977), 793.

225 *The Cambrian* (5 January 1839).

226 *Seren Gomer* (July 1842), 200–3.

227 For the religious revival accompanying the cholera epidemics, see C. B. Turner, 'Religion and popular revivals in Victorian and Edwardian Wales' (Unpublished Ph.D. thesis, University of Wales, Aberystwyth, 1973); and J. J. Morgan, *Dafydd Morgan a Diwygiad 1859* (Mold, 1906).

228 Pembrokeshire Records Office D/CT/162. *The Cambrian* (28 February, 24 March 1832).

229 *Cardiff and Merthyr Guardian* (24 November 1849).

230 *Cardiff and Merthyr Guardian* (9 June 1849).

231 *Carmarthen Journal* (10 August 1832).

232 *Cardiff and Merthyr Guardian* (16 June 1849).

233 *Cardiff and Merthyr Guardian* (18 August 1849); similar reports appeared on 16 June and 11 August 1849.

234 Rammell, *Report to the General Board of Health*, p. 46.

235 *Carmarthen Journal* (3 February 1832).

236 Glamorgan Archives Office Cardiff U/C 3 Cardiff Union Sanitary Committee Minute Book, Daily Meetings August–September 1849, 22, 29 August and 1 September 1849.

237 M. W. Flinn (ed.), *Edwin Chadwick's Report on the Sanitary Conditions of the Labouring Population of Great Britain* (Edinburgh, 1965), passim.

238 *Carmarthen Journal* (7 September 1832).

239 Ieuan Gwynedd Jones, *Mid-Victorian Wales*, p. 28.

240 *Caernarvon and Denbigh Herald* (8 December 1866).

241 Keith Kissack, *Victorian Monmouth*, p. 63.

242 R. Rees, *King Copper*, pp. 94–102; Thomas Williams, *Report on the Copper*

Smoke and its Influence on the Public Health and Industrial Diseases of
Coppermen (Swansea, 1854).

243 The Cambrian (7 July 1832).

244 Seren Gomer (1832), 282–4.

245 The Cambrian (18 February 1832).

246 Seren Gomer (September 1848), 396.

247 The Cambrian (28 January 1825).

248 Seren Gomer (May 1848), 392.

249 Seren Gomer, 16 (1832), 298.

250 DWB.

251 Ibid.

252 Many of these practices were used by doctors. Midwives and medics fought
a long battle in the nineteenth century to establish control of childbirth.
J. Donnison, Midwives and Medical Men: A History of Interprofessional
Rivalries and Women's Rights (London, 1977).

253 For William Richards see Seren Gomer (April 1853), 191; and North Wales
Chronicle (20 December 1846).

254 Seren Gomer, 204 (1832), 288.

255 Carmarthen Journal (24 August 1832).

256 Seren Gomer (September 1821), 257–8. On the craze for being buried alive see
Jan Bond, A Cabinet of Medical Curiosities (London, 1997), pp. 96–121.

257 J. F. C Harrison, 'Early Victorian radicals and the medical fringe', in W. F.
Bynum and R. Porter (eds), Medical Fringe and Medical Orthodoxy 1750–1850
(London, 1987), pp. 198–215; Cyril Bracegirdle, Dr William Price: Saint or
Sinner (Llanrwst, 1997), passim; and Ivan Waddington, The Medical Profession
in the Industrial Revolution (Dublin, 1984), pp. 1–5.

258 Richard Davenport-Hines, The Pursuit of Oblivion: A Social History of Drugs
(London, 2002); Virginia Berridge, Opium and the People: Opiate Use and Drug
Control Policy in Nineteenth and Early Twentieth Century England (London,
1981).

259 Ceri W. Lewis, Iolo Morganwg (Caernarfon, 1995), p. 56. Iolo in his autobiography, which is contained in his voluminous papers in the National Library,
wrote 'about 26 years of age I fell into the habit of taking Laudanum in which
I continue to this day. I took it at first [to] relieve a very troublesome cough, and
that in very large doses of nearly 300 drops at a time, which is I think more than
half an ounce'; Geraint Phillips, 'Math o wallgofrwydd: Iolo Morganwg,
opiwm a Thomas Chatterton', National Library of Wales Journal, 29 (1996),
391–410.

260 Quoted in D. Densil Morgan, Christmas Evans a'r Ymneilltuaeth Newydd
(Llandysul, 1981), 87.

261 University of Wales, Bangor MS 597. Medical Recipes of Christmas Evans,
31 December 1823. Many of his recipes contained opium.

262 NLW 12,165D.

263 David Edward Owen, British Opium Policy in China and India (London, 1933);
Peter Ward Fay, The Opium War 1840–42 (London, 1975); Barry Milligan,

Pleasures and Pains: Opium and the Orient in Nineteenth-Century British Culture (London, 1995).

[264] P. S. Brown, 'Medicines advertised in eighteenth-century Bath newspapers', *Medical History*, 20 (1976), 152–68; idem, 'The vendors of medicines advertised in eighteenth-century Bath newspapers', *Medical History*, 19 (1975), 352–69; Blanche Beatrice Elliott, *A History of English Advertising* (London, 1962). For an impression of the extent of the medical advertisements in the Welsh press see the front page of the *Cardiff and Merthyr Guardian* (25 February 1860), which included publicity for the following: 'Everyman his own doctor'; 'Dr La'Mer'd – Self Preservation and an Essay on Nervous Debility'; 'Dr Thomson's Tonic Elixir for Nervous and General Debility'; 'Dr Thomson's Invigorating Pills'; 'Mr Williams' Friendly Counsels, a popular treatise'; 'F. W. Joy and William Evans of Cardiff Neurotone'; Revd F. Russell, 'Gratis to sufferers, a clergyman having himself suffered from nervous debility . . . The Family Physician'; 'Know myself and what I'm fit for'; The 'Medical Friend and Marriage Guide or the Way to Health and Happiness'; 'Diseases and Self-Cure'. In *The Cambrian* in 1815 Dr Jones of Tenby offered a cure for all cancers and the King's evil. His elixir 'cures every species of ulcers, tumors etc. whether cancerous, scrofulous, scarbotic or syphilitic'.

[265] *DWB.*

[266] Ibid.

[267] *North Wales Chronicle* (1 January 1850).

[268] *The Cambrian* (20 August 1825).

[269] *Cardiff and Merthyr Guardian* (1 May 1858).

[270] Llew Llwyfo was scathing in his condemnation of 'Peleni Adfeiriol' Dr Hugh Smith, see Eryl Wyn Rowlands, *Y Llew Oedd ar y Llwyfan* (Caernarfon, 2001), p. 50. Brutus reserved some of his severest criticism for the false claims made by urine gazers. He related an anecdote in which he gave one a bottle of calf's urine to test. The charlatan insisted that the fluid was passed by a pregnant woman. To another, he gave a sow's urine and was told that the person who passed this water had yellow fever. He concluded 'dios bod dynion o'r natur hyn yn lladd llawer o gleifion yn eu hanwybodaeth, heblaw dinistrio iechyd cannoedd' ('undoubtedly men like these kill many through their ignorance, let alone destroy the health of hundreds'), p. 99. David Owen (Brutus), *Brutsiana* (Llandovery, 1855), pp. 97–100. J. H. Kilfer, 'Uroscopy, the artists' portrayal of the physician', *Bulletin of the New York Academy of Medicine*, 29 (1964), 759–66.

[271] *The Cambrian* (3 November 1838).

[272] *North Wales Chronicle* (28 December 1850).

[273] Roy Porter, *Quacks: Fakers and Charlatans in English Medicine* (Stroud, 2001), p. 194; H. Burger, 'The doctor, the quack and the appetite of the public for magic in medicine', *Proceedings of the Royal Society of Medicine*, 17 (1933), 171–6; J. Camp, *Magic, Myth and Medicine* (London, 1973).

[274] *The Cambrian* (12 January, 26 January, 2 February, 1 March, 8 March, 7 December 1839); T. G. Davies, 'Dau iachawr o Abertawe: y Baron Spolasco a James Rogers', *National Library of Wales Journal*, 25 (1987), 98–113.

[275] Some of the papers of the Harrises, Cwrt-y-cadno are in the Cwrtmawr collection in the National Library of Wales.

[276] Elwyn Bowen, *Vaynor: A Study of the Welsh Countryside* (Merthyr Tydfil, 1992), p. 384.

[277] *Cardiff and Merthyr Guardian* (23 June 1849).

[278] *Carmarthen Journal* (12 January 1846).

[279] *Cardiff and Merthyr Guardian* (9 June 1849).

4: Fear and Anger

[1] The story of the devil in Mary Ann Street, Cardiff, is told in *Y Cymro* (10 October 1968); *Western Mail* (17 July 1989). On fear in general see William G. Naphy and Penny Roberts (eds), *Fear in Early Modern Society* (Manchester, 1997); J. Delumeau, *Sin and Fear: The Emergence of Western Guilt Culture 13th–18th Centuries* (New York, 1990).

[2] E. Wyn James, *Dechrau Canu: Rhai Emynau Mawr a'u Cefndir* (Bridgend, 1987), p. 63.

[3] On William Williams, see Gomer M. Roberts (ed.), *Gwaith Pantycelyn* (Aberystwyth, 1960).

[4] Titus Lewis, *Llyfr Rhyfeddodau, neu Amlygiadau o waredigaethau rhyfeddol Duw i'w weision, a'i farnedigaethau trymion ar elynion* (Carmarthen, J. Evans, 1808); David Davies, *Dwy bregeth; yn gyntaf, ar ragluniaeth Duw; a'r ail, ar gyfiawnder Duw yn nghospedigaeth yr annuwiol* (Cardiff, 1842); Richard Lewis, *Cân newydd: yr hon sy'n dangos barn Duw yn y glawogydd a ddigwyddodd yn y cynhaeaf ac ar ôl hynny yn y flwyddyn 1821* (Merthyr Tydfil, 1822); T. J. Jones, *Cân neu gwyn ymostyngar, wrth ystyried yr hin a'r tywydd gwlyb, hyd fis Awst, yn y flwyddyn hon 1816* (Denbigh, 1816); Thomas Jones, *Cân newydd o ddiolchgarwch i Dduw am atal ei farnedigaeth yn amser y cynhaeaf, 1823* (Aberteifi, 1823); William Evans, *Pregeth yn dangos y modd y cyfiawnheir dyn gerbron Duw, yn myd gras, a'r angenrheidrwydd am weithredoedd da, erbyn dydd barn* (Crughywel, 1836); and Owen James, *Trugaredd a, neu, yn agos i dri chant o siamplau rhyfeddol o farnedigaethau Duw ar yr anuwiol, ac o drugaredd nodedig i'r duwiol mewn amryw wledydd ac oesoedd; gyda llawer o ystoriau buddiol eraill, wedi eu casglu allan o ysgrifeniadau gwyr dysg: er dychryn i'r drygionus, er cysur i'r daionus, ac er rhybydd i bawb* (Carmarthen, 1809).

[5] For an excellent example of a contemporary almanac see *Vox Stellarum: or, a loyal almanac, for the year of human redemption 1834* (London, 1834). William Augustus, Will Awst's *Husbandman's Perpetual Prognostication* was published by John Ross in 1794 at Carmarthen. He was widely consulted by the inhabitants of Cil-y-cwm, Carmarthenshire, for his weather forecasts.

[6] Gwen Emyr, *Sally Jones: Rhodd Duw i Charles* (Bridgend, 1986), pp. 31–5; and D. E. Jenkins, *Life of the Rev. Thomas Charles* (Denbigh, 1908).

[7] Walter E. Houghton, *The Victorian Frame of Mind* (New Haven, 1957), pp. 241–55.

[8] Ben Bowen Thomas, *Drych y Baledwr* (Aberystwyth, 1958), p. 98.

9   John Jones, *Cadach gwyn Miss Jones y Glyn: llofruddiaeth echryslawn; Fy nghariad ydwyt ti* (Llanrwst, 18??); D. Jenkins, *Galar Gân lofruddiaeth am Dafydd Lewis, gerllaw Trecastel ar Rhagfyr 6, 1844: a dienyddiad Thomas Thomas yn Aberhonddu, Ebrill 10, 1845* (Aberystwyth, 1845); Josiah Thomas Jones, *Llofruddiaeth ddychrynllyd a gymerodd le yn Duke St, Aberdar, nos Wener, Tachwedd 30ain, 1866, pryd y lladdwyd un Thomas Watkins gan Benjamin Jones, Labrwr, yr hwn sydd yn awr yn Ngharchardy Abertawy . . . Frightful murder in Duke Street, Aberdare on Friday evening, Nov. 30th, 1866, when one Thomas Watkins, a cattle-dealer, was murdered by Benjamin Jones, Labourer* (Aberdare, 1866); Ieuan Griffiths, *Cân alarus: er coffadwriaeth am y llofruddiaeth ddychrynllyd a gyflawnwyd gan Alice Hewitt ar ei mam, ac am y weithred ofnadwy cafodd hithau ei dienyddio wrth garchardy Caerleon, ar y 28ain o Ragfyr, 1863* (Cardigan, 1864); J. A. Sharpe, 'Last dying speeches: religion, ideology and public execution in seventeenth-century England', *Past and Present*, 107 (1985), 144–67; Michael Diamond, *Victorian Sensation: Or the Spectacular, the Shocking and the Scandalous in Nineteenth-Century Britain* (London, 2003), passim.

10   R. Leach, *The Punch and Judy Show: History, Tradition and Meaning* (London, 1985), p. 57.

11   M. G. R. Morris, 'Tavernspite: a meeting of the ways', *Journal of the Pembrokeshire Historical Society*, 5 (1992–3), 73.

12   NLW MS 204D. At the Carmarthenshire Assizes in April 1835, five death sentences were passed on a relatively short calendar of cases, *Seren Gomer* (April 1835). For the effect of hanging on people's fears see Steve Fielding, *Hangman's Record* (London, 1995); idem, *The Hangman's Record*, vol. 1, *1868–1899* (London, 1994); and Harry Potter, *Hanging in Judgment: Religion and the Death Penalty in England* (London, 1993). I am grateful to Dr Huw Walters for drawing these sources to my attention.

13   *Caernarvon and Denbigh Herald* (13 August 1853).

14   *Monmouthshire Merlin* (16 and 23 April 1852).

15   *The Cambrian* (5 December 1818).

16   Barry Davies and Gwyn Rhys (eds), *The Diary of William Thomas of Peterston Super Ely* (Cardiff, 1995), p. 413.

17   Lewis Lloyd, *The Port of Caernarfon* (Harlech, 1989), p. 170.

18   *The Cambrian* (13 May 1826).

19   *The Cambrian* (9 August 1817).

20   David Boorman, *The Brighton of Wales: Swansea as a Fashionable Seaside Resort c.1780–c.1830* (Swansea, 1986), p. 160.

21   V. A. C. Gatrell, B. Lenman and G. Parker (eds), *Crime and Law: The Social History of Crime in Western Europe since 1500* (London, 1980), pp. 282–3.

22   Robin Gwyndaf, 'Abergwesyn, Y Porthmyn a Ruth Watcyn', *Medel*, 1 (1985), 37.

23   D. L. Jones, *Y Ffraethebydd neu Cymhorth i Chwerthin* (Wrexham, n.d.), p. 107.

24   *Carmarthen Journal* (20 January 1832).

25   Quoted in Deirdre Beddoe, *Welsh Convict Women* (Barry, 1979), p. 50.

26   For a discussion see David Phillips, *Crime and Authority in Victorian England: The Black Country 1835–1860* (London, 1977), p. 41.

27 David J. V. Jones, *Crime in Nineteenth Century Wales* (Cardiff, 1992), pp. 30–65. See also A. A. Powell, 'Crime in Brecknockshire *c.*1733–1830 as revealed by the records of the Great Sessions' (Unpublished MA thesis, University of Wales, 1990).

28 PRO, HO 73/55. Report of 14 November 1839.

29 For example, see Henry Richard, *Letters and Essays on Wales* (London, 1866), pp. 56–78. Sir Thomas Phillips, *Wales: The Language, Social Condition, Moral Character and Religious Opinions of the People, Considered in Relation to Education* (London, 1849), p. 72, argued that Wales was not as bad as England and was in a much better condition if you took out Glamorgan and Monmouth (about half the Welsh population)! Blaming outsiders and strangers for crime is a feature of many communities, see A. Corbin, *Village of Cannibals: Rage and Murder in France, 1870* (Havard, 1993), p. 107.

30 Lytton Strachey, *Eminent Victorians* (London, 1988 edn), p. 33.

31 Carmarthen Record Office Felon's Register Accession 4,916, passim.

32 H. Zehr, *Crime and the Development of Modern Society* (London, 1982), chap. 5. For the Felons Register see Richard Ireland and Claire Breay, 'Hard labour on a hard disc: Carmarthen's register of felons on computer' *Carmarthenshire Antiquary*, 29 (1993), 61–6; and Richard Ireland, 'The felon and the angel copier: criminal identity and the promise of photography in Victorian England and Wales', in N. Knafla (ed.), *Policing and War in Europe* (Westport, CT, 2002).

33 David J. V. Jones, *Crime in Wales*, pp. 33, 19.

34 Keith Strange, 'In search of the celestial empire: crime in Merthyr, 1830–60', *Llafur*, 3, 1 (1980), 44–86.

35 David J. V. Jones, *Crime in Wales*, p. 71.

36 (T. J. Hogg), *Report on Certain Boroughs*, PP 1837–8, XXXV, pp. 37, 89.

37 V. A. C. Gatrell, 'The decline of theft and violence in Victorian and Edwardian England, 1834–1914', in V. A. C. Gatrell, B. Lenman and G. Parker (eds), *Crime and Law*, p. 240.

38 *North Wales Chronicle* (24 May 1836).

39 *Carmarthen Journal* (1 and 15 March 1829).

40 *The Cambrian* (3 February 1827).

41 *The Cambrian* (8 March 1829).

42 *The Cambrian* (2 July 1835).

43 *The Cambrian* (19 April 1817).

44 *North Wales Chronicle* (1 January 1850).

45 *The Cambrian* (29 April 1820, 15 March 1829, 23 August 1829, 2 January 1830).

46 *North Wales Chronicle* (1 January 1850).

47 *Carmarthen Journal* (28 December 1839).

48 *Carmarthen Journal* (9 December 1820).

49 *Carmarthen Journal* (2 March 1832).

50 *The Cambrian* (22 March 1827).

51 *Seren Gomer* (August 1832).

52 *The Cambrian* (17 and 24 March, 29 September 1810).

53 *The Cambrian* (7 October 1826).

54 *The Cambrian* (9 September 1826).

55   *The Cambrian* (17 November 1838).
56   *Carmarthen Journal* (21 July 1843).
57   *The Cambrian* (12 November 1825).
58   *The Cambrian* (24 March 1821).
59   NLW, Lochturfin 3. This is quoted at length in Glyn Parry, *Naid i Dragwyddoldeb: Trosedd a Chosb 1700–1900* (Aberystwyth, 2001), p. 13.
60   David J. V. Jones, *Crime in Wales*, pp. 128, 188.
61   *Cardiff and Merthyr Guardian* (24 November 1849).
62   *Carmarthen Journal* (28 December 1838, 8 and 15 August 1845).
63   *Carmarthen Journal* (3 November 1842).
64   *The Cambrian* (24 October 1817).
65   *The Cambrian* (28 December 1816).
66   *The Cambrian* (3 July 1820).
67   *The Cambrian* (23 January 1830).
68   Dafydd Owen, *I Fyd y Faled* (Denbigh, 1986), p. 200.
69   Evidence given to the *Reports for the Committee of Commons Inclosures* session 1 February–5 September 1844, vol. v (1844), p. 211.
70   *Carmarthen Journal* (22 July 1831).
71   E. Vaughan Jones, 'Sheep stealing at Llangelynin, 1792', *Journal of the Merioneth Historical and Record Society*, 7, 4 (1976), 401–2.
72   *The Cambrian* (18 December 1824).
73   On juvenile delinquency see J. Manton, *Mary Carpenter and the Children of the Streets* (London, 1976); and J. R. Gillis, *Youth and History: Tradition and Change in European Age Relations, 1770–Present* (London, 1974).
74   *Cardiff and Merthyr Guardian* (7 May 1853).
75   *Report on Employment of Children*, PP (1842), XVII, appendix, part ii, p. 506.
76   *Carmarthen Journal* (9 January 1846).
77   Glamorgan Record Office Cardiff, D/D Con C/3/5/2 Habitual Criminals Record Book.
78   *The Cambrian* (17 March 1827).
79   *Monmouthshire Merlin* (15 January 1831).
80   *The Cambrian* (24 March 1810).
81   *The Cambrian* (17 December 1814).
82   *The Cambrian* (5 August 1825).
83   *The Cambrian* (23 March 1833).
84   *The Cambrian* (4 May 1812).
85   Hywel Teifi Edwards, 'The eisteddfod poet: an embattled figure', in idem (ed.), *A Guide to Welsh Literature c.1800–1900* (Cardiff, 2000), p. 29.
86   *The Cambrian* (23 November 1822).
87   Francis Jones, *A Treasury of Historic Pembrokeshire* (Newport, 1998), p. 239.
88   For the duel see V. G. Kiernan, *The Duel in European History: Honour and the Reign of Aristocracy* (Oxford, 1989); and Robert B. Shoemaker, 'The taming of the duel: masculinity, honour and ritual violence in London, 1600–1800', *Historical Journal*, 45, 3 (2002). For Welsh duels see *The Cambrian* (2 March 1811, 31 August 1811, 25 January 1817, 14 June 1817, 20 June 1818, 21 March 1819, 15 May 1819, 28 August 1819, 24 March 1821, 5 January 1822, 23 November 1822) and *Seren Gomer* (June 1819, January 1834).

89 Dafydd Wyn Wiliam, 'Almanacwyr Caergybi', *Anglesey Antiquarian Society Transactions* (1984), 102.
90 E. G. Millward, *Ceinion y Gân* (Llandysul, 1983), pp. 11–12. For Cranogwen see Tegwyn Jones, *Anecdotau Llenyddol* (Talybont, 1987), p. 101.
91 *The Cambrian* (10 August 1866).
92 *The Cambrian* (5 January 1866).
93 E. Vaughan Jones, 'A Merioneth murder of 1812', *Journal of the Merioneth Historical and Record Society*, 6, 1 (1969), 66–104.
94 *The Cambrian* (25 September 1812).
95 *The Cambrian* (18 September 1812).
96 *The Cambrian* (29 September 1810).
97 *Carmarthen Journal* (5 August 1814).
98 *The Cambrian* (10 May 1817).
99 *The Cambrian* (19 February 1820).
100 *The Cambrian* (4 October 1829).
101 For a few murders see *Seren Gomer* (1836), 215–16, and (December 1848), 387, *Carmarthen Journal* (8 July 1864) and the *Cardiff and Merthyr Guardian* (31 March 1849). Some of the gorier murders have been retold in Peter Fuller and Brian Knapp, *Welsh Murders*, vol. 1, *1770–1918* (Llandybie, 1986); Bethan Phillips, *Dihirod Dyfed* (Cardiff, 1991); Eigra Lewis Roberts, *Llygaid am Lygad* (Llandysul, 1990); idem, *Dant am Ddant* (Llandysul, 1996); J. Towyn Jones, *Ar Lwybr Llofrudd* (Llandysul, 1990); and Gwylon Phillips, *Llofruddiaeth Shadrach Lewis* (Llandysul, 1986).
102 *Seren Gomer* (June 1848), 191–2.
103 *The Cambrian* (19 December 1818).
104 *The Cambrian* (12 August 1826).
105 For example, in the *Cardiff and Merthyr Guardian* (1 January 1853), and *Seren Gomer* (September 1842), 184–5.
106 *The Cambrian* (15 July 1826).
107 On domestic violence in the nineteenth century see S. D'Cruze, *Crimes of Outrage: Sex, Violence and Victorian Women* (London, 1998); L. Gordon, 'Family violence, feminism and social control', *Feminist Studies*, 12, 3 (1986), 376–96; idem, *Heroes of their own Lives: The Politics and History of Family Violence* (London, 1989); A. J. Hammerton, *Cruelty and Companionship: Conflict in Nineteenth-Century Married Life* (London, 1992); N. A. Jones, 'A torrent of abuse: crimes of violence between working-class men and women in London', *Journal of Social History*, 2 (1978), 328–45; and Russell Davies, 'Voices from the void: social crisis, social problems and the individual in south west Wales, c.1876–1920', in Geraint H. Jenkins and J. Beverley Smith (eds), *Politics and Society in Wales, 1840–1922* (Cardiff, 1988).
108 *Carmarthen Journal* (21 April 1843).
109 *Cardiff and Merthyr Guardian* (20 August 1853).
110 *The Cambrian* (19 April 1811); *Carmarthen Journal* (13 and 20 April 1811).
111 *The Cambrian* (19 July 1817).
112 *The Cambrian* (30 August 1829).
113 *The Cambrian* (30 August 1817).

[114] *Carmarthen Journal* (14 February 1814).

[115] *The Cambrian* (30 August 1817). For the murder of Tamar Edwards see 'Llofruddio mam gan ei mab', *Seren Gomer*, 25 (1842); and 'Dienyddiad Dic Tamar', *Seren Gomer* (September 1842), 203.

[116] *Seren Gomer* (14 September 1827); and *Caernarvon and Denbigh Herald* (4 January 1862).

[117] *Carmarthen Journal* (4 May 1849).

[118] *Carmarthen Journal* (24 July 1835).

[119] *Monmouthshire Merlin* (22 July 1837).

[120] *Carmarthen Journal* (3 August 1811).

[121] On crimes of violence against children in Wales see Richard W. Ireland, 'Perhaps my mother murdered me: child death and the law in Victorian Carmarthenshire', in C. Brooks and M. Lobban (eds), *Communities and Courts in Britain 1150–1880* (London, 1997), pp. 229–44; and idem, 'Confinement with hard labour: motherhood and penal practice in a Victorian gaol', *Welsh History Review*, 18 (1996–7), 621–38. For the British practice see Lionel Rose, *Massacre of the Innocents: Infanticide in Great Britain 1800–1939* (London, 1986).

[122] *Carmarthen Journal* (17 March 1848, 11 October 1850 and 30 April, 7 May and 15 July 1847).

[123] *The Welshman* (13 January and 24 March 1843).

[124] *Carmarthen Journal* (7 May 1847).

[125] *Caernarvon and Denbigh Herald* (31 March 1866).

[126] *The Cambrian* (12 April 1817).

[127] *Cardiff and Merthyr Guardian* (2 April 1859).

[128] *Cardiff and Merthyr Guardian* (12 March 1853).

[129] *North Wales Chronicle* (26 January 1836).

[130] *North Wales Chronicle* (14 June 1836).

[131] *Monmouthshire Merlin* (1 April 1837).

[132] *Carmarthen Journal* (6 August 1831); *The Cambrian* (6 August 1831).

[133] *Carmarthen Journal* (15 July 1864).

[134] *The Cambrian* (28 July 1838). For similar cases of concealment of birth and infanticide see *The Cambrian* (2 May 1817, Llanddeusant), (5 June 1839, Cardiff), (12 January 1833, Monmouth), (24 March 1833, Pembroke), (23 June 1832, Gwynfe), (21 May 1831, Swansea), (26 April 1817, Pwllheli), (17 April 1830, Presteigne), (17 April 1830, Pembrokeshire), (8 December 1827, Bridgend); *Carmarthen Journal* (16 July 1813, Kidwelly), (25 February 1814, St Ishmaels), (10 August 1811, Monmouth), (2 April 1847, Ystradgynlais); *Monmouthshire Merlin* (8 April 1837, Newport), (16 August 1862, Newport), *Seren Gomer*, 251, 254 (1826), (Denbigh), (January 1836), 30 (Llandeilo); (April 1836), 30 (Llandeilo Talybont), (April 1834), 126 (Llangamarch), (April 1834), 125 (Carmarthen), (January 1819), 3 (Swansea), 202 (1832), 224 (Tally), (May 1844), 151 (Mynydd Islwyn), 199 (1832), 123 (Pembrokeshire); *Cardiff and Merthyr Guardian* (20 January 1849, Cardiff), (10 March 1849, Cardiff); *Caernarvon and Denbigh Herald* (13 October 1866, Bethesda), (12 October 1872, Llandrindod Wells).

[135] Jennifer Green, *The Morning of her Day* (Liverpool, 1987); Patricia Parris,

'Mary Morgan: contemporary sources', *Transactions of the Radnorshire Society*, 53 (1983), 57–64. The quotation is from a letter Justice Hardinge wrote to the bishop of St Asaph in April 1805, published in John Nichols (ed.), *Illustrations of the Literary History of the Eighteenth Century*, vol. 3 (London, 1818), p. 126.

[136] *The Cambrian* (13 May 1815).

[137] *Cardiff and Merthyr Guardian* (28 July 1849).

[138] *Carmarthen Journal* (10 September 1813).

[139] *Carmarthen Journal* (28 April 1843).

[140] *Carmarthen Journal* (19 June 1829).

[141] *The Cambrian* (20 June 1822).

[142] *The Cambrian* (8 June and 7 September 1816).

[143] *The Cambrian* (27 August 1827).

[144] *The Cambrian* (16 May 1817).

[145] *Carmarthen Journal* (15 March 1814).

[146] *Carmarthen Journal* (18 June 1835); and *Seren Gomer* (July 1835), 218.

[147] *Seren Gomer* (March 1848), 96; David J. V. Jones, *Crime in Wales*, p. 74.

[148] *Cardiff and Merthyr Guardian* (11 March 1859).

[149] *North Wales Chronicle* (7 December 1850); *Seren Gomer* (September 1850), 316.

[150] *The Cambrian* and the *Carmarthen Journal* (10 July 1824).

[151] *North Wales Chronicle* (12 October 1850).

[152] *The Cambrian* (9 September 1826).

[153] *The Cambrian* (25 June 1825).

[154] *The Cambrian* (12 March 1831).

[155] *The Cambrian* (4 April 1818).

[156] *The Cambrian* (28 May 1831).

[157] *The Cambrian* (1 June 1833).

[158] *The Cambrian* (29 November 1814).

[159] *The Cambrian* (6 October 1821).

[160] *The Cambrian* (10 November 1827).

[161] *The Cambrian* (19 September 1818).

[162] *Seren Gomer* (August 1836), 254.

[163] *The Cambrian* (14 April 1838).

[164] *Seren Gomer* (June 1819).

[165] *Carmarthen Journal* (20 October 1835).

[166] *The Cambrian* (6 May 1829); Glyn Parry, *Naid i Dragwyddoldeb: Trosedd a Chosb 1700–1900* (Aberystwyth, 2001), p. 5.

[167] *Carmarthen Journal* (20 June 1862).

[168] *Seren Gomer* (December 1834), 373.

[169] *Seren Gomer* (August 1848), 251.

[170] *Seren Gomer* (August 1841), 253.

[171] *Monmouthshire Merlin* (11 February 1837).

[172] Ivor Waters, *Inns and Taverns of Chepstow and the Lower Wye Valley* (Chepstow, 1976), p. 71.

[173] *Monmouthshire Merlin* (1 April 1837).

[174] *Cardiff and Merthyr Guardian* (23 April 1853).

[175] For other Welsh murders involving drink see Glamorgan Record Office Cardiff O/D XBG 19, 13 February 1846 (in Caerphilly); *Carmarthen Journal* (21 August 1835, Chepstow), (30 January 1835, Swansea), (21 August 1835, Knighton); *North Wales Chronicle* (12 October 1850, Pen-y-groes, north Wales), (29 March 1856, a field in north Wales); *The Cambrian* (22 May 1830, Carmarthen), (12 January 1822, Carmarthen); *Seren Gomer* (August 1848), 256 (Pembrokeshire).

[176] *Seren Gomer* (January 1846), 30.

[177] *The Cambrian* (1 April 1826).

[178] *The Cambrian* (31 October 1854).

[179] Edward Pugh, *Cambria Depicta* (London, 1816), p. 75.

[180] *Monmouthshire Merlin* (16 August 1862).

[181] *Cardiff and Merthyr Guardian* (25 August 1849).

[182] *Cardiff and Merthyr Guardian* (29 January 1853).

[183] *The Cambrian* (19 April 1817).

[184] *North Wales Chronicle* (2 August 1856).

[185] *Carmarthen Journal* (7 January 1859).

[186] David J. V. Jones, *Crime in Wales*, pp. 93–7.

[187] On the *Ceffyl Pren* tradition see Rosemary Jones, 'Women, community and collective action: the *Ceffyl Pren* tradition', in Angela John (ed.), *Our Mother's Land: Chapters in Welsh Women's History 1830–1939* (Cardiff, 1991), pp. 17–42; and eadem, 'Separate spheres?' Women, language and respectability in Victorian Wales', in Geraint H. Jenkins (ed.), *The Welsh Language and its Social Domains 1800–1911* (Cardiff, 2000). For similar traditions in England see E. P. Thompson, 'Rough music: le charivari anglais', *Annales ESC*, 27 (1972), 285–312; and Martin Ingram, 'Ridings, rough music and the "reform of popular culture" in early modern England', *Past and Present*, 105 (1984), 79–113. For European traditions see Eugen Weber, *Peasants into Frenchmen: The Modernization of Rural France 1870–1914* (London, 1977), pp. 309–406.

[188] *Carmarthen Journal* (4 November 1864).

[189] *The Cambrian* (20 April 1839).

[190] *The Cambrian* (29 July 1833).

[191] *Monmouthshire Merlin* (1 April 1837).

[192] *The Cambrian* (16 November 1860).

[193] *Carmarthen Journal* (1 February 1812).

[194] *The Cambrian* (26 October 1866).

[195] *North Wales Chronicle* (10 August 1850).

[196] *Caernarvon and Denbigh Herald* (22 March 1862).

[197] *Monmouthshire Merlin* (27 December 1862).

[198] *The Cambrian* (15 and 28 April 1810).

[199] *The Cambrian* (24 August 1819).

[200] *The Cambrian* (1 April and 25 August 1826).

[201] For anti-Irish riots in Wales see Paul O'Leary, 'Anti-Irish riots in Wales', *Llafur*, 5 (1991), 27–36.

[202] *Cardiff and Merthyr Guardian* (9 July 1853).

[203] Elizabeth Inglis Jones, 'Memories of old Cardiganshire', *Ceredigion*, 4, 1 (1960), 73.

204 *Cardiff and Merthyr Guardian* (14 June 1834).

205 Quoted in David J. V. Jones, 'Distress and discontent in Cardiganshire 1814–9', *Ceredigion*, 5, 2 (1965), 280–9.

206 D. Parry Jones, *Welsh Country Upbringing* (London, 1948), p. 98.

207 For two contemporary views see John Henry Cliffe, *Notes and Recollections of an Angler* (London, 1860); and Griffith Evan Jones, *Confessions of a Welsh Salmon Poacher* (Holborn, 1877).

208 David J. V. Jones, 'The poacher: a study in Victorian crime and protest', *Historical Journal*, 22, 4 (1977), 825–60.

209 *Caernarvon and Denbigh Herald* (15 February 1862).

210 David J. V. Jones, 'The second Rebecca riots: a study of poaching on the River Wye', *Llafur*, 2, 1 (1976), 32–56. See also Harry Hopkins, *The Long Affray: The Poaching Wars in Britain* (London, 1986).

211 David J. V. Jones, 'Second Rebecca riots', 37.

212 David Howell, *The Rural Poor in Eighteenth Century Wales* (Cardiff, 2000), p. 197.

213 S. C. Ellis, 'Observations of Anglesey life in quarter sessions rolls', *Transactions of the Anglesey Antiquarian Society* (1986), 133.

214 G. Smith, *Smuggling in the British Channel 1700–1850* (Newbury, 1989), p. 92.

215 Thomas Pennant, *History of the parishes of Whiteford and Holywell* (London, 1796), p. 92.

216 S. C. Passmore, 'New Quay at the time of the 1851 Census', *Ceredigion*, 10, 3 (1986), 301–28.

217 *The Cambrian* (30 January 1821).

218 *The Cambrian* (17 April 1824).

219 *Cardiff and Merthyr Guardian* (1 January 1859).

220 G. I. Hawkes, 'Illicit trading in Wales in the eighteenth century', *Cymru a'r Môr/Maritime Wales*, 10 (1986), 104–5. See also James W. Dawson, *Commerce and Customs: A History of the Ports of Newport and Caerleon* (Newport, 1932), pp. 93–9.

221 *Carmarthen Journal* (3 November 1843).

222 *The Cambrian* (8 December 1832).

223 *Caernarvon and Denbigh Herald* (30 March 1835).

224 *The Cambrian* (16 February 1829).

225 *The Cambrian* (11 January 1816).

226 *The Cambrian* (4 October 1817).

227 *The Cambrian* (8 January 1820).

228 *The Cambrian* (1 February 1817).

229 *The Cambrian* (15 March 1806).

230 M. J. Baylis, 'A portrait of Thomas Makeig IV (1772–1838) of Little Scotland and Park y Pratt', *Ceredigion*, 5, 2 (1965), 221–2; and Tom Bennett, *Shipwrecks around Wales*, 2 vols, Newport, 1987, 1992), vol. 1, p. 63.

231 Huw Williams, *Canu'r Bobol* (Denbigh, 1978) has a discussion of the background of *Brad Dynarfon*. The Welsh wreckers met their match on the morning after the great hurricane of 25–26 October 1859 – the night of the loss of the *Royal Charter*. Rushing to the beach at Porth Colmon, the locals were

met with the terrifying sight of rough Spaniards, swords buckled to their belts, who looked as though they would cut a few throats at the slightest provocation. Dilys Gater, *Historic Shipwrecks of Wales* (Llanrwst, 1992), p. 12.

[232] *The Cambrian* (29 July 1833).

[233] David Howell, *The Rural Poor in Eighteenth-Century Wales*, p. 207.

[234] *Monmouthshire Merlin* (30 November 1839).

[235] *The Cambrian* (1 June 1827).

[236] *Carmarthen Journal* (8 May 1835).

[237] *Carmarthen Journal* (20 April 1832).

[238] *The Cambrian* (1 June 1827, 4 May 1833). On the Usk escapees see Brian Foster, 'The Usk houses of correction and the early days of the Usk county gaol', *Gwent Local History*, 94 (2003), 3–31; for other Welsh prisons see Hugh J. Owen, 'The common gaols of Merioneth during the eighteenth and nineteenth centuries', *Journal of the Merioneth Historical and Records Society*, 3, 1 (1957). For a general history of imprisonment see Christopher Harding, Bill Hines, Richard Ireland and Philip Rawlings, *Imprisonment in England and Wales: A Concise History* (Beckenham, 1985).

[239] *Carmarthen Journal* (5 March 1832).

[240] *The Cambrian* (8 September 1832).

[241] *The Cambrian* (13 February 1830).

[242] On Welsh juries see Richard Ireland, 'Putting oneself on whose country? Carmarthenshire juries in the mid-nineteenth century', in T. G. Watkin (ed.), *Legal Wales, its Past, its Future* (Cardiff, 2001).

[243] *The Cambrian* (19 April 1811).

[244] *The Cambrian* (5 January 1866); a similar incident happend at Monmouth, *Monmouthshire Merlin* (13 August 1831).

[245] R. C. B. Oliver, 'The Gwardole letters of 1843', *Transactions of the Radnorshire Society*, 62 (1992), 30.

[246] *Carmarthen Journal* (18 March 1843). Elwyn Davies and Brian Howells (eds), *Pembrokeshire County History*, vol 4, *Modern Pembrokeshire 1815–1974* (Haverfordwest, 1993), p. 315.

[247] R. W. Ireland, 'Putting oneself', p. 70.

[248] Thomas Edwards, *Tri Chryfion Byd*, ed. Norah Isaac (Llandysul, 1975). For a discussion of the characters and social context of the *anterliwtiau* see Saunders Lewis, 'Twm o'r Nant', in R. Geraint Gruffydd (ed.), *Meistri'r Canrifoedd* (Cardiff, 1973), pp. 280–98, and Rhiannon Ifans, *'Cân di Benill . . .?': Themâu Anterliwtiau Twm o'r Nant* (Aberystwyth, 1997).

[249] Ivor Waters, *Inns*, p. 81.

[250] Roy Porter, *English Society in the Eighteenth Century* (Harmondsworth, 1990 edn), pp. 130–42.

[251] For examples of the severe sentence meted out to coiners and forgers, see *The Cambrian* (13 February 1819, 10 April 1819, 12 June 1819, 10 July 1819, 11 February 1820, 2 September 1820, 12 January 1827), and the *Monmouthshire Merlin* (1 April 1837).

[252] David J. V. Jones, *Crime in Wales*, p. 115.

[253] *The Cambrian* (13 December, 25 December and 27 December 1817, and 28 March 1818).

[254] *Report of the Commissioners of Inquiry into the State of Education in Wales,* 1847 (870), xxvii, p. 31.

[255] Ibid.

[256] For the climate of fear in the heads of the valleys communities in the south-east see David J. V. Jones, *The Last Rising: The Newport Chartist Insurrection of 1839* (Oxford, 1985), pp. 161–5, 172.

[257] W. Lloyd Davies, 'The riot at Denbigh in 1795: Home Office correspondence', *Bulletin of the Board of Celtic Studies,* 4 (1928–9).

[258] David J. V. Jones, *Before Rebecca: Popular Protests in Wales 1793–1835* (London, 1973), pp. 52–3; David Howell, *Rural Poor,* pp. 204–5.

[259] Gareth Elwyn Jones, *Modern Wales: A Concise History c.1485–1979* (Cambridge, 1984), p. 229.

[260] David Howell, *Rural Poor,* p. 186.

[261] Hilary M. Thomas, *The Diaries of John Bird 1790–1803* (Cardiff, 1987), p. 131.

[262] For the heady, millenarian atmosphere see Gwyn A. Williams, *When was Wales?* (London, 1985), pp. 159–73; David Davies, *The Influence of the French Revolution on Welsh Life and Literature* (Carmarthen, 1926), pp. 22–79; and J. J. Evans, *Dylanwad y Chwyldro Ffrengig ar Lenyddiaeth Cymru* (Liverpool, 1928), pp. 73–85. For an excellent summary of the British context see Edward Royle, *Revolutionary Britannia? Reflections on the Threat of Revolution in Britain, 1789–1848* (Manchester, 2000).

[263] NLW, Great Sessions 4/628/5.

[264] NLW, Great Sessions 4/256/4.

[265] NLW, Great Sessions 4/753/1. For a discussion see Milwyn Griffiths, 'Denbighshire in the records of the Court of Great Sessions', *Denbighshire Historical Society Transactions,* 22 (1973), 117–20; and Geraint H. Jenkins, 'A very horrid affair: sedition and unitarianism in the age of revolution', in R. R. Davies and Geraint H. Jenkins (eds), *From Medieval to Modern Wales* (Cardiff, 2004), pp. 175–96.

[266] Iorwerth Peate, *Yr Hen Gapel, Llanbrynmair 1739–1939* (Llandysul, 1939); and idem, 'Traddodiad Llanbrynmair' *Transactions of the Honourable Society of Cymmrodorion* (1954), 10–17.

[267] NLW, Great Sessions, 4/196/1. Quoted in Melvin Humphreys, *The Crisis of Community, Montgomeryshire, 1680–1815* (Cardiff, 1996), p. 260.

[268] Hugh Jones, *Hymnau Newyddion: Ynghyd ag Ychydig Benhillion ar yr Amserau* (Chester, 1797), p. 6.

[269] Gwyn A. Williams, *Madoc: The Making of a Myth* (London, 1979), pp. 89–91; and Hywel M. Davies, 'Very different springs of uneasiness: emigration from Wales to the United States of America during the 1790s', *Welsh History Review,* 15 (1991), 373–5.

[270] For William Jones see Geraint H. Jenkins, *The Foundations of Modern Wales 1642–1780* (Cardiff and Oxford, 1987), pp. 301, 332, 387–8.

[271] J. B. Edwards, 'John Jones (Jac Glan-y-Gors): Tom Paine's Denbighshire henchman?', *Denbighshire Historical Society Transactions,* 51 (2002), 95–112; and E. G. Millward, *John Jones (Jac Glan-y-Gors)* (Cardiff, 2003).

[272] John Saunders Lewis, 'Jac Glan-y-Gors', *The Welsh Outlook* (1919), 238.

[273] On Richard Price see D. O. Thomas, *The Honest Mind: The Thought and Work of Richard Price* (Oxford, 1977); and Martin Fitzpatrick, 'Historical religion and radical political ideas in late eighteenth century England', in Eckhard Hellmuth (ed.), *The Transformation of Political Culture: England and Germany in the Late Eighteenth Century* (London, 1990), pp. 339–72.

[274] David Williams, *Autobiography: Incidents in My Own Life Which have been Thought of Some Importance* (1802?, Brighton, 1980 edn); J. Dybikowski, *On Burning Ground: An Examination of the Ideas, Projects and Life of David Williams* (Oxford, 1993); David Williams, 'The Missions of David Williams and James Tilly Matthews to England (1793)', *English Historical Review*, 53 (1938), 651–68.

[275] Geraint Dyfnallt Owen, *Thomas Evans, Tomos Glyn Cothi* (Swansea, 1967). The general atmosphere of the 1790s is well told in Gwyn A. Williams, 'Druids and democrats: organic intellectuals and the first Welsh nation', in idem, *The Welsh in their History* (London, 1982), pp. 31–64.

[276] David J. V. Jones, 'The Carmarthen riots of 1831', in idem, *Before Rebecca*, pp. 117–32; Pat Molloy, *A Shilling for Carmarthen: The Town they Nearly Tamed* (Llandysul, 1930); and idem, *Four Cheers for Carmarthen: The Other Side of the Coin* (Llandysul, 1981); for an interesting reaction to the riotous tradition of Carmarthen see the bad-tempered report of Superintendent Lewis to the magistrates after riots at the 1876 election. Carmarthenshire Record Office, Carmarthen Borough Police Report Book, 1876–1878.

[277] Gwyn A. Williams, *The Merthyr Rising* (London, 1978), passim.

[278] Owen R. Ashton, 'Chartism in mid-Wales', *Montgomery Collections*, 62, 1 (1971–2), 10–57.

[279] *Monmouthshire Merlin* (23 November 1839); David J. V. Jones, *The Last Rising*, pp. 153, 278.

[280] David Williams, *John Frost: A Study in Chartism* (Cardiff, 1939), passim; and Ivor Wilks, *South Wales and the Rising of 1839: Class Struggle as Armed Struggle* (London, 1984), passim.

[281] David J. V. Jones, 'More light on Rhyfel y Sais Bach', *Ceredigion*, 4 (1965); David Williams, 'Rhyfel y Sais Bach', *Ceredigion*, 2 (1952); D. Jenkins, 'Rhyfel y Sais Bach', *Ceredigion*, 1 (1951); W. J. Lewis, 'A disturbance on Llanrhystud Mountain', *Ceredigion*, 4 (1962); idem, 'The condition of labour in mid Cardiganshire in the early nineteenth century?, *Ceredigion*, 4 (1963); and David J. V. Jones, 'Distress and discontent in Cardiganshire 1814–1819', *Ceredigion*, 5, 3 (1966). For a contemporary comment see *The Cambrian* (8 July and 26 August 1826).

[282] Rosemary Jones, 'Popular culture, policing, and the "disappearance" of the *Ceffyl Pren* in Ceredigion, c.1837–1850', *Ceredigion*, 11 (1988–9), 19–39.

[283] Rebecca has been very fortunate in her historians. There are two classic accounts: David Williams, *The Rebecca Riots* (Cardiff, 1971 edn); and David J. V. Jones, *Rebecca's Children: A Study of Rural Society, Crime and Protest* (Oxford, 1989).

[284] This argument was powerfully put by Henry Richard, *Letters and essays on Wales* (London, 1866), pp. 52–70.

285 For the Liberation Society see Ieuan Gwynedd Jones, 'The Liberation Society and Welsh politics', in idem, *Explorations and Explanations: Essays in the Social History of Victorian Wales* (Llandysul, 1981), pp. 236–68; see also idem, *Communities: Essays in the Social History of Victorian Wales* (Llandysul, 1987).

286 Pembrokeshire Record Office D/CT/512.

287 David J. V. Jones, 'Second Rebecca riots', 32–56.

288 For disturbances in 1856 see *North Wales Chronicle* (8 and 22 March 1856).

289 Tim Jones, *Rioting in North East Wales* (Wrexham, 1997).

290 Jenny Griffiths and Mike Griffiths, *The Mold Tragedy of 1869* (Llanrwst, 2001).

291 *Monmouthshire Merlin* (23 November 1868).

292 Hywel M. Davies, 'Loyalism in Wales, 1792–93', *Welsh History Review*, 20, 4 (2001), 691.

293 E. D. Evans, *A History of Wales 1660–1815* (Cardiff, 1976), p. 224.

294 Hywel M. Davies, 'Loyalism', p. 707.

295 *The Cambrian* (3 July 1830); Edward Pearce, *Reform: The Fight for the 1832 Reform Act* (London, 2004).

296 *Seren Gomer* provides several examples of support for Queen Caroline; see, for example, December 1821, 336–7. For ballads showing her support see Dafydd Owen, *I Fyd y Faled* (Denbigh, 1986), p. 300.

297 For discussion of these themes see I. R. Christie, *Stress and Stability in Late-Eighteenth Century Britain* (Oxford, 1984); H. T. Dickinson, *British Radicalism and the French Revolution* (Oxford, 1985); J. R. Dinwiddy, *Radicalism and Reform in Britain, 1780–1850* (London, 1992); R. R. Pozier, *For King, Constitution and Country: the English Loyalists and the French Revolution* (Lexington, KY, 1983); I. McCalman, *Radical Underworld: Prophets, Revolutionaries and Pornographers in London, 1795–1840* (Cambridge, 1988); R. Reid, *Land of Lost Content: The Luddite Revolt, 1812* (London, 1986); E. P. Thompson, *The Making of the English Working Class* (Harmondsworth, 1968); R. Wells, *Insurrection: The British Experience, 1795–1803* (Gloucester, 1986); and David Snodin, *A Mighty Ferment: Britain in the Age of Revolution 1750–1850* (London, 1978).

298 For the use made by the common people of the Welsh courts see Melvyn Humphreys, *Crisis of Community: Montgomeryshire 1680–1815* (Cardiff, 1996), pp. 249–251; and Richard Suggett, 'Slander in early-modern Wales', *Bulletin of the Board of Celtic Studies*, 29 (1992), 119–49. See also C. W. Brooks, 'Interpersonal conflict and social tension: civil litigation in England, 1640–1830', in A. L. Beier, David Cannadine and James M. Rosenheim (eds), *The First Modern Society: Essays in English History in Honour of Lawrence Stone* (Cambridge, 1989), pp. 357–400; Rob Sindall, *Street Violence in the Nineteenth Century* (Leicester, 1990); and Mark Harrison, *Crowds and History: Mass Phenomena in English Towns, 1790–1835* (Cambridge, 1988).

299 *Carmarthen Journal* (21 May 1847).

300 Dot Jones, 'Did friendly societies matter? A study of friendly societies in Glamorgan, 1794–1910', *Welsh History Review*, 12, 3 (1985), 324–49. There were women's friendly societies at Cowbridge, Merthyr, Neath, Newbridge, Pyle,

St Bride's Bay, and Swansea. See also G. A. Williams, 'Friendly societies in Glamorgan, 1793–1832', *Bulletin of the Board of Celtic Studies*, 18 (1959), 275–83.

[301] Ian Gilmour, *Riot, Rising and Revolution: Governance and Violence in Eighteenth-Century England* (London, 1992), pp. 391–431.

[302] Peter Linebaugh, *The London Hanged: Crime and Civil Society in the Eighteenth Century* (Harmondsworth, 1993); V. A. C. Gatrell, *The Hanging Tree: Execution and the English People 1770–1868* (Oxford, 1996); E. P. Thompson, *Whigs and Hunters: The Origin of the Black Act* (London, 1975); Douglas Hay (ed.), *Albion's Fatal Tree: Crime and Society in Eighteenth Century England* (London, 1975).

[303] *Caernarvon and Denbigh Herald* (13 August 1853).

[304] *Seren Gomer* (April 1835), 127.

[305] Thomas W. Laquer, 'Crowds, carnival and the state in English executions 1604–1868', in A. L. Beier, David Cannadine and James M. Rosenheim (eds), *First Modern Society*, pp. 305–56.

[306] Roy Porter, *The Enlightenment: Britain and the Creation of the Modern World* (Harmondsworth, 2000), pp. 397–446; see also W. H. G. Armytage, *Heavens Below: Utopian Experiments in England 1560–1960* (London, 1961), p. 77.

[307] Robert Owen, *Report to the county of Lanark: A new view of society* (London, 1813, reprinted 1969), p. 170. Geoffrey Powell has recently argued that: 'Owen's thinking had more to do with the challenges of the religious culture of eighteenth-century Wales than with the Enlightenment elsewhere in Britain'. See idem, 'They shall no longer see us through a glass darkly: Robert Owen and the Welsh Enlightenment', *Montgomeryshire Collections*, 91 (2003), 53.

[308] Ieuan Gwynedd Jones, '1848 ac 1868: Brad y Llyfrau Gleision a Gwleidyddiaeth Cymru', in Prys Morgan (ed.), *Brad y Llyfrau Gleision* (Llandysul, 1991), p. 59;

[309] Norbert Elias, *The Civilizing Process*, vol. 1, *The History of Manners* (New York, 1978); vol. 2, *Power and Civility* (New York, 1982); vol. 3, *The Court Society* (New York, 1983); see also P. J. Corfield, *Power and the Professions in Britain 1700–1850* (London, 1995).

5: *Love, Lust and Loneliness*

[1] Lytton Strachey, *Eminent Victorians* (London, 1980 edn), p. i.

[2] Brian Harrison, 'Underneath the Victorians', *Victorian Studies* (1967), 239–62; Steven Marcus, *The Other Victorians: A Study of Sexuality and Pornography in Mid-Nineteenth Century England* (New York, 1966); Carol Zisowitz Stearns and Peter Stearns, 'Victorian sexuality: can historians do it better?', *Journal of Social History* (1985), 625–41; Peter Gay, *Education of the Senses*, vol. 1, *The Bourgeois Experience, Victoria to Freud* (New York, 1984); Carl N. Degler, 'What ought to be and what was: women's sexuality in the nineteenth century', *American History Review*, 79, 5 (1974), 1468–71; Steven Seidman, 'The power of desire and the danger of pleasure: Victorian sexuality reconsidered', *Journal of Social History*, 24 (1990), 47–63.

3   Derec Llwyd Morgan, *Y Diwygiad Mawr* (Llandysul, 1981); Eryn Mant White, *Praidd Bach y Bugail Mawr* (Llandysul, 1995); Edward Thomas, *Mamau Methodistaidd* (Wrexham, 1905); Edward J. Bristow, *Vice and Vigilance: Purity Movements in Britain since 1700* (Dublin, 1997); Muriel Jaeger, *Before Victoria: Changing Standards and Behaviour 1787–1837* (Harmondsworth, 1967); James Laver, *The Age of Illusion: Manners and Morals, 1750–1848* (London, 1972); and G. S. Rousseau and Roy Porter (eds), *Sexual Underworlds of the Enlightenment* (Manchester, 1988).

4   *The Cambrian* (29 January 1820).

5   Froom Tyler, 'Thomas Bowdler censor of Shakespeare', in Stewart Williams (ed.), *Glamorgan Historian*, vol. 8 (Barry, n.d.), pp. 194–204.

6   Roy Porter and M. Roberts (eds), *Pleasure in the Eighteenth Century* (London, 1996). For the Regency see T. A. J. Burnett, *The Rise and Fall of a Regency Dandy: The Life and Times of Scrope Berdmore Davies* (Boston, 1981); E. Beresford Chancellor, *The Lives of the Rakes*, vol. 6, *The Regency Rakes* (London, 1925); idem, *Life in Regency and Early Victorian Times: An Account of Brummell and D'Orsay 1800–50* (London, 1926); Rees Howell Gronow, *The Reminiscences and Recollections of Captain Gronow Being Anecdotes of Camp, Court, Clubs and Society 1810–60* (New York, 1964); Donald A. Low, *Thief's Kitchen: The Regency Underworld* (Glanster, 1982); Donald Pilcher, *The Regency Style 1800–30* (London, 1947); J. B. Priestley, *The Prince of Pleasure and his Regency 1811–20* (New York, 1969); and Maurice J. Quinlan, *Victorian Prelude: A History of English Manners 1700–1830* (New York, 1941).

7   Robert B. Shoemaker, *Gender in English Society 1650–1850: The Emergence of Separate Spheres?* (London, 1998); A. Henderson, *Disorderly Women in Eighteenth Century London* (London, 1999).

8   *Y Gymraes* (1851), 111.

9   R. Tudur Jones, 'Daearu'r Angylion: Sylwadau ar ferched mewn llenyddiaeth, 1860–1900', in J. E. Caerwyn Williams (ed.), *Ysgrifau Beirniadol XI* (Denbigh, 1999), pp. 191–226.

10 Matthew Sweet, *Inventing the Victorians* (London, 2001), pp. 177–81.

11 Norman Vance, *The Sinews of the Spirit: The Ideal of Christian Manliness in Victorian Literature and Religious Thought* (Cambridge, 1985); and J. A. Mangan and J. Walvin (eds), *Manliness and Morality: Middle Class Masculinity in Britain and America, 1800–1940* (Manchester, 1992).

12 Coventry Patmore, *The Angel in the House* (London, 1854–62).

13 In H. E. Thomas, *Traethawd ar Gymru a'r Cymdeithasau Llenyddol* (Birkenhead, 1854), p. 17. See also W. Gareth Evans, *Education and Female Emancipation: The Welsh Experience 1847–1914* (Cardiff, 1990), pp. 50–1, 279.

14 G. M. Young, *Portrait of an Age: Victorian England* (Oxford, 1976 edn), p. 80.

15 Jane Aaron, *Pur fel y Dur: Y Gymraes yn Llên Menywod y Bedwaredd Ganrif a'r Bymtheg* (Cardiff, 1998), p. 15.

16 R. Tudur Jones, 'Daearu'r Angylion', p. 193; *Y Frythones* (1879), 89.

17 Thomas Medwin, *The Angler in Wales: or Days and Nights of Sportsmen*, 2 vols (London, 1834), vol. 2, p. 120.

18 M. G. R. Morris, *Romilly's Visits to Wales 1829–1854* (Llandysul, 1998), p. xxvi.

19 Jacqueline Lewis, 'Passing judgements: Welsh dress and the English tourist', *Folk Life* (1994–5), p. 39.
20 Aaron, *Pur fel y Dur*, p. 167; R. Merfyn Jones, 'No barrier against agony: Elizabeth Gaskell's north Wales', *Journal of the Merioneth Historical and Records Society*, 11 (1990–3), 272–83; Edward Pugh, *Cambria Depicta* (London, 1816), pp. 189, 191; and P. Howell Williams, 'The causes and effects of tourism in North Wales' (Unpublished Ph.D. thesis, University of Wales, Aberystwyth, 2000), pp. 16, 25, 50, 175, 189.
21 Prys Morgan (ed.), *Brad y Llyfrau Gleision* (Llandysul, 1991), passim.
22 Keith Thomas, 'The double standard', *Journal of the History of Ideas*, 20, 2 (1959), 195–216.
23 Pembroke Dock was described as 'an area of clandestine prostitution', *Reports from Committees, Contagious Diseases Acts*, 3, IX (February–December 1882), p. lxxix.
24 Keith Thomas, 'Double standard', 214–16.
25 *The Cambrian* (25 May 1822).
26 W. Linnard, 'Gwragedd ar Werth yng Nghymru', *Medel* (1985), 18–21.
27 *Bye-gones* (1885), 159.
28 *The Cambrian* (17 April 1824).
29 *Cardiff and Merthyr Guardian* (7 March 1835).
30 Linnard, 'Gwragedd', 19.
31 D. Leslie Chamberlain, *Welsh Nicknames* (Pen-y-groes, 1981), p. 18.
32 The ballad is mentioned in Dafydd Owen, *I Fyd y Faled* (Denbigh, 1986), p. 205, and is available in full in Carmarthenshire Record Office, Carmarthenshire Antiquarian Society Scrapbooks, vol. 5. AB/1612–1830, 138.
33 T. Mardy Rees, *Hiwmor y Cymro: Hiwmor mewn Llenyddiaeth Gymraeg* (Liverpool, 1917), p. 79.
34 *Carmarthen Journal* (23 November 1832).
35 Dyfnallt Morgan (ed.), *Y Ferch o Ddolwar Fach* (Caernarfon, 1977), p. 77; Derec Llwyd Morgan, 'Emynau'r cariad tragwyddol', *Barddas*, 94 (1985), 6–7.
36 For a still controversial discussion of bloodshed and Methodism see E. P. Thompson, *The Making of the English Working Class* (Harmondsworth, 1979), pp. 402–19; see also A. M. Allchin, *Ann Griffiths: The Furnace and the Fountain* (Cardiff, 1987); idem, *Ann Griffiths* (Cardiff, 1976).
37 H. Turner Evans, *A Bibliography of Welsh Hymnology to 1960* (Caernarfon, 1977); Branwen Jarvis, 'Emynyddes bro'r Eisteddfod', *Y Casglwr*, 53 (1994), 20; and eadem, 'Mary Owen yr emynyddes', *Y Traethodydd*, 143 (1988), 45–53.
38 Daniel Evans, *Hymnau a Thonau er Gwasanaeth yr Eglwys yng Nghymru* (London, 1866), p. 34.
39 Ibid., p. 39.
40 Jane Aaron, *Pur fel y Dur*, pp. 44–7.
41 E. P. Thompson, *Making*, pp. 405–11.
42 Gomer M. Roberts (ed.), *Gwaith Pantycelyn* (Aberystwyth, 1960), pp. 167–8.
43 Arthur Mitzman, 'Privacy no more: historians in search of nineteenth century intimacy', *Journal of Social History* (1990), 359–70.
44 Amy Parry-Williams, 'Geiriau ein canu gwerin', *Canu Gwerin*, 2 (1979), 15, 23.
45 D. Roy Saer, *Caneuon Llafar Gwlad* (Cardiff, 1994), p. 52.

[46] Alan Llwyd, *Y Flodeugerdd o Ddyfyniadau Cymraeg* (Llandysul, 1988), p. 6.

[47] Huw Meirion Edwards, 'The lyric poets', in Hywel Teifi Edwards (ed.), *A Guide to Welsh Literature, c.1800–1900* (Cardiff, 2000), p. 103. Similar sentiments were expressed by Gwilym Mynech in his *Cwyn hen lanc o Kansas* (1876) quoted in Eirug Davies, *Gwladychu'r Cymry yn yr American West* (Llanrwst, 2003).

[48] *Royal Commission on Labour: The Agricultural Laborer*, PP 1893, vol. 11, Wales Report, pp. 151–2.

[49] D. Owen (Brutus), 'Boanerges', *Gwaedd Uwch Gwlad neu yr Udgorn yn chwythu ei sain o'r frwydyr, er casglu y buddinoedd ynghyd i ryfel yn erbyn y Bwystfil mawr sydd yn andwyo Cymru* (Llandovery, 1843), p. 15. Other outraged authors were Daniel Dafydd Amos, 'Anlladrwydd, neu buteindra', *Y Diwygiwr* (16 June 1851), 172; and 'Hen ffeiriwr' (John Beynon) 'Hanes Ffair y Cefn', *Y Diwygiwr*, (22 July 1858), 200–6. I am grateful to Dr Huw Walters for drawing these sources to my attention.

[50] *Seren Gomer* (1832), 322.

[51] Trefor M. Owen, 'Caru yn y ffeiriau yn y ganrif ddiwethaf', *Medel*, 2 (1985), 27–31.

[52] Wirt Sikes, *Rambles and Studies in Old South Wales* (London, 1881), p. 185.

[53] Ibid., pp. 195–6.

[54] Hefin Jones, *Dic Dywyll y Baledwr* (Llanrwst, 1995), p. 49. See also Stephen Jones, *Cân Newydd, sef dull marchnadoedd a ffeiriau Cymru* (1811).

[55] Hefin Jones, *Dic Dywyll*, p. 24.

[56] Trefor M. Owen, 'Three Merioneth valentines', *Journal of the Merioneth Historical and Record Society*, 4 (1961–4), 70–3.

[57] Idem, *The Story of the Love Spoon* (Swansea, 1973).

[58] Russell Davies, *Secret Sins: Sex, Violence and Society in Carmarthenshire 1870–1920* (Cardiff, 1996), pp. 165–6; Catrin Stevens, *Arferion Caru* (Llandysul, 1977), pp. 57–67. For a discussion of the advantages of courting in bed see *Ymddiddan Rhwng mab a merch ynghylch myned i garu'n y gwely* in J. D. Lewis's collection of ballads in the National Library of Wales (63ch).

[59] Amy Parry-Williams, 'Geiriau'.

[60] Ibid., 21.

[61] *The Cambrian* (21 June 1822).

[62] *The Cambrian* (8 April 1815).

[63] *Cardiff and Merthyr Guardian* (15 January 1853).

[64] Dafydd Owen, *I Fyd y Faled*, p. 207; J. D. Lewis collection of ballads (63ch).

[65] E. W. Jones, 'Carwriaeth y Cymry, eu cipdrem feddygol ar flynyddoedd cynnar y bedwaredd ganrif ar bymtheg yng Ngheredigion', *National Library of Wales Journal* (1966), 17.

[66] W. Bingley, *Excursions in North Wales* (London, 1804), pp. 282–3; Samuel J. Pratt, *Gleanings Through Wales*, vol. 1 (London, 1797), pp. 105–7.

[67] Herbert Williams, *Davies the Ocean: Railway King and Coal Tycoon* (Cardiff, 1991), p. 9.

[68] For the dangerous liaisons in Llanelli House see the *Cardiff and Merthyr Guardian* (16 August 1851). Evidence of Robert ap Gwilym Ddu's love child was uncovered by Guto Roberts, see *Y Cymro* (17 March 1999).

[69] Jennifer Green, *The Morning of her Day* (London, 1990), passim.

[70] Chris Evans, '*The Labyrinth of Flames': Work and Social Conflict in Early Industrial Merthyr Tydfil* (Cardiff, 1993), p. 124.

[71] A. H. Dodd, *The Industrial Revolution in North Wales* (Cardiff, 1933), p. 141; *DWB*.

[72] Richard Hough, *Captain James Cook*: A *Biography* (London, 1994), p. 392. For the epic adventures of Captain Meriweather Lewis see Stephen E. Ambrose, *Undaunted Courage: The Pioneering First Mission to Explore America's Wild Frontier* (London, 2003).

[73] *Annual Reports of the Registrar General* (1839–71).

[74] Quoted in Grace Hagen, 'Women and poverty in south west Wales, 1834–1914', *Llafur*, 7, 3/4 (1998–9), 30. See also Thomas Rees, *Letters on Wales* (London, 1859), p. 68.

[75] Daniel Owen, *Profedigaethau Enoc Huws* (Denbigh, 1891), p. 1. David M. Thomas (ed.), *Dylan Remembered* (Cardiff, 2003); *www.swansea.gov.uk/dylan-thomas* (accessed 21 April 2004).

[76] This argument is most notably put by Edward Shorter, *The Making of the Modern Family* (London, 1976). For bundling in Scotland see T. C. Smout, 'Aspects of sexual behaviour in nineteenth century Scotland', in Peter Laslett (ed.), *Bastardy and its Comparative History* (London, 1980), pp. 192–216; and idem, chap. 7 of *A Century of the Scottish People* (London, 1986), pp. 159–80.

[77] *North Wales Chronicle* (22 January 1850).

[78] *Caernarvon and Denbigh Herald* (4 January 1860).

[79] *Caernarvon and Denbigh Herald* (20 January 1872).

[80] For other cases see *North Wales Chronicle* (26 February and 7 September 1850, at Pwllheli) and *Cardiff and Merthyr Guardian* (10 September 1853).

[81] *Cardiff and Merthyr Guardian* (25 January 1851).

[82] *Merthyr Telegraph and Pontypridd Intelligence* (2 January 1858).

[83] West Glamorgan/Swansea Record Office, Solicitor's Day Books, 12 August 1841, D/D XCXI.

[84] M. G. R. Morris, *Romilly's Visits to Wales 1827–1854* (Llandysul, 1998), p. 94.

[85] *Monmouthshire Merlin* (5 April 1862).

[86] *The Cambrian* (17 and 24 April and 29 May 1830).

[87] *Seren Gomer* (1846), 123–4.

[88] For family advice see David Price, *Yr Adeiladydd Teuluaidd* (Denbigh, 1857); and Jonah Morgan, *Elfennau Teulu Dedwydd* (Aberdare, 1865). For the courtship of Thomas and Sally Charles see Gwen Emyr, *Sally Jones: Rhodd Duw i Charles* (Bridgend, 1996), pp. 10–21.

[89] M. Harriet Cope (trans.), *The Memoirs of Maria Stella (Lady Newborough) by herself* (London, 1914), p. 7.

[90] P. Branca, *Silent Sisterhood: Middle Class Women in the Victorian Home* (London, 1975), pp. 3–4.

[91] W. Rhys Jones, 'Gwenith Gwyn', 'The besom wedding in the Ceiriog valley', *Folk-lore*, 39, 2 (1928), 133–66.

[92] Roy Palmer, *The Folklore of Radnorshire* (Logaston, 2001), p. 82.

93 *Cardiff and Merthyr Guardian* (2 April 1853). John Pryse, *Cân ofidus sef hanes teimlad hen ferch weddw yn methu cael gwr* (Llanidloes, 18??).

94 *DWB.*

95 R. Tudur Jones, 'Daearu'r Angylion', p. 194.

96 *Seren Gomer* (July 1819), 237.

97 J. A. Banks, *Victorian Values: Secularisation and the Size of Families* (London, 1981), pp. 98–9.

98 D. Thomson, 'I am not my father's keeper: families and the elderly in nineteenth century England', *Law and History Review*, 2 (1984), 265–86.

99 Lawrence Stone, *The Family, Sex and Marriage in England 1500–1800* (Harmondsworth, 1979), pp. 254–302. For the treatment of children see Peter N. Stearns, 'Girls, boys, and emotions: redefinitions and historical change', *Journal of American History*, 80, 1 (1993), 36–74.

100 David J. V. Jones, *Crime in Nineteenth Century Wales* (Cardiff, 1993), passim.

101 James L. Clifford, *Hester Lynch Piozzi (Mrs Thrale)* (Oxford, 1952), p. 71; see also Katherine C. Balderston (ed.), *Thraliana: The Diary of Mrs Hester Lynch Thrale (Later Mrs Piozzi) 1776–1809* (Oxford, 1942); Marquis of Lansdowne (ed.), *Queeney Letters: Being Letters Addressed to Hester Maria Thrale by Doctor Johnson, Fanny Burney and Mrs Thrale-Piozzi* (London, 1934); and Mary Hyde, *Impossible Friendship: Boswell and Mrs Thrale* (Cambridge, MA, 1972).

102 *Registrar General's Report* (1845), p. xxv.

103 *North Wales Chronicle* (2 September 1830); *Seren Gomer* (April 1848), 125.

104 *North Wales Chronicle* (19 September 1830).

105 *Seren Gomer* (June 1842).

106 Roy Palmer, *Folklore*, p. 150.

107 Roy Saer, *Caneuon Llafar Gwlad*, vol. 1 (Cardiff, 1974), pp. 32–3, 60–1.

108 Ibid., pp. 44–5, 64–5.

109 J. C. Hughes *Oriau'r Bore* (Wrexham, 1872); Hugh Williams, *Canu'r Bobol* (Denbigh, 1978), p. 54.

110 Hefin Jones, *Dic Dywyll*, p. 29.

111 *Cardiff and Merthyr Guardian* (27 October 1849).

112 *The Cambrian* (18 February 1825).

113 Lawrence Stone, *Road to Divorce: England 1530–1987* (Oxford, 1992), p. 273.

114 Ibid., pp. 274–5.

115 *The Cambrian* (7 September 1822).

116 *The Cambrian* (20 January 1860).

117 Jacqueline S. Wilkie, 'Submerged sexuality: technology and perceptions of bathing', *Journal of Social History* (1986), 649–64.

118 Quoted in Cyril Pearl, *The Girl with the Swansdown Seat* (London, 1980).

119 T. G. Davies, *Neath's Wicked World: and Other Essays in the History of Neath and District* (Llandybïe, 2000), p. 68.

120 For Edith Williams see Trevor Fishlock, *Conquerors of Time: Exploration and Invention in the Age of Daring* (London, 2004), p. 17; Roy Saer, 'Canu llofft stabal', *Canu Gwerin*, 11 (1988), 20.

121 Ben Bowen Thomas, *Drych y Baledwr* (Aberystwyth, 1957), p. 127. Parents

often sought to place obstacles in the paths of their daughter's courtships. See for example: I. Davies, *Cerdd yn dangos fel y saethodd gwr darw ei gymydog yn lle cariad y ferch* (Trefriw, 1808); Richard Williams, *Cân newydd yn gosod allan garwriaeth Billy Williams a Hannah Johnson o Lanhafren* (Caernarfon, 18??); J. Jones, *Cân o hanes carwriaeth rhwng mab tylawd a merch ieuangc gyfoethog* (Trefriw, 1820); I. Davies, *Dwy gerdd diddan. 1. O hanes captain llong a ffansiodd ferch i wr bonheddig o'i gymdogaeth ai rhieni hi oedd yn erbyn iddo ei chael yn briod drwy fod un arall uwch ei râdd yn ei cheisio ond er maint y rhwystr ar gwrthwynebiadau fe gadwodd cariad ei le rhyngthynt a hwy a briodwyd; 2. Ymddiddan rhwng dyn a'i gydwybod bob yn ail penill* (Trefriw, 1810?).

122 Roy Palmer, *Folklore*, p. 127.

123 Catherine Brennan, *Angers, Fantasies and Ghostly Fears: Nineteenth Century Women from Wales and English Language Poetry* (Cardiff, 2003), p. 54.

124 Roy Porter, *Quacks: Fakers and Charlatans in English Medicine* (London, 2001), pp. 100, 140–8.

125 Quoted in Cyril Bracegirdle, *Dr William Price: Saint or Sinner* (Llanrwst, 1997), p. 81.

126 R. T. W. Denning (ed.), *The Diary of William Thomas of Michaelston-super-Ely near St Fagans, Glamorgan: 1762–1795* (Cardiff, 1995), p. 385.

127 Robert Dyer, *Nine Years of an Actor's Life* (Plymouth, 1833), pp. 122–3.

128 E. Trudgill, 'Prostitution and pater familias', in H. J. Dyos and M. Wolff (eds), *The Victorian City: Images and Realities* (London, 1973), pp. 693–4; E. M. Sigsworth and T. J. Wyke, 'A study of Victorian prostitution and venereal disease', in M. Vicinus, *Suffer and Be Still: Women in the Victorian Age* (Bloomington, IN, 1972), pp. 78–9; J. R. Walkowitz, 'The making of an outcast group: prostitutes and working women in nineteenth-century Plymouth and Southampton', in M. Vicinus (ed.), *A Widening Sphere: Changing Roles of Victorian Women* (Bloomington, IN, 1977), pp. 72–93; eadem, *Prostitution and Victorian Society* (Cambridge, 1980), pp. 21–31; J. R. Walkowitz, *Prostitution and Victorian Society: Women, Class and the State* (Cambridge, 1980); Stanley D. Nash, *Prostitution in Great Britain, 1485–1901: An Annotated Bibliography* (London, 1994); Trevor Fisher, *Prostitution and the Victorians* (Stroud, 1997); Paul McHugh, *Prostitution and Victorian Social Reform* (London, 1980).

129 *Cardiff and Merthyr Guardian* (18 June 1853).

130 *Cardiff and Merthyr Guardian* (22 May 1858); *Caernarvon and Denbigh Herald* (27 January 1872).

131 *Merthyr Telegraph* (1 July 1865).

132 *Monmouthshire Merlin* (4 January 1862).

133 Ronald Pearsall, *The Worm in the Bud: The World of Victorian Sexuality* (Harmondsworth, 1983), p. 420.

134 *Seren Gomer* (February 1841); Huw Walters, 'Gwawr Robyn Ddu Eryri', *Y Casglwr* (11 August 1980).

135 *Cardiff and Merthyr Guardian* (30 and 23 July 1853, 16 August 1851, 10 April 1852).

136 *Monmouthshire Merlin* (6 February 1864).

137 *Cardiff and Merthyr Guardian* (24 March 1860).

138 *Cardiff and Merthyr Guardian* (16 January 1858).

139 *The Cambrian* (8 June 1866).

140 *Cardiff and Merthyr Guardian* (16 July 1853).

141 *The Cambrian* (19 October 1833).

142 *Cardiff and Merthyr Guardian* (25 February 1860).

143 *The Cambrian* (13 January 1860).

144 David J. V. Jones, *Crime in Wales*, p. 195. Elizabeth James, Neathy, appeared before Glamorgan magistrates twice in one week, *The Cambrian* (4 May 1860); *Merthyr Telegraph* (10 September 1860).

145 *Merthyr Telegraph* (21 September 1866).

146 David J. V. Jones, *Crime in Wales*, p. 197.

147 Hefin Jones, *Dic Dywyll*, p. 12.

148 *Caernarvon and Denbigh Herald* (12 April 1862).

149 *Caernarvon and Denbigh Herald* (12 October 1872).

150 *Caernarvon and Denbigh Herald* (20 January 1872).

151 *Caernarvon and Denbigh Herald* (2 March 1867).

152 George G. Lerry, 'The policemen of Denbighshire', *Denbighshire Historical Society Transactions*, 2 (1953), 114–15.

153 *North Wales Chronicle* (25 October 1856).

154 Gerald Morgan (ed.), *Lle Diogel i Sobri: Hunangofiant Capelulo* (Llanrwst, 1982), p. 33.

155 *Caernarvon and Denbigh Herald* (23 February 1867).

156 *Carmarthen Journal* (8 June 1864).

157 *Carmarthen Journal* (8 August 1864).

158 *The Cambrian* (12 June 1860).

159 *The Cambrian* (28 December 1865).

160 *The Cambrian* (15 February 1866). For other detailed cases of prostitution in Swansea see *The Cambrian* (3 February, 22 June and 2 March 1860).

161 John Willett, *The First Report of the Cardiff Associate Institute for Improving and Enforcing the Laws for the Protection of Women* (Cardiff, 1860).

162 *Cardiff and Merthyr Guardian* (5 and 26 February 1853).

163 *Cardiff and Merthyr Guardian* (23 July 1853).

164 *Cardiff and Merthyr Guardian* (5 August 1853).

165 E. O'Neil, 'The Notorious Jack Matthews' (unpublished typescript, Cardiff Central Library); his obituary appeared in the *Cardiff Argus* (18 July 1888). For the atmosphere of the area see W. R. (Bodwyn) Owen, 'Tiger Bay: the street of the sleeping cats', *Glamorgan Historian*, vol. 7 (Barry, 1979), pp. 72–86.

166 *Cardiff and Merthyr Guardian* (25 February 1860).

167 Keith Strange, 'In search of the celestial empire: crime in Merthyr, 1830–60', *Llafur*, 3, 1 (1980), 44–86; and David J. V. Jones and Alan Bainbridge, 'The conquering of China: crime in an industrial community', *Llafur*, 2, 4 (1979).

168 For colourful reports of prostitutes and prostitution in Merthyr see *Merthyr Telegraph* (18 June and 10 September 1864); *Cardiff and Merthyr Guardian* (20 January 1849, 11 June 1853, 2 and 23 April 1853, 6 June 1849).

169 'Journal of a Scripture Reader', NLW MS 4,943B.

170 Ibid., p. 10.

171 Ibid., p. 42.
172 Ibid., p. 58.
173 For these places see *Monmouthshire Merlin* (7 June, 4 January, 4 August, 12 July, 4 January 1862); *The Cambrian* (26 January 1826). For prostitution in Newport see *Monmouthshire Merlin* (14 May 1852, 5 April 1862, 22 December 1849, 17 November 1849).
174 *Cardiff and Merthyr Guardian* (29 December 1849).
175 *Cardiff and Merthyr Guardian* (5 February 1859).
176 Clive Wood, *The Fight for Acceptance: A History of Contraception* (Aylesbury, 1970); Angus McLaren, *A History of Contraception* (London, 1990).
177 *Cardiff and Merthyr Guardian* (7 July 1849, 9 July 1853); *The Cambrian* (6 January 1860, 19 January 1811).
178 *Carmarthen Journal* (21 December 1849).
179 *DWB*.
180 *Carmarthen Journal* (16 July 1813).
181 *Seren Gomer* (October 1836), 228; *North Wales Chronicle* (2 August 1836).
182 *The Cambrian* (26 April 1817).
183 Richard William Leopold, *Robert Dale Owen: A Biography* (Newport, 1969), passim.
184 Michael Mason, *The Making of Victorian Sexuality* (Oxford, 1994), pp. 59, 283. See also idem, *The Making of Victorian Sexual Attitudes* (Oxford, 1994); and Roy Porter and Mikulas Teich (eds), *Sexual Knowledge, Sexual Science: The History of Attitudes to Sexuality* (Cambridge, 1994).
185 Roy Porter, ' "The Secrets of generation display'd": *Aristotle's* masterpiece in the Eighteenth Century', *Eighteenth Century Life*, 9, 3 (1985), 1–16; Janet Blackman, 'Popular theories of generation, the evolution of Aristotle's Works. The study of an anachronism', in John Woodward and Baird Richards (eds), *Health Care and Popular Medicine in Nineteenth Century England* (London, 1977), pp. 56–88.
186 Gerald Morgan, 'Dirgelwch Aristotle', *Y Casglwr*, 4 (1977), 8.
187 Advertised in *The Cambrian* (4 May 1821) and *North Wales Chronicle* (7 May 1850). Other advertisements offered Buckland's *Physiology* and Dr Reuben's *Physiological Mysteries and revelations in love, courtship and marriage: an infallible guide-book for married and single persons, in matters of the utmost importance to the human race.*
188 Matthew Sweet, *Inventing*, p. 107.
189 *Carmarthen Record Office*, CDX/308/12.
190 *Carmarthen Journal* (18 May 1811).
191 *North Wales Chronicle* (21 August 1850).
192 *Carmarthen Journal* (18 December 1835).
193 *The Cambrian* (16 November 1860).
194 *Caernarvon and Denbigh Herald* (25 June 1853).
195 *Cardiff and Merthyr Guardian* (23 June 1849, 1 May and 3 July 1858); *Monmouthshire Merlin* (4 January 1862).
196 Solomon's Adverts can be seen in the *Carmarthen Journal* (8 December 1810,

2 January 1846); *The Cambrian* (20 January 1816, 4 March 1811). For Dr Solomon's career see Roy Porter, *Quacks*, pp. 156–61.

[197] Lawrence Stone, *Family*, p. 379.

[198] Iwan Meical Jones, 'Datgelu'r Cymru: portreadau ffotograffig yn oes Fictoria', in Geraint H. Jenkins (ed.), *Cof Cenedl*, vol. 14 (Llandysul, 1999); Brian Foster, 'The Usk houses of correction and the early days of the Usk county gaol', *Gwent Local History*, 94 (2003), 23–4; see also Claude Quétel, *History of Syphilis*, trans. Judith Braddock and Brian Pike (Oxford, 1990).

[199] *The Cambrian* (1 April 1826, 17 February 1816). Other advertisements for products to cure venereal diseases appeared in the *Carmarthen Journal* (16 March 1811, 13 March 1846, 28 January 1862); in *The Cambrian* (27 January 1810, 1 August 1812, 28 July 1838); and in the *Monmouthshire Merlin* (14 January 1837).

[200] *The Cambrian* (27 January 1810).

[201] *North Wales Chronicle* (15 June 1850).

[202] Michael Mason, *The Making of Victorian Sexuality*, p. 189.

[203] Iain McCalman, *Radical Underworld: Prophets, Revolutionaries and Pornographers in London, 1795–1840* (Cambridge, 1988), p. 120.

[204] Ibid., p. 205.

[205] Ibid., pp. 219–22, 224–5, 231, 235–6.

[206] Liza Z. Sigel, 'Filth in the wrong people's hands: postcards and the expression of pornography in Britain and the Atlantic World', *Journal of Social History* (2000), 859–86. For some examples of their work see Chris Hart, *The Illustrated Book of Queen Victoria's Secrets* (London, 2000); and Christopher Peachment, *The Illustrated Book of Filthy Victorian Photographs* (London, 2001).

[207] Ronald Pearsall, *Worm*, pp. 466–8; Lynn Hunt (ed.), *The Invention of Pornography: Obscenity and the Origins of Modernity, 1500–1800* (New York, 1993).

[208] T. Mardy Rees, *Welsh Painters, Engravers and Sculptors 1527–1911* (Caernarfon, 1911), pp. 52–9; the quotation is from p. 58.

[209] Quoted in Ronald Pearsall, *Worm*, p. 608. For a discussion of popular reaction to the naked body see Catherine Gallagher and Thomas Laquer (eds), *The Making of the Modern Body: Sexuality and Society in the Nineteenth Century* (Berkeley, CA, 1987).

[210] Jacqueline Lewis makes this point about the intrusion of stereotypes into rural Wales in 'Passing judgements: Welsh dress and the English tourist', *Folk Life*, 33 (1994), 44. Not all Welsh women, of course, could afford to conform to the wasp-waisted fads of fashion. Edwin Roberts complained in 1852 that 'either the absence of stays or slovenliness, or want of tact, gives (Welsh women) an appearance of personal neglect; so that a young woman, who may be as perfect as a Vatican Venus, has no more shape than a matron of fifty'. Roberts was commenting on the women of the iron districts of Merthyr Tydfil, where a tight waist, together with the heat of the workplace, would have resulted in an epidemic of fainting women. See Edwin F. Roberts, *A Visit to the Iron Works and Environs of Merthyr Tydfil in 1852* (London, 1853), p. 11.

[211] Valerie Steele, *Fashion and Eroticism: Ideas of Feminine Beauty from the Victorian Era to the Jazz Age* (Oxford, 1985), pp. 161–75.

[212] Hefin Jones, *Dic Dywyll*, p. 22.

[213] J. D. Lewis collection of ballads. I'm grateful to Dr E. G. Millward and Dr Huw Walters for drawing my attention to the J. D. Lewis collection. For a discussion of similar themes see G. R. Quaife, *Wanton Wenches and Wayward Wives* (London, 1979); Anna Clark, *The Struggle for the Breeches: Gender and the Making of the British Working Class* (Berkeley, CA, 1995); and E. J. Burford, *Wits, Wenches and Wantons: London's Low Life: Covent Garden in the Eighteenth Century* (London, 1992).

[214] *Y Casglwr* (8 August 1979), 14.

[215] E. G. Millward, 'Ychwanegiadau at Brydyddiaeth Jac Glan-y-gors', *Bulletin of the Board of Celtic Studies*, 29 (1982), 666–7, reclaims some of the verses which had been censored by earlier editors; idem, 'Llenyddiaeth arall oes Victoria', *Y Casglwr*, 10 (1980); idem, 'Byd y Baledwr', *Y Faner* (19 May 1978), 17–18.

[216] Carmarthenshire Record Office, Coedmor papers D/LL/2661. I am grateful to the gentlemen on the office's staff for drawing this source to my attention.

[217] Roy Saer, *Caneuon Llafar Gwlad*, vol. 1 (Cardiff, 1974), pp. 34–5, 61.

[218] Meredydd Evans, 'Twll Bach y Clo', *Canu Gwerin*, 5 (1982), 5–8, idem, 'Twll Bach y Clo', *Y Casglwr*, 15 (1981), 12.

[219] Ronald Pearsall, *Worm*, p. 210.

[220] *Cardiff and Merthyr Guardian* (8 July 1858).

[221] *Monmouthshire Merlin* (5 April 1862). For a discussion of the prevalence of child sexual abuse see the painful evidence in Louise A. Jackson, *Child Sexual Abuse in Victorian England* (London, 2000); and Lionel Rose, *The Erosion of Childhood: Child Oppression in Britain 1860–1918* (London, 1991). For other cases in Wales see *Cardiff and Merthyr Guardian* (3 July 1858); *North Wales Chronicle* (15 March 1856, 25 October 1827); and *The Cambrian* (4 November 1820).

[222] David J. V. Jones, *Crime in Wales*, p. 79. For general assaults on women see Anna Clark, *Women's Silence, Men's Violence: Sexual Assaults in England, 1770–1845* (New York, 1987).

[223] *The Cambrian* (3 August 1866).

[224] *The Cambrian* (6 April 1860, 4 September 1830).

[225] For discussion of these themes see M. Chaytor, 'Husband(ry): narratives of rape in the seventeenth century', *Gender and History*, 10 (1995), 1–25; S D'Cruz, *Crimes of Outrage: Sex, Violence and Victorian Women* (London, 1998); L. Gordon, 'Family violence, feminism and social control', *Feminist Studies*, 12 (1986), 453–78; idem, *Heroes of their own Lives: The Politics and History of Family Violence* (London, 1989); and N. A. Tomes, 'A "torrent of abuse": crimes of violence between working-class men and women in London', *Journal of Social History*, 11 (1978), 328–45.

[226] *Seren Gomer* (September 1848), 282. For other cases in Wales see *Caernarvon and Denbigh Herald* (31 March 1866); *Carmarthen Journal* (15 April 1843); *The Cambrian* (1 May 1824, 7 September 1819 and 27 March 1830).

[227] Jan Bondeson, *The London Monster: Terror on the Streets* (London, 2003).

[228] P. Howell Williams, 'The causes and effects of tourism in north Wales 1750–1850' (Uunpublished Ph.D. thesis, University of Wales, Aberystwyth, 2000), p. 287.

229 *Report on Education*, PP 1847, Denbighshire, appendix A, pp. xxvii, 75.
230 David J. V. Jones, *Crime in Wales*, p. 80.
231 *Seren Gomer* (1831), 154. *Carmarthen Journal* (10 September 1831).
232 Carmarthen Record Office, Felon's Register Acc. 4,916, case nos 333 and 378.
233 Ibid., case nos 1130 and 1133.
234 Ibid., case no. 1357. The case is reported in the *Carmarthen Journal* (15 July 1870).
235 *Carmarthen Journal* (9 March 1866).
236 Elizabeth Mavor, *The Ladies of Llangollen: A Study in Romantic Friendship* (Harmondsworth, 2001 edn); see also Bridget Hill, *Women Alone: Spinsters in England 1660–1850* (New Haven, 2001).
237 Helen R. Hallesy, *Glamorgan Pottery (Swansea, 1814–38)* (Llandysul, 1995), p. 35.
238 Jane Aaron, *Pur fel y Dur*, p. 141–2.
239 T. Mardy Rees, *Welsh Painters*, p. 103.
240 John Frost, *The Horrors of Convict Life* (Preston, 1856), p. 40.
241 Robert Hughes, *The Fatal Shore* (London, 1987), p. 265.
242 Ronald Pearsall, *Worm*, pp. 549–53.
243 Ibid., pp. 561–8.
244 Ibid., p. 412.
245 Robert Meyrick and Neil Holland, *To Instruct and Inspire* (Aberystwyth, 1997), p. 3.
246 Gerald Morgan, *Nanteos: A Welsh House and its Families* (Llandysul, 2001), p. 103.
247 Glamorgan Record Office, Cardiff; Quarter Sessions Order Book, QS/M23 p. 190; *Cardiff and Merthyr Guardian* (8 July 1858).
248 *The Cambrian* (21 April 1827).
249 *The Cambrian* (25 May 1860).
250 Jan Bondeson, *London Monster*, pp. 76–7, 270.
251 *Cardiff and Merthyr Guardian* (1 January 1853).

6: *Worship and Wizards*

1 Quoted in David J. V. Jones, *The Last Rising: The Newport Chartist Insurrection of 1839* (Cardiff, 1999), p. 188.
2 Henry Tobit Evans, *Rebecca and her Daughters* (Cardiff, 1910).
3 Brian Foster, 'The Usk houses of correction and the early days of Usk county gaol', *Gwent Local History*, 94 (2003), 26–7.
4 Robin Gwyndaf, 'Religion in everyday life in Wales', p. 168. I am grateful to Robin for a typescript of this paper.
5 For an excellent example see David Davies, *Echoes from the Welsh Hills: Or Reminiscences of the Preachers and People of Wales* (London, n.d.) who claimed 'it is the Protestant Christianity of the Welsh people, as lived and taught by their religious teachers during the last two centuries and a half, that has preserved them from ignorance, lawlessness, and irreligion, and made of them one of the

most Scripturally-enlightened, loyal, moral, and religious nations on the face of the earth' (p. 176).

6   John Hughes, *Methodistiaeth Cymru: Sef Hanes Blaenorol a Gwedd Bresenol y Methodistiaid Calfinaidd yng Nghymru, o ddechreuad y cyfundeb hyd y flwyddyn 1850* (Wrexham, 1851); see also R. T. Jenkins, *Hanes Cymru yn y Ddeunawfed Ganrif* (Cardiff, 1973 edn).

7   T. M. Bassett, *Bedyddwyr Cymru* (Swansea, 1977); J. Morgan Jones (ed.), *Hanes ac Egwyddorion Annibynwyr Cymru* (Swansea, 1939); R. Tudur Jones, *Hanes Annibynwyr Cymru* (Swansea, 1966); and idem, *Yr Undeb: Hanes Undeb yr Annibynwyr Cymreig 1872–1972* (Swansea, 1975).

8   Ieuan Gwynedd Jones, 'The Merthyr of Henry Richard', in G. Williams (ed.), *Merthyr Politics: The Making of a Working-Class Tradition* (Cardiff, 1966), p. 28.

9   David Owen, Brutus, makes the point regarding the divisions in Nonconformity forcibly in several articles in *Yr Haul*; see, for example, 11, 127 (1846), 7. 'Yr Hen Bersoniaid Llengar' was a term devised by R. T. Jenkins in *Hanes Cymru yn y Bedwaredd Ganrif ar Bymtheg* (Cardiff, 1933) to describe a group of Anglicans which included John Jenkins (Ifor Ceri), Walter Davies (Gwallter Mechain), Evan Evans (Ieuan Glan Geirionydd), John Williams (Ab Ithel), and the 'father of Welsh history' Thomas Price (Carnhuanawc). See Bedwyr Lewis Jones, *Yr Hen Bersoniaid Llengar* (Denbigh, 1963); Dyfnallt Morgan (ed.), *Gwŷr Llên y Bedwaredd Ganrif ar Bymtheg* (Llandybïe, 1968).

10   D. Densil Morgan, *Christmas Evans a'r Ymneilltuaeth Newydd* (Llandysul, 1991), pp. 31, 106. See also R. Currie, *Methodism Divided* (London, 1968).

11   For a statistical analysis of Welsh religion see John Williams, *A Digest of Welsh Historical Statistics*, vol. 2 (Cardiff, 1985), p. 352.

12   *DWB*.

13   *Yr Haul* (January 1846), 6.

14   M. W. Thompson (ed.), *The Journeys of Sir Richard Colt Hoare . . . 1793–1810* (London, 1983), p. 177; Edward Morgan, *A brief memoir of the life and labours of the Rev. Thomas Charles, A. B. late of Bala, Merionethshire* (London, 1831); Thomas Charles, *The Welsh Methodists vindicated . . .* (London, 1802).

15   *North Wales Gazette* (22 July 1818).

16   Quoted in Peter Howell Williams, 'The causes and the effects of tourism in north Wales 1750–1850' (Unpublished Ph.D. thesis, University of Wales, Aberystwyth, 2000), p. 470.

17   D. E. Jenkins, *Life of Thomas Charles*, vol. 3 (Denbigh, 1908), p. 187.

18   Letter of John Elias to F. Carmichael, 25 October 1822. NLW MS 11,721C. For a discussion of these themes see I. M. Lewis, *Ecstatic Religion* (London, 1975).

19   P. Howell Williams, 'Causes'.

20   Roland Thomas, *Richard Price: Philosopher and Apostle of Liberty* (London, 1924); Walford Gealy, 'Richard Price, FRS (1723–91)', *Y Traethodydd*, 46 (1991), 135–45.

21   Whitney R. D. Jones, *David Williams and the French Revolution* (Rhymney, 1989); idem, *David Williams: The Anvil and the Hammer* (Cardiff, 1986); and J. Dybikowski, *On Burning Ground: An Examination of the Ideas, Projects and Life of David Williams* (Oxford, 1993).

22   Hywel M. Davies, 'Cymro, gelynol i bob gorthrech: Morgan John Rhys

(1760–1804)', in Geraint H. Jenkins (ed.), *Cof Cenedl: Ysgrifau ar Hanes Cymru* (Llandysul, 1994), pp. 63–96.

23   *North Wales Gazette* (27 March 1817).

24   C. B. Turner, 'Revivals and popular religion in Victorian and Edwardian Wales' (Unpublished Ph.D. thesis, University of Wales, Aberystwyth, 1979), p. 12. See also Edward Parry, *Llawlyfr ar hanes y diwygiadau crefyddol yng Nghymru* (Corwen, 1898).

25   *The Cambrian* (10 January 1829).

26   *Cardiff and Merthyr Guardian* (25 May 1860).

27   D. Williams, *Great Hymn Tunes of Wales*, NLW MS 12,621D.

28   Ieuan Gwynedd Jones (ed.), *The Religious Census of 1851: A Calendar of the Returns Relating to Wales*, vol. 2, *North Wales* (Cardiff, 1981), p. 13.

29   Ibid.

30   Ieuan Gwynedd Jones and David Williams (eds), *The Religious Census of 1851: A Calendar of the Returns Relating to Wales*, vol. 1, *South Wales* (Cardiff, 1977), p. 324.

31   Ibid., p. 256.

32   I. G. Jones, *Census: North Wales*, p. 292.

33   R. S. Thomas, *Collected Poems* (Llandysul, 1993).

34   I. G. Jones and D. Williams, *Census: South Wales*, pp. 417, 460.

35   Ibid., p. xxxi.

36   *The Cambrian* (15 January 1831).

37   I. G. Jones, *Census: North Wales*, p. 270. For the problems of the Church see Peter Virgin, *The Church in an Age of Negligence: Ecclesiastical Structure and Problems of Church Reform, 1700–1840* (Cambridge, 1988).

38   C. B. Turner, 'Revivals', p. 143.

39   E. Morgan (ed.), *Valuable Life and Letters of John Elias* (Caernarfon, 1847), p. 199. For a broader discussion see H. A. Kelly, *Towards the Death of Satan: The Growth and Decline of Christian Demonology* (London, 1969).

40   *Y Fraethebydd*, for example, contained several examples of how simple country folk confounded educated but unworldly ministers.

41   J. Vyrnwy Morgan, *Welsh Religious Leaders in the Victorian Era* (London, 1905).

42   Ibid.

43   D. T. Davies, *Coleg Dewi a'r Fro* (Lampeter, 1984).

44   I. G. Jones and D. Williams, *Census: South Wales*, p. xxxiv.

45   K. O. Morgan, *Freedom or Sacrilege? A History of the Campaign for Welsh Disestablishment* (Penarth, 1966).

46   The results for Wales have been tabulated and gathered in I. G. Jones and D. Williams (eds), *Census: South Wales;* and I. G. Jones (ed.) *Census: North Wales*.

47   I. G. Jones and D. Williams, *Census: South Wales*, vol. 1, p. 262.

48   I. G. Jones, *Census: North Wales*, vol. 2, p. 4.

49   Ibid., p. 338.

50   Ibid., p. 385.

51   I. G. Jones and D. Williams, *Census: South Wales*, vol. 1, p. 326.

52 Ibid., p. 288.
53 Gareth Elwyn Jones, *Modern Wales* (Cambridge, 1984), p. 273. For Mann's interpretation of the results see Horace Mann, 'On the statistical position of religious bodies in England and Wales', *Journal of the Royal Statistical Society*, 18 (1855), 155. For a criticism see W. S. F. Pickering, 'The 1851 religious census: a useless experiment', *British Journal of Sociology*, 18, 4 (December, 1967).
54 John Williams, *A Digest of Welsh Historical Statistics*, vol. 2 (Cardiff, 1985), p. 352.
55 I. G. Jones, *Census: North Wales*, vol. 2, p. 389.
56 William Rees, *Memoirs of the Rev. William Williams (Wern)* (London, 1846), p. 38.
57 Anthony Jones, *Welsh Chapels* (Stroud, 1996).
58 Elizabeth Phillips, *A History of the Pioneers of the Welsh Coalfield* (Cardiff, 1925), p. 94.
59 Herbert Williams, *Davies the Ocean* (Cardiff, 1991), passim.
60 'Hanes, cyfansoddiad, rheolau dysgyblaethol ynghyd â chyffes ffydd y corff o Fethodistiaid Calfinaidd yng Nghymru: a gytunwyd arnynt yn nghymdeithas Aberystwyth a'r Bala, yn y flwyddyn 1823', *Cyffes Ffydd*, 1, pp. 24–8.
61 W. R. Lambert, 'Some working class attitudes towards organized religion in nineteenth century Wales', *Llafur*, 2, 1 (1976), 4–17.
62 *The Cambrian* (13 November 1819).
63 *The Cambrian* (1 January, 6 May, 10 June and 24 June 1820).
64 *Carmarthen Journal* (1 May 1832).
65 *The Cambrian* (12 March 1825).
66 For other sacrilegious outrages see *Seren Gomer* (April 1841), 319, (January 1834), 31, (September 1855), 424, (June 1832), (February 1832), 64, (September 1819), 302; *Carmarthen Journal* (13 March 1835, 16 December 1864); and *The Cambrian* (9 December 1820, 10 March 1827, 12 March 1825, 23 February 1822).
67 *North Wales Chronicle* (26 October 1850).
68 *DWB*.
69 W. Alun Matthias, 'Cnoi Baco', *Y Casglwr*, 61 (1997).
70 *Tywysydd yr Ieuainc* (March 1848), 378.
71 *Y Diwygiwr*, 23 (1858), 147.
72 *Monmouthshire Merlin* (2 July 1862). For the guidance given to the Welsh people on living moral and virtuous lives see Arthur Jones, *Moesaddysg neu hyfforddiad er ymddygiad boddhaol* (Bangor, 1813); and Jonathan Edwards, *Cyfarwyddiadau ac annogaethau i gredinwyr, i roddi cwbl ddiwydrwydd i wneuthur eu galwedigaeth a'u hetholedigaeth yn sicr* (Bala, 1809).
73 *Seren Gomer* (August 1834), 231.
74 *The Cambrian* (28 July 1838).
75 Quoted in John Williams-Davies, *Cider Making in Wales* (Cardiff, 1984), p. 45.
76 *Yr Eurgrawn Wesleaidd* (February 1836), 45.
77 W. R. Lambert, *Drink and Sobriety in Victorian Wales c.1820–1895* (Cardiff, 1983), p. 129.
78 Ibid., p. 128.

[79] Ibid., p. 91.

[80] E. G. Millward (ed.), *Ceinion y Gân* (Llandysul, 1983), pp. 76–7.

[81] For example, *Seren Gomer* (September 1836), 251, (September 1842), 224, (May and September 1846). For a detailed discussion see Huw Walters, 'Y wasg gyfnodol Gymraeg a'r mudiad Dirwest, 1835–1850', *National Library of Wales Journal*, 28 (1993–4), 153–95.

[82] E. Jones, *The Bardic Museum* (London, 1802), p. xvi.

[83] On David Davies see Brinley F. Roberts, 'Davies y Binder', *Transactions of the Honourable Society of Cymmrodorion* (1985), 187–229; idem, 'The Revd David Davies: a Victorian bookbinder', in David A. Stoker (ed.), *Studies in the Provincial Book Trade of England, Scotland and Wales before 1900: Papers Presented to the British Book Trade Index, Seventh Annual Seminar, Aberystwyth, 11–13 July, 1989* (Aberystwyth, 1990), pp. 13–32; and idem, 'Diwylliant y ffin', in Hywel Teifi Edwards (ed.), *Cwm Tawe* (Llandysul, 1993), pp. 45–80; see also Benjamin Jones, *Temperance versus Teetotalism/Cymedroldeb/The Total Overthrow of Teetotalism/Llwyr-Ddymchweliad Titotaliediaeth* (Llanrwst, 1838), p. 77. I am grateful to Dr Huw Walters for the references.

[84] William Williams, *Cymeroldeb a Llwyrymatebiad: Sylwadau ar y Ddwy Egwyddor* (Caernarfon, 1836), p. 2.

[85] *Cardiff and Merthyr Guardian* (6 April 1839).

[86] W. R. Lambert, *Drink*, p. 46.

[87] W. W. Hart, *To Guard My People: An Account of the Origin and History of the Swansea Police* (Swansea, 1957), p. 67.

[88] J. O. Jones, *The History of the Carnarvonshire Constabulary* (Caernarfon, 1963), p. 88.

[89] Hywel Teifi Edwards (ed.), *A Guide to Welsh Literature c.1800–1900* (Cardiff, 2000), p. 45.

[90] Ibid., p. 219.

[91] Gareth Elwyn Jones, *Modern Wales*, p. 287.

[92] W. Llewelyn Jones, *Hanes yr Ysgol Sul yng Nghymru* (film, UW Aberystwyth).

[93] E. P. Thompson, *The Making of the English Working Class* (Harmondsworth, 1979), pp. 412–17.

[94] John Parry, *Rhodd Mam* (Wrexham, 1811). For the influence and importance but not the effect of *Rhodd Mam* see *Y Traethodydd* (1904), 446; and *Cymru* (O. M. Edwards), vol. 12 (1897), p. 229.

[95] Gareth Elwyn Jones, 'Llyfrau Gleision 1847', in Prys Morgan (ed.) *Brad y Llyfrau Gleision* (Llandysul, 1991), pp. 22–48.

[96] Lewis Lloyd, *The Port of Caernarfon 1793–1900* (Harlech, 1989), p. 146.

[97] For Welsh education see Leslie W. Evans, *Education in Industrial Wales 1700–1900* (Cardiff, 1971); C. E. Gittins, *Pioneers of Welsh Education* (Swansea, n.d.); M. G. Jones *The Charity School Movement* (Cowbridge, 1938); Geraint D. Owen, *Ysgolion a Cholegau'r Annibynwyr* (Llandysul, 1939); D. A. Pretty, *Two Centuries of Anglesey Schools 1700–1902* (Anglesey, 1977); and Jac L. Williams and G. R. Hughes (eds), *The History of Education in Wales* (Swansea, 1978).

[98] For the cultural vitality of Welsh religion see T. J. Morgan, *Diwylliant Gwerin*

(Llandysul, 1972); Gareth Williams, *Valleys of Song: Music and Society in Wales 1840–1914* (Cardiff, 1998).

[99] *The Cambrian* (13 February 1830).

[100] Olive Anderson, 'The incidence of civil marriage in Victorian England and Wales', *Past and Present*, 69 (1975), 74–5. For the tradition of besom or broom weddings see T. Llew Jones, 'Y Sgubell', *Llafar Gwlad*, 4 (1984); and Gwenith Gwynn (W. Rhys Jones), 'The besom wedding in the Ceiriog valley', *Folk-Lore*, 39, 2 (1928), 133–48.

[101] On the emotional impact and implication of religion see R. Marie Griffith, ' "Joy unspeakable and full of glory": the vocabulary of pious emotions in the narratives of American Pentecostal women, 1910–1945', and Kimberly L. Phillips, ' "Stand by me": sacred quartet music and emotionology of African American audiences, 1900–30', both in Peter N. Stearns and Jan Lewis (eds), *An Emotional History of the United States* (New York, 1998).

[102] Gwynn ap Gwilym and Ifor ap Gwilym, *Emynau Cymru/The Hymns of Wales* (Talybont, 1995).

[103] *Hymnau Hen a Newydd i'w Harfer Y'Ngwasanaeth yr Eglwys* (London, 1881).

[104] Ibid., p. 236.

[105] Ibid., p. 237.

[106] Ibid., p. 285.

[107] Ibid., p. 308.

[108] Ibid., p. 325.

[109] Ibid., p. 413.

[110] Ibid., p. 286; E. Wyn James, *Dechrau Canu: Rhai Emynau Mawr a'u Cefndir* (Bridgend, 1987).

[111] *Hymnau Hen*, pp. 530–1.

[112] Ibid., p. 253.

[113] Ibid., p. 528.

[114] *Seren Gomer* (December 1819), 301. For an interesting discussion on angels see T. Talwyn Phillips, *Angel y Nos a Phregethau Eraill* (Bala, 1903); and *Hymnau Hen*, pp. 530–1.

[115] *Hymnau Hen*, pp. 530–1.

[116] Derec Llwyd Morgan, *The Great Awakening in Wales*, trans. Dyfnallt Morgan (London, 1988), p. 255.

[117] Ibid., p. 251. H. Desroches, *Jacob and the Angel: An Essay in the Sociology of Religion* (Cambridge, MA, 1973); John Harvey, *The Art of Piety: The Visual Culture of Welsh Nonconformity* (Cardiff, 1995); idem, *Image of the Invisible: The Visualization of Religion in the Welsh Nonconformist Tradition* (Cardiff, 1999); Jeffrey Burton Russell, *A History of Heaven: The Singing Silence* (Princeton, NJ, 1997).

[118] *Seren Gomer* (December 1819), 391. For the Devil see Peter Stanford, *The Devil: A Biography* (London, 1997); and D. Walker, *The Decline of Hell* (Chicago, 1964). For a remarkable contemporary work see Beelzebub, *Yr Arweinydd Diogel i Uffern* (Swansea, 182?); Jeffrey Burton Russell, *The Prince of Darkness: Radical Evil and the Power of Good in History* (London, 1989); and

idem, *The Devil: Perceptions of Evil from Antiquity to Primitive Christianity* (London, 1977).

[119] *Seren Gomer* (May 1820), (March 1846), 69, (January 1846), 15–17. One of the most remarkable documents deposited in the National Library of Wales is Dr John Harries's Conjuring Book NLW MS 11,117B. This includes a 'recipe' and instructions 'to call forth Bael a King from the East and 66 Legions of inferior spirits' and Marehorsias 'a great and mighty Marquess with . . . dominion over 30 legions'.

[120] The protracted efforts of his family to have Thomas Price declared insane can be consulted in the Pembrokeshire Record Office, Haverfordwest D/JAM/50.

[121] Quoted in Kerry Davies, 'Sexing the mind: women, gender and madness in nineteenth-century Welsh asylums', *Llafur*, 7, 1 (1996), 37.

[122] *DWB*. On these themes see Charles Mackay, *Extraordinary Popular Delusions and the Madness of Crowds* (New York, 1932 edn); and David Cressy, *Agnes Bowker's Cat: Travesties and Transgressions in Tudor and Stuart England* (Oxford, 2000).

[123] Eirlys Gruffydd, 'Y diafol a'i ddilynwyr', *Llafar Gwlad*, 4 (1984) and 'Y diafol a'r werin', *Llafar Gwlad*, 2 (1983–4).

[124] Mr and Mrs S. C. Hall, *The Book of South Wales* (London, 1861), p. 325.

[125] Robin Gwyndaf, 'The past in the present: folk beliefs in Welsh oral tradition', *Fabula Journal of Folktale Studies*, 35 (1994), 231. I am grateful to Robin Gwyndaf for a typescript of this paper and for several other acts of generosity.

[126] *Seren Gomer* (August 1848), 252.

[127] *Cardiff and Merthyr Guardian* (7 July 1819).

[128] *Seren Gomer* (July 1832), 224.

[129] *Seren Gomer* (January 1848), 28.

[130] Richard Holland (ed.), *Bye-gones* (Llanrwst, 1992), pp. 106–11.

[131] Jonathan Ceredig Davies, *Folk-Lore of West and Mid Wales* (Aberystwyth, 1911), p. 273.

[132] P. Howell Williams, 'Causes', p. 61.

[133] D. Edmondes Owen, 'Pre-Reformation survivals in Radnorshire', *Transactions of the Honourable Society of Cymmrodorion* (1910–11), 92–114; Judith Devlin, *The Superstitious Mind: French Peasants and the Supernatural in the Nineteenth Century* (New Haven, 1987); Steven Wilson, *The Magical Universe: Everyday Ritual and Magic in Pre Modern Europe* (London, 2000).

[134] For a discussion on this theme see Keith Thomas, *Religion and the Decline of Magic* (Harmondsworth, 1981 edn); B. Malinowski, *Magic, Science and Religion and Other Essays* (London, 1974); and Stuart Clark and Prys Morgan, 'Religion and magic in Elizabethan Wales: Robert Holland's *Dialogue on Witchcraft*', *Journal of Ecclesiastical History*, 27 (1976), 31–46. For a contemporary view see John Hughes, *Methodistiaeth Cymru* (Wrexham, 1851).

[135] William Roberts, *Crefydd yr Oesoedd Tywyll* (Wrexham, 1852). See also Robert Davies, *Ar Ffolineb Swyngyfaredd a phob ofergoelion eraill* (Caernarfon, 18??); Peter Roberts, *Yr Hynafion Cymreig: neu Hanes am draddodiadau, defodau ac ofergoelion yr hen Gymry; yng nghyd a sylwadau ar eu dechreuad* (Carmarthen, 1823); Thomas Frimston, *Ofergoelion yr hen Gymry* (Llangollen, 1906); and

John Roberts, *Hyfforddiad ac annogaith i rodio yn ofn Duw ar hyd y dydd* (Bala, 1830).

[136] Evan Jones, *Facts, Figures and Statements: An Illustration of the Dissent and Morality of Wales: An Appeal to the English People* (London, 1849), p. 41.

[137] This has recently been republished by the University of Wales Press: John Harvey (ed.), *The Appearance of Evil: Apparitions of Spirits in Wales* (Cardiff, 2003).

[138] J. H. Davies (ed.), *The Life and Opinion of Robert Roberts, a Wandering Scholar as Told by Himself* (Cardiff, 1923), p. 49.

[139] Quoted in Robin Gwyndaf, 'Past in the present', 231.

[140] *Carmarthen Journal* (14 August 1824).

[141] Gomer M. Roberts, *Hanes Plwyf Llandybïe* (Cardiff, 1939), pp. 226–85. For Lodwick William see Huw Walters, 'Sherlyn Benchwiban, unig anterliwt Sir Gâr', in his *Cynnwrf Canrif: Agweddau ar Ddiwylliant Gwerin* (Swansea, 2004). I am grateful to Huw for a copy of a typescript of this book.

[142] J. H. Davies, *Rhai o Hen Ddewiniaid Cymru* (London, 1901); Kate Bosse Griffiths, *Byd y Dyn Hysbys* (Talybont, 1977); Stephen J. Williams, *Y Dyn Hysbys* (Aberystwyth, 1935); Elias Owen, *Welsh Folk Lore: A Collection of Folk-Tales and Legends of North Wales* (London, 1896); Jacqueline Simpson, *The Folk Lore of the Welsh Border* (London, 1976).

[143] D. E. Jenkins, *Beddgelert: Its Facts, Fairies and Folklore* (Porthmadog, 1899), pp. 56, 74.

[144] Brian John, *Pembrokeshire Witches and Wizards* (Newport, 2001), pp. 52–4, 57, 91.

[145] Ibid., p. 56.

[146] Ibid., pp. 48–50.

[147] Ibid., p. 31. See also Eirlys Gruffydd, *Gwrachod Cymru* (Caernarfon, 1980), p. 154; M. A. Murray, *The Witch Cult in Western Europe* (Oxford, 1971); and B. F. Roberts, 'Rhai swynion Cymraeg', *Bulletin of the Board of Celtic Studies*, 21, 3 (November 1965).

[148] Keith Kissack, *Victorian Monmouth* (Monmouth, 1988), p. 154.

[149] Jane Pugh, *Welsh Witches and Warlocks* (Llanrwst, 1987), p. 82.

[150] The Harrieses have attracted considerable historical attention, for example, J. Rowland, Giraldus, 'Dr Harries Cwrt y Cadno: the Carmarthenshire conjuror', in Arthur Mee (ed.), *Carmarthenshire Notes, Antiquarian, Topographical and Curious I* (1889), p. 29; A. Mee, *Magic in Carmarthenshire: The Harrieses of Cwrt y Cadno* (Llanelli, 1912); Ithiel Vaughan-Poppy, 'The Harries kingdom: wizards of Cwrt y Cadno' (1976), unpublished essay, National Library of Wales, Misc. Rec. 329; and Richard C. Allen, 'Wizards or charlatans – doctors or herbalists: an appraisal of the "cunning men" of Cwrt y Cadno Carmarthenshire', *North American Journal of Welsh Studies*, 1, 2 (2001).

[151] David Owen, Brutus, 'Ofergoelion yr oes', in *Brutusiana* (Llandovery, 1853), p. 71; idem, 'Cwrt y Cadno', *Yr Haul*, 5 (1840), 286.

[152] J. H. Davies, *Rhai o Hen Ddewiniaid*, pp. 154–7; Kate Bosse Griffiths, *Byd y Dyn Hysbys*, pp. 28–9.

[153] Anon, 'The Cwrt-y-Cadno library', *Carmarthenshire Antiquarian*, 23 (1932); see also NLW MS 11,119B.

[154] H. Elvet Lewis, *Sweet Singers of Wales* (London, 1889), p. 99.

[155] NLW MS 11,117B and 11,119B.

[156] Brian Luxton, 'William Jenkin, the wizard of Cadoxton-juxta Barry', *Morgannwg*, 24 (1980), 31–60.

[157] *The Cambrian* (7 November 1807).

[158] D. Rhys Phillips, *The History of the Vale of Neath* (Swansea, 1925), pp. 582–3. Robin Gwyndaf, 'Llanelian' Home Ground Fact Sheet HTV (Cardiff, 1997).

[159] NLW MS 11,190.

[160] Anon, 'Three Carmarthenshire conjurors', *Bye-Gones, Relating to Wales and the Border Counties*, 5 (1897), 209.

[161] H. Watney, 'A Welsh archimago', *Red Dragon*, 10 (1886), 282–3.

[162] NLW MS 11,119B.

[163] Amongst the books in the Harrieses' Library was *Synopsis Medicinae* (1685), NLW MS 11,119B.

[164] For their medical works see the following manuscripts in the National Library of Wales: Account Book MS 11,702F, Patients Day Book, 1815–29, MS 11,703E; and Prescription Book, MS97; Medical Lectures, MS 11,701C; Medical Prescriptions MS 11,704A and 11,705A; Treatises on Urine MS 11,710B.

[165] For the links between medicine and magic see Ronald Hutton, *The Triumph of the Moon: A History of Modern Pagan Witchcraft* (Oxford, 1999); Owen Davies, *Witchcraft, Magic and Culture 1736–1951* (Manchester, 1999), pp. 214–35; Wayland D. Hand, *Magical Medicine: The Folkloric Component of Medicine in the Folk Belief, Custom and Rituals of Europe and America* (Berkeley, CA, 1980); and idem, 'The folk-healer: calling and endowment', *Journal of the History of Medicine*, 26 (1971), 263–75.

[166] *Bye-Gones* (1894), 501–4, (1896), 249–57.

[167] Anne E. Jones, 'Folk medicine in living memory in Wales', *Folk Life*, 18 (1980), 54. Bob Bushaway, *By Rite, Custom, Ceremony and Community in England 1700–1880* (London, 1982); idem, ' "Tacit, unsuspected but still implicit faith": alternative belief in nineteenth century England', in T. Harries (ed.), *Popular Recreations in England, 1500–1850* (London, 1995).

[168] Timothy Lewis, *A Welsh Leech Book* (Liverpool, 1914), p. 100.

[169] Anne E. Jones, 'Folk medicine', p. 62.

[170] Ibid., p. 60.

[171] Francis Jones, *The Holy Wells of Wales* (Cardiff, 1954), p. 97.

[172] David Hoffman, *Welsh Herbal Medicine* (Abercastle, n.d.); Anne E. Jones, 'Folk Medicine', p. 63.

[173] Timothy Lewis, *Welsh Leech Book*, p. 39; A. Kiev (ed.), *Magic, Faith and Healing* (London, 1964).

[174] Hugh Davies, *Welsh Botanology* (London, 1813).

[175] Glyn Penrhyn Jones, 'Folk medicine in eighteenth century Wales', *Folk Life*, 7 (1969), 69.

[176] D. Williams, *Cofiant J. R. Jones o Ramoth* (Carmarthen, 1913), pp. 690–1.

[177] For adverts of almanacs and fortune-telling guidebooks see *Seren Gomer* (September 1819), 320 and (October 1819), 352.

[178] Examples of these have been preserved in the Museum of Welsh Life at St Fagans – see items no. F86. 155, F86. 176 and F83. 115.

[179] Roy Palmer, *The Folklore of (Old) Monmouthshire* (Little Logaston, 1998), pp. 152–3.

[180] Jonathan Ceredig Davies, *Folk Lore*, p. 9–10.

[181] Ibid., p. 12.

[182] T. Gwynn Jones, *Welsh Folklore* (London, 1979), p. 214.

[183] Paxton Hood, *Christmas Evans: The Preacher of Wild Wales* (London, 1881), p. 23.

[184] Huw Walters, 'Bwyta pechod yng Nghwmaman', *Y Geninen*, 28 (1978), 96–9.

[185] E. Tegla Davies, 'Diwylliant gwerin y bedwaredd ganrif ar bymtheg', *Denbighshire Historical Society Transactions*, 11 (1962), 106–7. For fictional accounts inspired by tales of Welsh sin eaters see Mary Webb, *Precious Bane* (London, 1924) and Margaret Attwood, *Dancing Girls and Other Stories* (London, 1982), pp. 213–24.

[186] I am grateful to Robin Gwyndaf for this reference which relates to an uncatalogued tape recording in the Museum of Welsh Life of evidence from Mr O. P. Hughes, Nebo, Caernarfon.

[187] Catrin Stevens, 'Marw ym Mhenfro', *Llafar Gwlad*, 13 (1986).

[188] George Borrow, *Wild Wales: Its People, Language and Scenery* (London, 1856), p. 301.

[189] Dafydd Evans, *Cân Newydd o hanes Dafydd Williams o Swydd Benfro yr hwn a gafodd ei argyhoeddi wrth weled canwyll gorph ei hun bedwar mis cyn ei farw a fu Ebrill 1, 1833* (Llanrwst, 183?).

[190] Owen Evans, *Dinbych ei Hynafiaethau a'i Henwogion* (Denbigh, n.d.), pp. 51–3.

[191] Edward Pugh, *Cambria Depicta: A tour through North Wales* (London, 1816), pp. 391–2.

[192] Edward Hamer and H. W. Lloyd, *The History of the Parish of Llangurig* (London, 1875), pp. 118–19.

[193] *The Cambrian* (10 December 1825); Brian Foster, 'The Usk houses of correction and the early days of the Usk County Gaol', *Gwent Local History*, 94 (2003), p. 12.

[194] Thomas Edwards, *Gweithiau Twm o'r Nant* (Llanuwchllyn, 1909–10), vol. 1, p. 87.

[195] *Carmarthen Journal* (19 January and 7 December 1811).

[196] Twm Elias, 'Dywediadau am y tywydd', *Llafar Gwlad*, 3 (1984).

[197] Eirlys Gruffydd, 'Coelion hen forwyr', *Llafar Gwlad*, 17 (1987), pp. 11–13.

[198] Lyn Davies, 'Coelion y glowyr', *Llafar Gwlad*, 9 (1987), 4–5; idem, 'Aspects of mining folklore in Wales', *Folklife*, 9 (1971), 79–107; and W. J. Lewis, 'The Cardiganshire miners' drinking song', *Ceredigion*, 2, 1 (1952), 53–4.

[199] Wirt Sikes, *British Goblins: Welsh Folklore, Fairy Mythology, Legends and Traditions* (Boston, 1881), p. 4; Hugh Evans, *Y Tylwyth Teg* (Liverpool, 1944); W. Jenkin Thomas, *The Welsh Fairy Book* (London, 1912); P. H. Emerson, *Welsh Fairy Tales and Other Stories* (London, 1894); idem, *Tales from Welsh Wales, Founded on Fact and Current Tradition* (London, 1894); Joseph Jacobs, *Celtic Fairy Tales* (London, 1891). For a superb account of fairy beliefs in

Ireland see Angela Bourke, *The Burning of Bridget Cleary* (London, 1999). See also Bingt Holbek, *Interpretation of Fairy Tales: Danish Folklore in a European Perspective* (Helsinki, 1987), p. 198; Diane Purkiss, *Troublesome Things: A History of Fairies and Fairy Stories* (London, 2000); and Marina Warner, *From the Beast to the Blonde: On Fairy Tales and their Tellers* (London, 1994).

[200] John Owen Hughes, *Y Tylwyth Teg* (Llanrwst, 1987), p. 46.

[201] For changelings see Jonathan Ceredig Davies, *Folk-Lore*, p. 116; and Wirt Sikes, *British Goblins*, pp. 59, 75, 88. Jonathan Ceredig Davies, *Folk-Lore*, p. 133.

[202] For a discussion on infanticide see Russell Davies, *Secret Sins: Sex, Violence and Society in Carmarthenshire c.1870–1920* (Cardiff, 1996), chap. 4.

[203] John Owen Hughes, *Y Tylwyth Teg*, pp. 49–50.

[204] Jonathan Ceredig Davies, *Folk-Lore*, p. 134, 102.

[205] Ibid., p. 144.

[206] Ibid., p. 147.

[207] Tony Roberts, *Myths and Legends of Pembrokeshire* (Abercastle, 1974), p. 9.

[208] *Seren Gomer* (February 1821), 64.

[209] W. Howells, *Cambrian Superstitions, Comprising Ghosts, Omens, Witchcraft, Tradtions etc.* (London, 1831), pp. 10–50; Brian John, *Pembrokeshire Ghost Stories* (Newport, 1999).

[210] Jonathan Ceredig Davies, *Folk-Lore*, pp. 154, 156.

[211] *Monmouthshire Merlin* (18 December 1869).

[212] Ibid. For other Welsh ghost stories see Gomer M. Roberts, 'Ysbrydion', *Y Genhinen*, 27, 3 (1977), 130–2.

[213] Robin Gwyndaf, *Straeon Gwerin Cymru* (Llanrwst, 1998); Thomas Thomas (Sarnicol), *Chwedlau Cefn Gwlad* (Aberystwyth, 1944); Myra Evans, *Casgliad o Chwedlau Newydd* (Aberystwyth, 1926); Evan Isaac, *Coelion Cymru* (Aberystwyth, 1938); John Jones (Myrddin Fardd), *Llên Gwerin Sir Gaernarfon* (Caernarfon, 1908); Trefor M. Owen, *Welsh Folk Customs* (Llandysul, 1987).

[214] D. E. Jenkins, *Beddgelert*, p. 156.

[215] For satiric responses to superstition see Rigdum Funnidos, *Drych y frad: Yn cynnwys yr asyn quadrupedaidd a'r asyn bipedaidd; Gwneuthur ymenyn a'r post; Cyfodi'r gwynt, alias puffiaeth; Y black art, Phenomena eglwysig; Hit my legs; Picking and stealing; ynghyd â dwy gân, un ar esgoriad Dic ar y cwic: a'r llall, Ymddiddaniad rhwng Diabolus a'i fab Cwic* (Crickhowell, 1843); John Jones, *Yr Oracl neu dynged-lyfr Buonaparte a'r dewin' sef hyfforddiadau i wneud dohell-droion (Conjuring) a phrawfion allfydawl* (Llanrwst, 1843); and idem, *Dehonglydd breuddwydion, a gymrwyd allan o ysgrifeniadau yr hen Gymry . . .* (Llanrwst, n.d.).

[216] Judith Devlin, *Superstitious Mind*, pp. 83–8, 185–214. There are innumerable highly interesting interpretations of folk tales, amongst the most bizarre and thought-provoking are: F. C. Bartlett, 'Psychology in relation to the popular story', *Folklore* (1920), 264–94; R. E. Blum, *The Dangerous Hour: The Love of Crisis and Mystery in Rural Greece* (London, 1970); H. Cox, *The Feast of Fools: A Theological Essay on Festivity and Fantasy* (New York, 1970); L. Dégh, 'Folk narrative', in R. Dorson (ed.), *Folklore and Folklife* (Chicago, 1972), pp. 53–84; Clodd Edward, *Twm Tit Tot: An Essay on Savage Philosophy in Folk-Tale*

(London, 1898); George Ewart Evans, *The Pattern under the Plough: Aspects of the Folk-Life of East Anglia* (London, 1971); Alessandro Falassi, *Folklore by the Fireside: Text and Context of the Tuscan Veglia* (London, 1980); E. S. Hartland, *The Science of Fairy Tales* (London, 1891); and Gustav Jahoda, *The Psychology of Superstition* (Harmondsworth, 1969).

7: Happiness and Humour

[1]   Quoted in Caroline Holland, *Notebooks of a Spinster Lady* (London, 1919), chap 21, 2 January 1900.
[2]   Gwyn Thomas, *A Welsh Eye* (London, 1964), p. 35.
[3]   Quoted in P. Howell Williams, 'The causes and effects of tourism in north Wales 1750–1850' (Unpublished Ph.D. thesis, University of Wales, Aberystwyth, 2000), p. 245.
[4]   Ibid., p. 169.
[5]   Samuel Rogers, *Pleasures of Memory* (London, 1792), p. 356.
[6]   P. Howell Williams, 'Causes', p. 200.
[7]   Quoted in Stella Margetson, *Leisure and Pleasure in the Nineteenth Century* (London, 1969), pp. 169–70.
[8]   Richard J. Moore-Colyer (ed.), *A Land of Pure Delight: Selections from the Letters of Thomas Johnes of Hafod, Cardiganshire (1748–1816)* (Llandysul, 1992), p. 6.
[9]   J. R. Walton, *The English Seaside Resort: A Social History 1750–1914* (Leicester, 1983), p. 283; Alain Corbin, *The Lure of the Sea* (Los Angeles, 1994); I. Wynne Jones, *Llandudno, Queen of the Welsh Resorts* (Cardiff, 1975).
[10] David Riseman, *The Lonely Crowd: A Study of Changing American Character* (New Haven, 1961), passim.
[11] *Anterliwtiau Twm o'r Nant* (Cardiff, 1964), p. 20.
[12] Peter Lord, *The Visual Culture of Wales: Imaging the Nation* (Cardiff, 2000), p. 213.
[13] David Dykes, *Wales in Vanity Fair* (Cardiff, 1989), p. 85.
[14] Ibid., pp. 84, 34.
[15] Robert Jones, 'Trebor Aled', *Pleser a Phoen* (Aberystwyth, 1908).
[16] Peter Quennell, *The Pursuit of Happiness* (Oxford, 1990), p. 169.
[17] G. J. Williams, *Iolo Morganwg* (Cardiff, 1956), p. 62.
[18] F. G. Payne, *Yr Aradr Gymreig* (Cardiff, 1975), p. 190.
[19] T. C. Evans, 'Ploughing with oxen in Glamorgan', *Canu Gwerin*, 14 (1991), 30–89; Huw Walters, 'Rhagor am ganu i'r ychen', *Canu Gwerin*, 22 (1999), 52–9.
[20] Osian Ellis, *The Harp in Wales* (Cardiff, 1991), p. 51.
[21] Hywel Teifi Edwards (ed.), *A Guide to Welsh Literature c.1800–1900* (Cardiff, 2000), p. 36.
[22] M. G. R. Morris (ed.), *Romilly's Visits to Wales 1827–1854* (Llandysul, 1998), p. 28.
[23] On the *eisteddfod* see Hywel Teifi Edwards, *Gŵyl Gwalia: Yr Eisteddfod yn Oes*

Aur Victoria 1858–1868 (Llandysul, 1980); idem, *Yr Eisteddfod* (Llandysul, 1976); and idem, *Codi'r Hen Wlad yn ei Hôl 1850–1914* (Llandysul, 1989).

24 *DWB.*

25 Gareth Williams, *Valleys of Song: Music and Society in Wales 1840–1914* (Cardiff, 1998); P. Crossley-Holland, *Music in Wales* (London, 1948); E. Mackerness, *A Social History of English Music* (London, 1964); J. Graham, *A Century of Welsh Music* (London, 1923); A. Ruff, *Welsh Hymns and their Tunes* (London, 1990); Huw Williams, *Canu'r Bobol* (Denbigh, 1978).

26 R. Pearsall, *Victorian Popular Music* (Newton Abbot, 1973); A. Croll, 'From bar-stool to choir-stall: music and morality in late nineteenth-century Merthyr', *Llafur*, 6, 1 (1992); Hywel Teifi Edwards, 'Y gân a ganai Morlais', in idem, *Codi'r Hen Wlad yn ei Hôl*. For an example of evocative plangent songs see Cass Meurig, 'Canu i gyfeiliant ffidil yng Nghymru'r ddeunawfed ganrif', *Canu Gwerin*, 24 (2001), 20–41. For contemporary views of *y cwrw bach* see Morgan Phillip, 'Cwrw Bach', *Seren Gomer*, 19 (May 1836), 137; and J. Gwili Jenkins (ed.), *Atgofion Watcyn Wyn* (Cardiff, 1907), p. 6. I am grateful to Dr Huw Walters for these references.

27 T. J. Morgan, *Diwylliant Gwerin* (Llandysul, 1972); R. D. Griffith, *Hanes Canu Cynulleidfaol Cymru* (Llandysul, 1948)

28 Huw Williams, 'Rhai o gymwynasau Ieuan Gwyllt', *Welsh Music*, 5, 7 (1972–8); idem, 'Cofio Ieuan Gwyllt', *Bwletin Cymdeithas Emynau Cymru* (1978); R. Griffiths, 'Y gymanfa ganu: ei gwreiddiau a'i natur', *Bwletin Cymdeithas Emynau Cymru*, 2, 9 (1986–7); I. Bradley, *Abide with Me: The World of Victorian Hymns* (London, 1997).

29 Keith Kissack, *Victorian Monmouth* (Monmouth, 1988), pp. 141–3.

30 Trevor Herbert, 'Late Victorian Welsh bands: taste, virtuosity and Cymmrodorion attitudes', in John Harper and Wyn Thomas (eds), *Welsh Musical History*, vol. 1 (Cardiff, 1996), pp. 92–102.

31 Richard Warner, *A Walk Through Wales in August 1797* (Bath, 1798), p. 114.

32 Thomas Christopher Evans, 'Yr hen Gymry a'i dawns', *Cymru*, 42 (1912), 221.

33 Emma Lile, *Troed yn ôl a Throed Ymlaen: Dawnsio Gwerin yng Nghymru* (Cardiff, 1999), passim.

34 Rhiannon Ifans, *Sêrs a Rybana: Astudiaeth o'r Canu Gwasael* (Llandysul, 1983), pp. 105–35.

35 Quoted in Emma Lile, *Troed*, p. 20.

36 *The Cambrian* (16 September 1815).

37 Peter Lord, *The Visual Culture of Wales: Industrial Society* (Cardiff, 1998), p. 102.

38 O. Llew Owain, *Hanes y Ddrama yng Nghymru 1850–1943* (Liverpool, 1947), p. 36.

39 Cecil Price, *The English Theatre in Wales* (Cardiff, 1948), pp. 54–6.

40 Ibid., pp. 86–7.

41 Ibid., p. 117.

42 *The Cambrian* (20 May 1820).

43 A. H. Dodd, *A History of Wrexham* (Wrexham, 1957), p. 247.

44 *Carmarthen Journal* (3 August 1832).

45 Cecil Price, *English Theatre*, p. 85.
46 A. H. Dodd, *History of Wrexham*, p. 247.
47 Cecil Price, *English Theatre*, p. 149.
48 O. Llew Owain, *Hanes*, pp. 26–37. On Matthews Ewenni see W. P. Griffith, 'Preaching second to no other under the sun: Edward Matthews, the Nonconformist pulpit and Welsh identity during the mid-nineteenth century', in Robert Pope (ed.), *Religion and National Identity: Wales and Scotland* (Cardiff, 2001); John James Morgan, *Cofiant Edward Matthews, Ewenni* (Mold, 1922).
49 Cecil Price, *English Theatre*, p. 80.
50 Ibid., p. 160.
51 Cecil Price, 'Portable theatres in Wales, 1843–1914', *National Library of Wales Journal*, 9 (1955–6), 65–93.
52 *The Cambrian* (13 May 1826).
53 *Carmarthen Journal* (13 September 1829).
54 Ricky Jay, *Learned Pigs and Fireproof Women* (New York, 1986); Raphael Samuel, *Theatres of Memory* (London, 1996); C. J. S. Thompson, *The Mystery and Lore of Monsters* (London, 1930).
55 Harold Carter, *The Towns of Wales: A Study in Urban Geography* (Cardiff, 1966); Andy Croll, *Civilizing the Urban: Popular Culture and Public Space in Merthyr, c.1870–1914* (Cardiff, 2000); M. J. Daunton, *Coal Metropolis Cardiff, 1870–1914* (Leicester, 1977); idem, 'Public place and private space: the Victorian city and the working class household', in D. Fraser and A. Sutcliffe (eds), *The Pursuit of Urban History* (London, 1983); Mark Girouard, *The English Town* (London, 1990).
56 *Cardiff and Merthyr Guardian* (30 June 1849).
57 *Cardiff and Merthyr Guardian* (24 March 1849).
58 *Cambrian Mirror* (1846), 176.
59 Peter Quennell, *Pursuit*, pp. 15, 52.
60 Huw Walters, 'Beirdd a phrydyddon Pontypridd a'r cylch yn y bedwaredd ganrif ar bymtheg: arolwg', in Hywel Teifi Edwards (ed.), *Merthyr a Thâf* (Llandysul, 2001), pp. 252–301. Richard Fenton, *Tours in Wales (1804–1813)*, ed. John Fisher (London, 1917), p. 155; E. G. Millward. *'Gym'rwch chi baned?': Traddodiad y Te Cymreig* (Llanrwst, 2000).
61 Brian Harrison, *Drink and the Victorians: The Temperance Question in England* (London, 1971), p. 40–1.
62 Richard Fenton, *Tours* p. 69.
63 P. Howell Williams, 'Causes', p. 267.
64 Keith Kissack, *Victorian Monmouth*, pp. 66–8.
65 John Williams Davies, *Cider Making in Wales* (Cardiff, 1984), pp. 43–7.
66 W. R. Lambert, *Drink and Sobriety in Victorian Wales c.1820–1895* (Cardiff, 1983).
67 *Cardiff and Merthyr Guardian* (8 September 1849).
68 *The Cambrian* (13 April 1839).
69 W. M. Williams, 'A slight historical and topographical sketch of the parish of Llanfechain', *Montgomeryshire Collections*, 5 (1872), 255–6.

70 W. R. Lambert, *Drink*, p. 11.
71 W. R. Lambert, 'Drink and work discipline in industrial south Wales c.1860–1870', *Welsh History Review*, 7, 3 (1975), 289–306.
72 L. J. Williams and J. Morris, *The South Wales Coal Industry 1841–75* (Cardiff, 1958), p. 209.
73 *The Cambrian* (7 September 1839).
74 David J. V. Jones, *The Last Rising: The Newport Chartist Insurrection of 1839* (Cardiff, 1999), p. 30.
75 Lewis Lloyd, *Pwllheli: The Port and Mart of Llŷn* (Caernarfon, 1991).
76 Gerry Evans, *Where Giants Dwell: A Sailor's Tale* (Auckland, 1999), p. 10.
77 *Piggot's Directory 1828–29* (London, 1829).
78 Lewis Lloyd, *The Port of Caernarfon* (Harlech, 1989), p. 159.
79 Kissack, *Victorian Monmouth*, p. 36.
80 Huw Roberts and Llew Roberts, *Telynorion Llanerch-y-medd, Teulu'r Britannia ac Eraill* (Beaumaris, 2000).
81 D. Wakin Morgan, 'The inns of Abercrave', *Brycheiniog*, 4 (1958), 116.
82 Herbert Williams, *Davies the Ocean: Railway King and Coal Tycoon* (Cardiff, 1991).
83 John Lyons, *The Old Parish Public Houses: Past and Present* (Bridgend, 1984); Ivor Waters, *Inns and Taverns of Chepstow and the Lower Wye Valley* (Chepstow, 1976).
84 Roy Marshall and Derek Gabriel, *The Great Pub Crawl: A History of Swansea Pubs* (Swansea, 1994), passim. Ronald Rees, *King Copper: South Wales and the Copper Trade 1584–1895* (Cardiff, 2000), p. 41.
85 *Carmarthen Journal* (20 February 1846).
86 *Monmouthshire Merlin* (1 April 1837).
87 W. R. Lambert, *Drink*, p. 18.
88 Ibid., pp. 16–17.
89 For the history of brewing see the entertaining account by Brian Glover, *Prince of Ales: The History of Brewing in Wales* (Stroud, 1993); and J. Morris, 'Evan Evans and the Vale of Neath Brewery', *Morgannwg*, 9 (1965), 38–60.
90 Quoted in Glover, *Prince of Ales*, p. 8.
91 David Dykes, *Vanity Fair*, p. 33.
92 Eirug Davies, *Y Cymry ac Aur Colorado* (Llanrwst, 2001), p. 54.
93 A. H. Dodd, *History of Wrexham*.
94 Glover, *Prince of Ales*, p. 61.
95 Ibid., p. 163.
96 David J. V. Jones, *Crime in Nineteenth Century Wales* (Cardiff, 1993), p. 90.
97 *The Cambrian* (31 December 1880). In all she was prosecuted 255 times.
98 *Caernarvon and Denbigh Herald* (20 January 1872).
99 *Cardiff and Merthyr Guardian* (11 June 1853); *The Cambrian* (13 January 1860).
100 Ivor Waters, *Inns*, p. 41.
101 *The Cambrian* (8 June 1816).
102 A. H. Dodd, *History of Wrexham*, p. 239.
103 *The Cambrian* (13 May 1826).
104 Francis Jones, *Treasury of Historic Pembrokeshire* (Newport, 1998), pp. 300–2.

[105] *Cardiff and Merthyr Guardian* (1 September 1849).

[106] *Cardiff and Merthyr Guardian* (7 May 1853).

[107] *Cardiff and Merthyr Guardian* (5 February and 18 June 1863).

[108] Peter Lord, *Hugh Hughes (1790–1863): Arlunydd Gwlad* (Llandysul, 1995), p. 60.

[109] P. Howell Williams, 'Causes', p. 336.

[110] *DWB*.

[111] For the painting see Peter Lord, *Visual Culture: Industrial Society*, p. 63. See also T. F. Holley, *Heads of the Valleys Tails: A Miscellany of Field Sports of the Area* (Merthyr Tydfil, 1985); idem, *Tails of Old Merthyr: A History of the Gelligaer Hunt, 1898–1939* (Merthyr Tydfil, 1983); idem, *Master of Hounds: Wyndham William Lewis, Esquire, The Heath, Cardiff* (Merthyr Tydfil, 1987); idem, *The Glôg Squires* (Merthyr Tydfil, 1995); Sydney F. Lloyd, 'The Anglesey Hunt 1757–1838', *Transactions of the Anglesey Antiquarian Society* (1954), 74–87; and idem, 'The Anglesey Hunt 1839–1955', *Transactions of the Anglesey Antiquarian Society* (1955), 29–45.

[112] Peter Lord, *Visual Culture: Imaging the Nation*, p. 195.

[113] For reports of Welsh races see *North Wales Chronicle* (17 May 1836); *The Cambrian* (22 September 1827, 31 July 1812, 10 September 1825). See also R. Moore Colyer, 'Field sports, conservation and the countryside in Georgian and Victorian Wales', *Welsh History Review*, 16 (1992–3), 308–30; and idem, 'Gentlemen, horses and the turf in nineteenth-century Wales', *Welsh History Review*, 16 (1992–3), 47–62.

[114] A. H. Dodd, *History of Wrexham*, p. 241.

[115] David Dykes, *Vanity Fair*, p. 81.

[116] *The Cambrian* (10 November 1838).

[117] *DWB*.

[118] A. H. Dodd, *History of Wrexham*, p. 242.

[119] Ivor Waters, *Inns*, p. 42.

[120] *The Cambrian* (19 July 1831).

[121] *The Cambrian* (2 July 1831).

[122] *Caernarvon and Denbigh Herald* (4 February 1843).

[123] A. H. Dodd, *History of Wrexham*, p. 243.

[124] Elizabeth Phillips, *A History of the Pioneers of the Welsh Coalfield* (Cardiff, 1925), p. 85. See also Owen Morien Morgan, *History of Pontypridd and Rhondda Valleys* (Pontypridd, 1903), p. 43.

[125] *Carmarthen Journal* (8 August 1845); *Monmouthshire Merlin* (14 October 1837). E. Wyn James, 'Baledi i'r "Clyw Cloff" ', *Canu Gwerin*, 15 (1992), 3–29; see also Tegwyn Jones, 'Rhagor o redwyr', *Canu Gwerin*, 16 (1993), 38–42.

[126] For Thomas Lloyd's bet see Major Francis Jones, 'Lloyd of Gilfachwen, Cilgwyn and Coedmore', *Ceredigion*, 8, 1 (1976), 94–5; *The Cambrian* (23 September 1814).

[127] Cardiff Central Library MS 4,683, Henry Murton, 'Recollections of Dowlais'.

[128] Eiluned Rees 'The Welsh book trade from 1718 to 1820', in Philip Henry Jones and Eiluned Rees (eds), *A Nation and its Books: A History of the Book in Wales* (Aberystwyth, 1998), pp. 123–5.

[129] Aled Gruffydd Jones, 'The newspaper press in Wales', ibid., p. 209.

[130] Huw Walters, 'The periodical press to 1914', ibid., p. 199; idem, 'The Welsh language and the periodical press', in Geraint H. Jenkins (ed.), *The Welsh Language and its Social Domains* (Cardiff, 1999).

[131] Huw Walters, *Llyfryddiaeth Cylchgronau Cymreig: A Bibliography of Welsh Periodicals 1735–1850* (Aberystwyth, 1993); idem, *Llyfryddiaeth Cylchgronau Cymreig: A Bibliography of Welsh Periodicals 1850–1900* (Aberystwyth, 2003).

[132] Boris Ford (ed.), *The Cambridge Cultural History: Victorian Britain* (Cambridge, 1992).

[133] W. D. Shaw, *The Lucid Veil: Poetic Truth in the Victorian Era* (Madison, WI, 1987); B. Richards, *English Poetry of the Victorian Period 1830–1890* (London, 1988); B. Hardy, *Forms of Feeling in Victorian Fiction* (London, 1986).

[134] Others who expressed in their memoirs their joy at reading were Nathanial Thomas (1818–83), Rosser Beynon, Asaph Glan Tâf (1811–76), and Richard Griffith Humphreys, Rhisiart o Fadog (1848–1924). *DWB*.

[135] Jonathan Rose, *The Intellectual Life of the British Working Class* (New Haven, 2003).

[136] Catherine Brennan, *Angers, Fantasies and Ghostly Fears: Nineteenth Century Women from Wales and English Language Poetry* (Cardiff, 2003), passim.

[137] Janet Davies, *The Welsh Language* (Cardiff, 1999).

[138] Peter Lord, *Visual Culture: Imaging the Nation*, pp. 191, 198.

[139] D. S. MacLeod, *Art and the Victorian Middle Class: Money and the Making of Cultural Identity* (Cambridge, 1996); J. Woolf and Seed (eds), *The Culture of Capital* (Manchester, 1989). On the religious iconography of Wales see Helen Ramage, 'Hoelion wyth – traed o glai', *Y Casglwr* (16 March 1982), 12–13.

[140] J. Maas, *Victorian Painters* (London, 1969); R. Strong, *And When did you Last See your Father? The Victorian Painter and British History* (London, 1978); C. Wood, *Victorian Panorama: Paintings of Victorian Life* (London, 1976).

[141] Hywel Teifi Edwards, *Gŵyl Gwalia*, pp. 53–112.

[142] *Monmouthshire Merlin* (18 December 1869). Christie Davies, *Welsh Jokes* (Barry, 1986); idem, *Ethnic Humor around the World: A Comparative Analysis* (Bloomington, IN, 1990); idem, 'Ethnic jokes and social change: the case of the Welsh', *Immigrants and Minorities*, 4, 1 (1985), 46–63; idem, *Jokes and their Relation to Society* (New York, 1998); idem, *The Mirth of Nations* (New Brunswick, NJ, 2002). I am grateful to Dr Huw Walters for drawing the work of Christie Davies to my attention.

[143] Huw Walters, *Llyfryddiaeth*; Benjamin Thomas (Myfyr Emlyn), *Dafydd Evans, Ffynonhenri* (Carmarthen, 1893); J. R. Hughes, *Humour Sanctified: The Memoir of Stephen Jenkins* (Tonypandy, 1902); E. G. Millward, 'Y Fictoriaid yn Gwenu', *Y Casglwr* (10 March, 1980).

[144] Emyr Wyn Jones, 'John Thomas, *Cambrian Gallery*, Ei atgofion a'i deithiau' *National Library of Wales Journal*, 4 (1961–4), 273.

[145] *Seren Gomer* (September 1848).

[146] *The Cambrian* (2 February 1839).

[147] For some examples of the historical treatment of humour see Theodore Zeldin, *France 1848–1945: Taste and Corruption* (Oxford, 1980), pp. 298–377; Jan Bremmer and Herman Roodenburg, *A Cultural History of Humour* (London,

1997); A. Dundes, *Cracking Jokes: Studies of Sick Humour Cycles and Stereotypes* (Berkeley, CA, 1987); F. K. M. Hillenbrand, *Underground Humour in Nazi Germany, 1933–1945* (London, 1995); L. E. Mintz (ed.), *Humor in America: A Research Guide to Genres and Topics* (New York, 1988); W. Schechter, *The History of Negro Humor in America* (New York, 1970); M. R. Townsend, *Forbidden Laughter: Popular Humour and the Limits of Repression in Nineteenth Century Prussia* (Ann Arbor, 1992); N. A. Walker, *A Very Serious Thing: Women's Humor and American Culture* (Minneapolis, 1988); and T. Wechsler, *A Human Comedy: Physiognomy and Caricature in Nineteenth Century Paris* (London, 1982).

[148] D. Leslie Chamberlain, *Welsh Nicknames* (Penygroes, 1981); Bedwyr Lewis Jones, 'Glasenwau gogleisiol', *Y Casglwr*, 3 (1984). *The Cambrian* (7 September 1839).

[149] Keith Thomas, 'The place of laughter in Tudor and Stuart England', *Times Literary Supplement* (21 January 1977); Sigmund Freud, *Jokes and their Relation to the Unconscious* (Harmondsworth edn, 1981); Barry Sanders, *Sudden Glory: A Brief History of Laughter* (London, 1996).

[150] This idea has been superbly documented in Stuart M. Tave's *The Amiable Humorist* (Chicago, 1960). See also Roy Porter, 'Architects of happiness', *BBC History* (December 2000).

[151] For the *Ceffyl Pren* and mocking, abusive laughter see *The Cambrian* (10 August and 23 March 1839); *Carmarthen Journal* (7 March 1856, 17 October 1862, 4 and 18 October 1861, 28 July 1837, 6 April 1838 and 22 March 1839); *Caernarvon and Denbigh Herald* (10 February 1870); and David J. V. Jones, *Crime in Wales*, p. 12.

[152] For *rhialtwch ffeiriau* see Ben Bowen Thomas, *Drych y Baledwr* (Aberystwyth, 1958), p. 121. On his journey through Wales, in 1777, Henry Penruddocke Wyndham remarked that 'such is the jolly debauchery of a Welsh fair' that 'the scene of riot and drunkenness is scarcely to be conceived'.

[153] Tegwyn Jones, 'Hiwmor yn y baledi', *Canu Gwerin*, 24 (2001), 3–16.

[154] William Davies, *Hanes Plwyf Llanegryn* (Peniarth, 2002), p. 185.

[155] *Telyn Egryn*, p. xii.

[156] *Twm o'r Nant* (Cyfres y Geiniog, Liverpool, n.d.), p. 76.

[157] *Seren Gomer* (April 1846), 96.

[158] For Shemi Wâd see Dewi Emrys, *Ysgrifau* (Wrexham, 1937), pp. 71–81; Derec Jenkins, 'Shemi Wâd: storiwr celwydd golau', *Y Casglwr* (March 1980), 5; and Robin Gwyndaf, 'Shemi Wâd', *Llafar Gwlad*, 5 (1986). For the tradition of the tall tale see idem, 'Personality and folklore in action: the folk speech and folk narrative of a Welsh joke-teller', *Fabula*, 31–2 (1990–1), 193–207.

[159] Bedwyr Lewis Jones, 'Cocosfardd Caernarfon', *Y Casglwr* (August 1977); Huw Ceiriog and Myrddin ap Dafydd, *Perlau Cocos: Casgliad o Farddoniaeth Talcen Slip* (Llanrwst, 1998).

[160] E. G. Millward, *Gym'rwch chi baned?*; Gerald Morgan, *Lle Diogel i Sobri Hunangofiant Capelulo* (Llanrwst, 1982).

[161] E. G. Millward, *Gym'rwch chi baned?*; Tegwyn Jones, *Anecdotau Llenyddol* (Talybont, 1987); Elwyn Edwards, *Yr Awen Lawen* (Llandybïe, 1989).

[162] *Carmarthen Journal* (31 May 1812).

163 Cecil Price, 'Portable theatres', 82.
164 The best guide to English Victorian humour is Ronald Pearsall, *Collapse of Stout Party: Victorian Wit and Humour* (London, 1975).
165 J. P. Mahaffy, *The Art of Conversation* (London, n.d.), p. 46.
166 *The Cambrian* (9 February 1839).
167 *Y Punch Cymraeg* (12 March, 9 July, 18 June 1864).
168 Pearsall, *Collapse*, p. 190.
169 Dewi Williams, 'Hiwmor diethr heddiw', *Y Casglwr*, 37 (March 1989).
170 Emyr Wyn Jones, 'Williams of Fron: cleric and satirist', *National Library of Wales Journal*, 14 (1965–6), 396–7.
171 Quoted in Keith Thomas, 'Place of laughter', p. 80.
172 D. L. Jones, *Y Ffraethebydd neu Cymhorth i Chwerthin* (Wrexham, n.d.), p. 112.
173 William Davies, *Casgliad o Ffraethebion Cymreig* (Treherbert, 1876), p. 73. See also Lewis Jones, *Gwreichion = Sparks* (Rhuthyn, 1904); John Lloyd Jones, *Hen yd y wlad: Sef casgliad o bert-ddywediadau a digrifion hen drigolion* (Blaenau Ffestiniog, 1911); and Lewis Jones, *Pobol od: Sef y cymeriadau hynod a welwyd o dro i dro yn Llandrindod* (Rhuthyn, 1903).
174 William Davies, *Ffraethebion Cymreig*, p. 91.
175 Ibid., p. 32.
176 Ibid., p. 78.
177 D. L. Jones, *Y Ffraethebydd*, p. 9.
178 William Davies, *Ffraethebion Cymreig*, p. 55.
179 Ibid., p. 98.
180 Ibid., p. 40.
181 Ibid., p. 30.
182 Ibid., p. 75.
183 Anonymous, *Cymhorth i Chwerthin: Sef Ystraeon Ysmala a Difyrus wedi eu Addurno a Lliaws o Ddarluniau Digrif* (Dowlais, 1876), p. 65.
184 William Davies, *Ffraethebion Cymreig*, p. 47.
185 Ibid., pp. 96, 85.
186 D. L. Jones, *Y Ffraethebydd*, p. 79.
187 William Davies, *Ffraethebion Cymreig*, p. 83.
188 D. L. Jones, *Y Ffraethebydd*, p. 29.
189 William Davies, *Ffraethebion Cymreig*, p. 76.
190 Ibid., p. 97.
191 *Y Punch Cymraeg* (2 July 1864).
192 William Davies, *Ffraethebion Cymreig*, p. 61.
193 D. L. Jones, *Y Ffraethebydd*, p. 107.
194 Ibid., p. 128.
195 *Y Punch Cymraeg* (14 April 1860).
196 D. L. Jones, *Y Ffraethebydd*, p. 70.
197 Ibid.
198 William Davies, *Ffraethebion Cymreig*, p. 39.
199 D. L. Jones, *Y Ffraethebydd*, p. 39.
200 R. W. Jones, *Ysgrifau John Puleston Jones*, p. 133, quoted in Tegwyn Jones, *Anecdotau Llenyddol* (Talybont, 1986), p. 112.

201 D. L. Jones, *Y Ffraethebydd*, p. 112.
202 William Davies, *Ffraethebion Cymreig*, p. 52.
203 Ibid., p. 94.
204 Ibid., p. 48.
205 Ibid., p. 24.
206 The book was published at Wrexham and ran to over 380 pages, evidence enough that Welsh religious leaders did have a sense of humour. For other examples of religious wit see T. Mardy Rees, *Hiwmor y Cymro: Sef Hiwmor mewn llenyddiaeth Gymraeg* (Liverpool, 1922); and Robert Jones, *Y Cydymaith Dyddanus* (Wrexham, 1872).
207 William Davies, *Ffraethebion Cymreig*, p. 61.
208 *Y Punch Cymraeg* (25 June 1864).
209 D. L. Jones, *Y Ffraethebydd*, p. 18.
210 *Y Punch Cymraeg* (13 Febraury 1864).
211 *Y Punch Cymraeg* (14 May 1864).
212 William Davies, *Ffraethebion Cymreig*, p. 58.
213 D. L. Jones, *Y Ffraethebydd*, p. 89.
214 *Y Punch Cymraeg* (20 February 1864).

Conclusion

1 Quoted in Joseph Roach, *Cities of the Dead: Circum–Atlantic Performance* (New York, 1996), p. 63.
2 For a discussion on these themes see Darren Oldridge, *Strange Histories: The Trial of the Pig, the Walking Dead, and Other Matters of Fact from the Medieval and Renaissance Worlds* (Abingdon, 2005) pp. 1–20; and Benedicta Ward, *Miracles and the Medieval Mind* (Aldershot, 1987), chap. 1.
3 For a discussion on the impact of technology on happiness and the alleviation of pain see Robert Darnton, *George Washington's False Teeth: An Unconventional Guide to the Eighteenth Century* (New York, 2003), pp. 89–107.
4 *Monmouthshire Merlin* (20 July 1844).
5 Written to his partner W. Allen, quoted in *The Oxford Dictionary of Quotations*, ed. Angela Partington (Oxford, 1996), p. 503. For an entertaining, if irreverent view of the historical profession see Peter Lamont, *The Rise of the Indian Rope Trick: How a Spectacular Hoax Became History* (London, 2004), pp. xiv–xx.
6 D. H. Lawrence, *Phoenix* (London, 1936), pp. 163–4.
7 Quoted in Theodore Zeldin, *France 1848–1945: Ambition and Love* (Oxford, 1979), p. 6.

Index

Learning Resources
Centre